KV-166-044

INTERNATIONAL CARRIAGE OF GOODS BY ROAD: CMR

AUSTRALIA

LBC Information Services
Sydney

CANADA and USA

Carswell
Toronto

NEW ZEALAND

Brooker's
Auckland

SINGAPORE AND MALAYSIA

Thomson Information (S.E. Asia)
Singapore

INTERNATIONAL CARRIAGE OF GOODS BY ROAD: CMR

THIRD EDITION

by

MALCOLM A. CLARKE,
M.A., LL.B, PH.D
University of Cambridge

LONDON
SWEET & MAXWELL
1997

Published in 1997 by
Sweet & Maxwell Limited of
100 Avenue Road, Swiss Cottage, London NW3 3PF
Computerset by Interactive Sciences Ltd, Gloucester
Printed and bound in Great Britain by
Hartnolls Ltd, Bodmin, Cornwall

No natural forests were destroyed to make this product:
only farmed timber was used and replanted

A CIP catalogue record for this book is available from the
British Library

ISBN 0 421 550708

Grateful acknowledgment is made for permission
to reproduce extracts from the *Law Reports*
(The Incorporated Council of Law Reporting for
England and Wales).

PREFACE TO THE THIRD EDITION

The CMR is not and nor was it intended to be a complete code of law regulating all aspects of the international carriage of goods by road. It was always understood that the regime would have to be completed by reference to relevant national law. In one country, however, entire books have been written on filling the gaps, which is regrettable because such work is beguiling and tends to draw courts through the gaps. Nonetheless, any account of the law of the CMR is incomplete without some kind of account of purely domestic law. In this, the third edition of what remains a book mainly on the CMR, rather than dig up bits of the substratum of English domestic law as and when required, I have brought it in by cross-reference; the cross-reference is to a second part of the book, in which I have sought to set out those rules of law in context, *i.e.* the context of the law of England (also the law of Scotland) governing the carriage of goods by road (solely) within the United Kingdom. So, the rules of the CMR itself are considered in the first and main part of this book, with English domestic law in the second part. My main aim is that the second part should complement the first but at the same time provide a coherent summary of English domestic law as it applies to contracts for the carriage of goods by road outside the scope of the CMR.

Cambridge, January 1, 1997

TABLE OF CONTENTS

2. THE CONTRACT OF CARRIAGE: DOCUMENTATION

3. THE JOURNEY

4. CLAIMS

A. THE CLAIMANT

B. LIMITATION OF ACTIONS

C. THE FORUM AND THE DEFENDANT

5. THE LIABILITY OF THE CARRIER

6. DEFENCES AVAILABLE TO THE CARRIER

7. THE SPECIAL RISKS

A. THE ONUS OF PROOF

B. THE RISKS

8. REMEDIES

A. COMPENSATION

[The next paragraph is paragraph 201.]

PART II: ENGLISH DOMESTIC LAW

9. THE CONTRACT OF CARRIAGE

10. THE JOURNEY

11. CLAIMS

12. THE LIABILITY OF THE CARRIER

13. DEFENCES

14. REMEDIES

APPENDIX A

APPENDIX B

APPENDIX C

APPENDIX D

APPENDIX E

TABLE OF CASES

(Alphabetical Order)

[References are to pages]

TABLE OF EUROPEAN CASES

(*Chronological Order*)

TABLE OF NON-EUROPEAN CASES

(Alphabetical Order)

TABLE OF STATUTES

TABLE OF ABBREVIATIONS

ADR	European Agreement concerning the International Carriage of Dangerous Goods by Road, 1957, Cmnd. 3769
ADSp	Allgemeinen Deutschen Spediteurbedingungen
Anson	Anson, *The Law of Contract* (25th ed.), Oxford 1979
B.T.	Bulletin des Transports, Paris
Benjamin	Benjamin, *Sale of Goods* (4th ed.), London 1992
C.L.J.	Cambridge Law Journal, Cambridge
CIM	International Convention concerning the Carriage of Goods by Rail, 1980
CMR	Convention on the Contract for the International Carriage of Goods by Road, 1956
Carver	Carver, *Carriage by Sea* (12th ed.), London 1971
Clarke, HR	Malcolm A. Clarke, *Aspects of the Hague Rules*, The Hague 1976
Clarke, Insurance	Malcolm A. Clarke, *The Law of Insurance Contracts*, London (3rd ed.) 1997
Clerk and Lindsell	Clerk and Lindsell, *Law of Torts* (17th ed.), London 1995
Costanzo	E. Costanzo, *Il Contratto di Trasporto Internazionale nella CMR*, Milan 1979
D.	Dalloz, Paris
Dicey	*Conflict of Laws* (12th ed.), London 1993
Donald	Alan E. Donald, *The CMR*, London 1981
E.C.E.	Economic Commission for Europe
E.T.L.	European Transport Law, Antwerp
Evans	M. Evans and M. Stanford, *Transport Laws of the World*, New York 1981
FIATA	Fédération Internationale des Associations de Transitaires Assimilés
FIATA Report	Report by FIATA ad hoc working group CMR Revision, November 1983
G.P.	Gazette du Palais, Paris
Giles	O.C. Giles, *Uniform Commercial Law*, Leyden 1970

Glass and Cashmore	D.A. Glass and C. Cashmore, *Introduction to the Law of Carriage of Goods*, London 1989
Greiter	I. Greiter, CMR-Gerichtsurteile, Eisenstadt 1986
Haak	K.F. Haak, *The Liability of the Carrier under the CMR*, The Hague 1986
Haak and Swart	K.F. Haak and E.C. Swart, *Road Carrier's Liability in Europe*, The Hague 1994 (part I) and 1995 (part II)
Herber/Piper	R. Herber and H. Piper, *CMR: Internationales Strassentransportrecht*, Munich 1996
Hill and Messent	A. Messent with D.A. Glass, *CMR: Contracts for the International Carriage of Goods by Road* (2nd ed.) 1995
J.B.L.	Journal of Business Law, London
J.C.P.	Juris-Classeur Périodique, Paris
J.M.L.C.	Journal of Maritime Law and Commerce, Silver Springs, Maryland
KVO	Kraftverkehrsordnung
Kahn-Freund	Otto Kahn-Freund, *The Law of Carriage by Inland Transport* (4th ed.), London 1965
Koller	I. Koller, *Transportrecht* (3rd ed.), Munich 1995
LMCLQ	Lloyd's Maritime and Commercial Law Quarterly, London
L.S.	Legal Studies, the Journal of the Society of Public Teachers of Law, London
Libouton	Libouton, *Convention on the Contract for the International Carriage of Goods by Road (CMR). Review of Court Decisions 1965–1971* (1973) 8 E.T.L. 1
Loewe	Roland Loewe, *Commentary on the Convention of 19 May 1956 on the Contract for the International Carriage of Goods by Road (CMR)* (1976) 11 E.T.L. 311
Mal. L.J.	Malayan Law Journal, Singapore
M.L.R.	Modern Law Review, London
McGregor	H. McGregor, *Damages* (15th ed.), London 1989
N.I.L.Q.	Northern Ireland Legal Quarterly, Belfast
N.J.W.	Neue Juristische Wochenschrift, Munich
Nickel-Lanz	M.-C. Nickel-Lanz, *La Convention relative au Contrat de transport international de Marchandises par Route (CMR)*, Lausanne 1976
O.J.L.S.	Oxford Journal of Legal Studies

Palmer	Norman E. Palmer, *Bailment* (2nd ed.), London 1991
Putzeys	Jacques Putzeys, *Le Contrat de Transport Routier de Marchandises*, Brussels 1981
Rodière	René Rodière, *Le Droit des Transports* (2nd ed.), Paris 1977
Rodière CMR	René Rodière, *Le CMR*, B.T. 1974.182–185, 206–208, 230–232, 242–244, 266–269, 278–280, 290–294, 314–316, 326–327, 338–341, 350–352, 362–364
Scrutton	Scrutton, *Charterparties and Bills of Lading* (19th ed.), London 1984
Stra GüV	Strassengüterverkehr, Vienna
Tetley	W. Tetley, *Marine Cargo Claims* (3rd ed.), Montreal 1988
Theunis	J. Theunis (ed.), *International Carriage of Goods by Road (CMR)*, London, 1987
Thume	K.-H. Thume and others, *Kommentar zur CMR*, Heidelberg 1995
TranspR	Transportrecht, Hamburg
Treitel	G.H. Treitel, *The Law of Contract* (9th ed.), London 1995
Tul.L.R.	Tulane Law Review, New Orleans
U.L.C.	Uniform Law Cases, published in Milan by the International Institute for the Unification of Private Law
U.L.R.	Uniform Law Review, published in Rome by the International Institute for the Unification of Private Law
VersR	Versicherungsrecht, Karlsruhe
Walker	D.M. Walker, *The Law of Contracts and Related Obligations in Scotland*, Edinburgh 1995
Yates	D. Yates, *Contracts for the Carriage of Goods*, London 1993
Zweigert and Kötz	K. Zweigert and H. Kötz (transl. Weir), *Introduction to Comparative Law*, Oxford 1989

Part I

THE CMR

CHAPTER 1

APPLICATION OF THE CMR

A. PROLOGUE

1. The origins of the CMR

"Having recognised the desirability of standardising the conditions governing the contract for the international carriage of goods by road, particularly with respect to the documents used for such carriage and to the carrier's liability",[1] nine European states (Austria, France, Luxembourg, Poland, Sweden, Switzerland, West Germany, the Netherlands and Yugoslavia) signed the Convention on the Contract for the International Carriage of Goods by Road, on May 19, 1956.[2] The Convention is generally known by the acronym for its title in French: Convention relative au Contrat de Transport International de Marchandises par Route: CMR. Carriage by road was one of the last types of transport to be the subject of uniform law, a reflection of the intensity of the conflict of interests involved.[3] The CMR came into force, as regards those states which had ratified or acceded to it, in October 1961. The United Kingdom acceded to the CMR on July 21, 1967, it having been given legislative expression as a Schedule to the Carriage of Goods by Road Act 1965, which came into force on October 19, 1967. That Act remains in force, as amended by the Carriage by Air and Road Act 1979. This book refers chiefly to the application of the CMR in England. In Wales, Scotland and Northern Ireland, to which the Acts also apply, the effect will for most purposes be the same.

In 1980 the Convention on International Multimodal Transport of Goods was concluded under the auspices of the United Nations. It is unlikely to come into force in the immediate future and, in any event, will not apply[4] to movements of goods within the scope of the CMR.

---

[1] The Preamble to the CMR.

[2] Generally see Loewe, paras. 1–8; Donald, "CMR—An Outline and Its History" [1975] L.M.C.L.Q. 420–421; Loewe 1996 U.L.R. 429.

[3] Vrebos (1966) 1 E.T.L. 678.

[4] Multimodal Convention, Art. 4.1.

2. The authors of the CMR

The CMR was largely the work of a committee[5] set up by a Working Party on Legal Questions, itself a subsidiary organ of the Inland Transport Committee of the United Nations Economic Commission for Europe (ECE).[6] A draft convention prepared by the committee was the basis of negotiations between national delegations during 1955 and 1956, conducted mostly in French,[7] as a result of which the final text was agreed. The draft was based partly on work done previously by the International Institute for the Unification of Private Law and partly on the International Convention on the Transport of Goods by Rail of October 14, 1890, which remains in force in its version of February 7, 1970, known as CIM. The CMR was drafted on the assumption that road and rail were in direct competition, that ultimately harmonisation of the various regimes would be necessary with a view to combined transport,[8] and that therefore, as far as possible, the liability regime and other rules should be the same.[9] In February 1972 the Inland Transport Committee of the ECE met to consider revising the CMR, but concluded[10] that it worked well enough, and that, although revision of some aspects might be desirable, it was not a matter of urgency.

B. INTERPRETATION[11]

3. The *Buchanan* case

The rules of interpretation appropriate to the CMR were discussed by the Court of Appeal[12] and, later, by the House of Lords[13] in

---

[5] Messrs Hostie (UNIDROIT), de Sydow (Sweden) and Kopelmanas (ECE Secretariat).

[6] For reference to *travaux préparatoires* see Haak, pp. 8 *et seq.* and Nickel-Lanz, pp. 187–188. The documents, which are in English and in French, are deposited in the Library of the United Nations at Geneva, under references such as those given in nn. 8 to 10, below.

[7] Loewe, Theunis, p. 145.

[8] E/ECE/TRANS/SC1/64 p. 9.

[9] For example, E/ECE/TRANS/SC1/116 p. 6; TRANS/WP9/11 p. 2; TRANS/WP9/22. Evidently some rules would differ as, for example, a railway is easy to contact through one of its stations, and a train easier to stop than a road vehicle, the driver of which has more commercial responsibility for the goods carried than the driver of a train.

[10] W/TRANS/SC1/438.

[11] In this book no distinction is intended between "construction" and "interpretation": on a possible distinction see Clarke, *Insurance*, para. 15–1.

[12] [1977] Q.B. 208, discussed by Hill, "The Interpretation of CMR in English Courts" [1977] L.M.C.L.Q. 212 and by Sacks and Harlow, "Interpretation, European-Style" (1977) 40 M.L.R. 578. Generally, see Jacobs and Roberts (eds.), *The Effect of Treaties in Domestic Law* (London, 1987); and Debattista, "Carriage Conventions and their interpretation in English Courts" [1997] J.B.L. 130.

[13] [1978] A.C. 141, discussed by Munday (1978) 27 I.C.L.Q. 450 and by Herman (1981) 1 L.S. 165.

James Buchanan & Co. v. Babco Forwarding & Shipping (U.K.):

> Whisky en route for Iran was stolen from the defendant carrier's vehicle before it had left the United Kingdom. In these circumstances the plaintiff sender had to pay £30,000 duty on the whisky, duty which would not have been exigible if the whisky had been successfully exported. It was admitted that the defendant was liable under the CMR in respect of the loss of the whisky; the question in dispute was the extent of that liability. The plaintiff sought to recover the amount paid as duty as an instance of "other charges incurred in respect of the carriage of goods" recoverable from the carrier under Article 23.4.[14] It was argued for the carrier that on "English" rules of interpretation the charge claimed must be a charge for carriage which, manifestly, the payment of duty was not. It was argued for the plaintiff that in an international convention a more liberal interpretation was appropriate, an interpretation whereby the "other charges" included charges consequent upon the carriage, thus including the duty that had become payable. Both the Court of Appeal and the House of Lords preferred the second argument and thus gave judgment for the plaintiff sender.

It was agreed, but with more emphasis in the Court of Appeal than in the House of Lords, that it was desirable that courts in different countries should interpret an international convention in an international and uniform manner, and that therefore consideration should be given to the decisions of courts in other countries.[15] That this might be difficult should not deter the attempt; non-uniformity leads to forum shopping and to the waste of both time and money. The basic approach to interpretation, upheld by the judgments of the House of Lords in *James Buchanan*, remains that of Lord Macmillan in *Stag Line v. Foscolo, Mango & Co.* in respect of the Carriage of Goods by Sea Act 1924[16]:

---

[14] On the meaning of Art. 23.4 see below, para. 97c.

[15] [1977] Q.B. 208, 213, *per* Lord Denning M.R., 221, *per* Roskill L.J., 222, *per* Lawton L.J.; [1978] A.C. 141, 168, *per* Lord Edmund-Davies; *Silber v. Islander Trucking* [1985] 2 Lloyd's Rep. 243, 245, *per* Mustill J.

[16] [1932] A.C. 328, 350 approved in the *James Buchanan* case [1978] A.C. 141, 152, *per* Lord Wilberforce and 160, *per* Lord Salmon; and in *Fothergill v. Monarch Airlines Ltd* [1981] A.C. 251, 282, *per* Lord Diplock, 285, *per* Lord Fraser and 293, *per* Lord Scarman. *cf.* Putzeys, para. 256: "La CMR s'interprète selon les principes généraux du droit national du juge saisie, sans rigorisme."

An important rule of English law in a domestic case is that the context of a statutory provision includes previous statutes in which the word or phrase to be interpreted has been used, with a presumption that the word or phrase has been used in the same sense in each statute: *Gosse Millerd v. Canadian Government Merchant Marine* [1929] A.C. 223, 230, *per* Lord Hailsham L.C. This is one of the "technical" rules of English law which need modification in the context of European uniform law: *James Buchanan* [1978] A.C. 141, 152, *per* Lord Wilberforce. It now appears that this has been accepted: *Fothergill v. Monarch Airlines* [1981] A.C. 251, 298–299, *per* Lord Roskill. However, when confronted with a gap in the CMR, resort to national law is permitted (below, n. 19); a lack of clear definition may be seen as a gap.

> "It is important to remember that the Act was the outcome of an International Conference and that the rules in the schedule [The Hague Rules] have an international currency. As these rules must come under the consideration of foreign Courts it is desirable in the interests of uniformity that their interpretation should not be rigidly controlled by domestic precedents of antecedent date, but rather that the language of the rules should be construed on broad principles of general acceptation."

This means, in the view of Lord Salmon,[17] that "words . . . should not be construed pedantically or rigidly but sensibly and broadly". One of the main purposes of uniform commercial law, the promotion of predictability and security in commerce,[18] is best achieved by broad interpretation of the law. This kind of approach is of particular importance for what has been described[19] as "the notoriously difficult CMR Convention".

The first task for the court is a search for the ordinary meaning of words in the CMR in their context, rather than an investigation of the intentions of the parties, which might take the court outside the text of the CMR. This is the golden rule, sometimes called the objective approach, and is as much applicable to a statute enacting an international convention as to any other kind of statute, although, as indicated above, account must be taken of the fact that such conventions tend to be more loosely worded than Acts of Parliament.[20]

However, the context of the CMR includes the Preamble of the CMR, by which the signatory states recognise the "desirability of standardising the conditions governing the contract for the international carriage of goods by road". The call for uniformity of law requires broad rules of construction, as indicated by Lord Macmillan (above), whose words are reinforced by the spirit if not the exact letter of the Vienna Convention on the Law of Treaties 1969.[21] Having ratified the Vienna Convention, the United Kingdom has an international obligation[22] to interpret later treaties as indicated in Articles 31 to 33 of that Convention. Although the CMR precedes the Vienna Convention, it is clear that the latter is

---

[17] [1978] A.C. 141, 160.

[18] Zweigert & Kötz, Vol. 1, p. 23.

[19] *Cummins Engine Co. v. Davis Freight Forwarding (Hull)* [1981] 2 Lloyd's Rep. 106, 109, *per* Mocatta J.

[20] *Silber v. Islander Trucking* [1985] 2 Lloyd's Rep. 243, 245, *per* Mustill J.

[21] Cmnd. 4140. Sinclair, *The Vienna Convention on the Law of Treaties* (2nd ed., Manchester, 1984), p. 115. Generally see Sinclair, Chap. 5; Kianti-Pampouki, Rev. Héllen, Dr. Internat., 144 (1991) 6. The approach authorised by Art. 31.1 of the Vienna Convention is broader than that of the golden rule in English domestic law.

[22] *Fothergill v. Monarch Airlines Ltd* [1981] A.C. 251, 283, *per* Lord Diplock. Unless, as in the case of the Vienna Convention on Contracts for the International Sale of Goods 1980, but not the CMR, the convention under interpretation lays down its own rules of interpretation: Honnold, *Uniform Law for International Sales* (1982, Deventer), para. 103.

not without influence on the general approach of the English courts to the CMR, as the provisions of the Vienna Convention codify already existing public international law.[23] From the Vienna Convention, it is evident that, although the search must start with the golden rule and with the text of the CMR, it does not stop there; courts are encouraged if not compelled to look beyond the strict confines of the text by means of (other) aids to interpretation.

4. Aids to interpretation

"Aids are not a substitute for the terms of a convention; nor is their use mandatory. The court has a discretion" and on appeal the court is not bound by the choice of aids made by the lower court.[24] As seen by commentators in Europe, English courts handle this discretion like a dangerous drug, to be dispensed with care in small quantities. In 1986 a German[25] observed that "reluctance to accept statutory derogations from the common law has probably led to the very restrictive approach in interpretation which is still to a certain extent predominant in English courts". And in the same year a Dutchman[26] observed that "in Britain the judiciary finds it difficult to deviate from a clear text even if that text would lead to unintended results". The aids to interpretation (or deviation) available to the English judge are as follows.

4a. Teleology: commercial purpose

Lord Denning M.R., in *James Buchanan*,[27] said that:

> "We must . . . put on one side our traditional rules of interpretation. . . . We ought, in interpreting this convention, to adopt the European method. . . . They adopt a method which they call . . . the 'schematic and teleological' method of interpretation. It is not really so alarming as it sounds. All it means is that the judges do not go by

[23] *Fothergill v. Monarch Airlines Ltd* [1981] A.C. 251, 282, *per* Lord Diplock. See Gardiner [1994] L.M.C.L.Q. 184. This is the practice in at least some other CMR states: see Jacobs and Roberts (*op. cit.*, n. 12 above), p. 74 (West Germany), p. 107 (Italy).
[24] *Fothergill v. Monarch Airlines Ltd* [1981] A.C. 251, 294–295, *per* Lord Scarman.
[25] Dr J.A. Frowein in Jacobs and Roberts (*op. cit.*, above, n. 21), p. 81.
[26] H.G. Schermers, *ibid.*, p. 117.
[27] [1977] Q.B. 208, 213. As regards the Vienna Convention (above, n. 21), the reference to "good faith . . . object and purpose" in Art. 31.1 of that convention is understood to include the principle of effectiveness, *ut res magis valeat quam pereat.*

> the literal meaning of the words or by the grammatical structure of the sentence. They go by the design and purpose which lies behind it. When they come upon a situation which is to their minds within the spirit—but not the letter—of the legislation, they solve the problem by looking at the design and purpose of the legislature—at the effect which it was sought to achieve. They then interpret the legislation so as to produce the desired effect."

Lawton L.J. agreed[28] with Lord Denning, "even though in so doing some strain may be put upon the grammar and literal meaning of the words". But in the same case the House of Lords, which clearly did not agree with Lord Denning, took a more traditional view. Lord Wilberforce thought[29] that the court must be "unconstrained by technical rules of English law, or by English precedent",[30] but that current English practice when interpreting international conventions was satisfactory and should be maintained. Viscount Dilhorne[31] knew "of no authority for the proposition that one consequence of this country joining the European Economic Community is that the courts of this country should now abandon principles of construction long established in our law". But he also thought[32] that "in construing a convention as in construing an Act where the language used is capable of two interpretations one must seek to give effect to the intentions of those who made it".[33] And in the later case of *Fothergill*[34] the House took a more "European" view of the interpretation of conventions: the English courts must "have recourse to the same aids to interpretation as their brother judges in other contracting states".

According to Article 31.1 of the Vienna Convention, the relevance of which has been accepted by the English courts,[35] the ordinary meaning of words must be sought not only in their textual context but also in the light of the "object and purpose" of

---

[28] *ibid.*, p. 222.

[29] [1978] A.C. 141, 152–153.

[30] He did not define what was technical.

[31] [1978] A.C. 141, 156. See also Munday (1978) 27 I.C.L.Q. 450, 454–455 who suggests that Lord Denning confused the interpretation of EEC law, in respect of which courts "must follow the European pattern" (*H. P. Bulmer v. J. Bollinger* [1974] Ch. 401, 426), and uniform law, to which the European pattern is not appropriate.

[32] [1978] A.C. 141, 157. See also *Silber v. Islander Trucking* [1985] 2 Lloyd's Rep. 243, 245, *per* Mustill J.

[33] Coke 4 Inst. 330. Viscount Dilhorne did not consider the possibility that the ambiguity may not appear until the intentions of the legislature have first been ascertained.

[34] *Fothergill v. Monarch Airlines Ltd* [1981] A.C. 251, 294, *per* Lord Scarman; see also 276, *per* Lord Wilberforce.

[35] *Fothergill v. Monarch Airlines Ltd* [1981] A.C. 251, 290, *per* Lord Scarman; Mann (1983) 99 L.Q.R.. 376, 377 *et seq.*; Gardiner (1995) 44 I.C.L.Q. 620. *idem* in Belgium: Bombeeck (1990) 25 E.T.L. 110, no. 27; in Germany: Brandi-Dohrn, TranspR. 1996. 45.

the text. Thus, for international law, reference to purpose is a primary rather than supplementary aid to interpretation.[35a] The design and purpose of a text, in what Lord Denning M.R. called the European method, may be sought both from the text itself and from evidence outside that text (extrinsic evidence). The implication from Viscount Dilhorne, that one can only look outside the text itself when the textual meaning is ambiguous, is open to question.[36] First, the plausibility of the textual or "plain meaning" approach depends upon its use within the confines of a system with established patterns for the use of language, strengthened by a symbiotic relationship between the approach to drafting and to interpretation.[37] Secondly, according to Article 32 of the Vienna Convention, the court shall have recourse to supplementary means of interpretation not only when the primary means in Article 31 fail to resolve an ambiguity but also:

(a) when they lead to "a result which is manifestly absurd or unreasonable",[38] and
(b) "to confirm the meaning resulting from the application of article 31".

The teleological or "purposive" approach to construction, based both on the evidence of the text itself and evidence outside it, is that which best promotes uniformity of construction[39] and, although some judges may use it only in cases of ambiguity,

---

[35a] *Fothergill* (above) at 279, *per* Lord Diplock; *Sidhu v. British Airways plc* [1997] 1 All E.R. 193, 202, *per* Lord Hope, H.L.

[36] "La première maxime générale sur l'interprétation est qu'il n'est pas permis d'interpréter ce qui n'a pas besoin d'interprétation" (Vattel) is, as Sinclair (above, n. 21) observes (p. 116), a *petitio principii.*

In *Fothergill* (above) Lord Wilberforce (at 272) and Lord Diplock (at 279), found the words unclear on a literal or textual approach before turning to the commercial purpose of the convention, while Lord Scarman (at 290) appeared to take both steps at once: in this case the ordinary literal meaning of a word ("loss") in the Warsaw Convention in question gave way to the meaning that fulfilled the commercial purpose of the provision.

Reference to the purpose of CMR is common in other jurisdictions: for example, *Lg Bremen 6.5.65*, quoted below, para. 5; see also *O.L.G. Düsseldorf 27.3.80*, (1983) 18 E.T.L. 89, 92.

[37] Honnold (above, n. 22), para. 90, citing support from *Fothergill* (above), 281–282, *per* Lord Diplock.

[38] The avoidance of an unreasonable result is a well established object of construction in English law: *Schuler AG v. Wickman Tool Sales Ltd* [1974] A.C. 235, 251, *per* Lord Reid; *Forsik. Vesta v. Butcher* [1989] 1 All E.R. 402, 418, *per* Lord Lowry. In *Silber v. Islander Trucking* [1985] 2 Lloyd's Rep. 243, 246 Mustill J. sought to find the natural meaning of CMR Art. 17.2, "whilst taking care to avoid any interpretation which produced an absurd result, or one inconsistent with the scheme of the Convention as a whole". He had already considered supplementary aids (*doctrine* and *jurisprudence*) but found them unhelpful.

[39] Haak, p. 17; Haak, Theunis, p. 228.

reference to purpose is now established in England.[40] The danger of the approach "is not, indeed, that the Judges become legislators, but that they may become legislators with widely differing, and perhaps unduly legalistic, views of the policy which is, or ought to be, behind the legislation".[41] This danger can be averted,[42] if the judge is willing to make reference to the other aids to interpretation. Moreover, as regards the Vienna Convention, the interpreter is expected to have recourse to *all* the evidence of the meaning to be attributed to a text: it is only when he considers all such evidence that he will be in a position to assess their relative value and weight.[43] This predicates attention to yet further aids to interpretation, as follows.

4b. Legislative history: travaux préparatoires

"Legislative history (like vintage wine) calls for discretion."[44] In the search for the purpose or true intention of the CMR Convention limited recourse may be had to the legislative history (travaux préparatoires) of the Convention. Objections to travaux are, first, that travaux may not reflect the intention of states acceding to the convention after its conclusion,[45] including in the case of CMR the United Kingdom; and, secondly, that people should not be bound by discussions or negotiations of which they may never have

---

[40] Notably as regards the Brussels Convention on carriage by sea: *The Hollandia* [1983] 1 A.C. 565, 575, *per* Lord Diplock; and as regards the Warsaw Convention: *Fothergill v. Monarch Airlines Ltd* [1981] A.C. 251; *Sidhu v. British Airways plc* [1997] 1 All E.R. 193, 202, *per* Lord Hope, H.L.; and *Corocraft v. Pan American Airways* [1969] 1 Q.B. 616, 654, *per* Lord Denning M.R., C.A.: "seeing that the French text is ambiguous and uncertain . . . it should be interpreted so as to make good sense among commercial men." Reference to the purpose of the CMR is common in other jurisdictions: for example, *Lg Bremen 6.5.65* quoted below, para. 5; see also *O.L.G. Düsseldorf 27.3.80*, (1983) 18 E.T.L. 89, 92.

In any event, the decisions lend colour to the scepticism of Professor Gutteridge (8 Tul.L.R. 1, 19): "one may be permitted to doubt whether the application of theories of the social purpose of the law to the clearing away of ambiguities of language has in practice any marked influence on the process of interpretation, . . . (the judge) will always try to put himself in the position of the legislator, whether in doing so he claims to be seeking for the social purpose of the rule, or merely confines himself to the declaration of what he believes to have been the intention of the legislator as evidenced by the phraseology of the rule itself and its context." For a more enthusiastic view of the usefulness of teleology, see Kahn-Freund, *Comparative Law as an Academic Subject* (Oxford, 1965).

[41] *Ulster-Swift v. Taunton Meat Haulage* [1977] 1 Lloyd's Rep. 346, 351, *per* Megaw L.J., C.A. See also *Buchanan* [1978] A.C. 141, 168–169, *per* Lord Edmund-Davies. Moreover, there is no single technique of teleology: Sacks and Harlow (1977) 40 M.L.R. 578. Generally see Giles, Chap. 1; Cohn (1955) 4 I.C.L.Q. 492. For criticism, similar to that of Megaw L.J., in cases in which no international convention was in issue: *Saloman v. Saloman* [1897] A.C. 22, 38, *per* Lord Watson; *Major & St. Mellons R.D.C. v. Newport Borough Council* [1952] A.C. 189, 191, *per* Lord Simmonds.

[42] Haak, p. 17.

[43] Sinclair (above, n. 21), p. 117.

[44] Honnold (above, n. 22), para. 91.

[45] *cf.* Sinclair (above, n. 21), p. 144.

heard.[46] In view of these objections, resort to travaux by English courts will be rare[47] and cautious.[48] Their use is more common and less restrained in other CMR states,[49] but in England will occur only when, travaux "clearly and indisputably point to a definite legislative intention"[50] and "the material involved is public and accessible".[51] In other words, it will not occur often, not least because the CMR was negotiated mostly in French, and very little of the relevant material has been published in English[52] or deposited in England.[53]

4c. Doctrine

As to writers, their commentaries are usually published after the conclusion of the convention in question, and

> "delegates cannot have taken them into account in agreeing on the text. To a court interpreting the Convention subsequent commentaries can have persuasive value only; they do not come into the same authoritative category as that of the institutional writers in Scots law. It may be that greater reliance than is usual in the English courts is placed upon the writings of academic lawyers by courts of other European states where oral argument by counsel plays a relatively minor role in the decision-making process. The persuasive

---

[46] *Fothergill v. Monarch Airlines Ltd* [1981] A.C. 251, 278, *per* Lord Wilberforce, 280, *per* Lord Diplock.

[47] *Fothergill*, (above, n. 46) at 278, *per* Lord Wilberforce. On the use of background materials relating to the Hague Rules see Tetley, *Marine Cargo Claims* (3rd ed., Montreal, 1988), pp. 70 *et seq.*

[48] *Fothergill*, (above, n. 46) at 278, *per* Lord Wilberforce, and 287, *per* Lord Fraser. Lord Wilberforce repeated his view in *Gatoil International Inc. v. Arkwright-Boston Manufacturers Mutual Ins. Co.* [1985] A.C. 255, 263 and Lord Fraser and Lord Roskill concurred with his judgment. See also *Sidhu v. British Airways plc* [1997] 1 All E.R. 193, 202, *per* Lord Hope, H.L. A more ready resort to travaux (of the Warsaw Convention) was made by Rogers J. in *S.S. Pharmaceuticals Co. v. Qantas Airways* [1989] 1 Lloyd's Rep. 319, 323 (S.C. N.S.W.).

[49] Jacobs and Roberts (above, n. 12), p. 23 (Belgium), p. 37 (Denmark), p. 75 (West Germany), p. 117 (Holland). In the case of the CMR see, for example, *B.G.H. 14.7.83*, 1986 U.L.R. I 596.

[50] *Fothergill* (above, n. 46) at 278, *per* Lord Wilberforce, who repeated his view in *Gatoil* (above, n. 48).

[51] *Fothergill* (above, n. 46) at 278, *per* Lord Wilberforce, and 287–288, *per* Lord Fraser. Lord Wilberforce repeated this view in *Gatoil* (above, n. 48). See also in this sense Sinclair (above, n. 21), p. 144.

However, accessible to whom? Perhaps this should mean accessible to persons, such as insurers, with specialised knowledge, rather than the man in the street: *Fothergill* (above, n. 46) at 302, *per* Lord Roskill; but *cf.* 288, *per* Lord Fraser.

[52] For reference to materials in other languages see Haak, pp. 8 *et seq.*

[53] The material, in English and French, can be found in the Library of the United Nations, Geneva. See above, n. 6.

effect of learned commentaries, like the arguments of counsel in an English court, will depend on the cogency of their reasoning,"[54]

and, perhaps, on the eminence and experience of the writer.[55] Unanimity among writers cannot be expected and their opinions should not, any more than those of the judges, be discarded simply because those opinions are diverse,[56] but considered on their merits. Attention was paid by the House of Lords to continental writers on the Warsaw Convention in *Fothergill*.[57]

4d. Case law

English courts will look at decisions of foreign courts[58] on uniform law, such as the CMR. The persuasive value of a decision depends, first, on the coverage of the national reporting system[59]: if the report of a case is too brief to give any reliable guide to its reasoning, it will be ignored.[60] Secondly, it depends on the deciding court's reputation and status,[61] and the extent to which its decisions are binding on other courts in the same jurisdiction.[62] It should be recalled that, although in its own country "a single decision of a German, French or Italian court is not a binding precedent, it is nevertheless of high persuasive authority".[63] Further, consistent case law[64] in such countries is accorded the same

---

[54] *Fothergill* (above, n. 46) at 283–284, *per* Lord Diplock. Thus a Dutch writer can say of the CMR: "Courts in their decisions process the results reached by academics": Haak, p. 18; repeated in Haak, Theunis, p. 228. Yet in Holland the HR appears to depend less on writers than, for example, the B.G.H., as the HR is considered to be fully informed by an opinion of the Procurer-General.

[55] *Fothergill* (above, n. 46) at 295, *per* Lord Scarman.

[56] *Silber v. Islander Trucking* [1985] 2 Lloyd's Rep. 243, 245, *per* Mustill J.

[57] Above n. 46. *idem*, *S.S. Pharmaceuticals Co. v. Qantas Airways* [1989] 1 Lloyd's Rep. 319 (S.C. N.S.W.).

[58] *Buchanan & Co. v. Babco Forwarding & Shipping (U.K.)* [1978] A.C. 141, 168, *per* Lord Edmund-Davies; *Fothergill v. Monarch Airlines Ltd* [1981] A.C. 251, 275, *per* Lord Wilberforce.

[59] *Fothergill* (above, n. 46) at 276, *per* Lord Wilberforce, 284, *per* Lord Diplock: care should be taken not to attach too much weight to a decision if it might be inconsistent with another unreported decision of a court of similar status in that country, notably where, as in Belgium, France and Germany, there are regional courts of appeal, whose decisions are not binding on each other.

[60] *Silber v. Islander Trucking* [1985] 2 Lloyd's Rep. 243, 246, *per* Mustill J.

[61] *Fothergill* (above, n. 46) at 275, *per* Lord Wilberforce, 284, *per* Lord Diplock, 295, *per* Lord Scarman. See also *Sidhu v. British Airways plc* [1997] 1 All E.R. 193, 203, *per* Lord Hope, H.L.

[62] *Fothergill* (above, n. 46) at 284, *per* Lord Diplock.

[63] Lipstein (1946) 28 *Journal of the Society of Comparative Legislation* (3rd ser.) 34, 36. See also Goodhart, (1934) 50 L.Q.R. 40; Honnold (above, n. 22) para. 92.

[64] *Gerichtspraxis, jurisprudence constante*. It should be recalled that a case is more likely in France than in England to be seen as raising a question of fact rather than law, hence the value of the decision as "precedent" is diminished.

Jurisprudence can be of value even though, inevitably perhaps, it is not unanimous or unequivocal: *cf. Silber v. Islander Trucking* [1985] 2 Lloyd's Rep. 243, 245, *per* Mustill J.

respect, comparable with that given to binding precedent, as custom or legislation.

Nonetheless, English judges may approach foreign decisions with caution, induced not only by the reserve inspired in many an Englishman by a foreign language but also by the awareness that courts, even the highest courts,[65] in other countries do not have a role that can be easily equated with that of the courts in England. As for courts in other CMR states, where judgments are traditionally short, such as in Belgium, France and Italy, no reference to foreign decisions is found or to be expected. It is different in Austria and Germany, where, as in England, judgments explain the decision at greater length. Further, as regards "the area of unification of private law and private international law, the widespread custom in Germany is to ask for advisory opinions from specialised institutes. These specialised institutes may well refer to foreign decisions which might then be used by the court itself."[66]

4e. Other conventions

For the interpretation of uniform law some writers[67] suggest the "comparative convention" method of approach. In these terms it is unlikely to appeal to the English judge, but as regards the CMR a limited approach of this kind in the form of reference to the CIM is justified as an instance of resort to other aids to interpretation: as the CMR was clearly derived from the CIM, reference to the corresponding provision of the CIM can be justified as part of the search for the purpose, or as part of the legislative history, of a provision of the CMR.[68] Be that as it may, courts[69] and commentators abroad have referred to the CIM to interpret the CMR and there are good grounds for the English court to do likewise.

4f. Good faith

Article 31.1 of the Vienna Convention[70] requires that the ordinary meaning of a treaty shall be sought "in good faith". The principle

---

[65] For a comparison of the House of Lords with the highest courts in other countries, see Tunc (1978) Rev.Int. de Dr.Comp. 5.

[66] Jacobs and Roberts (above, n. 12), p. 76.

[67] For example Haak, Theunis, p. 226.

[68] *ibid.*

[69] For example, *B.G.H. 21.12.73* (1975) 10 E.T.L. 91; *Amsterdam 4.6.74* (1975) E.T.L. 531; *B.G.H. 6.7.79* (1980) 15 E.T.L. 863; *B.G.H. 11.12.81* (1983) 18 E.T.L. 63, 69. In England in one CMR case comparative reference was made to uniform law, with which, perhaps, the court is more familiar, the Hague Rules: *Eastern Kayam Carpets v. Eastern United Freight* (Queen's Bench Div., December 6, 1983).

[70] See above, para. 3.

of good faith in this context is closely linked to the principle *pacta sunt servanda*. Although a doctrine of good faith in national law is more closely associated with the civil law countries,[71] the "basis obligation of good faith to observe promises and agreements —*pacta sunt servanda*—was originally enforced on grounds of conscience in the Court of Chancery in England".[72] As regards interpretation, the principle of good faith means that the court should "draw inspiration from the good faith which should animate the parties if they were themselves called upon to seek the meaning of the text".[73] For the CMR this includes the goal of uniformity found in the Preamble to the CMR and hence implies reference to techniques of interpretation which promote that goal, notably those aids to interpretation discussed here.

4g. The strict construction of exclusions

The chief basis in English common law for the strict construction of exclusions is the principle of construction *contra proferentem*, which assumes that the terms are drafted by the profferor, that he can be presumed to look to his own interests,[74] and that there was inequality of bargaining power when the terms were negotiated.[75] None of these assumptions can be made in relation to exceptions contained in CMR, notably the carrier's defences in Article 17. Exceptions in the Hague Rules have been construed strictly,[76] but neither the history of the CMR nor the balance of power between carriers and cargo are the same.

5. Gaps in the CMR

On certain points the CMR refers expressly to national law. It might be inferred that this was the limit of reference to national law, at least, within the scope of the CMR. But the area of intended unification is not sharply drawn,[77] and in practice courts

---

[71] Lücke, "Good Faith and Contractual Performance," in Finn (ed.), *Essays on Contract* (North Ryde), Chap. 5; Nicholas, *French Law of Contract* (2nd ed., London, 1992) pp. 153–154; Steyn [1991] Denning L.J. 131; Clarke (1993) 23 H.K.L.J. 318; Brownsword (1994) 7 J.C.L. 197.

[72] O'Connor, *Good Faith in English Law* (Aldershot, 1989), p. 99.

[73] Sinclair (above, n. 21), p. 120. As regards good faith in treaty relations between states, see Rosenne, *Developments in the Law of Treaties, 1945–1986* (Cambridge 1989), Chap. 3.

[74] Clarke, *Insurance*, para. 15–5C.

[75] *Tersons v. Stevenage Development Corp.* [1963] 2 Lloyd's Rep. 333, 368, *per* Pearson L.J., C.A. The form and content of the Rules, notably the exceptions in Art. IV, r. 2, "the marble table of Moses" for shipowners, were mostly the work of shipowners.

[76] *Foreman & Ellams v. Federal Steam Navigation Co.* [1928] 2 K.B. 424, 439, *per* Wright J. Tetley, at 74.

[77] Haak, pp. 10 *et seq.*, pp. 18 *et seq.*; Haak, Theunis, pp. 225–226.

have identified "gaps",[78] or restricted the scope of the CMR,[79] and resorted to rules of national law to settle disputes arising out of the international carriage of goods by road.

In England the courts have been reluctant to acknowledge the existence of gaps in law of this kind,[80] unless and to the extent that the court can be persuaded that the regime in question is not comprehensive.[81] In *James Buchanan*[82] the House of Lords concluded, differently from Lord Denning M.R. in the Court of Appeal, that there was no gap in Article 23.4 of the CMR. Typical is this statement from Lord Wilberforce[83]: "I cannot detect that this is a case of a gap in the legislation. The question simply is whether this loss is to fall on the owner or on the carrier. The words used must cover the case in one way or the other—we have to decide which: if they are not such as to impose liability on the carrier, the owner is left to bear the loss." If the House had found a gap, it is clear that the House would have worked its way around it rather than spanned it with a bridge of teleological construction; Viscount Dilhorne[84]: "The courts have rightly refused to encroach on the province of Parliament and have refused to engage in legislation." But in the case of uniform law like the CMR, the province of Parliament is to approve and purvey legislation drafted in other precincts. Whether it is called a gap, a gash or a gaffe, it is evident that a number of questions arising in connection with the international carriage of goods by road remain unanswered by the CMR.[85] What is to be done? In the Court of Appeal in *James Buchanan* Lord Denning M.R. had little hesitation in spanning the gap with what he considered to be appropriate European principles[86]: having described the principles,[87] especially the rule of teleology, he concluded that Europeans "fill in gaps quite unashamedly, without hesitation". Is this true?

There is a widely held view that, as far as possible, uniform law such as the CMR should be autonomous and should be interpreted only by reference to itself.[88] In the case of the CMR many courts

---

[78] Such instances are listed below, para. 64.

[79] Notably in Germany: below, paras. 65 and 66.

[80] As regards the CMR, see *James Buchanan & Co. v. Babco Forwarding & Shipping (U.K.)* [1978] A.C. 141. See further *Eastern Kayam Carpets v. Eastern United Freight* (Queen's Bench Div., December 6, 1983).

[81] Lipstein, "Common Law Courts in the Age of Statutes", *La Sentenza in Europa* (Milan, 1988), 42, 48 *et seq.*

[82] Above, n. 80.

[83] *Buchanan* above, n. 80 at 153; see also 156–157, *per* Viscount Dilhorne, 160, *per* Lord Salmon, and 166, *per* Lord Edmund-Davies.

[84] 156; see also 160–161, *per* Lord Salmon.

[85] See below, paras. 64 *et seq.*

[86] [1977] Q.B. 208, 213.

[87] Quoted above, para. 4.

[88] Haak, Theunis, p. 225; Piper, TranspR 1990.357. For the attitude of the Swiss courts, see Fischer, TranspR. 1995.424. In England, *cf.* Hill and Messent, p. 10. For a summary of academic opinion on the autonomous character of the CMR, see Haak, pp. 31 *et seq.*

have subscribed to this principle with apparent conviction, but finding that the CMR is not a complete and self-contained code,[89] have resorted nonetheless to contract terms or to national law on certain issues, for example, to identify the person responsible for loading.[90] A typical response comes from Holland[91]: "If and to the extent that the CMR is silent and a reply must be given to questions about the liability of the carrier arising in such a case, one must apply the rules of national law applicable on the basis of private international law." Again, in Austria the OGH has consistently referred to national law to fill perceived gaps in the CMR.[92] In Germany, however, although the courts have taken a restrictive view of the outer boundary of the CMR, within its field of play they have been reluctant to resort to national law, if assistance can be derived in any way by interpretation of the CMR itself.[93]

In *Lg Bremen 6.5.65*[94] the carrier agreed to carry goods from Italy to France and West Germany, but did not even collect the goods in question, having deployed his vehicles to perform other contracts of carriage. This was clearly a breach of contract, but not a breach regulated by Article 17 or by any other provision of the CMR.[95] In these circumstances the court responded thus[96]: "the CMR is to be interpreted according to its purpose and its underlying principles (*Sinn und Zweck*), by making the carrier liable in other matters by application of rules of national law which, subject to the application of the CMR, underlie the contract." Accordingly the court did not extrapolate from the CMR itself, but fell back on the German commercial code, Article 325.

Decisions like this suggest that, if a gap is found at the level of the CMR, that gap will be treated as a hollow rather than as a void: below the CMR there remains the substratum of existing

---

[89] See below, paras. 64 *et seq.*

[90] Austria: *OGH 12.12.84*, Stra GüV 1985/5 p. 12, Greiter 263. Belgium: *Brussels 17.12.84*, (1985) 20 E.T.L. 354; *Rb Leuven 5.4.88*, (1988) 23 E.T.L. 493. France: Chao B.T. 1986.373.

[91] *Rb Breda 16.12.69*, 1970 U.L.C. 298, 301.

[92] *OGH 18.12.84*, Stra GüV 1985/4 p. 34, Greiter 270: on the liability of the sender to the carrier for damage to the vehicle caused by defective loading: the court might have argued from the implications of Art. 10 of the CMR, but resorted to national law.

Likewise as regards breach of contract not involving loss, damage or delay to goods but the consequences (seizure of vehicle but not lateness of goods) of the driver's attempt to take alcohol into Saudi Arabia: *OGH 12.12.84*, Stra GüV 1985/6 p. 28, Greiter 239. See also on recourse to national law: *OGH 24.3.81*, Greiter 93; *OGH 18.5.82*, SZ 55/73, TranspR 1983.48, Greiter 154; *OGH 16.1.85*, Stra GüV 1985/8 p. 8, Greiter 275; *OGH 13.6.85*, Stra GüV 1985/12 p. 10.

[93] For example *B.G.H. 6.7.79*, (1980) 15 E.T.L. 863. But the courts have nonetheless felt obliged to apply national law, for example on the existence of a right of set-off: *B.G.H. 7.3.85* (1985) 20 E.T.L. 343.

[94] (1966) 1 E.T.L. 691; Rodière, para. 37.

[95] On this see below, para. 65.

[96] (1966) 1 E.T.L. 691, 687.

national law, to which the court may turn without usurping the function of the legislature and without the necessity to guess what the draftsmen of the CMR would have said, if the question had been put to them.[97]

6. The French text of the CMR

The English and the French texts of the CMR are of equal authority; they are set out in Appendix I and Appendix II of this book. English courts will refer to the French text in the circumstances set out in this passage from the judgment of Lord Wilberforce in *James Buchanan*[98]:

> "it is perfectly legitimate in my opinion to look for assistance, if assistance is needed, to the French text. This is often put in the form that resort may be had to the foreign text if (and only if) the English text is ambiguous, but I think this states the rule too technically. As Lord Diplock recently said in this House the inherent flexibility of the English (and, one may add, any) language may make it necessary for the interpreter to have recourse to a variety of aids: *Carter v. Bradbeer* [1975] 1 W.L.R. 1204, 1206. There is no need to impose a preliminary test of ambiguity.
>
> My Lords, I would not lay down rules as to the manner in which reference to the French text is to be made. It was complained—by reference to the use of the French text by Roskill L.J. and Lawton L.J.—that there was no evidence as to the meaning of the French text, and that the Lords Justices were not entitled to use their own knowledge of the language. There may certainly be cases when evidence is required to find the exact meaning of a word or phrase; there may be other cases when even an untutored eye can see the crucial point (*cf. Corocraft Ltd v. Pan American Inc.* [1969] 1 Q.B. 616 (insertion of 'and' in the English text)). There may be cases again where a simple reference to a good dictionary[99] will supply the key (see, *per* Kerr J. in *Fothergill v. Monarch Airlines Ltd* [1978] Q.B. 108 on 'avarie'). In a case, such as I think the present is, when one is dealing with a nuanced expression, a dictionary will not assist and reference to an expert might also be unhelpful, for the expert would have to direct his evidence to a two-text situation rather than simply to the meaning of words in his own language, so that he would be in the same difficulty as the court. But I can see nothing illegitimate in the court looking at the two texts and reaching the

---

[97] Passage cited with approval in *Eastern Kayam Carpets v. Eastern United Freight* (Queen's Bench Div., December 6, 1983).

[98] *James Buchanan & Co. v. Babco Forwarding & Shipping (U.K.)* [1978] A.C. 141, 152–153; see also 161, *per* Lord Salmon. The first sentence in the quotation from the judgment of Lord Wilberforce was quoted and applied in *O.L.G. Hamburg 28.2.65*, N.J.W. 1986.670.

[99] Reference to dictionaries and to expert evidence on the meaning of the French text was approved in *Fothergill v. Monarch Airlines Ltd* [1981] A.C. 251, 273–274, *per* Lord Wilberforce, 286, *per* Lord Fraser, 293, *per* Lord Scarman, 300, *per* Lord Roskill.

> conclusion that both are expressed in general or perhaps imprecise terms, so as to justify rejection of a narrow meaning."

Article 33.4 of the Vienna Convention provides that, if a comparison of the two texts "discloses a difference of meaning which the application of Articles 31 and 32 [of the Vienna Convention] does not remove, the meaning which best reconciles the texts, having regard to the object and purpose of the treaty, shall be adopted". This provision appears to rule out any preference for the French text, as being the language in which the negotiations leading to the CMR Convention were conducted.[1]

If the English courts are free to turn to the French text only if "assistance is needed",[2] when does the need arise? It is clear from the words of Lord Wilberforce quoted above that, in his view, "need" was not confined to a case of ambiguity in the English text. But Lord Edmund-Davies, while claiming that he was "not disposed to differ from . . . Lord Wilberforce, regarding the propriety of adverting to the French text" of the CMR, clearly thought differently: there must first be ambiguity in the English text, then (and only then) can resort be had to the French.[3] It is Lord Edmund-Davies whose view finds most support among the other judges in *James Buchanan*. Thus, in the Court of Appeal Roskill L.J. asked[4]:

> "Why, then, in those circumstances, when one is in doubt as to the true construction of the English text of the Convention, should one deprive oneself of the assistance that is ready to hand in its French text . . . in *Post Office v. Estuary Radio Ltd* [1968] 2 Q.B. 740 this court in a judgment delivered by Diplock L.J., at 760, said that it

---

[1] Bombeeck (1990) 25 E.T.L. 110, no. 34.

[2] In this sense in relation to the Warsaw Convention: *Fothergill v. Monarch Airlines Ltd* [1981] A.C. 251, 286, *per* Lord Fraser, who added that reference would also be made if counsel pointed to an apparent inconsistency between the English and the foreign text. See also 299 and 301, *per* Lord Roskill.

[3] *James Buchanan*, above, n. 98 at 167. Also in this sense: *Milor SrL v. British Airways plc* [1996] 3 All E.R. 537, 540 *per* Phillips L.J., C.A.

[4] [1977] Q.B. 208, 220. See also Lawton L.J. (at 223): "As there is a latent ambiguity in the word 'compensation' as used in what purports to be an exact reflection in English of what is in the French text, in my judgment this court can look at the French text to resolve that ambiguity." And Lord Salmon [1978] A.C. 141, 161: "If in a statute which is based on an international convention expressed in two different languages, there is some doubt as to its meaning in one language, it is permissible to seek help from the way in which it is expressed in the other." In *Saloman v. Commissioners of Customs and Excise* [1967] 2 Q.B. 116, 143, Diplock L.J. said: "if the terms of the legislation are not clear but are reasonably capable of more than one meaning, the treaty itself becomes relevant, for there is a prima facie presumption that Parliament does not intend to act in breach of international law, including therein specific treaty obligations; and if one of the meaning which can reasonably be ascribed to the legislation is consonant with the treaty obligations and another or others are not, the meaning which is consonant is to be preferred." The court then interpreted the Customs and Excise Act 1952 in the light of the European Convention on the Valuation of Goods for Customs Purposes 1950.

> was legitimate to look at the French and Spanish texts of the convention there in question to resolve an ambiguity in the English Order in Council. It seems to me that following this decision and being in doubt which is the right interpretation to put on the relevant English phrase, I am entitled to look at the French text."

So, if there is ambiguity in the English version,[5] the English courts may turn to the French text, even though the immediate task in hand is to interpret an English Act of Parliament, expressed only in English,[6] and even though authoritative interpretation of the French text may be difficult to undertake.[7]

7. Interpretation: summary

Placing *James Buchanan*[8] alongside other cases in which the English courts have construed English Acts of Parliament containing the substance of international conventions on uniform law, the position appears to be as follows.

(i) The court will seek in good faith the natural and ordinary meaning of the words in question in the context of the Act,[9] including its purpose as it appears from the Act itself.[10]
(ii) The words will be construed sensibly and broadly rather than pedantically or rigidly.[11]
(iii) If in the application of (i) and (ii) there appears to be an ambiguity[12] in the English text, and perhaps in any event, resort may be had to supplementary aids to interpretation.

Supplementary aids include the French text of CMR,[13] the purpose of the CMR as appears from extrinsic evidence,[14] the

---

[5] As a precondition of reference to the French text, this is said to be contrary to international law: Bombeeck (1990) 25 E.T.L. 110, no. 26.
[6] *James Buchanan & Co. v. Babco Forwarding & Shipping (U.K.)* [1977] Q.B. 208 at 220, *per* Roskill L.J., C.A.; [1978] A.C. 141, 152, *per* Lord Wilberforce, 158, *per* Viscount Dilhorne. See also *Salomon v. Commissioners of Customs and Excise* [1967] 2 Q.B. 116, 144, *per* Diplock L.J., C.A.
[7] See Lord Wilberforce in the passage quoted in the text. His brethren had doubts. Lord Edmund-Davies said ([1978] A.C. 141, 166), "I have misgivings about the Bench drawing solely upon its own knowledge of a foreign language in arriving at important conclusions." Viscount Dilhorne (158) confirmed his misgivings: "I do not regard my knowledge of the nuances of the French language to be a reliable guide to the meaning to be given to these English words."
[8] *James Buchanan & Co. v. Babco Forwarding & Shipping (U.K.)* [1978] A.C. 141.
[9] Above, para. 3.
[10] Above, para. 4a.
[11] Above, para. 3.
[12] Above, para. 4a.
[13] Above, para. 6
[14] Above, para. 4a.

travaux préparatoires,[15] commentaries,[16] decisions in other jurisdictions[17] and the CIM.[18]

C. THE CMR AND THE CONFLICT OF LAWS

8. A unilateral conflict rule

When a case falls within the scope of the CMR, the scope as defined by Article 1,[19] the forum applies the CMR to what is, *ex hypothesi*, an international contract, without resort to normal rules of the conflict of laws. In other words, like Article X of the Hague or Hague-Visby Rules,[20] Article 1 is a unilateral conflict rule in the *lex fori* of a contracting state: whenever a court in a contracting state characterises the case before it as a contract of the kind defined in Article 1.1, it applies the CMR as enacted in the *lex fori*. As for non-contracting states, the intention is that the courts of those states will apply the CMR as a result of the paramount clause, incorporating the CMR as terms of the contract, required by Article 6(1)(k).[21]

When a contract does not fall within the scope of Article 1.1, the parties may adopt the CMR, subject of course to the conflict rules of the *lex fori*. Whether the CMR applies *proprio vigore* or by adoption, it is incorporated into and becomes part of the contract of carriage.[22] The contract is its context and provides an important perspective when the CMR is unclear or incomplete; in particular, it is to the appropriate law of the contract that the court will turn on questions outside the scope of the CMR.[23]

9. The law of the contract apart from the CMR

What is the law of the contract, apart from the CMR? This question, although extensively discussed by writers in continental Europe,[24] has been largely ignored by the courts. Leading writers

---

[15] Above, para. 4a.
[16] Above, para. 4a.
[17] Above, para. 4a.
[18] Above, para. 4a.
[19] Below, para. 10.
[20] Clarke, H.R., pp. 14–15.
[21] Reinforced by Art. 7.3. See further Haak, p. 42.
[22] *James Buchanan & Co. v. Babco Forwarding & Shipping (U.K.)* [1978] A.C. 141, 152, *per* Lord Wilberforce. Rodière (1971) 6 E.T.L. 2, 4. Helm, VersR 1988.548. On whether a choice of the CMR will be allowed to displace mandatory rules of national law, see *HR 26.5.89* (1990) 25 E.T.L. 717.
[23] See above, para. 5.
[24] Haak, pp. 40–41; Rodière, paras. 268–269 and references cited; Rodière, CMR, para. 26.

prefer the *lex loci contractus*: there is only one such law in each case and its identity can be easily ascertained. The courts, however, may apply the *lex loci contractus*[25] or the *lex fori*, without discussion.[26] The latter course can often be justified on theoretical grounds when the *lex fori* is also the law of the place of performance (for example, where the accident occurred) or the law of the place of destination (for example, where the loss or damage was discovered and disputed). To avoid this uncertainty it is open to the parties to choose the law to govern issues outside the CMR, provided that the choice does not have the effect of ousting the CMR from its proper sphere.

In English common law the proper law of the contract is the law chosen by the contracting parties, chosen expressly or impliedly. In the absence of such a choice, the court localises the contract in the state whose system of law has the closest connection with the contract. In general terms, this may be true of both before and after the entry into force of the Contract (Applicable Law) Act 1990; the issue is controversial. The Act gives effect to the Rome Convention 1980, and it came into force on April 1, 1991.

(a) Although it has been doubted whether in modern conditions the place of contracting has any real significance,[27] it is a point of contact favoured in some other CMR states (above). It is a law that can be applied to all aspects of the contract of the carriage outside the scope of the CMR. Moreover, the *lex loci contractus* is not fortuitous, as the CMR carriage is commonly contracted in the place of sending between parties with businesses there.[28]

(b) The law of the place of destination, although attractive to the consignee, is less attractive to some carriers, and may change in the course of contract performance, if the sender exercises his right under CMR Article 12.1 to change the place of destination.

---

[25] *OGH 12.12.84*, Stra GüV 1985/5 p. 12; Greiter 263 concerning liability for breach of contract other than delay, loss or damage to goods regulated by CMR. See also *OGH 16.1.85*, Stra GüV 1985/8 p. 8; Greiter 275; and *OGH 13.6.85*, Stra GüV 1985/12 p. 10, concerning actions between Austrian carrier and sub-carrier in respect of breaches of contract concluded in Austria, breaches not governed by CMR: Austrian law applied.

[26] For example, *Rb Breda 16.12.69*, above, para. 5. *cf. O.L.G. Munich 3.5.89*, TranspR 1991.61, in which the court stated that, in the absence of an express choice of law, the court would apply the law of the place of the carrier's main establishment (Austria), as long as this was also the place of loading, of unloading or of the sender's main establishment. As none of these conditions were satisfied in this case, the court applied the lex fori as the parties had chosen the forum.

[27] *Encyclopedia of Comparative Law*, vol. III, Chap. 26, para. 32. *cf. Greer v. Poole* (1880) 5 Q.B.D. 272. *Roberts v. Underwriters at Lloyd's* 195 F.Supp. 168 (D Idaho, 1961).

[28] *cf. Amin Rasheed Shipping Corp. v. Kuwait Ins. Co.* [1984] A.C. 50, 62, *per* Lord Diplock.

(c) The use of a standard contract form, such as the IFF Standard Trading Conditions or the French Contrat Type,[29] to underlie the CMR regime, may be seen as a localising factor or, indeed, as an implicit choice of the legal system from which the form comes.[30]

(d) If the court finds that these indications are unhelpful, it may find assistance in Article 4.4 of the Rome Convention, whereby "if the country in which, at the time the contract is concluded, the carrier has his principal place of business is also the country in which the place of loading or the place of discharge or the principal place of business of the [sender] is situated, it shall be presumed that the contract is most closely connected with that country". The places of lading and discharge are those agreed at the time when the contract was concluded. The carrier is any person who contracts to carry, whether or not he performs the carriage himself. These points appear from the official report of Professors Giuliano and Lagarde. In the case of successive carriage, Article 4.4 offers little assistance.

10. Contracts of carriage: Article 1.1

The scope of the CMR is the subject of Article 1.1:

> "This Convention shall apply to every contract for the carriage of goods by road in vehicles for reward, when the place of taking over the goods and the place designated for delivery, as specified in the contract, are situated in two different countries, of which at least one is a Contracting country, irrespective of the place of residence and the nationality of the parties."

Article 1.1 is not exclusive: it does not forbid the widespread practice of contractual adoption of the CMR in cases in which the CMR would not otherwise have applied.[31]

---

[29] Le contrat type de transport public routier de marchandises (décret 14.3.86): B.T. 1986.373.

[30] Especially if the form is not much used outside that legal system: *cf. Amin* (above, n. 28) at 70, *per* Lord Wilberforce.

[31] As, for example, in *Versailles 13.11.85*, B.T. 1986.42, the carriage being from Turkey to Iraq; and in *James Buchanan* (above, para. 3) in which the CMR would not have applied *proprio vigore*, as the container was to be unloaded from the vehicle for carriage by sea: below, para. 14. See also *Bordeaux 21.12.94*, B.T.L. 1995.74.

It has been argued that a contractual term adopting the CMR, when the case is outside the scope of Art. 1, is a stipulation directly or indirectly derogating from the provisions of the CMR and thus null and void under the CMR itself, Art. 41.1 (below, para. 92). However, be that as it may, it is clear that in practice adoption is permitted: see Donald, nos. 36–37. Voluntary adoption of the CMR is also permitted in Belgium: Putzeys, no. 192; and in France: Rodière, CMR, para. 4.

cf. the (untenable) view held (nonetheless) in Italy that the CMR **only** applies when adopted by the parties: *Cass. 28.11.75*, 1976, U.L.R. I 247; and the view held in France that the CMR does not apply unless stated to so do in the consignment note: *Cass. 26.11.80*, (1983) 18 E.T.L. 70.

The CMR applies to contracts of carriage. One corollary of this limit is the position of the CMR carrier who damages other goods, *i.e.* goods that the carrier has not contracted to carry, such as those of third parties at the place of delivery. The carrier may be liable under, for example, local law but the carrier's liability is not governed by the CMR.[32] Contracts of carriage are contracts whereby one party, the carrier, agrees for reward to effect the carriage of goods from one place to another, whether personally or through the instrumentality of sub-contractors[33]; "a 'carrier' means someone who *contracts* to carry",[34] whether or not that person actually carries the goods. From such contracts distinguish (a) those of the traditional freight forwarder (below, paragraph 10a), whose duties to the goods owner at common law[35] are less onerous than those of a carrier under the CMR; (b) a possible hybrid of forwarding and carrier made by a "transportation contractor" (below, paragraph 10b); (c) contracts to hire vehicles (below, paragraph 10c); and (d) haulage contracts (below, paragraph 10d). A person may be a carrier although carriage is not a significant part of that person's business.[36]

10a. Freight forwarders

Traditionally, it has been said, the freight forwarder, also called a forwarding agent, "is not a carrier; he does not obtain possession of the goods; he does not undertake the delivery of them at the other end. . . . All that he does is to act as agent for the owner of the goods to make arrangements with the people who do carry—steamships, railways and so on—and to make arrangements so far as they may be necessary for the immediate step between the ship and the rail, the Customs, or anything else . . . ".[37] They "forward goods for you . . . to the uttermost ends of the earth. They do not undertake to carry . . . They are simply undertaking to get someone else to do the work, and as long as they exercise reasonable care in choosing the person to do the work, they have performed their contract."[38]

---

[32] *HR 15.4.94*, 1994 U.L.R. 379.

[33] *Rb Rotterdam 31.1.67*, S. & S. 1967, no. 56, reported by Haak, p. 55; *Cass. 13.2.78*, B.T. 1978, 210; generally see Hill (1976) 11 E.T.L. 182, 192.

[34] *Ulster-Swift v. Taunton Meat Haulage* [1977] 1 Lloyd's Rep. 346, 359, *per* Megaw L.J., C.A.; applied in *Eastern Kayam Carpets in Eastern United Freight* (H.C., December 6, 1983, unreported). Also in this sense T. *Supremo de España 14.7.87* (1995) 30 E.T.L. 678. *O.L.G. Düsseldorf 8.5.69* (1970) 5 E.T.L. 446, 474–475; *OGH 20.1.82*, EvBl 1982, no. 62, Greiter 122.

[35] Hill, *Freight Forwarders* (London, 1972), paras. 133 *et seq.*

[36] A proposal to limit the CMR to the contracts of a "commercial carrier" (*transporteur professionnel*) was rejected: E/ECE/TRANS/SC1/130 Annexe 4 p. 2.

[37] *Jones v. European & General Express Co.* (1920) 25 Com.Cas. 296, 298, *per* Rowlatt J. See also *Heskell v. Continental Express* [1950] 1 All E.R. 1033, 1037, *per* Devlin J.

[38] *Pisanz & Co. v. Brown, Jenkinson & Co.* (1939) 64 Ll.L.Rep. 340, 342, *per* Goddard J.

More particularly, the freight forwarder was defined by Hill[39] as, "any person which holds itself out to the general public to . . . provide and arrange transportation of property, for compensation, and which may assemble and consolidate shipments of such property, and performs or provides for the performance of breakbulk and distributing operations with respect to such consolidated shipments and assumes responsibility for the transportation of such property from point of receipt to point of destination and utilises for the whole or any part of the transportation of such shipments, the services of a carrier or carriers, by sea, land or air, or any combination thereof." Hill continued: "It can therefore be seen that the essential elements in this definition are the forwarding and/or consolidation of shipments and the subsequent carriage by one or more of the various methods of transportation commonly in use. In other words the forwarder does not generally offer to carry himself, he merely offers to act as professional intermediary between the consignor or consignee of goods and the carrier, though this does not preclude him from effecting part of the transit personally." However, a person who generally acts as a forwarder may in a particular case contract as a carrier.[40] As regards the CMR, the forwarder may be a traditional forwarder, *i.e.* an agent with no responsibilities under the CMR, or a carrier, or, in the case of one who consolidates the customers' goods into a single load for carriage by someone else, the forwarder may be in the position of a sender.[41]

A forwarding contract is governed not by the CMR[42] but by national law alone.[43] In practice the distinction between a contract of carriage and a forwarding contract may be difficult to make. Person A may contract as carrier for one stage of the transit, but having agreed also to arrange carriage for the next stage, A may be a forwarder for that.[44] Alternatively, the same movement may be seen as one with A as carrier for both stages, performing the first stage with A's own vehicles and the second stage with those of

---

[39] Hill, *Freight Forwarders* (London, 1972), para. 22. Forwarders, who are members of the British Institute of Freight Forwarders, generally operate under the Institute's Standard Trading Conditions.

[40] In *Langley, Beldon & Gaunt v. Morley* [1965] 1 Lloyd's Rep. 297, 306 Mocatta J. suggested that this was exceptional in relation to sea transit, but as editor of Scrutton (p. 42, n. 79) appears to have resiled from this view. In any event, it is not exceptional in relation to road transit.

[41] *idem* as regards carriage by sea: Scrutton, p. 43.

[42] Many terms of the CMR may be incorporated into a contract between a shipper and a freight forwarder at the parties' choice: Rodière, para. 257. A court, however, will be reluctant to imply the CMR conditions as a whole into such a contract, to which they are considered inappropriate: *Comm, 16.2.70*, J.C.P. 1970–II–16392, note Rodière J.C.P. 1968–II–15563.

[43] *Tetroc v. Cross-Con (International)* [1981] 1 Lloyd's Rep. 192, 195, *per* Judge Martin. As regards English law, see Yates, Part 7.

[44] As in *Walek & Co. v. Chapman & Ball* [1980] 2 Lloyd's Rep. 279. Kahn-Freund p. 332.

another person, a sub-contractor. Indeed, both at common law[45] and under the CMR[46] the contract of carriage is not personal to the carrier, and the carrier therefore may sub-contract the actual carriage of the goods. A person may operate a trailer, while sub-contracting for a tractor, and yet be a carrier under the CMR.[47] Moreover, a person may be a carrier even though he owns not a single tractor, not a single trailer, and must sub-contract each stage of the transport.

> In *Ulster-Swift v. Taunton Meat Haulage*[48] senders arranged with defendants A for the carriage of meat from Enniskillen to Basle, and A engaged B to perform the carriage. The argument that A were not carriers but forwarding agents, because they did not in fact perform the carriage, was rejected by the Court of Appeal, That a person may be a carrier, although he does not himself carry the goods, is implicit in Article 3, whereby "the carrier" is "responsible for the acts or omissions of his agents and servants and of any other persons of whose services he makes use for the performance of the carriage. . . " A carrier, it was held,[49] "means someone who *contracts* to carry", and who may perform the carriage himself or perform it through sub-contractors.[50]

A distinction has to be drawn therefore between one who contracts to carry (carrier) and one who contracts to arrange for

---

[45] *Homecraft Weavers v. Ewer & Co.* (1945) 78 Ll.L.Rep. 496; *Garnham, Harris & Elton v. Alfred Ellis* [1967] 2 Lloyd's Rep. 22, 27, *per* Paul J. Scrutton, 46. *Aliter* in the case of unusually valuable goods without express consent of the other party: *Garnham.*

[46] Art. 3.

[47] Hill, *op. cit.*, para. 31 and para. 136.

[48] [1977] 1 Lloyd's Rep. 346.

[49] At 359, *per* Megaw L.J.

[50] Also in this sense: *Cummins Engine Co. v. Davis Freight Forwarding (Hull)* [1981] 2 Lloyd's Rep. 106, 109, *per* Mocatta J.; *Tetroc v. Cross-Con (International)* [1981] 1 Lloyd's Rep. 192, 195, *per* Judge Martin.

Vestre Landsret 8.7.69, reported by Sevon: 1971, U.L.C. 291, 295; *The Hague 17.5.68* (1968) 3 E.T.L. 1227; *Brussels 19.10.72*, (1973) 8 E.T.L. 503, 508; *Brussels 19.10.72* (1974) 9 E.T.L. 608; *O.L.G. Hamm 6.12.93*, TranspR 1994.195. Putzeys, paras. 74–76; Piper, VersR 1988.201, 205. Contrary opinion in Holland is discussed and rejected by Haak, p. 77.

A different view has been found in France: a person who does not himself carry out any part of the transport has been traditionally regarded as a *commissionaire de transports* and not a carrier, and to his contracts the CMR does not apply: *Cass. 16.2.70* (1970) 5 E.T.L. 435, 438; *Paris 14.3.78* (1978) 13 E.T.L. 742; *Nîmes 26.5.82*, B.T. 1982.407, 408. Rodière, para. 698; Libouton, para. 14; But *cf. Cass. 25.6.79* (1980) 15 E.T.L. 79. Note: the *commissionaire*, sometimes called *spediteur*, is found in civil law jurisdictions, and is an agent to his principal, the consignor or consignee, but principal in relation to the carrier: Hill, *op. cit.*, para. 87.

Although decisions of the B.G.H. were in this sense, Art. 1 KVO was amended in 1978, so that as regards internal transport the forwarder (*Spediteur*) could be treated as a carrier only when employing the carrier's own vehicle (*Kraftfahrzeug*). Although the same rule has been applied to international transport (for example, *O.L.G. Munich 4.4.79*, VersR 1979.713), most courts have declined to apply it in that context: *O.L.G. Hamburg 6.12.79*, VersR 1980.290; *O.L.G. Munich 14.1.81*, VersR 1981.562; *B.G.H. 10.2.82*, (1983) 18 E.T.L. 32; and cases cited by Haak, p. 72. On the role of the *Spediteur* today, see *O.L.G. Munich 12.4.90*, TranspR 1990.280.

someone else to do it (forwarder),[51] and it must be drawn not in general but in each case. In each case we must characterise not the person, carrier or forwarder, but the contract[52] or the part of the contract. At the same time, it is relevant nonetheless to consider the role the person has played in the past in dealing with the other,[53] as it may be supposed that that person expects and is expected to play the same role again. What counts, most of all, is the role that the person has led the customer to expect.[54] The question has been said to be one of impression[55]; however, while no single factor is decisive, certain factors have been influential as a "guide".[56]

10a(*i*). Form and substance

The English courts attach little weight to the descriptions of themselves used by the parties, such as "freight forwarder",[57] "principal",[58] "agent",[59] "forwarding agent",[60] or even to the name written in the consignment note as that of the carrier.[61] The CMR consignment note, including the way the parties describe them-

---

[51] *TPI Amsterdam 8.4.64*, 1964 U.L.C. 169, 173.

[52] *Elektronska v. Transped* [1986] 1 Lloyd's Rep. 49, 52, *per* Hobhouse J. *Rb Breda 23.2.65*, S. & S. 1965.86, quoted by Haak, pp. 65–66. Hill & Messent suggest (p. 20) that "the status of the parties to a contract which is potentially governed by the CMR can only be established *ex post facto* and *pro hac vice*". For example, *Aqualon (U.K.) Ltd v. Vallana Shipping Corp.* [1994] 1 Lloyd's Rep. 669. Also in this sense: *Paris 20.1.81*, BT 1982.38. Brunat 1982.422; and Herber/Piper, Art. 1, 26; *cf.* Koller, Art. 1, 2.

[53] *Lee Cooper v. Jeakins & Sons* [1964] 1 Lloyd's Rep. 300, 308, *per* Marshall J.; *Marston Excelsior v. Arbuckle, Smith & Co.* [1971] 2 Lloyd's Rep. 306, 311, *per* Phillimore L.J. C.A.; *Moto Vespa S.A. v. MAT (Britannia) Express* [1979] 1 Lloyd's Rep. 175, 177–178, *per* Mocatta J.; *Zima v. m/v Roman Pazinski* 493 F.Supp. 268, 273 (S.D. N.Y., 1980); Porter, Va.J.Int.Law. 171, 184 *et seq.* (1984). In the same sense in Holland: *TPI Amsterdam 8.6.64*, 1964 U.L.C. 169, 172; and in Germany: Thume, Art. 1, 65 *et seq.*

[54] *Paris 20.1.81*, BT 1982.38.

[55] *Tetroc v. Cross-Con (International)* [1981] 1 Lloyd's Rep. 192, 198, *per* Judge Martin, citing *Hair & Skin Trading Co. v. Norman Airfreight Carriers* [1974] 1 Lloyd's Rep. 443, 445, *per* Bean J.

[56] *Tetroc*, above, n. 55, at 195. For an account of the factors that have influenced the Dutch courts see Haak, pp. 65–68; and the German courts: *ibid.*, pp. 68–74.

[57] *Tetroc v. Cross-Con (International)* [1981] 1 Lloyd's Rep. 192, 196, *per* Judge Martin; *Lee Cooper v. Jeakins & Sons* [1964] 1 Lloyd's Rep. 300, 308, *per* Marshall J. *idem*; *s' Hertogenbosch 21.12.65*, 1966 U.L.C. 119; *O.L.G. Munich 12.4.90*, TranspR 1990.280. See also Loewe, para. 21.

[58] *Davis (Metal Brokers) v. Gilyott & Scott* [1975] 2 Lloyd's Rep. 422, 424, *per* Donaldson J.; *Tetroc*, above n. 57.

[59] *Harris v. Continental Express* [1961] 1 Lloyd's Rep. 251, 257, *per* Paull J. *cf. Marston Excelsior v. Arbuckle, Smith & Co.* [1971] 2 Lloyd's Rep. 306, 311: Phillimore L.J. looked at notepaper headings.

[60] Scrutton, p. 42. "Freight forwarder" and "forwarding agent" are terms sometimes used interchangeably: *Tetroc*, above, n. 57.

[61] *Tetroc*, above n. 57 at 196 and 198, *per* Judge Martin; *The Hague 9.1.70* (1970) 5 E.T.L. 587. Loewe, para. 67.

selves and their duties, although relevant evidence,[62] is "in no way conclusive"[63]; but an express reference to the CMR, which, as we have seen, applies to contracts of carriage, is an important, even decisive, sign of a contract of carriage.[64]

What counts, in general, is the substance of the obligation undertaken. If the person is held out as willing to act as a carrier,[65] or makes representations amounting to a guarantee that the goods will reach destination, and the customer reasonably relies on those representations, the court will be inclined to hold that person to that promise.[66]

> In *Tetroc v. Cross-Con (International)*[67] the defendants were sued in respect of machinery found damaged at destination, and argued that they were not carriers but freight forwarders, to whom the CMR did not apply. They pointed, in particular, to a letter from the plaintiff saying: "Will you kindly *arrange* onward transport . . . ".[68] Judge Martin was not impressed by this letter[69]: "I think one has to be careful not to attribute too much to a rather vague word such as 'arrange' used by a businessman in this context. I agree it could mean that the defendants should arrange for other people to affect [*sic*] at p. 28 onward transport. On the other hand, it could mean that the defendants should arrange to do it themselves. I do not attach very much importance to it." Nor did he derive assistance from correspondence referring to the sub-contractors as "the carriers". Having considered other factors,[70] the judge concluded[71] that the defendants were not agents but principals and carriers.

Form has more importance in France and in Belgium.[72] In France the court looks to the *persona* which the contractor

[62] *Texas Instruments Ltd v. Nason (Europe) Ltd* [1991] 1 Lloyd's Rep. 146, 149, per Tudor Evans J.; *Zima v. m/v Roman Pazinski* 493 F.Supp. 268, 273 (S.D. N.Y., 1980). *Aqualon (U.K.) Ltd v. Vallana Shipping Corp.* [1994] 1 Lloyd's Rep. 669, 676 *per* Mance J. Porter (1984) Va.J.Int. Law. 171, 184 *et seq.*

[63] *Elektronska v. Transped* [1986] 1 Lloyd's Rep. 49, 50, *per* Hobhouse J., especially if, as in that case, the note only came into existence after the contract was made (51). In the same general sense: *OGH 8.9.83*, (1985) 20 E.T.L. 282, 287–288; see also *OGH 25.4.84*, Greiter, 223, 227.

[64] *O.L.G. Munich 5.7.89*, TranspR 1990.16, in which, however, the court also pointed to other factors suggesting that the contract was a contract of carriage.

[65] *Claridge, Held & Co. v. King & Ramsay* (1920) 3 Ll.L.Rep. 197.

[66] Holloway, 17 J.M.L.C. 243, 247 (1986).

[67] [1981] 1 Lloyd's Rep. 192. See also *Brussels 25.5.72*, 1974 U.L.R.I. 338.

[68] Emphasis added. *cf. Rb Antwerp 26.6.69* (1969) 4 E.T.L. 1026.

[69] At 196. Also in this sense *Texas Instruments* above n. 62 at 151. Still, more weight may be given to what has been written for the contract or the particular customer, such as the content of the present or past invoices, than to printed standard forms or headings: *Elektronska v. Transped* [1986] 1 Lloyd's Rep. 49, 53, *per* Hobhouse J.

[70] Arrangements (below, para. 10a(*ii*) and charges (below, para. 10a(*iii*)).

[71] At 198.

[72] Perhaps also in Germany: Helm, VersR 1988. 548, 551; Herber/Piper, Art. 1, 26; and Thume, Art. 1, 65 *et seq.* There is also a difference with England, if the person is found to be a forwarder: "the forwarder under most Continental systems, while remaining liable to his client as agent, does for some purposes contract with the actual carrier as a principal . . . [the forwarder] does not create privity of contract between his customer and the carrier. . . . The only contractual redress will thus be against the forwarder, and

assumes, notably in the documentation.[73] Even so, what is essentially a contract of carriage does not cease to be a contract of carriage because the parties have called it something else[74]; carriers do not cease to be carriers simply because they have called themselves something else: "l'habit ne fait pas le moine".[75]

In Belgium, deciding[76] that the claimant was a carrier (*commissionaire de transports assimilé au transporteur*), the court looked at[77] "the terms used by the parties when doing business with each other, the headings on the documents they exchanged and on their notepaper". In another case[78] the customer's instructions to the defendant confirmed that the latter would receive the following day crates marked in a certain way, which would have to be delivered to Iseghem "by your groupage lorry". As these instructions were accepted by the defendant (who then subcontracted the carriage) without comment or protest, the court held that the defendant stood in the position of a carrier. In a third case[79] the court was more cautious. It took the words used by the parties at face value, but was ready to look behind the appearances if the common intention of the parties was different.[80] Moreover,

---

because that contract is not a contract of carriage, it will not be subject to CMR." (Hill and Messent, p. 30). Concerning the *Spediteur* in Germany, see Herber, Art. 1, 34 *et seq.* Koller, part A; Thume, general note to Art. 1, 70 *et seq.*

Moreover, in France the *commissionaire de transport* is distinguished from the *transitaire*: "Entre commissionnaire et transitaire, la différence de statut porte essentiellement sur l'étendue des obligations, le commissionnaire, tenu d'une obligation de résultat, étant garant de la bonne exécution du transport, alors que le transitaire, qui est juridiquement un mandataire, ne répond que de ses fautes prouvées" (Brunat B.T. 1982.422). The *commisionnaire*, unlike the *transitaire*, is responsible for the failure of those whom he engages to undertake the transport, and in this respect he looks like a carrier: Haak, p. 61, who argues therefore (p. 62) that the *commissionnaire* should be treated as a CMR carrier, while conceding that this conclusion has been rejected by a majority of French decisions.

[73] *Paris 20.10.81*, B.T. 1982.38; *Cass. 21.6.82*, B.T. 1982.427; note Brunat B.T. 1982.422; *Paris 22.9.86*, B.T. 1987.139, 140; *Grenoble 4.2.88*, B.T. 1988.699; *Versailles 30.11.95*, B.T.L. 1996.191. But it has been stressed that it is only a (rebuttable) presumption that the person named in the consignment note as carrier is really the carrier: *Cass. com. 1.12.92*, B.T.L. 1992, 790.

[74] For example, *un contrat de service: Aix 15.1.88*, B.T. 1988.276.

[75] *Cass. 22.11.88*, B.T. 1989.209, applying Art. 41. Also in this sense: Pesce, Theunis, p. 11.

[76] *T.C. Brussels 12.2.77*, (1978) 13 E.T.L. 285. In Belgium a distinction is drawn between *un commissionnaire de transport*, who is seen as a carrier whether the actual carrier or not, and *un commissionnaire-expéditeur*, who is not a carrier, but whose function (*cf.* liability) is like that of a traditional forwarder in England: Putzeys, paras. 69–70. The position in Holland is similar to that in Belgium: Haak, p. 65. On the role of the *commissionnaire de transport* in France, see B.T. 1990.87.

[77] At 289. *Paris 27.6.79*, B.T. 1979.440; *Paris 10.5.78*, B.T. 1979.157; *Paris 24.11.78*, B.T. 1979.137; *Cass. Belge 17.9.87* (1988) 23 E.T.L. 201, 203. Likewise *Amsterdam 6.1.66*, (1969) 4 E.T.L. 151 in which the court looked closely at the wording of the agent's receipt, as well as at the agent's advertising material and at the terms of correspondence between the parties.

[78] *Brussels 23.12.71*, (1972) 7 E.T.L. 865. Also in this sense *Brussels 24.1.69*, (1969) 4 E.T.L. 943.

[79] *Brussels 19.10.72*, (1973) 8 E.T.L. 503. Weerdt (1989) 24 E.T.L. 523, para. 71.

[80] At 507. See also *Cass. Belge 17.9.87* (1988) 23 E.T.L. 201, 204.

although the general conditions of Belgian forwarding agents (*expéditeurs*) were printed on the agents' notepaper, that was not decisive, as it did not show that the customer had agreed to the conditions.

10a(*ii*). Arrangements

In deciding that the defendants in *Tetroc*[81] were carriers bound by the CMR, the judge was impressed by the fact that "the defendants did not tell the plaintiffs . . . what arrangements they had made on their behalf".[82] Nonetheless, a contract which contains a stipulation concerning the kind of vehicle to be used, is likely to be seen as a contract of carriage.[83]

10a(*iii*). Charges

Again, in deciding that the defendants in *Tetroc*[84] were carriers, the court was impressed by the fact that they charged an all-in fee.[85] In *Elektronska v. Transped*, the practice was "to agree different freights with the actual carrier on the one hand and the goods' owner on the other, making a profit which was the difference between the two freights". The court observed that this "is a

---

[81] *Tetroc v. Cross-Con (International)* [1981] 1 Lloyd's Rep. 192, above, para. 9a(*i*).

[82] At 198. See also in this sense: *Brussels 19.10.72* (1973) 8 E.T.L. 503, 507–508; *T.C. Genoa 27.9.88*, (1989) 14 E.T.L. 70. In *Brussels 24.1.69* (1969) 4 E.T.L. 937, 940, 1970 U.L.C. 17, 18 the court said, holding that the respondent was liable as a carrier: "The respondent, who holds himself out as one who arranges daily transport services by road between Paris and Antwerp and who stipulates general conditions in which there is more about transport than about forwarding matters, not only did not tell (the customer) that he did not undertake transport commissions himself, but also sent an invoice for 'transport freight' to the customer, as well as all types of other charges to do with transport." *cf.* Muth/Glöckner, p. 90.

[83] *O.L.G. Munich 5.7.89*, TranspR 1990.16.

[84] *Tetroc v. Cross-Con (International)* [1981] 1 Lloyd's Rep. 192, 195. *cf. Texas Instruments* above, n. 62 at 152.

[85] This factor was also important in *The Hague 17.5.68* (1968) 3 E.T.L. 1227; *Brussels 24.1.69*, 1970 U.L.C. 17; *Vestre Landsret 8.7.69*, 1971, U.L.C. 291, 295; *O.L.G. Bremen 12.2.76*, VersR 1976.584; *O.L.G. Frankfurt 20.1.81*, VersR 1981.1131; *OGH 7.11.81*, Stra GüV 1984/3 p. 10, 11; *OGH 25.4.84*, Greiter 223, 227–228; *O.L.G. Hamm 14.11.85*, TranspR 1986.77; *Cass. Belge 17.9.87* (1988) 23 E.T.L. 201, 204; *O.L.G. Hamburg 18.5.89*, TranspR 1990.188; *O.L.G. Munich 5.7.89*, TranspR 1990.16; *O.G.H. 14.7.93*, TranspR 1994.189. Also in this sense: Pesce, Theunis, pp. 10–12.

In Germany the HGB para. 413 provides that a forwarder who agrees a fixed sum (*Fixkostenspediteur*) with the consignor for the entire transport is treated as the carrier, and thus subject to the CMR: *B.G.H. 5.6.81* (1982) 17 E.T.L. 301; *B.G.H. 21.11.75*, VersR 1976.434; *O.L.G. Munich 12.4.90*, TranspR 1990.280; *O.L.G. Munich 23.7.96*, TranspR 1997.33. Koller, Art. 1, 3.

cf. Amsterdam 6.1.66, (1969) 4 E.T.L. 151, 160–161. Haak (p. 66) argues that in Holland the charge factor is not of "determinative significance". See also *Brussels 23.6.66* (1967) 2 E.T.L. 1006.

typical contract and sub-contract situation and would need very clear evidence to make it reconcilable with an agency".[86] By contrast, if in a proper account the person could charge the customer only the amount paid to the actual carrier, plus a distinct amount as (agency) fee, the person is a forwarder.[87]

10a(*iv*). Proof

If a claimant wishes to establish liability under the CMR, it is for the claimant to show that the CMR applies[88] and, therefore, that the defendant has made a contract of carriage within the meaning of Article 1.1; this conforms to the usual burden of proof in contracting states. Fearing that it might become an automatic defence to assert status as a forwarding agent or freight forwarder and that this defence might be difficult for a claimant to dismantle, some Belgian courts have suggested that the onus should be on the defendant, in what is otherwise a CMR case, to prove that they have not made a contract of carriage.[89] This development seems mistaken. First, it finds no support in the CMR itself. Secondly, it exaggerates the difficulties of proof faced by the claimant. If the claimant had to show that the defendant carried on the business of carrier on a regular basis, it might be difficult indeed, but it is not so. The cases referred to above show that what is required of the claimant is to show that the defendant purported to be a carrier in the particular case and with the particular claimant. That, he should be able to do.

10b. The transportation contract

In *Evans & Sons (Portsmouth) v. Andrea Merzario*[90] a case of multimodal transport in which the dispute concerned the sea stage, Kerr J. said: "The defendants were not carriers or any other type of bailee in relation to the sea carriage, but merely transportation contractors. The sea carriage was merely one incident of the contract as a whole which they properly arranged as transportation contractors." By reference to this case the transportation

---

[86] [1986] 1 Lloyd's Rep. 49, 52, *per* Hobhouse J. Also in this sense: *Harris (Harella) Ltd v. Continental Express* [1961] 1 Lloyd's Rep. 251, 259, *per* Paull J.; *Davis (Metal Brokers) v. Gilyott & Scott* [1975] 2 Lloyd's Rep. 422, 424–425, *per* Donaldson J.; *Zima v. m/v Roman Pazinski* 493 F. Supp. 268, 273 (S.D. N.Y., 1980). Porter, VaJ.Int.Law. 171, 184 *et seq.* (1984). This element has also been influential in a wider context, for instance to distinguish one who sells as principal from one who sells as agent; *Re Nevill, ex p. White* (1871) 6 Ch.App. 397.

[87] *Marston Excelsior v. Arbuckle, Smith & Co.* [1971] 2 Lloyd's Rep. 306, 310, *per* Lord Denning M.R., C.A.

[88] *Rb. Antwerp 27.2.67*, (1968) 3 E.T.L. 1244; *Cass. 5.2.85*, B.T. 1986.350.

[89] Libouton, para. 7. For a similar onus on the "carrier" who alleges that the contract is one of hire: *Cass. 5.2.85*, B.T. 1986.350.

[90] [1976] 2 All E.R. 930, C.A.

contractor has been identified by one writer[91] as a category of person, not altogether new but yet distinct from that of forwarder or carrier. The transportation contractor, it is said, does not have the liability of a carrier, but is liable for loss or damage to goods, if it "was in some way due to a breach of his contract to procure carriage".[92] But in *Evans* this person was little more than a forwarder acting in relation to multimodal transport. According to the record of the evidence, the defendants carried on "business in London as forwarding agents and carriers" and, although what counts is a person's role in the particular contract,[93] on appeal in that case Lord Denning M.R. simply referred to them as "forwarding agents".[94] However, Roskill L.J., having begun to describe the defendants as if they were forwarders,[95] continued in different terms[96]: "The work which they do is performed by them through many sub-contractors; the particular sub-contractors who carried this container. . . were shipowners known as EUR." Thus, in his view the defendants performed contractual work through carriers, but were not themselves (actual) carriers. While true as a description of what actually happened, it is submitted that in law, if the work that they performed through other persons was the international carriage of goods by road, work that they were contractually obliged to perform, the defendants were carriers: whatever their title, for the purpose of the CMR it is the work promised that counts. Hence, if the promise is one of carriage, the contractor is a carrier, even though the operation is sub-contracted to other carriers.[97]

10c. Vehicle hire

The contract for the carriage of goods by road has been distinguished from a contract to hire a vehicle and driver, to which the CMR does not apply.[98]

In France, courts have looked, first, to the nature of the documents[99] and, then, to the kind of remuneration. They have held that to provide for payment according to the distance covered

[91] Holloway, 17 J.M.L.C. 243, 248 (1986). A decision in this sense, *Rb Amsterdam 5.12.79*, S. & S. 1980.96, is reported by Haak, p. 77.
[92] At 252.
[93] Above, para. 10a(*i*).
[94] [1976] 2 All E.R. 930, 932.
[95] At 934: "The defendants are not carriers; they are forwarding contractors who arranged for the transport of goods, in this case from Milan, by rail no doubt by the Rhine Valley to Rotterdam and thence by sea to this country."
[96] *ibid.*
[97] See *Ulster-Swift v. Taunton Meat Haulage* [1977] 1 Lloyd's Rep. 346, C.A., above, para. 10a and cases there cited.
[98] *Cass. com. 17.12.96*, B.T.L. 1997.19.
[99] Chao and de Fos Colette, B.T. 1986.340, 341; Tilche B.T.L. 1992.798 and B.T.L. 1993.114. Haak, p. 81.

points to a contract of hire,[1] whereas to deliver goods for a fixed charge (and within an agreed time) is transport.[2] But, to operate a vehicle in the colours and markings of the sender, which suggests hire, is, it has been held,[3] perfectly consistent with a contract of carriage. The decisive question must be whether the contract fits the description in Article 1 of the CMR; in particular, whether it contains a "place designated for delivery" in a country different from that in which the goods are to be taken over. In cases of doubt, there is presumed to be a contract of carriage, it being for the owner of the vehicle to prove that the contract was really one of hire and thus not subject to the CMR.[4]

In Austria, the feature of a hire contract (*Lohnfuhrvertrag*) is that a manned vehicle is put at the disposal of the hirer,[5] who gives directions as to what it carries and where it goes,[6] but here too the way in which charges are assessed has some importance.[7]

In England, the court might be tempted to make the distinction between hire and CMR carriage by analogy with that between voyage charters and time charters; this is probably unsafe.[8] On the one hand, the CMR contract gives the sender a degree of commercial control over the movement of the vehicle,[9] which is not found in the typical voyage charter; on the other hand, a time charter may be a trip time charter.[10] However, in so far as the decisive difference is the kind of payment (periodical hire), the analogy may be of assistance. More helpful, perhaps, is the distinction drawn in respect of "owner-drivers", between a contract of carriage and a contract of service in English law.[11]

If the contact is one of hire, the CMR does not apply and the liability of the owner of the vehicle is less strict,[12] for example in

---

[1] *cf. Cass. 13.10.80*, B.T. 1980.598.

[2] *Aix 15.1.88*, B.T. 1988.276.

[3] *Paris 22.2.80*, B.T. 1980.239.

[4] *Cass. 5.2.85*, B.T. 1986.350.

[5] In this sense in Belgium: *Rb Antwerp 28.1.85*, 1986 U.L.R. II 624, affirmed on other grounds: *Antwerp 15.3.89* (1989) 24 E.T.L. 574. Also, Putzeys as regards *l'affrètement* (para. 45) and *la location de véhicule avec équipage* (para. 62).

[6] *OGH 8.9.83*, (1985) 20 E.T.L. 282, 287. Herber, Art. 1, 42; Koller, Art. 1, 3. Also in this sense: Pesce, Theunis p. 11, for whom the end pursued (*causa*) in the hire contract is the availability of transportation with a vehicle in suitable condition.

[7] Thus a standing charge plus 12 schillings per kilometre indicated a contract of hire: *OGH 8.9.83*, (1985) 20 E.T.L. 282, 287.

[8] In the case of road transport the distinction is less clear: Putzeys, para. 43.

[9] Below, para. 32.

[10] Wilford, Coghlin, Healy and Kimball, *Time Charters* (4th ed., London, 1995) p. 531.

[11] Below, para. 49.

[12] The "Contrat type de location d'un véhicule industriel avec conducteur pour le transport routier de marchandises" was brought into being by Décret du 14.3.1986. For commentary see Chao and de Fos Colette in B.T. 1986.340.

Whereas the carrier undertakes *une obligation de résultat*, the charter contract gives rise to *une obligation de moyens*: Putzeys, para. 45. A further distinction is made between the charter contract, *l'affrètement*, and *la location de véhicule avec équipage*: Putzeys, paras. 62 *et seq.*

case of theft,[13] than that of a carrier under the CMR.[14] If, however, the hirer agrees to carry goods for third parties the hirer's role may become that of a CMR carrier[15] and, as in the case of the maritime charterer, the hirer may step aside and leave the vehicle owner and customer in the relationship of carrier and sender under the CMR.[16]

10d. Haulage contracts

A haulage contract is a contract whereby the owner of a tractor or locomotive unit places it at the disposal of another for the carriage of goods on a trailer supplied by the latter.[17] As regards the present issue (whether the CMR applies to the case at all) this is not a separate category, but is governed by the criteria that separate a contract of carriage from a contract of hire.[18] However, if the CMR applies, there is a further question about the extent of its application: whether not only the goods laden but also the trailer itself are goods under the CMR.[19] If the owner of the trailer loads the goods of a third party, the answer is likely to be negative, the former having the role of carrier as regards the latter,[20] but the overall picture if far from clear.

11. Goods

The scope of the CMR is limited to contract to carry goods. Goods are not defined in the CMR and one might resort to national law for assistance. English law has no single definition of goods. The most developed statement is found in the Sale of Goods Act 1979, section 61(1):

> " 'goods' includes all personal chattels other than things in action and money, and in Scotland all corporeal moveables except money; and in particular 'goods' includes emblements, industrial growing

---

[13] *Cass. 5.2.85*, B.T. 1986.350.

[14] Below, para. 75a.

[15] Haak, p. 78.

[16] *The Hague 5.1.79*, S. & S. 1980.10, reported by Haak, p. 79.

[17] Putzeys, para. 56: "Le contrat de traction est un contrat par lequel un professionnel, appelé tractionnaire, met à la disposition d'un entrepreneur de transport sa force de traction d'un ensemble routier non pourvu de moyens de déplacement par lui-même, pour un temps ou une opération définis et moyennant un prix fixé d'avance ou fixable selon des critères déterminés."

[18] Above, para. 10c. As regards the position in Belgium, France and Holland, see Haak, pp. 82 *et seq.*; Putzeys, paras. 55 *et seq.*

[19] An affirmative answer was given in *Rb Amsterdam 16.4.75*, S. & S. 1975.81, *The Hague 31.3.78*, S. & S. 1980.10, *HR. 5.10.79*, S. & S. 1979.117, reported by Haak, p. 84; *Cass. Belge 2.2.90*, B.T.L. 1992.141. Also in this sense, Putzeys, para. *56bis*, contending that the trailer should be considered as a kind of packing.

[20] Putzeys, para. 57. *cf. The Hague 5.1.79*, above, para. 10c.

> crops, and things attached to or forming part of the land which are agreed to be severed before sale or under the contract of sale."[21]

Other English statutes refer broadly to personal chattels[22] or look more narrowly to "goods in the nature of merchandise".[23] However, Article 1.4 excludes certain things from the CMR, such as funeral consignments,[24] which are clearly not merchandise; this exclusion would not be necessary if the narrower meaning had been intended.[25] Although a definition of goods, such as that found in the Sale of Goods Act, would be a viable definition, as things in action and land are not carried by road, the meaning of "goods" depends primarily on the context in which the word is used.[26] In the interests of uniformity resort to any national notion of "goods" is best avoided, and the CMR applied to everything that is in fact carried by road, except those things specifically excluded by Article 1.4. Moreover, the CMR should be applied to goods in fact carried by road, even goods moving on their own wheels[27] and whether or not the goods have commercial value, except passengers' luggage.[28]

In Belgium, it has been held[29] that containers are not goods within the meaning of the CMR Article 1.1 and thus that damage to containers in which goods are packed is not governed by the CMR. A similar decision has been reached there concerning a tanker trailer.[30] But it is generally thought that goods in any particular case include their packing,[31] as Article 23 refers to the gross weight,[32] and perhaps the same should be true of the container or trailer, if in the same ownership as the contents.[33]

12. Excluded goods

Certain things, which might otherwise have been regarded as goods to which the CMR applied, are excluded from the CMR by Article 1.4:

---

[21] See further, Benjamin, para. 1–077.
[22] Benjamin, para. 1–078.
[23] Marine Insurance Act 1906, Sched. 1, r. 7; Factors Act 1889, s. 1(3); Merchant Shipping Act 1894, s. 492.
[24] Below, para. 12.
[25] Loewe, para. 25.
[26] *The Noordam (No. 2)* [1920] A.C. 904, 908–909, P.C.
[27] Helm, VersR 1988.548.
[28] Fischer, TranspR 1995.326; Koller, Art. 1, 4; Thume, Art. 1, 3. Passengers' luggage is not carried under a contract for the carriage of goods by road but under the contract of passage.
[29] *Rb Antwerp 7.1.77* (1977) 22 E.T.L. 420.
[30] *Rb Antwerp 27.10.71* (1972) 17 E.T.L. 1054, 1056.
[31] Helm Art. 23 Anm 5; Nickel-Lanz, para. 108 and para. 158; Putzeys, para. 891; *idem* in England under the Sale of Goods Act: *Wormell v. RHM Agriculture* [1986] 1 All E.R. 769; reversed on different grounds: [1987] 3 All E.R. 75, C.A.
[32] Nickel-Lanz, *loc. cit.*
[33] See further Fischer, TranspR 1995.326, 332.

"This Convention shall not apply:
(a) to carriage performed under the terms of any international postal convention;
(b) to funeral consignments;
(c) to furniture removal."

12a. Funeral consignments

Funeral consignments include the transport of human remains and of animal remains, if intended for burial.[34] It has been suggested that the exclusion would not apply to a commercial consignment of funeral fittings, such as coffins.[35]

12b. Furniture removal

When the CMR was drafted, a number of categories of exclusion were considered.[36] The main explanation of those finally listed in Article 1.4 was that postal movements and funeral consignments were already subject to international agreements.[37] Removals were excluded from the CMR because it was held that the application of the CMR to removals would be time-consuming and inappropriate,[38] and that special rules were required, which would soon be contained in a special convention,[39] as in the case of postal movements and funeral consignments. No such convention was concluded, however, and it may be doubted today whether furniture, which is often moved in containers like other kinds of goods, requires special treatments.[40]

Nonetheless, the CMR requires a distinction to be drawn between the carriage of goods and the removal of furniture. If the convention on removal had come into force, that convention as *lex specialis* might have drawn the line of demarcation. As no line has been drawn, orthodoxy mandates a search for the intention of the draftsman of the CMR; however, the evidence is that there was no clear intention but a failure to agree a satisfactory definition.[41]

---

[34] In any event, it is doubtful whether human remains are goods in English law: see Benjamin, para. 1–087.

[35] Loewe, para. 35.

[36] Proposals by the United Kingdom delegation, to exclude carriage for military authorities, factory removals, theatrical removals, carriage of passengers' unaccompanied baggage, and of exhibits for international fairs and exhibitions, were rejected: TRANS/WP9/35 p. 2; TRANS/WP9/65 p. 4.

[37] Haak, p. 51.

[38] Loewe, para. 36.

[39] CMR—Protocol of Signature, Art. 2.

[40] Rodière (1970) 5 E.T.L. 620, 622.

[41] Loewe (1976) 11 E.T.L. 503.

One possible answer turns less on the things carried than the operation in hand. This, it is said,[42] was the intention of the draftsman in view of the more diverse duties and skills that might be required of the remover. This is the inference from the French *déménagement* and (although not an official language of the CMR) the German *Umzugsgut*. In France removal is distinguished from transport by reference to the nature of the contractor's obligation, and the degree to which the contractor is required not simply to move the goods but to pack and prepare them.[43] Thus, the CMR has been applied[44] in Belgium to the carriage of household effects in two containers because it was "an ordinary transport by road" and the move did not concern "a removal in the ordinary sense of the word, . . . taking things out and dealing with their wrapping at collection and delivery". However, the type of vehicle used does not determine the issue.[45]

Another possible answer focuses on "Removal", and suggests a change of establishment, thus ruling out carriage in association with a contract of sale or display at an exhibition. A consignment of furniture from London, to furnish an office being opened in Paris by a buyer of that furniture, would be governed by the CMR.[46] A movement of used furniture from a London firm to its Paris office would be excluded from the CMR by Article 1.4[47]; but, although it is argued that the movement of personal effects alone are within the exception,[48] the movement of household furniture for private non-commercial purposes might yet be goods subject to the CMR.[49]

> In *O.L.G. Hamburg 28.2.85*[50] persons with their principal home in Germany sent household items to their second home in Greece. The court held that this was not within the exception because some of the items were new, and had not been part of the home in Germany, and in any event as regards other items, it was not a case of changing dwelling but of moving some things from one home to another, while retaining the first.

---

[42] Nickel-Lanz, para. 16. See also Fischer, TranspR 1996. 407.

[43] Thume, Art. 1, 53; Rodière, para. 232 and cases cited; and *Cass. 19.6.57*, D.58.113, note Rodière.

[44] *Rb Antwerp 1.4.80*, (1980) 15 E.T.L. 461, 469. However, this decision appears to have been influenced by national (Belgian) law, that whether the movement of household effects is characterised as carriage or not depends on whether carriage is the essential or central part of what the contractor has promised: Putzeys, para. 102*bis*.

[45] Herber/Piper, Art. 1, 61; Koller, Art. 1, 10, citing *O.L.G. Hamburg 3.7.80*, VersR 1980.1075.

[46] Also in this sense: Pesce, Theunis, p. 12. *O.L.G. Hamburg 28.2.85*, (below).

[47] *cf. O.L.G. Hamburg 28.2.85*, (below).

[48] Koller, Art. 1, 10; but *cf.* Thume, Art. 1, 54.

[49] Herber/Piper, Art. 1, 64; Thume, Art. 1, 51.

[50] N.J.W. 1986.670. Fischer, TranspR 1995.326, 328. *cf.* Donald, "CMR—An Outline and Its History" (1975) L.M.C.L.Q. 420, 422. As regards mixed consignments, *cf.* Herber/Piper, Art. 1, 65; and Koller, Art. 1, 10.

13. Multimodal transport: application of the CMR

By Article 1.1 the CMR applies to international carriage by road. If by road, carriage will not be outside the scope of the CMR as regards parts of the operation that take place off road, notably taking over and delivery. Further, provided that the goods remain on the road vehicle,[51] and subject to one exception,[52] the CMR applies to a transport of goods which is partly by road and partly by sea, rail, inland waterway or air, whether or not the non-road stage is shorter, in distance or in time, than the stage by road.[53] That is also subject to the condition that the relevant stages taken separately or together involve an international movement of goods from one state to another.[54] Most international and multimodal movements of goods fall into one of three patterns.

(i) If there is carriage by road within state B followed by a non-road stage, for example carriage by sea, to state C without vehicle (whether or not followed by road or rail carriage to a final destination within state C), the CMR does not apply. It does not apply to the road stage in state B, because that stage was entirely within state B. Moreover, although the sea stage was from one state to another, the CMR does not apply to that stage, or to the land and sea stage together, because the vehicle did not go with the goods.

(ii) If there is carriage by road from state A to state B, followed by a sea stage without vehicle to state C, the CMR applies to the initial road stage between states A and B.[55] But, as in case (i), the CMR does not apply to the sea stage, because the vehicle did not go with the goods.

(iii) If, however, in either case (i) or case (ii) the goods were carried by sea from state B to state C without being unloaded from the vehicle used for the initial road stage, the CMR applies to the entire journey. This is the effect of Article 2.1, introduced in 1950 at the request of the United Kingdom[56] and described[57] 35 years later as the "English nightmare":

---

[51] Below, para. 14.

[52] When another regime, such as the Hague Rules, must be applied: below, para. 15.

[53] So, the CMR may apply to the carriage of goods on a trailer from Birmingham (U.K.) to Birmingham (Alabama): Theunis, Theunis, pp. 246–247.

[54] Below, para. 18.

[55] For example, *O.L.G. Düsseldorf 8.5.69* (1970) 5 E.T.L. 446. Generally, see *Antwerp 23.9.75* (1976) 11 E.T.L. 279; *Rb Antwerp 4.1.77* (1977) 12 E.T.L. 843; Fitzpatrick, "Combined Transport and the CMR" [1968] J.B.L. 311.

An early draft of the CMR was limited to carriage by road, but extension to non-road, notably sea, stages was proposed by the delegation of the United Kingdom. For an account of the *travaux préparatoires* see Haak, pp. 94 *et seq.*

[56] Haak, p. 94; Muth/Glöckner, p. 94. Generally on Art. 2 see Bombeeck, Hamer and Verhaegen, "La Réponsabilité du Transporteur Routier dans le Transport par Car-Ferries," (1990) 25 E.T.L. 110; Czapski, "La Résponsabilité du Transporteur Routier Lors du Transroulage et du Ferroutage" (1990) 25 E.T.L. 172; Ramberg, Theunis, Chap. 2; Theunis, Theunis, Chap. 16.

[57] Theunis, Theunis, p. 256.

> "Where, in addition to a road stage, the vehicle containing the goods is carried over part of the journey by sea, rail, inland waterways or air, and . . . the goods are not unloaded from the vehicle, this Convention shall nevertheless apply to the whole of the carriage."

This provision is qualified by an important proviso, which is discussed below.[58]

14. Goods not unloaded: ro-ro and piggyback transport

According to Article 1.1, the CMR applies to contracts for the carriage of goods "in vehicles". Thus, if goods, such as motor-cars, are sent under their own power, the CMR does not apply,[59] although it may apply, of course, if the motor-cars are sent in or on other road vehicles.[60] Moreover, by Article 2.1. the CMR applies to multimodal transport, only if the goods "are not unloaded from the vehicle", by implication, not unloaded for the purpose of transfer to the next mode of transport.[61] Article 2.1. excludes, therefore, lo-lo transport: the movement of goods or unit loads, which are lifted from the vehicle and placed in a ship, train, barge or aircraft.

By contrast, if the goods remain on the vehicle and both goods and vehicle are loaded on to a ship (ro-ro transport), train (piggyback transport),[62] or barge, the goods have not been unloaded from the vehicle and, *ceteris paribus*, the CMR applies.

In this connection, what counts is the initial intention[63] and agreement of the parties. If, without the assent of the customer, the CMR carrier alters the mode of transport from ro-ro to lo-lo, the contract remains subject to the CMR.[64] However, it has been held by a majority of the members of the Supreme Court of Denmark[65]

---

[58] Para. 17.
[59] Haak, p. 94; Muth/Glöckner, p. 90.
[60] For example, *O.L.G. Düsseldorf 8.5.69* (1970) 5 E.T.L. 446, below, para. 81.
[61] Haak, p. 97.
[62] There are not many reported cases. Such a case is found in *Cass. 30.11.82*, B.T. 1983.129. There are no reported cases of the application of the CMR to transport with an air stage, as goods are generally unloaded for this stage. The most common case concerns a stage of carriage by sea. Hovercraft were not contemplated by the draftsman of the CMR, but presumably Art. 2.1 would be applied if part of the journey were by hovercraft: Loewe, para. 53.
[63] *Rb Antwerp 9.12.77* (1978) 13 E.T.L. 110, 119; *Cass. 30.11.82*, B.T. 1983.129, discussed below, para. 15. The same is true of the international character of the journey: it is the initial intention that counts; see below, para. 18.
[64] *Rb Antwerp 9.12.77* (above). Ramberg, Theunis, p. 25. As regards the effect of unauthorised transhipment, see below, para. 30a.
[65] *Supreme Court of Denmark 28.4.89* (1989) 24 E.T.L. 345.

that, if customer and carrier have an umbrella agreement for a series of consignments, whereby the carrier can choose the mode and thus the legal regime, the CMR will apply or not according to the mode chosen by the carrier. There is some attraction in the minority view in that case, that this arrangement should be enforceable against the customer only if the carrier gives the customer sufficient notice of the mode chosen for each consignment.

Unloading ends or prevents the application of the CMR, only if the purpose of unloading is either delivery to the consignee or transfer to a different mode of transport without vehicle.[66] Unloading for other purposes does not have that effect.

14a. Operational convenience: inspection, storage and transhipment

The application of the CMR is not prevented by the unloading of goods for inspection,[67] reconditioning or restowage, provided that they continue their journey on a road vehicle, not necessarily the original vehicle. Moreover, the application of the CMR is not prevented by storage of goods, if that storage is incidental to the continued performance of the contract of carriage. It is otherwise, however, if the storage is because the carrier is unable to carry out the contract in accordance with its terms, a situation envisaged by Article 16.2, whereby at that moment "the carriage shall be deemed to be at an end".[68]

The application of the CMR is not prevented by the unloading of goods from the vehicle, if the transfer to another vehicle of the carrier or of a sub-contracted carrier is made for reasons of operational convenience.[69] If, for example, a trailer has travelled Felixstowe–Zeebrugge–Brussels, where its load is transferred to another trailer for carriage on to Liège, all this under a single contract of carriage, the entire movement would be governed by the CMR. Even if the stage from Brussels to Liège were subcontracted to a local carrier, whose contract with the main carrier was governed by local law,[70] not only the relations of the main

[66] *cf. Supreme Court of Denmark 28.4.89* (1989) 24 E.T.L. 345: transfer of a container from a vehicle to a special ship's trailer, a trailer used only during the sea stage, takes the case outside the CMR.

[67] Ramberg, Theunis, p. 25.

[68] Below, para. 33c(*ii*).

[69] *'s Hertogenbosch 21.12.65* (1966) 1 E.T.L. 698; *Antwerp 8.3.93* (1994) 29 E.T.L. 104.

[70] Libouton, para. 23.

carrier and customer but also those of the local carrier and customer would be governed by the CMR.[71]

14b. Necessity

If in terms of Article 14, "it is or becomes impossible to carry out the contract in accordance with the terms laid down in the consignment note before the goods reach the place designated for delivery", the carrier is then required to ask for instructions from the person entitled to dispose of the goods[72] or, if unable to get instructions from that person within a reasonable time, to "take such steps as seem to him to be in best interests" of that person. To do that, evidently, unloading and perhaps transfer to another vehicle may be a matter of necessity, and in that case Article 2.1 provides that, although the goods have been unloaded from the (original) vehicle, nonetheless the CMR shall apply.

> In *Moto Vespa v. MAT (Britannia Express)*[73] lathes were carried by road, apart from the inevitable sea crossing, from Birmingham to Madrid. Just short of Madrid the vehicle was involved in an accident and the lathes were transferred to another vehicle for the final miles to Madrid. The contract of carriage was governed by the CMR, notwithstanding the change of vehicle.

From a literal reading of Article 2.1 it might be inferred (*expressio unius*) that unloading does not prevent the application of the CMR only when it is a case of prevention (Article 14), and then, in view of the context of the saving provision in Article 2 on multimodal transport, only in a case which was in any event, apart from the circumstances preventing performance, a case of multimodal transport. A literal interpretation of this kind would rule out the cases of unloading for operational convenience,[74] and has not been followed.

15. Multimodal transport: exclusion of the CMR

If, in a case of multimodal transport, typically road–sea–road, loss, damage or delay occurred during the road stage, the CMR is

---

[71] *T.C. Verviers 7.4.79* (1979) 14 E.T.L. 664, 670: carriage Belgium-Rochdale, with sub-contract on the last stage Sheffield-Rochdale in a different vehicle; *Lyon 18.10.85*, B.T. 1986.744: carriage Sarezzo (Italy) Sochaux (France), with sub-contract on last stage Lyon-Sochaux: the CMR governs the rights of the sender in respect of damage on the last stage, although the sub-contract may well be governed by local law. See also Rodière (1970) 5 E.T.L. 620, 624. The same was held in *Cass. 18.3.86*, B.T. 1986.607: carriage by road Condeville-Le Havre, rail Le Havre–Italy, governed as to the road stage by the CMR.

[72] On Art. 14, see below, para. 33.

[73] [1979] 1 Lloyd's Rep. 175. See also *Brussels 19.12.68* (1969) 4 E.T.L. 948.

[74] Above, para. 14a.

applied. If the stage during which the loss, damage or delay occurred is unknown, again, the CMR is applied. If, however, it is known to have occurred on the sea stage, although the goods have not been unloaded from the vehicle, the liability of the road carrier to the goods owner will be governed not by the CMR but by the law appropriate to the sea stage, if the case falls within the proviso to Article 2.1:

> "Provided that to the extent that it is proved that any loss, damage or delay in delivery of the goods which occurs during the carriage by other means of transport was not caused by an act or omission of the carrier by road, but by some event which could only have occurred in the course of and by reason of the carriage by that other means of transport, the liability of the carrier shall be determined not by this convention but in the manner in which the liability of the carrier by the other means of transport would have been determined if a contract for the carriage of the goods alone had been made by the sender with the carrier by the other means of transport in accordance with the conditions prescribed by law for the carriage of goods by that means of transport. If, however, there are no such prescribed conditions, the liability of the carrier by road shall be determined by this Convention."

The actual carrier "by other means of transport", typically a sea carrier,[75] is a sub-contractor from the main carrier, the road carrier,[76] and the sub-contract will be governed by the legal regime for the sea stage. The purpose of the proviso is, first, to bring the legal regime of the main contract, between customer and road carrier, into line with that of the sub-contract, between road carrier and sea carrier, as regards events occurring during the sea stage; and, secondly, to do so on the basis of rules designed and "prescribed" for carriage by that means of transport.[77] The assumption is that liability in multimodal transport will be based on the "network"

---

[75] *Ceteris paribus* the same considerations would apply to a non-road stage by rail, air or inland waterway.

[76] *Thermo Engineers v. Ferrymasters* [1981] 1 Lloyd's Rep. 200, 204, *per* Neill J.

[77] Ramberg, Theunis, pp. 19, 27. Theunis, Theunis, p. 236: while protecting the goods interest through an action against the CMR carrier for what occurs on the sea stage. Also in this sense Bombeeck (above, n. 56) paras. 51 *et seq.*, contending persuasively that the second purpose is more important than the first.

In any case, a difficulty of alignment (the first purpose) arises with groupage. The road carrier, who has consolidated shipments, is liable on the basis of the description or value of the goods in each consignment note, and can recover from the sub-contractor for carriage by sea only on the basis of the maritime transport document; unless the latter enumerates the individual consignments within the consolidated load, the right of recovery will be appreciably less than the liability: *Toulouse 8.12.83*, B.T. 1984.457. Further, the sea carrier may contend that, for the purpose of Art. IV.5 of the Hague or Hague-Visby Rules, the unit is the trailer or vehicle, plus load.

system,[78] and has the obvious drawback that, as the proviso does not apply in every case, the customer may not know in time the degree of compensation recoverable from the carrier[79] and hence the insurance cover that is required.

The person, most often the carrier,[80] who alleges that loss, damage or delay occurred on any particular stage of the journey, must prove it.[81] If there is no allegation that it occurred on the sea stage, it has been held[82] that the CMR applies to that stage, even if the facts bring the case within the proviso; however, there is force in the observation[83] that in such a case the court should apply the proviso, whether the parties invite the court to do so or not. In any event, for the proviso to apply, there are three "cumulative conditions".[84]

(i) *The end of the road*

The first condition is that the loss, damage or delay must have occurred "during the carriage by the other means of transport", during the sea stage.

> *Aix 30.5.91*[85] concerned a trailer of shirts and trousers, which was contracted for carriage from Casablanca to inland Marseilles but stolen from the quay at Marseilles while still in the charge of the stevedore. Although there is nothing particularly maritime about the theft of a trailer[86] standing on *terra firma* (*cf.* below, (iii)), the court held that the liability was maritime because, the trailer not having been handed over by the sea carrier's agent (the stevedore), the sea stage had not yet finished.[87]
>
> *Thermo Engineers v. Ferrymasters*[88] concerned the carriage of a heat exchanger on an open trailer from Aylesbury to Copenhagen, with a sea stage commencing at Felixstowe. The trailer was left in the custody of the dock company at Felixstowe which sought to load

---

[78] On the basis that this is the approach most likely to attract enough support for a degree of uniformity. Moreover, it seems appropriate to some that events which occur at sea should be governed by the legal regime designed for carriage by sea: Bombeeck (above, n. 56) para. 7.

[79] Haak, p. 99. Evidently, the customer may not see the lower level of liability under the Rules as an adequate protection, and there is some pressure on carriers to neutralise the scheme of Art. 2 by insuring the goods on behalf of the customer with a non-recourse policy: Theunis, Theunis, p. 257.

[80] Except, for example, in cases of delay in which the liability of the carrier under Art. 23.5 of the CMR is likely to be lower than that under other regimes.

[81] Haak, p. 57.

[82] *T.C. Paris 11.3.83*, B.T. 1984.74 note Brunat.

[83] Brunat, *loc.cit.* It is enough, in terms of Art. 2.1, that "it is proved that" the loss, etc., falls within the proviso, whether the consequent application of the proviso is claimed by the parties or not.

[84] *Thermo Engineers v. Ferrymasters* [1981] 1 Lloyd's Rep. 20, 204, *per* Neill J.

[85] B.T.L. 1992.281.

[86] In this sense: Herber/Piper, Art. 2, 18.

[87] However, the court also held that Art. 2 was concerned only with the liability of the carrier and did not affect prescription, which was at all times governed by CMR Art. 32, with the result that the action was out of time.

[88] [1981] 1 Lloyd's Rep. 200; [1981] 1 All E.R. 1142; (1990) 25 E.T.L. 194.

> the trailer on the lower cargo deck of a ro-ro vessel by means of a tugmaster vehicle. In the course of this manoeuvre the top of the heat exchanger struck the deck head at the lower end of the ramp down to the cargo deck; the heat exchanger was damaged. The court held that the damage had occurred during the sea stage.

In that case the claimant argued that the CMR applied because, although at the time of the damage, the trailer was on a ship, the trailer was moving on its own wheels, and the ship was stationary and was not the "effective" means of transport. The argument was rejected. There being "force in the submission that CMR was intended to fit in with other conventions"[89] and there being no rule (in the CMR) about when the land stage ended, the court inferred that the land regime (CMR) had ended because the sea regime (the Hague-Visby Rules) had begun.

While it must have been intended that the CMR should fit with other conventions, *i.e.* that there should be a clear and predictable line between them, it is less clear that the CMR was intended to fit *in* with or give way to other conventions.[90] Nor is it clear that the states party to the CMR had any particular line in mind in 1956, as many of those states were also party to the sea convention (Hague Rules) and did not then agree on the point at which the sea regime began. For example, in English law the Rules begin to apply not at a predetermined point in space, such as the ship's rail, but when the carrier begins to perform his duties under the particular contract of carriage by sea, so that the sea carrier is responsible under the Rules for that part, often the whole part, of the loading operation for which he has assumed responsibility.[91] But in 1956 French law had a different rule, whereby the Rules applied partly by reference to a point in space, the ship's tackle.[92] Nonetheless, whereas the general object of Article 2 was to extend the scope of the CMR to multimodal transport, one of the purposes of the proviso was to preserve the scope of the non-road regime as *lex specialis* in a network of legal regimes for multimodal transport, and when it is clear that an event is within the scope of the Rules, the Rules and not the CMR should apply. Be that as it may, the pattern of opinion, judicial and academic, seems to be exemplified by *Aix 30.5.91* (above) and one with which the *Ferrymasters* case is not inconsistent. Carriage by sea as well as carriage by road

[89] At 204.

[90] On the contrary, the further requirement of the proviso that the event must be one "which could only have occurred in the course of and by means of" carriage by sea, suggests that primacy may have been intended for the CMR.

[91] Hague Rules (and now Hague-Visby Rules) Art. 1(e) as viewed in *Pyrene Co. v. Scindia Navigation Co.* [1954] 2 Q.B. 402. *Pyrene* was approved on this point in *Renton & Co. v. Palmyra Trading Corp.* [1957] A.C. 149.

[92] By reference to Art. 1 of a law of April 2, 1936, which purported to give effect to the Rules. That law was repealed by a law of June 18, 1966, whereby the carrier is liable from the time that he takes over the goods (article 27).

under CMR begins and ends when the carrier in question receives or relinquishes custody and control of the goods.[93]

(ii) *Road carrier not responsible*

The second condition is that the loss, damage or delay "was not caused by an act or omission of the carrier by road". If, for example, stowage by that carrier is such that the load breaks loose during a non-road stage, the road carrier is liable under the CMR.[94]

Although the party contending that the proviso applies must prove conditions (i) and (iii) in accordance with the general rule of proof, as regards condition (ii), the onus is reversed: it is presumed that loss, etc., was not caused by the carrier's act or omission, unless the contrary is shown.[95]

Condition (ii) is clear until it is read with another provision of the CMR. Under Article 3 the road carrier is responsible, not only for the acts or omissions of that carrier's own employees, but also for those of the carrier's agents, including therefore all sub-contractors and, in particular, it would appear, a carrier on a sea stage. If so, the road carrier would be responsible in most cases of loss, damage or delay on a sea stage and the proviso would operate in very few: only those cases in which the loss was caused neither by the road carrier nor by the sea carrier, or their employees or agents; for example, in a collision with another vessel which was entirely to blame. Hence, a literal reading of the condition appears to defeat the purpose of Article 2.1 of the CMR.[96] To avoid this result, Neill J. in *Thermo Engineers v. Ferrymasters* construed condition (ii) on the basis that Article 3 did not apply.[97] Whereas the road carrier might be responsible for the driver of the tug-master, a man employed by the dock company, and the road carrier remains responsible for servants and agents acting in performance of carriage by road, he is not responsible for the sea carrier or those employed by the sea carrier.

---

[93] Herber/Piper, Art. 2, 17; Thume, Art. 2, 126; but *cf.* Koller, Art. 2, 8b. As regards CMR on this point, see below.

[94] *Cass. 30.11.82*, B.T. 1983.129 (road-rail). *idem* in the case of a sea stage: *Paris 23.3.88*, B.T. 1988.265; DMF 1898.229 (bad stowage of the goods in the trailer by the road carrier).

[95] *Paris 13.10.86*, B.T. 1986.689.

[96] *Thermo Engineers v. Ferrymasters* [1981] 1 Lloyd's Rep. 200, 204, *per* Neill J. The purpose is to bring the liability of the road carrier to the customer in line with that of the sea sub-carrier to the road carrier: see above at n. 77.

[97] *ibid.* In this sense: Rodière B.T. 1973.458, 461. The judge also said (*ibid.*): "A construction which imposed a wide responsibility on the carrier by road would, in my view, . . . be inconsistent with paragraph 2 of that article."

Art. 2.2 provides: "If the carrier by road is also himself the carrier by the other means of transport, his liability shall also be determined in accordance with the provisions of paragraph 1 of this article, but, as if, in his capacities as carrier by road and as carrier by the other means of transport, he were two separate persons."

(iii) *Perils of ships and planes and trains*
The loss, damage or delay must have been caused by an event which *could only* have occurred in the course of and by reason of the other means of transport. For English lawyers brought up on Scrutton, the obvious temptation in the case of a sea stage is to equate this condition with the concept of perils of the sea, that is, something which is peculiar to the sea or to ships at sea, not merely a peril *on* the sea, but a peril *of* the sea. Whether the equation is correct or not, the operation of the condition depends on the particularity with which the event is classified or described.

For example, in a case such as *Thermo Engineers v. Ferrymasters*[98] it might be thought that the CMR applied because the loss (impact damage) or the event (collision with an overhead obstruction) is not a peril peculiarly, still less "only", associated with carriage by sea. Put like that, there was no apparent difference between collision with the deck head of the ship, as occurred in that case, and collision with a bridge on the road to Felixstowe.

> In *Cass. 30.11.82*[99] a mechanical digger was to be carried by road and sea from Grugliasco (Italy) to Hatfield (United Kingdom). While still in Italy the tractor failed and the trailer carrying the digger was transferred to the railway. In France the load broke loose and damaged installations of the S.N.C.F. at Compiègne. The liability of the sender, carrier and third party responsible for loading the digger was governed not by the legal regime for carriage by rail (CIM) but by the CMR.

In *Thermo Engineers v. Ferrymasters*,[1] however, the judge was more specific about what had happened, and thus reached a different result: "It seems to me that any adequate description of the relevant events in this case would have to include a statement to the effect that a collision with the *bulkhead of a ship had taken place in the course of loading the ship*."[2] Put like that, the event could only have occurred at sea.

Interpreted in this way, the third condition will be satisfied easily in most cases and, given condition (i), that loss, damage or delay must occur during the other means of transport, such as sea

---

[98] See above, 15b(*i*). Also *Aix 30.5.91*, *ibid.*
[99] B.T. 1983.129.
[1] Above, n. 98.
[2] At 205 (emphasis added). The same might be said of *Aix 1.10.87*, B.T. 1988.559: the court applied the Rules to a case of damage to fruit, the temperature of which was allowed to rise during sea transit, because the sea carrier failed to plug the trailer into the ship's electricity supply in order to operate the refrigeration unit. The appropriate description of what happened (the "event") does not appear to have been discussed. See also *HR 14.6.96*, S. & S. 1996 no. 138.

transport, the third condition is largely redundant[3] and, incidentally, the equation of condition (iii) with perils of the sea is unsound.[4] However, the effect of that decision is to widen the scope and promote the purpose of the proviso, and to restrict the application of the CMR.

15a. Conditions prescribed: the application of the Hague-Visby rules to a sea stage

If the proviso applies, the carrier's liability[5] is determined not by the CMR but according to Article 2.1,

> "in the manner in which the liability of the carrier would have been determined if a contract for the carriage of goods alone had been made by the sender with the carriage by the other means of transport in accordance with the conditions prescribed by law for the carriage of goods by that means of transport."

As regards carriage by sea, application of the Hague or Hague-Visby Rules is only compulsory for contracts for the carriage of goods by sea (Article II), which are international (Article X), and which are evidenced by a bill of lading or similar document of title (Article I(b)). Sometimes a bill of lading or similar document is issued,[6] but often it is not, notably when it is replaced by a sea waybill, which is nether a bill of lading nor a similar document of title: below 15a(*i*). Further, the Rules do not apply to authorised deck carriage: below, 15a(*ii*). When the Rules do not apply,[7] it is unclear what law does apply: below, 15a(*iii*).

---

[3] Also in this sense: Bombeeck (above, n. 56), para. 12. *cf.* Koller, Art. 2, 8b.

[4] On the judge's approach, the rupture of a ship's pump used to pump up the ship's main boilers, when the pump became overcharged, is a peril of the sea. However, in the leading case of *The Inchmaree, Thames & Mersey Marine Insurance Co. v. Hamilton, Fraser & Co.* (1887) 12 App.Cas. 484, the House of Lords held that this was not a peril of the sea, for (*per* Lord Bramwell at 492–493) "the same thing would have happened had the boilers and engines been on land, if the same mismanagement had taken place". In *Stott (Baltic) Steamers v. Marten* [1916] 1 A.C. 304 a ship was damaged when it was struck by an item of cargo that was being loaded on; the House of Lords held that this event was not a peril of the sea.

[5] *cf.* questions of prescription which, it has been held in France, are still governed by the CMR: Chao, B.T.L. 1992.281.

[6] As in *Thermo Engineers v. Ferrymasters* [1981] 1 Lloyd's Rep. 200, (above, para. 17).

[7] These are not the only cases in which such issues arise. In *The Hague 19.12.79*, S. & S. 1980 no. 33, as reported by Haak, p. 102, the court refused to apply the Hague Rules to the sea carrier's fault (delay), as this occurred in the period prior to loading which, in the opinion of the court, was not subject to the mandatory application of the Rules. Also in this sense: Bombeeck (above, n. 56), para. 10. It is submitted, however, that that opinion is incorrect: *The Captain Gregos* [1990] 1 Lloyd's Rep. 310, C.A. Clarke [1989] L.M.C.L.Q. 394 and [1990] L.M.C.L.Q. 314.

15a(*i*). Sea waybills

Sea waybills take the case outside the compulsory application of the Hague-Visby Rules. The waybill evidences a contract of carriage and is also a non-negotiable receipt,[8] but it has no role in relation to title, and hence is not a bill of lading. As "*only*... contracts of carriage covered by a bill of lading or any similar document of title"[9] are subject to the Rules,[10] it is commonly assumed[11] and has been held[12] that the Rules do not apply to waybills, unless adopted expressly in the waybill.[13]

This assumption has been challenged by Professor Tetley,[14] whose argument proceeds from the public policy behind the Rules, and from an apparent contradiction between Article II and Article VI. The contradiction, he argues, creates an ambiguity that authorises a purposive construction, whereby the Rules apply to every kind of carriage by sea satisfying Article X,[15] unless excepted by Article VI.[16] The exception in Article VI applies to non-negotiable receipts marked as such for non-commercial shipments, and not therefore to non-negotiable receipts for commercial shipments, waybills. As that is the only exception, waybills are governed by the Rules. Further, he argues, if the only documents to which the Rules applied were the bills of lading and similar documents mentioned in Article II (and Article I(b)), it would be unnecessary to have Article VI to exclude non-negotiable receipts. Hence, the waybill must be governed by the Rules. The difficulties about these arguments are as follows.

---

[8] Tetley, pp. 941–942, adopting the definition stated by the Economic Commission for Europe: "a non-negotiable document which evidences a contract for the carriage of goods by sea and the taking over or landing of the goods by the carrier, and by which the carrier undertakes to deliver the goods to the consignee named in document." The consignee obtains delivery, not by producing the waybill, but by (any satisfactory) proof of his own identity.

[9] Emphasis added.

[10] Art. I(b).

[11] For example, Tinayre B.T. 1990.571, 572; Williams [1979] L.M.C.L.Q. 297; Putzeys B.T. 1991.87; Humphreys [1992] J.B.L. 453; Thume, Art. 2, 116; Law Commission, Report no. 196 (1991), paras. 5.6 *et seq.*

[12] *Antwerp 15.3.89* (1989) 24 E.T.L. 574. See also *Harland & Wolff v. Burns and Laird Lines* and *The European Enterprise* (below at nn. 23 and 26).

[13] This possibility is provided for by section 1(6)(b) of the Carriage of Goods by Sea Act 1971, if the waybill "expressly provides that the Rules are to govern the contract as if the receipt were a bill of lading".

[14] At 941 *et seq.* His thesis has been adopted by Czapski (above, n. 56), p. 176.

[15] Under Art. X of the Hague-Visby Rules (*cf.* Art. X of the Hague Rules), the Rules apply if (a) the bill of lading is issued in a contracting State, (b) the carriage is from a part in a contracting State, or (c) the contract contains a Paramount clause adopting the Rules. Art. X is a unilateral conflicts provision giving the court a connecting factor, which authorises application of the Rules as part of the *lex fori*: see Clarke, HR, Chap. 1, para. 4.

[16] Argument rejected by the Court of Session: *Harland & Wolff v. Burns & Laird Lines* (1931) 40 Ll.L.Rep. 286, 288 *per* Lord Clyde, discussed below.

(a) If Article VI alone determines the types of document (and thus indirectly the types of contract) which were excluded from the Rules, what is the purpose of the reference to documents (bills of lading and similar documents of title) in Article I(b)? To find a central role for Article VI, Article I(b) has to be put to one side. As regards documents, the central provision in the mind of the draftsman was, surely, Article I(b), to which Article VI was no more than a corollary. In 1924 it may have been seen as a complete corollary, but the subsequent emergence of the waybill has opened a gap on which the Rules have nothing to say.

(b) The purpose of the Rules was directed mainly at documents affecting title, which the waybill, unlike the "bill of lading or any similar document of title", does not. It is true that the French text of Article I(b), which refers to documents "formant titre pour le transport des marchandises par mer", is wider and would be construed as embracing any kind of transportation document, including the waybill.[17] However, the main purpose of the Rules was to ensure a uniform minimum level of liability for carriers, less for the benefit of the consignor or consignee than for that of persons, notably bankers,[18] interested in the security of documents in international trade,[19] notably documents of title. Documents of title give the holder the right to possession, and are therefore transferable[20]; they include bills of lading but not waybills,[21] which did not and do not play that kind of part in trade. In the mind of the draftsman of 1924, the references to documents in Article I(b) and Article VI were, it is submitted, complementary and complete. There was no gap, no contradiction, and no ambiguity.

(c) If, contrary to point (b), there is a gap in the Rules, it is a fissure forced by modern developments in the movement of goods in short sea trades, for which the Rules have no catch-all provision. This seems to be the general assumption of the moment, which has prompted bodies such as the CMI to seek to regulate the

---

[17] CMI, Uniformity of the Law of Carriage of Goods by Sea in the Nineteen Nineties, 14–16. The fact that it must be "similar" to the bill of lading does not necessarily mean that it should have similar legal characteristics, but could mean that it has a similar function (*ibid.*). See also Colinvaux, *The Carriage of Goods by Sea Act 1924* (London, 1954), p. 30. *Contra: Hugh Mack* (below), at 383; *The Maurice Desgagnes* (below), *loc. cit.*

[18] If not originally, by 1921: the Rules were based on a draft prepared by the International Law Association at The Hague in 1921, where bankers' interests were prominently represented.

[19] *Hugh Mack & Co. v. Burns & Laird Lines* (1944) 77 Ll.L.Rep. 377, 382, *per* Andrews L.C.J. (C.A. N.I.); *The Maurice Desgagnes* [1977] 1 Lloyd's Rep. 290, 295, *per* Dube J. (F.C. Canada). Aubrun, D.1937.4.1 no. ID; Scrutton, p. 409; Guyon, *Les Transports Régis par la Loi du 2 avril 1936* (Paris, 1959), para. 10; Marais, *Les Transports Internationaux de Marchandises par Mer* (Paris, 1949), p. 14; Williamson & Payne, *The Carriage of Goods by Sea Act 1924* (London, 1934), p. 2.

[20] Colinvaux (above, n. 17).

[21] Benjamin 18–010. Delivery of goods depends not on production of the waybill but on proof of identity: P. & I. International, April 1987, p. 3; Tetley, p. 986.

situation,[22] and the General Council of British Shipping to offer a standard waybill as if the Rules did not apply.

(d) Last but not least, there is some authority for the view that it is not Article VI but Article I(b) that determines scope as regards documents, so that the Rules do not apply to a document outside Article I(b) and do not, therefore, apply to waybills.

> In *Harland & Wolff v. Burns & Laird Lines*[23] there was a "sailing bill" which functioned as evidence of a contract of carriage. The Court of Session[24] held that it fell outside the scope of the Rules because a bill of lading or similar document of title, as envisaged by Article I(b), was alien to the purpose of the contract, as this was "not mercantile—for the goods were neither sold nor for sale—but was limited to the transport of the machinery".

So, the essential characteristic of the documents mentioned in Article I(b) is that they are mercantile documents, *i.e.* created with a view to the sale of goods, a sale in which the carriage document might be required to play a part.[25] The waybill is not such a document. More recently, the same assumption, that the waybill is not a bill of lading or similar document of title, was made in England in *The European Enterprise*[26] and in Holland in *HR 29.6.90*.[27]

15a(*ii*). Deck carriage and Paramount clauses

Unauthorised deck carriage is subject to the compulsory application of the Rules[28] but, in general, authorised deck carriage[29] is not. An exception might arise when authorised deck carriage is the subject of a Paramount clause, a clause adopting the Rules, which is valid under Article X(c). The difficulty about any such exception is that Article X is concerned with and, apparently, limited to the

---

[22] At its conference in Paris, June 1990, the CMI agreed a document, entitled "Uniform Rules for Sea Waybills", for voluntary adoption by the parties to a contract of carriage by sea "not covered by a negotiable bill of lading or similar document of title".

[23] (1931) 40 Ll.L.Rep. 286.

[24] At 287.

[25] *ibid.*

[26] *Browner International Transport Ltd v. Monarch SS. Co. Ltd* [1989] 2 Lloyd's Rep. 185, noted by Debattista [1989] L.M.C.L.Q. 403. In this case the non-negotiable receipt could be governed by the Rules, only if the case fell within section 1(6)(b) of the Carriage of Goods by Sea Act 1971 which, in the event, it did not. Section 1(6) reads: "the Rules shall have force of law in relation to . . . (b) any receipt which is a non-negotiable document marked as such if the contract contained in or evidenced by it is a contract for the carriage of goods by sea which expressly provides that the Rules are to govern the contract as if the receipt were a bill of lading."

[27] See below, n. 35.

[28] Scrutton, p. 430. Achard, DMF 1989.219, 223 and cases cited.

[29] Art. I(c) excludes from the Rules: "cargo which by the contract of carriage is stated as being carried on deck and is so carried."

carriage of "goods" and, arguably, the effect of Article I(c) is that authorised deck cargo is not "goods" within the special meaning of the Rules.[30]

Even if that difficulty can be dismissed as pedantic, a further difficulty derives from the argument that, for the Rules to apply, they must be the "conditions prescribed by law for the carriage of goods" by sea (Article 2.1, CMR), and that if the Rules are brought in not by the objective connecting factors in Article X(a) or in Article X(b) but by a Paramount clause under Article X(c), the Rules are not prescribed by law but prescribed by the parties to the contract of carriage. Hence, it is argued, the proviso to Article 2.1 of the CMR does not apply. Although this was the decision of the French Court of Cassation in *The Anna-Oden*,[31] the argument is unsound. When the Rules are prescribed by law, it is indeed by Article X, but all of Article X. The opening words of Article X, "The provisions of these Rules shall apply", operate as much in the case of the Paramount clause, Article X(c), as they do in the case of Article X(a) and of Article X(b). This was the view of the Paris court in a later case, *The Radbod*,[32] and, it is submitted, that the later view is the better view.

---

[30] The function of Art. X(c) and the Paramount clause is to apply the Rules, not to cases falling outside other Rules, such as Art. I(c), but to cases outside Art. X(a) and Art. I(b).

cf. the argument that, even if a case falls under the Rules, a trailer is a case of "particular goods" within Art. VI, in respect of which the sea carrier is "at liberty to enter into any agreement in any terms as to the responsibility and liability of the carrier for such goods": Theunis, Theunis, pp. 252 *et seq.*

[31] *Cass. 5.7.88*, DMF 1989.227; (1989) 24 E.T.L. 49, rejecting the contrary view in *Paris 13.10.86*, DMF 1988.101; B.T. 1986.689. In this case a ferry from Gothenburg to Ghent met bad weather, and goods (shoes) in trailers on deck were damaged. The road carrier wanted his liability to the claimant to be governed by the Rules, so that he could plead perils of the sea, rather than the CMR which would require him to raise the more difficult defence of unavoidable circumstances (below, para. 74). The court held that the Rules were not prescribed conditions in the sense of Art. 2 of the CMR, so the CMR applied to the sea stage.

The difficulty was of the courts' own making, for both the Court of Cassation and the Paris court (DMF 1988.101, 105) appear to have assumed (incorrectly) that *all* deck carriage was outside the scope of the Rules and that therefore but for the Paramount clause the contract would not have been subject to the Rules. However, it was not disputed there had been no agreement that the goods should be carried on deck, nor any statement to that effect in the bill of lading; hence the contract was apparently one of unauthorised deck carriage subject to the Rules anyway, as it is only authorised deck carriage that is excluded by Art. 1(c), and the Rules applied *proprio vigore* by virtue of the connecting factor in Art. X(a), the issue of a bill of lading in a contracting State (Sweden): the Paramount clause was unnecessary.

[32] *Paris 23.3.88*, DMF 1989.229, 237; (1990) 25 E.T.L. 215: Rules applied to a trailer swept from the deck of a ferry between Gothenburg and Ghent. See also Achard, DMF 1989.219, 225.

The decision has been criticised by Achard (p. 221) for its effect, to increase significantly the chance that the road carrier's rights against the sea carrier will not correspond with his liability to the consignee in the frequent short sea movements between countries party to the CMR. However, as he also points out (p. 224, citing Gaillet, DMF 1972.515), the practical difficulty of identifying in advance the cargo that

15a(*iii*). In default of conditions prescribed, the applicable regime

If, as submitted,[33] contracts evidenced by sea waybills are not subject to the compulsory application of the Hague-Visby Rules, it appears that in many cases, notably carriage across the English Channel and the North Sea, there are no "conditions prescribed" for that stage; so, what law applies? To this question there is no clear answer.

One answer might be that, if one of the purposes of the proviso to Article 2.1 is to ensure correspondence between the liability of the sea carrier under the sub-contract and the liability of the main road carrier under the main contract, the latter should be based on the former, whatever that liability might be. Thus in *Paris 13.10.86*[34] the court assumed that, if the sender had contracted with the sea carrier, he would have made the same contract with him as did the CMR road carrier. The court looked at the actual contract between the road carrier and the sea carrier and, finding a Paramount clause adopting the Rules, applied the Rules.[35]

The trouble with this answer is that it would allow the road carrier and the sea carrier to agree whatever terms they pleased, terms which might not be so pleasing to the sender. It was to prevent this that the authors of the CMR referred in Article 2 to "conditions prescribed by law",[36] and not, therefore, conditions, for example, drawn up by the sea carrier.

A second answer[37] is to apply the proviso literally and seek the hypothetical contract: liability is *as if* the sender had contracted with the sea carrier *in accordance with the conditions prescribed by law* for that stage, *i.e. as if* the Rules applied, which means *ex hypothesi*, and fiction it is, as if the case fell within the scope provisions of the Rules,[38] which would then apply *proprio vigore*.

---

will be carried on rather than under deck and obtaining the consent of the shipper in question, so that the case is one of authorised deck carriage and thus excluded from the Rules by Art. I(c), is such that the problem in *The Anna-Oden* should not arise very often.

[33] Above, para. 15a(*i*).

[34] B.T. 1986.689, 691.

[35] *HR 29.6.90* (1990) 25 E.T.L. 589, 630; U.L.R. 1990.I.457.

[36] Czapski (above n. 56), p. 175; Loewe, para. 56; Putzeys (1990) 26 E.T.L. 107, 108. *Contra*: Theunis, Theunis, p. 256. See also Herber, TranspR 1994.375.

[37] "Le contrat fictif"—Bombeeck (above, n. 56), no. 38. In *Thermo Engineers v. Ferrymasters* [1981] 1 Lloyd's Rep. 200, the facts did fall within the scope provisions of the Rules but Neill J. (at 206) took the fiction one stage further, and looked for any increase in liability, above the usual minimum set by the Rules, the maritime carrier might have agreed in the particular case five years earlier. This inquiry has little to commend it: see Hill & Messent, p. 51; Ramberg, Theunis, p. 29.

[38] The Rules apply to a contract for the carriage of goods by sea covered by a bill of lading or similar document of title (Art. I) in relation to the loading, handling, stowage, carriage, custody, care and discharge of the goods (Art. II), with certain (mostly geographical) connecting factors stated (Art. X), except non-commercial shipments of particular goods (Art. VI).

In essence, this is the answer suggested in the first edition of this book,[39] and is based on an analogy with the commonplace model of a reference to foreign law minus the conflicts rules of that legal system. It will be recalled that the scope provisions of uniform law have been described as unilateral conflicts rules[40]; that, in the case of the Rules, once a case has been characterised as falling within the scope provisions of the Rules, the rest of the Rules, the "conditions prescribed by law" for carriage by sea,[41] govern the case. A voluntary reference (Paramount clause) to the law of state A is generally a reference to the substantive rules of that legal system, its conflicts rules excluded. So it is with Article 2 of the CMR, which, in the case of a sea stage, contains a reference to the substantive rules of the Hague or Hague-Visby Rules, whether the actual facts come within the scope provisions of the Rules, especially a bill of lading, etc. (Article I(b)) issued in a state party to the rules (Article X(a)), or not.[42]

> In *HR 29.6.1990*[43] Volvo sent engines and other vehicle components on trailers. Some of these were stowed on deck for the crossing from Göteborg to Rotterdam and, during hurricane force winds, the goods suffered considerable damage. The claimant insurer, subrogated to the rights of Volvo (both sender and consignee), argued that the case was governed by the CMR. The defendant (road) carrier argued that the case was governed by the Rules. At first instance[44] the tribunal held that, as the parties to the carriage by sea had used not a bill of lading but a waybill, the Rules were not prescribed by law; voluntary adoption of the Rules did not change this. The case was governed by the CMR. From this decision the case was taken on appeal directly to the Supreme Court of Holland (Hoge Raad). Against the advice of the Advocate-General, the Hoge Raad allowed the appeal. The Rules applied. The Hoge Raad was reluctant to provide an answer which would mean that in practice the Rules would rarely apply. In effect it adopted a solution similar to the second answer suggested here, whereby the appropriate regime is determined without regard to the facts of the case and thus, in particular, without regard to the fact that the parties had used a waybill and not a bill of lading. Conditions prescribed by law, said

---

[39] The suggestion has qualified support from Bombeeck (above, n. 56), para. 61.

[40] Above, n. 15.

[41] A reference not to the scope provisions but to the substantive provisions of the Rules is, it is submitted, a more comfortable reading of the words, "conditions prescribed by law *for* the carriage of goods" by sea (emphasis added), which, moreover, sits more easily with Art. II of the Rules: ". . . under every contract of carriage of goods by sea", as defined in Arts. I and X, "the carrier . . . shall be subject to the responsibilities and liabilities, and entitled to the rights and immunities hereinafter set forth". It is the latter that are the "conditions prescribed by law".

[42] Herber/Piper, Art. 2, 22. *cf.* Benjamin, para. 21–058 which looks for the fictional contract, but whose search is heavily handicapped by the premise that the hypothesis can only be applied by satisfying the scope provisions of the Rules.

[43] (1990) 25 E.T.L. 589; TranspR 1991.132.

[44] *Rb Amsterdam 18.11.87* (1990) 25 E.T.L. 251.

the court, meant simply the appropriate uniform law (not for the particular transport that took place) but for that mode of transport, in this case international carriage by sea.[45] Accordingly, the CMR gave way in this case to the version of the Rules in force in Göteborg (Sweden).

This answer is a clear answer, but does not fully serve the purpose of the proviso in Article 2.1. It ensures that the sea stage is subject to a regime tailored for carriage by sea, but does not ensure an alignment between the regimes governing main contract and sub-contract. A further objection[46] is that the court may be unable to identify the law prescribed for the sea stage. For an English court, the only regime, described by the French text of Article 2 as *les dispositions impératives de la loi*, is found in the Rules; however, for other courts, such as those in Belgium,[47] the answer may be less clear.

A third answer proceeds from the general perspective that the proviso is an exception[48] to the main rule in Article 2.1, to be strictly construed, and that the CMR applies unless a case falls clearly within the proviso. If not, the CMR governs the non-road stage.[49] This was the solution adopted by the court below but rejected in *HR 29.6.90* (above). One difficulty about this argument is that, although the proviso may be an exception, the applicability of the conditions prescribed, such as the Rules, is not a condition of the scope of the exception, but a consequence of the exception, and should not therefore be strictly construed.

The third answer finds support in the French text[50] of the CMR: "the conditions prescribed by law for the carriage of goods by that means of transport" are translated as "les dispositions *impératives* de la loi concernant le transport de marchandises par le mode de transport autre que la route",[51] suggesting more clearly than the English version a reference to law that is compulsory,[52] and hence to the CIM, the Hague-Visby Rules, or the Warsaw Convention

---

[45] At 628.

[46] Also raised in the first edition of this book, and underlined by Bombeeck (above, n. 56), para. 49 and paras. 55 *et seq.*

[47] Theunis, Theunis, pp. 249–250.

[48] *Radbod*, *Paris 23.3.88*, DMF 1989.229, 235.

[49] This kind of argument was rejected in *Paris 13.10.86*, B.T. 1986.689.

[50] English courts have been reluctant to look at the French text, unless they can be persuaded to see ambiguity in the English text: above, para. 6.

[51] Emphasis added. This emphasis is also found in a German translation in common use, which speaks of "zwingended Vorschritten".

[52] Theunis, Theunis, p. 250. Note, that, as a matter of the interpretation of treaties, it does not follow, because the French text is clearer than the English text, that the French text should prevail: Bombeeck (above, n. 56) para. 32. *cf.* Czapski (above, n. 56) pp. 179–181, expressing a preference for the English text. By the same token, conditions voluntarily adopted, even those permitted by the Rules, cannot be prescribed: Hill and Messent, p. 52. *Contra*: Theunis, p. 255.

—*when* they are compulsory. Otherwise, the CMR applies. Moreover, if the difference in the texts cannot be resolved, it will be recalled that courts are instructed[53] to interpret the words in the sense which best takes into consideration the object of the convention. As that object is generally assumed to be uniformity of law over the widest area,[54] this too suggests a narrow view of the proviso, as suggested by the text in French.[55]

16. "Vehicles"

According to Article 1.2, "vehicles" means motor vehicles, articulated vehicles, trailers and semi-trailers, defined in accordance with Article 4 of the Convention on Road Traffic of September 19, 1949[56]:

(a) "Motor vehicle" means any self-propelled vehicle normally used for the transport of persons or goods upon a road, other than vehicles running on rails or connected to electric conductors. This definition will have to be reconsidered, if development of vehicles designed to run on both road and rails is successful.

(b) "Articulated vehicle" means any motor vehicle with a trailer having no front axle and so attached that part of the trailer is superimposed upon the motor vehicle and a substantial part of the weight of the trailer and its load is borne by the motor vehicle. Such a trailer shall be called a "semi-trailer".

(c) "Trailer"' means any vehicle designed to be drawn by a motor vehicle.

(d) *cf.* swapbodies which have no wheels and cannot therefore be drawn along the road without being placed on something else which does have wheels such as a trailer. Although some courts in Germany have treated these as vehicular units to

---

[53] Vienna Convention, Art. 33: above, para. 6.

[54] For example, Bombeeck (above, n. 56) paras. 28 *et seq.*; Thume, Art. 2, 106.

[55] However, the legislative history of the provision suggests that the English version is a more accurate expression of the intention: Herber/Piper, Art. 2, 22; Koller, Art. 2, 8(c).

[56] It is intended that this definition should eventually be replaced by that in Art. 48 of the Convention on Road Traffic of November 8, 1968, which came into force for states party to it in 1977. However, a number of states, including the United Kingdom, have not ratified the Convention (December 31, 1989) and hence English law refers to the Convention of 1949. As the CMR refers only to the 1949 version, *semble* that should apply, whether the version of the CMR being applied derives from a state that has adopted the 1967 version or not: Haak, p. 49. *Contra*: Loewe, paras. 30–32.

which the CMR applied,[57] this interpretation has been rejected by commentators.[58]

17. "For reward"

The CMR applies only to carriage for reward, from which the self-evident conclusion has been drawn[59] that it does not apply to unremunerated carriage. However, it has been suggested[60] that the reward need not take the form of cash. This appears to have been the intention of the authors of the CMR, who were concerned that parties might seek to evade the CMR by contracting for remuneration in kind.[61] This part of Article 1.1 has given rise to little difficulty or litigation.

18. International character

The CMR applies, in the words of Article 1.1,

> "when the place of taking over of the goods and the place designated for delivery, as specified in the contract, are situated in two different countries, of which at least one is a Contracting country, irrespective of the place of residence and the nationality of the parties."

As uniform law, the CMR is intended to avoid conflicts of law arising out of the international carriage of goods. International carriage is identified without regard to two connecting factors, expressly rejected by Article 1.1,[62] the nationality of the parties and their place of residence.[63] Implicit also is rejection of reference to domicile and to place of business.[64] Moreover, it makes no difference that one party is state controlled: Article 1.3:

---

[57] *e.g. O.L.G. Hamburg 13.3.93*, TranspR 1994.193.

[58] Herber/Piper, Art. 1, 22; Koller, Art. 1, 5 and Thume, Art. 1, 33 *et seq.*

[59] Muth/Glöckner, p. 91.

[60] Loewe, para. 27.

[61] TRANS/WP9/11, p. 30.

[62] To avoid the kind of judicial amendment that has occurred with regard to some other conventions, for example, the Hague Rules; Clarke, HR, Chaps. 4–9.

[63] Courts have applied this to the letter; see, for example *O.L.G. Karlsruhe 24.5.67* (1968) U.L.C. 289, 293; *Bremen 6.5.65* (1966) 1 E.T.L. 691; *Limoges 2.6.67*, B.T. 67.273; *O.L.G. Nuremburg 14.6.65* (1971) 6 E.T.L. 247, 258; *Rotterdam 27.4.71*, 1974, U.L.R. II. 224, 227–228.

[64] *O.L.G. Nuremburg* (above), *O.L.G. Celle 13.1.75* (1975) 10 E.T.L. 410, 415; Costanzo, p. 7. There is no exact equivalent in German law of the English concept of domicile, but it is clear that this kind of factor is irrelevant to the application of the CMR.

> "This Convention shall apply also where carriage coming within its scope is carried out by States or by governmental institutions or organizations."

International carriage is identified by reference to the movement of the goods. The criterion is territorial, as indicated by the contract.[65] If the contract provides for the movement of goods from one state to another, the CMR applies even though, delivery having been impossible at the destination contracted for, the goods are brought back to the place at which they were taken over by the carrier[66] or most of the transit is inside one state[67]; or the goods are moved by the road vehicle itself in only one of the two states[68]; or the goods do not reach the place intended for delivery; or even if the goods never leave the state in which they were taken over; what counts is contractual intention, whether the intention is carried through or not.[69]

A purely national road stage is governed by the CMR, if followed[70] or preceded[71] by a stage to or from another country, provided that the entire movement is the subject of a single contract. This is true whether the national stage is performed by the international carrier or by a local sub-carrier. But, if the first[72] or

---

[65] *OGH 14.1.76*, S.Z. 49 no. 3, Greiter 40, 42. Putzeys, paras. 232 *et seq.* If a carrier purports to conclude with one sender two contracts to carry one load of goods, the first from Marseilles to the Italian border and the second from there to Milan, this is likely to be seen as a single contract for international carriage: Putzeys, para. 236. *cf. Paris 23.10.96*, B.T.L. 1997.104, in which the carrier signed a contract to carry from Angers to Tunisia but later the same day signed a contract to carry on the first stage from Angers to Vitralles (France); the former prevailed.

[66] *Paris 25.10.95*, B.T.L. 1995.831.

[67] *cf.* the idea of "from frontier" carriage, which is not international: *HR 16.3.1979*, S. & S. 1979 no. 64, discussed by Haak, pp. 45 *et seq.*, in which the transit to Ebersdorf (Germany) began 250 metres inside Dutch territory, and the Hoge Raad rejected application of the CMR. Also *Cass. 25.3.1997*, B.T.L. 1997. 276.

[68] Provided that, in accordance with Art. 2, the goods remain on a road vehicle during the non-road stage, for example, carriage from Scheveningen on the Dutch coast to Haverhill inland United Kingdom: *Rb Rotterdam 3.6.83*, S. & S. 1983 no. 111.

[69] For example, when a consignment from Port-de-Bouc (France) to Jersey (United Kingdom) via Dieppe was stolen before it had left French soil, the case was governed by the CMR: *Aix 31.5.85*, B.T. 1986.740. See also *Cass. 18.3.86*, B.T. 1986.607; *TGI Nancy 15.1.87*, B.T. 1987.565; *Paris 18.5.79*, B.T. 1989.577; *Paris 28.11.79*, B.T. 1990.378. Rodière (1970) 5 E.T.L. 620, 624. *cf.* Fitzpatrick [1968] J.B.L. 311, 317.

[70] *BGH 27.1.82* (1985) 20 E.T.L. 349: Selm-Frondenberg (Germany) to Belgium; *Cass. 18.3.86*, B.T. 1986.607: by road within France Condeville-Le Havre, by rail Le Havre-Sottrici-Vares (Italy); *Paris 28.11.89*, B.T. 1990.378: Romans-La Courneuve (France) to Brussels.

[71] *'s Hertogenbosch 21.12.65* 1966 U.L.C. 119; Saltzgitter-Venlo-Maastricht; *Lyon 18.10.85*, B.T. 1986.744: Sarezzo (Italy)-Lyon-Sochaux (France) under a single contract and consignment note: last stage governed by the CMR as regards the rights of the customer.

[72] *Versailles 15.1.86*, B.T. 1986.741, criticised by Chao B.T. 1986.733, 734, in which the court distinguished a feeder stage from local collection within the Paris area, "une tournée de ramassage préparatoire au déplacement international", to which it applied local law. There is a suggestion that, if the vehicle had not been returning to its Paris depot before heading for Belgium, the decision might have been different.

last[73] stage is purely national and the subject of a separate contract, this feeder service is governed not by the CMR but by local law,[74] even if the stage is executed by the carrier who performed the international stage.[75] If, however, the designated consignee of international carriage refuses the goods and the carrier then obeys the instructions of the sender, given under Article 15 (below, paragraph 33b), to carry the goods on to another consignee in the same state, the latter movement is in performance of the original (international) contract of carriage and is governed by the CMR.[76]

The usual evidence of contractual intention about the place of departure and the place of destination[77] is the consignment note.[78] In the absence of a consignment note indicating the place of departure and the place of destination, other evidence of the intention of the parties will suffice.[79] In the event of conflict between the designation in the consignment note and other clear evidence of the intention of the parties to the contract, it has been suggested that the latter should prevail.[80]

18a. Movements within the United Kingdom

Article 1.1 is qualified as regards the United Kingdom. By a reservation in the Protocol of Signature, the CMR convention does not apply to traffic between the United Kingdom of Great Britain and Northern Ireland and the Republic of Ireland. As regards "(a) the Isle of Man; (b) any of the Channel Islands; (c) any colony; (d) any state or territory which is for the time being a protectorate or protected state for the purposes of the British Nationality Act 1948", section 9 of the Carriage of Goods by Road Act 1965 provides that the CMR may be extended to these places by Order

---

[73] *Cass 21.6.82*, B.T. 1982.427: Nîmes-London-Hull; *Paris 27.1.86*, B.T. 1986.742: Antwerp-Roubaix-Attiches (France); *Dijon 22.11.88*, B.T. 1989.566: Hamburg-Corbas-Vaulx (France).

[74] *Lyon 3.3.83*, B.T. 1983.359: London-Lyon-Villeurbanne (France). See also *Paris 15.10.86*, B.T. 1987.72 and *Versailles 15.1.86* (above, n. 72). The feeder service is also national as regards the carrier's liability insurance: *Poitiers 18.1.89*, B.T. 1990.101.

But if the last stage were a matter of metres, that would be seen as ancillary to the international movement and governed by the CMR: *Paris 14.12.77*, B.T. 1978.289.

[75] *Paris 27.1.86* (above, n. 73).

[76] *O.L.G. Munich 12.4.91*, TranspR 1991.298.

[77] The requirement of Art. 1.1. is that "at least one is a contracting country". *Venice 31.10.74* (1975) 10 E.T.L. 242.

[78] *Aix 31.5.85*, B.T. 1986.740; note Chao; Paris 2.7.92, B.T.L. 1992.639. *cf. T.C. Paris 23.4.82*, B.T. 1982.383: goods were carried from London to Pantin (France) and, after customs clearance and the removal of other goods, were stolen before being carried on to final destination in France by the same vehicle. It was held that the final stage, during which the theft occurred, was not subject to the CMR, being governed by a separate contract from the international carriage, which ended at Pantin, the destination mentioned in the consignment note.

[79] *Rouen 16.6.72* (1972) 7 E.T.L. 1040.

[80] Loewe, para. 47.

in Council, subject to such exceptions, adaptations and modifications as may be specified in the Order. The Act came into operation on June 5, 1967.[81] The parties to the CMR and the territories in respect of which they are parties was stated by Order in that same year.[82]

The United Kingdom has extended the CMR to Gibraltar, the Isle of Man and Guernsey.[83] The territory does not therefore include the remainder of the Channel Islands, notably Jersey. This left the way clear for an argument that a movement of goods between the mainland of the United Kingdom and Jersey was a carriage of goods to which the CMR applied, because the mainland United Kingdom was party and the movement international.

This argument was rejected in *Chloride Industrial Batteries Ltd v. F. & W. Freight Ltd*[84]: Sheen J. considered[85] that the issue turned on the meaning of "country" in the context of the CMR. Having noted argument that the use of the word "country" in Article 1.1. and in Article 31.3 suggested that "country" meant a state capable of contracting with other states, and evidence that the external relations of Jersey were the responsibility of the government of the United Kingdom, he concluded[86] that there was "no doubt that for the purposes of the convention Jersey is not a different country from the United Kingdom and that the contract of carriage is not in respect of international carriage".

On appeal the decision of Sheen J. was affirmed,[87] but with more emphasis on the construction of the relevant documents, the CMR convention itself and the legislation giving effect to the CMR in the United Kingdom. Dillon L.J. pointed out[88] that it would make a nonsense of the scheme of accession, whereby the United Kingdom reserved a power of extension to Guernsey and Jersey, if Jersey were a country which could itself apply independently to accede to the convention. He concluded[89] that in the case of the CMR "each country's dependencies are to be regarded as part of that country".

---

[81] S.I. 1967 No. 819. The Convention came into operation in the United Kingdom on October 19, 1967: S.I. 1967 No. 1683 Schedule.

[82] S.I. 1967 No. 1683. As regards France, the territory to which the CMR applies includes not only Metropolitan France, but also France d'Outre-Mer. However, the CMR applies to transport between France and Monaco: *Paris 16.4.90*, B.T. 1991.13; *Cass. 3.11.92*, B.T.L. 1992.727; 1992 U.L.R. II 319.

[83] Gibraltar: S.I. 1967 No. 820, as amended by S.I. 1981 No. 604. Isle of Man: S.I. 1981 No. 1543. Guernsey: S.I. 1986 No. 1882.

[84] [1989] 1 All E.R. 481 (carriage of batteries from Manchester to Jersey).

[85] At 483, *per* Sheen J.

[86] At 484.

[87] [1989] 3 All E.R. 86, C.A.

[88] At 88.

[89] At 89.

18b. Contracting states

The following countries are states party to the CMR convention[90]: Austria,[91] Belgium, Bulgaria, Czechoslovakia, Denmark, Finland, France, Germany, Greece, Hungary, Ireland, Italy, Luxembourg, The Netherlands, Norway, Poland, Portugal, Romania, Russia, Spain, Sweden, Switzerland, Turkey, the United Kingdom and Yugoslavia.

D. THE CMR REGIME IN OUTLINE

19. The liability of the carrier

Under Article 17.1 of the CMR, the carrier is liable for loss of or damage to the goods occurring between the time when they were taken over by the carrier and the time of delivery, as well as for delay in delivery: below, Chapter 5. To be excused liability, the carrier may plead one of two kinds of defence. The first, set out in Article 17.2, is that the loss or damage was caused by fault on the part of the claimant, by inherent vice or by unavoidable circumstances: below, Chapter 6. The second, set out in Article 17.4, is the existence of special circumstances which raise a presumption that the carrier is not liable for the loss or damage unless, in accordance with Article 18.2, the claimant proves that it can be attributed not to the special circumstances but to the carrier: below, Chapter 7. The special circumstances, such as the fact that loading was carried out by the sender, are listed. If the carrier is unable to establish one of these two kinds of defence, the carrier may fall back on Article 32 and the defence that the claim against him is out of time (Chapter 4, part B) or that the amount of liability is limited (Chapter 8 (paragraphs 97 *et seq.*)). These further defences will fail, however, if the claimant can establish wilful misconduct on the part of the carrier: Chapter 8 (paragraphs 101 *et seq.*). Wilful misconduct removes the limits of the amount of liability and extends the period of limitation.

20. Supplementing the text of the CMR

Behind the provisions of CMR is, first, by inference from the CMR itself, a residual duty of care: Chapter 7 (paragraph 79). This infer-

[90] According to information dated December 31, 1989, published by the Secretary General of the United Nations, the depositary for instruments of ratification and accession.

[91] With effect from July 28, 1990, the CMR also applied to purely national transport in Austria: civil code Art. 439A. See further, Fischer, TranspR 1994.365. See also Haak and Swart, part 2.

ence arises from many of the cases in which (in accordance with Article 18.2) the claimant is able to prove that the loss or damage is attributable not to the special circumstance pleaded by the carrier (under Article 17.4) but to an act of neglect by the carrier: it is breach of the residual duty that justifies the attribution. The residual duty of care appears also as the corollary of the defence of unavoidable circumstances (Article 17.2): only if a certain level of care has been shown by the carrier, can it be said that the circumstances leading to loss or damage were unavoidable. The level of care required, described as "utmost care", is high.

Behind the provisions of CMR is, secondly, the liability of the carrier at common law:

(a) The central obligation of the CMR itself, set out in Article 17.1, is the corollary of the contractual obligation, if not express then usually implied by common law, to carry the goods to the agreed destination on time and deliver them there in the same good order and condition in which they were taken over.
(b) CMR is silent on certain matters, for example who is obliged to load the goods or, another example, the meaning of "inherent vice", and the English court must resolve these matters by reference to common law.
(c) The scope of the CMR is limited to what occurs to the goods after they have been taken over by the carrier: the carrier in breach of a contractual promise to take the goods is liable not under the CMR but under common law. Similarly, if the carrier has undertaken any obligations after the point of delivery, these too are a matter not for the CMR but for common law. In any event the carrier may incur a liability in tort.

All these issues of common law are considered in Part II of this book.

CHAPTER 2

THE CONTRACT OF CARRIAGE: DOCUMENTATION

21. Formation of the contract of carriage

The CMR is silent on the rules governing the formation of contracts of carriage. The court applies the appropriate rules of national law. For the relevant rules of English law, see below, Chapter 9.

22. The consignment note

No particular form is required of contract of carriage.[1] However, Article 4 of the CMR does require the issue of a consignment note, which functions as a receipt for the goods, and as evidence of the contract of carriage, but has no role as a document of title. Article 4 continues:

> "The absence, irregularity or loss of the consignment note shall not affect the existence or the validity of the contract of carriage which shall remain subject to the provisions of this Convention."

In *Rouen 16.6.72*[2] there was a consignment of veneer from Villers Cotteret (France) to Leeds, carriage to be effected by the claimant carrier, who sub-contracted the first stage on French soil to the defendant. During that stage the goods were damaged in an accident, before being carried on to Leeds on another vehicle. The defendant contended that the CMR did not apply to the first stage of the movement because a consignment note was not issued until after the accident, at a time when the defendant had ceased to carry the goods. This contention was rejected by the court.[3]

---

[1] *Lg Bremen 6.5.65* (1966) 1 E.T.L. 691, 696.

[2] (1972) 7 E.T.L. 1040. For an example of an "irregular" consignment note see *Brussels 16.11.77* (1978) 15 E.T.L. 319, 330 where the court applied Art. 4 in respect of an air waybill badly adapted for use in road transport.

cf. the Hague-Visby Rules which apply only if a bill of lading or similar document of title has been issued: see above, para. 15a(*i*).

[3] *Rouen 16.6.72* (above, n. 2), at 1043. See also *Brussels 19.12.68* (1969) 4 E.T.L. 948, 950–951; *Cass. 17.2.70* (1970) 5 E.T.L. 439; *B.G.H. 27.1.82* (1985) 20 E.T.L. 349.

The authors of the CMR considered it unrealistic to expect the road transport industry to issue a consignment note in all cases, and that it was not practicable to enforce any such requirement with penalties.[4] Although a consignment note is not essential, its absence may cause difficulties. First, in the absence of a single document covering the entire movement, a claimant may have difficulty in persuading a court that the carriage is international in the sense required by Article 1.1; it may, for example, enable the first carrier to disclaim responsibility for what occurs on later stages.[5] Secondly, if the CMR applies to a case, the operation of certain of the CMR rules depends on the existence of a consignment note. For example, the sender who wishes to dispose of goods already in transit may do so only on production of a consignment note: Article 12.5.[6] It is unlikely that for the purpose of Article 12.5 the consignment note must be a document that complies with all the features required of a consignment note by the CMR, such as signature[7] and contents.[8] However, it is evident that if a note does not have these features or has not been issued at all, the role of the note as a receipt is lost and these matters will have to be proved by the claimant by some other means. Thirdly, quite apart from the CMR, failure to provide a consignment note may be a breach of the contract of carriage.[9]

23. The form of the consignment note

No particular form of consignment note is required by the CMR but a form has been drawn up by the International Road Union (IRU) with the CMR in mind. Although the CMR does not identify the party with the responsibility for preparing the consignment note, in practice[10] and perhaps also in theory[11] it is the sender (or forwarder on the sender's behalf), who obtains a blank standard form of note and fills it out. It has been argued, however, that

---

[4] TRANS/WP9/11 p. 31.

[5] It may also enable a defendant carrier to argue that the CMR does not apply because the carrier did not know that the movement was international; see above, para. 18 and below, para. 50.

cf. Rouen 16.6.72 (above, n. 2), where the foreign destination was mentioned in a note handed to the defendant sub-carrier on taking over the goods: the court held that the CMR applied.

[6] Below, para. 32. A consignment note is also necessary to raise the limits on the amount of compensation: below, para. 100.

[7] Art. 5: below, para. 23. Generally see Helm, VersR 1988.548, 550.

[8] Art. 6: below, para. 24.

[9] See below, para. 202.

[10] See also below, para. 202. *cf.* Loewe, para. 68, who points out that, according to Art. 5.1, a consignment note must be handed to the sender. However, the practice in relation to bills of lading for the carriage of goods by sea suggests that the formal issue of the bill of lading by the sea carrier is not conclusive that the document is his responsibility. The same is probably true of carriage by road.

[11] Fos Colette B.T. 1987.161, 177; Rodière, para. 336.

failure to issue a consignment note may make the carrier liable.[12] In any event, it seems that the importance of the consignment note is such that refusal by one party to the contract of carriage by road to co-operate in the creation of a consignment note would justify the other party in electing to terminate the contract of carriage[13] or, in terms of English law, to refuse to perform his side of the contract.[14] Moreover, if a note is prepared, theory and practice agree that the sender has the responsibility for the accuracy of particulars in the consignment note, even when entered by the carrier at the sender's request.[15]

As regards the number of consignment notes, Article 5.2 provides:

> "When the goods which are to be carried have to be loaded in different vehicles, or are of different kinds or are divided into different lots, the sender or the carrier shall have the right to require a separate consignment note to be made out for each vehicle used, or for each kind or lot of goods."

Article 5.1 requires three copies of each such consignment note, one to be handed to the sender, one to accompany the goods and the third to be retained by the carrier. This reflects the practice with regard to bills of lading for carriage by sea: the intention was that the consignment note might be used, like the bill of lading, as a document of title, if permitted by national law. However, this is generally considered to be superfluous in view of the relative rapidity of carriage by road.[16]

In other contexts, English law recognises signatures[17] that are printed or stamped,[18] and will probably permit them in consignment notes governed by the CMR.[19] The absence of a signature required by Article 5.1 does not invalidate the contract of carriage, but it may make it difficult to show that the person, who has not signed the consignment note, is a party to the contract.[20] However, in the absence of a note or of a signature, the court will consider other evidence that the carrier received the goods stated in the

---

[12] Mercadal, Theunis, p. 33, citing *Paris 9.7.80*, B.T. 1980.449. The suggestion is that, to take over the goods without appropriate acknowledgment is a kind of fraud or negligence; *sed quaere*.

[13] Loewe, para. 69.

[14] Below, para. 104.

[15] Art. 7.2. *Paris 15.12.77*, B.T. 1978.53. See below, para. 26.

[16] Loewe, para. 49. See below, para. 202.

[17] Including, of course, signatures of agents and thus, in the case of the sender, signature by a forwarder.

[18] For example, see *Goodman v. Eban* [1954] 1 Q.B. 550.

[19] They are permitted under French law; see Mercadal, Theunis, p. 40; Rodière (1970) 5 E.T.L. 620, 625; Rodière, CMR, para. 11.

[20] *OGH 4.10.83*, Stra GüV 1984/12 p. 26, Greiter 210. *Paris 27.1.71*, 1971, U.L.C. 151; *TC Paris 12.10.71*, 1973 U.L.C. 268, 273; *Paris 11.6.74*, B.T. 1974. 319, 320.

note[21] and seek to establish the relevant facts, as usual, on the balance of probabilities.

24. The contents of the consignment note: Article 6

Article 6 lists the matters to be mentioned in the consignment note. A distinction is drawn between matters listed in Article 6.1, which must be mentioned in all cases, and matters listed in Article 6.2, which must be mentioned if applicable to the particular case, and matters referred to in Article 6.3, the mention of which is optional. Article 6 reads:

> "1. The consignment note shall contain the following particulars:
> (a) the date of the consignment note and the place at which it is made out;
> (b) the name and address of the sender;
> (c) the name and address of the carrier[22];
> (d) the place and date of taking over of the goods and the place designated for delivery[23];
> (e) the name and address of the consignee;
> (f) the description in common use of the nature of the goods and the method of packing, and, in the case of dangerous goods, their generally recognised description[24];
> (g) the number of packages and their special marks and numbers;
> (h) the gross weight of the goods or their quantity otherwise expressed[25];
> (i) the charges relating to the carriage (carriage charges, supplementary charges, customs duties and other charges incurred from the making of the contract to the time of delivery)[26];

---

[21] *City Vintages Ltd v. SCAC Transport International* (High Court, December 1, 1987, unreported). This also appears to be the position in Germany: *B.G.H. 9.2.79* (1980) 15 E.T.L. 215, 220.

[22] The insertion of a name in the consignment note is not decisive that the person named is the carrier under the CMR: *Tetroc Ltd v. Cross-Con (International) Ltd* [1981] 1 Lloyd's Rep. 192, 196, 198, *per* Judge Martin, in which the defendant's denial of carrier status, pointing to the name of another firm in the consignment note, was rejected by the court. *idem* as regards the identity of the sender, in the absence of signature: *Paris 6.1.71*, 1971 U.L.C. 149, in which the French seller, sued by the carrier for carriage charges, successfully defended on the basis that the seller was not a party to the contract of carriage, but had contracted it as agent for the buyer in Ireland. See further above, para. 10a(*i*).

[23] In *Rb Antwerp 3.4.77* (1977) 12 E.T.L. 411, summarised [1978] L.M.C.L.Q. 92, the note named Antwerp as the place of delivery from Amsterdam, but the court admitted evidence that the place intended was a suburb of Antwerp, and that therefore the short stage from Antwerp centre to the suburb was international, not domestic, carriage.

[24] As regards the consequences of failure to give information about dangerous goods, see below, para. 73a.

[25] The requirement is in the alternative, even though compensation under Art. 23.3 must be by reference to weight; hence senders are encouraged to mention gross weight in all cases: Donald, para. 202.

[26] By the very nature of the charges, notably customs charges, it may be impossible to enter this information when the consignment note is first issued. A proposal, that the charges be restricted to those payable by the consignee, was rejected: TRANS/WP9/35 p. 7.

(j) the requisite instructions for Customs and other formalities;
(k) a statement that the carriage is subject, notwithstanding any clause to the contrary, to the provisions of this Convention."

The statement required by paragraph (k), known as the "Paramount clause", is to promote the application of the provisions of the CMR,[27] as the proper law of the contract[28] or as terms of the contract of carriage, in the courts of non-CMR states. If the note does not contain the clause, and as a result the claimant receives an amount of compensation lower than that recoverable in such a case under the CMR from the court of a non-contracting state, the claimant may sue the carrier under Article 7.3:

> "If the consignment note does not contain the statement specified in article 6, paragraph 1(k), the carrier shall be liable for all expenses, loss and damage sustained through such omission by the person entitled to dispose of the goods."

Article 6 continues:

> "2. Where applicable, the consignment note shall also contain the following particulars:
> (a) a statement that transhipment is not allowed[29];
> (b) the charges which the sender undertakes to pay;
> (c) the amount of "cash on delivery" charges[30];
> (d) a declaration of the value of the goods and the amount representing a special interest in delivery[31];
> (e) the sender's instructions to the carrier regarding insurance of the goods;
> (f) the agreed time-limit within which the carriage is to be carried out[32];
> (g) a list of the documents handed to the carrier.[33]
> 3. The parties may enter in the consignment note any particulars which they may deem useful."[34]

---

[27] *TPI Breda 23.2.65*, 1966, U.L.C. 98, 102–103. According to *Cass.It. 28.11.75*, 1976 U.L.R. I. 247, and 26.11.80 (1983) 18 E.T.L. 70, absence of the statement prevents the application of the CMR; this is unlikely to be followed in other CMR states.
[28] Putzeys, para. 239.
[29] See below, para. 30a.
[30] Such a term, like other terms referred to in Art. 6.2, will be enforced, although omitted from the consignment note: *B.G.H. 10.12.82* (1983) 18 E.T.L. 32, 39. On the meaning of delivery C.O.D., see below, para. 38.
[31] See Arts. 23.6, 24 and 26, discussed below, para. 100.
[32] See below, para. 58a.
[33] This might include, for example, documents to satisfy customs formalities expected during the transport; see Art. 11.1.
[34] It is particularly useful to record the party responsible for loading and unloading the goods: *OGH 25.9.68* (1973) 8 E.T.L. 309, 315. Below, para. 28. Other examples of such particulars include detail of the nature of dangerous goods in addition to that required for the purposes of Art. 6.1(f), jurisdiction clauses and arbitration clauses; Loewe, para. 88.

Failure to mention in the consignment note one of the matters listed in Article 6 will have consequences which vary from case to case. The general picture is as follows. Failure to mention a matter referred to in Article 6.1 and Article 6.2 is an irregularity of the consignment note which, according to Article 4, does not "affect the existence or validity of the contract of carriage". However, if omissions cause loss, damage or delay, the sender may be liable under Article 7.[35] Moreover, it is obvious that omission may reduce the efficacy of the note as a receipt for goods or as a record of the contract.

In *O.L.G. Stuttgart 24.1.67*[36] grape juice carried from Perpignan to a point in Germany arrived in poor condition. The carrier pleaded that this was the result of the nature of goods of that kind and claimed exoneration under Article 17.4(d).[37] The claimant replied that the real cause of damage was that the journey had taken too long and pointed to the fact that delivery had taken place later than a delivery date agreed by the parties and proved by the claimant. The court, however, refused to attach significance to this date as it had not been mentioned in the consignment note. But in *B.G.H. 10.2.82*[38] the carrier was instructed to deliver the goods only against payment by the consignee, a term which was proved to have been part of the carriage and was applied, although it had been omitted from the consignment note.

The Stuttgart decision caused some surprise,[39] and it is the later decision of the B.G.H. that is likely to be imitated, especially in England. English decisions on the function of a bill of lading suggest that transport documents of this kind are evidence of the contract of carriage, but not the contract itself; thus, collateral terms may be proved and enforced although not mentioned in the document.[40] English courts and, perhaps, French courts are likely to take a similar view of consignment notes governed by the CMR:

In *Paris 12.11.86*[41] Novatrans pleaded a limitation clause in its standard terms for piggyback carriage. In spite of a strict rule of French law, that requires actual awareness and acceptance of contract terms and militates against constructive knowledge of contract

[35] Below, para. 26.

[36] 1968 N.J.W. 1054. Also *O.L.G. Hamm 12.11.73*, 1974 U.L.R. II 212 (carrier unable to recover from consignee charges not stated in the consignment note).

[37] See below, para. 89.

[38] (1983) 18 E.T.L. 32, 39.

[39] Libouton, para. 26; Thume, Art. 6, 34. *cf.* Loewe, para. 85; and Herber/Piper, Art. 6, 24 who mention the decision without comment.

[40] See, for example, *Ardennes (S.S.) (Owners of Cargo) v. Ardennes (S.S.) (Owners)* [1951] 1 K.B. 55.

[41] B.T. 1987.59.

terms,[42] the court inferred knowledge of the term from documents relating to other contracts of carriage concluded between the same parties in the same period.

25. The effect of statements in the consignment note: Article 9

There is a presumption[43] that the carrier has taken over the goods mentioned in the consignment note[44] in the condition and quantity there stated. This is the effect mainly of Article 9.2, which amplifies Article 9.1, and assumes performance by the carrier of an "obligation" stated in Article 8 to check certain features of the goods.[45] The presumption from Article 9 is limited to the apparent condition of the goods.[46] Article 9 reads:

> "1. The consignment note shall be prima facie evidence of the making of the contract of carriage, the conditions of the contract and the receipt of the goods by the carrier.
> 2. If the consignment note contains no specific reservations by the carrier, it shall be presumed, unless the contrary is proved, that the goods and their packaging appeared to be in good condition when the carrier took them over and that the number of packages, their marks and numbers corresponded with the statements in the consignment note."

In the absence of a consignment note acknowledging receipt of the goods, there is no presumption about the quantity and condition of the goods received by the carrier, and the claimant must find other evidence to support the allegation that loss or damage was sustained while the carrier was responsible for the goods.[47]

---

[42] Chao B.T. 1986.357 and cases cited. A decision such as that in *Kendall v. Lillico* [1969] 2 A.C. 31, whereby a party is taken to know of standard terms on past invoices, is less likely in France: *Cass. 24.11.80*, B.T. 1981.74; *Cass. 20.6.86*, B.T. 1986.367. So is a decision such as that in *Thompson v. LMS Ry* [1930] 1 K.B. 41, C.A., that a party is bound by terms the existence of which he is taken to know: *Cass. 3.12.85*, B.T. 1986.367. Again, a decision such as *British Crane Hire v. Ipswich Plant Hire* [1975] Q.B. 303, C.A., below para. 203, that persons operating in a commercial context are taken to know that other operators in that context have standard terms intended to be part of the contract, is not likely in Belgium: Putzeys, paras. 192 *et seq.*

[43] For example, *Rb Breda 16.12.69*, 1970, U.L.C. 298, 303.

[44] The presumption does not apply to matters mentioned not in the consignment note but in other documents, to which it may be annexed, such as customs documents provided by the sender under Art. 11: Putzeys, para. 444.

[45] Below, para. 25b.

[46] Below, para. 25a.

[47] *B.G.H. 9.12.79* (1980) 15 E.T.L. 215. *cf. Limoges 2.6.67*, B.T. 1967, 273, where it was held that, even in the absence of a consignment note, the carrier was presumed to have received the merchandise in good condition. In the absence of a consignment note, an inference might be drawn from the failure of the carrier to make reservations, that the goods appeared to be in good condition; but this kind of argument was rejected by the B.G.H. (above, at 220): Art. 9.2, said the court, reverses the burden of proof, and if there is no note and Art. 9.2 cannot be invoked, the normal burden remains on the claimant to prove that loss or damage occurred during transit.

The rule is the same in the case of a note lacking the signature required by Article 5.1[48]: if other proof cannot be found, the allegation fails, as a note proves nothing against a carrier who has not signed it.[49]

If the presumption arises, it may be rebutted by the carrier, not only as regards the sender but also as regards the consignee.[50] The carrier may rebut the presumption by proof that, in spite of the absence of reservations in the consignment note about the quantity or condition of the goods when they were taken over, loss or damage occurred before that,[51] when the carrier was not responsible for the goods.

25a. Apparent condition

The meaning of the "apparent condition" of the goods has been litigated in the analogous context of carriage by sea, and this is likely to influence courts in England. The apparent condition refers to what is discernible externally on a reasonable examination, "so far as met the eye".[52] Similarly, in France "un dommage est apparent lorsqu'au moment de la délivrance le réceptionnaire peut s'en rendre compte par un examen rapide, mais cependant suffisant, à l'aide des sens dont chacun dispose, éventuellement complété par des moyens normaux".[53] A stricter view would put an unreasonable burden of examination on the carrier.[54] Moreover, the scope of the statement about apparent condition turns on and, in practice, is limited by the knowledge and experience of the person actually receiving the goods, often the driver.[55] At the same

---

[48] *City Vintages Ltd v. SCAC Transport International* (High Court, December 1, 1987, unreported). See above, para. 23.

[49] *idem* in the case of a sender: for example, a seller could deny being the "sender" liable for failure to declare the dangerous nature of the goods sent: *Douai 11.3.82*, B.T. 1982.199 and cases cited.

[50] *TC Paris 13.3.72*, B.T. 1972. 230; *Paris 17.5.74*, B.T. 1974. 297; *Cass. com. 29.10.91*, B.T.L. 1991.735.

This rule is seen in Belgium (Putzeys, paras. 398 *et seq.*) as *une présomption simple*, which assumes that the truth of the matters has not yet been verified by the carrier. If, however, there is *une vérification contradictoire*, the presumption (*irréfragable*) cannot be rebutted against the sender.

cf. also Art. 3.4 of the Hague-Visby Rules which allows no rebuttal against a consignee.

[51] *O.L.G. Düsseldorf 8.5.69* (1970) 5 E.T.L. 447, 466.

[52] In this sense for carriage by sea: *The Peter der Grosse* (1875) 1 P.D. 414, 420, *per* Sir Robert Phillimore.

[53] *Paris 9.7.59*, DMF 1959.680; see also *Paris 3.12.1984*, DMF 1986.287. In Belgium, Putzeys, para. 387: "ce qui saute aux yeux d'une personne normalement avertie . . . La vérification doit cependant être non seulement attentive, mais encore minutieuse." *idem* in Germany: Thume, Art. 9, 9; and in Holland: *Amsterdam 2.11.89*, S & S 1990 no. 298.

[54] *Rb Antwerp 13.10.72* (1973) 8 E.T.L. 330, 331.

[55] In this sense for carriage by sea: *Moine Comte v. East Asiatic Co.* (1954) 20 Mal.L.J. 113; Shachar 10 J.M.L.C. 74 (1978); *cf. The Hoyanger* [1979] 2 Lloyd's Rep. 79 (Canadian Federal Court).

time, all carriers, including road carriers,[56] are expected to have some knowledge about the characteristics of the goods normally carried.

The carrier is not obliged to test the strength of ropes or packaging used by the sender,[57] still less to assess the quality of the goods as such. In particular, the carrier is not required to check that goods have been consigned at an appropriate (core) temperature.[58] However, apparent condition extends not only to goods but also to their packaging[59] and external temperature.[60] Moreover, an acknowledgment that the goods were taken over apparently in good condition implies that the goods appear to be fit to withstand the intended journey, and to be fit for use or consumption at the time of delivery and for a reasonable time thereafter.[61]

The acknowledgment is underpinned by Article 8, which requires the carrier to look: he has an "obligation to" check the goods,[62] which arises when he takes them over, and applies even when loading or stowage is carried out by the sender.[63] Moreover, although the extent of the presumption[64] raised by Article 9.2, in the absence of reservations, goes mainly to the matters to be checked in accordance with Article 8 but not to the quality of the loading or stowage as such,[65] in some circumstances, inferences about the ability of the goods to withstand the journey must carry implications about the quality of the sender's loading, stowage or packing.[66] Thus the French courts have refused to allow the carrier to plead defective packing (Article 17.4(b)), if the defect was such as to have been apparent when the goods were taken over, unless the carrier entered reservations under Article 8.2 at the time.[67] In England, however, Article 9.2 "renders difficult any reliance upon Article 17.4(b) if no special reservation was made by the driver at the time the [merchandise] was collected. That having been said, it

---

[56] *OGH 25.9.68* (1973) 8 E.T.L. 309, 315.

[57] Putzeys, para. 388.

[58] *Ulster-Swift v. Taunton Meat Haulage* [1975] 2 Lloyd's Rep. 502; affirmed [1977] 1 Lloyd's Rep. 346, C.A.; *O.L.G. Hamm 11.6.90*, TranspR 1990.375.

[59] This is expressed in both Art. 9.2 and Art. 8.1.

[60] W/TRANS/SC 1/438 no. 36, p. 9.

[61] At common law: *Dent v. Glen Line* (1940) 45 Com.Cas. 244. In this sense under the CMR: Brunat B.T. 1982. 174, 175, citing *Paris 11.7.79* (unreported), and *Cass. 15.2.82*, B.T. 1982.182, which concerned fresh meat.

[62] Below, para. 25b.

[63] *Colmar 10.7.70*, 1971 U.L.C. 137.

[64] Above, para. 25.

[65] *Paris 3.11.70* (1971) 6 E.T.L. 264, 271–272; *Paris 27.1.80*, B.T. 1970.100; *Lyon 19.3.75*, B.T. 1975.169, affirmed by *Cass. 14.6.76*, B.T. 1976.342. As to a duty to check the sender's loading or stowage as it concerns safety or roadworthiness, a duty which is quite distinct from Arts. 8 and 9, see below, para. 87.

[66] *Silver v. Ocean S.S. Co.* [1930] 1 K.B. 416, 440, *per* Slesser L.J., C.A., concerning carriage by sea. Under the CMR see *Liège 6.5.70* (1970) 5 E.T.L. 716, 723; *Rb Antwerp 10.10.80* (1982) E.T.L. 64. *Contra*: Haak, p. 186.

[67] *Cass. 12.10.81* (1982) 17 E.T.L. 294; B.T. 1981.576; *TC Toulouse* 8.3.82, B.T. 1982.247.

should perhaps be added that Article 9(2) relates only to the burden of proof. If a court decides that it was the defective packaging of the goods which caused them to be damaged, then the carrier is entitled to rely upon Article 17.4(b) even if the driver failed to make reservations as to the state of the packaging."[68]

25a*(i)*. Containers

In the case of containers packed by the sender, the carrier may not see the contents of the container at all. If the carrier acknowledges receipt of specified goods inside the container, he is bound by his statement, but if he acknowledges receipt of "one container", the carrier admits no more than that,[69] except to the extent that something on or about the outside of the container, perhaps a temperature gauge, indicates something about the contents.[70] Exceptional cases apart, the claimant can prove (as required by Article 17.1) that loss or damage to the contents of "one container" occurred during transit, only if the carrier has been required to weigh the container, including the goods, and there is disparity between that weight and the delivered weight, or if the claimant can bring scientific evidence that the nature of damage is such that it must have occurred during transit.[71]

In general, it is doubtful whether the driver can be expected to open a container and examine the contents on behalf of the carrier, unless required to do so by the sender under the power given to him by Article 8.3.[72] At common law, however, as regards carriage by sea,[73] there may be a duty to inspect the contents of a container, if there is (a) a trade custom to do so, *e.g.* in the case of certain hazardous goods, (b) a special agreement to do so, or (c) if the carrier is put on inquiry by circumstances (such as a visibly damaged container or leaking contents) suggesting that the goods have

---

[68] Hardingham [1981] L.M.C.L.Q. 306, 312. See also Putzeys, para. 391. There remains, however, the issue whether the carrier who fails to take steps to remedy patent defects is in breach of his general duty of care: below, paras. 79 and 84.

[69] Schmitthoff and Goode (eds.), *International Carriage of Goods* (London, 1988), p. 70. *idem* France as regards containers sent by sea: *Cass 22.2.83*, DMF 1983.660. As to the note that mentions contents but is qualified "said to contain," see below, para. 25b.

[70] Loewe, para. 97; Putzeys, para. 389.

[71] For instances in cases of carriage by sea, see Schmitthoff and Goode, *op. cit.*, at 79 *et seq.*

[72] This is the implication of Art. 8.3 itself: below, para. 25b. In this sense as regards the CMR: Costanzo, p. 28. It is also the common law rule for marine carriage: *The Esmeralda I* [1988] 1 Lloyd's Rep. 206.

But as regards the CMR *cf. O.L.G. Karlsruhe*, 24.5.67, 1967 U.L.C. 289 in which the court required the driver to enter a refrigerated container and check the contents with a thermometer: this decision was criticised by Willenburg: 1968 N.J.W. 1020, 1021. But the same decision was reached in *Paris 30.5.73*, B.T. 1973.304, 305 and in *Paris 20.11.79*, B.T. 1980.190, 191.

[73] Schmitthoff and Goode, *op. cit.*, pp. 71 *et seq.*

been or will be damaged.[74] As regards the CMR, it is submitted that (a) is possible, while (b) might occur as a "requirement" by the sender under Article 8.3,[75] and (c) would be true as an instance of the carrier's general duty to take care of the goods during transit.[76]

25b. Checks and reservations

The carrier's "obligation" to check the goods, and enter reservations about their quantity and condition is the subject of Article 8:

> "1. On taking over the goods, the carrier shall check:
> (a) the accuracy of the statements in the consignment note as to the number of packages and their marks and numbers, and
> (b) the apparent condition of the goods and their packaging.
> 2. Where the carrier has no reasonable means of checking the accuracy of the statements referred to in paragraph 1(a) of this article, he shall enter his reservations in the consignment note together with the grounds on which they are based. He shall likewise specify the grounds for any reservations which he makes with regard to the apparent condition of the goods and their packaging. Such reservations shall not bind the sender unless he has expressly agreed to be bound by them in the consignment note.
> 3. The sender shall be entitled to require the carrier to check the gross weight of the goods or their quantity otherwise expressed. He may also require the contents of the packages to be checked. The carrier shall be entitled to claim the cost of such checking. The result of the checks shall be entered in the consignment note."

Article 8.1 underpins the presumption against the carrier expressed in Article 9,[77] but Article 8.2 also gives the carrier a chance to escape the presumption when unable to make the checks. However, in that case the carrier must not only mention in the consignment note that checks were not possible but state the reasons. Further, if in spite of a chance to check—thus taking the case outside Article 8.2—the carrier has doubts about the accuracy of the number, etc. the carrier must also say so in the consignment note (this is an inference from Article 9.2) but does not have to give grounds. By contrast with Article 8.2, which limits the presumption against the carrier, Article 8.3 extends the scope of the presumption in certain circumstances.

---

[74] *e.g. Aix 12.5.92*, B.T.L. 1993.328.

[75] Under Art. 8.3, the sender may require the carrier to check "the contents of packages".

[76] Below, para. 79.

[77] Above, para. 25.

25b*(i)*. The nature of the carrier's obligation to check

Non-fulfilment of the "obligation" imposed on the carrier by Article 8.1 does not give rise to liability for breach of the contract of carriage, but affects the onus of proof[78] in cases of loss or damage. However, the carrier may nonetheless be liable for failure to remedy defects that would have been observed, if the carrier had made the checks exhorted by Article 8, liable not for breach of Article 8 but for breach of the basic duty as carrier under Article 17.[79]

25b*(ii)*. The mode and effect of reservations

Reservations under Article 8.2 must be made at the right time, which is the time of "taking over" and hence the time at which the carrier assumes responsibility for the goods under Article 17.[80] To establish the facts, it is important that any reservations, whether by the carrier on taking over or by the consignee on delivery, are made on the copy of the consignment note which is relinquished by the person making the reservations.[81]

If for any reason a driver wishes to enter a reservation about goods being taken over but is unable to enter it upon the consignment note, he should contact his employer so that the latter may take the appropriate steps.[82]

The effect of reservations by the carrier depends on whether the sender has agreed to be bound by them or not. If, in the words of Article 8.2, he "has expressly agreed to be bound by them", he is not allowed to dispute the truth of the reservations.[83] It has been argued[84] that the sender's signature of the note, required by Article 5.1, does not amount to such agreement. If that is correct, it

---

[78] Muth/Glöckner, pp. 108 *et seq.* As is clear in German domestic law, the requirement is *eine Sollvorschrift. cf.* Loewe, para. 96, who refers to it "not as a recommendation, but rather an obligation", yet admits that the only consequences of breach lie in the effect on Art. 9 and Art. 10.

[79] See below, paras. 54, 79, 84 and 87.

[80] Below, paras. 27 and 54.

[81] *Antwerp 21.10.75* (1976) 11 E.T.L. 271, 274–275; "it is appropriate that the consignee should write reservations on the carrier's copy and that the carrier should write reservations on the sender's copy. However, carrier's reservations on the consignee's copy, which remains in the carrier's possession are not appropriate." In such a case it may be difficult to prove that they were made at the time when the carrier became responsible for the goods.

[82] *Liège 6.5.70* (1970) 5 E.T.L. 716, 723.

[83] In practice, it is unrealistic to expect the sender's express agreement: Buyl, Theunis, p. 281.

[84] Hill and Messent, p. 77; Loewe, para. 104. This appears strange to the common lawyer, accustomed to the binding force of signed documents. However, Loewe argues from the CMR: the sender is obliged by Article 5.1 to sign the note in all cases, whether he accepts the reservations or not, so it does not follow from signature that he has agreed to any particular reservation.

follows that mere silence in the face of reservations is neither agreement to be bound by them nor an admission of the truth of the reservations.[85] In such cases reservations would not be without effect: the wording of Article 8.2 suggests that valid reservations may nonetheless destroy the presumption in Article 9,[86] and any claimant must prove by other means that loss or damage occurred during transit. This is disputed, however, and a totally different view has been expressed,[87] that in such cases the reservations are without any effect and the carrier is left with no choice but to abandon the contract and unload the goods.

Whether the carrier has "reasonable means" of checking the accuracy of the information is a question of fact.[88] In the case of a consignment note listing the contents of a container, the carrier's response may be a clause "said to contain" or "STC". The French courts have held[89] that a bill of lading notation of this kind is "une réserve insuffisamment motivée"; and a Belgian court,[90] has held that the same is true of a case governed by Article 8.2 of the CMR. If so, the opinion, that the carrier who fails to enter reservations in the consignment note, when he has genuine doubts about its accuracy, commits a serious breach of contract *vis-à-vis* the consignee,[91] is not attractive, not least because in one study of 7,000 cases of loss or damage, the carrier had entered reservations in only two.[92] In practice, drivers are less keen on making reservations than on taking rest and recuperation. Bearing in mind that, unlike the Hague-Visby Rules, the CMR allows the carrier to rebut the presumption that the goods were received as stated, perhaps this practice is ultimately in the interests of all concerned, and should not be disturbed.

25b*(iii)*. Optional checks: Article 8.3

Checks on "gross weight of the goods or their quantity otherwise expressed" and on "the contents of the packages" are not required

---

[85] Also in this sense: Putzeys, para. 420.

[86] Haak, p. 188. *Contra* Putzeys, para. 417. The Haak view is also that suggested by the analogy with carriage by sea.

[87] Muth/Glöckner, p. 111: leaving unresolved the question, who pays for the cost.

[88] Putzeys, para. 385, suggesting for example (para. 386) that, when packages are machine loaded by the sender, the carrier lacks reasonable means of checking their number.

[89] *Cass. 29.1.80*, DMF 1981.267, approved by Rodière: B.T. 1980.183. Other writers have been critical: for example, Achard DMF 1981.259; Putzeys, para. 416; Mercadel DMF 1982.371, 376.

[90] *Rb Antwerp 8.5.73*, JPA 1973.245. *Contra: Rb The Hague 14.1.81*, S & S 1981, no. 65, reported by Haak, p. 189. Also in the latter sense: Putzeys, paras. 410 *et seq.*

[91] Putzeys, para. 429; Rodière, CMR, para. 19. *cf.* Nickel-Lanz, para. 60: in general Art. 8 concerns the onus of proof and in general the carrier is not liable in damages for failure to check the goods. In England *cf. Brown, Jenkinson & Co. v. Percy Dalton (London)* [1957] 2 Q.B. 621, C.A.: the carrier who knows that the document is false in this regard commits the tort of deceit.

[92] Buyl, Theunis, p. 280.

of the carrier by the CMR, unless they are required by the sender. This is because some members of the ECE working party felt that to require such checks in every case might involve excessive delay.[93] Accordingly, the decision to have such checks is made by the sender, the one who stands to lose most as a result of any delay that the checks might cause, and who by Article 8.3 must pay the cost of checks. The carrier cannot be required to check the quality of the goods.[94] And if, after the checks have been made, the sender and the carrier are unable to agree that the statements in the note are accurate, it is open to the carrier to enter reservations in the note.[95]

Whereas Article 9.2, whereby the goods are presumed to be as stated in the consignment note,[96] refers specifically to matters which the carrier *must* check to satisfy Article 8.1, it does not refer at all to the additional matters which the carrier *may* be required to check under Article 8.3. Does that mean, therefore, that the presumption is confined to the former? On the contrary, it is contended, the silence of Article 9.2 is because a mere presumption would understate the effect of the checks that the carrier may be required to make under Article 8.3. Such checks, it is said, amount to proof which may only be rebutted by contesting the method or accuracy of the checking.[97]

As the apparent condition of the goods includes their fitness for the journey,[98] a carrier, who takes over goods which should have been pre-chilled, must consider their apparent temperature. If the time and the equipment are available, the carrier is well advised, although not obliged by Article 8, to go beyond "what meets the eye" and to check the internal temperature of the goods before assuming responsibility for them[99]; also to record the temperature in the consignment note. If so, what is the effect of a statement in the consignment note by the carrier that is voluntary, that is, a statement not required by Article 8.1 or Article 8.2, and not required by the sender under Article 8.3? Professor Rodière argued[1] that, being a statement of a kind not mentioned in Article 8 or Article 9, it produces neither proof nor presumption.[2] This might also be true in England, if the CMR contained in the Carriage of Goods by Road Act were a complete and self-contained expression of English law on the matter. As it is not,

[93] Loewe, para. 95.
[94] Putzeys, para. 393; that would be contrary to Art. 41: Zapp, TranspR 1991.371.
[95] Putzeys, para. 394.
[96] Above, para. 25.
[97] For example, by showing that the scales on which the goods were weighed had not been properly adjusted at the time: Loewe, paras. 95 and 105; Rodière (1970) 5 E.T.L. 620, 628.
[98] Above, para. 25a.
[99] See Chao, Theunis, pp. 116–117.
[1] (1970) 5 E.T.L. 60, 629.
[2] So held in *Lg Offenburg 21.1.69* (1971) 6 E.T.L. 283, 288–289.

common law is likely to be brought in, and the effect of voluntary statements would depend on the circumstances in which the statement was made and, in particular, the basis on which the carrier made them and whether their accuracy was acknowledged by the sender. In the event of such a statement being reasonably relied upon by a third person, such as a consignee, then it is likely that the carrier would be estopped by what he had said.[3]

26. The liability of the sender for information

26a. Statements in the consignment note

Although Article 8 provides that the carrier should check certain statements in the consignment note,[4] many statements in documents relating to the transport, including the consignment note itself, are based on information supplied by the sender, information which the carrier is neither obliged nor, perhaps, able to verify. These statements include the address of the consignee, the precise description of the goods, the number of packages, when the carrier lacks reasonable means to check it as provided in Article 8.2,[5] and the weight of the goods or quantity otherwise expressed, when the sender has not required the carrier to check it under Article 8.3.[6]

By Article 7.1 the sender is "responsible for all expenses, loss and damage sustained by the carrier by reason of the inaccuracy or inadequacy" of certain of the statements required by Article 6 to be made in the consignment note.[7] The selected statements (set out in Article 7.1) are in fact all of the statements required by Article 6, in respect of which inaccuracy or inadequacy is likely to cause loss, damage or expense.[8] For example, the carrier, who was penalised for operating unknowingly a vehicle that was overloaded, was able to recover the amount of the fine from the sender.[9] The CMR does not limit the liability of the sender: the limits in Article 23 apply only to the liability of the carrier.

26b. Customs documents

Article 11.1 imposes a duty on the sender to provide documents or information for the customs or other authorities. The documents

---

[3] *C.N. Vascongada v. Churchill & Sim* [1906] 1 K.B. 237.
[4] Above, para. 25b.
[5] Above, para. 25b(*ii*).
[6] Above, para. 25b(*iii*).
[7] Above, para. 24.
[8] See the full text of Art. 7 in Appendix A.
[9] *Colmar* 16.6.72, B.T. 1972.320. *Sed quaere* in view of the carrier's responsibility to check the roadworthiness of his loaded vehicle: below, para. 87b.

must be attached to the consignment note or placed at the disposal of the carrier[10] and, in this connection, the sender "shall furnish him with all the information which he requires".

Article 11.2 provides that the "carrier shall not be under any duty to enquire into either the accuracy or the adequacy of such documents and information". However, as the consignment note must contain a list of the documents handed to the carrier,[11] it has been suggested[12] that there is a presumption that the carrier has received the documents listed, if the carrier does not protest at the appropriate time. Article 11.2 continues:

> "The sender shall be liable to the carrier for any damage caused by the absence, inadequacy or irregularity of such documents and information, except in the case of some wrongful act or neglect on the part of the carrier."

An obvious example is loss of revenue while the vehicle is detained.[13] The exception suggests the case in which the carrier causes or compounds the "absence, inadequacy or irregularity".[14]

> In *Paris 27.1.71*[15] a vehicle en route from France to West Germany arrived at the border on time, but was detained there for several days because the documents relating to the goods were in French rather than in German. The sender sued the carrier, pointing out that the carrier had advised him about the documents required, but had failed to inform him that they must be in German. The carrier simply pointed to Article 11, whereby responsibility for such documents was put on the sender. The court agreed[16] with the carrier, taking the view that, if the carrier undertook responsibility for the documents, this stipulation would be invalid as it would derogate from the provisions of the CMR, contrary to Article 41.

The court in that case appears to have overlooked the exception of "wrongful act or neglect on the part of the carrier" in Article 11.2 and, although it was not clear on the facts of the case that the carrier had been negligent, it must be open to a court to reach a different conclusion on comparable facts.

---

[10] It may suffice for the sender to send the documents directly to the appropriate customs post: Nickel-Lanz, para. 55.

[11] Art. 6.2(g).

[12] Nickel-Lanz, para. 56.

[13] *Paris 2.12.81*, B.T. 1982.73, 74–75. For other early examples see Mercadal, Theunis, pp. 38–39.

[14] For example, see *Cass. 10.6.76*, B.T. 1976.402. The formalities referred to are those in respect of import or export regulations or of exchange control: Loewe, para. 113.

[15] 1971, U.L.C. 151; B.T. 1971.115.

[16] At 153.

In *O.L.G. Düsseldorf 12.2.81*[17] the sender failed to provide a TIR Carnet, but the carrier raised no objection and organised one himself. This proved to be defective, and the court held that the carrier had to bear the consequences.

26c. Dangerous goods

In the case of "goods of a dangerous nature" the sender is required by Article 22 "to inform the carrier of the exact nature of the danger and indicate, if necessary, the precautions to be taken". To the extent that this information is apparent from the "generally recognised description" of the goods, it must be entered in the consignment note, as a matter of Article 6.1(f), but the rest of the information may also be entered as a matter of Article 6.3. If not, the sender must prove "by some other means" that "the carrier knew the exact nature of the goods". The meaning of dangerous goods and liability for dangerous goods is discussed below.[18]

---

[17] VersR 1982.302.
[18] Para. 73.

CHAPTER 3

THE JOURNEY

27. Taking over the goods

The CMR contemplates that goods will be taken over by the carrier and delivered to the consignee, and implies that a journey will occur in between, but has little to say about any of these matters, although they are essential to any contract of carriage and central to the liability of the carrier: the carrier is liable under Article 17.1 of the CMR for loss or damage occurring between the time of taking over and the time of delivery.[1] These are matters for the contract nonetheless, but matters left largely to the agreement of the parties.[2] Likewise, if the carrier fails to take over the goods at all, that is a breach of the parties' contract and the consequences are governed not by the CMR but by national law.[3]

The goods are taken over by the carrier when they come into the custody and control of the carrier[4] or, as appears to be the same, when they are received by the carrier for the purpose of performing the contract of carriage.[5] Hence, if the carrier leaves a trailer on the sender's premises for the sender to load, the carrier has yet to take over the goods.[6] But, if the goods are sent to the carrier's depot for temporary storage prior to loading and transport, the carrier has taken over the goods.[7] "Taking over" is the obverse of "delivery".[8]

A contrary view[9] is that control "must be control for the purposes of carriage and not for other purposes such as warehousing

---

[1] On Art. 17.1 see below, para. 54. On delivery see below, para. 37.
[2] Kahn-Freund, p. 302.
[3] Below, para. 65.
[4] Glass and Cashmore, para. 3.40; Haak, p. 181; Putzeys, para. 372; Tilche, B.T.L. 1992.50. A change in custody and control marks a significant change in risk, and hence it is generally at that moment that insurance cover for the journey begins: Clarke (1988) 23 E.T.L. 645.
[5] *The Hague 15.6.79* (1980) 15 E.T.L. 871, 881; *O.G.H. 3.7.85*, Stra GüV 1986/2 pp. 10, 13. Putzeys, para. 369: "La prise en charge est l'acte juridique par lequel le transporteur accepte une marchandise au transport et dès lors en assume la responsabilité."
[6] Donald, para. 42.
[7] This is true, in particular, of groupage, and is implicit in Art. 19.
[8] Below, para. 37.
[9] Hill and Messent, p. 104.

or packing prior to the commencement of carriage. Only when such ancillary purposes are completed will the carrier be deemed to take over the goods for the purposes of the CMR." However, in so far as packing and warehousing are ancillary to a contract of carriage and are obligations assumed by the carrier *in* the contract of carriage, as the CMR applies *to* the contract of carriage (Article 1), the carrier's liability for breach of those obligations should be governed by the CMR. It is the contract, not the physical operation, which determines the scope in time of the carrier's obligations under the CMR, and indicates the moment at which the carrier takes over the goods.[10] So, it is submitted, if the contract requires the carrier to take over the goods prior to loading, and store them for a short time first, all this is subject to the CMR.[11] If, however, the contract requires loading to be undertaken by the sender, the carrier does not usually take over the goods and assume liability under the CMR until loading is complete[12] and custody and control pass.

In *Paris 16.5.69*,[13] to determine responsibility for damage to a machine caused in part by bad stowage, the court looked to the scope of the duty undertaken in the contract[14]: "la formule 'prise en charge sur camion' signifie que le transporteur prend en charge la marchandise à partir du moment où elle est chargée sur un camion; que ce chargement constitue une opération distincte de l'arrimage lequel, *sauf convention particulière* ou circonstance spéciale tenant notamment à la nature de la marchandise transportée, incombe au transporteur." Although the carrier in this case remained responsible for stowage, the court accepted that the goods were not taken over by the carrier until loading on had been completed.

Compare Lyon 5.5.1995[15]: the carrier took over goods from F at place A, then proceeded to place B to take over more goods from F. For this purpose, the vehicle together with the goods taken over at A was handed over to F for loading, while the driver went off for a meal. At this point, vehicle and goods (both those loaded at A and those loaded at B) were stolen. The court held that the carrier was not liable as the carrier was not in charge of the goods. *Sed quaere*: as regards the goods loaded at A, surely, F was an agent of the carrier

---

[10] By analogy with the English solution to a similar problem under the Hague Rules: *Pyrene Co. v. Scindia S.N. Co.* [1954] 2 Q.B. 402, 405, *per* Devlin J.; *Renton & Co. v. Palmyra Trading Corp.* [1957] A.C. 149, 170, *per* Lord Morton.

Also in the sense of the text: *OGH 3.7.85*, Stra GüV 1986/2 pp. 10, 13. Putzeys, paras. 373, 377–378.

[11] *The Hague 15.6.79* (1980) 15 E.T.L. 871. Putzeys, para. 378. *H.R. 6.4.90*, S. & S. 1990, no. 78. *cf. H.R. 22.1.93*, S. & S. 1993, no. 58.

[12] *OGH 3.7.85*, Stra GüV 1986/2 pp. 10, 13.

[13] (1969) 4 E.T.L. 896.

[14] At 903 (emphasis added). See also *Rb Antwerp 4.3.69* (1969) 4 E.T.L. 1030.

A further distinction has been drawn between stowage and wedging, but the usefulness of this distinction has been doubted: Libouton, para. 48.

[15] B.T.L. 1995, 451.

whose custody and control should have been treated as that of the carrier.

28. Loading

As the CMR does not settle responsibility for loading (and unloading),[16] this is governed by national law,[17] in practice the law of the place of contracting or of performance.[18] It follows from what has been said above[19] that, if taking over by the carrier may occur after the goods have been loaded, loading is not necessarily his responsibility. If the moment of taking over (and delivery) may be determined by the contract, so also the responsibility for loading (and for unloading). This is the rule in Austria,[20] Belgium[21] and, perhaps, France.[22] If, however, it is the carrier who is responsible for loading, liability is determined under the CMR.[23]

If the contract does not allocate responsibility for loading, in France, for example, the general view is that loading must be carried out by the carrier: the carrier is the party likely to have the experience to know what should be done and the skill to do it.[24] The exception is when loading involves special gear which the sender has but the carrier has not,[25] or, a related situation, when the goods are above a certain weight.[26] However, in Germany loading is made the responsibility of the sender by statute[27]; and in Austria, where the issue has arisen relatively frequently, the OGH has stated[28] that, if not settled by the contract, loading is the

---

[16] The draftsman considered it unwise to provide general rules, as much turned on the particular case and the particular place: Nickel-Lanz, para. 50.

[17] *OGH 18.12.1984*, Stra GüV 1985/4 pp. 34, 35; Greiter 270, 273. *Rb Leuven 5.4.88* (1988) 23 E.T.L. 493. *Contra*: Putzeys, para. 792, adopting the view of Loewe, para. 161.

[18] Nossovitch B.T. 1982.102, 103.

[19] Para. 27.

[20] *OGH 25.9.68*, Greiter 19, 24; *OGH 29.4.82*, TranspR 1984.105, Greiter 151, 153; *OGH 14.9.82*, SZ 55 no. 123, TranspR 1984.195, Greiter 174, 178; *OGH 8.10.1984*, Stra GüV 1985/6 p. 28, Greiter 239, 242. *OGH 18.12.1984*, Stra GüV 1985/4 pp. 34, 35, Greiter 270, 274.

[21] *Brussels 17.12.84*, (1985) 20 E.T.L. 354. Responsibility remains with the party concerned, whether the operation is actually carried out by that party's servants or agents or those of the other party to the contract of carriage: *Brussels 13.1.72* (1972) 7 E.T.L. 585; *TC Brussels 26.10.72* (1973) 8 E.T.L. 516. *cf. T. Civ. Charleroi 1.10.68*, 1969 U.L.C. 327. Putzeys, para. 793.

[22] Nossovitch B.T. 1982.102, 103.

[23] *O.L.G. Hamm 14.11.85*, TranspR 1986.77, VersR 1987.609.

[24] Rodière (1970) 5 E.T.L. 620, 630–631; Nossovitch B.T. 1982.102, 103. It is the same in Belgium and Spain: Rodière CMR, para. 27.

[25] *T. Civ. Charleroi 1.10.68*, quoted below, n. 31.

[26] Nossovitch B.T. 1982.102, 103.

[27] Art. 17 KVO.

[28] *OGH 21.3.77*, SZ 50 no. 43, TranspR 1982.111, 1978 U.L.R. II 292, 297, Greiter 50, 53; *OGH 2.9.87*, 1988 U.L.R. II 724.

responsibility of the sender. More recent statements by the court[29] have been more flexible and point to the party who, bearing in mind the kind of goods and the kind of vehicle, is best qualified to be responsible for loading; only if doubt remains is loading the responsibility of the sender.[30] In any event, a distinction has been drawn in some cases between loading and stowage: even when loading is to be carried out by the sender, stowage remains the responsibility of the carrier.[31]

The importance of the question arises from the special risk in Article 17.4(c)[32] whereby, if loading is by the sender and the loss or damage could have been caused by the operation of loading, it is for the sender to prove that it was not so caused. However, the connection is disputed by some writers, who argue[33] that for the purpose of Article 17.4(c) the question is not who was legally responsible for loading but who actually did it; or if both did it, who was in charge of the operation.[34]

29. Sub-contracting

The contract of carriage may contain a term permitting the carrier to sub-contract the whole or part of the journey. If not, permission will usually be implied, unless the terms of the contract forbid it or the nature of the contract suggests otherwise. The CMR is silent on this point which will be determined by national law.[35]

---

[29] *OGH 3.7.1985*, Stra GüV 1986/2 pp. 10, 13. See also in this sense *OGH 21.3.1977*, TranspR 1982.111, Greiter 50, 53; *OGH 8.10.1984*, Stra GüV 1985/6 p. 28, Greiter 239, 242; *OGH 18.12.1984*, Stra GüV 1985/4 pp. 34, 35, Greiter 270, 274; *OGH 21.2.1985*, Stra GüV 1985/10 pp. 18, 19, Greiter 285, 288.

In any case, it appears that it is the responsibility of the carrier to ensure that the safety of the vehicle and hence of the goods is not imperilled: Austria: *OGH 25.9.1968*, Greiter 19, 24; *OGH 29.4.82*, TranspR 1984.105, Greiter 151, 153. Belgium: *Rb Leuven 5.4.88* (1988) 23 E.T.L. 493; also *Brussels 9.6.70*, B.T. 70.343; *Liège 2.10.85*, BRH 87.56. Unloading is also the responsibility of the carrier: *Gent 20.11.75* (1976) 11 E.T.L. 231. Generally, see below, para. 87b.

[30] In such circumstances it would be irrelevant that the driver lent a hand: *OGH 3.7.1985*, Stra GüV 1986/2 pp. 10, 13.

[31] For example, in *T. Civ. Charleroi 1.10.68*, (1969) U.L.C. 327, 330, the court said: "stowage must be dissociated from loading; if in certain cases loading requires lifting gear and is thus the sender's duty, the same is not true of stowage, which is a different operation and necessary to properly effected transport and to the safety of the vehicle and of other road users; consequently, this operation may be carried out by the carrier if it does not involve any special difficulty; so in each case it is purely a question of fact". See also *Paris 16.5.68* (1969) 4 E.T.L. 896, 903 quoted above, para. 27; and *Corbeil-Essones 18.4.69* (1969) 4 E.T.L. 988. *cf. O.L.G. Düsseldorf 27.11.68* (1971) 6 E.T.L. 115, 123.

[32] Below, para. 85.

[33] Loewe, para. 161; Nickel-Lanz, para. 144; Putzeys, paras. 792 *et seq.*

[34] Nickel-Lanz, para. 51. See *O.L.G. Koblenz 6.10.89*, TranspR 1991.93.

[35] See below, para. 208.

30. The vehicle

Prima facie, it is for the carrier to choose a vehicle which will get the contract goods to destination in the same good order and condition in which the goods were received. The choice of vehicle and ancillary equipment is influenced by the needs of the particular cargo, a matter of which the sender usually has more knowledge than the carrier, although rarely to a degree that relieves the carrier of all responsibility in the matter.[36] Sensible parties will get together prior to the carriage and agree what is required, but this does not always happen. Disputes about the suitability of vehicle and equipment arise.

The context of a dispute may be Article 18.4,[37] when the "carriage is performed in vehicles specially equipped to protect the goods". Alternatively, the context may be Article 17.2, when the carrier defends on the basis that the damage could not have been avoided,[38] or that it was the fault of the sender,[39] and the sender replies that the carrier cannot be exonerated under Article 17.2 because in the terms of Article 17.3 there was a "defective condition of the vehicle",[40] the assumption being that an unsuitable vehicle is a defective vehicle.[41] The questions that may have to be asked are as follows.

First, is there any express term of the contract of carriage governing the type of vehicle or special equipment to be used? Secondly, is there any implied term of the contract of carriage governing the type of vehicle or special equipment to be used?[42] If it is clear that sensitive goods (for example, mushrooms) are to be carried at a specified (low) temperature, it can be inferred that the carrier must ensure that the vehicle used by him is capable of the task in hand.[43] Again, if it is obvious that the goods are vulnerable to the elements, the carrier must ensure that the vehicle is one that can be covered.[44] Moreover, the driver, too, must be capable of performing the task in hand. The driver must have the necessary information and the basic language "skills" necessary to deal with problems that might arise, especially in far places where it may be difficult to obtain instructions from the sender or consignee. If not,

---

[36] For example, he must inform the sender about the modes of transport he has available: *Antwerp 13.12.89* (1990) 25 E.T.L. 319. Thume, TranspR 1992.1, 2.

[37] Below, para. 75f.

[38] Below, paras. 74 and 75f.

[39] Below, para. 70.

[40] Below, para. 75f.

[41] For example Helm, p. 474; Hill and Messent, p. 126; Putzeys, para. 770*bis*: "est assimilable à la défectuosité du véhicule, son inaptitude." *Contra*: Haak, p. 151.

[42] As to English law, see below.

[43] *O.L.G. Nuremburg 14.6.65* (1971) 6 E.T.L. 247, 262. On this, however, see discussion of the third question (below).

[44] *Paris 18.12.92*, B.T.L. 1993.52.

it has been held[45] that the carrier will be liable for consequent loss, as the loss was one that might have been avoided[46] if the driver had been better qualified to deal with the situation.

Thirdly, is there a trade custom on the matter? If there is a well-established practice to carry a certain kind of goods in a certain kind of vehicle, a term to that effect will be implied in the contract. For example, it is customary to transport motor vehicles in transporters or other open vehicles.[47]

Prima facie, this rule reinforces the implication, suggested above, for sensitive goods such as mushrooms; but the truth is less clear. The question is whether it is primarily the responsibility of the sender, perhaps as agent of the customer consignee, to protect them by suitable packing, or that of the carrier to provide protection by means of the vehicle. The problem comes to a point in these cases of sensitive goods.[48] Article 18.4 provides that "*If* the carriage is performed in vehicles specially equipped to protect the goods", the carrier must take reasonable steps to select and maintain, etc., the equipment[49]; the CMR does not lay down when special equipment or special vehicles must be used.

One view is that there is neither an implied term nor a custom that sensitive goods should be carried in a vehicle specially equipped to protect those goods; if the sender wants that, he must stipulate for it. If not, the goods are at sender's risk and if the goods suffer, that is not the responsibility of the carrier.

> In *Aix 10.11.76*[50] Swiss cheese, carried from Berne to Marseilles in hot weather and mostly in unrefrigerated transport, was damaged on arrival. The carrier pleaded the sensitivity of the goods, a special risk under Article 17.4(d). The court asked whether it was for the sender or the carrier to see that the mode of transport was appropriate to the nature of the goods and concluded[51] from Articles 17.4 and 18.4 taken together that "if the goods were of a kind exposed . . . to one of the risks in question, special instructions to reduce the risk were obligatory and it was for the sender to give them".

In other cases[52] too, mostly in France, it has been held that, if the sender wants a refrigerated vehicle, the sender must contract

---

[45] *OGH 27.8.81*, Greiter 97, 102: heavy load caught in sandstorm in Saudi Arabia, driver unable to speak English or Arabic.

[46] Hence no defence under Art. 17.2: below, para. 74.

[47] *O.L.G. Düsseldorf 8.5.69* (1970) 5 E.T.L. 446; below, para. 80.

[48] For the meaning of sensitive goods, see below, para. 89.

[49] (Emphasis added). On this provision see below, para. 89b.

[50] B.T. 1977.248.

[51] At 249. See also *Ag Basel 8.4.92*, TranspR 1992.408.

[52] *Aix 20.12.77*, B.T. 1978.245, 246 (apples); *Versailles 29.4.84*, B.T. 1984.249, 250 (pineapples, Paris to Switzerland in July). Also in this sense *Venice 31.10.74*, summarised in (1975) 10 E.T.L. 242 (bananas, Belgium to Italy in summer), approved by Helm, p. 474.

for one expressly and, if not, the carrier is not responsible for the deterioration suffered by perishables in an unrefrigerated vehicle. However, it is doubtful whether an allocation of risk like this relieves the carrier of the general duty to care for the goods[53] and, in particular, in certain cases to take measures against the effects of defective packing by the sender.[54]

This leads to a second, different and, it is submitted, better view, which can also be found in France. If the carrier is presented with goods packed in such a way that it is obvious that they will be damaged in transit, the carrier must either decline to take the goods over, or must provide a vehicle specially equipped to carry the goods safely as they are.[55] *A fortiori*, if the carrier has contracted to carry goods known to be sensitive goods, it is the carrier's responsibility in any event to provide a suitable vehicle.[56] Similarly, the carrier must provide a vehicle that is large enough to carry a load of goods (whether sensitive or not) in safety.[57] But if the carrier does not do so, and this is evident to the sender who allows the goods to be taken over nonetheless, the sender may have to share some of the responsibility.[58]

> In *The Hague 15.6.79*[59] the carrier was held liable for deterioration in flowers occurring because the boxes in which the flowers were packed were loaded too tightly and with insufficient flow of air for effective refrigeration. The carrier argued that he had been compelled to load tightly to get all the boxes into the vehicle. The court rejected this argument because[60] the carrier "could have told the (sender) that the quantity offered for carriage could not be loaded onto one refrigerated vehicle . . . by accepting the load offered and loading it onto one refrigerated vehicle he accepted the risk that tight loading could cause damage".

---

53 Below, para. 79.

54 Below, para. 84.

55 *Paris 10.2.84*, B.T. 1984.558.

56 See also *Ag Basel 8.4.92*, TranspR 1992.408. *Nîmes 18.5.88*, B.T. 1988.472 (wine from Vaucluse to Munich in January); *Cass. com. 22.2.94*, B.T.L. 1994.263 (paintings by Magritte in a standard vehicle that was more suitable for furniture).

57 *Aliter* if the sender does not provide the carrier with the relevant information.

58 This is suggested in *Nîmes 18.5.88* (above) where the court felt obliged to point out that the sender in that case was not on notice of the inadequacy of the vehicle's equipment. However, when a sender saw or should have seen a physical defect in the vehicle, the sender will have to share some of the responsibility (for example, *Paris 26.5.82*, B.T. 1982.503) and in principle the same should be true of manifest unsuitability. In this sense Haak, p. 153; Putzeys, para. 770*ter*.

59 (1980) 15 E.T.L. 871.

60 At 894. Moreover, the flowers were in boxes of standard size, and the court may have thought that the carrier had enough information in advance to realise that his vehicle would be too small for the load.

cf. O.L.G. Hamm 19.2.73 (1974) 9 E.T.L. 753: the amount of meat to be loaded by the sender was greater than the carrier was led to expect and greater than could be transported safely, *i.e.* with sufficient ventilation to avoid deterioration. It was held that the carrier had no liability at all for the damage that occurred.

In *Paris 10.11.81*[61] the court required the carrier to employ persons having some familiarity with the goods of the kind being loaded, and in *Cass. 15.2.82*[62] the court made it clear that, if it was apparent that the goods (meat) could not last the journey even in the refrigerated vehicle provided, the carrier should decline to carry it or bear the consequences. The Paris court, however, appeared to go further, by placing on the carrier in this regard *un devoir de conseil*, a view that is supported by some decisions in France[63] but not by others.[64]

Much depends on the facts of the case and the express or implicit (for example, customary) allocation of responsibility for protecting the goods in question, or ensuring that the vehicle is suitable.[65] In general, it is submitted that the second view (above) is preferable; and that we can conclude with Loewe[66] that the vehicle is defective in the sense of unsuitable, with consequent liability under Article 17.1 and 3, "in cases where the carrier is aware of the unsuitability (because, for instance, the sender has drawn his attention to some particular requirements arising from the nature of the goods to be carried), or where he should have been aware of it (for instance, where carriage of goods of that nature is so commonplace that the unsuitability should have been obvious to any carrier knowing his trade)". We must repeat, however, that even if the vehicle is not defective in this sense, the carrier will be liable for failure to respond to a threat to the goods, and thus for failure to fulfil the general duty to take care of the goods.[67]

30a. Transhipment

Transhipment from one road vehicle to another road vehicle, for the operational convenience of the carrier, is allowed,[68] unless, as

---

[61] B.T. 1982.183.

[62] B.T. 1982.182.

[63] *Cass. 15.2.82*, B.T. 1982.182. See also *Cass. 13.1.81*, B.T. 1982.309, (1983) 18 E.T.L. 13 in which the court censured a decision, which exonerated the carrier in respect of deterioration to nectarines, when the carrier knew that the refrigerated unit was incapable of preserving the nectarines, if set, as it was set, at the temperature stipulated by the sender.

A fortiori, to the extent that goods are damaged because transport is delayed, in breach of contract, the carrier cannot blame the sender for not having packed the goods in a way that would have protected them from the effects of the delay: *Cass. 5.12.89*, B.T. 1990.310.

[64] Notably *Cass. 12.10.81*, B.T. 1981.576; Brunat B.T. 1982.174.

[65] For example, *Cass 5.7.76*, 1977, U.L.R. II 204; it was the carrier's responsibility to see that the vehicle and load would not exceed the weight limit imposed in the country of destination (U.K.), for he was best placed to ensure that the limit was not exceeded in respect of any particular consignment.

[66] Para. 157.

[67] Below, para. 79.

[68] For example, cases cited above, para. 14.

contemplated by Article 6.2(a), transhipment is prohibited by the terms of contract.

Transhipment from road vehicle to a non-road vehicle is a breach of the contract of carriage,[69] unless contemplated by the contract of carriage or unless the case falls within Article 14: if circumstances allow the carriage to be carried out only in a way different from that permitted by the consignment note, the carrier is unable to obtain instructions within a reasonable time from the person entitled to dispose of the goods, and transhipment appears to be in the best interests of the latter, transhipment is allowed.[70]

In *OGH 10.2.81*[71] the driver of goods from Switzerland to the island of Bahrein, finding that no ferry could take a vehicle of the size of the one used, unloaded the goods and had them carried to Bahrein by dhow. The court held that he was entitled to do this.

If, however, the transhipment is in breach of the contract of carriage, the liability of the carrier is determined by the CMR, even though the unauthorised mode of transport is by rail or by water.

In *Cass 30.11.82*[72] a mechanical digger was to be carried by road and sea from Grugliasco (Italy) to Hatfield (United Kingdom). While still in Italy the tractor failed and the trailer carrying the digger was taken on by rail, apparently without the knowledge or consent of the sender, who had loaded and stowed the digger on the trailer. In France the load broke loose and damaged installations of the SNCF at Compiègne. The sender's contention, that by changing the mode without seeking instructions under Article 14 the carrier was in breach of the contract and of the CMR, was not denied by the Court of Cassation, but the Court refused to interfere with the decision of the court below (that the sender was partly responsible) because the change of mode played no part in the cause or extent of the damage, and had caused no loss to the sender.

In answering other (unsuccessful) arguments of the sender in that case, the Court of Cassation accepted the premise of those arguments, that liability for damage occurring during the unauthorised rail stage was governed by the CMR. This is not because agreed carriage road-rail would have been subject to the CMR but

---

[69] *Paris 15.2.82*, B.T. 1982.141: a load from Lyons (France) to Riyadh (Saudi Arabia) was to be sent entirely by road, and was insured on this basis; however, the carrier took it by road to Marseilles and from there by sea to Latakia (Syria). This led to delay while further documents were obtained for the sea stage. The court held that the carrier was in breach of contract and liable for the consequential loss. See also *Rb Antwerp 9.12.77* (1978) 13 E.T.L. 110. In this sense, Loewe, para. 57. See also above, para. 13.

[70] Below, para. 33a.

[71] Greiter 88.

[72] B.T. 1983.129.

because, once the CMR applies, the carrier cannot change the regime and thus the contract without the consent of the other party.

The suggestion has been made[73] that transfer to an unauthorised mode of transport is not only a breach of contract but a deviation at common law,[74] which deprives the carrier of all defences in the contract of carriage, including those defences derived from the CMR. But the application of the common law doctrine of deviation would be a blow to the uniformity sought by the CMR. Other countries in Europe may not have such a rule[75] and hence in some cases, such as *Cass. 30.11.82* (above),[76] courts apply CMR defences in spite of an unauthorised change of mode. Hence, it is submitted that the doctrine of deviation should not apply to contracts governed by the CMR: this submission is advanced in greater detail in connection with change of route.[77]

31. The route

The CMR is silent on the question of the route that should be taken by the vehicle between departure and destination.[78] The route is the route agreed by the parties to the contract of carriage. A route may be agreed, however, not only expressly but also implicitly. If there is a usual route, it is normally that route which is implied. The usual route is normally the shortest route, unless the carrier normally takes a different route and the customer is aware of that.

> *Paris 18.10.73*[79] concerned the transport of theatrical properties for a ballet company on tour in Switzerland. Finding in early May 1971 that the direct route over the San Bernadino pass, although open to vehicular traffic, was in poor condition, both the bus carrying the company and the lorry carrying the properties took a longer

---

[73] Hill and Messent, p. 45.

[74] Strictly speaking, this should be "quasi-deviation" or "fundamental breach", as deviation in English common law refers to a departure from the contract route: Kahn-Freund, pp. 284 *et seq.* below.

[75] Generally in civil law countries the carrier loses his defences only in cases of *dol* or *faute lourde*: Tetley, pp. 104 *et seq.*; Nicholas, *French Law of Contract* (2nd ed., Oxford, 1992), p. 228. These doctrines are provided for by the CMR, and discussed below, paras. 101 *et seq.*

[76] The defendant carrier was allowed to plead the defence in Art. 17.4(c) and the apportionment of liability authorised by Art. 17.5.

[77] Below, para. 31a.

[78] An early draft of the CMR required the route to be stated in the consignment note, but this was deleted, as being a "matter of no great importance" to be left to the private agreement, if any, of the parties to the contract: TRANS/WP/14/42 p. 6.

[79] B.T. 1973.488; 1976 U.L.R. I 242. See also *OGH 27.8.81*, Greiter 97: having taken local advice, the driver chose to proceed across the desert in Saudi Arabia, rather than take the coast road, and the transport was halted by a sandstorm. The carrier was held liable for resultant loss, not because the driver had deviated but because loss had occurred which the carrier had not proved to be unavoidable under Art. 17.2.

route from Lugano to Bienne, and the lorry arrived too late for the properties to be set up for the next performance. The carrier was held liable for the loss caused by the delay; however, the contention that the carrier's breach amounted to a *faute lourde* which, if accepted, would have removed the limitation on the amount of the carrier's liability,[80] was rejected.

If the vehicle leaves the agreed route, what are the consequences in law? First, as we have seen, there may be liability for delay.[81] Secondly, it has been suggested that, as in carriage by road within the United Kingdom,[82] a departure from the route should be treated as a common law deviation, with the consequences that the carrier would be unable to plead any exemptions or other defences in the contract of carriage, including those which derive from the CMR.

31a. Common law deviation

Certainly, common law deviation may apply to the sea stage of a CMR contract, when that stage is governed not by the CMR but by the appropriate maritime regime. Moreover, the doctrine of deviation has been applied in cases of carriage by rail governed by common law.[83] But in *Silber*,[84] a CMR case a century later, there was no suggestion that to stop for two hours and assist another of the carrier's vehicles rather than seek local assistance, even in Italy, is a breach of the contract of carriage, still less a breach so bad that the carrier would lose his limitations and defences. The better view, it is submitted, is that the common law doctrine of deviation does not apply to contracts governed by the CMR.

First, the premise of the maritime rule is that the (insurance) risk has changed, and unless extended, there is no insurance cover.[85] Whether or not that is still true of carriage by sea, it is not generally true of carriage by road. Although it is said[86] that the doctrine of deviation applies to uniform maritime law, the Hague or Hague-Visby Rules, that view can be justified by reference to Article IV.4 of the Rules and to their common law background. No parallel rule is found in the CMR and no parallel argument can be made for the application of the doctrine to international carriage by road. Secondly, other countries party to the CMR do not

---

[80] On this see below, para. 102c.

[81] *Paris 18.10.73* (above, n. 79). As to the meaning of delay, see below, para. 58; and for the extent of liability in cases of delay, see below, para. 97c.

[82] See below, para. 210a.

[83] See below, para. 210a.

[84] *Silber v. Islander Trucking* [1985] 2 Lloyd's Rep. 243. This case is discussed in some detail below, paras. 74 *et seq*.

[85] *Tate & Lyle*, below, n. 88.

[86] Tetley, p. 746.

have special rules for deviation, and to apply the common law rules to CMR carriage would damage uniformity. The CMR has special rules in Article 29 for serious breach of contract, called wilful misconduct,[87] which displace certain of the carrier's defences in the case of wilful misconduct and, by implication, in no other case. Finally, as regards not only the CMR but common law at large, in recent years the doctrine of deviation has been seen by some as a doctrine *sui generis*,[88] something which should be put back in the sea from which it came.[89] If doubt remains, the carrier by road could imitate the response of the carrier by sea, by contracting a liberty clause,[90] which permits departure from the direct or usual route. Such liberty clauses will be construed strictly in the light of the commercial purpose of the entire adventure; however, it is submitted that they do not infringe the CMR.

31b. Reasonable dispatch

The CMR has rules about delay in delivery,[91] and is thus concerned with the duration of the transport, once the goods have been taken over, but does not expressly require the carrier to collect and carry the goods with reasonable dispatch. Can a duty of that kind be implied?

At common law,[91a] the English court would hold that a carrier must send his vehicle to collect the goods with reasonable dispatch, either by analogy with the duty imposed on the carrier by sea or on the basis of an implied term of the contract of carriage necessary to give business efficacy to the contract. However, as regards the movement of goods, the CMR is concerned less with means than with ends: if the goods are delivered within the time allowed in the quantity and condition in which they were taken over, the carrier has performed the contract of carriage. In so far as the CMR carrier has a residual duty to mitigate loss or damage occurring en route, that duty is set not at the level of reasonable care but of "utmost" care.[92] Accordingly, the existence of a duty of

---

[87] See below, para. 101.

[88] *Tate & Lyle v. Hain SS. Co.* (1936) 55 Ll.L. Rep. 159, 173, *per* Lord Atkin; *Photo Production v. Securicor Transport* [1980] A.C. 827, 845; Coote [1970] C.L.J. 221.

[89] Clarke [1978] L.M.C.L.Q. 472. For a persuasive argument that, in any event, a distinct doctrine of deviation has not survived the decision in *Photo Production Ltd v. Securicor Transport* [1980] A.C. 827, see Debattista [1989] J.B.L. 22. *Contra*: Treitel, pp. 209 *et seq*.

[90] At common law, as the doctrine of deviation was said to rest on the intention of the parties, the doctrine could be modified or displaced by a clear expression of that intention: *Gibaud v. G.E. Ry Co.* [1921] 2 K.B. 426, 435, *per* Scrutton L.J., C.A.

[91] Below, para. 58.

[91a] See above (Part I), Chap. 2.

[92] See below, para. 74e. As an aspect of that duty, if a delay occurs, the carrier may be required to inform the person entitled to dispose of the goods so that, for example, appropriate arrangements can be made: *O.L.G. Munich 12.4.90*, TranspR 1990.280.

reasonable dispatch in the case of carriage governed by the CMR is very doubtful.[93]

32. Disposal of the goods

Although the contract of carriage may stipulate that the goods shall be delivered to person A at place X, the CMR provides for the alteration of these terms of the contract, and for delivery to a different person or to a different place. This right unilaterally to alter the terms of the contract is referred to as the right of disposal and is governed by Article 12; it has been distinguished from a variation of the terms of the contract which, as such, has to be agreed by both parties and to which Article 12 does not apply.[94]

32a. Disposal by the sender

The right of disposal is linked to possession of the consignment note. If, therefore, the sender has no consignment note, the sender has no right of disposal. This will be so if goods are grouped to be sent. In that case the sender receives not a consignment note but a certificate of shipment in respect of the sender's goods. Information relating to all the senders concerned and their goods is recorded on a consignment note that travels with the goods, as well as being telexed or faxed to the carrier's agent at the place of destination. Moreover, if the terms of the consignment note confer the right to dispose of the goods on the consignee, the consignee alone has that right. If it does not, the sender has the right to dispose of the goods, in accordance with Article 12.1 and Article 12.2, until the second copy of the consignment note has been handed (by the carrier) to the consignee, or the goods have arrived at destination and the consignee has required delivery of the goods in accordance with Article 13.

These rules start in Article 12 from the position that the right of disposal lies with the sender, who consigns the goods and who settles the terms of the consignment note. By Article 12.1 the sender may designate a new consignee or a new destination, including return to sender.[95] *Ceteris paribus*, the exercise of the right of disposal does not discharge the contract of carriage but alters its terms.[96] Unilateral alteration of the terms of the contract in this way poses obvious practical problems for the carrier, and

---

[93] *cf. Paris 22.6.82*, below, para. 33a.
[94] *O.L.G. Hamburg 7.4.94*, TranspR 1994.444.
[95] For example, *Brussels 6.4.77* (1977) 12 E.T.L. 881; goods just short of destination were damaged in a roard accident and were sent back to the sender for repair.
[96] *Brussels 6.4.77* (above). Maccarone, Theunis, p. 64; Pesce, p. 162.

Article 12 puts conditions, both positive and negative, on the right of disposal, conditions aimed mainly at protecting the position of the other persons concerned. The exercise of the right of disposal, therefore, is subject to a number of conditions, as follows.

(a) To carry out the new instructions must, in the words of Article 12.5(b), be "possible at the time when the instructions reach the person who is to carry them out".[97] Something is possible if it is "reasonable and possible".[98] The allocation of the onus of proving that this condition is satisfied (or not) is unclear.[99] On the one hand, the carrier may be the person best placed to produce evidence of what was possible and what was not. On the other hand, the B.G.H. had held that, in accordance with the general rule that he who wishes to rely on a provision must prove his right to do so, the onus is on the person seeking to exercise the right of disposal[1] in accordance with new instructions and, indeed, the feasibility of carrying out the instructions concerned does appear from the text of Article 12 to be a condition of the right of disposal. In the opinion of the B.G.H.,[2] this conclusion is reinforced by the role of these conditions, which is to protect the carrier.

(b) The person exercising the right of disposal must produce, as required by Article 12.5(a), "the first copy of the consignment note", *i.e.* the one originally handed to the sender,[3] "on which the new instructions to the carrier have been entered". New instructions given solely by telephone or by telefax will not do. Production of the note proves a person's right of disposal; the note is not, however, a negotiable instrument or a document of title.[4]

If no consignment note has been issued, evidently none can be produced but the B.G.H. has held[5] that, nonetheless, the carrier is obliged to obey the instructions of the sender.[6] The purpose of production, said the court,[7] is to protect both the person truly entitled to dispose of the goods, and also the carrier himself, from

---

[97] If so, the carrier must "immediately notify" the person who gave him the instructions: Art. 12.6.

[98] Maccarone, *loc. cit.* below, adopting the view of FIATA. The measure of what is possible is, it is submitted, the same as that of what is possible by way of delivery under Art. 14; see below, para. 33a(*i*) *in fine*.

[99] Maccarone, Theunis, p. 73, states that it is for the carrier to show that fulfilment is not possible. *Contra*: Pesce, p. 167.

[1] *B.G.H. 27.1.82* (1985) 20 E.T.L. 349, 353.

[2] *ibid.*

[3] Art. 5.1.

[4] Loewe, para. 119. The right to dispose of the goods is distinguished from ownership of the goods: Maccarone, Theunis, p. 62.

[5] *B.G.H. 27.1.82*, TranspR 1982.105; (1985) 20 E.T.L. 349. For the facts of this case, see below, para. 32c.

[6] The B.G.H. pointed out (at 352) that it was clear from Art. 15, for example, that production of a consignment note was not required in all cases in which the carrier was obliged nonetheless to obey the instructions of the sender.

[7] At 352. *cf.* Muth/Glöckner, p. 117, who sees these conditions as mainly a protection for the carrier.

the danger that the carrier might follow instructions from a person not entitled to dispose of the goods. When there is no consignment note and the carrier knows this, the carrier also knows that there is no note whereby a person other than the sender might acquire the right of disposal under Article 12.3, and therefore the danger does not arise. In these circumstances, the only person in a position to give the carrier instructions is the sender, whose instructions should be obeyed, whether the sender produces a consignment note or not. Were it otherwise, failure by the carrier to issue a consignment note would deprive the sender not only of the right of disposal but also of any right to stop carriage or change delivery instructions, a situation that the B.G.H. was reluctant to endorse.[8]

(c) The person exercising the right of disposal must, as required by Article 12.5(a), give the carrier an indemnity[9] against all expenses, loss or damage involved in carrying out the new instructions. It has been contended[10] that this includes lost operating profits as consequential loss or damage.

(d) In the case of the sender, the right of disposal is lost if the carrier has delivered the second copy of the consignment note to the consignee.[11] If this occurs, it usually occurs at the same time as delivery of the goods to the consignee. However, not always: as Maccarone points out,[12] under the terms of Article 13.1, the consignee is entitled to the second copy immediately after the "arrival" of the goods, which may be earlier than delivery or, if the goods have been transferred en route to a vehicle operated by the consignee, later than delivery.[13] Moreover, in practice, although not entitled to it, the consignee may persuade the carrier to hand over the second copy prior to arrival, thus ending the sender's right of disposal.[14]

(e) In the case of the sender, the right of disposal is lost if the consignee has required delivery of the goods[15] or if, knowing that the goods have been lost or delayed, the consignee has taken

---

[8] *B.G.H. 27.1.82* (1985) 20 E.T.L. 349, 353.

[9] The form of indemnity is not specified. Loewe (para. 121) has suggested that it may be an advance payment or adequate security for payment.

[10] Maccarone, Theunis, p. 74.

[11] Art. 12.2 by reference to Art. 13.1.

[12] Theunis, p. 71.

[13] Delivery is discussed below, para. 37.

[14] Earlier drafts of the CMR prohibited this possibility, but the final draft does not: Nickel-Lanz, para. 69.

[15] Art. 12.2 by reference to Art. 13.1. In *OLG Munich 23.4.93*, TranspR 1993.348, the driver obeyed the order of the consignee to deliver at place X, a place other than the contractual destination, when the consignee had yet to acquire the right of disposal. Although this was an interference with the right of the sender to dispose of the goods, in the absence of any evidence that the sender wished to dispose of the goods to anyone other than the consignee, delivery at place X was treated as delivery to the consignee in accordance with the contract.

steps[16] to establish a claim against the carrier.[17] Together with condition (d), condition (e) is an elaborate way of saying that, in these circumstances, it is too late for the sender to dispose of them to someone else.

(f) The right of disposal cannot be exercised if, in the words of Article 12.5(b), the fulfilment of the new instructions interferes[18] "with the normal working of the carrier's undertaking" or prejudices the senders or consignees of other consignments.[19] This will be the case if fulfilment would cause undue delay in delivery of other consignments[20] or, perhaps, if the vehicle will have to return empty from the new destination.[21] However, if, as has been also suggested,[22] loss of operating profit is a loss in respect of which the carrier has a right to indemnity from the person giving the instructions, the carrier cannot refuse to comply with instructions on this ground. As regards the onus of proving interference, see above in relation to condition (a).

(g) The instructions must not result in a division of the consignment: Article 12.5(c). According to Loewe,[23] if a load travels in one vehicle under more than one consignment note, the right of disposal may be exercised in respect of each note and hence each part of the load, so that the carrier may be obliged to deliver different parts of the load to different destinations. Hill and Messent object[24] that Loewe has misread "consignment" in Article 12.5(c) as "consignment note", and that this possibility exposes the carrier to a much extended journey, which he did not envisage when he contracted it. However, what the passer-by may see as one vehicle bearing a single consignment may be seen by those involved as one vehicle bearing a number of consignments. Even if "consignment" is ambiguous, it might be argued that a carrier, who contracts one load under more than one consignment note, who knows that there is a right of disposal and a right to recover the cost of obeying instructions,[25] should envisage the possibility of multiple instructions and an extended journey. Moreover, if the instruction is unreasonable or outrageous, the carrier can refuse to comply on the basis of impossibility under condition (a) or of interference under condition (f).

---

[16] Below, paras. 60–61.

[17] Helm, Art. 12 Anm. 6.

[18] Loewe (para. 122) suggests that the interference must be "serious". See also Pesce, p. 167, n. 166.

[19] If so, the carrier must "immediately notify" the person who gave him the instructions: Art. 12.6.

[20] Helm, Art. 12 Anm. 11.

[21] Putzeys, para. 492.

[22] Maccarone, Theunis, p. 74. But *cf*. Herber/Piper, Art. 12, 32.

[23] Para. 123, apparently accepted by Helm Art. 12 Anm. 12; and Thume, Art. 12, 28.

[24] At p. 85.

[25] Pesce, p. 167.

(h) In the case of the sender, the right of disposal is lost if that right has passed to the consignee under Article 12.3: see below, paragraph 32b.

32b. Disposal by the consignee

First, the consignee acquires the right of disposal with the help of the sender, in the terms of Article 12.3 "from the time when the consignment note is drawn up, if the sender makes an entry to that effect in the consignment note" and, as the consignee must satisfy the appropriate conditions for the exercise of the right of disposal,[26] if the sender transmits to the consignee that copy[27] of the consignment note for production by the consignee to the carrier: Article 12.5(a). In the exercise of this right of disposal, the consignee may order "the delivery of the goods to another person", but "that other person shall not be entitled to name other consignees": Article 12.4.

If, as required by Article 12.3, the sender enters the consignee's right of disposal in the consignment note, the right cannot be exercised by the consignee until the note can be produced by the consignee, and it appears that the entry alone does not terminate the sender's right of disposal; the sender may have a change of mind, delete the entry and exercise the right. If, however, the sender transmits the copy to the consignee, so that the consignee can produce it, there is a time, the time of transmission, during which neither can exercise the right, as neither can produce the note. Again, if the sender transmits the note, but omits to make the required entry, the right of disposal cannot be exercised by the sender, because the sender cannot produce the note, and it cannot be exercised by the consignee, because no entry has been made.[28] So, Loewe suggests[29] that there may be "a break in continuity—in other words, a time when no one can dispose of the goods". The

---

[26] Above, para. 32a.

[27] *i.e.* what is called by Art. 12.5(a) the "first" copy: this is the one handed to the sender: Art. 5.1.

[28] In this case Hill and Messent (p. 84) suggest a solution in England, whereby delivery of the first copy by sender to consignee might be seen as an assignment, presumably an equitable assignment, of the right of disposal. Delivery of the note with intention to assign the right of disposal would suffice: *Le Feuvre v. Sullivan* (1855) 10 Moo.P.C. 1, 13, *per* Knight-Bruce L.J., P.C. However, assignment is not effective against the debtor (carrier), unless the debtor has been given informal but clear notice of the assignment: *Brandt's Sons & Co. v. Dunlop Rubber Co.* [1905] A.C. 454, 462, *per* Lord Macnaghten. It appears that presentation of the note by the consignee to the carrier could constitute notice. Usually, at that same time the consignee receives the second copy of the note, which has travelled with the goods, and that triggers Article 12.2, whereby the carrier must obey the orders of the consignee anyway. So the solution and perhaps also the problem are academic.

[29] Para. 119. See also Maccarone, Theunis, p. 67.

same problem would arise in the unlikely event that the note is pledged to a bank.[30]

Secondly, the consignee acquires the "right of disposal", regardless of the co-operation of the sender, when the carriage is effectively over,[31] by following the procedure set out in Article 13.1. In these circumstances, the consignee does not in terms acquire a "right of disposal", but the sender's right of disposal is defeated and the carrier must "obey the orders of the consignee": Article 12.2.[32]

32c. The liability of the carrier

As regards disposal of the goods, the carrier's duty is neither determined nor affected by the contract of sale. It is a tradition of civil law systems, reflected in the CMR, that the right of disposal under the contract of carriage is independent of rights, especially rights of property, arising under an associated or underlying contract, such as sale.[33] So, a sender, who has lost his right of disposal under the CMR but seeks to exercise the right of stoppage under the Sale of Goods Act 1979,[34] has no right of action against the carrier who follows the orders of the consignee, as required by the contract of carriage (and the CMR), rather than those of the sender/seller, as might be required by the Sale of Goods Act.[35] However, a sender who has lost the right of disposal of the goods under the CMR has not thereby lost any right of action against the carrier under the CMR in respect of loss, damage or delay.[36]

As regards disposal of the goods, the liability of the carrier is governed by Article 12.7 of the CMR. The carrier is liable (a) "if he has not carried out the instructions given under the conditions

---

[30] Maccarone, Theunis, p. 67: there is little evidence of any practice of using the consignment note as security.

[31] However, note that, if the carrier lets the consignee have the second copy earlier than delivery, the consignee has the right of disposal from that earlier time: Nickel-Lanz, para. 69. But see the following note.

[32] It has been suggested that the orders the consignee may give under Art. 12.2 are no different from those the consignee may give under Art. 12.3, hence subject to the same conditions: Nickel-Lanz, para. 84 and references cited. However, exercise of the right of disposal under Art. 12.3 is conditional on production of the first copy of the consignment note, whereas this does not appear to be necessary in order to comply with Art. 13.1: the consignee can be identified to the carrier by whatever means are available.

[33] Maccarone, Theunis, p. 64 note 8, and pp. 65–66. Maccarone (p. 67) supports a proposal in the FIATA Report (p. 13) that the words "right to dispose" be replaced by the words "right to give new instructions to the carrier".

[34] ss. 44–47.

[35] Benjamin, para. 21–056; Glass and Cashmore, para. 3.30; Maccarone, Theunis, pp. 66–67.

[36] Below, para. 41. Thus, if goods damaged during transit are delivered to the consignee/buyer, who obtains compensation from the sender/seller under the contract of sale, the latter has a right of action against the carrier in respect of the damage: for example, *B.G.H. 10.4.74* (1975) 10 E.T.L. 83, in which the carrier's argument, that the sender who lost the right of disposal also lost the right of action, was rejected.

provided for" in Article 12,[37] or (b) if he "has carried them out without requiring the first copy of the consignment note to be produced".[38] Liability is to the "person entitled to make a claim for any loss or damage caused thereby".[39]

> In *B.G.H. 27.1.82*[40] handbags to be carried from Germany to Belgium reached the carrier's groupage depot in Germany, when the sender instructed the carrier to hold them there. Nonetheless the goods were sent on and delivered to the consignee/buyer, who did not pay the sender/seller the purchase price. The sender recovered the amount of the price from the carrier.[41]

As regards the principles governing an award of damages, the B.G.H. saw this case as one of loss of goods under Article 17 of the CMR,[42] the amount of damages being governed by Articles 23 and 29 and, in particular, limited by Article 23.3.[43] By contrast, most writers[44] state that there is no such limit[45] on the amount recoverable under Article 12.7, and for the following reasons.

(a) As a matter of construction of the CMR, the operation of Article 23.3 is confined to actions arising under Chapter IV of the CMR,[46] Articles 17 *et seq.*, in which Article 23.3 is placed.

(b) By its own terms Article 23 operates (only) when "a carrier is liable for compensation in respect of total or partial loss of goods", and clearly "loss" includes the "loss" for which the "carrier is liable" under Article 17, the very first provision of Chapter IV.[47] On one view, taken by the B.G.H., "loss" has the same meaning not only in Article 23.3 and Article 17 but also in Article

---

[37] Above, para. 32a. *Paris 22.6.82*, B.T. 1982.432, described below, para. 33a, adds that the carrier will be liable if he does not carry out the instructions with reasonable diligence. *Sed quaere*, as in general the level of the duty of the carrier to perform the contract of carriage is higher than one of reasonable diligence: below, paras. 33a(*i*), 74e and 79.

[38] For example, *Cass. 29.10.1985*, B.T. 1986.165, in which the carrier, who had obeyed the instructions of the consignee without requiring production of the consignment note, was liable to the *commissionnaire* to the extent of the latter's liability to the sender for loss of market.

[39] Maccarone, Theunis, pp. 74–75. As to entitlement to make a claim, see below, para. 40.

[40] TranspR 1982.105; (1985) 20 E.T.L. 349.

[41] For the precise amount to be awarded to the claimant in the case further evidence was required.

[42] At 351, citing in the same sense: *B.G.H. 27.10.78*, N.J.W. 1979.2473. Nickel-Lanz argues (by reference to E/ECE/TRANS/SC 1/130 annexe 4, no. 23, p. 18) that unless the case falls within Chap. 4, the intention of the draftsman was that liability under Art. 12.7 was to be based on national law.

[43] At 353. On Article 23.3, see below, para. 97.

[44] Glass and Cashmore, para. 3.30; Helm, Art. 12 Anm. 13; Herber/Piper, Art. 12, 40; Hill and Messent, p. 86; Koller, Art. 12, 9; Loewe, para. 124; Putzeys, para. 497. Thume, Art. 12, 52.

[45] If correct, presumably the claim would be subject to common law limits.

[46] Putzeys, para. 497. Chap. IV includes Art. 17, under which the *B.G.H. 27.1.82* placed the action in that case (above, n. 40).

[47] *B.G.H. 27.1.82* (above, n. 40).

12.7. However, other courts[48] have distinguished "loss" in Article 17 and Article 23.3 from "loss" in Article 12.7, which concerns, in their view, a specific kind of economic loss, quite different from the more general use of the word[49] in the later provisions of the CMR.

(c) Finally, the CIM, from which the CMR is derived, contains a provision which corresponds to Article 12.7, and which states that the action against the carrier is subject to a limit, that "any compensation shall not exceed that payable in the event of loss of the goods".[50] No such limit is expressed in Article 12 of the CMR.

33. Difficulties on the road

If the transport becomes more difficult or more expensive to achieve than expected, the carrier is obliged, nonetheless, to perform the contract,[51] and to bear the extra cost. If, however, the contract becomes impossible to perform in accordance with its terms, is not the contract automatically discharged. Article 14 and Article 15 make provision for events that render performance as originally envisaged impossible: Article 15 as regards events preventing delivery and Article 14 as regards events occurring earlier.[52] However, if these events occur, the carrier has by Article 16.2[53] the power to bring the "carriage" to "an end", and for most if not all purposes this also discharges the contract.[54]

33a. Impossibility of performance: Article 14

By Article 14.1, if it "becomes impossible to carry out the contract in accordance with the terms laid down in the consignment note",[55] the carrier must ask for instructions from the person with

---

[48] For example, *OGH 14.11.84*, Greiter 245, 248. In a similar vein, Helm Art. 12 Anm. 13 suggests that Art. 17 and Art. 23 concern loss of or damage to the claimant's goods, but that Art. 12.7 governs loss to other parts of the claimant's patrimony as a result of the carrier's breach of Art. 12.

[49] Discussed below, paras. 55 and 56.

[50] Art. 30.3 (CIM 1970); a similar provision is found in earlier versions, for example, Art. 23.4 (CIM 1961).

[51] Helm, Art. 14 Anm. 2; Loewe, para. 128; Muth/Glöckner, p. 121; Rodière (1971) 6 E.T.L. 2, 3–4.

[52] Helm, Art. 14 Anm. 1.

[53] Below, para. 33c(*ii*).

[54] On the general effect of discharge of contract, see below, paras. 104–105.

[55] As attention is focused on the consignment note, in the event of conflict between the terms of the contract and the terms of the note, it is with the latter that Art. 14.1 is concerned: Helm Art. 14 Anm. 2, who also suggests, however, that, if no consignment note has been issued, Art. 14.1 will be applied by analogy to the terms of the contract.

the right of disposal.[56] Relevant terms include a time-limit for delivery, or a route to be followed.[57] By inference, however, Article 14 is not concerned with the impossibility of performance of other terms relating to delivery,[58] as this is specifically dealt with by Article 15.[59]

The carrier must ask for instructions within a reasonable time and give enough information, if it is available, to enable appropriate instructions to be given.[60] If instructions are forthcoming, the rights of the parties are then governed[61] by the rules about disposal in Article 12.[62] The instructions must be reasonable to the extent dictated by Article 12.5(b). While awaiting or executing instructions, the carrier has the same liability for the goods, the liability of Article 17, as under the original contract of carriage.

> In *Paris 22.6.82*[63] carriage became impossible because the load of cauliflowers had become unstable. The carrier was instructed by the sender to continue and to deliver the load as soon as possible, which necessitated transhipment to another vehicle. However, the carrier delayed transhipment pending the outcome of a new discussion of liability for the cost of transhipment. As a result of the extra delay the time for delivery passed, the consignee refused to accept the cauliflowers, and for this the carrier was held liable to the sender.

33a(*i*). Impossibility

"Impossible" in Article 14, like "prevent" in Article 15[64] and "unavoidable" in Article 17.2,[65] must be given a sensible meaning rather than a narrow or literal meaning.

First, impossibility may occur regardless of cause, in particular, regardless of whether it was caused by the fault of the carrier.[66] If the carrier was indeed at fault, the carrier may be liable under Chapter IV of the CMR but that is not something with which Article 14 is concerned.

---

[56] As to the person with the right of disposal, see above, para. 32.
[57] Loewe, para. 128.
[58] Also in this sense: Helm, Art. 14 Anm. 1.
[59] See below, para. 33b.
[60] Rodière (1971) 6 E.T.L. 2, 4.
[61] Helm, Art. 14 Anm. 3. Rodière (1971) 6 E.T.L. 2, 4, infers this, although in his view the CMR "does not provide for the case where the person entitled does give instructions to the carrier".
[62] This proposition assumes that, in the words of Article 14.1, "instructions from the person entitled to dispose of the goods in accordance with the provisions of article 12", the final phrase "in accordance, etc." depends mainly not on "persons entitled" but on "instructions". Generally on Art. 12, see above, para. 32.
[63] B.T. 1982.432.
[64] Below, para. 33b.
[65] Below, para. 74.
[66] Rodière (1971) 6 E.T.L. 2, 3, pointing to the opening words of Art. 14.1: "If *for any reason* it is or becomes impossible . . . " (emphasis added).

Secondly, impossibility is assessed in the light of the steps that the carrier can be expected to initiate to overcome the difficulties. In *Liège 18.12.67*[67] the court concluded that the carriage had become impossible when the driver discovered that his load had become unbalanced. This may well have been true, but the court did not feel it necessary to explain. It was certainly impossible without remedial action by the carrier, but if this alone made performance impossible, then much of the responsibility to deal with the difficulties that arise during carriage would pass from the carrier to the person from whom the carrier must seek instructions. Clearly, some independent initiative and response are expected of the carrier when things go wrong.[68] Moreover, the impossibility is described by German commentators as objective impossibility[69]: performance is not impossible if the carrier can overcome the obstacle by employing someone else to do what is required.[70] Consequently, carriage is not impossible under Article 14, until the carrier has taken steps to overcome the problem, or it is clear that any steps would be futile. The problem ceases to be one solely for the initiative of the carrier, and becomes one for instructions under Article 14, when it becomes impossible "to carry out the contract in accordance with the terms".[71]

Thirdly, impossibility is not absolute. Impossibility is relative to the contract: in the words of Article 14.1, it must have become "impossible to carry out the contract in accordance with the terms laid down in the consignment note". If the contract indicates a particular customs post, a strike at that post may make performance impossible, but if the contract does not indicate any particular post, a strike at the post on the direct route does not make it impossible to carry out the contract if a detour can be made to another post where the officers are not on strike.[72]

Further, performance may be impossible, even though the carrier has not done absolutely everything possible to overcome the obstacle. As is also true of the carrier's basic duty as carrier under Article 17,[73] the level of the carrier's duty is not absolute. Under Article 17 the carrier is excused if loss, damage or delay is unavoidable, the obverse of which is that the carrier's duty is not absolute and strict but is a duty to exercise "utmost" care to

[67] (1969) 4 E.T.L. 965, 973; see the critical note at 974.

[68] See below, paras. 33c, 75 and 79.

[69] Helm, Art. 14 Anm. 2, points out that Art. 14.1 speaks not of impossibility for the carrier but simply of impossibility.

[70] Unless, of course, it is a term of the note that the work shall not be subcontracted.

[71] Thus the decision in *Liège 18.12.67* would be easier to understand if the consignment note had contained a time-limit which, as a result of the need to rearrange the cargo, had become impossible to keep.

[72] *Paris 27.5.80*, B.T. 1980.45.

[73] Below, para. 79.

perform the contract.[74] Although Article 14 is not directly concerned with the carrier's liability for failure to perform, but with what should be done next when it becomes impossible to perform, there is both sense and symmetry in an alignment of the two requirements.[75] If the carrier has exercised utmost care to avoid delay, the delay is unavoidable under Article 17.2, and the carrier is not liable for the delay under Article 17.1 but must seek instructions about what to do next, because performance on time has become impossible in the sense of Article 14.

33b. Prevention of delivery: Article 15

By Article 15.1, if "circumstances prevent delivery of the goods after their arrival at the place designated for delivery", the carrier must seek instructions from the sender.[76] As in the cases governed by Article 14.1, Rodière contends[77] that the carrier must ask for instructions within a reasonable time and give the sender enough information to enable the sender to give appropriate instructions.

> In *Montpellier 8.1.87*[78] a seller of clothes sent 21 parcels of clothes to a buyer in Andorra, who refused delivery. The carrier did not inform the sender or seek instructions, and the sender made no inquiries about the clothes. The clothes remained in the carrier's warehouse for a year, and the carrier was held liable in part of the depreciation in the value of the clothes, the remainder being attributed to the fault of the sender. The carrier was obliged, said the court,[79] to ask for instructions within a reasonably short period of time.

If prevention is alleged, the first question is whether there has been a prevention of delivery at all. As with impossibility under Article 14,[80] prevention is not absolute but relative. First, it is relative to the terms of the contract. For example, if the contract provides for delivery at A or B, and it has become impossible at A,

---

[74] Below, para. 74e.

[75] Together with that of Art. 12.5(b): above, para. 32a.

[76] *cf.* Art. 14 (above, para. 33a) which requires the carrier to seek instructions from the person entitled to dispose of the goods. If the prevention occurs after the consignee has given an order for the goods to be delivered to another person in accordance with the consignee's right of disposal under Art. 12, the role of the sender in Art. 15 is assumed by the consignee: Art. 15.3.

[77] (1971) 6 E.T.L. 2, 5; also that the sender's right to give instructions is subject to the limits in Art. 12: *ibid.*, p. 6.

[78] B.T. 1987.589.

[79] At 590. See also *Cass. 23.5.77*, B.T. 1977.388 in which the carrier who took no action, neither contacting the sender nor exercising powers under Art. 16.3, when the goods (frozen fish) were refused by the consignee, was liable for deterioration in the goods.

[80] Above, para. 33a(*i*).

delivery has not been prevented.[81] Secondly, the carrier does not have to do absolutely everything possible to deliver the goods. For example, if the consignee refuses to take over the goods, the carrier does not have to linger on the slight chance that the consignee will change his mind: delivery has been prevented if the consignee refuses to take over the goods *promptly*.[82] However, delivery has not been prevented merely because the carrier has not got the precise or correct address for delivery. The carrier must make inquiries, even though this takes time and may be inconvenient.[83]

When prevention occurs, Article 15.1 draws a distinction between prevention of delivery because the consignee has refused the goods, whatever the reason for refusal,[84] and prevention with some other cause, for example, prevention because the necessary equipment is not available or because the consignee cannot be found.

If the cause of prevention is refusal by the consignee, the requirements of Article 12 on disposal are relaxed by the second sentence of Article 15.1: "the sender shall be entitled to dispose of them without being obliged to produce the first copy of the consignment note". The relaxation is necessary because the first copy may have been sent to the consignee. However, if the consignee has a change of mind and requires delivery before the carrier has received instructions to the contrary from the sender, it appears[85] that the carrier must deliver to the consignee after all: Article 15.2.

If the cause of prevention is some cause other than the refusal of the consignee, the inference has been drawn,[86] *a contrario*, that the sender can give instructions only in accordance with Article 12: in particular, the sender must produce the first copy of the consignment note, as required by Article 12.5(a). If the sender cannot do so, there appears to be a hiatus in which the carrier is obliged to ask the sender for instructions but the sender is not entitled to give them. In practice, the first copy is likely to be with the consignee, who is in a position to untie the knot by exercising the right of disposal under Article 12 or, if the consignee does not oblige, the

[81] Helm, Art. 15 Anm. 2.

[82] *Kg Rotterdam 24.5.66* (1966) 1 E.T.L. 729.

[83] *O.L.G. Hamburg 25.2.88*, VersR 1988.909.

[84] For example, because the goods have been damaged en route: *Moto-Vespa v. MAT* (below, para. 37f). This would also include a case in which the consignee wanted delivery but refused to pay charges due: Loewe, para. 134; Putzeys, para. 534.

[85] Article 15.2 states that the consignee "may . . . require delivery" but does not state that the carrier must comply with that requirement.

[86] Rodière (1971) 6 E.T.L. 2, 6, who suggests that the practical solution would be for the sender to "instruct" the carrier to address himself to the consignee for "instructions"; however, *ex hypothesi*, the carrier would not be obliged to follow the "instructions" of either sender or consignee.

carrier can bring the carriage to an end by exercising the powers under Article 16.2.[87]

A further hiatus may occur if the carrier asks the sender for instructions, but the sender, who perhaps has lost interest in the goods, declines to give any instructions.[88] Whereas Article 14 has a default provision in paragraph 2 for the situation in which the carrier "has been unable to obtain instructions in reasonable time", there is no such default provision for prevention of delivery under Article 15. In this situation the carrier may wish to exercise the powers in Article 16.[89]

33c. Interim and other measures decided by the carrier

Although in the cases governed by Article 14[90] and Article 15[91] the carrier is obliged to ask for instructions, the carrier has immediate powers under Article 16 to unload and sell the goods: below, paragraph 33c(*ii*). Moveover, if the carrier asks for instructions under Article 14.1, but is unable to obtain them within a reasonable time, the carrier has a duty under Article 14.2 to take reasonable steps, steps which may amount to alternative performance of the contract of carriage: below, paragraph 33c(*i*).

33c(*i*). Reasonable steps: alternative performance

If the carrier seeks instructions, as required by Article 14.1, Article 14.2 provides that if, first, circumstances are such as to allow "the carriage to be carried out under conditions differing from those laid down in the consignment note" and if, secondly, the carrier "has been unable to obtain instructions in reasonable time"[92] in accordance with Article 12,[93] then he must "take such steps as seem to him to be in the best interests of the person entitled to dispose of the goods". When taking such steps the carrier is acting as an agent of necessity.[94]

The steps include unloading. Distinguish, however, unloading under Article 16.2,[95] whereby the carriage is "at an end": this is

---

[87] Below, paras. 33c(*i*) and 33c(*ii*).

[88] In this situation Rodière (1971) 6 E.T.L. 2, 6 suggests that the sender may be held liable for damage to the goods which would result from absence of instructions. However, given the carrier's general duty of care for the goods (below, para. 79), and the reluctance of English courts to impose civil liability of any kind for inactivity such as silence, the sender's silence is unlikely to be seen as the cause of any damage to the goods.

[89] Above, para. 32c.

[90] Above, para. 33a.

[91] Above, para. 33b.

[92] He must prove that he was unable to do so: *Rb Arnhem 28.1.71*, 1977 U.L.R. II 207.

[93] Above, para. 32.

[94] Rodière (1971) 6 E.T.L. 2, 5.

[95] Below, para. 33c(*ii*).

hardly a step "such as to allow the carriage to be carried out" in terms of Article 14.2.[96] Yet, unloading the goods, for example to reload them an hour later on another vehicle, may be very much a reasonable step under Article 14.2. Hence it will be a question of fact whether unloading occurs as one of the steps taken under Article 14.2 to carry out the carriage[97] or as an act under Article 16.2 which brings the carriage to an end.

Steps also include contracting for on-carriage by another carrier. If on-carriage is by the same mode and within the terms of the consignment note, there is no impossibility within the sense of Article 14.1.[98] However, if it is contrary to the terms of the consignment note, for example on-carriage by a different mode of transport,[99] the decision must be justified as a reasonable step under Article 14.2.

> In *OGH 10.2.81*,[1] nearing the end of carriage from Switzerland to Bahrein, the driver found that, through no fault of his employer or of the forwarder, the vehicle was too heavy to cross from Al Khobar to Bahrein in the expected way (ferry). Having failed over a period of six hours to make telephone contact with the sender in Switzerland, and fearing theft if the goods were left on the vehicle, the driver had the goods sent on by dhow. In application of Article 14.2, the court said that the reasonable time for obtaining instructions depended on the circumstances of the case, that in this case the driver was justified in the steps that he took, and that the carrier's claim for expenses succeeded.

In such cases, given the initial contract of carriage whereby the carrier promises to carry to final destination, as well as the liberty of the carrier to sub-contract,[2] although *ex hypothesi* the terms of the consignment note have been changed, the better view is that the carrier remains responsible for the entire carriage, while the actual on-carrier is a sub-carrier.[3] The alternative view,[4] that the carrier is a forwarding agent who arranges a new contract of carriage, fits less easily with Article 14.2, which imposes a duty on the carrier, a duty which would not have fallen upon him but for

---

[96] The power given by Art. 16.2 to unload the goods, end the carriage and entrust the goods to a third party (conduct which may be eminently in the interests of the person entitled to dispose of the goods) is given only by reference to Art. 14.1; however, since the reference in Art. 16.2 is to the "cases" in Art. 14.1, it could be argued that the powers in Art. 16.2 also exist in connection with "reasonable steps" under Art. 14.2.

[97] For example, to unload the goods (in the desert) in order to go back and get advice and assistance does not end the carriage: *OGH 27.8.81*, Greiter 97, 102.

[98] Above, para. 33a(*i*).

[99] Helm Art. 14 Anm. 4.

[1] Greiter 88.

[2] Above, para. 29.

[3] In this sense Glass and Cashmore, para. 3.34. This appears to have been presumed without discussion in *OGH 10.2.81* (above, n. 1).

[4] Hill and Messent, p. 95, who offer this as a possible alternative.

the original contract of carriage. Although Article 14.1 speaks of impossibility to carry out the contract, while Article 14.2 speaks of carrying out not the contract on different terms but the carriage under different conditions, the more natural inference is of alternative performance of the original contract rather than its truncation, and of continuation on an entirely new basis.[5]

It has been contended[6] that, if a carrier responds to one obstacle (cause A) by taking reasonable steps under Article 14.2, which *ex hypothesi* involve a change in the carriage originally contracted for, if then the carrier meets another kind of obstacle (cause B), the latter is outside the scope of the CMR Articles 14 *et seq.*, as it is no longer an Article 14 case of impossibility "to carry out the contract in accordance with the terms laid down in the consignment note". However, this can hardly have been the intention of those who drafted the CMR. With this in mind a court may take the view that Article 14 applies, not to a carrier who is carrying out the original contract, as the contention assumes, but to a situation in which it is impossible to do so. If suspension trouble in the refrigerated vehicle contracted for (cause A) is dealt with by transfer to an unrefrigerated vehicle, which is then involved in a road accident (cause B), the accident is as much a cause of impossibility to carry out the original contract on time as the breakdown. More difficult is the case in which, for example, the carrier, advised of a strike of contract delivery depot A, heads for depot B, only to find that a sympathy strike has been called at B: the strike at B is not a cause of impossibility to perform a contract to deliver at A.[7] Nonetheless, a court may conclude that *ex hypothesi* the contract cannot be carried out in strict accordance with its original terms, but that it is still in essence the same contract that is being carried out, and that therefore Article 14.2 applies.

33c(*ii*). Unloading: ending the carriage

Article 16.2 provides that, in cases under Article 14 or Article 15, the carrier "may immediately unload the goods for account of the person entitled to dispose of them and thereupon the carriage shall be deemed to be at an end".[8] It is clear that the carrier may do this without waiting for instructions and, perhaps, without needing to

[5] Especially when the on-carriage takes place entirely within the boundaries of one country and hence the CMR does not apply to a new contract in those circumstances: above, para. 20.

[6] Hill and Messent, p. 95.

[7] Unless, of course, the strike at B is seen as part of the strike at A.

[8] *Aliter*, if unloading is done as a step under Article 14.2: above, para. 33c(*i*).

concern himself with whether such unloading is likely to be compatible with instructions.[9] If the unloading is undertaken on the initiative of the carrier, the cost of unloading is expressed by Article 16.2 to be "for account of the person entitled to dispose" of the goods, but the cost of subsequent storage is not mentioned. If storage is confirmed by instructions from that person, that person bears the cost[10]; but, if not, the carrier may have to exercise the power of sale to recover the cost of storage.[11]

If the carriage ends under Article 16.2, the unloading has the effect of delivery[12] under Article 17. Moreover, Article 16.2 provides that the carrier "shall then hold the goods on behalf of the person" entitled to dispose of them. The carrier is liable for loss of or damage to the goods under national law,[13] such as the law of bailment in England.[14]

The CMR does not require the carrier to inform the person entitled to dispose of the goods that the goods have been unloaded, or where they are. However, in the terms of Article 16.2, it is the carriage that is "deemed to be at an end" and not the contract[15] or, therefore, the application of the CMR.[16] As the decision to unload must be made in cases governed by Article 14.1 and Article 15, and although the carrier's liability for the safety of the goods is now governed not by the CMR but by national law, the unloading does not nullify the carrier's duty to seek and carry out instructions under those provisions, and it is difficult to see how the carrier can properly seek instructions without stating what has happened to the goods.[17]

---

[9] *cf.* Hill and Messent, p. 95: the goods can only be unloaded and stored, if that is in the best interests of the person entitled, apparently a reference to the duty of the carrier to take reasonable steps under Art. 14.2. Certainly, the carrier cannot unload and store in disregard of his implied duty to take reasonable care of the goods: Putzeys, para. 536; see also below, para. 79. However, it has been argued (above, para. 33c(*i*)) that the duty to take steps in the best interests of the goods under Art. 14.2 and the right to unload under Art. 16.2 do not arise in the same circumstances.

[10] *Paris 21.12.82*, B.T. 1983.233.

[11] *Paris 22.12.83*, B.T. 1984.486.

[12] Loewe, para. 139; Helm, Art. 16 Anm. 2. Except perhaps that, as the goods are unloaded "for account of" the person entitled to dispose of them, that person bears the cost of unloading, whether or not unloading was his responsibility under the original contract of carriage: Hill and Messent, p. 98.

[13] Helm., Art. 16 Anm. 2; Hill and Messent, p. 98. Herber/Piper, Art. 16, 21; Koller, Art. 16, 7; Loewe, para. 139; Thume, Art. 16, 19. See *Düsseldorf 26.10.78*, below, para. 66; and *O.G.H. 15.4.93*, TranspR 1993.425.

[14] *Stephenson v. Hart* (below, para. 35).

[15] *Contra*: Helm, Art. 16 Anm. 2. Whereas it makes sense that the carrier's vehicle should not be tied up with the goods, it is more surprising that the carrier should have a unilateral power to end the contract, even in the circumstances proscribed by Art. 14 and Art. 15.

[16] The CMR applies not to carriage as such but to the contract of carriage: above, para. 10.

[17] Such a duty is confirmed by common law: below, para. 211. *cf.* Glass and Cashmore, para. 3.37.

If, as is likely, the CMR carrier wishes to be rid of the goods and warehouses them, Article 16.2 states that the carrier may entrust the goods to a third party, and that "in that case he shall not be under any liability except for the exercise of reasonable care in the choice of such third party". At this point it is clear that the carrier is beyond any instructions, as well as any liability for failure to carry out those instructions, in the sense of Article 12. The carrier is also beyond the scope of the CMR: the carrier's liability, if any, will be determined by national law.[18]

33c(*iii*). Selling the goods

Article 16.3 gives the carrier a power of sale, sale according to a procedure determined by the law[19] or custom of the place where the goods are situated: Article 16.5. Local law may require notice of the sale to the sender or consignee, but the CMR does not.

Article 16.3 cannot be read in isolation: it does not give the carrier a power to sell at will, but must be construed in context as confined to the case of impossibility (Article 14) or of prevention (Article 15). Even in these cases the circumstances in which the carrier is entitled to sell the goods are limited.

If "the goods are perishable or their condition warrants such a course", or "when the storage expenses would be out of proportion to the value of the goods", evidently cases in which time is against deliberation, the carrier may sell the goods "without awaiting instructions from the person entitled to dispose of them" or, presumably, from the sender.[20]

In other cases, the carrier must first seek instructions. If, however, the carrier has asked for instructions from the person entitled to dispose of the goods under Article 14 or from the sender under Article 15[21] and "after a reasonable period he has not received from the [appropriate person] instructions to the contrary which he may reasonably be required to carry out",[22] the carrier may sell the goods.

---

[18] As to English common law, see below, Chap. 12

[19] Excluding the conflicts rules of that place: Loewe, para. 145.

[20] In the circumstances of Art. 15.1 when the sender is entitled to give instructions but is not the person entitled to dispose of the goods.

[21] In the circumstances of Art. 15.1 when the sender is entitled to give instructions but is not the person entitled to dispose of the goods.

[22] Presumably, the "reasonable period" is measured from the time that the carrier asked for instructions. The intention was that the reasonable period be governed by the "law of the place in which the goods were held": E/ECE/TRANS/SC1/130 Annexe 4 p. 8.

Although there is no reference to Art. 12, in practice if not also in principle the instructions must be instructions which, like instructions given under Art. 14 and Art. 15 comply with Art. 12.5: Herber/Piper, Art. 16, 33; Koller, Art. 16, 9; Loewe, para. 143; Thume, Arts. 16, 32. *cf.* Hill and Messent, p. 100.

In each case Article 16.4 provides that "the proceeds of sale, after deduction of the expenses chargeable against the goods", such as the charges due under the consignment note[23] and, where relevant, the cost of requesting and carrying out instructions,[24] "shall be placed at the disposal of the person entitled to dispose of the goods. If these charges exceed the proceeds of sale, the carrier shall be entitled to the difference". Although the obligation of the carrier in cases of impossibility and prevention are distinct from the carrier's general duty to carry and care for the goods, an action by the carrier for expenses may be defended on the ground that the sale was necessitated by damage to the goods, for which the carrier was responsible under Article 17.[25]

33d. Liability

33d(*i*). Damages

The liability of the carrier for loss caused[26] by failure to fulfil the obligations in Articles 14–16 is assumed.[27] However, the basis of that liability is not clear, as there is no reference in Articles 14–16 to the nature or extent of liability for their breach.[28]

> In *O.L.G. Hamm 11.3.76*[29] a seller sent a machine from Germany to a buyer in Austria, but short of destination at Salzburg, where the consignee should have provided customs documents for import to Austria, the carrier obeyed the order of the consignee/buyer to deliver it to another firm for importation and on-carriage, during which the goods were damaged. The carrier sued for carriage charges, and the sender counterclaimed in respect of the damage, for which it was held the carrier was responsible in part.

The opinion of the court was that the carrier's compliance with the order of the consignee was a breach of contract (*Vertragsverletzung*), for the following reasons. The carrier was obliged to

[23] Art. 16.2.

[24] Arts. 16.1 and 16.2.

[25] *The Hague 24.6.87*, S. & S. 1988, no. 73.

[26] *Cass. 30.10.82*, B.T. 1982.129: when the lorry broke down and could not be repaired, the trailer bearing a badly stowed machine was transferred by the carrier from road to rail, without consultation with the sender, and the machine was damaged when the machine broke loose on the rail stage. The sender complained *inter alia* that the carrier had made no attempt to obtain instructions as required by Art. 14; but the court held that the transfer to rail and hence the breach of Art. 14 were not a cause of loss or damage to the sender. *cf. OLG Hamm 11.3.76* (below, n. 29).

[27] For example, Rodière (1971) 6 E.T.L. 2, 5.

[28] Except to the extent of the reference back to Art. 12 and hence to Art. 12.7. It is not entirely clear that the reference includes a reference to Art. 12.7. Even if it does, it is still not clear whether liability under Art. 12.7 is affected by Art. 23 of the CMR on the amount of compensation recoverable: above, para. 32c.

[29] N.J.W. 1976.2077.

carry to destination without deviation, unless the seller/sender consented to something different, and in this case this obligation was broken by the carrier's compliance with the instructions of the consignee. No consignment note having been issued, the consignee did not have the right to give instructions or to dispose of the goods.[30] When the consignee failed to hand over the requisite customs documents at Salzburg, the contract could not be performed in strict accordance with its terms, and the carrier should have sought the instructions of the sender in accordance with Article 14. Although the carrier's breach of Article 14 occurred between the time of taking over the goods and delivery, Articles 17 *et seq.* of the CMR did not apply. The court pointed out, first, that the contractual liability under the provisions of the CMR is not exclusive,[31] and did not rule out altogether other grounds of liability. Secondly, in this case Articles 17 *et seq.* did not apply because, although the breach occurred before delivery, the *damage* occurred after delivery by the carrier.[32] So the court applied national law, whereby there was a breach of the carrier's basic, essential and customary duty of care to be found in BGB Article 276, and the carrier was liable on that basis. The approach taken in this case poses a number of difficulties.

First, it is difficult to believe that it is the intention behind the CMR that the uniform regime can be avoided by the unilateral and wrongful decision of the carrier to deliver, and thus end the carriage, sooner than the contract required; that a carrier can proscribe both the carriage and the CMR by dumping the goods on the pavement outside the consignee's warehouse, from where they are later stolen, and the plead a liability limit in standard conditions lower than that in the CMR.[33] Indeed, that would not be "delivery",[34] and the loss of or damage to the goods in a case like that would occur before true delivery, and the liability of the carrier would be governed by the CMR.

In *The Hague 27.5.83*[35] the carrier's driver delivered by pumping the load into a tank on the consignee's premises, as he had done

---

[30] Nor could such a right be implied from the terms of the sale contract, "*frei Deutsche Grenze*"; such terms concerned the allocation of transport costs between seller and buyer, and were without effect on the contract of transport.

[31] At 2078, pointing to the possibility of delictual liability mentioned in Art. 28 and citing *B.G.H. 23.3.66*, N.J.W. 1967.42, a decision on the liability of the carrier in German domestic law, that provisions of the BGB governing the contract of carriage do not exclude or limit the (concurrent) operation of provisions, such as Art. 823.1 BGB, concerned *inter alia* with (delictual) liability for negligence causing damage to the property of other people.

[32] The same view has been taken of cases in which loss or damage occurs before the goods are taken over, notably in cases in which the carrier fails to take the goods over at all: below, para. 65.

[33] *cf.* Muth/Glöckner, p. 121: if, faced with surmountable difficulties, the carrier abandons the carriage, national law applies.

[34] Below, para. 37.

[35] S. & S. 1984, no. 68.

before, but without checking with the consignee that this was still the right place. The tank was full and much of the load overflowed and was lost. The carrier's contention, that the loss occurred at a time and place for which the carrier was not responsible for the goods, was brushed aside by the court. The carrier was held liable under the CMR.

Secondly, the decision in *O.L.G. Hamm 11.3.76* (above) depends on a strict interpretation of the CMR, notably Article 17,[36] whereby the carrier is liable for loss or damage "occurring between the time when he takes over the goods and the time of delivery", and not, at least as far as the CMR is concerned, if it occurs outside that period. In some cases there will be the usual argument over when loss or damage actually occurred, and over the rule to apply to damage that begins before delivery but continues to develop after delivery.[37] Subject to that, the strict interpretation is probably correct, but the results may be curious.

It is a rudiment of the CMR regime that the carrier is not liable for consequential loss of market at the place of destination.[38] However, if the carrier's vehicle breaks down and the goods are transferred to a vehicle sent by the consignee, delivery occurs at the point of transfer, the operation of the CMR regime ends at the point of transfer and, if the goods reach destination late, the original carrier may be liable in full for consequential loss on the basis that it occurred after delivery and is governed by national law.

Also curious is one result of the associated view,[39] that liability for breach of Articles 14–16 is outside the CMR regime, not *ratione temporis*, as in *O.L.G. Hamm 11.3.76*, but *ratione materiae*, and thus governed by national law. On the one hand, a carrier who delays carriage in breach of his initial contract is liable under Chapter 4 of the CMR for the consequences of his delay, but his liability is limited by Article 23.5 to the amount of the carriage charges. On the other hand, if the carrier delays compliance with instructions given under Articles 14–16 or, indeed, Article 12, his liability for the same or very similar loss is governed by national law, and is likely to be much greater.

---

[36] It is also the inference of Art. 11.3 concerning the consequences arising from the loss or incorrect use of documents. Whereas liability under Art. 11.3 is expressly limited to the amount "payable in the event of loss of the goods", *i.e.* the amount payable under Chap. 4 of the CMR, Art. 12.7 and still less Arts. 14–16 contain no such qualification. Accordingly, these cases will be left to national law.

[37] See insurance cases, for example: *Mayer & Sherratt v. Co-operative Ins. Sy.* [1939] 2 K.B. 627 (C.A.—insurer liable for loss commencing during period of cover and continuing to develop thereafter); *Fooks v. Smith* [1924] 2 K.B. 508 (loss occurring during period was covered, but not later loss to which the goods were thereby exposed); *Hough v. Head* (1885) 55 LJQB 43, 44 (Lord Esher M.R.: if loss is caused inside the period but does not occur until later, the loss is not covered).

[38] In general, such loss is not recoverable under the CMR: below, paras. 97 and 97c.

[39] Rodière (1971) 6 E.T.L. 2, 4–5.

In conclusion, it appears that, first, if breach of Articles 14–16 results in loss or damage occurring between taking over and delivery, the case falls within Article 17, and the liability of the carrier is governed by Chapter 4 of the CMR and therefore limited by Article 23.[40]

Secondly, if loss or damage occurs between taking over and delivery and gives rise to the impossibility or the prevention envisaged by Articles 14–16, the carrier's subsequent breach of Articles 14–16 is also a breach of the carrier's residual duty of "utmost" care in responding to emergencies en route[41] and, as such, is governed by the CMR.

> For example in *Cass. 23.5.77*[42] the carrier who took no actions, neither contacting the sender nor exercising powers under Article 16.3, when the goods (frozen fish) were refused by the consignee, was liable for deterioration in the goods as carrier. The goods had remained on this vehicle during the delay, and the court stressed that the carriage had not ended.

Thirdly, in other cases of breach of Articles 14–16, such as that in *O.L.G. Hamm 11.3.76* (above), the liability of the carrier will be governed by national law.

33d(*ii*). Expenses

If the carrier obtains and obeys instructions, Article 16.1 states that the carrier may recover, presumably from the party giving the instructions,[43] the cost of obtaining and executing those instructions. In the amount of expenses, the carrier is not allowed to include a profit component. This conclusion follows from the language of Article 16.1 and as a matter of inference from the application of Article 12.5, which allows the carrier to decline to follow instructions which "interfere with the normal working of the carrier's undertaking".[44] So, in a case in which the designated consignee refused delivery of the goods and the carrier obeyed the instruction of the sender to take the goods on a further journey to another consignee,[45] the carrier was not allowed to recover for the latter more than expenses even though, if that phase had been

---

[40] For example, *Amiens 28.10.92*, B.T.L. 1992.767. Moreover, in *Lyon 24.3.83*, B.T. 1984.166, it appears that, but for *une faute lourde* by the (*commissionnaire* treated as the) carrier, the court would have applied Art. 23 to a breach of Art. 15.

[41] Below, para. 79.

[42] B.T. 1977.388. See also *O.L.G. Saarbrücken 21.11.74* (1976) 11 E.T.L. 261, below, para. 88; *Metz 28.10.87*, B.T. 1988.168; but *cf. O.L.G. Hamburg 31.3.94*, TranspR 1995.245.

[43] So held in *Paris 21.12.82*, B.T. 1983.233.

[44] Koller, Art. 16, 2; Thume, Art. 16, 6.

[45] *O.L.G. Munich 12.4.91*, TranspR 1991.298.

contracted for initially, the carrier's charge would have included an extra profit element for that phase.

Not surprisingly, Article 16.1 makes an exception when the expenses were caused by the wrongful act or neglect of the carrier himself. The cause may be an act or neglect giving rise to impossibility (Article 14) or to prevention of delivery (Article 15), or it may be one which increases the cost of dealing with an impossibility or prevention for which the carrier was not originally responsible[46]: in each case the carrier must bear the cost himself.

If, in breach of contract, the carrier does not ask for and obtain instructions, but nonetheless takes steps which are in the best interests of the goods, it has been held[47] that the carrier is not entitled to recover the expense.

If the carrier is unable to obtain instructions, it might be inferred[48] that the expense of taking steps in the best interests of the goods, as required by Article 14.2, is recoverable by the carrier. However, doubt exists, as the right to recover expenses is apparently limited to "the cost of his request for instructions, and any other expenses entailed in carrying out such instructions": Article 16.1. In other cases, it appears that the carrier has no right to recover the (extra) cost of taking steps: hardly an inducement to act, as required by Article 14.2, in the best interests of the person entitled to dispose of the goods. In Germany it has been suggested[49] that such expenses may be recoverable under national law; however, it has been held[50] in France that the only course open to the carrier is to exercise the power to sell the goods,[51] and deduct the costs incurred from the proceeds.

As regards security for expenses, Article 16.2 provides that, if the carrier unloads and holds the goods as bailee or deposits the goods with a third party, the charges and expenses "shall remain chargeable against the goods".[52] Otherwise, Article 16 makes no mention of any security for expenses, except in so far as the reference to instructions implies a reference to Article 14, which in

---

[46] Loewe, para. 138; Rodière (1971) 6 E.T.L. 2, 7.

[47] *Grenoble 4.2.88*, B.T. 1988.699.

[48] From *Grenoble 4.2.88*, B.T. 1988.699.

[49] Helm, Art. 14 Anm. 4; Muth/Glöckner, p. 122.

[50] *Paris 22.12.83*, B.T. 1984.486: the consignee, the person interested, having refused delivery and so refused to give instructions, could not be held liable for storage charges.

[51] Above, para. 33c(*iii*).

[52] Loewe, para. 141 argues that this "provision is not intended to apply to any costs incurred only after performance of the contract of carriage proper has come to an end: this is clear from the use of the word 'remain'." However, it is submitted that the phrase in which "remain" occurs means that expenses shall continue to be chargeable, whether new expenses or old expenses, and that this is the more reasonable interpretation.

turn refers[53] to Article 12: under Article 12.5(a) a person is only entitled to dispose of the goods under Article 12 if that person "indemnifies the carrier against all expenses, loss and damage involved in carrying out such instructions". However, in the case of disposal under Article 12, the argument for security is stronger,[54] for in the situation of Article 16, the carrier can resort to the proceeds of sale of the goods. Hence, it is doubtful whether the carrier can demand a security, except as provided by Article 16.2.

34. Destination

Article 6.1(d) requires the consignment note to state "the place designated for delivery". Subject to any modification by the person entitled to dispose of the goods,[55] the destination will be the one mentioned in the consignment note or, in the absense of a note, the one agreed with the carrier when the contract is concluded. If goods are brought to a place of delivery, for example a named city, but the precise point of delivery has not been specified, English law implies a duty to deliver at the consignee's place of business there.[56]

If the destination is the place of business of the carrier, from where the goods are to be collected by the consignee, it can be argued that delivery occurs when the consignee collects the goods or, perhaps the better view,[57] when the goods have arrived at the carrier's place and are at the disposal of the consignee. In such circumstances it has been argued[58] in England that, if the contract is silent on the point, the carrier has an implied duty to give the consignee notice of arrival. Only when effective notice has been given are the goods at the disposal of the consignee, so that the carrier can argue that delivery has occurred,[59] that his liability as carrier has ceased and his liability as warehouseman (on his own terms and conditions) has begun. If the carrier is unable to give

---

[53] See discussion of the ambiguity in the reference in Article 14.1 to Article 12, above, para. 33a.

[54] Loewe, para. 143: "the carrier cannot be required to carry out instructions which are so unreasonable that they would obviously involve the loss of or at any rate some serious deterioration in the value of the goods, since the carrier might in such case suffer loss from the fact that he would no longer be able to consider the goods as sufficient security for his expenses".

[55] Above, para. 32.

[56] Below, para. 212.

[57] Below, para. 212.

[58] Kahn-Freud, p. 303.

[59] This possibility is discussed below, para. 212.

effective notice to the consignee, because, for example, he lacks information about the consignee, it appears that this is a situation in which delivery has been prevented and which is therefore governed by Article 15.[60]

35. The consignee

Article 6.1(d) requires the consignment note to state the name of the consignee. Article 13.1 entitles the consignee to require delivery of the goods against a receipt. The consignee has no document, such as the bill of lading for goods carried by sea, which demonstrates the consignee's right to the goods. It suffices that the consignee can be identified in some other way as the person to whom the carrier has been instructed to deliver the goods, but the question arises, what must the carrier do to check that the person demanding the goods is indeed the consignee?

If the carrier delivers the goods to a person who, to the carrier's actual knowledge, has no right to receive the goods, the carrier commits an act of wilful misconduct,[61] which deprives the carrier of defences under Article 17. In France the same has been held of the carrier who delivered goods to a person without any attempt to check that that was the right person.[62]

If the carrier delivers the goods to a person in circumstances which should arouse the carrier's suspicion or put him on inquiry, he commits a breach of the contract of carriage. At common law, the carrier fulfils his duty by delivery of the goods at the correct address to a person who has apparent authority to receive them: it is enough that the carrier has not been negligent. Under the CMR, it appears that this is not enough.[63] The carrier has contracted to carry the goods and to deliver them to the right person. If he hands them over to the wrong person, he has not handed them over to the right person and delivery has not occurred. If the goods are disposed of by the wrong person, this is a loss to the right person which occurs between the time of taking over and delivery, so the carrier's liability is based on Article 17 of the CMR. That liability is not absolute, but nor is it pegged at the lower level of reasonable

---

[60] Above, para. 33b.

[61] See below, para. 101. In French law such a breach constitutes *une faute lourde: Cass. 12.6.50*, G.P. 50. II. 195; *Paris 23.3.29*, G.P. 29. II. 129. It is a fundamental breach in English law: see below, para. 240. However, it has been suggested that that doctrine has no application to liability governed by the CMR: above, para. 31a.

[62] *Cass. 12.12.89*, B.T. 1990.283. It is uncertain whether an English court would reach the same decision: below, para. 102c.

[63] *cf.* the first edition of this book, para. 35.

care, but at the intermediate level of "utmost" care required, for example, in cases of theft and robbery en route.[64] Both sense and symmetry suggest that the level of care required of the carrier to avoid robbery en route should also be required of him to avoid more devious kinds of dishonesty at destination.[65]

36. Unloading

As the CMR does not settle responsibility for (loading and) unloading, this is governed by national law. As to the appropriate national law, opinion is divided between the law of the contract and the law of the place in which unloading is to take place.[66] If English law is found to be the governing law, there is still no clear answer. In most respects the matter is governed by the same considerations as loading.[67]

Just as loading must be distinguished from the act of taking over the goods, the point at which liability under Article 17 commences, so also unloading must be distinguished from delivery,[68] the point at which liability comes to an end.

37. Delivery

Delivery takes place in accordance with the terms of the contract of carriage, including any custom of the trade which can be read into the contract,[69] as well as with Article 13 of the CMR. Article 13.1 provides:

> "After arrival of the goods at the place designated for delivery, the consignee shall be entitled to require the carrier to deliver to him, against a receipt, the second copy of the consignment note and the goods."

No form is prescribed for the receipt. The second copy of

[64] Below, para. 75a.
[65] If the carrier's breach lies in failure to carry out instructions as to the disposal of the goods, which may involve a change of destination or of consignee, the matter is affected by Art. 12.7: above, paras. 32c and 33d(*i*).
[66] Rodière (1970) 5 E.T.L. 620, 632–633(*i*).
[67] Above, para. 28.
[68] Below, para. 37.
[69] For example, in *Paris 4.3.85*, B.T. 1985.396, below, para. 37a. For more recent French decisions, see B.T.L. 1992.145.

the consignment note is the copy that travels with the goods,[70] the third having been retained by the carrier and the first by the sender.[71] Although possession of a consignment note may be essential, if the consignee is to exercise rights of disposal under Article 12,[72] the consignee does not need it in order to exercise rights under Article 13,[73] notably, the right to require delivery of the goods and the right to enforce the contract.

Article 13.2 provides:

> "The consignee who avails himself of the right granted to him under [Article 13.1] shall pay the charges shown to be due on the consignment note, but in the event of dispute on this matter the carrier shall not be required to deliver the goods unless security has been furnished by the consignee."

As to the charges, the contract of carriage being quite separate from any contract of sale between sender and consignee, the consignee must pay these charges to the carrier regardless of any defect or shortage in the goods for which the sender (and not the carrier) is responsible. As to the range of charges, they are those "shown to be due on the consignment note".[74] Arguably, although not specified by Article 13, the CMR has the CIM rule that the charges extend not only to charges owed by the consignee personally but to any charge concerning that particular consignment.

As to the security, Loewe contends[75] that, in spite of the French text (*caution*, which in French law is limited to the deposit of a sum of money), security should be read as any kind of security which safeguards the rights of the carrier.

Delivery is important as it marks the point at which the carrier's responsibility as carrier[76] under Article 17.1 ends. As delivery is not defined by the CMR, courts turn to the terms of the contract,[77] if any, and to national law.[78] The rules of national law in leading CMR states are similar.

---

[70] Art. 5.1. Above, para. 23.

[71] Unless it has been sent to the consignee to facilitate his right to dispose of the goods under Art. 12.3.

[72] Above, para. 32b.

[73] Glass and Cashmore, para. 3.31.

[74] According to Art. 6 these charges are charges relating to the carriage (carriage charges, supplementary charges, customs duties and other charges incurred from the making of the contract to the time of delivery); charges which the sender undertakes to pay; and cash on delivery charges.

[75] Para. 127.

[76] Below, para. 54.

[77] See below, paras. 40a *et seq.*

[78] *AG Hamburg 21.6.77*, VersR 1977.1048. See also Helm, Art. 17 Anm. 2; but *cf.* Haak, pp. 180 and 182.

Delivery must be in the right place[79] and to the right person.[80] Delivery occurs when the goods pass from the control of the carrier or his agent to that of the consignee or his agent.[81] If the consignee has control, actual possession[82] is unnecessary if the goods are in the hands of another person who holds them for the consignee. The key concept, therefore, is control.[83] Delivery is a question of fact for the carrier to prove by any means available.[84]

Delivery is unaffected by whether the carrier has given to the consignee notice of arrival,[85] or whether the consignee has had a satisfactory opportunity to inspect the goods at that time[86] or whether the consignee has received the second copy of the consignment note.[87] A consignee may have notice but no goods. He may have goods but no knowledge of their defects. The key concept is control.

Delivery may not coincide with unloading,[88] as unloading may be the task of the consignee,[89] who thus gains control of the goods on the vehicle and thus takes delivery at latest when unloading

---

[79] See above, para. 34.

[80] *O.L.G. Munich 27.3.81*, VersR 1982.264. As to the identity of the right person, see above, para. 35.

[81] Custody in the sense of safe-keeping (*der Gewahrsam*) and control (*die tatsächliche Gewalt*) but not necessarily actual possession (*den Besitz des Gutes körperlich zu ergreifen*): Willenberg N.J.W. 1968.1022, citing *Lg Frankfurt am Main 14.5.65*, and *O.L.G. Zweibrücken 23.9.66* (below, n. 97). Also in this sense: *O.L.G. Hamm 11.3.76*, N.J.W. 1976.2077, 2078 col. 1; *AG Hamburg 21.6.77*, VersR 1977.1049. This conception of delivery under the CMR is evidently based on the rule in the HGB Art. 429: Helm, Art. 17 Anm. 2; Muth/Glöckner, p. 118, citing *O.L.G. Düsseldorf 27.4.55*, N.J.W. 1955.1322; see also *O.L.G. Nürnberg 21.12.89*, TranspR 1991.99. *idem* in *Austria: O.G.H. 4.11.81*, TranspR 1982.80; Greiter 103; *O.G.H. 11.12.86*, Stra GüV 1987/5 p. 18; *O.G.H. 7.7.89*, VersR 1990.1180; *O.L.G. Hamburg 14.5.96*, TranspR 1997.101.

This is also the point at which transit insurance of goods normally ends: Clarke (1988) 23 E.T.L. 645. This provides a strong argument for a coincidence in the change of risk and liability regime.

[82] Haak, p. 181.

[83] Haak, *loc. cit.*; Loewe, para. 149.

[84] *Cass. 5.7.88*, B.T. 1988.530. Putzeys, para. 517.

[85] Notice does not amount to delivery: *The Hague 10.5.78* (1978) 13 E.T.L. 607. *O.L.G. Hamburg 14.5.96*, TranspR 1997.101. On the possibility of a common law duty to give notice, see above, para. 34.

[86] *Rotterdam 15.1.71* (1971) 6 E.T.L. 417. This can be inferred from Art. 30.1, which contemplates delivery in the case of non-apparent damage. *cf.* however, *Paris 15.6.84*, below, para. 37a in which the absence of oppoortunity to check the goods was one element that led the court to decide that there had been no delivery.

Lack of opportunity to examine the goods may mean that the consignee will be unable to enter reservations in the case of apparent damage in time to destroy the presumption of conforming delivery and thus make it harder to show that the carrier is liable for damage occurring while the goods were in the carrier's charge; this should be in the mind of the consignee when agreeing to the time and place of delivery. If the consignee chooses to take control of the goods in a place where it is difficult to check the goods, or through the agency of a third party who lacks the expertise to check the goods, so be it; but it is not a reason for prolonging the liability of the carrier under Art. 17.

[87] *O.L.G. Nürnberg 21.12.89*, TranspR 1991.99.

[88] *Brussels 24.1.69* (1969) 4 E.T.L. 937; *Brussels 17.6.71* (1972) 7 E.T.L. 595. Haak, p. 183; Loewe, para. 149; Putzeys, para. 508.

[89] As to responsibility for unloading, see above, para. 36.

begins.[90] Nor is there any necessary coincidence between delivery and arrival at the place of destination: the goods may be left there on a wharf,[91] or in a customs shed,[92] or on a vehicle which it is the carrier's duty to unload,[93] or in a warehouse of the carrier[94] or of a third party. Here too there has been no delivery, unless the carrier or third party are holding the goods for the consignee in the circumstances of Article 15.2.[95] Conversely, delivery may occur before arrival at destination if the consignee obtains control of the goods from the carrier on the road.[96]

> In *O.L.G. Zweibrücken 23.9.66*[97] peaches left Italy for Germany but the carrying vehicle broke down en route. The peaches were transferred at the point of breakdown to a lorry sent out by the consignee. The court held that this was delivery, saying[98] "By delivery within the meaning of (Article 17.1) is to be understood the process by which the carrier gives up the care of the goods transported by agreement with the consignee and puts the latter in a position to exercise actual control over the goods."

For control to pass to the consignee, there must be co-operation on the part of the consignee, which some systems of law call *réception*[99]: no co-operation, no *réception* and prima facie no delivery. If the vehicle has arrived at the right place, the carrier

---

[90] *AG Hamburg 21.6.77*, VersR 1977.1048; *Cass. 22.11.88*, 1988 U.L.R. II 744. Putzeys, para. 509. This appears correct in principle; however, as has been pointed out (Loewe, para. 149; Hill and Messent, p. 105), if custody and control pass to the consginee and thus delivery occurs prior to unloading by the consignee, the designation of unloading by the consignee as a special risk in Art. 17.4(c) would be superfluous.

[91] *Brussels 24.1.69* (1969) 4 E.T.L. 937.

[92] *Cass. 24.11.87*, B.T. 1988.42; or freeport: *O.L.G. Hamburg 14.5.96*, TranspR 1997.101.

[93] *Gent 20.11.75* (1976) 11 E.T.L. 231; *Paris 15.6.84*, B.T. 1984.545. *idem* even though the vehicle is on the consignee's premises: *Antwerp 13.2.85* (1986) 21 E.T.L. 183; or when the carrier handed the goods over to a third party to unload the goods, but that party was acting for the carrier, whose duty it was in that case to unload, there had been no delivery to the consignee: *Gent 20.11.75* (1976) 11 E.T.L. 231.

[94] *Paris 31.1.84* B.T. 1984.543. Or even a warehouse belonging to the consignee, if the carrier retains control of the goods: *Arnhem 6.12.78*, S. & S. 1979 no. 14; see also in this sense *Paris 15.6.84*, discussed below, para. 37a.

[95] Above, para. 33c.

[96] For example by sending a vehicle or that of an agent, such as another carrier, to receive the goods from the first carrier: *O.L.G. Hamm 11.3.76*, N.J.W. 1976.2077. This is so, even if delivery is a breach of contract with the sender, who has the right of disposal: *ibid.*; also in this sense: *O.L.G. Munich 23.4.93*, TranspR 1993.348. On the right of disposal, see above, para. 32.

[97] N.J.W. 1966.1717; VersR 1967.1145;

[98] At 1718, col. 1.

[99] Putzeys, para. 507: "La livraison est l'acte juridique par lequel le transporteur se décharge de la responsabilité d'une marchandise . . . entre les mains d'un destinataire qui la reçoit . . . A la livraison coincide en principe la réception; encore qu'il n'y ait livraison effective qu'à l'instant de la réception par le destinataire, il s'agit de démarches distinctes." And para. 523: "La réception est l'acte juridique par lequel le destinataire accepte la livraison de la marchandise par le transporteur et le décharge ainsi de sa responsabilité. La réception suit la livraison, il ne peut y avoir réception, s'il n'y a pas eu livraison." See also Libouton, Theunis, p. 79.

may find it impossible or impractical to deliver and thus be rid of the goods and of liability under Article 17. Clearly, the carrier is not allowed to dump the goods outside the consignee's warehouse, for this is not delivery "by agreement with the consignee"[1]: although the carrier has relinquished control of the goods, the consignee has not acquired it.[2] However, it would be enough in the absence of the consignee's personnel to deliver into the premises or to deliver liquid goods into the appropriate tank[3]: the carrier relinquishes control and the consignee acquires it, albeit passively. It has been suggested[4] that at common law tender of delivery is treated as delivery if through no fault of his own the carrier is unable to effect actual delivery. This may be true of common law but it is not the position under the CMR.[5] Under the CMR, the first question is whether and when the carrier is entitled to deliver: below, paragraphs 37a to 37c. If the carrier is unable to deliver in accordance with the contract, then contract delivery has been prevented and the position is governed by Article 15[6] and Article 16.[7] In practice the position depends on the impediment to delivery, which varies according to whether the consignee does not want the goods at all, does not want them yet, or does want them but is not there to receive them.

37a. Justifiable postponement of delivery

If the consignee justifiably declines to take immediate delivery, but postpones it perhaps to a more convenient time, the carrier remains responsible for the goods under Article 17 until delivery later. One possibility is that, on arrival at the agreed place of delivery, the consignee in the proper exercise of the right of disposal[8] instructs the carrier to proceed with the goods to a different place: delivery does not take place until the instruction has been

---

[1] *Cambrai 12.9.78*, B.T. 1978.445 (goods left on public highway near consignee's premises). See also *Cass. 20.5.86*, B.T. 1986.446. *Aix 15.11.95*, B.T.L. 1996.133. *cf. O.G.H. 11.12.86*, below, para. 37c.

[2] *O.L.G. Nürnberg 21.12.89*, TranspR 1991.99.

[3] *The Hague 27.5.83*, S. & S. 1984, no. 68; however, in this case, the tank, into which the driver had previously pumped the liquid, was full and it overflowed and the liquid was lost. The court held that the carrier should have consulted the consignee and was liable for the loss. Nonetheless the court proceeded on the basis that delivery had occurred. But *cf. Antwerp 19.11.91* (1992) 26 E.T.L. 127; delivery had occurred in such circumstances but the liability of the carrier was governed by the CMR.

[4] Glass and Cashmore, para. 1.67.

[5] Unless the contract defines delivery in this way: below, para. 37e.

[6] Above, para. 33b.

[7] Above, para. 33c.

[8] Above, para. 32b.

carried out.[9] Another possibility is that the carrier arrives at the agreed place of delivery, and the consignee wants to take control of the goods there, but not yet. Within reason the carrier must wait upon the consignee's convenience.

In *O.G.H. 16.3.77*[10] a loaded vehicle arrived at the premises of the consignee in Milan at 11.45 a.m. but the driver was turned away because the midday break was due to begin at noon and continue until 2 p.m. The driver went to a nearby restaurant to telephone his employer and have lunch but, in order to do so, had to leave his vehicle and trailer in a side street two blocks away. When he went to return to the vehicle at 2 p.m., he found that it had been stolen. The carrier was held liable[11] not under Austrian national law but under Article 17.1 of the CMR, as the loss had occurred between the time that the goods had been taken over and the time of delivery.

In *Paris 15.6.84*[12] the consignee's warehouse was in the *gare internationale routière de Paris Terminal*, and the load arrived within the Terminal at 4 p.m. in July. In view of the lateness of the hour the goods were not unloaded that day. The driver departed with the traction unit, leaving the trailer outside the warehouse but within the enclosed precinct of the Terminal, from where it was stolen overnight. The carrier's argument, that by placing the goods at the disposal of the consignee at 4 p.m., delivery had been effected and the carrier's liability under the CMR was at an end, was rejected by the court. Noting that the consignee had neither received nor acknowledged the goods, or been put in a position to make reservations about shortage or damage, the court concluded[13] that neither the carriage nor the carrier's liability under the CMR had come to an end at the time of the theft.

In *Paris 4.3.85*[14] there was proof of a French custom, of which the carrier was aware, that vehicles carrying foodstuffs were to be unloaded in the morning, so that the goods could be distributed to customers in the afternoon. In these circumstances it was held that the consignee was entitled to refuse to take delivery of a load, which had arrived at 3 p.m., until the next morning, and the carrier was liable under Article 17.1 for deterioration in the goods which occurred overnight when the vehicle's refrigeration unit failed, even

[9] *O.L.G. Düsseldorf 1.2.68*, cited by Willemberg N.J.W. 1968.1022. See also *O.L.G. Nürnberg 21.12.89*, TranspR 1991.99.

[10] 1978 U.L.R. I 370; Greiter 46.

[11] The driver had failed to display the "utmost care which was possible and reasonably to be expected in the circumstances", the carrier could not be exonerated on the ground of unavoidable circumstances within the meaning of Art. 17.2: see below, para. 75a.

[12] B.T. 1984.545.

[13] At 546–547.

[14] B.T. 1985.396. Also in this sense *Nîmes 29.10.80*, 1981 U.L.R. I 267, in which apples were delayed because the carrier failed to deliver during market hours and had to await the end of "le weekend anglais".

though the goods might have been saved if they had been immediately transferred from the vehicle to the consignee's coldstore.

37b. Goods to be "kept until called for"

Distinguish three possibilities. If the carrier is to keep the goods at the place of destination, and to contact the consignee and arrange collection, but is unable to make contact with the consignee, it is a case of the missing consignee,[15] to which Article 15[16] and Article 16[17] of the CMR apply. In two other cases the CMR and common law concur that the carrier holds as carrier until the consignee can be expected to collect the goods.[18] First, if it is agreed that the carrier shall wait until contacted by the consignee, the carrier holds as carrier under Article 17 until the consignee collects, thus obtaining control of the goods and ending carriage, or until a reasonable time has passed without collection, after which the carrier holds not as carrier but under national law.[19] Secondly, if there is no such agreement and the carrier is able to contact the consignee, the carrier must do so[20]: once again the carrier holds as carrier under Article 17, until the consignee collects or a reasonable time has passed without collection, after which in the latter case the carrier holds under national law. In each case, the shorter the period of transit the shorter the time in which it is reasonable to require the carrier to hold the goods as carrier.[21]

37c. Delivery, as agreed, without the consignee

Exceptionally, the contract may provide for delivery without the immediate presence or co-operation of the consignee. In this case delivery occurs in accordance with the contract.

In *O.G.H. 11.12.86*[22] the carrier agreed to carry goods to a trade fair in Cologne by February 22 at latest, and was given an exact location (hall, stand, etc.) for delivery. The goods were left at that

---

[15] Below, para. 37a.
[16] Above, para. 33b.
[17] Above, para. 33c.
[18] Subject to the terms of the particular contract.
[19] See below, Chap. 12.
[20] A duty to give notice may be implied: above, para. 34. In *HR 20.4.79*, S. & S. 1979 no. 83, discussed by Haak, pp. 182–183: the delay in collection was the fault of the carrier, and it was held that delivery did not occur until actual delivery to the consignee, even though the carrier's consequent liability (under CMR Art. 23.5) was *less* than it would otherwise have been.
[21] Glass and Cashmore, para. 1.67.
[22] Stra GüV 1987/5 p. 18.

location on February 22 by a sub-contractor provided by the organisers of the fair. The consignee was not there to take charge of them, but was advised by telephone. Some of the goods were stolen. The OGH held that for delivery it sufficed[23] that the goods were put at the disposal of the consignee at an agreed place; and that therefore the carrier in this case was not liable under Article 17.

The OGH was influenced by the facts of the case, notably that the contract was precise as to time and place, and that the rules of the fair allowed delivery later than February 22 but at a higher charge, but that the consignee/exhibitor, who was also the sender, had chosen to stay in Vienna and, presumably, carry on business there and to arrive at the fair shortly before it opened, after the goods had arrived. Nonetheless, this kind of decision might be found again, if it can be said that the consignee has agreed to the mode of delivery in question and has thus agreed to assume the risks involved. Agreement may be express or based on a local custom[24] to that effect, this providing a definition of delivery for the particular case, which the CMR itself lacks.

37d. Consignee missing

Delivery without the consignee present in person or through an agent[25] is exceptional. Generally, delivery requires the cooperation of the consignee.[26] Without this there can be no delivery, so prima facie no consignee, no delivery. However, if the carrier brings the goods to the consignee's address and, finds it impossible to contact the consignee, he may unload the goods at an appropriate place. At that point, the carriage ends, and there is therefore a notional delivery. In this situation Article 15.1 of the CMR applies if "circumstances prevent delivery of the goods after their arrival at the place designated for delivery".[27] For the carrier, one possibility in that situation is to "immediately unload the goods for account of the person entitled to dispose of them and thereupon the carriage shall end", the carrier holding the goods for that person, or entrusting them "to a third party, and in that case he

[23] At 19.

[24] In this sense Putzeys, para. 519, citing a term used by Belgian carriers. In *O.G.H. 11.12.86* (above, n. 22), although the sub-contractor's conditions of carriage provided that the liability of the sub-contractor ended when the goods were deposited at the appropriate stand whether the exhibitor was there to receive them or not, the decision was based on general rules.

[25] Above, para. 37c.

[26] Above, para. 37.

[27] Above, para. 33b.

shall not be under any liability except for the exercise of reasonable care in the choice of such third party".[28]

37e. Wrongful refusal of delivery

As in the last case of the missing consignee, if the carrier tenders the goods at the consignee's place of business and the consignee wrongfully refuses to take delivery, the consignee cannot thereby tie the carrier to the cost and inconvenience of holding the goods and to continued liability under Article 17. Refusal is a circumstance preventing delivery and the situation is governed by Article 15 and Article 16.

As the CMR does not define delivery,[29] it can be argued that it is open to the parties to define delivery in the contract of carriage, provided that the parties' definition is not inconsistent with the CMR. One possibility, convenient for carriers, is to extend the meaning of delivery to include a "tender of delivery"[30] so that, if delivery is tendered, in the sense that the carrier offers to transfer control to the consignee, that is deemed to be delivery in the sense that carriage ends and liability under Article 17 ends too. However, it is submitted that the contract cannot terminate carriage any more abruptly than permitted by the CMR,[31] notably Article 16. Thus, for example, if the goods are still on the vehicle at the time of tender, the effect of Article 16.2 is that carriage does not end until the carrier has unloaded the goods at an appropriate place.[32]

37f. Refusal of damaged goods

If the goods have been damaged en route, and the carrier is ordered to stop or, when the carrier reaches destination, the consignee refuses to take delivery, one possible scenario is that carriage ends in accordance with Article 16.2.[33] A second is that the consignee, while rejecting the goods as consignee/buyer, takes delivery of the goods on behalf of the sender and holds the goods

[28] Art. 16.2: above, para. 33c(*ii*). It can be argued that a provision, such as RHA Conditions of Carriage 1991, cl. 6(2)(b), whereby in such circumstances transit is deemed to continue beyond that time, is contrary to Art. 41.

[29] Above, para. 37.

[30] For example, RHA Conditions of Carriage 1991 condition 6(2): "Transit shall (unless otherwise previously determined) end when the consignment is tendered at the usual place of delivery at the Consignee's address within the customary cartage hours of the district."

[31] Art. 41, below, para. 92.

[32] Above, para. 33c(*ii*).

[33] Above, para. 33c(*ii*).

to the sender's instructions.[34] A third is that the carrier may be ordered back to the place of consignment and that, until the goods have been returned to the sender, there has been no delivery and the carrier remains liable under Article 17.[35]

In *Moto Vespa v. MAT (Britannia Express)*[36] goods being carried from Birmingham to Madrid were damaged in an accident just short of Madrid. They were carried on to Madrid, where they were rejected by the consignee and, without being unloaded, taken back to Barcelona and eventually returned to Birmingham. Mocatta J. held[37] that this was a case to which Article 15 applied, a case in which circumstances prevent delivery and the carrier must act on any instructions from the sender. Hence he held that there was no delivery at Madrid within the meaning of Article 32.

In that case, Mocatta J. rejected the idea that there had been delivery in Spain but did not explicitly consider whether there had been (re)delivery back in Birmingham. This possibility was raised by Parker J. in a later case, *Worldwide Carriers v. Ardtran International*,[38] in which damaged goods had been returned to sender. He said: "Under art. 12(1) the sender has the right to dispose of the goods, in particular by asking the carrier to stop the goods in transit, to change the place at which delivery is to take place or to deliver the goods to a consignee other than the consignee indicated in the consignment note . . . If, therefore, on hearing of damage the sender requires the goods to be returned to him he is doing no more than stop the goods in transit, change the place of delivery and change the consignee. When these instructions are carried out it appears to me that, at least in some cases, there will have been delivery under the contract and thus that art. 32(1)(a) applies."

Compare *'s Hertogenbosch 21.12.65*[39]: the carrier, employed by the consignee to carry a machine from a place in Germany to the consignee's address in Maastricht, took it first to the carrier's depot in Venlo and then had it taken on to Maastricht by a sub-carrier. On this final stage of the journey the machine was damaged and, on arrival in Maastricht on February 16, the consignees said that they did not want it. It was taken back to the carrier's depot in Venlo, where it remained until the consignees had decided that it was, after all, worth having the machine repaired and the machine was again taken to them in Maastricht where it arrived on February 23. Whether the period of limitation, within which action must be

---

[34] C.A. for Western Sweden 9.4.74, reported by Wetter [1979] L.M.C.L.Q. 404, 405.

[35] Putzeys, para. 532, criticising decisions in Belgium and France to the contrary.

[36] [1979] 1 Lloyd's Rep. 175.

[37] At 180.

[38] [1983] 1 Lloyd's Rep. 61, 65. *cf. Brussels 28.6.69*, 1970 U.L.C. 115: a load of glass was damaged en route and brought back to the place from which it had been sent. For the purpose of Art. 32 the court held that delivery had never taken place.

[39] 1966 U.L.C. 119. See also *H.R. 24.3.95*, S. & S. 1995, no. 74.

brought, had expired, depended on whether delivery had taken place on February 16, or on February 23. The carrier pointed to the earlier date, contending that the final journey to Maastricht on February 23 was the subject of a separate agreement and a thing apart from the carriage in respect of which action had been instituted. However, the court noted that the machine had been sent back to Venlo on February 16 to await the consignee's instruction, something contemplated as part of the contract of carriage by Article 16.2[40] and concluded[41]: "For the commencement of prescription by virtue of Article 32 of the CMR the only thing that counts is the delivery of the goods, for reasons which are obvious, moreover, because it is only then that the consignee is in a proper position to know the nature and extent of the damage." Delivery occurred on February 23.

38. Cash on delivery

The contract of carriage may require[42] the carrier to collect "cash on delivery" charges. If so, this is a matter required by Article 6.2 to be mentioned in the consignment note,[43] but agreement on delivery C.O.D. may be proved against the carrier by other means.[44] If, however, the point arises against the consignee, the consignee is obliged by Article 13.2 of the CMR to pay the charges "shown to be due on the consignment note".

In *OLG Hamm 12.11.73*[45] the claimant carrier delivered goods to the defendant consignee under a consignment note which did not state whether charges, such as freight and ancillary expenses, were to be paid by the sender or by the consignee, and it was these that the carrier sought to recover from the consignee. The carrier contended that, by accepting the goods and an invoice for the charges together with the consignment note, the consignee became liable to pay the charges. This contention was rejected by the Landgericht, and the appeal against that decision was dismissed, because the only charges which the consignee was obliged to pay under the CMR were in terms of Article 13.2 those "shown to be due on the consignment note".

---

[40] *Semble* the proposition was correct, but by reference to Art. 12: if the goods were unloaded at Venlo, under Art. 16.2 that would end carriage, and that would be inconsistent with the court's decision that delivery did not occur until the later date of 23 February.

[41] At 125.

[42] On the words needed to impose the obligation, see Mercadal, Theunis, p. 41.

[43] See above, para. 24.

[44] For example, a letter recording some or all of the instructions to the carrier and thus the terms of the contract of carriage: *'s Hertogenbosch 13.1.70* (1971) 6 E.T.L. 817. See also *O.L.G. Düsseldorf 13.12.90*, TranspR 1991.91.

[45] 1974 U.L.R. II 212; N.J.W. 1974.1056. Muth/Glöckner, p. 154.

Although it is difficult to fault the decision as a matter of construction of Article 13, the result sits uncomfortably with Article 21: while the consignee is obliged by Article 13.2 of the CMR to pay only charges "shown to be due on the consignment note", by Article 21 the carrier is liable to the sender for failure to collect those charges which the carrier should have collected "under the contract of carriage". If a contractual duty to collect a charge is not recorded in the note, and the decision is correct, the carrier may be obliged to collect from the consignee a charge which the consignee is not obliged by the CMR to pay. In these circumstances, a court may be willing to seek grounds outside the CMR on which to compel the consignee to pay.[46] The court in that case implied that a person, such as the sender, might be obliged to pay other charges under the terms of the contract of carriage, but stressed that the consignee was not a party to the contract of carriage. If this issue arises in England, the result is likely to be the same. In some cases the consignee will be a party to the initial contract of carriage.[47] In other cases the carrier must argue, like the sea carrier before him, that a *Brandt*[48] contract can be implied between road carrier and consignee, whereby the carrier agrees to deliver on the terms of the initial contract of carriage, in consideration for which the consignee agrees to pay certain charges.

If the carrier is obliged to collect cash on delivery and the consignee is obliged to pay, but the consignee refuses to pay and so the carrier refuses to deliver, delivery has been "prevented" and the situation is governed by Article 15.[49]

If the carrier is obliged to collect cash on delivery and the consignee is obliged to pay, but the consignee does not pay, and nonetheless the carrier delivers the goods to the consignee, the carrier is liable to the sender under Article 21:

> "Should the goods have been delivered to the consignee without collection of the 'cash on delivery' charge which should have been collected by the carrier under the terms of the contract of carriage, the carrier shall be liable to the sender for compensation not exceeding the amount of such charge without prejudice to his right of action against the consignee."

The carrier is liable under Article 21 only to the sender or one for whom the sender has stipulated.[50] Moreover, the carrier is

---

[46] A similar problem arises when there is no consignment note at all: the carrier will be liable for failure to collect, it has been held, if the duty is proven by other means: *'s Hertogenbosch 13.1.70* (1971) 6 E.T.L. 817.

[47] Below, para. 216a.

[48] See below, para. 217.

[49] Above, para. 33b.

[50] *O.G.H. 5.5.83*, TranspR 1984.42; Greiter 185.

liable only when it is the carrier, and not a third party such as a bank, who is obliged to collect cash on delivery.

In *Eastern Kayam Carpets v. Eastern United Freight*[51] the carrier disregarded the sender's instruction to deliver only "cash against documents", the sender was not paid by the consignee/buyer, and sought compensation from the carrier in breach. On the scope of Article 21 the carrier's argument, that "charge" in Article 21 referred only to freight, warehousing charges and the like, was rejected. Hirst J. accepted the sender's argument and the decision in *Rb Breda 16.12.69*[52] that the protection of Article 21 was mainly for the seller and that a "charge" could include payment of the price of the goods. It would be odd, said the court, if the only liability of carrier to sender under Article 21 would be for failure to collect freight and warehousing charges, charges for which it was usually the sender or consignee who was liable to the carrier. It would also be odd, if the carrier were liable for wrongful delivery under Article 12.7, because the carrier had failed to obey an instruction received after performance of the carriage had begun,[53] but not liable under Article 21 for failure to obey an instruction stipulated in the contract from the beginning. All this suggested that Article 21 applied to failure to collect a purchase price to be collected by the carrier. However, the case before the court concerned "cash against documents", a charge to be collected by a bank, which generated the appropriate documents showing that payment had been made and against which the goods were to be delivered[54]: delivery "cash against documents" is not governed by Article 21.[55]

39a. The form of payment

Article 21 speaks of "cash on delivery", but as the CMR does not define this phrase, the court hearing the case will turn to the national law governing payment,[56] which in the case of English law is the law of the place of payment[57] and thus in most cases the place of delivery. The phrase is well known in commerce and "cash" is understood to mean payment. As to the meaning of payment, while there is some uniformity of approach in states party to the CMR, there is no uniformity of result.

---

[51] High Court, December 6, 1983, unreported.

[52] Below, para. 38a.

[53] Above, para. 33d.

[54] See also in this sense: *Paris 21.10.70*, 1971 U.L.C. 141, 143; B.T. 1970.307 ("contre documents pour solde de notre facture"). On the theoretical basis, and futility, of the distinction between "cash against delivery" and "cash against documents", see Putzeys, para. 715.

[55] *Toulouse 18.2.92*, B.T.L. 1992.781. *O.L.G. Düsseldorf 21.4.94*, TranspR 1994.391. Libouton (1973) 8 E.T.L. 2, 55.

[56] *B.G.H. 10.2.82* (1983) E.T.L. 32, 40. Mercadal, Theunis, p. 38; Muth/Glöckner, p. 154; Putzeys, para. 719.

[57] Dicey, *The Conflict of Laws* (12th ed., London, 1993), pp. 924 *et seq.*

> In *Rb Breda 16.12.69*[58] goods were carried from Rotterdam to Nantes. The driver was given a sight draft for the goods, together with a consignment note which said "Unloading solely and exclusively after the (draft) has been accepted by signature". The driver delivered the goods without obtaining the required signature. The sender brought an action against the carrier, relying on Article 21. The carrier's contention, that this was not a case for Article 21, as it was not a case of cash, was rejected.

The court said[59]:

> "To judge by its purpose, the 'cash on delivery' clause is one whereby the consignee of goods must satisfy a particular duty of payment—which need not necessarily comprise payment of all or part of the sale price of the goods—before being able to obtain, by delivery, the right to dispose of the consignment intended for him; the carrier's duty, most usually expressed in the 'cash on delivery' clause not to hand over the goods except against payment of a sum of money, may be replaced by an obligation imposed on the carrier not to permit delivery except against acceptance of a sight draft signed by the consignee, a draft which, in France even more than in Holland, fulfils a role which is tantamount to payment with legal tender."

While this is indeed true of France[60] and Belgium[61] there is the difference that, while in France the carrier is in no way obliged to ensure that a cheque is honoured, in Belgium the carrier is liable to the sender if the cheque is not honoured. Moreover, in Germany, as a cheque is not regarded as providing the sender with sufficient security, a cheque cannot be accepted as payment "cash on delivery" at all.[62]

In England the original rule, which survives[63] as a faint presumption, is that cash refers to legal tender at the place of delivery. In business, however, payment is now generally seen as "comprehending any commercially recognised method of transferring funds the result of which is to give the transferee the unconditional right to the immediate use of the funds transferred".[64] A method of transfer is commercially recognised if it is in accord with the

---

[58] 1970. U.L.C. 298; (1970) 15 E.T.L. 67.

[59] At 300.

[60] *Paris 31.1.83*, B.T. 1983.183; *Paris 23.6.94*, B.T.L. 1994.692; *Cass. com. 6.6.95*, B.T.L. 1995.474; Tilche, B.T.L. 1994.684.

[61] Putzeys, para. 719. A cheque is acceptable: *Cass. Belge 18.2.94* (1994) 27 E.T.L. 464.

[62] *B.G.H. 10.2.82* (1983) 18 E.T.L. 32, 40. Helm, p. 492 Anm. 2; Muth/Glöckner, p. 154. See also *O.L.G. Düsseldorf 21.4.94*, TranspR 1994.391; *B.G.H. 25.10.95* (1996) 31 E.T.L. 404. Concerning the possibility that payment by such a method has been agreed or is customary in the trade context, see *O.L.G. Hamburg 18.4.91*, TranspR 1991.297. Herber/Piper, Art. 21, 6 and 21; Koller, Art. 21, 1; Thume, Art. 21, 39 *et seq.* The question was left open in *O.L.G. Düsseldorf 21.4.94* (above).

[63] *Pollway v. Abdullah* [1974] 2 All E.R. 381, 383, *per* Roskill L.J. with whom the other members of the Court of Appeal agreed.

[64] *The Brimnes* [1973] 1 W.L.R. 386, 400, *per* Brandon J., the decision on this point being affirmed: [1975] Q.B. 929, C.A.

commercial practice of the parties, the place or the context.[65] In England, commercial practice usually allows buyers to pay by cheque[66] and the same is likely to be held of the CMR consignee. In any case, payment by cheque is good tender, if no objection is raised by the payee.[67] However, while it is good tender, it is only conditional payment and it is not generally regarded as actual payment until it has been honoured by the drawee.[68] The form of payment appropriate to the case may be affected by exchange control better handled between banks; this consideration has encouraged "delivery against documents",[69] but as we have seen, this practice is outside the scope of Article 21.

39b. The nature and extent of the carrier's liability

If the carrier fails to perform an undertaking to collect cash on delivery, the carrier is liable under Article 21, and the nature of the liability is said[70] to be strict, although Article 21 says nothing on the matter. The amount of liability, says Article 21, is "for compensation not exceeding the amount of such charge". The indications are that, although Article 21 is in Chapter 4 of the CMR, the liability is not affected by Articles 23 *et seq*., also in Chapter 4,[71] but like other heads of economic loss caused by the carrier[72] is governed by national law. However, Article 29, also in Chapter 4, provides that the "carrier shall not be entitled to avail himself of provisions of this chapter which exclude or limit liability" in the case of wilful default, etc., and it is thought[73] that the provisions in question include Article 21. Moreover, claims under Article 21 are also affected by Article 32 in Chapter 5.[74]

When national law applies, it may limit the sender to the amount of loss that the sender proves to have been actually caused by the carrier's breach of Article 21.[75] However, the French text, whereby "le transporteur est tenu d'indemniser l'expéditeur à concurrence du montant du remboursement", suggests that the carrier is always liable for the amount that should have been

---

[65] Goode, *Payment Obligations in Commercial and Financial Transactions* (London, 1983), p. 25; see also p. 11. Mann, *The Legal Aspect of Money* (5th ed., Oxford, 1992), pp. 74 *et seq.*

[66] *Benjamin*, para. 9–026, n. 36.

[67] *Cohen v. Roche* [1927] 1 K.B. 169, 180, *per* McCardie J.

[68] *D & C Builders v. Rees* [1966] 2 Q.B. 617, C.A.

[69] Tilche B.T.L. 1992.780.

[70] Helm, p. 492 Anm. 3: *eine reine Erfolgshaftung. idem: Toulouse 18.2.92*, B.T.L. 1992.781; *Paris 23.6.94*, B.T.L. 1994.692. Herber/Piper, Art. 21, 15; Koller, Art. 21, 4; Thume, Art. 21, 125 *et seq. cf.* Tilche, B.T.L. 1992.781.

[71] *O.G.H. 13.6.85*, Stra GüV 1986/12. Helm, p. 492 Anm. 5; Loewe, para. 185.

[72] See above, para. 33d(*i*).

[73] Article 29, discussed below, para. 107. In this sense Nickel-Lanz, para. 64.

[74] *'s Hertogenbosch 13.1.70* (1971) 6 E.T.L. 817.

[75] Muth/Glöckner, p. 154.

collected.[76] Although there is no evident ambiguity in the English text of the kind likely to send an English court to the French text,[77] it has also been suggested[78] that the French text allows a more practical solution.

The carrier's liability is stated by Article 21 to be "without prejudice to his right of action against the consignee". It has been suggested that this right is not a right of the sender to which the carrier is subrogated but an independent right arising out of Article 21[79] or out of the contract of carriage,[80] and thus a right free of any defences that the consignee might have had in that regard against the sender.[81]

---

[76] Libouton (1973) 8 E.T.L. 2, 55. I have been advised by Dr Edward James of the Department of French in the University of Cambridge that this is correct: whereas some dictionaries translate "à concurrence de" as "not exceeding", the better view is that this is not accurate. The phrase is an abbreviated version of "jusqu'à (la) concurrence de". This is explained by *Le Petit Robert* as "jusqu'à ce qu'une somme parvienne à égaler une autre"; and by *Trésor de la Langue Français* (Imbs, 1977) as "jusqu'à la rencontre, à la coincidence finale avec un chiffre déterminé, en particulier une somme d'argent due; jusqu'à la limite extrême de". In older books the idea is clearly that of a figure reached by an accretion or aggregation of smaller sums, but reached fully in each case.

[77] On the role of the French text see above, para. 66.

[78] Hill and Messent, p. 173. This is in line with the French domestic law view, that the carrier pays the sender not damages but the sum in question in place of the consignee, from whom he may later seek to recover the same amount: Brunat B.T. 1982.56. See further Putzeys, paras. 721 *et seq.*

[79] Putzeys, paras. 727 *et seq. cf.* Helm, p. 493 Anm. 6: the right is not based on Art. 21, but on Art. 13.2.

[80] Brunat B.T. 1982.56.

[81] *Paris 8.12.81*, B.T. 1982.61. Brunat B.T. 1982.56; Mercadal, Theunis, p. 38, citing *Paris 19.11.81*, B.T. 1982.62, in which the same rule was applied in a case of delivery against documents.

CHAPTER 4

CLAIMS

A. THE CLAIMANT

40. Action against the carrier by the consignee: Article 13

Although Article 13.1 entitles the consignee to sue the carrier, Article 13 contains a particular rule aimed at a particular problem,[1] and it is widely assumed[2] that the CMR contains no general or definitive rule governing the identity of the person or persons entitled to sue the carrier. Subject to Article 13, courts tend to apply the *lex fori*,[3] and the identity of other persons entitled to sue the carrier, notably the sender, is considered below.[4] The first sentence of Article 13.1 deals with the consignee's right to delivery of the goods,[5] and continues:

> "If the loss of the goods is established or if the goods have not arrived after the expiry of the period provided for in article 19, the consignee shall be entitled to enforce in his own name against the carrier any rights arising from the contract of carriage."

Prima facie, the consignee entitled to sue under Article 13.1 is the person mentioned as consignee in the consignment note,[6] whether the original consignee or the person to whom that consignee has ordered the goods to be delivered,[7] and whether the

---

[1] *B.G.H. 21.12.73* (1975) 10 E.T.L. 91, 94–95: below, para. 40a.

[2] *O.L.G. Karlsruhe 24.5.67*, 1967 U.L.C. 289, 295, quoted below, para. 41; Rodière, para. 573.

[3] For example, in France Art. 101 c.com. In Germany, see *B.G.H. 21.12.73* (1975) E.T.L. 91, 95. Moreover, if the consignee has assigned the right of action (in this instance to the sender), the validity of this assignment is governed by the appropriate national law (in this instance the law of the carrier's place of business): *B.G.H. 28.4.1988* (1989) 24 E.T.L. 89.

[4] Para. 41.

[5] As to the consignee's right to delivery see above, para. 37. The conditions of delivery, receipt of goods and consignment note are not conditions of the right of suit in the second sentence of Art. 13.1: *Cass. Belge 13.6.80* (1980) 15 E.T.L. 851, 861.

[6] *Paris 2.12.81*, B.T. 1982.73.

[7] Art. 124. Above, para. 32b.

consignee has suffered loss or not.[8] In practice, it is less simple, as in some CMR states national law may entertain the argument that behind the nominal consignee is the "real" consignee, the person really entitled to sue.[9] Whoever that is, under Article 13.1 the consignee is entitled to sue, whether or not the consignee has taken delivery of the goods or of the second consignment note.[10] The only condition is that the charges must have been paid: Article 13.2.[11]

40a. Actions in respect of damage

Under Article 13.1 the consignee is entitled to sue for loss or delay,[12] but there is no mention of damage. It was argued in Austria[13] that, as other provisions of the CMR distinguish loss and damage, the distinction must have been deliberate in Article 13, and that therefore the consignee has a right of suit in respect of loss and delay but not damage. The argument was rejected[14]: the consignee's right to delivery of the goods under Article 13.1 is a right to have the goods in their entirety and undamaged, a right not intended to be without remedy. The same argument has been convincingly rejected in Germany.[15] The B.G.H. explained the reference to loss and delay in Article 13.1 as intended to ensure a right of suit in cases of loss or delay in those countries in which that right is denied to a consignee who has received no consignment note. There was no intention to exclude an action for damage.

40b. The consignee's rights

If the contract is concluded by the consignee personally or by the sender as agent for the consignee,[16] the words of Article 13.1, that the consignee may enforce not only rights stated in the consignment note[17] but "any rights arising from the contract of carriage",

---

[8] *Cass. Belge 13.6.80* (1980) 15 E.T.L. 851, 861: the carrier's argument that the consignee, having been promised replacement goods by the sender, had suffered no loss, was rejected as defence to a claim by the consignee.

[9] In *B.G.H. 6.5.81* (1982) 17 E.T.L. 313 the nominal consignee was an agent of the buyer, and the buyer justified entitlement to sue the carrier not *qua* real consignee under Art. 13 but by reference to rules of national law. *cf.* also the "real" sender under the CMR: *Aix 25.10.82*, B.T. 1983.591; below, para. 41a.

[10] Pesce, p. 164.

[11] Below, para. 40c.

[12] Art. 19: below, para. 58.

[13] *O.G.H. 17.2.82*, SZ 55 Nr. 20, Greiter 127.

[14] Greiter 134. Also in this sense *O.G.H. 22.11.84*, Greiter 253, 258.

[15] *B.G.H. 21.12.73* (1975) 10 E.T.L. 91, 94–95; *B.G.H. 24.9.87*, 1988 U.L.R. II 713, 716. Piper, TranspR 1990.357, 358 and cases cited.

[16] Below, para. 41a(*ii*).

[17] Hill, "Carriage of Goods by Road to the Continent", (1976) 11 E.T.L. 182, 187.

restate a right enjoyed by the consignee in many cases as a party to the original contract of carriage.[18] In cases of doubt in which the CMR provides no answer, the courts may turn to national law to determine the scope of the consignee's rights and duties under that contract.

If the contract of carriage is not concluded by or for the consignee but by the sender, the consignee is nonetheless entitled under Article 13 to enforce "any rights arising from the contract of carriage" concluded by the sender, rights of which the consignee may be unaware when the consignee agrees to buy the goods carried or accepts delivery of them.

40b(*i*). The effect of concessions by the sender

If by contracting personally the sender "creates" rights for the consignee to enforce later under Article 13.1, can the consignee also abandon rights, which have arisen under the contract of carriage, by making concessions to the carrier which bind not only the sender but also the consignee?

If the right has been created or conferred by the CMR itself, although the concession is not a "stipulation" in the original contract, which might be forbidden by Article 41,[19] a concession may be contrary to the spirit of Article 41. For example, as the carrier is forbidden to contract out of liability for theft (Article 17 and Article 14), it would be absurd if the carrier could achieve the same result the day after contracting by persuading the sender to concede an undertaking not to enforce the right to compensation in case of theft, and later pleading that concession as a defence to an action by the consignee.

If the right has been created or conferred not by the CMR but by the contract of carriage, the concession cannot offend Article 41, and the effect of the concession depends on the role of the sender, and on national law.

If the sender is acting as the agent of the consignee, the consignee is bound by any concession within the actual or apparent authority of the sender under the applicable national law: see below.

If the sender is not acting as the agent of the consignee, the position is less clear. Some writers[20] speak of the consignee's rights as being "independent" of those of the sender; however, the consignee's rights "arise" out of a contract of carriage made by the sender, and the real question, perhaps, is one of the proper construction of Article 13.1 and the point in time at which the rights

---

[18] Below, para. 41a(*ii*).

[19] Below, para. 92.

[20] Maccarone, Theunis, p. 70.

"arise" for the consignee. Prima facie, the consignee acquires those rights arising at the time that he acquires them,[21] and hence subject to any variation or waiver agreed by the sender since the contract was first formed.

The answer is likely to be different if the consignee had been led (whether by sender or carrier) to expect rights different from those actually in force between sender and carrier or if the consignee is not led to expect anything in particular because, as is commonly the position of consignees of goods by road, the consignee receives no document of any kind.

> In France in *The Anna Oden* the maritime phase of a transport from Sweden to France was carried out with the trailers on deck, where the contents were damaged. The defendant carrier relied, first, on Article 2.1 of the CMR, that the carrier's liability to the consignee should be determined as if he had made with the consignee a contract for the carriage of goods by sea[22]; and, secondly, on a bill of lading evidencing such a contract, which allowed deck stowage and which, being subject to the Hague Rules, exonerated the carrier for damage caused, as in this case, by perils of the sea. This defence was successful in the Paris court[23] but not in the Court of Cassation.[24]

The main point of disagreement between the two courts in *The Anna Oden* concerned whether the Rules applied *proprio vigore* to carriage on deck.[25] If they did, as held by the Paris court, the consignee could not overcome the carrier's defence of perils of the sea. If, however, as held by the Court of Cassation, the Rules applied to the case only by reason of voluntary incorporation, exoneration in respect of perils of the sea under the Rules was, like any other exclusion clause, a mere term of the contract, a term to which the consignee had not agreed[26] and of which the consignee did not have notice. This being so, the carrier could not plead that term to defend an action by the consignee. In that case, unlike *Leduc v. Ward* in England,[27] it does not appear that the consignee had received a transport document which led the consignee to expect any one contract term rather than another. Nonetheless, the decision supports the proposition that the consignee is not affected

---

[21] This might be inferred from the existence of the sender's right of disposal under Art. 12.

[22] Above, para. 31.

[23] *Paris 13.10.86*, DMF 1988.101.

[24] *Cass.5.7.88* (1989) 24 E.T.L. 49.

[25] See above, para. 15a(*ii*).

[26] The appellant carrier had failed to prove "*l'acceptation . . . de la clause*" on the part of the consignee (p. 51).

[27] Below, para. 216c.

by any terms agreed by the sender with the carrier which are not customary or of a kind that the consignee should expect.[28]

40c. The consignee's duties

If, as we have seen,[29] the consignee may enforce rights under the contract of carriage against the carrier, is the carrier entitled to enforce rights against the consignee?

Article 13.1 entitles the consignee to enforce rights against the carrier but, with one reservation, makes no mention of enforcement by the carrier of rights against the consignee. The reservation is that, while not speaking of enforcement, it is a condition of entitlement to sue the carrier that the consignee should pay the charges mentioned in Article 13.2:

> "The consignee who avails himself of the rights granted to him under paragraph 1 of this article shall pay the charges shown to be due on the consignment note, but in the event of dispute on this matter the carrier shall not be required to deliver the goods unless security has been furnished by the consignee."[30]

On a strict interpretation of this provision, if there were no payment, there could be no suit by the consignee. The Venice court[31] has held that the payment of charges was a precondition of the right to delivery but not of the right of suit. An English court might be tempted to interpolate the common law rule that tender of payment amounts to actual payment and thus permit the tendering consignee to sue.[32]

Subject to this reservation about charges, the CMR appears to give no reciprocal right of action to the carrier against the consignee. The inference[33] is that liabilities of the sender are not passed on with the goods to the consignee, like hot potatoes. Article 22.2 states the liability of the sender for dangerous goods. Article 7.1 states the liability of the sender for inaccurate or

---

[28] Lack of consent on the part of the consignee also troubled the court in *O.L.G. Hamm 12.11.73* (above, para. 38); and in *Cass. 10.7.89*, B.T. 1989.619: the consignee is not bound by the (limitation) clauses of a document signed at the time of delivery, and which the consignee had not seen before: *ibid.* That case involved a sea stage followed by a road stage inside France. For the same rule applied to CMR carriage, see *Paris 19.11.81*, B.T. 1982.62. Nickel-Lanz, paras. 67 *et seq.*

cf. Loewe (para. 242): the "jurisdiction agreed upon between the principal and the carrier is binding on all parties whose rights derive from the contract of carriage, for example, the consignee". But on this Art. 31.1 refers to "agreement between the parties", and in English eyes, unless the consignee is a party to the contract containing that agreement the consignee is free to bring suit elsewhere.

[29] Above, para. 40b.

[30] For the nature of the charges, see above, para. 38.

[31] *31.10.74* (1975) 10 E.T.L. 242 (summary).

[32] *Startup v. Macdonald* (1843) 6 Man. & G. 593. Treitel, pp. 669–670.

[33] In this sense Pesce, p. 163, n. 156. *Dubitante*: Maccarone, Theunis, pp. 69–70.

inadequate information. The liability of the consignee for these things is excluded by implication under the CMR. The possibility remains, however, that the carrier will have enforceable rights against the consignee on some ground outside the CMR, perhaps lien[34] or implied contract but then the question arises whether the rights acquired by the carrier against the consignee derogate from the CMR and, therefore, are null and void under Article 41.[35]

41. Title to sue: rules of national law

If the sender is also the consignee, as such the consignee has a right of action under Article 13.1.[36] If the sender is not the consignee, the CMR is silent on the sender's right, if any, to sue the carrier. The general view is that under the CMR the consignee's right of action is not exclusive throughout,[37] that the CMR does not exclude an action by the consignee[38] or by someone other than the consignee, assumed for discussion to be the sender, based on rules of national law.

If a right, of action is acquired by the consignee,[39] is a right of action still available to the sender concurrently with that of the consignee and, if so, on what terms? A second and related question is whether the carrier can be made to pay twice over, once to the sender and once to the consignee. The answer of the courts is negative. "The misgivings entertained by the defendant, that it might have to face a second claim from the sender, are without foundation. If the consignee has had its rights to compensation in respect of damage to the goods upheld, the carrier may, if sued by the party with which it has contracted—the sender—resist the action on the ground that it has fulfilled its duty under the contract of transport to pay compensation and is therewith discharged."[40] But on what ground?

One answer, found in Germany, is that the person entitled to sue is the person entitled to dispose of the goods.[41] As there can be

---

[34] Below, para. 106.

[35] Below, para. 42.

[36] Above, para. 40.

[37] *O.L.G. Karlsruhe 24.5.67*, 1967 U.L.C. 289, 295, quoted below, para. 41b. Haak, p. 257; Koller, Art. 13, 8; Libouton, para. 33; Rodière, para. 573; Thume, Art. 13, 26. *cf.* Helm, Art. 17 Anm. 30, that a general principle of suit based on the right of disposal is sufficiently clear from the CMR itself: this view was rejected by *B.G.H. 21.12.73* (1975) 10 E.T.L. 91. *cf.* also Herber/Piper, Art. 13, 30.

[38] As in *Texas Instruments v. Nason (Europe) Ltd* [1991] 1 Lloyd's Rep. 146: the court considered first title to sue at common law and secondly title under Art. 13.

[39] Above, para. 40.

[40] *B.G.H. 6.7.79* (1980) 15 E.T.L. 863, 869–870.

[41] *B.G.H. 6.7.79* (above). See also below, para. 41b.

only one such person at any one time,[42] double exposure of the carrier is avoided.

Another answer might have been that a person can sue only if and to the extent that that person has suffered loss. Although we are concerned here with rights of action under national law, this answer sits uncomfortably with the CMR, which clearly countenances actions by persons who have not suffered loss themselves.[43] The "party formally entitled to claim compensation does not necessarily have to be the party that has sustained the loss, indeed it is often the case with the carriage of goods that the one formally entitled to sue and the one who has suffered loss are not the same person, as happens frequently in practice, for example, when the sender or consignee named in the consignment note is a forwarder (*Spediteur*)."[44]

Although loss is neither the basis of title to sue nor a condition of entitlement to sue on some other ground, loss is relevant when a court must choose between two claimants, each of which is entitled to sue on some other ground: a claimant recovers only if and to the extent that that claimant has suffered loss.[45] Loss does not determine title to sue, but it may determine how much can be recovered. Loss means financial loss, whether it be suffered by the claimant whose goods have been lost or damaged or by the carrier who, having discharged his liability to the goods owner, adopts the role of sender in an action to recover the amount of that liability from the sub-contractor who lost or damaged the goods.[46]

Subject to this, concurrent rights of action against the carrier have been recognised, for example, in Austria,[47] Belgium,[48] and

---

[42] Above, para. 40.

[43] This is true of the consignee's right of action under Article 13: *Cass. Belge 13.6.80* (1980) 15 E.T.L. 851, 861: the carrier's argument that the consignee, having been promised replacement goods by the sender, had suffered no loss, was rejected as defence to a claim by the consignee.

[44] *OGH 22.11.84*, Greiter 253, 258. See also in this sense: *Lyon 5.2.82*, B.T. 1982.154; *B.G.H. 20.4.89* 1989 U.L.R. II 806; *O.L.G. Linz 27.11.89*, TranspR 1990.154. In some countries the agents have an independent right of action against the carrier: Haak, pp. 270 *et seq.*

The requirement of loss is sometimes equated with title to sue for the person at whose risk the goods are carried, and so, as regards the contract of carriage, is rejected on the basis that any contract whereby the goods are sold is separate from and without influence on the contract of carriage: *Poitiers 7.2.83*, B.T. 1983.455, 456. Haak, pp. 268 *et seq.*; Putzeys, para. 1057.

cf. Maccarone, Theunis, p. 74 as regards an action under Art. 12.7: the claimant must be the "person who has been damaged by the non-fulfilment of the instructions *and* who is party to the contract of carriage" (emphasis added).

[45] *Brussels 16.11.77* (1980) 15 E.T.L. 319, 329; *Brussels 5.12.68* (1969) 4 E.T.L. 958; *B.G.H. 10.4.74*, (1975) 10 E.T.L. 83. Haak, p. 270; Piper, VersR 1988. 201, 202.

[46] *O.L.G. Munich 5.7.89*, TranspR 1990.16.

[47] *OGH 12.4.84*, Stra GüV 1984/10 p. 10; Greiter 215, 220.

[48] *Brussels 5.12.68* (1969) 4 E.T.L. 958; *Rb Antwerp 7.12.73* (1976) 11 E.T.L. 295, 299; *Brussels 30.10.75* (1976) 11 E.T.L. 238, 243; *Brussels 16.11.77* (1980) 15 E.T.L. 319. Libouton, para. 33; Putzeys, para. 1056.

France,[49] although, as we have seen, generally not in Germany.[50] The nature of the two claimants' title to sue may not be the same, but they may not be mutually exclusive.[51] Apart from Article 13.1 of the CMR, title to sue may be based on the following grounds.

41a. The party to the contract

The person who contracts with the carrier is entitled to sue the carrier.[52] The identity of that person varies from case to case.

41a(*i*). The sender

The person who appears to make the contract of carriage and can therefore sue is the sender,[53] whether he be also the seller of the goods or not. Indeed, the sender has been identified as the person who makes the contract of carriage,[54] but who is not necessarily the person who actually consigns the goods.[55] The exception is when an apparent sender contracts on behalf of another person, such as the consignee.[56] This is common in England[57] and also perhaps in France.

In *Aix 25.11.82*[58] the Italian seller (*vendeur au départ*) of frozen seafood, unpaid for by the buyer in France, sued the carrier in respect of damage to the goods. The seller's action, which was based on the contract of carriage,[59] failed for, although the seller was

---

[49] *Paris 10.2.84*, B.T. 1984.558; Rodière, para. 363.

[50] *B.G.H. 6.7.79* (1980) 15 E.T.L. 863. *Contra*: Muth/Glöckner, p. 119, citing Dutch cases. Even in Germany, however, it has been held that the sender who has indemnified the consignee/buyer in respect of damage to goods in transit has a right of action against the carrier responsible for the damage: *B.G.H. 10.4.74* (1975) 10 E.T.L. 83.

[51] In this sense Putzeys, para. 1056; "there is room for a multiplicity of persons entitled to claim"—Haak, p. 265, with an impressive multiplicity of supporting citations from writers and Dutch cases. Also in this sense *Brussels 30.10.75* (1976) 11 E.T.L. 238, 243.

[52] *Cass. 27.10.75*, B.T. 1975.526; *O.L.G. Linz 27.11.89*, TranspR 1990.154, 156: whether that person has suffered loss or not. Piper, TranspR 1990.357; Rodière, para. 571. *cf.* the English position discussed below. But *cf.* Van Ryn (1966) 1 E.T.L. 638, 652.

[53] *Brussels 30.10.75* (1976) 11 E.T.L. 238, 243. For example the *commissionnaire de transport: Cass.com. 25.6.91*, B.T.L. 1992.4; or the *Spediteur: B.G.H. 20.4.89* 1989 U.L.R. II 806.

[54] Brunat, B.T. 1983.592; Cashmore, "Who are Consignors and Consignees for the purposes of a Contract of Carriage", [1990] J.B.L. 377; Haak, p. 253. Attempts by the authors of the CMR to define "sender" were abandoned, as the task proved to be too difficult: TRANS/WP9/35 p. 3.

[55] Haak, *loc.cit.*

[56] Below, para. 41a(*ii*).

[57] Below, para. 42.

[58] B.T. 1983.591.

[59] Brunat, *loc.cit.*, n. 54, suggests that the seller would have succeeded with an action in quasi-delict: art. 1384 al.5 C.Civ.; for example, *Reims 8.6.82*, B.T. 1983.382.

mentioned as sender in the consignment note, the true sender was the buyer and it was he who had concluded the contract of carriage, and at whose risk the goods had travelled.

Equally, when goods are consigned by an agent whose name appears in the consignment note, it is not he (or not only he[60]) but (also) the person for whom he is acting, who is the real sender and who is entitled to sue the carrier as party to the contract of carriage.

41a(*ii*). The consignee

The consignee is a party to the contract when an apparent sender or other agent contracts with the carrier on the consignee's behalf.[61] Even if the contract of carriage is contracted by the sender personally in some CMR states the consignee also becomes a party to the contract: the consignee is said to "adhere" to the contract concluded by sender and carrier.[62] In Belgium, for example, the person entitled to sue is the person whose rights have been infringed,[63] and this points to those party to the contract of carriage, which may include the consignee.[64] Rights of action may be concurrent, but recovery is limited to the amount of actual loss suffered by each.[65] The result is not unlike that found in England, when the *Brandt* rule[66] is applied.

41b. The person with the right of disposal

Title to sue may be based on the right to dispose of the goods in question. Normally there is only one such person, hence sender

[60] *HR 7.12.73* (1974) 9 E.T.L. 724, 728–729, discussed by Putzeys, para. 1059: the claimant bought goods from F and sold them to G, but under the terms of the second contract of sale the claimant retained during carriage risk but not ownership. The claimant contracted for carriage by the defendant and, although the consignment named F as sender and G as consignee, it was held that the claimant, although not a sender within the terms of Art. 12 or Art. 13, was entitled to sue the carrier under the contract of carriage. A very similar opinion is reported as *HR 13.2.73* (1974) 9 E.T.L. 602, 607.

[61] See *Aix 25.11.82*, above, para. 41a(*i*).

[62] In France the consignee becomes a party to the contract by accepting delivery of the goods: *Paris 19.11.81*, B.T. 1982.62; *Cass. 10.7.89*, B.T. 1989.619. Nickel-Lanz, paras. 67 *et seq.*

[63] Putzeys, paras. 1055 *et seq.*

[64] Haak, p. 266. As to how the consignee becomes party to the contract, see above, para. 40.

[65] *Brussels 5.12.68* (1969) 4 E.T.L. 958; *Brussels 16.11.77* (1980) 15 E.T.L. 319. Whether or not the consignee is regarded as a party to the contract of carriage, the consignee may have a right of action under art. 1121 of the Belgian civil code as a third party beneficiary of the contract of carriage: *TC Brussels 22.6.73* (1974) 9 E.T.L. 330.

[66] *Brandt v. Liverpool, Brazil & River Plate S.N. Co.* [1924] 1 K.B. 575, C.A. On this device, see below, para. 217.

and consignee may qualify in turn but not at the same time.[67] The sender's own right of action flows from the fact that he has contracted with the carrier and that, by virtue of the CMR Article 12.1, he has the right to dispose of the goods until that right is extinguished as provided in [Article 12.2]. In the circumstances of the case one must conclude that the right of disposal was extinguished when the goods which escaped theft were delivered to the consignee."[68]

A right of suit linked to the right of disposal is expressly stated in the CIM,[69] but not in the CMR, and this might suggest a different principle for the CMR.[70] The difference between the texts of the CMR and the CIM, as Haak put it,[71] "can be explained in two ways: non-adoption of article 42(3) CIM emphasises the difference with the CMR (B.G.H. in 1973 and 1974)[72] or alternatively is superfluous as a result of the model function of the CIM (B.G.H. in 1979).[73] He affirmed that the legislative history shows that the first conclusion is correct, and indeed this is so.[74] Nonetheless, the CIM rule has been applied to the CMR, particularly in Austria,[75] Germany,[76] and Switzerland,[77] and in some cases it has been adopted on the basis that the rule is justified by the CMR itself. For example, *O.L.G. Karlsruhe 24.5.67*:

> "Under the provisions of the CMR it is the person with the right to dispose of the goods who may claim in respect of damage to them. In the absence of an express rule in (the CMR) . . . it may be inferred from Article 27.1 [*sic*]. If the contracting parties to the CMR had intended a different rule, it would have been proposed that the convention say so expressly, particularly at any rate in two signatory states (Switzerland and West Germany between which the transport

[67] Above, para. 32.

[68] *Brussels 30.10.75* (1976) 11 E.T.L. 238, 243.

[69] Art. 16.3 (CIM 1952); Art. 42.3 (CIM 1960); Art. 54.3 (CIM 1980). Rodière, para. 573.

[70] *B.G.H. 10.4.74*, VersR 1974.796, reported by Haak, pp. 259–260.

[71] At 263, citing legislative history of the CMR.

[72] *B.G.H. 21.12.73* (1975) 10 E.T.L. 91; *B.G.H. 10.4.74*, VersR 1974.796.

[73] *B.G.H. 6.7.79* (1980) 15 E.T.L. 863.

[74] TRANS/WP9/35 pp. 16–17.

[75] *OGH 17.2.82*, SZ 55 Nr. 20, Greiter 127; *OGH 9.9.82*, TranspR 1984.11, 42, Greiter 170, 174 citing Helm, Art. 17 Anm. 30; *OGH 12.4.84*, Stra GüV 1984/10 p. 10, Greiter 215, 220; *OGH 22.11.84*, Greiter 253, 258. *Contra* in Austria: *O.L.G. Linz 27.11.89*, TranspR 1990.154, 155. In any event, the right is not exclusive: a seller could sue, even though the right of disposal had passed to the consignee: *OGH 12.4.84* (above).

[76] *O.L.G. Hamm 4.11.71* (1974) 9 E.T.L. 499, 501; *B.G.H. 6.7.79* (1980) 15 E.T.L. 863. Helm, Art. 17 Anm. 30. In the opinion of Haak, pp. 263–263, the right of disposal remains the main qualification for a right of action after the decision in *B.G.H. 6.7.79* (1980) 15 E.T.L. 863.

cf. B.G.H. 21.12.73 (1975) 10 E.T.L. 91, 94 that, while the right of disposal was decisive in branches of national law, this is not true of the CMR. See also *B.G.H. 10.4.74* (1975) 10 E.T.L. 83, 85.

[77] Nickel-Lanz, para. 210 and cases cited.

in question took place) . . . where it is the person with the right to dispose of the goods who may claim in respect of damage to them."[78]

This view was adopted by the B.G.H. in 1979[79]: although not express, it could be inferred from the text of the CMR itself that the proper claimant was the person with the right of disposal. But this inference depends on the German version of the CMR, which differs from the English and the French, and in which the "claimant" has been translated[80] as the "person with the right of disposal" (*Verfügungsberechtigte*). The inference also depends[81] on the close association in Article 13 of the consignee's right of action and the consignee's possession of the second consignment note (and thus the right of disposal); but association is not the same as interdependence and it is submitted that Article 13 does not link the right of action to possession of the second note.[82]

A right of suit by reference to the right of disposal has the superficial attraction that the logical consequence[83] is that the carrier faces suit from only one person, the one with the right of disposal. However, this is simplicity at a price. So, in 1974[84] the B.G.H., generally favourable to the person with the right of disposal, decided that when that person, the consignee, had been compensated under the terms of the contract of sale by the sender/seller, the latter had a right of action against the carrier, although lacking the right of disposal. Moreover, in other countries, such as Belgium,[85] the right of disposal is recognised as but one ground among others for a title to sue.

41c. The owner of the goods

Action may be brought by the person who owns the goods. However, title to sue on this ground is based on the assumption that the owner is the person who, because of his ownership, concluded the contract of carriage. Hence, ownership is not a distinct basis for

[78] 1967 U.L.C. 289, 295.

[79] *B.G.H. 6.7.79* (1980) 15 E.T.L. 863. *cf. B.G.H. 21.12.73* (1975) E.T.L. 91, in which the court appeared to take the opposite view that while the right of disposal gave the right of action, this had to be justified by national law rather than the CMR. These cases are discussed by Haak, pp. 258 *et seq.*

[80] Art. 17.2, Art. 18.2, Art. 20 and Art. 27. The French "ayant-droit" and the Dutch "rechthebbende" are, like the English "claimant", less specific.

[81] For example *B.G.H. 6.7.79* (1980) 15 E.T.L. 863, 868–869.

[82] Also in this sense: Haak, p. 263; Pesce, p. 164.

[83] Haak, p. 263 and p. 267.

[84] *B.G.H. 10.4.74*, VersR 1974.796, reported by Haak, pp. 259–260.

[85] *Brussels 30.10.75* (1976) 11 E.T.L. 238, 243. See also writers outside Germany, such as Haak, p. 265 and Putzeys, para. 1058, who recognise that the right of disposal gives rise to a right of action, but assert that it is not exclusive.

title to sue.[86] This position is found in England[87] and Italy, [88] but has been rejected in Belgium.[89] Further, it should be recalled that the owner at the time of loss or damage has a right of action in England in tort.[90]

42. Title to sue in England at common law

At common law, it is clear that action lies at the suit of the person who has contracted for the carriage and, although less clear, the presumption is that it is the owner of the goods who has contracted with the carrier.[91]

B. LIMITATION OF ACTIONS

43. The one-year period of limitation: Article 32

Article 32 sets the period of limitation. In the French version it is referred to as the period of prescription[92]; nonetheless, the intention appears to have been to bar the remedy rather than to extinguish the right,[93] and it follows that the limitation must be specially pleaded.[94] Alternatively, one can say that this is one of the aspects of limitation on which the CMR is silent and which therefore is governed by national law; and in the national law of most European countries limitation must be specially pleaded.[95] Article 32 provides:

> "The period of limitation for an action arising out of carriage under this Convention shall be one year. Nevertheless, in the case of wilful

---

[86] See above, para. 41a: title to sue *qua* party to the contract of carriage.
[87] Below, para. 42.
[88] Maccarone, Theunis, p. 65: title to sue is, however, linked to the right of disposal which, in his view, "can only belong to the owner".
[89] References to ownership or to risk were rejected in *Brussels 16.11.77* (1980) 15 E.T.L. 319; *Cass. Belge 13.6.80* (1980) 15 E.T.L. 851, 862. As regards risk *cf.* Libouton, para. 33. Moreover, risk was a factor in favour of title to sue in *HR 7.12.73* (1974) 9 E.T.L. 724, discussed by Putzeys, para. 1059.
[90] Below, para. 229.
[91] See below, Chap. 11.
[92] Whereas limitation is procedural and the right itself is not extinguished, the effect of prescription is not only to bar the right but also to extinguish the right.
[93] Haak, p. 293; Putzeys, para. 1116, this being the case in most European countries.
[94] Halsbury, *Laws of England* (4th ed., London, 1982), Vol. 28, para. 647. Haak, p. 293; Putzeys, para. 1116.
[95] In this sense Loewe, para. 258 and Loewe, Theunis, p. 156. For example, *OGH 14.1.76* SZ 49/3, Greiter 40, 44; 1976 U.L.R. II 366.

misconduct, or such default as in accordance with the law of the court or tribunal seised of the case, is considered as equivalent to wilful misconduct, the period of limitation shall be three years. The period of limitation shall begin to run:

(a) in the case of partial loss, damage or delay in delivery, from the date of delivery;

(b) in the case of total loss, from the thirtieth day after the expiry of the agreed time-limit or where there is no agreed time-limit from the sixtieth day from the date on which the goods were taken over by the carrier;

(c) in all other cases, on the expiry of a period of three months after the making of the contract of carriage.

The day on which the period of limitation begins to run shall not be included in the period."

The period of limitation is one year, excluding the commencement date.[96] The period is short. On the one hand, the carrier "who, in the course of business, carries a great deal of merchandise must be protected from being surprised by a complaint some considerable time after the transaction is completed. . . . For reasons of equity, the short period of limitation has also been granted to the consignee."[97] On the other hand, the period is so short that the necessity to make a claim may not become apparent until it is too late. An example is found in the consequences of careless handling of customs documents by the carrier.[98] Be that as it may, the purpose of Article 32 is to protect the parties, especially the carrier,[99] by promoting certainty and predictability.[1] Ironically, Article 32, which is based[2] on Article 46 of the CIM (1952),[3] is probably the most litigated provision of the CMR.[4]

---

[96] For the commencement dates, see below, para. 44. There are three possibilities listed (a) to (c) in Art. 32.1, and the next sentence excluding the commencement date applies not just to (c) but to all three: *KG Delft 13.5.65*, 1966 U.L.C. 104, 107; *Brussels 16.11.77* (1980) 15 E.T.L. 319.

[97] Loewe, Theunis, p. 155.

[98] Schmid/Kehl, TranspR 1995.435.

[99] *OGH 12.2.85*, Stra GüV 1985/9 p. 21, Greiter 280. Muth/Glöckner, p. 178.

[1] That firms in the transport industry should know where they stand: *ICI plc v. MAT Transport* [1987] 1 Lloyd's Rep. 354, 360, *per* Staughton J. Also in this sense: *B.G.H. 11.12.81* (1983) 18 E.T.L. 63, 68; *OGH 10.11.81*, SZ 54/165, TranspR 1982.111, Greiter 108; *OGH 2.4.82*, SZ 55/49, TranspR 1984.43, Greiter 148, 150; *OGH 12.2.85*, Stra GüV 1985/9 p. 21, Greiter 280.

[2] *B.G.H. 28.2.75* (1975) 10 E.T.L. 523, 524. Wetter, "The Time Bar Regulations in the CMR Convention", [1979] L.M.C.L.Q. 504. Consequently, it is assumed that the rules are intended to be the same: *B.G.H. 11.12.81* (1983) 18 E.T.L. 63, 69.

[3] This explains the complexity of Art. 32. There have been calls for reform: for example, Haak, p. 312; Wetter (above), p. 509.

[4] Loewe, Theunis, p. 152. Brunat: B.T. 1984.340.

43a. The scope of Article 32: actions arising out of carriage

Article 32 applies whether the action is brought by or against the carrier. In *Amsterdam 4.6.74*[5] it was argued[6] that Article 32 applied only to actions against the carrier, because Article 32 appears in a chapter which follows a chapter concerned with the carrier's liability; because there are special reasons for having a short period for suit in such a case; and because Article 32.2 on the suspension of limitation[7] refers only to claims *against* carriers. In reply it was argued, successfully, that Article 32 appears in a chapter headed generally "Claims and Actions"; that the reasons for a short period are valid whether suit was by or against the carrier; and that the CMR imposes liability not only on the carrier but also on the sender. The absence of any reference to an action by the sender or consignee in Article 32 was, said the court,[8] because it was based on the corresponding provisions of the CIM in which reference to such an action would have been inappropriate. Article 32 applies to actions not only against carriers but also by carriers.

Further, Article 32 applies to any "action arising out of carriage under" the CMR. It applies therefore whether the action is based in contract or in tort,[9] and whether the action is based on a duty imposed by the CMR itself or on some other contractual duty "arising out of carriage" subject to the CMR. For example, Article 32 has been applied in Germany to an action by the goods interest to recover carriage charges paid in advance,[10] and to an action by a carrier for *Standgeld*[11] in respect of the detention of the vehicle

---

[5] (1975) 10 E.T.L. 531. See also *B.G.H. 28.2.75*, 1975, U.L.R. II 373, N.J.W. 1975.1075, (1975) 10 E.T.L. 523 in which Art. 32 was applied to a claim for carriage charges against the sender; and in this same sense: *B.G.H. 11.12.81* (1983) 18 E.T.L. 63, 67; *Reims 10.10.84*, B.T. 1985.271; *O.L.G. Düsseldorf 26.1.95*, TranspR 1995.288. But *cf. O.L.G. Munich 12.4.91*, TranspR 1991.298.

[6] (1975) 10 E.T.L. 531, 535–536.

[7] Below, para. 45.

[8] (1975) 10 E.T.L. 531, 538. See also *Brussels 28.6.69* (1969) 4 E.T.L. 925; *B.G.H. 18.2.72* (1972) 7 E.T.L. 860, 1973 U.L.C. 264; and *B.G.H. 28.2.75* (above, n. 5).

[9] Art. 28.1: the carrier may use CMR provisions to defend "an extra-contractual claim". In the German version this has been translated literally but paraphrased by some courts as "Ansprüche aus unerlaubter Handlung": for example, *O.L.G. Düsseldorf 8.5.69* (1970) 5 E.T.L. 446, 462.

For example from the cases, a damage claim against a carrier sub-contractor: *OGH 27.9.83*, TranspR 1984.191, Greiter 205. See also *OGH 10.11.81*, TranspR 1982.111, Greiter 108; *O.L.G. Hamburg 9.2.89*, TranspR 1990.191.

[10] *B.G.H. 18.2.72*, N.J.W. 1972.1003 (1972) 6 E.T.L. 860, 1973 U.L.C. 264; *OGH 14.1.76*, SZ 49/3, Greiter 40, 1976 U.L.R. II 366; *OGH 2.4.82*, SZ 55/49, TranspR 1984.43, Greiter 148.

Also to an action in respect of consequential economic loss (of business): *B.G.H. 27.10.78*, N.J.W. 1979.2473; and an action for failure to collect C.O.D. charges: *'s Hertogenbosch 13.1.70* (1971) 6 E.T.L. 817; *Supreme Court of Denmark 22.4.71*, 1971 U.L.C. 307.

[11] Translated by Collins (and by Loewe, Theunis, p. 153) as "stallage", but this is not the sense of the word here. Better is one of the equivalents offered by Wildhagen, such as "demurrage" or "detention".

at a customs post in Teheran[12]; and in France[13] Article 32 has been applied to an action by a carrier to recover the cost of dealing with customs formalities in Istanbul.[14]

Although a uniform law such as the CMR should be given as wide a sphere of operation as its language allows,[15] a literal construction of Article 32 may go too far. For example, as it would be an action arising out of carriage, a negligence action by a pedestrian struck by the vehicle might be subject to Article 32. However, in Austria[16] Article 32 has been limited to actions by persons entitled to claim[17] under the contract of carriage. And in Germany, although it might be said that the presence of goods warehoused prior to being taken over by the carrier is a circumstance arising out of carriage, it has been held[18] that Article 32 does not apply to a claim in respect of goods lost from a warehouse.[19] More controversial is the applicability of Article 32 (and of the CMR as a whole) to an action against the carrier for failure to take goods over from the warehousemen in order to commence the journey contacted for.

If a contract of carriage governed by the CMR has been concluded, any action to enforce that contract is an action "arising out of carriage under" the CMR, and, prima facie, the period of limitation set by Article 32.1(c) may commence, even though performance of the contract has not been commenced. However, in Austria and Germany decisions on this point differ, and the courts are at odds with the leading writers.

> In *B.G.H. 18.2.72*[20] a contract was concluded between carrier and sub-carrier to carry machine parts from Germany to Spain in several instalments, and a dispute arose concerning the number of journeys that had been made by the sub-carrier. The carrier sought to recover money paid to the sub-carrier in respect of a journey

---

[12] *B.G.H. 11.12.81* (1983) 18 E.T.L. 63, TranspR 1982.153.
Also to an action by a carrier for carriage charges: *Muller Batavier v. Laurent Transport Co.* [1977] 1 Lloyd's Rep. 411. Also in this sense *Rb Amsterdam 24.5.72*, 1974, U.L.C. II. 229, 231; *Amsterdam 4.6.74*, 1975 U.L.R. I 271; *B.G.H. 28.2.75*, 1975, U.L.R. II. 373, N.J.W. 1975.1075; *OGH 5.11.80*, Greiter 79.

[13] *Lyon 6.7.83*, B.T. 1984.339 note Brunat. *idem*, *O.L.G. Nuremburg 26.11.74*, N.J.W. 1975.501.

[14] In spite of the argument that French law sees the task as a *mandat* distinct from the contract of carriage. The effect of the decisions is that the operation arises out of the carriage only as long as it is undertaken by the carrier personally as a duty to the other party to the contract of carriage. If the carrier had commissioned an agent to handle the customs formalities, the agent's action against the carrier would not have arisen out of the carriage and would have been governed by the *droit commun* with a longer prescription period (10 years): *Orléans 24.3.87*, B.T. 1987.662.

[15] *OGH 10.11.81* (below).

[16] *OGH 10.11.81*, SZ 54/165, TranspR 1982.111, Greiter 108. Thume, Art. 32, A18.

[17] Above, paras. 40 *et seq.*

[18] *B.G.H. 13.1.78*, (1978) 13 E.T.L. 402.

[19] As to when such ancillary stages or operations are part of the contract of carriage and hence subject to the CMR, see above, para. 10d.

[20] (1972) 7 E.T.L. 860, 1973 U.L.C. 264.

which, alleged the carrier, had not been made. The court below decided that the dispute did not arise out of carriage, as the claim was founded on the allegation that there had been no carriage, and applied not Article 32 but the shorter limitation period in the contractual conditions. The B.G.H. disagreed[21] with the premise that the claim was founded on an allegation of (total) non-performance. The dispute was over the number of journeys which *had* been performed and hence the amount of the charges due. It did not, however, challenge the assumption that, if the case were one of non-performance, the CMR limitation period did not apply.

This assumption is contrary to the opinion of writers in Germany[22] and to the decision in Austria in *OGH 12.2.85*,[23] in which the court, rejecting the view of Loewe,[24] applied Article 32 to a case of non-performance. The assumption is consistent with the view taken in Germany[25] that cases in which the goods have not been taken over by the carrier are outside the scope of the basic liability of CMR Article 17. But, whereas Article 17.1 makes the carrier liable for loss or damage occurring *after* the goods have been taken over by the carrier,[26] the scope of Article 32 is wider: a claim is, surely, one "arising out of carriage" in the terms of Article 32 whether performance of the carriage has been commenced or not. Moreover, the assumption produces odd results. If the shipper, who has goods warehoused in London, contracts for their carriage, but the carrier does not collect and the goods rot, Article 32 applies if the warehouse has attorned to the carrier,[27] but Article 32 does not apply if it has not. The ordinary meaning of Article 32, the context of Article 32, a convention applicable to contracts for the carriage of goods by road,[28] and the purpose of Article 32, to protect the carrier, indicate an intention that the actions barred should not be limited to those arising out of breach of Article 17 but should include all actions of any kind arising out of the contract of carriage. As Saville J. observed in *Shell Chemicals UK Ltd v. P & O Road Tanks Ltd*,[29] the CMR

[21] At 863.
[22] Helm, Art. 32 Anm. 1, by reference to Art. 31, Anm. 3. See also Herber/Piper, Art. 32, 3, 5; Koller, Art. 32, 1.
[23] Stra GüV 1985/9 p. 21, Greiter 280. See also *O.G.H. 22.2.90*, VersR 1991.127; TranspR 1992.357.
[24] Professor Loewe was unrepentant: Loewe, Theunis, p. 153.
[25] Below, para. 65.
[26] As the goods have not been taken over by the carrier, there has been no loss or damage "occurring between the time when he takes over the goods and the time of delivery," as required by Article 17.
[27] In these circumstances the warehouse holds for the carrier, and the carrier has thus taken the goods as over in the sense of Article 17.1; and as the storage is ancillary to the movement of goods, the goods have been taken over in performance of the contract of carriage: above, para. 27.
[28] Art. 1.1; above, para. 10.
[29] [1993] 1 Lloyd's Rep. 114.

> "deals with certain aspects of carriage of goods by road. So far as liability for loss of or damage or delay to consigned goods is concerned, I am prepared to assume for the purposes of the argument that the intent was to provide a complete code for the period stipulated in art. 17.1; but it does not begin to follow that the intent was therefore to exclude every other type of possible liability which is unrelated to loss of or damage to the consigned goods unless expressly included elsewhere in the Convention. To my mind therefore the only relevant provision in the present context is art. 32(1)(c) which does provide a special limitation period for *all cases other than those of loss of or damage or delay to the consigned goods*."[30]

43b. Exception: the three-year period for wilful misconduct

An exception to the one-year period is provided in the second sentence of Article 32.1[31]:

> "in the case of wilful misconduct, or such default as in accordance with the law of the court or tribunal seised of the case, is considered as equivalent to wilful misconduct, the period of limitation shall be three years."

Wilful misconduct or equivalent default also affects the amount of liability; this is the effect of Article 29, discussed below.[32] The equivalent of wilful misconduct in English law, in terms of its effect on the limitation period, is fraud.[33] Fraud includes not only common law fraud[34] but also "conduct which, having regard to some special relationship between the two parties concerned, is an unconscionable thing for the one to do towards the other".[35] However, as regards Article 32 and Article 29 of the CMR, the reference to equivalent misconduct is irrelevant in states, such as

[30] At p. 116 (emphasis added). The context was that of a carrier that collected the right tank (of liquid chemical) and carried it most of the way but did not deliver the right tank to the consignee, with consequent damage to the consignee's refinery occurring after delivery.

[31] *cf. B.G.H. 11.12.81* (1983) 18 E.T.L. 63, 69: Prima facie the exception applies to all cases otherwise subject to the general one-year rule, but it was held by the B.G.H. that, while the exception applies to actions concerning obligations arising under the CMR itself, other actions "arising out of carriage" under the CMR, while subject to the one-year period set by the first sentence of Article 32.1, are not affected by the exception in the second. An English court is not likely to take this view.

[32] Para. 101. See, for example, *Cass. 8.1.74* (1974) 9 E.T.L. 314.

[33] Limitation Act 1980, s.32.

[34] A false statement "made (1) knowingly, or (2) without belief in its truth, or (3) recklessly, careless whether it be true or false": *Derry v. Peek* (1889) 14 App.Cas. 337, 374, *per* Lord Herschell.

[35] *Kitchen v. Royal Air Force Association* [1958] 1 W.L.R. 563, 573, *per* Lord Evershed M.R., C.A.; *Applegate v. Moss* [1971] 1 Q.B. 406, C.A.

the United Kingdom, where there is a concept of wilful misconduct.[36]

Under Article 32 the period is extended "in the case of" wilful misconduct, whereas under Article 29 the amount of liability may be increased only if the damage was "caused by" wilful misconduct.[37]

> In *Paris 25.3.88*,[38] a case of wilful misconduct (*dol*) in the form of deception, the deception lay in the name given by the carrier and used in the consignment note, a name similar to that of another company with the same registered address, which made it not impossible but more difficult for the claimant to commence action within the one-year period. The court applied the three-year period. However, as to the amount of compensation, the damage to the goods was not caused by the deception but by a road accident, so Article 29 did not apply.

English law usually requires some connection in fact between reprehensible conduct and the legal right which is affected by that conduct, and the degree of connection depends mainly on the degree of disapproval of the misconduct in question. If the conduct is sufficiently serious, the connection may be slight. If, for example, the vehicle carries heroin, the court is likely to refuse enforcement of the contract of carriage even though the nature of the cargo had no real causal connection with the particular loss, damage or delay in respect of which compensation is sought.[39] Nonetheless, a causal connection of some kind is required, however tenuous.

No other exception to the one-year period is allowed. Both the construction of Article 32 and the purpose[40] of Article 32 indicate that the only exception is the case of wilful misconduct or equivalent default. Hence, no exception is made for the claimant in respect of loss which has not materialised until after the limitation period has run—at least in a case in which the claimant should have expected some loss of that kind.

> In *Paris 25.3.82*[41] the claimant, a *commissionnaire de transport*, contracted for the carriage of coffee from Trieste to Le Havre. The coffee was stolen before it had left the region of Venice. The carrier was liable. As the commissionnaire could not prove that the coffee had left Italy, the commissionnaire was required to pay import duty, but no demand was made for the duty until 15 months after the theft. He subsequently claimed this sum from the carrier at a time

---

[36] Below, para. 102.
[37] Below, para. 101d.
[38] B.T. 1989.46.
[39] Below, para. 243b.
[40] Above, para. 43.
[41] B.T. 1982.434.

when the prescription period had passed, contending that the period had not run against him until he had had documentary evidence of the amount of the duty. This contention was rejected by the court, as he knew or should have known from the time of the theft that, unless the coffee was recovered and exported, the duty would have to be paid.[42]

Moreover, no exception is made because the defendant's breach of contract is a breach of the criminal law, unless the case is also one of wilful misconduct or equivalent default.

43b(*i*). Criminal compensation

In theory, the claimant barred by Article 32.1 might recover compensation by joining a penal action against the carrier, to which the one-year limitation period does not apply. In France this avenue has been closed,[43] because the actions are essentially different: the one (CMR) being generally for a limited amount and the other (criminal compensation) being for full compensation. The result, described as "shocking",[44] is that, whereas in general a prosecution must be brought sooner than a civil suit, here the position is reversed: the civil action must be pursued more promptly than the prosecution. Moreover, speed required in the civil action will be difficult to achieve, if the documentary evidence needed for the civil action is tied up in the prosecution.[45] In England, a similar question has arisen, although not in connection with the CMR.[46]

---

[42] Also in this sense: *B.G.H. 11.12.81* (1983) 18 E.T.L. 63, 68–69.

[43] *Cass. 7.4.87*, B.T. 1987.343: a tanker with wine from France was stopped at the border with Germany, and the wine destroyed as unfit for consumption. The carrier was prosecuted for having carried wine in a tanker previously used for the carriage of industrial chemicals. The owner of the wine sought to be made *partie civile* to the criminal proceedings brought against the carrier and thus benefit from a longer limitation period (three years instead of one). In line with an earlier decision on the same point regard the Warsaw Convention (*Cass. 24.2.78*, Gaz.Pal. 1978.331) the Court of Cassation censured the court below for having applied the longer period.

[44] Rodière, Gaz.Pal. 1978.331. For a comparable reaction to a similar possibility in English law, see Atiyah [1979] Crim.L.R. 504.

[45] Rodière, para. 672. The solution in France would be that a mere application for a compensation order (*se constituer partie civile*) in the penal process would be enough to suspend the period of limitation in the civil process, the outcome can be awaited without prejudice to the civil suit, and in practical terms the difference between the periods would be attenuated: Rodière, Gaz.Pal. 1978.331, 332.

[46] In England, the civil CMR action is generally limited in amount, while a compensation order, if sought in the Crown Court, is unlimited in amount: *Jackson's Machinery of Justice* (Cambridge, 1989), p. 281. However, in practice the order is discretionary and the amounts awarded are small. Moreover, restitution is not the only factor affecting the court's discretion: it must also consider the offender's means, and the moral and criminological elements of the case. These considerations make this a process fundamentally different from civil suit. See further on this matter the second edition of this book, para. 45b(*i*).

Clearly, a CMR claim is not what Parliament had in mind, still less a claim that is out of time. Add the need to promote uniformity under the CMR, and it is nonetheless clear that the period in Article 32 should not be outflanked by a compensation order in criminal proceedings.

43c. The commencement of proceedings

What constitutes the commencement of an action in any particular case "must depend upon the procedural law of the country where the action is commenced".[46a] The same is true of a counterclaim.[47] The distinction between a defence to the action and a counterclaim is also a matter for national law.[48] In England, an action in the courts commences on the date of issue of the writ.[49]

> In *Impex Transport v. Thames Holdings*[50] the last of a number of consignments of fruit was delivered in England on January 11, 1974. On August 2, 1974, the claimant carriers issued and served a writ on the defendant consignees in respect of freight and certain other expenses. On October 18 of that year the defendants filed an affidavit in which facts giving rise to a counterclaim for damage to the goods were deposed. On March 12, 1975, and hence after the end of the period of limitation for a claim or counterclaim in respect of damaged goods, the defendants served their defence and counterclaim. Robert Goff J. held that the counterclaim had been brought too late.

In that case the judge said[51] that by

> "the procedural law of the country where the right of action is exercised, in the present case English law . . . certain informal steps—such as the notice of counterclaim . . . or correspondence . . . are insufficient to constitute a 'setting up' of a counterclaim for the purpose of the old Ord. 21, r. 10 . . . In no case has it been decided that an affidavit in opposition to a summons for judgement under Ord. 14 is sufficient for this purpose. . . .
>
> [T]here are dicta in the cases which support the view that to constitute the 'setting up' of a counterclaim under the old Ord. 21, r. 16, the service of a pleading containing a counterclaim, or some

---

[46a] *Impex Transport v. Thames Holdings* [1981] 2 Lloyd's Rep. 566, 569, *per* Robert Goff J.

[47] At 569–570, *per* Robert Goff J.

[48] *Cass. 8.1.85*, B.T. 1985.169: the defendant's response to the carrier's claim for carriage charges, to point to the loss that he, the defendant, had suffered because the goods were delivered late, was not a *défense du fond*, as held by the Rouen court, but a counterclaim caught by Art. 32.4.

[49] *Impex*, above, n. 46a at 569.

[50] [1981] 2 Lloyd's Rep. 566.

[51] [1981] 2 Lloyd's Rep. 566, 569–573.

equivalent formal document, is necessary. . . . I can see no reason to apply any different construction to the present Ord. 15, r. 2(3). . . . An action is, of course, commenced by the formal step of the issue of a writ; one would expect to find a similar formal step for the initiation of a counterclaim, and the only comparable step appears to be the service of a counterclaim, either together with or subsequently added to the defence, or the service of some other document which, by virtue of some order of the Court, is to stand as a counterclaim, as for example when the Court makes an order dispensing with pleadings."[52]

As for arbitration, in England arbitration commences for the purpose of limitation when one party serves on the other a notice requiring the appointment of an arbitrator.[53] The procedure for service of notice is regulated by the Arbitration Act 1996[54]:

Application of Limitation Acts

13.—(1) The Limitation Acts apply to arbitral proceedings as they apply to legal proceedings.

(2) The court may order that in computing the time prescribed by the Limitation Acts for the commencement of proceedings (including arbitral proceedings) in respect of a dispute which was the subject matter—

(a) of an award which the court orders to be set aside or declares to be of no effect, or

(b) of the affected part of an award which the court orders to be set aside in part, or declares to be in part of no effect,

the period between the commencement of the arbitration and the date of the order referred to in paragraph (a) or (b) shall be excluded.

(3) In determining for the purposes of the Limitation Acts when a cause of action accrued, any provision that an award is a condition precedent to the bringing of legal proceedings in respect of a matter to which an arbitration agreement applies shall be disregarded.

(4) In this Part "the Limitation Acts" means—

(a) in England and Wales, the Limitation Act 1980, the Foreign Limitation Periods Act 1984 and any other enactment (whenever passed) relating to the limitation of actions;

---

[52] At 574 the judge indicated that, although not enough to constitute a counterclaim, the affidavit might amount to written notice of a kind which suspends the period of limitation; see below, para. 45.

[53] This is the effect of the Carriage of Goods by Road Act 1965, s.7(2)(a), in which the original reference to s.27 of the Limitation Act 1939 has been superseded by reference to s.34 of the Limitation Act 1980. s.7(2) contains equivalent provisions for Northern Ireland and for Scotland.

[54] The matter was previously regulated by s.34 of the Limitation Act 1980, which section has been repealed. Generally, see Merkin, *Arbitration Act 1996* (London, 1996).

(b) in Northern Ireland, the Limitation (Northern Ireland) Order 1989, the Foreign Limitation Periods (Northern Ireland) Order 1985 and any other enactment (whenever passed) relating to the limitation of actions.

Commencement of arbitral proceedings

14.—(1) The parties are free to agree when arbitral proceedings are to be regarded as commenced for the purposes of this Part and for the purposes of the Limitation Acts.

(2) If there is no such agreement the following provisions apply.

(3) Where the arbitrator is named or designated in the arbitration agreement, arbitral proceedings are commenced in respect of a matter when one party serves on the other party or parties a notice in writing requiring him or them to submit that matter to the person so named or designated.

(4) Where the arbitrator or arbitrators are to be appointed by the parties, arbitral proceedings are commenced in respect of a matter when one party serves on the other party or parties notice in writing requiring him or them to appoint an arbitrator or to agree to the appointment of an arbitrator in respect of that matter.

(5) Where the arbitrator or arbitrators are to be appointed by a person other than a party to the proceedings, arbitral proceedings are commenced in respect of a matter when one party gives notice in writing to that person requesting him to make the appointment in respect of that matter.

Service of notices, &c

76.—(1) The parties are free to agree on the manner of service of any notice or other document required or authorised to be given or served in pursuance of the arbitration agreement or for the purposes of the arbitral proceedings.

(2) If or to the extent that there is no such agreement the following provisions apply.

(3) A notice or other document may be served on a person by any effective means.

(4) If a notice or other document is addressed, pre-paid and delivered by post—

(a) to the addressee's last known principal residence or, if he is or has been carrying on a trade, profession or business, his last known principal business address, or

(b) where the addressee is a body corporate, to the body's registered or principal office,

it shall be treated as effectively served.

(5) This section does not apply to the service of documents for the purposes of legal proceedings, for which provision is made by rules of court.

(6) References in this Part to a notice or other document include any form of communication in writing and references to giving or serving a notice or other document shall be construed accordingly.

A telex notice is effective on receipt.[55] In the case of notice served by post, "unless the contrary intention appears, the service is deemed to be effected by properly addressing, pre-paying and posting a letter containing the document and, unless the contrary is proved, to have been effected at the time at which the letter would have been delivered in the ordinary course of post.[56]

44. The commencement of the period of limitation

Apart from a special rule in Article 39.4 for recourse between carriers,[57] commencement of the period of limitation is governed by Article 32.1, set out above.[58] There are three rules for three cases:

(a) In the case of partial loss, damage or delay in delivery,[59] the limitation period runs from the date of delivery.[60] Delay in delivery implies that delivery occurs, so delay such that the goods are not delivered at all is not a case for rule (a) but for rule (c), as is the case in which, although the goods were delivered, they were delivered by another carrier and not by the carrier against which the claim is made.[61]

(b) In the case of total loss,[62] evidently there is no delivery from which the limitation period can run, and a rule different from rule (a) is required. In the case of total loss, the period runs from the thirtieth day after the expiry of the agreed time-limit or, where there is no agreed time-limit, from the sixtieth day from the date when the goods were taken over by the carrier. The time-limit is the time-limit agreed for delivery. Goods are taken over by the carrier when the carrier acquires control of the goods from the sender.[63] When control is transferred from one carrier to another in the course of the performance of a single contract of carriage, it is unclear from which taking over the 60-day period runs.[64]

---

[55] *The Pendrecht* [1980] 2 Lloyd's Rep. 56. See also below, para. 202.
[56] Interpretation Act 1978, s.7.
[57] Below, para. 44b.
[58] Para. 43.
[59] As to the meaning of delivery, see above, para. 37. Rule (a) applies even though the consignee could have taken delivery at an earlier time: Loewe, para. 261.
[60] An instance in England is *Impex*, discussed above, para. 43c.
[61] *O.L.G. Hamburg 9.2.89*, TranspR 1990.191.
[62] For the meaning of total loss see below, para. 56. In the context of Art. 32.1(b) total loss refers to the total loss of goods of the claimant under the particular contract of carriage, even though other goods, grouped and carried with the goods lost but carried under different contracts of carriage, have not been totally lost: *TC Brussels 28.2.75* (1975) 10 E.T.L. 419, 426; *Brussels 16.11.77* (1980) 15 E.T.L. 319, 329.
[63] On this point, see above, para. 27.
[64] Hill and Messent, p. 240.

(c) In all other cases, the limitation period starts to run "on the expiry of a period of three months after the making of the contract of carriage".

Other cases include cases in which the carrier has performed the contract of carriage, and claims to recover charges, such as carriage charges,[65] as well as damages for the detention of a vehicle at a customs post.[66] Other cases also include claims by the sender or consignee, which do not fit rule (a) because there has been no delivery, and do not fit rule (b) because there has been no total loss.[67]

In the case of an umbrella contract for a series of transports over a period of time, a literal application of rule (c) would mean that time had expired before the claim arose or even before the particular movement of goods had been requisitioned. A purposive interpretation of rule (c) suggests that the period should run from the commencement of the particular carriage or taking over, or from the date of the requisition that initiated it,[68] but the matter has not been resolved in the courts.[69]

A single movement of goods may give rise to claims and cross claims with different limitation dates, not only because they may have different commencement dates for the period of limitation but also because the period for one claim may have been suspended under Article 32.2,[70] but the period for another claim may not. The suggestion, that all claims arising out of one movement should have the same limitation period[71] or that, if there is a damage claim, any freight claim should be brought within the

---

[65] *Muller Batavier v. Laurent Transport Co.* [1977] 1 Lloyd's Rep. 411. Also *Brussels 13.9.68* (1969) 4 E.T.L. 1153; *Rb Mechelen 14.2.73* (1973) 8 E.T.L. 630; *Amsterdam 4.6.74* (1976) 11 E.T.L. 266; *B.G.H. 28.2.75* (1975) 10 E.T.L. 523, 524–525 where the B.G.H. was impressed by the more explicit terms of the corresponding provision in the CIM, Art. 47.2.

[66] *B.G.H. 11.12.81* (1983) 18 E.T.L. 63.

[67] For example *Shell Chemicals UK Ltd v. P & O Road Tanks Ltd* [1993] 1 Lloyd's Rep. 114, discussed above, para. 43a. See also *Brussels 28.6.69* (1969) 4 E.T.L. 925: a claim for damages; *'s Hertogenbosch 13.1.70* (1971) 6 E.T.L. 817, 822–823: a claim for the amount of a "cash on delivery" charge, which the carrier had failed to collect from the consignee; *B.G.H. 18.2.72* (1972) 7 E.T.L. 860: a claim for repayment of advance charges; *OGH 2.4.82*, SZ 55 no. 49, TranspR 1984.43, Greiter 148: a claim to recover charges overpaid; *O.L.G. Hamburg 9.2.89*, TranspR 1990.191: a claim for the cost of employing another carrier to deliver the goods, which the defendant had failed to deliver.

[68] In this sense: Wetter (above, n. 2), p. 506. Another tactic open to a claimant is to rely on an extension of the period under national law, as permitted by Article 32.4. In some states an extension will be granted in cases of hardship, but not in England: below, para. 45f.

[69] *cf. B.G.H. 11.12.81* (1983) 18 E.T.L. 63 in which the court was unsympathetic to the argument that the limitation period might run from an instruction given under Art. 16.

[70] Below, para. 45.

[71] Costanza, pp. 45 *et seq.* who argues for co-extensive periods, preferably on the basis of the shorter applicable period.

same period as the damage claim, has not been followed. Indeed, there is force in the argument[72] that the time in which the carrier must commence an action for carriage charges, which is governed by rule (c), should not be shortened to the period for a damage claim, especially if the damage claim has the short antecedent period in case (a), as the carrier may have insufficient notice that counterclaims will be made.[73] If this is right, rule (c) generally gives a later date of commencement and hence a longer period in which to bring suit than rules (a) and (b), and claimants will seek to expand the sphere of rule (c) at the expense of the other two. The controversial case is that of goods damaged but undelivered.

44a. Goods damaged but not delivered

Lines have been drawn over the relatively common case of goods, not destroyed, but damaged to such an extent that they are not taken on and delivered to the consignee but sold as scrap, or returned to sender for repair and perhaps resale. The case has been variously seen as one of case (a), case (b), case (c), or, in the first decision on the point in England, as a case falling outside this part of the CMR altogether.

In *Moto Vespa v. MAT (Britannia Express)*[74] lathes had been damaged en route for Madrid, where they arrived but were not delivered, so it was not a case for rule (a). Rule (b), for cases of total loss, was not seriously considered. However, as "other cases" meant "case other than partial loss, damage, or total loss and here there was undoubtedly damage", it was not, said the court,[75] a case for rule (c). Therefore, the court held that, as regards the period of limitation, the case fell outside the CMR altogether, and applied the six-year period of the English Limitation Act.

The view that the CMR limitation period does not apply to such a common case is curious. The conclusion is also unfortunate, for, if the case is governed by the differing provisions of national law, the position of the parties is less predictable than was intended by the authors of the CMR. Moreover, the conclusion is mistaken,[76] for it rests on an interpretation of Article 32.1, whereby rule (c) refers only to cases that lack *any* of the *individual* features found in cases falling within rule (a) and rule (b). But on a very ordinary

---

[72] Wetter (above, n. 2), p. 506.

[73] However, if the claim for charges takes the form of a counterclaim, that is what happens by the operation of Art. 32.4: see below, para. 45g.

[74] [1979] 1 Lloyd's Rep. 175.

[75] At 180.

[76] The conclusion has been widely criticised in terms varying from "unhappy" (Haak, p. 298) and "unfortunate" (Hardingham (below, n. 81), p. 364) to "nonsensical" (Loewe, Theunis, p. 155).

and literal interpretation of Article 32.1, which is no less obvious than that adopted in *Moto Vespa*, rule (c) refers to cases without either of the *combinations* of features found in rule (a) or rule (b), *i.e.* cases that are neither *case* (a) nor *case* (b). Add the teleological factor that Article 32 was intended to be comprehensive, to cover all claims arising under the CMR, and it is no surprise that the interpretation in *Moto Vespa* was later rejected in England in *Worldwide Carriers v. Ardtran International*.[77]

A second view found in England is that the case of goods damaged but not delivered is a case for rule (b). In *ICI Fibres v. MAT Transport*[78] nylon yarn en route from Harrogate to consignees in the south of France was damaged near Calais and sent back to Harrogate. Staughton J. considered that, although the goods had not suffered total loss in the ordinary sense of the CMR,[79] and thus prima facie the case was not within rule (b), the matter was affected by Article 20: if the goods are not delivered within 60 days of their being taken over, "the person entitled to make a claim may thereupon treat them as lost". The claimant carrier stated that he did not wish to treat the goods as lost in this case. But the judge concluded[80]: "I would be reluctant to accept that for all purposes the owner is obliged to treat the goods as lost, and that if they were found before he received compensation he could not claim them. . . . But so far as limitation and the running of time are concerned, it seems to me that the parties are entitled to know where they stand. For that purpose at any rate non-delivery within 60 days is conclusive evidence binding on both parties that there has been a loss of the goods." As the goods had never been delivered to the consignees in the south of France, still less within 60 days of their having been taken over, he held that it was case (b).

The decisive point was that the case is one of total loss. In other words, that a delay, which is treated by Article 20 as total loss for the purpose of compensation under Article 23, is also treated as a case of total loss for the purpose of limitation under Article 32, a view that has support in the courts[81] but not among writers.[82] The special meaning in Article 20 and Article 23 is to promote certainty,[83] notably, to indicate when missing goods can be regarded as lost under Article 23 and so to enable the claimant to recover

[77] *Worldwide Carriers v. Ardtran International* [1983] 1 Lloyd's Rep. 61, 65, *per* Parker J.; Chitty, para. 3273.

[78] [1987] 1 Lloyd's Rep. 354.

[79] At 358. On the meaning of loss, see below, para. 56.

[80] At 360.

[81] *Worldwide Carriers v. Ardtran International* [1983] 1 Lloyd's Rep. 61, 65, *per* Parker J. Also *TC Paris 14.3.78* (1978) 13 E.T.L. 742, 746. *Contra: Brussels 28.6.69* (1969) 4 E.T.L. 925, 928. Hardingham, "Aspects of the Limitation of Actions under the CMR", [1979] L.M.C.L.Q. 362, 363.

[82] Opinions of this interpretation include "remarkable" (Haak, p. 299) and "somewhat strained" (Glass [1984] L.M.L.Q. 30, 42).

[83] Below, para. 57.

compensation when the fate of the goods (and hence the extent of any economic loss) is unknown. Article 32 on limitation, in a different chapter of the CMR, uses different language,[84] and does not require a special meaning for "loss" in order to ensure certainty in matters of limitation: if the goods are missing, and if, therefore, it is unknown whether they will eventually be delivered and come under case (a) or be totally lost and come under case (b), certainty is safeguarded simply by treating the case as case (c). Hence there appears to be insufficient justification for the application of Article 20 out of context, and for thus giving "total loss" in Article 32 anything other than its ordinary meaning.

A third view found in a Belgian decision[85] and favoured by most writers,[86] is that the case of goods damaged but not delivered is not case for rule (a), as there is no delivery, and is not a case for rule (b), as damage is not total loss, but must therefore be an "other case", governed by rule (c). On the premise that the situation is governed by neither rule (a) nor rule (b), this is correct; however, there is a fourth view, which disputes the premise as regards rule (a).

The fourth view which some but not all commentators see as one standing with but qualifying the third, is that, if the damaged goods are returned to sender or delivered to a third party on the instructions of the sender, that is (re)delivery (to the sender) or third party and the events amount to case (a).[87] On this view, the conclusion is the same in the related situation of goods which are lost for the period of time in Article 20.1, found and eventually delivered to the consignee.[88] The view was entertained in England, as a tentative and alternative ground for decision, in *Worldwide Carriers v. Ardtran International*[89]:

> "Under art. 12(1) the sender has the right to dispose of the goods, in particular by asking the carrier to stop the goods in transit, to

---

[84] Art. 20 says that non-delivery of the goods within 60 days of taking over shall be "evidence of loss" and that the claimant "may thereupon treat them as lost". Art. 32.1(b) applies simply "in the case of total loss".

[85] *Brussels 28.6.69* (1969) 4 E.T.L. 925, 928. The view was also taken, but apparently without discussion, in *O.L.G. Munich 5.7.89*, TranspR 1990.16.

[86] Glass [1984] L.M.C.L.Q. 30, 44; Haak, p. 299; Hardingham (above, n. 81), p. 364; Herber, Art. 32, 17; Loewe, Theunis, p. 155; Putzeys, para. 1128; Wetter (above, para. 43, n. 2), p. 505.

[87] If the carrier does not return the goods but unloads and stores them, prima facie this is a situation in which delivery to the designed consignee has been prevented, a situation governed by Art. 15 and Art. 16. The effect of unloading (Art. 16.2) is that "the carriage shall be demeed to be at an end. The carrier shall then hold the goods on behalf of the person" entitled to dispose of them. This too, in the view of the commentators, is a kind of delivery: see above, para. 33c(*ii*). If, however, the goods are stored temporarily with a view to being sent on to destination, as contracted for, Art. 15 does not apply: See *O.L.G. Düsseldorf 23.11.89* (below, n. 92).

[88] See *O.L.G. Düsseldorf 23.11.89* (below, n. 92).

[89] [1983] 1 Lloyd's Rep. 61, 65, *per* Parker J. Also in this sense Anon. note to *Brussels 28.6.69* (1969) 4 E.T.L. 925, 930; and Hardingham (above, n. 81), p. 364.

> change the place at which delivery is to take place or to deliver the goods to a consignee other than the consignee indicated in the consignment note . . . If, therefore, on hearing of damage the sender requires the goods to be returned to him he is doing no more than stop the goods in transit, change the place of delivery and change the consignee. When these instructions are carried out it appears to me that, at least in some cases, there will have been delivery under the contract and thus that art. 32(1)(a) applies."

This view deserves serious consideration. The purpose of this part of Article 32 is to fix an ascertainable point in time from which it is reasonable that time should run against the claimant. Delivery is the prime point fixed by case (a), as the transfer of custody from carrier to recipient marks a point at which, for most goods claims, the extent of loss or damage can and should be assessed.[90] Delivery is most appropriate as the point of commencement, when it is delivery to the person most likely to make a claim against the carrier. In many if not most cases delivery is made to the person at whose risk the goods travel; that could be either sender or consignee but if the consignee has refused delivery, the likely claimant is the sender and, if the consignee takes delivery as agent of the sender, the consignee may also make a claim as agent for the sender.[91] The fourth view, that the case falls within rule (a), has support especially in Germany.

> In *O.L.G. Düsseldorf 23.11.89*[92] a groupage consignment included a piece of electrical machinery which was warehoused en route and mislaid. It was found over a year later, rusty and useless. The court held[93] that it was not a case of actual total loss, because the piece was just one item of the goods subject to the contract of carriage, but that, in any case, as the goods had eventually been found, it was not a case of loss. This, it was held, was a case of delay in delivery under rule (a).

In a case like this, the court considered that it should be open to the consignee to accept delivery of the goods and claim in respect of damage, a course that would be closed if the consignee could not afford to wait, lest his action be barred, but were compelled to treat non-delivery on time as a case of total loss under rule (b).

Of these four views, the first is plainly wrong and has little support. The second is less plainly wrong than the first, and has a little more support. Although the third view merits consideration

---

[90] In this sense: *'s Hertogenbosch 21.12.65*, 1966 U.L.C. 119, 125, discussed above, para. 37f.

[91] Below, para. 45a.

[92] TranspR 1990.63. The view, that return to sender is a case of delivery, was taken, as an alternative ground for the decision, in *O.L.G. Munich 5.7.89*, TranspR 1990.16, 17; Herber, Art. 32, 17; Koller, Art. 32, 4; Thume, Art. 32, 27. Also in this sense: Putzeys, para. 532. *Contra*: Helm, Art. 32 Anm. 5.

[93] At 66.

and has support from writers, the better view, for which there is growing support in the courts, is the fourth.

44b. Claims between successive carriers

As regards claims between successive carriers, Article 39.4 states that these are governed by the provisions of Article 32, but provides a special rule for the commencement of the period of limitation:

> "The period of limitation shall, however, begin to run either on the date of the final judicial decision fixing the amount of compensation payable under the provisions of this Convention, or, if there is no such judicial decision, from the actual date of payment."

The person seeking to rely on the extended period provided by Article 39.4, the carrier seeking recourse, must prove the date of the judicial decision or the date on which payment was made.[94] The range of claims governed by this provision is limited to claims which are for compensation[95] and which are between carriers.

44b(*i*). Claims between carriers

Although the opening words of Article 39.4 refer to "claims between carriers", they appear in Chapter 6, headed "Provisions Relating to Carriage Performed by Successive Carriers", and it has been argued that Article 39.4 is concerned only with successive carriers and does not apply to sub-carriers. If carrier A performs part of the carriage but sub-contracts, for example, the second part of the carriage to carrier B, A and B are successive carriers and, if carrier B is held liable to the consignee for damage occurring during the first part, carrier B may have a recourse action against carrier A, an action regulated under Chapter 6. But, it has been argued, if carrier A sub-contracts the entire carriage to carrier B, the sub-contract is between A as sender and B as carrier,[96] and any claim between them is not a claim "between carriers": Chapter 6 does not apply.[97] This argument has been rejected in England. In *Ulster-Swift*[98] A, who had contracted to carry meat to Basle, sub-contracted the entire movement to B. Having been held liable for damage to the meat, A brought a recourse action against B which

---

[94] *Gent 20.6.86* (1986) 21 E.T.L. 371.

[95] Below, para. 44b(*ii*).

[96] Loewe, Theunis p. 158. This analysis of the relationship is supported by *O.L.G. Düsseldorf 12.2.81*, VersR 1982.302; *O.L.G. Munich 5.7.89*, TranspR 1990.16.

[97] See below.

[98] *Ulster-Swift v. Taunton Meat Haulage* [1977] 1 Lloyd's Rep. 346.

was out of time unless Article 39.4 applied. In a single judgment read by Megaw L.J. the Court of Appeal held that Article 39.4 applied.

In this case counsel for B argued that A was not a carrier, and referred the court to the Carriage of Goods by Road Act 1965, in which section 14(2)(c) applies the Act and the CMR to "any carrier who, in accordance with Article 34 or otherwise is party to a contract of carriage". The purpose of section 14(2)(c) appears to have been precautionary, and the court concluded that A was a carrier.[99] This, of course, is true of A when A contracts with the (original) sender for the carriage, which A eventually subcontracts entirely to B. It does not, however, follow from this that A is a carrier in A's relations with B: B may have no knowledge that A has contracted with an (original) sender and no idea whether A's role in relation to the goods is that of seller, agent or carrier. On the contrary, it has been held in Germany[1] that on questions of liability in a recourse claim by A against B, B has the role of carrier and A has the role of the sender. The question in *Ulster-Swift* was not answered by section 14(2)(c), and the court had to return to Article 39.4 itself.

When reading uniform law such as the CMR, words must be given their natural and ordinary meaning *in context*,[2] and the context includes not only the somewhat distant shape of section 14(2)(c) but also the more immediate shadow of the heading[3] of the chapter in which Article 39.4 is found: "Provisions relating to Carriage Performed by Successive Carriers." But, said the court[4]; "we do not think that is a sufficient reason for reading Art. 39, para. 4, as meaning only 'claims between successive carriers, within the meaning of Article 34' ", and referred back to section 14(2)(c). Section 14(2)(c), it has been submitted above, is unhelpful. The most it can do is to create ambiguity which justifies further inquiry.

If there is ambiguity, the court can look at secondary aids to interpretation, including the purpose of the draftsman.[5] The purpose of Article 39.4 was to give the carrier, who has paid compensation for loss, damage or delay caused by another carrier, a

---

[99] At 360, *per* Megaw L.J.

[1] For example, *O.L.G. Düsseldorf 12.2.81*, VersR 1982.302; *O.L.G. Munich 5.7.89*, TranspR 1990.16.

[2] Above, para. 3.

[3] English law gives less weight to headings than appears to be required for uniform interpretation. Lewison, *The Interpretation of Contracts* (London, 1989), para. 6.02: "In order to arrive at the true interpretation of a document, a clause must not be considered in isolation, but must be considered in the context of the whole document." But (*ibid.*) "the context of a document as a whole will not usually override the plain meaning of the words used". Nonetheless, the court will give some weight to headings; for example, as regards the Law of Property Act 1925, *Beswick v. Beswick* [1968] A.C. 56, 77, *per* Lord Reid.

[4] At 630, *per* Megaw L.J.

[5] Above, para. 4a.

reasonable time in which to bring a recourse action. Commonly, a claim is not brought against a carrier until the end of the limitation period, and as it may well be unreasonable to expect the carrier to make a recourse claim within what remains of the period, the carrier is given more time by Article 39.4. If that is true in the case of successive carriers, it is also true in the case of sub-carriers, and it is on this ground, it is submitted, that the decision in *Ulster-Swift*[6] might attract support and, indeed, Chapter 6 has been applied to the sub-carrier in both France[7] and Germany.[8]

44b(*ii*). Claims for compensation

As the special rule of commencement in Article 39.4 concerns claims which may be settled by a judicial decision fixing the amount of "compensation", it has been inferred that, if the claim is not for compensation (damages for breach of contract) but for carriage charges (performance of contract), the case is outside Article 39.4 and it is Article 32.1 alone which applies.[9] While the English version of Article 39.4 (first sentence) speaks loosely of "claims", the nature of the rule appears clearly from the equivalent words in French and German[10]: Article 39.4 is concerned only with actions to recover sums in compensation that the claimant has had to pay to a third party.

Although a logical inference from the language of Article 39.4, this limit on the scope of Article 39.4 presents a trap for the carrier who is owed carriage charges. Let us suppose that A contracts carriage and sub-contracts the second stage to B but has yet to pay B, and that damage occurs on the second stage. Claims that are time barred may not be exercised by way of counterclaim or set-off,[11] and B's claim for charges against A may be time barred before a damage claim is brought against B by the consignee. So, a "carrier who is owed charges by another carrier, but who fears

---

[6] Above, n. 98.

[7] In France Arts. 34 *et seq.* have been applied to the sub-contractor in *Paris 17.11.83*, B.T. 1984.390. No reasons were given, and the decision has been severely criticised by a commentator (*ibid.*), whose strictures have been adopted by Haak, p. 310 and by Loewe, Theunis, p. 158. Another such decision is *Cass. 25.1.72*, B.T. 1972.148, 1973 U.L.C. 282; but the opposite has been decided in some lower courts: *Agen 29.6.81*, B.T. 1981.433; *TGI Metz 10.11.81*, B.T. 1982.38; *TGI Valence 18.11.81*, B.T. 1982.211. The opposite view has also been taken in Belgium: *Antwerp 8.11.89* (1990) 25 E.T.L. 83.

[8] Decisions applying Arts. 34 *et seq.* to sub-carriers include *Lg Duisberg 10.5.68*, (1969) 4 E.T.L. 979, 986, affirmed on this point by *O.L.G. Düsseldorf 8.5.69* (1970) 5 E.T.L. 446, 464–465: the sub-carrier was liable to the claimant cargo interest on the basis that, being a successive carrier within the terms of Art. 34, the sub-carrier was liable under Art. 17.1.

[9] *Muller Batavier v. Laurent Transport Co.* [1977] 1 Lloyd's Rep. 411, 414, *per* May J.

[10] Respectively, "recours" and "Rückgriffsansprüche"; likewise the Dutch word "verhaal": Haak, p. 310; and the Italian words "azioni di regresso".

[11] Art. 32.4: below, para. 45g.

that a claim for an indemnity by that other carrier in respect of a cargo claim may be a possibility, should therefore consider carefully whether he should let matters rest or whether he should alternatively initiate proceedings for his charges before such proceedings become time barred".[12]

45. Suspension of the period of limitation

Suspension of the period of limitation is regulated by Article 32.2:

> "A written claim shall suspend the period of limitation until such date as the carrier rejects the claim by notification in writing and returns the documents attached thereto. If a part of the claim is admitted the period of limitation shall start to run again only in respect of that part of the claim still in dispute. The burden of proof of the receipt of the claim, or of the reply and of the return of the documents, shall rest with the party relying upon these facts. The running of the period of limitation shall not be suspended by further claims having the same object."

Were it otherwise, the recipient of a claim might play soft music to smooth the passage of time and with it the period of limitation. Extension of the period of limitation is generally governed by the *lex fori*;[13] and Article 32.2 was included in the CMR to deal with possible deficiencies in the *lex fori.*[14] In case of conflict between Article 32.2 and (other) rules of the *lex fori*, it is clear from the wording of Article 32.3 that Article 32.2 is to prevail in cases falling within Article 32.1. Further, another purpose of Article 32.2 is said[15] to be to allow the claimant "to wait and see whether the claim is going to be paid amicably without the need for legal proceedings to be instituted".

If these are the reasons for suspension of the period of limitation by Article 32.2, that rule should apply whether the claim is against the carrier or by the carrier. However, the wording of Article 32.2 indicates that there may be suspension under Article 32.2 only when the claim is against the carrier.[16] To a claim brought by the carrier Article 32.2 does not apply.[17] In the case of a dispute over

---

[12] Hardingham (below, n. 15), p. 365, who points out that the first carrier can cover his position by the issue of a writ, for service later if the need arises.

[13] Art. 32.2; below, para. 45f.

[14] *B.G.H. 28.2.75* (1975) 10 E.T.L. 523, 525.

[15] Hardingham, "Aspects of the Limitation of Actions under CMR", [1979] L.M.C.L.Q. 362, 366–367.

[16] *B.G.H. 28.2.75* (1975) 10 E.T.L. 523; *OGH 22.5.78*, TranspR 1980.143, Greiter 66; *Paris 24.8.87*, B.T. 1987.424.

[17] But there can still be suspension under the *lex fori*: Art. 32.3. *B.G.H. 28.2.75* (1975) 10 E.T.L. 523, 525.

carriage charges, it may be quite fortuitous whether a claim is brought by the carrier to recover charges, or by the goods interest to recover charges alleged to have been overpaid; it is thus equally fortuitous whether the suspension is governed by the CMR or by national law, although the difference between the CMR period of limitation and the national period of limitation may be great.[18]

For the suspension of the period of limitation, the claim must be such that the content of the claim[19] and the identity of the claimant[20] make it apparent to the carrier that the claim should be taken sufficiently seriously to merit response, however short.

45a. The claimant

To suspend the period of limitation, the claim does not have to come from the sender mentioned in the consignment note.[21] The claim must come or appear to come from a person who might have reason to claim and against whom time may run under Article 32.[22] It must be a claim "made by the plaintiff or by someone authorized to act on his behalf".[23]

> In *Aix 8.11.68*[24] goods were totally lost and the action, which was brought one year and 60 days after the goods had been taken over, was out of time, unless the running of time had been suspended under Article 32.2. Suspension there was, if a written claim by underwriters, made before they had indemnified their insured (claimant), was a "written claim" within Article 32.2. The court said[25] that the underwriters, "being a third party not in legal relationship with the carrier, not a party to the contract of transport, could not suspend the running of time". The claimant replied that the underwriters acted as agents of the claimant, whose legal relationship with the carrier was not in doubt, and that there was nothing in the CMR to suggest that a party could not act through an agent. However, the court pointed out[26] that "in their letter of April 30, 1966 [the underwriters] stated that their claim was made as the insurer of [the sender]. They did not rely at all on any mandate given to them by the [sender]. . . . As a matter of principle the suspension or prescription, like its interruption, of a debt can only occur on the

[18] For example, in *Paris 18.11.87*, B.T. 1988.393 the court applied the French *droit commun* to an action by a carrier for carriage charges, and the period available to the claimant carrier was 30 years, although the commentator (at 394) argued that it should have been 10 years!

[19] Below, para. 45b.

[20] Below, para. 45a.

[21] *Aix 11.3.69*, 1970 U.L.C. 122; B.T. 1969.389.

[22] Libouton, para. 91.

[23] *Jones v. Bencher* [1986] 1 Lloyd's Rep. 54, 61, *per* Popplewell J.

[24] 1970 U.L.C. 119, (1969) 4 E.T.L. 918, B.T. 1968.18. See also *Aix 11.3.69*, 1970 U.L.C. 122; B.T. 1969.389 (carrier represented by his insurer).

[25] (1969) 4 E.T.L. 918, 922.

[26] At 922–923.

demand of the creditor against whom time is running, and not on the demand of a third party."

cf. TC Mons 9.11.76,[27] in which the *Aix* decision (above) was referred to, but the tribunal held that a claim sent by a damage assessor "in the name of and on behalf of the persons interested in the goods" was a "written claim" within Article 32.2, for the assessors were agents of those persons.

The issue of authority is governed by the usual rules of English agency,[28] coloured perhaps with the sentiment that a claimant wishing to benefit from suspension under Article 32.2 should be diligent. The agent must have actual or apparent authority to make the written claim on behalf of the claimant. Apparent authority to bind the claimant arises when, although lacking actual authority to do so, the agent is held out as having that authority by the principal. Apparent authority matters most when the principal seeks to deny being bound by the act of the alleged agent, so this kind of authority is unlikely to be in issue in the context of Article 32.2. If the agent does not have authority, a more likely response by the claimant is to ratify the agent's act.[29] Actual authority is determined by the relationship between the claimant and the agent, a relationship the nature or even existence[30] of which may be unknown to the recipient of the claim; so the recipient ignores a claim at some peril.

In *Moto Vespa v. MAT (Britannia Express)*[31] H sold lathes to the claimants in Spain, and carriage by the defendants was contracted for the claimants by ES, who had contracted with the defendant carriers many times before without indicating whether they were contracting as principals or agents. Mocatta J. held that a written claim made by ES for the claimants, undisclosed principals, could be effective under Article 32.2, even though it referred mistakenly to H and not to the claimants as "our principals". In this case the purposes of Article 32.2 were fulfilled, for there was a "clear warning of a claim pending",[32] from a person who, whatever the appearance, had actual authority to act on behalf of the claimants.

Actual authority to make a written claim under Article 32.2 may be express or implied. Authority is express when the agent is

---

[27] (1977) 12 E.T.L. 300, 303.

[28] For example, whether claimant A can suspend the running of time for claimant B in respect of the same journey and the same carrier, is a question for national law: *B.G.H. 24.10.91*, TranspR 1992.177.

[29] But if there is to be ratification, the agent must have purported to act for the claimant, although without necessarily naming the claimant, at the time of making the written claim.

[30] If there is actual authority, the existence of the principal need not be disclosed: *Moto Vespa v. MAT (Britannia Express)* [1979] 1 Lloyd's Rep. 175; *Keighley, Maxted & Co. v. Durant* [1901] A.C. 240.

[31] [1979] 1 Lloyd's Rep. 175.

[32] At 180.

specifically instructed to make the written claim. Authority is implied from the kind of relationship that exists between claimant and agent, as when the agent is a forwarder,[33] a consignee on behalf of the sender,[34] or a damage assessor.[35]

If an insurer of goods is subrogated to the rights of the insured against a carrier, the insurer may claim directly against the carrier,[36] and there may be an issue of fact whether the insurer is acting in subrogation or as agent in a claim by the insured. In any event, in England the insurer has no right of subrogation and hence no direct claim until the insurance money has been paid in full.[37] However, a right of subrogation is distinct from authority to make a claim.[38] Although an insurer who has not paid the insurance money dos not in general have authority to claim against the carrier, the insurer may have specific authority to conduct suit against a third party at fault and hence to make written claims against the carrier, even though the insurer has yet to pay insurance money,[39] and has yet to acquire rights in subrogation against the carrier.[40]

45b. The claim

To suspend the limitation period, there must be a written[41] claim: Article 32.2. On the nature and content required of the written

---

[33] Or *commissionnaire de transport: Aix 8.11.68* (above, n. 24), p. 120. But see n. 39 (below).

[34] *O.L.G. Düsseldorf 13.1.73* (1973) 8 E.T.L. 620, 629. But not when the claim is sent by the consignee, but the claimant is a carrier who, having sub-contracted the entire movement and compensated the sender, brings a recourse action against the sub-carrier: *TGI Valence 18.11.81*, B.T. 1982.211.

[35] *TC Mons 9.11.76* (1977) 12 E.T.L. 300, 303: *des commissaires d'avarie au nom et pour le compte des intéressés à la marchandise.*

[36] *Moto Vespa v. MAT (Britannia Express)* [1979] 1 Lloyd's Rep. 175, 181, *per* Mocatta J.; *Aix 11.3.69*, 1970 U.L.C. 122, 124; B.T. 1969.389; *Rb Antwerp 17.2.74* (1974) 9 E.T.L. 504.

[37] *Page v. Scottish Ins. Corp.* (1929) 33 Ll.L.Rep. 138, C.A. Clarke, *Insurance*, para. 31–3b.

[38] Also in this sense: Haak, p. 306.

[39] In England this is an aspect of the relationship between the underwriter and insured, and may be regulated by the contract of insurance. *Semble* in some other countries the insurer may have no right or authority to make a written claim until he is subrogated to the rights of the insured: for example, Belgium: Putzeys, para. 1144. Germany: *BGH 21.11.96*, TranspR 1997.164.

Compare also the *commissionnaire de transport*: although he stands guarantor to the sender of performance by the carrier (*Cass. 4.5.82*, B.T. 1982.332), it has been held that he is not entitled to bring suit or make written claims under Art. 32.2 until he has indemnified his principal, the sender: *Cass. 4.10.82*, B.T. 1982.549. *Contra: Lyon 5.2.82*, B.T. 1982.154.

[40] *Antwerp 30.6.82* (1983) 18 E.T.L. 84. *cf.* Loewe, Theunis p. 158.

[41] According to Sched. 1 to the Interpretation Act 1978, writing includes "typing, printing, lithography, photography, and other modes of representing or reproducing words in visible form". This clearly includes a telex: *Rb Antwerp 18.6.68* (1968) 3 E.T.L. 1237; and *Cass. Belge 12.12.80* (1981) 16 E.T.L. 250.

claim there is little guidance from the CMR, and courts apply rules of national law.

45b(*i*). The nature of the claim

Article 32.2 indicates that the claim must contain something which the carrier may wish to "reject". It is not enough, for example, to make reservations at the time of a joint survey,[42] thus reserving the possibility of action later without resolving to take it. Again, it is not enough merely to request performance of the contract: "a straightforward request by one carrier against another, or by the carrier against the consignor for payment of the freight" is not a claim.[43]

In *Muller Batavier v. Laurent Transport Co.*[44] on Article 39.4, it was held that "claims" by a carrier "means claims by one carrier against another . . . in respect of that other's responsibility for something that has gone wrong in the course of carriage, for breach by that other of his obligation . . . which has resulted in damage and a claim for compensation at the end of the line".[45] In England, therefore, a written claim under Article 32.2 includes "a general intimation of intention to hold the carrier liable".[46] In France, it is "une demande d'indemnisation justifiant une prise de position du transporteur".[47] In Germany, it includes a demand that the carrier make good the loss or damage.[48] In Holland, it includes a letter stating that, unless by return of post the carrier admits liability to pay the (precise) amount mentioned by the claimant, a writ will be issued.[49] Moreover, it may be enough just to forward a damage survey,[50] especially if that was the form taken by the claim on a previous occasion on which the carrier paid compensation for damage.[51]

---

[42] *Rb. Antwerp 18.6.68*, 1969 U.L.C. 161, 162, (1968) 3 E.T.L. 1237 (also reported in (1969) 4 E.T.L. 1064); *B.G.H. 9.2.84* (1985) 20 E.T.L. 274, 280; *O.L.G. Koblenz 6.10.89*, TranspR 1991.93, 96. *Contra:* Loewe, Theunis p. 145.

[43] *Muller* (below), at 416, *per* May J.

[44] [1977] 1 Lloyd's Rep. 411.

[45] At 415, *per* May J. See also in this general sense: *B.G.H. 9.2.84* (1985) 20 E.T.L. 274, 280. Haak, p. 303. *idem* concerning a charterparty: *A/S Rendal v. Arcos* (1937) 58 Ll.L.Rep. 287, 298–299, *per* Lord Maugham, H.L.

[46] *Moto Vespa v. MAT (Britannia Express)* [1979] 1 Lloyd's Rep. 175, 180, *per* Mocatta J. Also in this sense *William Tatton & Co. v. Ferrymasters* [1974] 1 Lloyd's Rep. 203, 207, *per* Browne J.

[47] *Aix 7.2.90*, B.T. 1990.698, 699.

[48] *O.L.G. Hamburg 9.2.89*, TranspR 1990.191; *O.L.G. Koblenz 6.10.89* (above, n. 42).

[49] *'s Hertogenbosch 21.12.65*, 1966 U.L.C. 119, 125–126. See also *Rb Amsterdam 24.5.72*, 1974 U.L.R. II 229.

[50] *O.L.G. Düsseldorf 13.1.73* (1973) 8 E.T.L. 620, 628.

[51] *Toulouse 26.3.69* (1971) 6 E.T.L. 131.

45b(*ii*). Form: documents

Article 32.2 speaks of a claim with "documents attached thereto". Although the documents are not specified, the inference, it has been argued, is that the claim in writing must be accompanied by documents in support. In France the argument has been rejected[52] and, in England, the submission that "written claim" "involved a semi-formal claim with documents attached" or that it meant a "documented" claim has been rejected.[53]

Documents must be attached only in so far as they are essential for the purpose of a written claim. As the purpose is not the immediate settlements of the dispute but to alert the carrier that a dispute has arisen, "it does not mean a precisely formulated claim with full details, but it must be such a notice as will enable the party to whom it is given to take steps to meet the claim by preparing and obtaining appropriate evidence for that purpose". This statement, made by Lord Wright[54] in relation to a charter-party claim, has been applied to a CMR case,[55] and suggests that what counts is not the form, such as claim plus documents attached, but the content.[56] In *Muller Batavier v. Laurent Transport Co.*[57] May J. spoke of "the almost universal practice . . . to make a claim . . . and to support it by relevant documents, such as survey reports", the purpose being to enable "the persons alleged to be responsible, to consider whether or not in their view they adequately support the claim". No doubt this is one of the best ways of making a claim, but the judge does not suggest that it is the only one.[58]

If documents are required in a particular case, the intention of the authors of the CMR was that the documents should be original documents. This was because they were thinking of the CIM, in particular of Article 46.2 of CIM 1952, which is in the mould of its ancestor, Article 45.3 of CIM 1933. Loewe explains[59]: "At the time when [the CIM], and also the CMR, were drawn up, photocopies were unknown or fairly rare. There were difficulties in the

---

[52] In *Paris 25.3.82*, B.T. 1982.434; appeal dismissed *Cass.20.7.83*, B.T. 1984.236.

[53] *Moto Vespa v. MAT (Britannia Express)* [1979] 1 Lloyd's Rep. 175, 180, *per* Mocatta J. The point was left open by Staughton J. in *ICI Fibres v. MAT Transport* [1987] 1 Lloyd's Rep. 354, 360. A stricter view is found in *Rb Rotterdam 5.4.74*, 1975 U.L.R. I 274, 275–276, requiring all possible documentation, and reasons for holding the carrier liable; but an earlier decision of the same court was that documentation was not required: *Rb Rotterdam 12.4.72*, 1976 U.L.R. I 252, 258.

[54] *A/S Rendal v. Arcos* (1937) 58 Ll.L.Rep. 287, 292, H.L.

[55] *ICI Fibres v. MAT Transport* [1987] 1 Lloyd's Rep. 354, 360. In this general sense: Loewe, Theunis, p. 157, stating it to have been the intention of the authors of the CMR that documents need be attached only so far as they are essential for the carrier to be able to reply to the claim.

[56] *Aix 11.3.69*, 1970 U.L.C. 122; B.T. 1969.389.

[57] [1977] 1 Lloyd's Rep. 411, 416.

[58] *cf.*, however, *Microfine Minerals & Chemicals Ltd v. Transferry Shipping Co. Ltd* [1991] 2 Lloyd's Rep. 630.

[59] Theunis, p. 160. Also in this sense: Haak, p. 304, and cases cited.

production of copies of long documents and the law of procedure of many countries required the time-consuming and expensive business of certification. It was therefore quite normal practice to send the carrier original documents." However, it is far from normal or practical in relation to modern carriage by road, not least because it has been decided that in the case of successive carriage a claim sent to one carrier does not count as a claim against another carrier involved[60]: to require the claimant to send original documents "does not sit easily with the idea that several claims should be made more or less at the same time".[61] A requirement of originals is not explicit in Article 32.2, and is likely to be ignored in the age of facsimile transmission and EDI: information can be transmitted and authenticated in other ways.[62]

45b(*iii*). Content

One opinion is that it is enough to give intimations of the most general kind, such as "goods received in damaged condition", but a stricter school of thought requires more detail and more information.[63] However, some of the cases cited for[64] and against[65] the stricter view concerned the validity of reservations under Article 30, and the purpose of a reservation under Article 30 is not the same as that of a written claim under Article 32.[66] The sparse case law on the point under Article 32 suggests that the stricter view is to be preferred,[67] and that the carrier must be given enough information to realise that a response is required and to be able to make one. The claims should therefore indicate the nature of the

---

[60] Below, para. 45c.

[61] Glass, "CMR: Putting Practice into Theory", [1984] L.M.C.L.Q. 30, 47.

[62] Loewe, *loc. cit.* (reporting a decision of the *Supreme Court of Denmark* to this effect); Helm, Art. 32 Anm. 8; Hill and Messent, p. 259; Walden and Savage, "The Legal Problems of Paperless Transactions", [1989] J.B.L. 102. On authentication of EDI, see Reed, "Authenticating Electronic Mail Messages—Some Evidential Problems", (1989) 52 M.L.R. 648. *cf.* May J. in *Muller Batavier v. Laurent Transport Co.* [1977] 1 Lloyd's Rep. 411, 416: "It is only sensible . . . to provide that . . . while the relevant documents are in the hands of the person alleged to be responsible, to consider whether or not in their view they adequately support the claim, the period of limitation is suspended. It is suspended because the evidence appertaining to the claim is in the hands of the opposite party. It is impractical, one may think—and quite clearly the framers of the Convention thought—to allow a limitation period, let alone a limitation period so short as one year, to run whilst all a party's evidence is in the hands of the other party or parties whom he may have to sue. All they have to do is to sit on it for nine months, and by the time it is returned the limitation period has expired and one is in no position thereafter to sue."

[63] Loewe, Theunis, pp. 145–146, 157.

[64] For example, *Antwerp 15.11.78* (1979) 14 E.T.L. 660.

[65] For example, *Cass. 19.4.75*, 1977 U.L.R. I 334.

[66] *B.G.H. 9.2.84* (1985) 20 E.T.L. 275, 280.

[67] For example, in *O.L.G. Düsseldorf 8.5.69* (1970) 5 E.T.L. 446, 472–473 it was not enough to claim in respect of damage to vehicles transported without identifying the vehicles in question. Also in this sense: *Toulouse 22.11.89*, B.T. 1990.437.

responsibility alleged, and enable the recipient to decide whether to notify the relevant insurer.[68]

45b(*iv*). Quantification

In *Moto Vespa*[69] Mocatta J. accepted the opinion of Browne J.[70] that the word "claim" did not necessarily mean a quantified claim; in some cases the main issue is the existence or liability rather than the amount. Even then, however, Belgian and French decisions indicate that rough quantification is required. In France it has been stated[71]: "Attendu que s'il n'est pas nécessaire que la réclamation soit chiffrée de façon définitive avec une totale précision, encore faut-il que le tansporteur sache que l'ayant droit entend rechercher sa responsabilité et puisse 'avoir une idée' des sommes qui lui sont réclamées." In many cases the carrier's response to the claim, rejection, acceptance or compromise, will depend on the amount of the claim, and this information must be given,[72] unless the relevant information is already in the recipient's possession.

In *Antwerp 30.5.79*[73] cigarettes had been stolen during transport. As regards a written claim, it was held[74] to be enough that "the telex mentions the ground, *viz.* leaving the lorries without a guard, on which the carrier is held liable; . . . an estimate of costs, expenses and loss is absolutely superfluous, since the point at issue is not compensation for damage to part of the goods carried, but the disappearance of the entire contents of a lorry and the claim is for the equivalent of the value of the stolen goods, which value was shown on the waybills which are in the carrier's possession". The appeal to the Court of Cassation was rejected, but, like the Antwerp court, the Court did not say simply that quantification was superfluous, but that it did not have to be explicit in the written claim, as the carrier had the necessary information already.[75]

If quantification is not possible with any accuracy because, for example, a complete survey of damage or investigation of loss has

---

[68] *O.L.G. Munich 24.4.92*, TranspR 1992.360. Putzeys, para. 1147.

[69] *Moto Vespa v. MAT (Britannia Express)* [1979] 1 Lloyd's Rep. 175, 180.

[70] *William Tatton & Co. v. Ferrymasters* [1974] 1 Lloyd's Rep. 203, 207. Also in this sense: *O.L.G. Düsseldorf 13.1.73* (1973) 8 E.T.L. 620, 628; and *O.G.H. 29.8.94*, TranspR 1995.110; (1995) 30 E.T.L. 211.

[71] *Aix 7.2.90*, B.T. 1990.698, 699; also in this sense, *Toulouse 22.11.89*, B.T. 1990.437. This is stated by Loewe, Theunis, p. 157, to have been the intention of the authors of the CMR.

[72] Also in this sense: Glass and Cashmore, para. 3.72.

[73] (1979) 14 E.T.L. 924. See also *Brussels 20.9.95*, B.T.L. 1995.794.

[74] At 930. See also *Rb Antwerp 7.12.73* (1976) 11 E.T.L. 295; *Rb Antwerp 3.3.76* (1977) 12 E.T.L. 437.

[75] *Cass. Belge 12.12.80* (1981) 16 E.T.L. 250, 255. Hence in *TC Liège 25.11.82* (1982) 17 E.T.L. 843, 848, while the tribunal accepted as a written claim a letter that did not mention the amount of the claim, it did so only because "that omission was put right" by an expert a few weeks later, and supported its conclusion by reference to Putzeys, para. 1147, requiring *inter alia* quantification.

not been possible, the question then is whether the claimant is entitled to make the claim and suspend the period of limitation, or must wait and allow time to run until the survey or investigation has occurred. The answer depends on the case and on what the particular carrier needs to know about the particular claim in order to determine his response. In any event, in Belgium the claimant who claims an amount can regard it as a provisional figure and revise it later in the light of further information about the actual amount of loss.[76]

45c. Receipt by the right person

The communications between claimant and carrier referred to in Article 32.2 are effective only on receipt by the person to whom they are sent[77]: "The burden of proof of the *receipt* of the claim . . . shall rest with the party relying on these facts."[78] In general, therefore, communications must be sent to the correct address.[79] If, however, they have reached the address, postal or electronic, held out by the recipient as the proper address to which communications should be sent.[80] they have been received, whether or not the communication reaches the desk or the attention of the appropriate person in the recipient firm. The person who sends a communication "chooses the medium and route of communication and consequently must bear the attendant risks, but the risks incident to the addressee's own zone of influence must be borne by the addressee".[81]

The usual recipient of the written claim is the carrier. However, it may also be the authorised agent of the carrier, including underwriters,[82] even though the underwriters have yet to pay the insured

---

[76] *TC Brussels 2.4.90* (1991) 26 E.T.L. 541.

[77] *TC Paris 25.6.79*, B.T. 1979.403; *Paris 25.3.82*, B.T. 1982.434. Loewe, para. 264 and Theunis, p. 159; Putzeys, para. 1145.

cf. Cass. 20.7.83, B.T. 1984.236 (note Brunat) which held that it was sufficient to prove that a written claim under Art. 32.2 was sent. This is consistent with a legal tradition that attaches more importance to intention than to communication of that intention: *Cass. 17.12.58*, D 1959.33; Nicholas, *The French Law of Contract*, Chap. 3; but as regards the CMR the decision ignores the wording of Art. 32.2, and has been doubted in France as inconsistent with the purpose of the provision, which is to safeguard the position of the recipient.

[78] Art. 32.2 (emphasis added).

[79] In *Paris 25.3.82*, B.T. 1982.434 the defendant carrier argued that the claim had not been sent to the correct address, but it was enough, it was held, that it had been sent to the address given by the carrier's driver.

[80] *Paris 25.3.82* (above). See below, para. 202.

[81] Zweigert and Kötz, p. 42, speaking of contract formation in German law.

[82] Or even the agent of the underwriters, in a case in which the agent's address was also the registered address of the carrier: *Antwerp 17.2.74* (1974) 9 E.T.L. 504. *Contra:* Helm, Art. 32 Anm. 8. *cf.* also France, where the cargo interest has a direct right of action against the insurer (*Cass. 28.3.39*, D 1939.1.68), so notice to the insurer may not be regarded as notice to the carrier.

carrier or to admit liability under the insurance contract.[83] Even so, the safer course is to send the claim not to the underwriters but to the carrier.

In *Poclain v. SCAC*[84] the issue was whether the carrier's underwriters had authority to receive the written claim. It was stated[85] and not contested, that the "legal burden of proof lies fairly and squarely on [the claimant]. Initially the same is true of the evidential burden, but this can shift." As a matter of implied actual authority, the underwriters would not "necessarily have been given authority to receive the written claim, if all that had happened was that they had been notified of the incident by [the carrier], had been given authority to make inquiries and had been told, either expressly or by reference to a course of dealing, that [the carrier] either did not intend to claim or had not yet decided whether to do so".[86]

If the carriage is performed by two carriers, A and B, the claim must be sent to the right carrier, the one ultimately to be held responsible. If that is carrier B, notice to carrier A, who ignores it, is ineffective to suspend the period against carrier B.[87] In any event, the claimant will be well advised to send written claims to all likely defendants.

45d. The effect of a written claim

The effect of a valid written claim is to suspend the limitation period. The limitation period, says Article 32.1, "shall begin to run" from one of the points in time there set out,[88] and the time before that has been called the "antecedent period".[89] Under Article 32.2 a "written claim shall suspend the period of limitation until such date as the carrier rejects the claim . . .". On an ordinary interpretation of these words, a written claim can "suspend the

[83] *Poclain* (below). *Aliter*, if the underwriter flatly denied liability and declined to handle the claim.

[84] [1986] 1 Lloyd's Rep. 404, C.A.

[85] At 406, *per* Sir John Donaldson M.R.

[86] However, on the evidence in the case, that could not be inferred, *i.e.* it was for the defendant carrier and the carrier's underwriters "to give some evidence revealing such a state of affairs", which they did not. The evidence before the court was that the carrier had notified the underwriters of the incident as soon as it happened, and that the carrier had left all negotiations to the underwriters, that the underwriters had discussed the claim with the claimant's surveyors and "virtually agreed the amount". The court held that the underwriters had authority to deal with the claim and that this included receiving a written claim.

[87] *Worldwide Carriers v. Ardtran International* [1983] 1 Lloyd's Rep. 61, 66, *per* Parker J. Both the practicality and fairness of this conclusion has been doubted: Glass (above, para. 45b(*ii*)), pp. 45 *et seq.*; Haak, p. 303.

[88] Above, para. 44.

[89] *ICI Fibres v. MAT Transport* [1987] 1 Lloyd's Rep. 354, 361, *per* Staughton J.

period of limitation" only after the period has commenced[90]: no commencement, no suspension. In other words, a written claim can suspend the limitation period but not the antecedent period, and can only do so prior to rejection.

The interpretation of words in their ordinary sense may give extraordinary results. In *Brussels 28.6.69* the court added to the limitation period of one year a 21-day suspension period, although the claim, which began the suspension, and the rejection, which ended it, had both occurred entirely during the antecedent period[91]: the suspension period was itself held in suspense until the limitation period had commenced. This possibility was criticised but left open by the English court in *ICI Fibres v. MAT Transport*,[92] but it is difficult to square with the wording of Article 32.2.

Less difficult is the sequence, claim-commencement-rejection, because in this sequence, unlike that in *Brussels 28.6.69* (above), rejection to stop suspension does not occur until the period of limitation has commenced. Although the words of Article 32.2 suggest that the effect of a claim—suspension—is immediate, this is not explicit, and the wording does not rule out the possibility of delayed suspension in consequence of a written claim made before the limitation period has begun. This was the decision of Staughton J. in *ICI Fibres v. MAT Transport*[93]: "I can think of no rhyme or reason why the Convention should have that result, or why the owner of the goods should lose his rights if he makes a claim too early but retain them if he makes the claim later. . . . In my judgment a written claim, unrejected, suspends the limitation period as soon as it begins to run. The case is one a fortiori."

One thing is clear: a written claim effective to suspend the period of limitation can have this effect only once. If the period, having been suspended by a valid written claim, starts to run again, because the carrier has rejected the claim, the claimant cannot halt the period by simply repeating that claim: the fourth sentence of Article 32.2 provides that "The running of the period of limitation shall not be suspended by further claims having the same object."[94]

---

[90] Loewe, para. 263; Libouton, para. 89, n. 177; Putzeys, para. 1145. *cf.* Hill and Messent, p. 250.

[91] This decision is supported by the decision of *OGH 1.7.81*, TranspR 1984.193, Greiter 168, that rejection of a claim is without effect until the period of suspension has commenced.

[92] Above, n. 89.

[93] Above, n. 89, at 361. He continued: "The words 'shall start to run again' in Art. 32(2) are insufficient to deflect me from that conclusion. It would have been unduly cumbersome to say ' . . . shall start to run, or to run again, as the case may be.' "

[94] See, for example, *B.G.H. 9.4.84* (1985) 20 E.T.L. 275; *O.L.G. Hamburg 9.2.89*, TranspR 1990.191.

45e. Rejection of the claim by notification in writing

Suspension of the period of limitation ends, according to Article 32.2, when "the carrier rejects the claim by notification in writing and returns the documents", if any,[95] sent with the claim. The rejection must be unambiguous, as its effect is to end the suspension of time: the claimant must not be left in doubt that the time has come to decide whether to pursue the claim through the courts or other legal procedures.[96] In many cases it is clear that a communication is a rejection, but it is not always so, or for reasons of the passage of time, a carrier may seek to argue that an earlier communication amounted to a rejection. In *Zerowatt SpA v. International Express Co.*[97] Webster J. agreed that a rejection must be unambiguous as such but thought that in this regard a communication should be construed not as a lawyer would but as would a businessman. If the carrier responded to a claim that response might fall into one of four categories: acceptance, non-acceptance in the sense of non-admission, rejection and a communication of some other kind.[98]

> In *Zerowatt SpA v. International Express Co.*[99] the first letter in question fell into the second category of non-acceptance mainly because, although the carrier purported to "refute any liability", the cause of damage was uncertain and the carrier awaited a report from a surveyor; this, said the court, would indicate to the claimant that the carrier was still considering his position. The second letter to be considered, which purported to "repudiate all liability", did not amount to a rejection either, for the same kind of reason and also because the letter was headed "Without prejudice": "everyone knows that letters written under this rubric form part of exchanges of communication between parties who are not at that stage, for the purpose of those communications, entirely at arm's length, but are willing to make statements which might be treated as admissions or concessions".

A claim may be rejected not only by the carrier himself but also by his authorised agents,[1] such as an insurer[2] and an insurance

[95] See above, para. 45b(*ii*).

[96] *Zerowalt SpA v. International Express Co.*, October 6, 1989, *per* Webster J.

[97] *ibid.*

[98] An acknowledgment of receipt is not a rejection: *Microfine Minerals and Chemicals Ltd v. Transferry Shipping Co. Ltd* [1991] 2 Lloyd's Rep. 630. See also in this sense: *O.L.G. Nuremburg 12.4.91*, TranspR 1992.63.

[99] Above, n. 96.

[1] *Toulouse 26.3.69* (1971) 6 E.T.L. 131, 136; *Paris 23.5.1979*, B.T. 1979, 522. *cf. Lyon 2.3.78*, B.T. 1978.382 which interpreted the CMR restrictively and required communication by the carrier himself.

[2] *Aix. 10.2.88*, B.T. 1988.347; *Aix 14.12.95*, B.T.L. 1996.521; *Grenoble 4.12.96*, B.T.L. 1997.120. However, in France the claimant may have a distinct and direct action against the insurer, and a rejection by the insurer may concern that action only, and have no effect on the claimant's position with the carrier.

broker.[3] Like the written claim,[4] rejection is effective on receipt.[5] However, the OGH has held[6] that rejection of a claim cannot take effect until the period of suspension has commenced.

As to the content of the rejection, it is enough that it shows whether and to what extent the carrier rejects the claim, to this end it has been held that the contents of the rejection must relate to the points made in the written claim.[7]

According to Article 32.2, the carrier must return the documents attached to the written claim and prima facie this means all such documents. The argument that this refers only to any original documents that might have been sent with the claim and does not refer to any photocopies of originals, surely the more likely case, has been rejected.[8] The carrier must send back whatever pieces of paper have been sent with the claim.[9] However, some courts have relaxed this requirement in another way by holding that the carrier is obliged to return only documents which the claimant needs[10] in order to pursue his claim in the courts. If, for example, the carrier admits part of the claim, he is not obliged to return documents relating solely to the part of the claim that he has admitted.[11] The Belgian Court of Cassation has held,[12] however, that all documents must be returned, whether the claimant needs them or not. Whereas it has been held[13] in France that, if the claimant provides photocopies of documents, the carrier is obliged to return none of them with his rejection, on the assumption that the claimant still has the originals, the Belgian Court[14] took a literal view of Article

---

[3] *The Hague 2.4.76* (1976) 11 E.T.L. 767.

[4] Above, para. 45c.

[5] Haak, p. 304; Loewe, para. 264. Or, perhaps, the day after receipt: Putzeys, para. 1148.

[6] *OGH 1.7.81*, TranspR 1984.193, Greiter 168.

[7] *Antwerp 30.5.79* (1979) 14 E.T.L. 924, 930.

[8] *Microfine Minerals and Chemicals Ltd v. Transferry Shipping Co. Ltd* [1991] 2 Lloyd's Rep. 630.

[9] *ibid.*, at 632, *per* Judge Kershaw Q.C.

[10] *Rb Roermond 15.10.70* 6 E.T.L. 839.

[11] *O.L.G. Celle 13.1.75* (1975) 10 E.T.L. 410, 417. *cf. Reims 22.3.76*, B.T. 1976.260; *Paris 21.12.78*, B.T. 1979.84. It may be difficult to identify partial admission. For example, Haak (p. 305) argues, with reference to decisions in Holland, that an admission of liability but not of the extent of liability is not a partial admission for this purpose.

[12] *Cass. Belge 27.9.84*, 1984 U.L.R. 406; criticised by Putzeys, para. 1149.

[13] *Paris 22.5.75*, B.T. 1975.320, 322: "the 'documents' in question (in Art. 32.2) must mean exclusively those which justify the claim"; the court held that the carrier did not have to return a photocopy of an *expertise*, for the claimant retained the original with which he could bring an action. Also in this sense, Muth/Glöckner, p. 180.

[14] *Cass. Belge 27.9.84*, 1984 U.L.R. 406. Also in this sense *Reims 22.3.76*, B.T. 1976.260 where the court reached that conclusion because (at 261) "the provisions of the CMR are *de droit étroit* and must be interpreted restrictively". Even in France such interpretation has been condemned (Rodière CMR, paras. 149–150) and it does not accord with the courts' approach to uniform law such as the CMR: above, para. 4a. See also *O.L.G. Munich 10.10.90*, TranspR 1991.138, 141.

32.2 and required the return of copies; and in *Microfine Minerals*[15] a similar view was taken in England.

45f. Extension of the period of limitation

Extension of the period of limitation is regulated by Article 32.3:

> "Subject to the provisions of [Article 32.2] the extension of the period of limitation shall be governed by the law of the court or tribunal seised of the case."

In England, when the court orders that an arbitration award be set aside or, if arbitration has commenced, the court orders that the arbitration agreement shall cease to have effect with respect to the dispute in question, section 13(2) of the Arbitration Act 1996 provides[16] that the court *may* also order that "in computing the time prescribed by the Limitation Act for proceedings (including arbitral proceedings) . . . the period between the commencement of arbitration and the date of the order . . . shall be excluded". This operates as a provision for extension of a period which has begun to run prior to the commencement of arbitration, and is valid under Article 32.3.

In England, extension of the CMR limitation period by agreement is not authorised by the Limitation Act.[17] Is it allowed by the CMR? Party agreement in the contract of carriage that the period of limitation shall be extended beyond that provided by Article 32 is said to be[18] contrary to Article 41 of the CMR, but that an agreed extension after a claim has arisen is allowed. The distinction is unwarranted: Article 41 invalidates stipulations derogating from the provisions of the CMR,[19] whether or not, it appears, the offending stipulation is found in the contract of carriage or some other related agreement. The draftsman was concerned less with form than with effect, and to ensure that the CMR was not defeated by collateral agreements. However, the draftsman allowed derogation from the limitation period if an extension is

---

[15] Above.

[16] This section is set out more fully above, para. 43b.

[17] ss.27 *et seq.* of the Limitation Act 1980 provide for extension, but s.39 provides that "This Act shall not apply to any action or arbitration for which a period of limitation is prescribed by or under any other enactment", including therefore the Carriage of Goods by Road Act, enacting the CMR. However, it has been suggested (Hill and Messent, p. 169) that CMR actions may still be subject to the general equitable jurisdiction, for example in relation to fraud, on which the 1980 Act is based.

[18] Hill and Messent, p. 255; Wetter, "The Time Bar Regulations in the CMR Convention," [1979] 504, 508. The distinction is rejected by Haak, p. 308. Generally see Herber/Piper, Art. 32, 52; and Koller, Art. 32, 20.

[19] Below, para. 92.

authorised by the *lex fori*.[20] Surely, the general ban on derogation contained in Article 41 is qualified by the special licence in Article 32, and it is submitted that extension by agreement, if permitted by the *lex fori*, is permitted by the CMR, whether it is agreement in advance or agreement after the claim in question has arisen.[21] Even so, the obvious point must be repeated, that the greater the intervention of the *lex fori* the greater the impairment to uniformity and hence to the certainty sought by the CMR.

In England, although extension is not provided for by statute, extension agreements are valid at common law.[22] Moreover, if, as appears,[23] the court is not obliged to raise CMR limitation *ex officio* and the parties agree expressly or tacitly not to do so themselves, the effect is that time is extended, and to a degree the same effect can be achieved by waiver or estoppel. In *Zerowalt SpA v. International Express Co.*[24] Webster J. upheld a tacit agreement of the parties that the running of time should be suspended pending a report which it had been expressly agreed, would resolve a technical difference between them.

45f(*i*). Waiver and estoppel

The time limitation will not be enforced against the claimant if the other party has waived the period or is estopped from pleading it.[25] Any such waiver or estoppel must be unequivocal.[26] Concerning English law on waiver and estoppel, see below, para. 218c.

45g. Counterclaim and set-off

Article 32.4 provides that, a "right of action which has become barred by lapse of time may not be exercised by way of counterclaim or set-off".[27] For there to be a relevant counterclaim, "claim

---

[20] It is subject to Art. 32.2 on suspension. As Art. 32.3 expressly allows extension, the rule of the *lex fori* will be "subject to" Art. 32.2, if it does not remove or inhibit suspension under the latter.

[21] For example, some states allow extra time if the claimant has been unable to make his claim on time.

[22] *Lubovsky v. Snelling* [1944] K.B. 44, C.A.

[23] Above, para. 43.

[24] (1991) 26 E.T.L. 530.

[25] A possibility similar in effect has been recognised in Austria: *OGH 22.5.78*, TranspR 1980.143, Greiter 66.

[26] *Microfine Minerals & Chemicals Ltd v. Transferry Shipping Co.* [1991] 2 Lloyd's Rep. 630.

[27] This provision is more restrictive than the corresponding law in many CMR states: Haak, pp. 308–309. Moreover, there can be no exact equivalent in England to *la demande reconventionnelle ou d'exception* or *die Widerklage oder die Einrede*. On the relationship between counterclaim and set-off, see *The Leon* [1985] 2 Lloyd's Rep. 470, 474, *per* Hobhouse J. Generally, see Derham, *Set-Off* (Oxford, 2nd ed., 1996).

and crossclaim must arise out of the same contract or transaction and must also be so inseparably connected that the one ought not to be enforced without taking account of the other".[28]

As time runs for a claim without regard to the running of time for other claims or counterclaims, and as their commencement dates may differ, Article 32.4 contains a trap for the customer who, perhaps preferring to avoid the cost and confrontation of a claim in court, decides not to claim against the carrier,[29] but to withhold all or part of the carriage charges. For example, the carrier's period of limitation may be under rule (c) and hence start three months after contract, whereas the customer's claim for damage may be under rule (a) and have started to run at the (earlier) date of delivery. Hence there may come a time when the carrier can claim for carriage charges but the customer has lost the right to (counter) claim for damage to the goods, or vice versa.[30]

To spring the trap, one move might be to meet the carrier's claim for charges by resort to the doctrine of deduction or abatement, but the efficacy of this move is doubtful. The first doubt is whether the doctrine is distinct from counterclaim and set-off[31] and thus untouched by Article 32.4. The second doubt is whether the case of carriage by road is untouched by the rule for carriage by sea, that a carrier's claim for freight is to be paid in accordance with the contract of carriage and cannot be subject to any deduction or abatement in respect of alleged loss or damage to goods.[32]

In *R.H. & D. International v. IAS Animal Air Services*[33] it was argued, in defence of a claim for carriage charges, that Article 32.4 "plainly contemplated that a right of action that was not barred by a lapse of time could be exercised by way of counterclaim or set-off, and that, as some of the periods of limitation prescribed in Article 32(1) applied to claims by consignees, the article read as a whole suggested that a claim by a consignee which was not barred by lapse of time could properly be exercised by way of set-off".[34]

---

[28] *Dole Dried Fruit & Nut Co. v. Trustin Kerwood Ltd* [1990] 2 Lloyd's Rep. 309, 311, *per* Lloyd L.J., C.A.

[29] Wetter (above, n. 18), p. 509.

[30] Especially when time in the damage claim has been suspended under Art. 32.2: see above, para. 45.

[31] Although the doctrine of deduction or abatement "is often described as an 'equitable set-off', it would, I think, be more accurately stated to be an 'equitable defence' . . . "—*The Brede* [1973] 2 Lloyd's Rep. 333, 337, *per* Lord Denning M.R., C.A.; see also at 340, *per* Cairns L.J. The judgments in *The Brede* were approved by the House of Lords in *The Aries* [1977] 1 All E.R. 398 and *The Dominique* [1989] 1 Lloyd's Rep. 431, H.L., where Lord Brandon (at 436) also referred to the doctrine as a defence. See also Derham, pp. 127 *et seq.*

[32] See below, para. 219.

[33] [1984] 2 All E.R. 203, 205.

[34] *cf. B.G.H. 7.3.85* (1985) 20 E.T.L. 343, holding that contract terms (Art. 32 ADSp) against set-off applied to a CMR case, as the CMR was silent on the question whether a right of set-off existed and hence this question was governed by national law.

The claimant carrier replied with precedent, six unreported cases applying the maritime rule and in which the claimants had obtained summary judgment for unpaid CMR carriage charges, despite the fact that the defendants made counterclaims for loss of or damage to the goods.[35] Neill J. decided for the claimant, as [36] "it would be wrong for me as a judge or first instance to introduce uncertainty into this branch of law by reaching a decision in conflict with the earlier decisions . . . which now extend over a period of $6\frac{1}{2}$ years". So, from out of the digital darkness came a great light for the comfort and clarification not only of the commercial Bar, who had seen the light in their screens for some time, but for the rest of commercial mankind.

If, as it now appears, the maritime rule applies to carriage by road, there is some comfort for the consignee in that the rule may be modified or excluded by the contract of carriage[37]; and that, unless the consignee abuses a dominant economic position, the court is unlikely to exercise its discretion to award the carrier interest on unpaid carriage charges, "because the basic reason for an award of interest is to compensate a party for the *wrongful* detention of his money".[38]

C. THE FORUM AND THE DEFENDANT

46. Jurisdiction: Article 31

When a dispute arises out of a contract of carriage governed by the CMR, jurisdiction is determined in the first instance at international level.[39] It is determined not by the local rules of the *lex fori*,[40] but by other rules, which although part of the *lex fori*,[41]

---

[35] Listed by Neill J. [1984] 2 All E.R. 203, 205. In only one of the cases (*Seawheel v. Henry Collins*, May 8, 1979) was reference made to Art. 32 and there the argument based on Art. 32.4 was rejected by Mustill J.: the draftsman "has done no more than contemplate the possibility of a set-off. I find it impossible to transfer that into a contractual right of set-off when it would not otherwise exist."

[36] At 206.

[37] See below, para. 219.

[38] *The Khian Captain (No. 2)* [1986] 1 Lloyd's Rep. 429, 434, *per* Hirst J.

[39] *i.e.* as a matter of agreement between CMR states concerning the states with jurisdiction in CMR cases. See *Smith v. Canadian Pacific Airlines*, below, n. 52, para. 46a.

[40] Haak, p. 277; Helm, Art. 31 Anm. 1; Loewe, para. 235. In particular Art. 57 of the Brussels Convention on Jurisdiction and the Enforcement of Judgments in Civil and Commercial Matters 1968, enacted in England by the Civil Jurisdiction and Judgments Act 1982, excludes from its operation matters governed by particular conventions, such as cases subject to CMR Art. 31. For example, *Harrison & Sons Ltd v. R.T. Stewart Transport Ltd* (1993) 28 E.T.L. 747 (Commercial Court, 1992). However, there is disagreement whether the Brussels Convention is totally excluded or whether it applies to matters on which the CMR is silent: Haak, p. 277.

[41] *O.L.G. Karlsruhe 24.5.67*, 1968 U.L.C. 289, 293.

have been agreed between states party to the CMR and stated in Article 31 and, as regards recourse actions, Article 39.[42]

If the courts of England have jurisdiction under Article 31 or Article 39 of the CMR, determination of the appropriate court in England is a matter for English law and is easy, as the High Court, the court of first instance in CMR cases, has territorial competence in such matters throughout the state. Not so, for example, in France, Holland or Germany: if the courts of Germany have jurisdiction in a CMR case, there remains the further problem, less easily resolved than in England, to identify the German court with jurisdiction in the particular case.

In Germany, the question has come before the B.G.H.[43] Clearly, Article 31 of the CMR governs jurisdiction at international level. If in a particular case Article 31 points to Germany, because, for example, the place of delivery (Z) is in Germany, it has performed its function; it is for the law of Germany to indicate the court within Germany in which suit must be brought.[44] Article 31 points not to the court at Z but to the "courts or tribunals" of the "country within whose territory . . . the place designated for delivery is situated". The question whether delivery at Z gives jurisdiction to the local court or to some other court in Germany with jurisdiction in transport cases is not answered by the CMR. The answer must be found in German law.

If, however, German law did not provide an answer, the view of some courts in Germany[45] is that in such a case Article 31 also operates at the second level and indicates not only the state but also the court within that state which has jurisdiction: reference to Z as the place of delivery means that the court for that region has jurisdiction under Article 31. To make Article 31 work, it is said,[46] each CMR state has an obligation to ensure that that indication is given effect within the state; if that is not done, the CMR must fill

---

[42] Below, para. 53.

[43] *B.G.H. 6.2.81* (1982) 17 E.T.L. 50, N.J.W. 1981.1902, VersR 1981.633.

[44] Helm, Art. 31 Anm. 5; Loewe, Theunis, p. 150; Muth/Glöckner, p. 175; Putzeys, para. 1096. French decisions to this effect include *Riom 18.11.77*, B.T. 1977.560; *Paris 15.12.77*, B.T. 1978.53; *Cass. com. 17.1.95*, B.T.L. 1995.90.

[45] For example, *Lg Hamburg 22.1.79*, 1980 U.L.R. I 266; VersR 1979.246. For decisions of this kind in France, see *Aix 3.3.94*, B.T.L. 1994.451; and *Angers 4.12.95*, B.T.L. 1996.337.

[46] Loewe, para. 245: "It was not the intention of the authors of the Convention to permit actions to be brought before the courts or tribunals mentioned in paragraph 1(a) and (b) only in cases where the national law—apart from CMR—itself provided that they were competent. The situation, on the contrary, is that CMR compels contracting States to place their courts or tribunals at the disposal of the parties in cases covered by subparagraphs (a) and (b), on the understanding that it is for the national law to determine which court or tribunal will be competent *ratione materiae* and *ratione loci*." See also in this sense: Haak, pp. 285 *et seq.*; Helm, Art. 31, Anm. 5; Loewe, Theunis p. 151. This, admittedly extensive, interpretation of Art. 31 is said to be justified to fill a gap and to promote uniformity of law: Kropholler NJW 1981.1904.

the gap. However, the latter view was rejected by the B.G.H.: Article 31 operates at the international level only,[47] and if German law did not indicate the court with jurisdiction in Germany, suit could not be brought there; and, in the case of a designation of German courts by the parties, the designation would be void.[48]

46a. *Forum non conveniens*

In England jurisdiction may be disputed not only when action is brought in England, but also when, in connection with such an action, a person seeks to serve notice on a third party outside the jurisdiction of the English court. A number of grounds on which notice may be served are stated in the Rules of the Supreme Court, Order 11, rule 1. Order 11, rule 1(1) permits the granting of leave to serve "if the action begun by the writ is brought under . . . the Carriage of Goods by Road Act 1965", which contains the CMR. If such an action is brought, that is the only ground in Order 11, rule 1 on which leave may be granted, as "the Rules of the Supreme Court take effect subject to any relevant statutory provision. . . . The Act and CMR must be treated as paramount. Further, . . . provisions such as this are intended to be a self-contained code within which a plaintiff must found his assertion of jurisdiction."[49] Jurisdiction in a CMR case can be founded only under Article 31 or Article 39.2.[50] However, although the CMR is paramount and its jurisdiction exclusive, this does not rule out the possibility that the court will exercise its inherent discretion to decline jurisdiction on the ground of *forum non conveniens*.

Forum non conveniens refers to the discretionary power of the court "to decline to exercise a possessed jurisdiction whenever it appears that the cause before it may be more appropriately tried elsewhere".[51] This has occurred under the parallel provision of the

---

[47] *B.G.H. 6.2.81* (1982) 17 E.T.L. 50, 54. Also in this sense: *Hg Vienna 3.4.84*. TranspR 1984.152; and H.R. 16.11.90, S. & S. 1991, no. 54. A similar view has been taken of Art. 28 of the Warsaw Convention: *Smith v. Canadian Pacific Airlines Inc.* 452 F. 2d 798 (2 Cir., 1971).

[48] *B.G.H. 6.2.81*, *loc. cit.*

[49] *Arctic Electronics Co. (U.K.) v. McGregor Sea and Air Services* [1985] 2 Lloyd's Rep. 510, 513–514, *per* Hobhouse J., citing Roskill L.J. in *Rothmans of Pall Mall (Overseas) v. Saudi Arabian Airlines Corp.* [1981] Q.B. 368, 385, C.A., which concerned the equivalent provisions of the Warsaw Convention and is discussed below, para. 46b(*i*). In *Arctic*, having failed to found jurisdiction under Ord. 11, r. 1(1) and Art. 39, the applicant sought to found jurisdiction under Ord. 11, r. 1(g) on the basis that the (fourth) party had broken the contract of carriage within the jurisdiction, but the argument was rejected.

[50] Also in this sense: *Bordeaux 7.11.83*, B.T. 1984.492. Putzeys, para. 1086.

[51] Blair, (1929) 20 Col.L.Rev. 1.

Warsaw Convention, Article 28, in the United States[52] where, however, the doctrine of *forum non conveniens* is better established than in England.[53] The possibility that the English court would decline to accept a designation of jurisdiction in a CMR case is real but, if it occurs, it would be regrettable, as bashfulness of this kind is not part of the civil law tradition[54] and would result in a lack of uniformity of approach to CMR cases. It must be doubted whether the exercise of the discretion to decline jurisdiction is consistent with the underlying scheme of Article 31 of the CMR.[55]

46b. Objective jurisdiction

Article 31 governs proceedings "arising out of carriage under" the CMR. From this it is clear that Article 31 applies whether the rules of law applied in the dispute are found in the CMR itself or in some other source, such as the English law of tort,[56] provided that the dispute is between parties to a contract of carriage as described in the CMR, Article 1.[57]

The inference has been drawn that Article 31 does not apply to a contract of carriage unless carriage has actually commenced, and does not apply, therefore, to an action against a carrier who has failed to perform his promise to take over the goods. This has been said[58] to be "because Article 31.1(b) refers to the place where the goods were taken over as against the place designated for delivery, requiring that the goods have actually been carried . . .". However, the conclusion does not follow from the premise, as the places mentioned in Article 31.1(b) are alternatives to those mentioned in

---

[52] *Smith v. Canadian Pacific Airlines Inc.* 452 F. 2d 798 (2 Cir., 1971): "We hold that in a Warsaw Convention case there are two levels of judicial power that must be examined to determine whether suit may be maintained. The first level, on which this opinion turns, is that of jurisdiction in the international or treaty sense under Art. 28(1). The second level involves the power of a particular United States court, under federal statutes and practice, to hear a Warsaw Convention case—jurisdiction in the domestic law sense. It is only after jurisdiction in both senses is had that the question of venue is reached and a determination made regarding the appropriateness and convenience for the parties of a particular domestic court." See also *Trivelloni-Lorenzi v. Pan American World Airways Inc.* 821 F. 2d 1147 (5 Cir., 1987).

[53] On the position in England see *Spiliada Maritime Corp. v. Cansulex Ltd* [1987] A.C. 460.

[54] Herzog (1976) 65 Rev.Crit.Dr.Int. Privé 1.

[55] See below, paras. 46b and 46e. Also doubtful: Glass, "CMR: Putting Practice into Theory", [1984] L.M.C.L.Q. 30, 39, n. 23.

[56] Loewe, paras. 235 and 238. See also the interpretation placed on similar words in Art. 32.1, above, para. 43. But *cf.* the narrow construction put on the scope of Art. 31 by some Dutch decisions, described by Haak, pp. 278–279.

[57] Thus excluding actions against the carrier in tort brought by third parties, for example, in respect of road accidents: Loewe, para. 239. For discussion of the same phrase in Art. 32, see above, para. 43a.

[58] Loewe, Theunis, p. 148, whose opinion was adopted in *Hg Vienna 3.4.84*, TranspR 1984.152. Also in this sense: Hill and Messent, p. 225.

Article 31.1(a): place of residence, etc. These and other points of contact mentioned in Article 31 are contacts regarded as significant in the private international law of CMR states.[59] There is nothing in Article 31 to suggest that it applies only when the claimant is in a position to bring an action in *any* one of the places mentioned. On the contrary, Article 31 as a whole is expressed to apply to "legal proceedings arising out of carriage under this Convention" and, in context, the reference to carriage under the Convention is a reference to contracts of carriage, as defined in Article 1.[60] Hence, the more widespread view is that Article 31 applies to a CMR contract, whether the goods have been taken over or not,[61] even though the court with jurisdiction may consider that the liability of the carrier is governed not by Article 17 of the CMR but by national law.[62] Article 31.1 provides:

> "In legal proceedings arising out of carriage under this Convention, the plaintiff may bring an action in any court or tribunal of a contracting country designated by agreement between the parties and, in addition, in the courts or tribunals of a country within whose territory:
>
> (a) The defendant is ordinarily resident, or has his principal place of business, or the branch or agency through which the contract of carriage was made,[63] or
>
> (b) The place where the goods were taken over by the carrier or the place designated for delivery is situated,
>
> and in no other courts or tribunals."

Although the forum, if any, designated by the parties[64] must be that of a state party to the CMR, the courts specified in Article 31.1(a) and (b), in which action may also be brought, do not have to be in a CMR state, except that, if the CMR and Article 31 are to apply at all, *ex hypothesi*, one of the courts specified in Article 31.1(b) must also be in a CMR state.[65] This is consistent with the scheme of the CMR to encompass transport between CMR states and non-CMR states, and to promote the application of the CMR in the former as *lex fori* through Article 1.1 and in the latter as contract terms through Article 7.3 and a paramount clause.[66]

---

[59] *B.G.H. 6.2.81* (1982) 17 E.T.L. 50, 54–55.

[60] Putzeys, para. 1088, pointing to Art. 1: see above, para. 10.

[61] This is also the view of Haak, p. 281; Helm, Art. 31 Anm. 3; Herber/Piper, Art. 31, 5; Koller, Art. 31, 1; Putzeys, para. 1088; Thume, Art. 1, 2.

[62] Below, para. 62.

[63] As to contract formation, see below, para. 202.

[64] Below, para. 46c.

[65] If the contract is within the scope of the CMR, a question regulated by Art. 1, then one of these two places must be in a contracting country; hence there is a reasonable chance that the forum will apply the CMR.

[66] On the paramount clause, see above, para. 24.

However, a claimant is well advised to choose a court in a contracting state, if possible, as only in that event will judgment be enforceable under the CMR in the other contracting states: Article 31.3.[67] Apart from the possibility of a forum in a state not party to the CMR, Article 31 is very similar to the corresponding provision of the Warsaw Convention: Article 28.1.

46b(*i*). Ordinary residence

Residence[68] and, particularly, "ordinary residence" imply some degree of permanence but have different meanings in different areas of the law.[69] In Article 31 of the CMR it seems that only a natural person can have an "ordinary residence".

In *Rothmans*[70] the question was whether the foreign carrier, who had an office in central London, was "ordinarily resident" there in the sense of Article 28 of the Warsaw Convention.[71] Mustill J. said[72] that:

> "For both persons and companies, the criterion for service at common law is presence within the jurisdiction. This concept is not easily adapted to the case of a foreign corporation. Not infrequently, the test of presence has been expressed by asking whether the company 'resides' or 'carries on business' within the jurisdiction. . . . Is that kind of presence sufficient to found judgment under the Convention? I think it unlikely that this is what was intended. International conventions of this kind tend to prescribe jurisdiction in narrow terms, on the assumption that the case where the defendant has insufficient assets to satisfy claims in any of the stipulated countries is catered for by the ready availability of enforcement in other countries which is available via the various conventions on mutual recognition of judgments. . . . Furthermore, on this wider interpretation [of Article 28] the concepts of residence and place of business are almost, if not exactly, the same. Yet the possession of a place of business in a country was plainly not intended to found jurisdiction on its own, since Article 28 lists a *principal* place of business as one of the four hallmarks of jurisdiction.

---

[67] Below, para. 46e.

[68] Generally, see Dicey, pp. 162 *et seq*.

[69] It is submitted that tax cases, in which residence is attributed to a corporation and often located in the place of central management and control, are of little assistance: the purpose of such decisions and the desire to avoid double taxation create a different perspective from the present. In *Rothmans* (below) Roskill L.J. (at 385) preferred to ignore analogies in national law altogether.

[70] *Rothmans of Pall Mall (Overseas) v. Saudi Arabian Airlines* [1981] Q.B. 368.

[71] A provision very similar to Art. 31 of the CMR.

[72] At 374–375. *cf.* Putzeys, para. 1096*bis*: in Belgium residence is where the company does business.

> In these circumstances, I consider that the words 'where the carrier is ordinarily resident' must be more narrowly construed. The following appear to be the possible readings: (i) the words do not apply to bodies corporate at all; (ii) they mean the place where the body is incorporated; (iii) they mean the place where the central administration and power of decision of the company is to be found . . ."

In *Rothmans*[73] the carrier did not satisfy any of these tests and the proceedings against it were set aside. On appeal, the judgment was affirmed: a branch office was not an "ordinary residence", for if it were, the "principal place of business", as a ground of jurisdiction, would be redundant. In the case of companies, the "ordinary residence" would normally coincide with the "principal place of business",[74] and the words must have been intended to mean something else. By inference,[75] ordinary residence refers to natural persons. 80 years after St Exupéry the idea of an unincorporated air carrier seems strange, but less so the idea of a one-man carrier by road.[76]

46b(*ii*). The principal place of business

The "principal place of business" referred to in Article 31.1(a) is the head office, that is, the place from which the business is principally conducted. There can be only one head or principal office. If the executive and managerial work is done in one place but the registered office[77] or the carrier's depot[78] is in another place, the principal place of business is the former. That is "the centre from which instructions are given, and from which control is exercised, and the centre from which the company is managed *without any further control* except such control as every company

---

[73] Above, n. 70.

[74] Dicey, p. 511.

[75] Glass and Cashmore, para. 3.70. By the evidence also of history: this appears to have been the intention of the draftsman of Art. 28: see *Rothmans* (above) at 387, *per* Roskill L.J.; *cf.* Shawcross and Beaumont (below, n. 78), para. 139: "Despite the uncertainties produced by the judgments in the *Rothmans* case, it is submitted that the seat of the board of directors remains the most appropriate test for the ordinary residence of a corporation, and that there is nothing in the special context of Art. 28 which requires that this test be discarded."

[76] A survey in the United Kingdom in 1995 indicated that 80 per cent of road hauliers operated no more than five vehicles.

[77] Loewe, Theunis, p. 150. But *cf.* Hill and Messent, p. 227 who suggest that it should be possible to bring an action in "either the statutory or actual place of business".

[78] *idem* as regards Art. 28 of the Warsaw Convention: Shawcross and Beaumont, *Air Law* (4th ed., 1993) Div. VII, para. 140, citing, *inter alia*, *Cesena Sulphur Co. v. Nicholson* (1876) 1 Ex.D. 428 (manufacture in Italy, control in London).

or the directors of a company are liable to by the larger body which they represent, the share-holders of the company".

The emphasis in this quotation from Swinfen Eady L.J.[79] was added by Leggatt L.J. in a shipping case, *The Rewia*.[80] In that case the Court of Appeal held that, although the ship was registered in Liberia and the day-to-day management was in Hong Kong, all that was done in Hong Kong was subject to the control of the directors in Hamburg, which was, therefore, the principal place of business.

46b(*iii*). The branch or agency

The "branch or agency through which the contract of carriage was made" is the branch or agency where the original contract is made, no account being taken of where any subsequent variations of the contract were agreed.[81] "Branch or agency", particularly "agency", might be read as a reference either to an establishment controlled by the defendant or to one independent of the defendant and subject only to the terms of a particular mandate.

An interpretation of Article 31.1(a) in compliance with comity[82] requiring a significant connection with the place of jurisdiction suggests that a contractual relationship of agency, perhaps for only one transaction, is not enough. Yet it appears that the scheme of the CMR does not depend on the sufficiency of the defendant's assets within the jurisdiction seised of the case, but on multiple grounds of jurisdiction and on enforcement, if necessary, in other CMR states.[83]

From the reference to the courts "of a country within whose territory . . . the defendant . . . *has* his principal place of business, or the branch or agency through which the contract of carriage was made",[84] it has been inferred[85] that in some sense the branch or agency must be the defendant's own branch or agency rather than an independent one merely mandated to make the contract of

[79] *The Polzeath* [1916] P. 241, 245, C.A.
[80] [1991] 1 Lloyd's Rep. 324, 334, C.A.
[81] So held under Art. 28 of the Warsaw Convention: *Boyar v. Korean Airlines* 664 F.Supp. 1481 (D.C., 1987). *Quaere*, if additional carriage charges are agreed.
[82] *International Shoe Co. v. Washington* 326 U.S. 310, 316 (1945).
[83] Mustill J. in *Rothmans*, quoted above, para. 46b(*i*). On enforcement, see below, para. 46e.
[84] Art. 31.1(a), with emphasis added.
[85] Hill and Messent, p. 227; Loewe, para. 243. This is assumed by Muth/Glöckner, pp. 174–175. But *cf.* Putzeys para. 1096*bis*, disputing that the words "branch of agency" depend on "has" and hence refer to the carrier: the branch or agency might be that of the sender. However, as Hill and Messent (*loc. cit.*) point out, on that interpretation the second part of Art. 31.1(a), lacking a verb, makes no sense.

carriage. Moreover, although a firm may have an independent *agent* in London, to have an *agency* there means to have the faculty of agency or to have an establishment where business is done not so much for the defendant but by the defendant for other people.[86] This implies some degree of establishment (and thus permanence) as well as control.[87] However, as in the case of airlines, times and practices have changed to accommodate contracts through agencies more distant in every sense than in the past, and today a purely literal interpretation of these words is not satisfactory.[88]

46b(*iv*). The place of take-over or delivery

The place, referred to in Article 31.1(b), "where the goods were taken over by the carrier" is the place at which the custody and control of the goods is transferred[89] to the carrier in question. The carrier may take over the goods personally or through agents. Thus, if the carrier contracts to carry over two stages, performs stage B but stage A is performed through a sub-carrier, the carrier

---

[86] O.E.D.

[87] This has been the interpretation of the words "branch, agency or other establishment" in Art. 5.5 of the Brussels Convention on Jurisdiction and the Enforcement of Judgments in Civil and Commercial Matters 1968, enacted in England by the Civil Jurisdiction and Judgments Act 1982; Dicey, Chap. 11.

For the purpose of service of a writ out of the jurisdiction it has been held that a person has a place of business through a "sole agent" who also acted for another firm: *Saccharin Corp. v. Chemische Fabrik von Heyden* [1911] 2 K.B. 516, C.A. However, this was a "borderline case" (At 520, *per* Vaughan Williams L.J.), and other decisions have been more stringent: *Okura & Co. v. Forsbacka Jernverks* [1914] 1 K.B. 715, C.A.; *Vogel v. Kohnstamm* [1973] Q.B. 133.

[88] The wider view is also that preferred by the German commentaries: Herber/Piper, Art. 31, 15; Koller, Art. 31, 3; Thume, Art. 31, 21. An instance of the same problem, more difficult because of interline agency arrangements, arose under Art. 28 of the Warsaw Convention with regard to the words "where [the carrier] has a place of business through which the contract has been made". See *Berner v. United Airlines Inc.* 157 N.Y.S. 2d 884 (1956), affirmed 170 N.Y.S. 2d 340 (1957) where, however, the agent's duties went "very far beyond the usual conception of mere principal and sales agent relationships" (at 881). The court went further in *Eck v. United Arab Airlines* 360 F. 2d 802 (2 Cir., 1966), [1966] 2 Lloyd's Rep. 485, 490 *et seq.*, holding (at 492) that "the defendant has a place of business in that country at which it regularly issues tickets even though the injured passenger's ticket is purchased at the office of another airline and confirmed abroad on the ground that the office that issued the ticket to the passenger should be regarded as a 'place of business' of the defendant airline 'through which the contract has been made'. This holding, which imports concepts of agency into the meaning of 'place of business' in Art. 28(1)'s third provision is not novel." See also *Boyar v. Korean Airlines* 664 F.Supp. 1481 (U.S.D.C. D.C., 1987). Shawcross and Beaumont (above, n. 78), para. 141, consider that Eck would not be followed by English courts, which would require that under Art. 28 the contract be made by one of the carrier's "establishments".

[89] See above, para. 27.

takes over the goods at the beginning of stage A,[90] not the beginning of stage B.[91] In other words,[92] the place of take-over "refers to the place where the contract of carriage commenced . . . and cannot be repeated down the line where successive carriers have participated at various stages".

The place, also referred to in Article 31.1(b), "designated for delivery" is the place where the carrier is intended to transfer the custody and control of the goods to the consignee.[93] If the actual place of delivery is different from the designated place, because something has gone wrong, it is the latter not the former which founds jurisdiction under Article 31.1(b).[94] The designated place is the place agreed between the parties initially or, perhaps, the place to which the carrier is instructed to proceed when the right of disposal[95] is exercised under Article 12.

46c. Jurisdiction agreed by the parties

In addition to the courts indicated by Article 31.1(a) and (b),[96] an action may be brought in "any court or tribunal of a contracting country designated by agreement between the parties". Designation of a court or tribunal in a non-contracting state would be contrary to Article 41.1.[97] The designation may be in the consignment note, or in the contract of carriage apart from the consignment note, or it may be the subject of a separate or subsequent agreement. In principle, the validity of the separate or subsequent agreement is a matter for national law.[98]

In general, the designation of a court or tribunal by agreement between sender and carrier will not bind the consignee or a successive carrier unless the latter has notice of the designation.

---

[90] *Moto Vespa v. MAT (Britannia Express)* [1979] 1 Lloyd's Rep. 175, 181, *per* Mocatta J., who thought that this follows from the rule that a carrier who sub-contracts a stage is nonetheless a CMR carrier for that stage: *Ulster-Swift v. Taunton Meat Haulage* [1977] 1 Lloyd's Rep. 346, C.A. See above, para. 44b(*i*).

[91] The contrary suggestion by Hill and Messent, p. 228, overlooks the fact that "taking over" is primarily an assumption of responsibility (as a CMR carrier under Art. 17) rather than a physical act, although of course a particular act signals the assumption of responsibility. The suggestion is also rejected by Herber, Art. 31, 17; and Loewe, Theunis, pp. 149–150.

[92] *Cummins Engine Co. v. Davis Freight Forwarding (Hull)* [1981] 2 Lloyd's Rep. 402, 409, *per* Connor L.J., C.A.

[93] See above, para. 37.

[94] *Paris 24.10.91*, B.T.L. 1991.779.

[95] *O.L.G. Hamburg 7.4.94*, TranspR 1995.115. Concerning the right of disposal, see above, para. 32.

[96] Above, para. 46b.

[97] Below, para. 92. The choice may also be ineffective unless not only the jurisdiction but also the court (*cf.* above, para. 46) is indicated: *Rouen 28.1.93*, D.M.F. 1993.403.

[98] It has been suggested that jurisdiction on disputes over the validity of such agreements may be governed by the Brussels Convention: Helm, Art. 31, Anm. 4. *Sed quaere*. See below, para. 46e.

In *Paris 14.11.69*[99] it was argued that in a contract to carry works of sculpture from Berlin to Paris the sender and the carrier agreed that the courts of Berlin should have jurisdiction. The carrier further argued[1] that "in taking delivery of the sculptures (the consignees) . . . have accepted the arrangement (*stipulation pour autrui*) concluded for their benefit in the contract of transport". The court rejected the argument because it found insufficient evidence of the existence of the alleged agreement. It also stated[2] that, even if the agreement existed, it would still be necessary to bring the jurisdiction clause to the knowledge of the consignee.

In England, it is doubtful whether the phrase in Article 31.1 "agreement of the parties" would be satisfied if the consignee has made a timely objection to a choice of jurisdiction. Further, it has been suggested[3] that, when unaware of them, the consignee may get rights under the contract of carriage but not duties. Does a designation contain a right or a duty? In so far as a consignee is more likely to sue than be sued and the designation is one of a number of courts in which the consignee may choose to sue, the designation has more of right than duty.[4] However, it is submitted that the consignee is not bound by a designation of which the consignee does not have actual or constructive notice,[5] with two exceptions. The consignee is bound by the designation if, as is commonly the case in England, it is part of a contract agreed by the sender as agent for the consignee,[6] or if the consignee has accepted a document containing the term when taking delivery of the goods.[7]

The designated court or tribunal does not have exclusive jurisdiction. When a dispute arises, it is just one option, in addition, to the courts mentioned in Article 31.1(a) and (b).

In *Rb Dordrecht 18.5.66*[8] carriage from Holland to Austria was agreed on standard terms which said: "Jurisdiction shall be where the carrier has his place of business." One place in which the carrier

---

[99] 1970 U.L.C. 133, B.T. 1969.159.

[1] 1970 U.L.C. 133, 134.

[2] *ibid.* Also in this sense: *Paris 29.3.69*, 1970 U.L.C. 125, B.T. 1969.159. However, Loewe, Theunis, p. 149, describes the decision on this point in *Paris 14.11.69* as "not quite comprehensible", and objects that the CMR does not require the designated forum to be mentioned in the consignment note. This is true, although Art. 6.3 envisages that it might be mentioned there. In any case, that is not the real point, which is whether and when a designation is made "by agreement between the parties".

[3] Above, paras. 40b and 40c.

[4] This is an issue only when the consignee is sued by the carrier in the designated court. The consignee as plaintiff is not in any event restricted to action in the designated court, but can sue in one of the other courts specified in Art. 31.1 or can adopt the designated court, thus, it might be said, designating it by a separate agreement with the carrier.

[5] Also in this sense: Muth/Glöckner, p. 175; Putzeys, para. 1094. *cf.* Hill and Messent, p. 226; Loewe, para. 242.

[6] Above, para. 42.

[7] *Paris 14.11.69* (above, n. 99).

[8] 1968 U.L.C. 155; (1968) 3 E.T.L. 416.

did business but which was not his principal place of business was Bregens. The tribunal held that, as the clause did not say that the place of business (Bregens) should be the only or exclusive place, it was just one possible forum together with those mentioned in Article 31.2(a) and (b).

The implication of this decision is that, if the clause had made the chosen jurisdiction the exclusive jurisdiction, action could not have been brought anywhere else. This is difficult to reconcile with the wording of Article 31.1, which talks of the place designated by the parties "and, in addition" the places mentioned in sub-paragraphs (a) and (b); the French text does not have exactly equivalent words, but the implication is the same.[9] A clause which chooses the jurisdiction of state X but excludes the jurisdiction of courts in the places mentioned in Article 31.1(a) and (b) is a clause "which would directly or indirectly derogate from" Article 31.1 and is thus "null and void" under Article 41.[10] The general view,[11] therefore, is that a designation cannot be exclusive, unless, it has been suggested,[12] the designation is found in an agreement concluded after the dispute has arisen, an agreement separate from the contract of carriage and thus unaffected by Article 41. However, it is difficult to believe that a court would allow Article 41 and the CMR to be sidestepped so easily.[13]

46d. Duplication of actions

By Article 31.1, the plaintiff has a choice of courts in which to start an action. To avoid duplication of actions Article 31.2 provides that, if an action is "pending" before a court competent under Article 31.1, "no new action shall be started between the same parties on the same grounds", except when judgment in the action pending would not be enforceable in the state in which the new action is started—notably when the action pending has been commenced in a non-CMR state.[14]

---

[9] En dehors de = besides.

[10] Glass (above, para. 46a), p. 38. This may be the explanation of the decision in *Rb Antwerp 23.9.75* (1976) 11 E.T.L. 279, 287–288 where the tribunal refused to follow the choice of jurisdiction in a combined transport bill of lading and accorded jurisdiction to the court of the place of delivery by virtue of the "imperative provisions of Art. 31". See also *Antwerp 5.4.77* (1978) 13 E.T.L. 478. By contrast, it has also been held that Art. 31 limits the range of options: suit cannot be brought in any jurisdiction not chosen by agreement or mentioned in Art. 31.1: above, para. 46.

cf. The decision in *The Morviken* [1983] 1 A.C. 565 in respect of jurisdiction under the Hague Rules.

[11] Haak, p. 282; Helm Art. 31 Anm. 4; Herber/Piper, Art. 31, 20; Koller, Art. 31, 5; Loewe, para. 79; Loewe, Theunis p. 149; Putzeys, para. 1090; Thume, Art. 31, 27.

[12] Putzeys, para. 1095; Thume, Art. 31, 33.

[13] See above, para. 45f(*i*).

[14] Helm, Art. 31, Anm. 6. Enforcement under CMR. Art. 31.3 is confined to judgments obtained in CMR states: below, para. 46e.

In *TC Brussels 28.2.75*[15] the defendant resisted the claim in Brussels by reference to Article 31.2 and to a previous claim begun but not brought to judgment in Italy. This defence was rejected by the Brussels court, because[16] "the two claims do not relate to the same parties and because the claim in the Italian court was concerned only with the right of recourse between carriers" whereas the claim in Brussels involved the person whose goods had been damaged.

The "same grounds" are a poor indicator of duplication, as an action in England for breach of the contract of carriage, such as failure to take over the goods, might be restarted in Germany on a different basis, such as delict.[17] It has been suggested[18] that the words "same grounds" should be read in the light of the French text and the words "pour la même cause".

Article 31.2 applies only to "an action . . . pending before a court or tribunal" and not, therefore, to arbitration. However, a similar object may be achieved under section 9 of the Arbitration Act 1996. If proceedings are commenced in England, any party to an agreement to arbitrate the relevant dispute abroad may apply for a stay of the proceedings in England.[19]

46e. The enforcement of judgments and awards

Article 31.3 provides that, when a judgment entered by a court or tribunal of a contracting state in an action arising out of CMR carriage "has become enforceable in that country, it shall become enforceable in each of the other contracting States, as soon as the formalities required in the country concerned have been complied with. These formalities shall not permit the merits of the case to be re-opened."

Evidently, the "country concerned" is the other contracting state in which the judgment is to become enforceable.[20] Article 31.3 is a crucial component of the scheme whereby actions may be

---

[15] (1975) 10 E.T.L. 419.

[16] At 425.

[17] Below, para. 65.

[18] Loewe, Theunis, p. 152.

[19] See Mustill and Boyd, *Commercial Arbitration* (London, 1982), Chap. 30.

[20] For actions arising out of CMR carriage Art. 31 operates alongside and in place of other bilateral or multilateral treaties affecting the enforcement of judgments, such as the Brussels Convention on Jurisdiction and the Enforcement of Judgments in Civil and Commercial Matters 1968 (enacted in England by the Civil Jurisdiction and Judgments Act 1982): Helm, Art. 31 Anm. 2; Loewe, para. 256; Loewe, Theunis, p. 152; Putzeys, para. 1105.

cf. Cass. 21.6.82, B.T. 1982.513 (below, para. 53), which applies the Brussels Convention to a CMR recourse action. This is an error: Haak, p. 278.

On the enforcement of foreign judgments in England, see Dicey, Chap. 14. However, it is accepted that CMR actions can be enforced only in accordance with Art. 31: Dicey, p. 568.

brought in a number of different states, even though the defendant's assets there may be insufficient for the enforcement of a judgment.[21] The mode of enforcement in England is governed by the Foreign Judgments (Reciprocal Enforcement) Act 1933,[22] which applies[23] to any judgment which has been given in a CMR state in any action referred to in Article 31.1 and which is enforceable in that state.

Article 31.4 provides that Article 31.3 "shall apply to judgments after trial, judgments by default and settlements confirmed by an order of the court, but shall not apply to interim judgments or to awards of damages in addition to costs against a plaintiff who wholly or partially fails in his action". The awards of damages mentioned are awards that might be made against a plaintiff for vexatious litigation.[24]

Arbitration awards as such are not reciprocally enforceable under Article 31, which refers only to judgments. If, however, judgment has been entered abroad on an arbitration award there, that judgment can be enforced like any other judgment.[25] Moreover, an arbitration award comes within the operation of the 1933 Act,[26] as well as the Arbitration Act 1996 and the New York Convention on the Recognition and Enforcement of Arbitral Awards 1958.[27]

46f. Costs

Article 31.5 provides that security for costs "shall not be required in proceedings arising out of carriage under this Convention from nationals of contracting countries resident or having their place of business in one of those countries". This provision is a corollary of the preceding provisions, which are thought adequate to ensure that an award of costs against a party is enforceable like a judgment or as part of a judgment. Moreover, it promotes uniformity[28] and rules out a possibility of anti-competitive discrimination.[29]

Doubt has been raised[30] whether a national can benefit from Article 31.5 in the courts of that person's "home" state, and it has

---

[21] See *Rothmans* above, para. 46b(*i*), and the quotation from the judgment of Mustill J.
[22] On the 1933 Act.
[23] By virtue of s.4 of the Carriage of Goods by Road Act 1965.
[24] Putzeys, para. 1107*bis*.
[25] See Mustill and Boyd (above, n. 19), pp. 372 *et seq.*
[26] This is the effect of the Carriage of Goods by Road Act 1965, s.4 and s.7(1).
[27] Mustill and Boyd (above, n. 19), pp. 375 *et seq.*
[28] Muth/Glöckner, p. 176.
[29] In *Berkeley Administration Inc. v. McClelland* [1990] 1 All E.R. 958, C.A., the court considered whether an order in respect of security for costs under R.S.C., Ord. 23, r. 1 against an EEC company resident abroad might be contrary to Art. 7 of the EEC Treaty.
[30] Helm, Art. 31 Anm. 8.

been suggested that this is a matter for the law of that state.[31] However, the objects of the CMR as uniform law are best served by evenhandedness between litigants from the countries mentioned.[32]

47. Arbitration: Article 33

As regards arbitration, Article 33 provides:

> "The contract of carriage may contain a clause conferring competence on an arbitration tribunal if the clause conferring competence provides that the tribunal shall apply this Convention."

The interpretation of an arbitration clause is a matter for the proper law of the contract in which the clause is contained. Thus, in one case[33] it was held that, although a contract of carriage was governed by the CMR as *lex fori* (English law), the arbitration clause in that contract was to be construed in accordance with the proper law of the contract (Swedish law). Even so, the clause thus construed must comply with Article 33 of the CMR[34] and, if it does not, it will be invalid under Article 41,[35] unless, it has been suggested,[36] the clause was not part of the contract of carriage but the subject of a separate and subsequent agreement reached after the dispute had arisen. However, this suggestion is doubtful.[37]

Article 33 requires that the clause shall "provide" that the arbitral tribunal shall apply the CMR. On the ordinary meaning of this requirement, it has been held[38] that there must be an express provision to that effect, and it does not suffice that the same effect is achieved in other ways, for example, by choosing arbitration in a CMR state or by choosing the law of a CMR state.[39] This was the intention of the draftsman because, if a tribunal which should apply the CMR does not do so, "under many legal systems this constitutes no grounds for nullity of the decision. If, however, the arbiters go beyond the express desire of the parties, they exceed

---

[31] Loewe, para. 255.
[32] Helm, *loc. cit.*
[33] *Bofors-UVA v. Skandia Transport* [1982] 1 Lloyd's Rep. 410.
[34] As part of English law, the *lex fori: Bofors-UVA* (above), at 412, *per* Bingham J. s.1 of the Carriage of Goods by Road Act 1965 together with Art. 1 of the CMR operate as a unilateral conflicts rule in favour of the CMR as part of the *lex fori*. The same is true of the Hague Rules: *The Hollandia* [1983] A.C. 565. Clarke, H.R. pp. 14–15.
[35] *Bofors-UVA* (above). *idem: Rb Rotterdam 10.11.70* (1971) 6 E.T.L. 273, 278; *Paris 27.6.79*, B.T. 1979.440, criticised for this by Putzeys, para. 1110.
[36] Herber/Piper, Art. 33, 2; Loewe, para. 269; Putzeys, para. 1109; Thume, Art. 33, 4.
[37] See above, paras. 47f(*i*) and 46c.
[38] *Bofors-UVA* (above, n. 33), at 413, *per* Bingham J.
[39] Herber/Piper, Art. 33, 2; Thume, Art. 33, 3.

their powers, and under many legal systems this constitutes grounds for nullity."[40]

Whether a consignee is bound by an arbitration clause will depend, as it does with a jurisdiction agreement, on whether it is part of the consignee's contract.[41] If a person is bound by an arbitration clause which is valid under Article 33, can that person nonetheless ignore the clause and bring suit in a court with jurisdiction under Article 31? This question is not answered by the CMR, but by the law of the court in which the matter arises, *i.e.* the court seised under Article 31. If that is the English court, the court proceedings will be stayed under the Arbitration Act so that the arbitration may proceed.[42] Further, the arbitration clause must be valid under the rules of the court in which the clause is questioned. In particular, English law requires the possibility of appeal on points of law to the ordinary courts.[43]

48. Responsibility for the acts of others

A carrier is responsible for the servants or agents that the carrier employs to perform the contract. This is the rule in national law; it is also the rule under the CMR.[44] For the avoidance of doubt, Article 3 provides:

> "For the purposes of this Convention the carrier shall be responsible for the acts and omissions of his agents and servants and of any other persons of whose services he makes use for the performance of the carriage, when such agents, servants or other persons are acting within the scope of their employment, as if such acts or omissions were his own."

Article 3 is designed to forestall a defence available in some countries, that the carrier is not liable for the acts or omissions of the carrier's servants or agents.[45] For English law on this matter, see below, paragraphs 234–235.

[40] Loewe, Theunis, p. 164. Also in this sense: Helm, Art. 33 Anm. 1.
[41] See above, para. 46c.
[42] *Bofors-UVA* (above, n. 33), at 413, *per* Bingham J.
[43] See *The Nema* [1982] A.C. 724. Treitel, pp. 407 *et seq.*
[44] Loewe, para. 61. *The Hague 9.1.70* (1970) 5 E.T.L. 587; *cf. Kg Rotterdam 21.11.69* (1970) 5 E.T.L. 79, criticised by Libouton, para. 24. See also above, para. 24.
[45] To explain the presence of Art. 3 in the CMR, Loewe, para. 61, simply observes that "similar provisions are found in almost all conventions dealing with the liability of a contractor since, in enterprises of a certain size, damage is hardly ever caused by the contractor personally". For example, CIM (1960) Art. 39 and, substantially the same, CIM (1980) Art. 50. However, a similar provision does not appear in the Hague Rules or the Warsaw Convention.

49. The scope of employment

In English law an employer, such as a carrier, is vicariously liable for the acts or omissions of the employer's (servants) and not for those of agents in the sense of independent contractors; but that is not a liability in contract, such as that under the CMR, but a liability in tort, and is considered in Part II of this book in connection with the carrier's liability in English domestic law.[46]

50. The choice of defendants: successive carriage

For the sender, the obvious target for suit is the carrier who made the initial contract to carry the goods in question. For the consignee, the obvious target is the carrier who delivered the goods. The carrier who contracted and the carrier who delivered may be the same carrier, but not necessarily: there may be others, as it is common for all or part of the journey to be sub-contracted.

The claimant's rights against the sub-contractor depend on the pattern of practice among the carriers concerned. One pattern, said to be common in the Benelux countries,[47] is for the initial and principal contractor to remain responsible for the entire journey under a single contract of carriage and to issue separate notes to each sub-contractor.[48] As regards the latter, the principal contractor has the role of sender,[49] and in English law the sub-contractor would generally have no contractual rights against or liability[50] to the original sender or the consignee although, of course, there may be liability in tort.[51] The other pattern, said to be common in cross-Channel movements,[52] is for the initial and

---

[46] Below, para. 234.

[47] Putzeys, para. 288, n. 200/1.

[48] If the sub-contract is international, it may be governed by the CMR: Muth/Glöckner, p. 182; if not it is governed by national law: De Weerdt (1989) 24 E.T.L. 523, para. 77. For a useful general study, see Marchand (1995) 30 E.T.L. 577.

[49] For example, *O.L.G. Düsseldorf 12.2.81*, VersR 1982.302; *O.L.G. Munich 5.7.89*, TranspR 1990.16.

[50] Unless the last carrier becomes liable to the consignee under the *Brandt* rule: below. Or, for example, in Belgium, if the sub-contractor issues a consignment note, it may be inferred that he has "adhered" to the contract of carriage with the (original) sender to whom he thereby becomes contractually liable: *Cass. Belge 17.9.87* (1988) 23 E.T.L. 201. Generally, see De Weerdt, *op. cit.* (n. 48), paras. 68 *et seq.*

[51] English law allows an action by the goods owner as bailor against the sub-contractor as bailee, but the latter is entitled to defend not only by pleading CMR exclusions and limitations (Art. 28, below, para. 68) but also any terms of the sub-bailment agreed with the contractor: see below.

[52] Perhaps because the intervention of water between the United Kingdom and the rest of Europe encourages the intervention of sub-contractors for convenient stages of the international journey. In any event, this part of the CMR has attracted more interest in England (see Hill and Messent, Chap. 11) than in other CMR states. It has aroused little enthusiasm across the Channel, having been described in Belgium as the scene of "great confusion" and in Holland as "extremely complicated and very unclear": Haak, pp. 106–107.

principal contractor to remain responsible for the entire journey under a single contract, but for a consignment note for the whole journey to be passed with the goods like a baton or, as some would say, like a rod for his back from carrier to carrier. Here the subcontractor has liability, to the sender or consignee not only in tort but also in contract, by virtue of Chapter VI, Articles 34–40, of the CMR.

The "cross-Channel" pattern is called successive carriage, and in this situation the claimant has a selection of targets: "the first carrier, the last carrier or the carrier who was performing that portion of the carriage during which the event causing loss, damage or delay occurred". Only these may be sued,[53] one or more. The legal basis of the right of action is found in Article 34[54]:

> "If carriage governed by a single contract is performed by successive road carriers, each of them shall be responsible for the performance of the whole operation, the second carrier and each succeeding carrier becoming a party to the contract of carriage, under the terms of the consignment note, by reason of his acceptance of the goods and the consignment note."

In short, the defendant's liability is based on a contract incorporating the terms of the CMR: consent to that contract, the link with the claimant, and assumption of responsibility, are found in the defendant's "acceptance" of the goods and of the consignment note in respect of the single contract of carriage.[55] By acceptance, the successive carrier is bound by the contract and thus by the CMR, even though the relevant stage of the carriage may occur entirely within the boundaries of one state.[56]

In Article 34 we find, said Rodière,[57] "a bold concept for which there is no equivalent in any other convention on transport". The claimant may sue whichever of these carriers it is most convenient to sue.[58] If the claimant is the sender, this may be the first carrier, with whom the sender contracted. If the claimant is the consignee,

[53] *SGS-ATES Componenti Elettronici SpA v. Grappa* [1978] 1 Lloyd's Rep. 281, 284, *per* Robert Goff J.; *OGH 12.4.84*, Stra GüV 1984/10 p. 10, Greiter 215.

[54] Haak (p. 106) maintains that Art. 34 is not based on any provision of the CIM but on Art. 432 HGB. But *cf.* Helm, Art. 34 Anm. 1 who points to CIM (1960) Art. 26 and Art. 49 to Art. 52.

[55] If a consignment is split into two or more parts to be carried by two or more carriers, with a consignment note for each part, it has been held, not surprisingly, that this is not successive carriage as understood in Art. 34; *Arctic Electronics Co. (U.K.) v. McGregor Sea & Air Services Ltd* [1985] 2 Lloyd's Rep. 510.

[56] Loewe, para. 275 by reference to the legislative history of the CMR. Also in this sense: Muth/Glöckner, p. 182.

[57] Rodière (1971) 6 E.T.L. 574, 580. See also the similar provision in CIM (1960) Art. 43.3 and CIM (1980) Art. 35.2.

[58] Further, if the claimant himself is sued by a carrier not mentioned in Art. 36, the same article allows any relevant counterclaim or set-off available to be raised in respect of that carrier's action.

this may be the last carrier, who delivered the goods. The consignee would be poorly placed if, as maintained by some[59] but not all[60] authorities in Belgium, the consignee's only right of action was against the first carrier, whose assets might be no more than an office in another country.

The carrier sued is liable jointly and severally with the others[61]: "responsible for the performance of the entire operation" on the basis of the CMR, as if the other carriers involved were that carrier's own servants or agents.[62] As Bingham L.J. observed,[63] "that carrier cannot escape liability by showing that he has delegated or sub-contracted performance to a non-CMR carrier who was actually responsible. By Article 34, a successor CMR carrier makes himself responsible for the whole operation and he remains responsible for a non-CMR carrier or delegate under art. 3. Any other interpretation would, I think, frustrate the CMR scheme."

An exception is made for multimodal transport. When Article 34 states that each carrier "shall be responsible for the performance of the whole operation", the "operation", it has been held, refers only to carriage by road, and a successive road carrier has no responsibility for a stage by rail or by sea.

> In *Antwerp 15.3.89*,[64] having contracted to carry goods from Wilrjik (Belgium) to Stockholm and Malmö, A sub-contracted the entire carriage to B, who sub-contracted the first (road) stage from Wilrjik to Ghent to C, and the second (sea) stage from Ghent to Gothenberg to D. The goods were damaged at sea. It was held that, as C was not a principal contractor, like A or B, "but merely a substitute sub-contractor for the sector from Wilrjik to Ghent, it cannot be held liable for damage suffered in the course of the maritime sector of the journey".[65] Unlike B, C could not be liable to the goods claimant for the sea stage.

---

[59] *Antwerp 8.10.86*, BRH 1987.65. De Weerdt (1989) 24 E.T.L. 523 No. 78. Also in this sense: certain decisions in Holland, cited by Haak, p. 112; and Loewe, para. 276.

[60] *cf. Cass. Belge 30.5.80* (1983) 18 E.T.L. 79.

[61] This is implied by Art. 37: *TC Brussels 28.2.75* (1975) 10 E.T.L. 419; *Ghent 20.11.75* (1976) 11 E.T.L. 231. Also in this sense: Haak, p. 113; Hill and Messent, p. 286. In German law it is described as *die gesamtschuldnerische Haftung:* Muth/Glöckner, p. 182. In the same sense: Helm, Art. 34 Anm. 4; Herber/Piper, Art. 34, 12; Koller, Art. 34, 6; Thume, Art. 34, 7.

[62] Hence, for example, the carrier is liable for their wilful default (Art. 29). Also in this sense: Hill and Messent, p. 280; but *cf.* Hardingham, "Actions against Successive Carriers under CMR", [1978] L.M.C.L.Q. 499, 504.

[63] *ITT Schaub-Lorenz Vertriebgesellschaft mbH v. Birkart Johann Internationale Spedition GmbH* [1988] 1 Lloyd's Rep. 487, 493, C.A. Also in this sense "as a general rule": *Thermo Engineers v. Ferrymasters* [1981] 1 Lloyd's Rep. 200, 204–205, *per* Neill J.

[64] (1989) 24 E.T.L. 574.

[65] At 588. Also in this sense Helm, Art. 34 Anm. 2; Muth/Glöckner, p. 181; Putzeys, para. 291. Note that some courts in Belgium, including perhaps the Antwerp court in this case, do not see B as a successive carrier, whereas most CMR courts would have seen him as a successive carrier (below, para. 50a) and, like B but unlike A, not liable for the sea stage.

50a. Successive carriers

The right of action given by Article 36 is against the first carrier, the last carrier and the performing carrier.

50a(*i*). The first carrier

Although Article 34 speaks of a contract "performed by successive road carriers", and Article 37 speaks of the recourse against carriers who have "taken part in the carriage", the first carrier is not necessarily the one who is the first to handle the goods, but the first to contract with a sender as carrier, whether he handles the goods physically or not. This proposition is disputed, but it has been held in England,[66] as well as in Austria,[67] Denmark,[68] France,[69] Germany[70] and Switzerland[71] that, if A contracts to carry but sub-contracts the entire operation to B, B is a carrier successive to A, who is also a carrier under the CMR. Both A, as first carrier, and B, as performing carrier, are liable to the goods interest on the basis of Article 34 of the CMR, provided that B accepts the goods and the consignment note as required by that Article.[72] This interpretation reflects less the ordinary or obvious meaning[73] of Article 34 than the courts' perception of the purpose of this part of the CMR, to give the claimant, sender as well as consignee, a choice of targets and hence a target which the claimant can spot and identify. The task should not be made more difficult because the initial carrier has sub-contracted.[74]

50a(*ii*). The performing carrier

The performing carrier is "the carrier who was performing that portion of the carriage during which the event causing the loss, damage or delay occurred": Article 36. The performing carrier is

---

[66] *Ulster-Swift v. Taunton Meat Haulage* [1975] 2 Lloyd's Rep. 502, 508, *per* Donaldson J.; [1977] 1 Lloyd's Rep. 346, 359–360, *per* Megaw L.J., C.A. Also in this sense: *Arctic Electronics Co. (U.K.) v. McGregor Sea & Air Services* [1985] 2 Lloyd's Rep. 510, 513, *per* Hobhouse J. Hill and Messent, p. 278.

[67] *OGH 12.4.84*, Stra GüV 1984/10 p. 10, Greiter 215; *OGH 4.6.87* (1988) 23 E.T.L. 714. See also *OGH 20.1.82*, Greiter 122.

[68] *Copenhagen 17.7.76*, 1987 U.L.R. II 730.

[69] *TC Paris 14.3.78* (1978) 13 E.T.L. 742; *Paris 17.11.83*, B.T. 1984.390.

[70] By implication: *B.G.H. 28.4.88* (1989) 25 E.T.L. 89, 95. Other decisions in Germany to this effect are cited by Haak, p. 112 and Helm, Art. 34 Anm. 2. Koller Art. 36, 2.

[71] *Trib. Fed. 22.11.83*, (1995) 30 E.T.L. 675.

[72] See below, para. 50b.

[73] *Ulster-Swift v. Taunton Meat Haulage* [1975] 2 LLoyd's Rep. 502, 507, *per* Donaldson J.; *Muller Batavier v. Laurent Transport Co.* [1977] 1 Lloyd's Rep. 411, 415, *per* May J. *OGH 12.4.84*, Stra GüV 1984/10 p. 10, Greiter 215, 221.

[74] *OGH 12.4.84*, (above) *loc. cit.* Muth/Glöckner, p. 181.

identified on the evidence. This is sometimes a matter of great difficulty, especially with transport in containers, and has given rise to the suggestion[75] that there is a presumption that the carrier responsible is the carrier in charge of the goods at the time that loss or damage was discovered, so that if "the following carrier makes reservations as to the state or quantity of the goods, the preceding carrier from whom he has taken the goods over will be 'the carrier responsible', even if the loss or damage could possibly have taken place while in the hands of an earlier carrier, unless evidence to this effect can be produced".[76] The rule suggested is like that of the common law of bailment. It is a sensible rule, but there is no warrant for this interpretation of the words of the CMR. Moreover, the courts have shown considerable ingenuity in tracking the source and moment of loss and damage to containerised goods.[77] It is submitted, therefore, that the performing carrier must be identified by the claimant in the usual way.

50a(*iii*). The last carrier

The last carrier is identified easily when the goods arrive at destination; but, if they do not? If carriage is to be performed successively by A, B and C, and total loss occurs while the goods are in the charge of B, it has been held[78] in Belgium that B is not only the performing carrier when loss occurred, but also the last carrier, so that C cannot be sued. Against this, Professor Rodière argued[79] that the last carrier is the last one envisaged, even if that carrier never takes over the goods at all, for two reasons: first, this is clearly the rule in the corresponding provision of the CIM, on which Article 36 is based.[80] Secondly, it is of overriding importance that the consignee should be provided with a convenient defendant. Certainly, it has been held that, when goods *do* arrive in the hands of a sub-contractor, the last carrier is the sub-contractor rather than the (absent and perhaps hard to identify)

---

[75] Hill and Messent, pp. 292–293.

[76] *ibid.*

[77] Goode and Schmitthoff (eds.), *International Carriage of Goods* (London, 1988), Chap. 4. This task has become easier with the use of the Stirnes "black box", the evidence of which has been accepted in some cases, for example, *TC Nanterre 5.1.89*, B.T. 1990.87.

[78] *Rb Antwerp 28.1.85* (1985) 20 E.T.L. 117, 1986 U.L.R. II 624; affirmed on different grounds: *Antwerp 15.3.89* (1989) 24 E.T.L. 574. See also *Paris 10.3.1992*, B.T.L. 1992.278.

[79] (1971) 6 E.T.L. 574, 583; but *cf.* Glass and Cashmore, para. 3.75, adopting Hill and Messent, p. 284, who conclude against Rodière precisely because the CMR differs from the CMR on this point.

[80] The influence of the CIM on this part of the CMR is disputed; see above, para. 50.

contractor for the last stage.[81] Rodière admitted that the language of the CMR differs from that of the CIM, and that there is some doubt about his solution. Indeed, doubt there is, as it is difficult to fault the general view that the last carrier suable under Article 36 must be a successive carrier under Article 34,[82] and hence a carrier who has accepted the goods and the consignment note[83]: *ex hypothesi*, C has not.

50a(*iv*). Other carriers

As many as 10 carriers may be involved in the movement of a single consignment of goods, but the claimant's range of targets is limited by Article 36 to the first carrier, the last carrier and the performing carrier. By clear implication, Article 36 excludes[84] legal proceedings against any other carrier involved "in respect of liability for loss, damage or delay". Construed literally and in isolation, this might mean any liability at all: another carrier may be liable in a recourse action under Article 37, but never in a direct action by the goods interest. However, construed in context, the liability referred to in Article 36 might be read as CMR liability, leaving open the possibility of a direct action under national law other than the CMR, such as the law of tort in England.[85]

50b. Acceptance of the goods and the consignment note

Under Article 34, a successive carrier "becomes a party to the contract of carriage . . . by reason of his acceptance of the goods and of the consignment note". This must be the original consignment note: a new consignment note will not do.[86] In practice, although not necessarily in theory, the carrier[87] accepts the goods when taking over the goods. The carrier accepts the consignment

---

[81] *Cass. com. 3.5.94*, B.T.L. 1994.390; (1995) 30 E.T.L. 685. But it has also been held that the contractor can be sued as the person responsible (under Art. 3) for the sub-contractor: *Cass. com. 9.7.96*, B.T.L. 1996.536. *cf.* also para. 50a(*i*) above: the contractor may also be sued as the first carrier.

[82] *Rb Antwerp 28.1.85* (above), at 627.

[83] See below, para. 50b.

[84] Above, para. 50. Concerning the liability of sub-contractors there have been conflicting decisions of the Italian Court of Cassation and the B.G.H., discussed by Grohe, ZEuP 1993.141.

[85] Concerning tort, see below, para. 229.

[86] *Harrison & Sons Ltd v. RT Stewart Transport Ltd* (1993) 28 E.T.L. 747 (Commercial Court, 1992). Herber, Art. 34, 10.

[87] *Semble*, the use of the word "acceptance", rather than the words "taking over" as found in Art. 17.1, suggests any manifestation of consent to assume responsibility for the goods on the terms of the consignment note. However, it has been assumed that the carrier accepts the goods when taking them over, for example, in *SGS-ATES Componenti Elettronici v. Grappa* [1978] 1 Lloyd's Rep. 281, 284, *per* Goff J. *cf.* the *Brandt* contract in English law: below, para. 217.

note when taking possession of it and accepting to be bound by it,[88] by its terms and by what it says about the quantity and condition of the goods: without acceptance of this kind, there can be no liability to suit as a successive carrier.[89] This requirement has been relaxed in Belgium[90] and, indeed, there is force in the argument against giving strict effect to the requirements of Article 34. The transport industry is not punctilious about formalities; the CMR scheme would be better promoted by adherence less to the letter than to the spirit of Article 34, and it should be enough, therefore, that the successive carrier demonstrated willingness to be "associated" with the single international contract of carriage; but that is not the generally held view.

Acceptance of the goods must be without reservation or, at least, without reservations amounting to a denial of responsibility. Absence of any reservation at all, as a condition precedent of any acceptance at all,[91] goes too far: if a subsequent carrier with reservations can never be a successive carrier, the reference in Article 35 to reservations makes little sense. The effect of any reservations on acceptance (of the goods and responsibility for them) depends, as it does when an initial carrier takes over goods, on the nature of the reservation and the terms in which it is expressed.[92]

Acceptance may be without reservations but it is not without limits. A successive carrier accepts responsibility to a degree that depends not only on what that carrier sees or should see of the

---

[88] *TC Brussels 11.5.87* (1988) 23 E.T.L. 720, 725: the tribunal held that the fact that the driver was in possession of the note and presented it to the consignee's agent did not amount to acceptance of a "very special and sometimes onerous legal regime", given that the carrier in question had issued his own consignment note as well.

[89] *Cass. It. 19.12.78*, Foro. it. 1979 I. 1512; *OGH 17.2.82*, S.Z. 55 Nr. 20, Greiter 127; *B.G.H. 9.2.1984* (1985) 20 E.T.L. 275; *B.G.H. 25.10.84* (1985) 20 E.T.L. 268, 271–272 *OGH 16.1.85*, Stra GüV 1985/8 p. 8, Greiter 275; *OGH 4.6.87* (1988) 23 E.T.L. 714; *B.G.H. 28.4.88* (1989) 25 E.T.L. 89; *OGH 13.4.89*, TranspR 1990.152; *B.G.H. 10.5.90*, TranspR 1990.418; *O.L.G. Munich 21.12.90*, TranspR 1991.96; *O.L.G. 6.3.93*, TranspR 1993.340. See also *Rotterdam 13.4.73*, 1977 U.L.R. I 338. Haak, pp. 109–111; Helm, Art. 34 Anm. 2; Herber, Art. 34, 10; Koller, Art. 34, 3; Putzeys, para. 288; Thume, TranspR 1991.85 *cf. O.G.H. 28.11.90*, TranspR 1991.135 in which the court refused to apply the CMR between carriers because, although there was a consignment note, it has not been signed by the sender and was not, therefore, a CMR consignment note.

[90] *TC Brussels 6.4.84*, 1986 U.L.R. II 607, 614: acceptance of the note is not essential, being just one indicator of consent to the contract of carriage. In the same sense in Belgium in the absence of a consignment note: Muller (1988) 23 E.T.L. 726, 730 and references cited. But *cf. Antwerp 3.4.77* (1977) 12 E.T.L. 411 which takes the general view in other countries. For further discussion of the Belgian decision to this effect, see Haak, p. 110.

Courts in Belgium have sometimes been influenced by Art. 4 (above, para. 22), that the absence of a consignment note does not affect the validity of the contract of carriage; however, Art. 4 is not relevant to Art. 34, as demonstrated by Hill and Messent, p. 268, citing *Colodense v. Gelders U.K. Transport* and *SGS-ATES Componenti Ellettronici v. Grappa* [1978] 1 Lloyd's Rep. 281, 284, *per* Robert Goff J.

[91] As suggested in *TC Brussels 1.5.87* (1988) 23 E.T.L. 720, 724.

[92] Above, para. 25b(*ii*).

goods[93] but also to a degree that depends on what the carrier knows or should know about the contract of carriage. For this, the successive carrier needs not only a consignment note but one that indicates the obligations which are being assumed.[94] If the carrier on a purely national stage receives a note that does not indicate that the carriage is governed by the CMR, it can be argued[95] that there is no acceptance at all in the sense of Article 34. This argument has support in the *travaux préparatoires*[96]: the requirement of Article 34 that the successive carrier should accept not only the goods but also the consignment note was included to deal with the objection that, otherwise, the sub-carrier for a purely national stage in an international movement governed by the CMR would not know what was involved. So, the successive carrier is only bound by those terms of the contract of carriage of which the carrier knows or should know, and in this perhaps there is symmetry for, it has been contended,[97] the same is true on the other side of the contractual fence of the consignee.

50b(*i*). The position of sub-contractors

The requirement of acceptance of both goods and note, as a condition of liability as a successive carrier under Chapter VI, gives rise to difficulties when A, the principal contractor and liable as such, sub-contracts the entire contract to B, and B likewise sub-contracts the entire contract to C.

The first problem is that in many cases, as has been held in Belgium[98] and Germany,[99] B does not appear to accept the goods and note and cannot therefore be a successive carrier under Article 34. In a physical sense, there is acceptance by C alone. One solution to this problem is "that the consignment note is, like the goods—indeed normally with the goods—accepted when it is taken over by the carrier concerned, by himself or *through his servant or agents*".[1] Thus, the suggestion has been put[2] that C

---

[93] Art. 35. On what the carrier should observe, see above, para. 25a.

[94] *B.G.H. 25.10.84* (1985) 20 E.T.L. 268, 272.

[95] Glass and Cashmore, para. 3.74.

[96] As reported by Haak, p. 107.

[97] Above, para. 40c.

[98] *Cass. Belge 30.6.95* (1996) 31 E.T.L. 545.

[99] *B.G.H. 25.10.84* (1985) 20 E.T.L. 268, 271–272, reversing the decision of the court below on this point. See also *B.G.H. 24.10.91*, TranspR 1992.177. This possibility does not seem to have been discussed in *ITT Schaub-Lorenz Vertriebgesellschaft mbH v. Birkart Johann Internationale Spedition GmbH* [1988] 1 Lloyd's Rep. 487, C.A., although the carrier was a sub-contractor who sub-contracted the carriage. Concerning conflicting decisions of the Italian Court of Cassation and the B.G.H., see Grohe, ZEuP 1993.141.

[1] *SGS-ATES Componenti Elettronici SpA v. Grappo* [1978] 1 Lloyd's Rep. 281, 284, *per* Robert Goff J. (emphasis added).

[2] Glass and Cashmore, para. 3.74; Hill and Messent, p. 267.

accepts the goods and the note also on behalf of B, the sub-contractor higher up the chain of delegation.

The second problem is that, as has been held in Germany,[3] C cannot be a successive carrier in the sense of Article 34 unless the note has been issued not by C but by someone higher up the chain, such as A or B. In England in *Ulster-Swift v. Taunton Meat Haulage*,[4] the note was issued by the sub-contractor, but the point was not taken and the sub-contractor was held, nonetheless, to be a successive carrier under Article 34.[5] The English court saw in Article 34 the creation of "an artificial statutory contract between the actual carrier and the owner of the goods . . . an unnecessary operation in terms of English law, where the owner of the goods would always have a right in bailment".[6] Being perhaps disinclined to make a fatal mountain out of a foreign molehill, the English court might have been persuaded to see the issue of the consignment note by C as an act done as agent for A and B[7]; however, imputed agency like this does little to recommend English law to lawyers abroad.

50b(*ii*). Entries on the consignment note

Article 35 requires the second or subsequent carrier to "enter his name and address on the second copy of the consignment note", the copy which accompanies the goods.[8] This serves the obvious function of providing the consignee with information with which to identify a potential defendant. A further function, it has been argued, is to evidence acceptance of the note (and hence of responsibility) by the successive carrier. However, the associated argument, that for that reason entry is a condition precedent to the liability of the successive carrier under Articles 34 and 36, has been rejected in Belgium[9] and also in England.

---

[3] *B.G.H. 284.88* (1989) 25 E.T.L. 89, 95. Also in this sense: *B.G.H. 25.10.84* (1985) 20 E.T.L. 268, 272.

[4] [1977] 1 Lloyd's Rep. 346, C.A.

[5] At 360, *per* Megaw L.J.

[6] At 361, *per* Megaw L.J., quoting Donaldson J. at first instance: [1975] 2 Lloyd's Rep. 502, 507. *cf.* Glass and Cashmore, para. 3.74: "By issuing the consignment note the subcontractor binds himself by its terms." However, this does not relate to the pre-existing contract of carriage, the single contract envisaged by Art. 34, or distinguish successive carriage from ordinary sub-contracting (above, para. 50), unless, as these writers suggest, it is issued with the authority of the previous contractor.

[7] Hill and Messent, p. 274.

[8] Art. 5.1.

[9] *TC Brussels 11.5.87* (1988) 23 E.T.L. 720, 724. Muller (1988) 23 E.T.L. 726, 729. Also in this sense: Loewe, para. 275 by reference to the legislative history of the CMR. The contrary view was pressed by the Dutch delegate during the drafting of the CMR, and clearly rejected by the other delegates: Haak, pp. 106–107.

> In *SGS-ATES Componenti Elettronici v. Grappa*[10] a reactor and components were sent by road from London to Catania under a single contract carried out in two stages with a different carrier for each stage. The second carrier did not enter its name in the consignment note as required by Article 35. The question arose whether this omission prevented that carrier from being a "last carrier" within the meaning of Article 36. Goff J. held[11] that the company was indeed a last carrier if it could be said to have accepted the goods and the consignment note within the meaning of Article 34, whether or not it had complied with Article 35.

This conclusion, which is supported by the legislative history of the CMR,[12] was reached after close attention to the words of the CMR. Giving the words of Article 34 their natural and ordinary meaning,[13] "the consignment note is, like the goods . . . accepted when it is taken over by the carrier concerned . . . with a view to carrying out the next part of the carriage of the goods pursuant to the terms of the consignment note. I can . . . see no reason to qualify this simple meaning by requiring compliance with the provisions of Art. 35." The judge pointed out that, in Article 35, the duty is required of "a carrier accepting the goods", suggesting that he is still "accepting" whether he complies with Article 35 or not. The requirements of Article 35 are not conditions but consequences of acceptance. This view of the matter is to be preferred, not only for the reasons just stated but, as the judge pointed out,[14] because the contrary view would allow carriers to evade CMR liability to consignees by the simple expedient of "forgetting to write their name and address in the consignment note.

51. Recourse: the basis of liability between carriers

If carrier B is a successive carrier under Article 34 from carrier A, and damages the goods, B's liability to the claimant is based on the CMR, even if the journey was purely national, for example, Felixstowe–Cardiff.[15] If, in respect of the same journey, the claimant is

---

[10] [1978] 1 Lloyd's Rep. 281.

[11] At 284.

[12] A proposal that the second and succeeding carriers should not be liable under the CMR unless they had entered their name and address in the second copy of the consignment note was rejected by the authors of the CMR: TRANS/WP9/35 p. 20.

[13] At 284. Goff J. also rejected the argument that the absence of name and address was an "irregularity" in the consignment note which, according to Art. 4, did not "affect the existence or the validity of the contract of carriage". His reason was that, unlike certain other provisions outside Chap. VI, "the provisions of Art. 4 were not expressly made applicable to the relations between successive carriers" (at 264). See also Hill, "Carriage of Goods by Road to the Continent", (1976) 11 E.T.L. 182, 197–198.

[14] At 284–285.

[15] Loewe, para. 275 by reference to the *travaux préparatoires*. This was, in effect, the situation in *Cummins Engine Co. v. Davis Freight Forwarding (Hull)* [1981] 3 All E.R. 567, C.A.

compensated by A, A may then sue B in the framework of Chapter VI[16]; the basis of B's liability is the CMR[17] unless and to the extent that A and B have agreed on a different liability, as is allowed by Article 40.

If carrier B is not a successive carrier under Article 34, although A's liability to the claimant may be based on the CMR, B has no liability to the claimant, except in tort. B may be liable to A, but that liability will be based solely on the sub-contract,[18] outside the scope of the CMR and Chapter VI, and be governed by the appropriate national law: in the case of a movement Felixstowe–Cardiff, by English law.[19] If, however, B's stage is international in the sense of Article 1, for example Rotterdam–Cardiff, for that stage B has the role of carrier and A the role of sender[20] and, although, *ex hypothesi*, Chapter VI does not apply, B's liability is governed by the CMR,[21] but it is liability not to the person ultimately interested in the goods but to A.

52. Recourse: indemnity and contribution under Article 37

The effect of section 5 of the Carriage of Goods by Road Act 1965, to which the CMR is scheduled, is to exclude national legislation "relating to contribution and indemnity between persons jointly or concurrently liable for the same loss or damage in the three parts of the United Kingdom, so leaving the way clear for the operation of the special provisions of CMR relating to such matters".[22] A carrier, who has been held "responsible for the performance of the whole operation" under Article 34,[23] may seek indemnity[24] or contribution from one or more of the other carriers involved in accordance with Chapter VI of the CMR.

The CMR contemplates two distinct kinds of legal proceedings, the first and main action by the goods interest followed by a

---

[16] Above, para. 50a.

[17] See above, para. 18.

[18] *Lyon 18.10.85*, B.T. 1986.744.

[19] *Rb Antwerp 25.11.74*, J.P.A. 1975.70, as reported by Hill and Messent, p. 263; *Lyon 18.11.85*, B.T. 1986.744.

[20] *O.L.G. Düsseldorf 12.2.81*, VersR 1982.302; *O.L.G. Munich 5.7.89*, TranspR 1990.16.

[21] One curious result is that, unlike the situation in which they relate as successive carriers, to which Art. 40 applies, A as sender and B as carrier cannot agree rights and duties *inter se* which derogate from the CMR: Art. 41, below, para. 92.

[22] *Cummins Engine Co. v. Davis Freight Forwarding (Hull)* [1981] 3 All E.R. 567, 571, *per* Brandon L.J., C.A.; *ITT Schaub-Lorenz Vertriebgesellschaft mbH v. Birkart Johann Internationale Spedition GmbH* [1988] 1 Lloyd's Rep. 487, 494, *per* Bingham L.J., C.A.

[23] See above, para. 50.

[24] Including not only the amount paid to the goods interest but also legal costs: Muth/Glöckner, p. 185, citing *Lg Hamburg 5.1.81*, VersR 1981.969.

second and consequential recourse action.[25] Any "inconsistency between CMR and English procedural rules must be resolved in favour of the CMR, which is paramount".[26] However, "where the procedure of the Court in which the first and main action is brought allows claims by a defendant for contribution or indemnity to be added to the main action by way of third party proceedings . . . there is no good reason in principle why what is contemplated by CMR as the second and consequential action should not be brought by way of such third party proceedings".[27]

As regards the recourse action, unless the carriers provide otherwise, this being allowed by Article 40, Article 37 applies:

> "A carrier who has paid compensation in compliance with the provisions of this Convention shall be entitled to recover such compensation together with interest thereon and all costs and expenses incurred by reason of the claim, from the other carriers who have taken part in the carriage . . . "

The context of Article 37, Chapter VI, indicates that only a carrier who is a principal or successive carrier under Article 34 has a right of recourse under Article 37.[28] Further, the wording of Article 37 "makes it quite clear that a carrier must pay [the claimant] before enforcing his right to recover against another carrier".[29]

Article 39.1 provides:

> "No carrier against whom a claim is made under Articles 37 and 38 shall be entitled to dispute the validity of the payment made by the carrier making the claim if the amount of the compensation was determined by judicial authority after the first mentioned carrier had been given due notice of the proceedings and afforded an opportunity of entering an appearance."

The effect of this provision is that a successive carrier B, against whom carrier A claims under Chapter VI, is "estopped" from

---

[25] *Cummins Engine Co. v. Davis Freight Forwarding (Hull)* [1981] 3 All E.R. 567, 574, *per* Brandon L.J. C.A.; *ITT Schaub-Lorenz Vertriebgesellschaft mbH v. Birkart Johann Internationale Spedition GmbH* [1988] 1 Lloyd's Rep. 487, 494, *per* Bingham L.J., C.A.

[26] Bingham L.J., 493–494.

[27] Brandon L.J., *loc. cit.*, cited with approval by Bingham L.J. in *ITT*, at 494 and applied by the Court of Appeal in that case.

[28] *B.G.H. 25.10.84* (1985) 20 E.T.L. 268, 273; *OGH 16.1.85*, Stra GüV 1985/8 p. 8, Greiter 275.

cf. the *obiter dictum* of Megaw L.J. in *Ulster-Swift v. Taunton Meat Haulage* [1977] 1 Lloyd's Rep. 346, 360, that the kind of carrier referred to elsewhere in Chap. VI, Art. 39, was not limited by being in Chap. VI or by Art. 34 to a successive carrier.

[29] *ITT Schaub-Lorenz* (above, n. 25), at 494, *per* Bingham L.J. Also in this sense: *OGH 19.10.78*, Greiter 72; *OGH 16.1.85*, Stra GüV 1985/8 p. 8, Greiter 275.

disputing the matters settled by judicial authority[30] in the action against A by the goods claimant. This explains the requirement of notice.[31]

As it concerns a recourse action, Article 37 provides that the maximum amount recoverable is the amount of compensation paid to the goods claimant, together with interest, costs and expenses. But it does not necessarily follow that the carrier A will recover in full. Although carrier B is barred by Article 39.1 (above) from disputing the validity of the payment made by carrier A, that does not prevent B's disputing B's own liability in that regard[32]: B may be able to raise a defence which carrier A could not or did not raise to the goods claimant.

52a. Defences between carriers

Generally, "the legal relations of carriers are to be governed (in the absence of alternative agreed conditions) by the same criteria as those governing the relations of carrier and the person entitled to make a claim".[33] So, in an action under Article 37(a) between the carrier who has paid and the carrier alleged to be solely responsible, the former assumes the role of a goods claimant and must prove that the loss, damage or delay occurred while the goods were in the hands of the latter. The consignment note and its contents are intended[34] to play the same evidentiary role as in an action by the goods claimant.[35] If, for example, the second carrier enters no reservations in the consignment note when accepting the goods from the first carrier, there is a presumption in accordance with Article 35.2 and Article 9 that the goods and their packaging appeared to be in good condition and that the number of packages, their marks and numbers corresponded with the statements in the consignment note.[36] However, it should be stressed that this presumption operates in a dispute between successive carriers, but is irrelevant to an action against one of those carriers by the sender or the consignee, to whom that carrier is responsible for the entire operation.[37]

---

[30] A judicial authority probably includes a properly appointed arbitrator: Loewe, para. 287.

[31] As to notice see *Cummins Engine Co. v. Davis Freight Forwarding (Hull)* [1981] 3 All E.R. 567, 575, *per* Brandon L.J., C.A.

[32] Hill and Messent, p. 301.

[33] Glass, "CMR and Hired Trailers—A Tilt Too Far?", [1981] L.M.C.L.Q. 384, 385, with reference to the basis of discussion in *Walek & Co. v. Chapman & Ball* [1980] 2 Lloyd's Rep. 279.

[34] See Art. 35 which applies to the relations of carrier and successive carrier the provisions of Art. 9 and Art. 8.2, but not Art. 8.1 or Art. 8.3: on the possible significance of these omissions, see Hill and Messent, pp. 282–283.

[35] Above, para. 25.

[36] For example, *Paris 10.2.84*, B.T. 1984.558; *Cass. 5.7.88*, B.T. 1988.546.

[37] Art. 34: above, para. 50.

52b. The carrier responsible: Article 37(a)

In Article 37 the right of recourse is subject to the provisions of sub-paragraphs (a) to (c), which concern the identity of the carrier or carriers liable to the carrier who has paid, and the extent of recovery.

Article 37(a) provides that "the carrier responsible for the loss or damage shall be solely liable for the compensation whether paid by himself or by another carrier".

"The carrier responsible" means the carrier or carriers on whose stage of the journey the loss, damage or delay occurred or is presumed to have occurred.[38] Being "solely" liable, only the carrier responsible can be sued under Article 37[39] unless that carrier is insolvent, in which case Article 38 provides for apportionment between the other carriers.[40]

"Loss or damage" covers what is referred to elsewhere in the CMR, for example Article 17.1, as "loss, damage or delay": there is no reason to think that a different rule of recourse was intended in the case of delay.

Common sense suggests that, unless the carrier responsible can be identified with confidence and in any case, perhaps, if there is any likelihood that the carrier responsible is insolvent,[41] action should be brought against all or any of the carriers involved, not only to determine responsibility but also to ensure that the action against the carrier(s) ultimately liable to contribute is commenced in time.

52c. Apportionment of liability between carriers: Article 37(b) and (c), Article 38

Article 37(b) provides that, "when the loss or damage has been caused by the action of two or more carriers, each of them shall pay an amount proportionate to his share of liability; should it be impossible to apportion the liability, each carrier shall be liable in proportion to the share of payment for the carriage which is due to him".[42]

---

[38] *Cummins Engine Co. v. Davis Freight Forwarding (Hull)* [1981] 2 Lloyd's Rep. 106, 110, *per* Mocatta J., affirmed [1981] 3 All E.R. 567, 574, *per* Brandon L.J., C.A.; *ITT Schaub-Lorenz Vertriebgesellschaft mbH v. Birkart Johann Internationale Spedition GmbH* [1988] 1 Lloyd's Rep. 487, C.A. Donald, para. 143; Loewe, para. 283; Rodière (1971) 6 E.T.L. 574, 585.

[39] *Cummins Engine* (above); *Cass. Belge 30.5.80* (1983) 18 E.T.L. 79 and not, as in this case, one of the other successive carriers involved. Also in this sense: *OGH 16.1.85*, Stra GüV 1985/8 p. 8, Greiter 275.

[40] Below, para. 52a.

[41] *ibid.*

[42] Applied in *Walek & Co. v. Chapman & Ball* [1980] 2 Lloyd's Rep. 279, 283.

Article 37(c) provides that, "If it cannot be ascertained to which carriers liability is attributable for the loss or damage, the amount of the compensation shall be apportioned between all the carriers as laid down in (b) above."

The situation that appears to fall between Article 37(b) and (c) is that in which proportionate apportionment or attribution can be made in part but there remains an area of uncertainty. As the primary provision is Article 37(b) and the primary part of that is the first sentence, in which apportionment is based on the causal contribution of the carriers concerned, it can be inferred that, if between carriers A, B and C, C can show that C was not responsible but it cannot be shown which of A and B are responsible, liability is apportioned under Article 37(c) between A and B, excluding C.[43]

Further, Article 38 provides:

> "If one of the carriers is insolvent, the share of the compensation due from him and unpaid by him shall be divided among the other carriers in proportion to the share of the payment for the carriage due to them."

The primary meaning of "insolvent" is not that any formal steps have been taken to declare the carrier bankrupt or to put the corporate carrier into liquidation, but simply inability to pay.[44] Article 38 applies not only when enforcement against the carrier has failed but also when it is obvious in advance that enforcement will be of no avail.[45] The "other carriers" are those also liable under Article 37,[46] excluding therefore any carrier not liable in the recourse action.

Muth and Glöckner point out[47] that this kind of guarantee is good for the public image of the transport industry, and that, if a carrier does not like the rule, he must choose with care those with whom he works, or contract out of Article 38, as permitted by Article 40.

53. Recourse: jurisdiction under Article 39

Whereas the competence of courts to decide the goods claimant's action is dealt with in Article 31, jurisdiction in a recourse action

---

[43] This is also the conclusion reached by Hill and Messent (1st ed.), p. 220 and by Rodière (1971) 6 E.T.L. 574, 586; Rodière CMR, para. 135. In the second edition Hill and Messent (p. 295) seem to be less sure. *cf.* Thume, Art. 37, 5 that in practice the wording of paragraph (b) does not give rise to any problems.

[44] O.E.D. The same is true of *insolvable* in the French version and in the German version of *zahlungsunfähig*.

[45] Evans, p. 71.

[46] Helm, Art. 38 Anm.

[47] p. 186.

is governed by Article 39, and not by Article 31, except as regards Article 31.3 and Article 31.4, which are brought into play by Article 39.3.[48] Article 39.2 provides that a carrier who wishes to take proceedings to enforce his right of recourse under Article 37:

> "may make his claim before the competent court or tribunal in which one of the carriers concerned is ordinarily resident, or has his principal place of business or the branch or agency through which the contract of carriage was made. All the carriers concerned may be made defendants in the same action."

Although Article 39.2 states that the carrier seeking recovery *may* claim in the courts mentioned, to claim at all, the carrier *must* claim there,[49] as there is no other forum under the CMR for recovery of compensation in accordance with Article 37.[50] The courts indicated by Article 39.2 are the same as some but not all of those available to the goods claimant under Article 31.1(a).[51] Reference to a court designated by agreement, specified in Article 31.1 but not in Article 39, is ruled out by implication.[52]

Obviously, it serves the convenience of the claimant carrier if all concerned can be brought before one court but, equally obviously, a court which has jurisdiction over one carrier, whose principal place of business is there, does not have jurisdiction on that same ground over another carrier involved if the latter's principal place of business is in another state. What is convenient for the claimant carrier may be less convenient for the other carriers concerned.

In *Cummins*[53] the last (road) stage of carriage from Lanarkshire to Amsterdam was sub-contracted by the defendant carrier, whose

---

[48] The argument that a recourse action could be brought on the basis of jurisdiction in Art. 31 was rejected by Brandon L.J. in *Cummins Engine Co. v. Davis Freight Forwarding (Hull)* [1981] 3 All E.R. 567, 575, C.A.

cf. Cass. 21.6.82, B.T. 1982.513 discussed below, in which the court appeared to ignore Art. 39, and applied the Brussels Convention.

[49] *Cummins, loc. cit.* below, n. 53. See also in this sense *Harrison & Sons Ltd v. RT Stewart Transport Ltd* (1993) 28 E.T.L. 747 (Commercial Court, 1992). In *Cummins* Eveleigh L.J. (at 576) left this point open, as Art. 39.2 does not contain the words "and in no other courts or tribunals" found in Art. 31. His doubts were shared by Hobhouse J. in *Arctic Electronics Co. (U.K.) v. McGregor Sea & Air Services* [1985] 2 Lloyd's Rep. 510, 514, who added a reason of his own for differing with Brandon L.J.: Art. 39.1 "contemplates that the successive carrier may voluntarily join a Chapter V action. Such an action may or may not be in a jurisdiction authorised by art. 39.2. Therefore, to give art. 39.2 a compulsory and exclusive effect would not be consistent with the proceedings contemplated and authorised by art. 39.1."

[50] For the meaning of the specified points of contact, see above, para. 46b.

[51] Moreover, Art. 40 provides that "carriers shall be free to agree among themselves on provisions other than those laid down in articles 37 and 38", but not, by implication, Art. 39. Also in this sense Hill and Messent, p. 303. *cf.* Loewe, para. 288; "In the light of article 40, it was unnecessary to draft a provision expressly permitting the designation of competent tribunals or courts."

[52] Loewe, para. 288.

[53] *Cummins Engine Co. v. Davis Freight Forwarding (Hull)* [1981] 3 All E.R. 567, C.A.

principal place of business was in England, to A, by A to B and by B to C: the goods were damaged while being carried by C in Holland. Before the English court, the defendant sought to serve third-party notices against A, B and C. Notices were set aside as regards A and B, because "neither was the carrier responsible for the loss or damage to the goods so as to entitle [the defendant] to sue them for an indemnity" under Article 37[54]; and against A, B and C because under Article 39.2 the defendant was "not entitled to bring proceedings against them, whether by way of third party proceedings or separate action, in an English Court".[55] Although, as Brandon L.J. admitted,[56] that was inconvenient for the defendant, "that consideration cannot be allowed to distort what I regard as the clear meaning of art. 39, para. 2. It may also be observed that the difficulty would have been avoided if the [the plaintiff goods owner] had sued all four defendants in the Netherlands, although I recognize that it is unlikely that they would have chosen to do so."

Under the first sentence of Article 39.2, a recourse claim may be made before the competent court in the country in which is the principal place of business of "one of the carriers concerned". On a wide view of these words, they include the carrier seeking recourse, and hence in a case like *Cummins* the English court would have jurisdiction not only over the English defendant but also over C, whose principal place of business was in Holland. On a narrow view of these words, they were limited to the carrier or carrier *against* which the recourse claim is brought. Reading the words in context, "a situation in which one carrier, who has been made primarily liable to a sender or a consignee, is seeking to recover over against one or more other carriers", Brandon L.J.[57] had no doubt that the narrower view was correct. One reason was the mention of "the carriers concerned" in the second sentence of Article 39.2, where they are referred to as "*defendants* in the same action".[58] The carrier seeking recourse could not be a "defendant in the same action" (second sentence) because the "same action" was the very action for recourse in which that carrier was plaintiff. So, that same carrier could not be a "carrier concerned" with a

---

[54] At 574, *per* Brandon L.J., with whom Eveleigh L.J. agreed (at 576): as Art. 36 limits recourse to the first carrier (the defendant), the last carrier (C) or the carrier who was performing that portion of the carriage during which the event causing loss, damage or delay occurred, that ruled out A and B.

[55] *ibid. cf.* Loewe, para. 288, who refers to "recovery as between carriers" and continues: "Since in the case of an action for recovery, the carriers prosecuted are joint debtors, the competence of a court or tribunal to hear an action brought against any one of them always includes the competence of the same court or tribunal to hear an action brought against the others."

[56] At 575. See also O'Connor L.J. (at 576).

[57] At 574, in accord with the "clear and impressive judgment of Mocatta J." at first instance: [1981] 2 Lloyd's Rep. 106.

[58] Emphasis added. Also in this sense: Connor L.J. (at 576); and *Arctic Electronics Co. (U.K.) v. McGregor Sea & Air Services* [1985] 2 Lloyd's Rep. 510, 513, *per* Hobhouse J.

principal place of business founding jurisdiction (first sentence) without conceding that the words "carrier concerned" meant something different in two successive sentences of the same provision (Article 39.2). This, understandably, Brandon L.J. was reluctant to accept. The "carriers concerned", he concluded, could only be the carriers defending the action for recourse.

The resulting business inconvenience, which Brandon L.J. conceded would follow, might have been avoided by a more purposive view of the provisions. Some warrant for that comes from section 14(2) of the Carriage of Goods by Road Act which, perhaps with the perceived imperfections of the CMR in view, provided that the "persons concerned in the carriage of goods by road to which the Convention applies" are not only the defendants to the action in recourse but also the sender, the consignee and, as well as assignees and servants and agents of carriers under Article 3, significantly, "*any carrier* who, in accordance with article 34 . . . or otherwise, is a *party to the contract* of carriage".[59] Clearly, the carrier seeking recourse in a "carrier concerned" in this sense and, given that the words appear only in twice in Chapter VI, *i.e.* in Article 39.2, it is regrettable that Brandon L.J. did not explain why he was giving section 14(2) so little effect. The explanation may be that section 14(2) is aimed solely at the interpretation of the Act and not at that of the Convention; but that is not clear either, because the main effect of the Act is to apply the CMR to "persons concerned in the carriage of goods by road": section 1 (which, apart from section 14(2) itself, is the only section in which that phrase appears). So, in contrast in the more recent case of *Harrison*,[60] Gatehouse J., having found that the interpretation of the text of the CMR in Chapter VI led to a narrow and "curious" view, felt able to reach a broader and more "natural" view based on section 14(2).[61]

Whatever the correct meaning of "carriers concerned", they do not *all* have to have a relevant connection with the forum as long as *one* of them does. The effect of Article 39.2, in the connection of Hill and Messent[62] is that if the first carrier, A, having compensated the goods interest, brings a recourse action against the third and last carrier, C, in the latter's principal place of business, B, the second carrier may be joined in the action, for example to defend the allegation that the damage occurred during B's stage, even

---

[59] Emphasis added.

[60] *Harrison & Sons Ltd v. RT Stewart Transport Ltd* (1993) 28 E.T.L. 747 (Commercial Court, 1992).

[61] *Viz.* that the carriers concerned included not only successive carriers, *i.e.* carriers having accepted a consignment note as required by Art. 34 but also carriers actively participating in carriage without such acceptance. Gatehouse J. found support on this point in a dictum of Megaw L.J. in *Ulster-Swift Ltd v. Taunton Meat Haulage Ltd* [1977] 1 Lloyd's Rep. 346, 360 (C.A.).

[62] At 303. In this sense, see *Harrison* (above).

though that action is brought in a jurisdiction with which B has no connection mentioned in Article 39.2.

> In *Arctic Electronics*[63] the plaintiff employed defendant A, who in turn employed B, to transport video game machines from Taipei to London. After an air stage to Luxembourg, the goods were carried by road vehicle to London in three lots by sub-carriers C, D and E. Machines in each lot were found to be damaged. The defendant A claimed indemnity from third party B, who sought to bring in C, D and E as fourth parties by fourth-party notices. C, whose only relevant connection was with Luxembourg, successfully contested the jurisdiction of the English court.

In that case C relied on *Cummins*, in which the "carriers concerned" did not include the claimant carrier and in which the carrier contesting jurisdiction had, like C, no relevant connection in England. In *Arctic*, B sought to distinguish *Cummins* because D, one of the *other* "carriers concerned", was resident in England. B's argument failed not because the argument was unsound but because a premise of the argument was false: D was not, as the argument assumed, a carrier concerned. This was because D's consignment to London was quite separate from C's consignment to London. "None of the other fourth parties were successive carriers for that consignment . . . successive carriers are successive carriers under a single consignment."[64] This was clear from Article 34, which states the scope of Chapter VI, which includes Article 39, as "carriage governed by a single contract of carriage . . . performed by successive road carriers"; and also from Article 38, which provides that, if one of the carriers concerned is insolvent, "the share of the compensation due from him and unpaid by him shall be divided among the other carriers *in proportion to the share of the payment for carriage due to them*".[65] The possibility remains, however, that the Hill and Messent argument might have succeeded if D's involvement had been in the carriage of the same consignment in succession to C.

> In *Cass 21.6.82*,[66] carrier A, registered in Iran, agreed to carry goods from Germany to Iran. A sub-contracted to B, registered in France, which sub-contracted to C, registered in Germany, which sub-contracted to D. C ordered part of the goods to the wrong consignee with consequent delay. A brought a recourse action against B and C, and B brought a recourse action against C. C disputed the jurisdiction of the French courts without success.

[63] *Arctic Electronics Co. (U.K.) v. McGregor Sea & Air Services* [1985] 2 Lloyd's Rep. 510.
[64] At 51, *per* Hobhouse J.
[65] Emphasis added.
[66] B.T. 1982.513.

The Court of Cassation observed first that, as A was obliged by contract with B to sue B in France, where without doubt the courts had jurisdiction between A and B, and as A's claims against B and C were closely connected, the court had jurisdiction in that matter as regards C. Secondly, as regards B's action against C the court dismissed C's objection not, however, by reference to Article 39.2 but because, a view rejected by the English courts,[67] the rules of jurisdiction in the CMR were not exclusive and hence the court had jurisdiction under Article 6 of the Brussels Convention.[68] This reasoning has been questioned[69] and, it is submitted, the decision would have had a surer basis, as suggested by the Hill and Messent argument and by an earlier French decision,[70] in Article 39.2.

---

[67] Above, para. 46.

[68] "A person domiciled in a Contracting State may also be sued:

(1) Where he is one of a number of defendants, in the courts for the place where any one of them is domiciled;

(2) as a third party in an action . . . in any third party proceedings, in the court seised of the original proceedings, unless these were instituted solely with the object of removing him from the jurisdiction of the court which would be competent in his case."

[69] Haak, p. 278. But the decision is defended by Batiffol, Rev.Crit.D.I.P. 1983.80, 85, on the basis that the words of Art. 39.2 ("may make his claim") are permissive not obligatory.

[70] *Paris 29.3.69*, 1970 U.L.C. 125; B.T. 1969.159.

CHAPTER 5

THE LIABILITY OF THE CARRIER

54. The liability of the carrier: Article 17.1

Although Article 17 was based on the firm and familiar footing of the CIM,[1] the CIM was largely unknown in England and at least one senior English judge came to the CMR for the first time without enthusiasm:

> "So we set out our journey through articles 17 and 18. It is a journey which we fear may be long and tedious. But the elaborate wording and the complexity of the articles do not provide a direct or a well-surfaced road to the destination."[2]

If the destination is a decision based on the CMR, the first step is to apply Article 17.1:

> "The Carrier shall be liable for the total or partial loss of the goods and for the damage thereto occurring between the time when he take over the goods and the time of delivery, as well as for any delay in delivery."

In the case of total loss, the claimant proves that the goods were taken over by the carrier. Then it is for the carrier, in order to be exonerated, to prove that the goods were delivered; otherwise total loss will be presumed.[3] In the case of partial loss or damage, it is for the claimant to prove that it occurred between taking over and delivery. In a particular case, the claimant may be able to prove that during that period specific events occurred which caused loss or damage. More often the proof is that on arrival at destination there was a difference between the quantity or condition of the goods taken over,[4] the goods which the carrier promised to deliver, and the quantity or condition of the goods actually

---

[1] E/ECE/TRANS/SC1/116 Art. 18.

[2] *Ulster-Swift v. Taunton Meat Haulage* [1977] 1 Lloyd's Rep. 346, 351, *per* Megaw L.J., C.A.

[3] *O.L.G. Hamm 2.12.91*, TranspR 1992.179; Koller, Art. 17, 12; Herber/Piper, Art. 17, 168.

[4] Below, paras. 60 *et seq.*

delivered, and the court is invited to infer that the goods suffered loss or damage between those two points in time. In the case of delay, the claimant proves a difference between the promised time of delivery and the actual time of delivery.[5]

If the claimant makes a case of this kind against the carrier, the carrier may seek exoneration by raising the defences in Article 17.2[6] and Article 17.4.[7] If these defences fail, the carrier will seek to limit liability to the amount indicated by Article 23.[8]

54a. The basis of liability

As in the more familiar case of carriage by sea, if it appears[9] that loss, damage or delay has occurred while the carrier was responsible for the goods, there is a prima facie case of breach of the contract of carriage, breach of a strict contractual duty to deliver the goods to the right person at the right destination, and in the order and condition in which they were taken over.[10] Like the Hague or Hague-Visby Rules on carriage by sea, the liability provisions of the CMR are seen in England as terms of a contract of carriage, with a substratum of bailment.

In Belgium[11] and in France,[12] the CMR carrier, like any other carrier under a contract of carriage, has *une obligation de résultat: une obligation de résultat de bonne fin de livraison de son chargement*,[13] which requires delivery of the goods to the right person and in the appropriate condition.[14] If there is loss, damage or delay, the carriage faces *une présomption de responsabilité*. As in England, the provisions of the CMR are seen as terms of the contract of carriage.[15]

---

[5] Below, para. 58.

[6] Below Chap. 6: paras. 69 *et seq.*

[7] Below Chap. 7: paras. 76 *et seq.*

[8] Below, paras. 93 *et seq.*

[9] But to make it "appear" so, the claimant must rebut a presumption established by Art. 30.1 that the goods have been delivered in accordance with the contract of carriage: see below, paras. 61 *et seq.*

[10] *idem* as regards carriage by sea under the Hague Rules, for example, *Albacora SRL v. Westcott & Laurance Line* [1965] 2 Lloyd's Rep. 37, 46, *per* Lord Cameron, Ct.Sess.

[11] *TC Liège 13.12.77*, 1980 U.L.R. I 270; *Brussels 31.12.79*, JT 1980.388; also cases cited by Buyl, Theunis, p. 276; Libouton, Theunis, p. 79. Putzeys, paras. 377, 652; Van Ryn (1966) 1 E.T.L. 638, 655.

[12] *Nancy 20.2.81.*, B.T. 1981.330; *TC Paris 9.6.83*, B.T. 1983.457; *Paris 10.2.84*, B.T. 1984.558. Gottrau B.T. 1986.706. Rodière, CMR para. 62.

[13] *TC Paris 9.6.83*, B.T. 1983.457, 459.

[14] Rodière, para. 527, pointing as regards French domestic law, to Art. 1784 c.civ.: "Ils sont responsables de la perte ou dess avaries des choses qui leur sont confiées, à moins qui'ils ne prouvent qu'elles ont été perdues ou avariées par cas fortuit ou force majeure."

[15] For example, Rodière (1971) 6 E.T.L. 2, 4–5 as regards Art. 14 to 16: "the obligations attributed to a contract by law (or by international convention) are not legal but contractual; if it is impossible to carry them out, they will therefore be open to censure according to the rules of contractual responsibility."

To courts in Austria[16] and in Germany,[17] CMR liability, looks like *eine Gefährdungshaftung*, a kind of strict liability, limited in amount and imposed by statute, for potentially dangerous things such as animals and railway trains.[18] Although different from the *présomption de responsabilité* of French law, the *présomption* is so hard to rebut that, it has been said,[19] the two are "almost identical". However, although German courts speak of the carrier's "contractual" liability under the CMR,[20] *Gefährdungshaftung* is associated with risk theory,[21] has a tortious flavour, and is different from the contractual conception of the CMR found in England, and from the contractual liability which the carrier may have in Austria and Germany under the contract of carriage, in addition to *Gefährdungshaftung*. Indeed, as in English law, in German law the principal obligation of the carrier is a contractual obligation to deliver the goods to the right consignee.[22] However, whereas the English judge is inclined to see the CMR as an integral part of the contract of carriage, the German judge perceives a tension between the CMR, as a special regime, and the ordinary contractual liability (*Vertragsverletzung*),[23] and is inclined to apply the latter at the expense of the CMR.[24]

If the special rules for special risks (Article 17.4)[25] are put aside, and the basic liability of Article 17.1, which in England is a strict

[16] For example, *OGH 27.8.81*, Greiter 97, 101. But *cf.* below, n. 26.

[17] For example, *B.G.H. 21.12.66*, N.J.W. 1967.499, 1967 U.L.C. 283, (1969) 4 E.T.L. 88; *O.L.G. Hamm 11.3.76*, N.J.W. 1976.2077; *O.L.G. Frankfurt 25.10.77*, VersR 1978.535.

[18] From the first half of the nineteenth century there was liability, if the loss or damage was caused "through the operation" of the railway, *i.e.* if it was caused or contributed to by sudden braking, collapse of the track, sparks from the trains, signal failure, or other incidents of the technical operation of running a railway. There was exoneration only in case of *höhere Gewalt*: external and elemental forces of nature or the conduct of third parties, the effects of which could not have been prevented even by the most extreme precautions: Zweigert & Kötz, vol. II, pp. 347–348. For a select bibliography see Markesinis, *The German Law of Torts* (3rd ed., Oxford, 1994), p. 692; and Zweigert & Kötz, vol. II, p. 340 and p. 353.

[19] Zweigert & Kötz, vol. II, p. 345.

[20] For example, *B.G.H. 27.10.78*, N.J.W. 1979.2473, 2474.

[21] In view of the chance that harm will occur: Honoré, *Encyclopedia of Comparative Law*, vol. XI, Chap. 7, paras. 94 *et seq.*; Lawson and Markesinis, *Tortious Liability for Unintentional Harm in the Common Law and the Civil Law*, vol. I, pp. 123 *et seq.*

[22] *B.G.H. 27.10.78*, N.J.W. 1979.2473. Helm, Art. 17 Anm. 4 argues that the concept of *Gefährdungshaftung* has no place in the modern contract of carriage. Other commentators too take a more nuanced view: Herber/Piper Vor, Art. 17, 3; Koller, Art. 17, 13; Thume, Art. 17, 3 *et seq.*; and, in particular, 9 *et seq.*

[23] Piper, VersR 1988.201, 208. Together with the tradition, for example in the case of people or things damaged while being carried by rail, of a claim both under the special statute (*Gefährdungshaftung*) and under the general civil law: Lawson and Markesinis, p. 159. The distinction is also marked in many standard contracts of liability insurance, whereby CMR liabliity is insured separately from other kinds of liability which the carrier may incur under the contract of carriage: Verheyen, Theunis, p. 263.

[24] Notably in the case of abandonment of the transport. See below, para. 66.

[25] For these rules, see below, Chap. 7.

contractual liability, is qualified by the defences in Article 17.2, the net result in England is a level of duty which is less than absolutely strict but greater than that of an ordinary duty of reasonable care.[26] The level is set by the key defence,[27] unavoidable circumstances,[28] and the net result is that the carrier has a duty to exercise, what has been called,[29] "utmost care" to perform the contract of carriage.

54b. The scope of liability in time

Although the CMR applies to the contract of carriage, as defined in Article 1.1, Article 17.1, the chief source of the carrier's liability under the CMR, applies only to loss or damage occurring *between* taking over and delivery, a period which may be shorter than the period to which the contract of carriage relates. The carrier's contractual liability for what occurs in the margin before the take over and after delivery is governed not by the CMR but by the contract and by national law. However, the importance of the margin depends on the meaning given to "taking over" and "delivery". If, as suggested above,[30] the goods are taken over by the carrier when they come into the carrier's control, and the goods are delivered when control passes in accordance with the terms of the contract to the consignee, the margin may well be slight: loss or damage occurring during stages ancillary to movement of the goods, such as storage and groupage, are within the scope of the CMR—if the goods are then in the control of the carrier.

Problems remain in respect of the precise moment at which loss or damage occurs in relation to the period of control. The carrier

---

[26] So, also, the level in Belgium and France is not the *présomption de faute* but the *présomption de responsabilité*: *Rennes 19.11.1930*, Dor Sup 9.18; *TC Charleroi 1.10.68*, 1969, U.L.C. 327, 330; *Colmar 11.1.72*, B.T. 1972.90, 1973 U.L.C. 276; *Brussels 12.12.77*, 1978 U.L.R. I 376, 379; *Paris 4.7.84*, B.T. 1985.158. Buyl, Theunis, p. 276; Van Ryn (1966) 1 E.T.L. 638, 659. *cf.* Putzeys, para. 655 who sees as regards the movement of the goods *une présomption de responsabilité*, which can be rebutted by the carrier by proof that the non-performance could not be imputed to him, but as regards the state of the goods *une présomption de faute*, which can be rebutted (more easily) by proof that he was not at fault. In Germany, Helm, Art. 17 Anm. 4 describes it as *in die Gruppe der Haftungen für vermutetes Verschulden . . . allerdings mit verschärften Sorgfaltsanforderungen*, but concedes that this is not the general view in Germany: for example, *B.G.H. 28.2.75*, N.J.W. 1975.1957, 1975 U.L.R. II 370. But *semble* Helm has support in *O.G.H. 15.12.81*, Greiter 119; *O.G.H. 10.7.91*, TranspR 1991.412 and *O.G.H. 12.11.96*, TranspR 1997.104. In Sweden Ramberg (1974) 9 E.T.L. 3, 14 refers to a synthesis of international opinion in favour of an "alternative placed between the principle of exculpation and the strict liability principle".

[27] Muth/Glöckner, p. 129: *Gefährdungshaftung*, but qualified by the possibility of a successful defence by reference to unavoidable circumstances (Art. 17.2).

[28] Below, para. 76.

[29] This description is taken from the judgment of Mustill J. in the *Silber* case, below, para. 75a.

[30] Paras. 27 and 37.

may argue that damage perceived during that period is attributable to an event before the period began,[31] while the claimant may argue that damage first perceived after that period is attributable to events during the period. Problems like this come to a point in the case of misdelivery.

> In *Eastern Kayam Carpets v. Eastern United Freight*[32] Hirst J. decided that misdelivery of the goods was outside the scope of Article 17.1, because "the very earliest moment at which the loss occurred was immediately after delivery, *i.e.* when the goods first got into the hands of the buyers"; and that there was therefore a gap in the CMR regime to which the common law applied. Some years later in *The Captain Gregos*[33] Hirst J. reached a similar decision in relation to carriage by sea, that misdelivery was outside the scope of the Hague-Visby Rules, but in this case his decision was reversed.[34]

In *The Captain Gregos*, Hirst J. decided that the scope of the Rules[35] was bracketed in time by the operations of loading and discharge. In the *Carpets* case, he took a similar view of "taking over" and "delivery" under Article 17.1 of the CMR. In each case, he decided that delivery, although to the wrong person, marked the end of the carrier's period of responsibility and control. But in the Court of Appeal in *The Captain Gregos*, Bingham L.J. objected,[36] that a "bailee does not properly and carefully carry, keep and care for goods if, whether negligently or intentionally, he fails to discharge them and so converts them to his own use". What is true of the carrier by sea is no less true of the carrier by road: he too has a duty to care for the goods.[37] It would be odd, surely, if the carrier could dump the goods on the road, dumping the CMR at the same time, and retreat behind standard terms of contract.[38] It would also be contrary to the clear implications of the first sentence of Article 16.2,[39] whereby carriage does not end unless and until there is delivery in accordance with the contract of

---

[31] Below, para. 74.

[32] December 6, 1983, unreported.

[33] *Cie Portorafti Commerciale SA v. Ultramar Panama Inc.* [1989] 2 All E.R. 54; [1989] L.M.C.L.Q. 394.

[34] [1990] 1 Lloyd's Rep. 310; [1990] L.M.C.L.Q. 314.

[35] Under the Rules, Art. II, the "responsibilities and liabilities" of the carrier are applied "in relation to the loading . . . and discharge" of goods. By contrast, for the application of Art. 17 the loss or damage must occur between taking over and delivery.

[36] At 315.

[37] The duty has been implied: below, para. 79.

[38] In this sense *Cambrai 12.9.78*, B.T. 1978.445. See also *OGH 27.8.81*, Greiter 97, in which the load was left but not immediately abandoned in the desert of Yemen: the issue of liability for loss of the goods and for the cost of a (negative) salvage report was governed by the CMR.

[39] That provision authorises the carrier, in cases in which delivery in accordance with the contract has been prevented, to unload the goods for account of the person entitled to dispose of them, and continues that "there-upon the carriage shall be deemed to be at end". On this provision, see above, para. 33c(*ii*) and 37d.

carriage.[40] It is submitted, therefore, that delivery does not occur and liability under Article 17 does not end until the goods are handed over to the right person; that delivery to the wrong person is not delivery at all, and the consequences are governed by Article 17 of the CMR.[41]

A further problem is whether, for the application of Article 17.1, all the loss or damage must "occur" between the time of taking over and the time of delivery, or whether, if some loss or damage, such as decay in perishable goods, occurs before delivery but continues to develop thereafter, the full and final amount of damage of that kind may be the subject of a CMR claim. The analogy of insurance cover[42] suggests an affirmative answer and, although CMR decisions differ[43] it is submitted that this is indeed the answer under the CMR.

> In *B.G.H. 27.10.78*[44] two consignments of dwarf beans sent on the same vehicle to different consignee/buyers were mixed up and some were delivered to the wrong buyer. The buyer who received the wrong beans stopped doing business with the claimant/sender, who claimed compensation from the carrier for loss of business. Noting that the cause of action was not the loss of the goods but the delivery of the wrong goods, and that the claimant's loss was not a consequence of loss, damage or delay governed by Article 17, the court applied not the CMR but German law relating to *positive Vertragsverletzung*.[45] The implication, however, is that, if loss, damage or delay occurs before delivery, its consequences may be the subject of a CMR claim, although they were not felt until after delivery.

In summary, Article 17.1 applies if, between the time of taking over and delivery, the period of control, the goods suffer any partial loss (below, paragraph 55), total loss (below, paragraph 56), or damage (below, paragraph 57). Article 17.1 also applies if there is any delay in delivery (below, paragraph 58).

---

[40] Thus in *O.L.G. Düsseldorf 23.11.89*, TranspR 1990.63, goods were mislaid by the carrier and found a year later. As they had not been delivered, the carrier's liability for deterioration in their condition was governed by the CMR.

[41] Even on the narrow construction of Art. 17.1, in the *Carpets* case (above, n. 32), the "delivery" does not occur until the act of delivery is complete, and it is not complete until the goods are in the hands of the (wrong) person; or placed at that person's disposition: see also above, para. 37. By this time the claimant, the rightful consignee, has suffered (at least some) loss: economic loss or, as seems to be the sense of Art. 17.1, loss of the goods themselves. On the meaning of loss, see below para. 56.

[42] Clarke, *Insurance*, para. 18–1B.

[43] In *OGH 27.8.81*, Greiter 97, the Art. 23 limit was applied not only to loss of goods prior to delivery, but also to the subsequent cost of assessing whether salvage was possible. But *cf. O.L.G. Hamm 11.3.76*, N.J.W. 1976.2077, above para. 33d(*i*), where the whole issue is discussed at greater length.

[44] N.J.W. 1979.2473.

[45] At 2474. However on the question of limitation the court applied Art. 32 of the CMR, as this provision was not limited in its application to loss, etc. before delivery, but applied to actions arising out of CMR carriage: see above, para. 43a.

55. Partial loss

The CMR draws a distinction between partial loss and total loss. The distinction affects both the commencement of the limitation period[46] and the amount of compensation recoverable by the claimant from the carrier.[47]

There is partial loss when goods taken over by the carrier are delivered to the agreed destination in a quantity, weight or volume less than that taken over.[48] The loss is partial because it is less than total.[49] A loss is partial or total not by reference to the quantity to be carried under the load on the vehicle but to the relevant contract of carriage and, if one has been issued, the consignment note that records it; hence, in the case of groupage there may be total loss of part of the load, if that part is the sole subject of a contract of carriage.[50]

The CMR also draws a distinction between partial loss and damage. This distinction does not affect the commencement of the limitation period but does affect the amount of compensation recoverable by the claimant from the carrier. Whereas partial loss concerns the weight, quantity or volume of goods, damage concerns the state or condition of goods.[51] The distinction is difficult to draw, if a deterioration in quality, prima facie an instance of damage, gives rise to a loss in weight or volume.[52]

56. Total loss

There is total loss when none of the goods, which have been taken over by the carrier in performance of a contract of carriage, have been delivered. In cases of total loss, the location of the goods is often unknown, however, this is not an essential feature of total loss under the CMR. For example, if the carrier can provide a map reference for the location of the goods—at the bottom of a ravine, there may still be total loss. The same may be true if the goods have been confiscated.[53] Nor is it essential that the goods have been destroyed or even damaged: there may be total loss if the

---

[46] Art. 32.1: above, para. 44.

[47] Arts. 23 *et seq.*: below, paras. 95 *et seq.*

[48] Rodière, para. 502; B.T. 1972.240.

[49] Below, para. 56.

[50] *Brussels 16.11.77* (1980) 15 E.T.L. 319. Herber/Piper, Art. 17, 4; *cf.* Thume, Art. 17, 72.

[51] Below, para. 57.

[52] Haak, p. 200. In particular, it may be difficult to distinguish a case of dessication within Art. 17.4(d): *Supreme Court Hungary 32 989/1974*, 1976 U.L.R. II 391.

[53] Thume, Art. 17, 67.

goods have been mislaid,[54] stolen, or delivered to the wrong person:

In *B.G.H. 27.10.78*[55] beans were delivered to the wrong person. Rejecting the view of the court below, that the goods had not been lost, the court stated that, whereas the location and possible recovery of the goods might affect the amount of compensation, it did not prevent the case being one of loss.[56] Although the court referred to Article 20.1,[57] whereby delay may be treated as total loss, it did so not as the sole basis of its decision, but to clarify the meaning of loss in a case which, even without Article 20.1, would have been seen as one of loss. Equally, as in *B.G.H. 18.5.95*,[58] goods which the carrier wrongfully sold by auction were goods that had been delivered to the wrong person and were lost. In contrast, goods, which it was no longer possible or appropriate to deliver to the consignee and which were brought back to the sender, were goods which, in the circumstances, had been handed over to the right person and were not goods that had been lost: *O.L.G. Düsseldorf 16.6.92*.[59]

From cases like that, the step is small to a notion of loss rather like that of frustration of contract[60] at common law: there is total loss if the goods are simply not available to the consignee as contemplated by the contract of carriage:

In *B.G.H. 3.7.74*[61] 1,000 cartons of deep frozen fish were brought from Cuxhaven to Boulogne but import permission was refused by the French inspector because about 5 per cent of the cartons had begun to defrost. It was suspected, but not established, that as a result of the insufficient refrigeration the entire consignment was

[54] Rodière, para. 501. This kind of loss has been discussed in insurance cases. In *Holmes v. Payne* [1930] 2 K.B. 301, 310 Roche J. said: "Uncertainty as to recovery of the thing insured is, in my opinion, in non-marine matters the main consideration on the question of loss. In this connection it is, of course, true that a thing may be mislaid and yet not lost, but, in my opinion, if a thing has been mislaid and is missing or has disappeared and a reasonable time has elapsed to allow of diligent search and of recovery and such diligent search has been made and has been fruitless, then the thing may properly be said to be lost." In *Webster v. GAFLAC* [1953] 1 Q.B. 520, 532 Parker J. said: "The test is whether, after all reasonable steps to recover a chattel have been taken by the assured, recovery is uncertain."

However, if the goods are later found, the CMR claimant may be entitled to treat the case as one of delay: *O.L.G. Düsseldorf 23.11.89*, TranspR 1990.63.

[55] N.J.W. 1979.2473 (also discussed above, para. 54b). Also in this sense *B.G.H. 13.7.79*, VersR 1979. 1154. Herber, Art. 17, 3; Muth/Glöckner, p. 133; Thume, Art. 17, 68. *idem* at common law: in *Skipworth v. G.W. Ry Co.* (1888) 59 L.T. 520, 522 delivery to the wrong person by a worker in a railway cloakroom was held to be "loss within the meaning of an exemption clause". See also *Hearn v. L.S.W. Ry Co.* (1855) 10 Ex. 801.

[56] *cf. O.L.G. Frankfurt 30.3.77*, VersR 1978.169 in which the court held that delivery to the wrong person could amount to loss, if they could not be recovered.

[57] Below, para. 56b.

[58] TranspR 1995.383.

[59] TranspR 1993.17.

[60] See Treitel, pp. 784 *et seq.*

[61] 1974, U.L.R. II 216.

unfit for human consumption. In these circumstances, the load could not remain in Boulogne and was sent back to Cuxhaven via Rotterdam where, after examination, it was deep frozen again, and sold to another buyer for the price originally agreed with the buyer in Boulogne. To assess the amount of compensation, the lower courts treated the case as one of partial loss, but on appeal the B.G.H. held that it was a case of total loss. The court accepted the contention of the sender that it was for the entire consignment that import permission was refused and that it was the entire consignment that was sent back. The B.G.H. inferred from Article 25.2 of the CMR that damage to part might deprive an entire load of any value[62] and this was what had happened. Moreover, to the sender with a customer in Boulogne the load was completely useless.[63] So the claimant recovered under Article 23.4 freight for the journey to Boulogne and back, the cost of warehousing and deep freezing on the return of the fish and the fees of experts who examined it—all on the basis of total loss.

56a. Damage amounting to total loss

As to the meaning of total loss, The English judge brings his experience of the Marine Insurance Act 1906, in which total loss is of two kinds, actual total loss and constructive total loss (CTL).

As regards CTL, there is CTL under the 1906 Act when the thing "is reasonably abandoned on account of its actual total loss appearing to be unavoidable, or because it could not be preserved from actual total loss", notably by repairing the thing and forwarding it to destination, "without an expenditure which would exceed its value when the expenditure has been incurred".[64] But, in *ICI Fibres v. MAT Transport*[65] Staughton J. decided that the common law concept of CTL does not apply to the CMR.[66] Indeed, there is scant sign that the notion of CTL, as such, has

[62] At 218.

[63] At 220. But *cf*. Putzeys, para. 693: if the goods are returned to the sender, whatever the cause, there is no total loss.

[64] s.60. Arnould, *Marine Insurance* (16th ed., London, 1981), para. 1169.

[65] [1987] 1 Lloyd's Rep. 354, 358. With respect, this seems right. First, provisions such as Art. 25 suggests that "damage" and "total loss" are mutually exclusive ideas covering the entire field of harm so that there is no gap to be filled by national rules of law: Hardingham, "Aspects of the Limitation of Actions under CMR", [1979] L.M.C.L.Q. 362, 363. Secondly, a concept as complicated as CTL cannot reasonably be implied into the CMR on the ground of "interpreting" the idea of "total loss", and, as Staughton J. observed (pp. 358–359), it cannot be assumed that the authors of the CMR had this concept in mind.

[66] Also in this sense: Demuth, TranspR 1996.257; Glass and Cashmore, para. 3.65; Putzeys, para. 690.

been applied to insurance other than marine insurance,[67] still less of application in other areas of law.

As regards actual total loss, in the same case, Staughton J. turned to the 1906 Act, in which section 57(1) provides that, where (a) the thing is destroyed, or (b) the thing is so damaged as to cease to be a thing of the kind insured, or (c) the insured is irretrievably deprived thereof, there is an actual total loss. In his judgment total loss in the CMR includes (a) and (c) but, a point that he did not have to decide, it is "very arguable" that it does not include (b). The argument against (b) has succeeded in other cases:

> In *William Tatton & Co. v. Ferrymasters*[68] a textile machine worth £32,700 was being carried from England to Italy, when the trailer on which it stood overturned and the machine was seriously damaged; it was subsequently worth only £9,000 as a source of spare parts. Browne J. stated[69] that counsel "for the plaintiffs, says that these goods were damaged to such an extent that they really had only scrap value left, and accordingly there was what he calls a constructive total loss. It seems to me that in the ordinary sense in which the words 'loss' and 'damage' are used in connection with the carriage of goods, this was plainly a case of damage, it is true very serious damage, and not of loss." Subsequently, in *Worldwide Carriers v. Ardtran International*,[70] in which steelcord being sent from France to England was so damaged that it had only scrap value, this statement was adopted by Parker J.

Compare cases cited by Seltmann.[71] The first is that of fruit, only part of which has been spoiled, but of which the rest cannot be extracted from the refrigerated vehicle without being "infected" and spoiled, too. The second is that of the chess set, two pieces of which are missing. These are cases of total loss.

Finally, it has been argued that, if there is delivery of the receptacle in which the goods were contained when taken over, but empty of its contents, the goods have not been totally lost.[72] The

---

[67] Clarke, *Insurance*, para. 16–2A2.

[68] [1974] 1 Lloyd's Rep. 203.

[69] *ibid.*, 205–206. Also in this sense: Haak, p. 200; and Putzeys, para. 692, by reference to unpublished decisions in Belgium: goods which have lost all economic value are nonetheless not a total loss. *cf. Paris 18.9.91*, B.T.L. 1991.655; Pesce, p. 196.

[70] [1983] 1 Lloyd's Rep. 61, 64. *cf. Thermo Engineers v. Ferrymasters* [1981] 1 Lloyd's Rep. 200, 206, in which, having held that the CMR did not apply, Neill J. said that, if he were wrong about that, the plaintiff should recover in full in respect of a machine having only scrap value. He said this without reference to Art. 25.1 (which concerns damage as opposed to loss) or to the *William Tatton* case (above, n. 68). In *ICI Fibres v. MAT Transport* [1987] 1 Lloyd's Rep. 354, 359 Staughton J. expressed a preference for the view taken by Browne J. and Parker J.

[71] Thume, Art. 17, 72. Also in this sense: Herber/Piper, Art. 17, 7.

[72] Putzeys, para. 690; Rodière, para. 501.

force of this argument depends on whether the container is itself part of the consignment of goods.[73]

56b. Delay amounting to total loss: Article 20.1

Article 20.1 provides that goods may be treated as lost when they "have not been delivered within thirty days following the expiry of the agreed time-limit, or if there is no agreed time-limit, within sixty days from the time when the carrier took over the goods".[74]

The importance of this provision is that, if delay is treated as total loss, the ceiling on recoverable loss is not the amount of the carriage charges[75] but the value of the goods[76] and, further, that there is a different commencement date for the period of limitation.[77]

The main objective of Article 20.1 is certainty,[78] to meet the need of parties in commerce to "know where they stand", while admitting that "better late than never" is a platitude of the pub and not the production line. The point is poignant in cases in which goods have been damaged en route and consequently returned to the sender. By reason of Article 20,[79] this is a case of total loss for the commencement date under Article 32.1(b). From a practical and commercial point of view, goods awaiting repair by the sender or goods delivered to the wrong person[80] may be as lost to the consignee as goods at the bottom of the North Sea, and to treat the goods as lost under Article 20.1 for the purpose of liability and compensation seems right. Less obviously, perhaps, the same may be true for the sender: although the goods have been sent back to the sender, as regards the movement of the goods to a particular consignee the goods (and the underlying transaction) may have been totally lost.[81]

If there is delay to the degree set by Article 20.1, but eventually the goods arrive at destination, whereas certainty suggests that it is total loss nonetheless,[82] flexibility and, perhaps, equity might suggest that the situation reverts to one of delay: that the purpose

---

[73] Above, para. 11.

[74] In modern conditions 60 days from the time of taking over is thought to be a short period, for example, for a trip to the Middle East. Parties would be well advised to agree a (longer) limit: Donald, paras. 238 *et seq.*

[75] Art. 23.5: below, para. 97c.

[76] Art. 23.1: below, para. 94.

[77] Art. 32.1: above, para. 44.

[78] *O.L.G. Düsseldorf 23.11.89*, TranspR 1990.63, 66. Hardingham, "The Delay Provisions of CMR", [1979] L.M.C.L.Q. 193, 194; Helm, Art. 20 Anm. 1.

[79] This conclusion has been criticised: see above, para. 44a.

[80] *B.G.H. 27.10.78*, N.J.W. 1979.2473, above para. 56.

[81] See *B.G.H. 3.7.74*, above, para. 56, in which the goods were held to be lost, but without reference to Art. 20.1.

[82] Helm, Art. 20 Anm. 1.

of Article 20.1 is to fix a rule when it is unknown whether the goods will arrive, that the presumption of total loss is not irrebuttable,[83] and that therefore on arrival of the goods, however late, the case reverts to one of delay rather than total loss.[84] However, if, as the law may require,[85] the consignee has sought to mitigate loss by obtaining alternative goods, the consignee should not be compelled to take the original goods which are late and, perhaps, of no use: this is the clear implication of Article 20.2–4, whereby the consignee obtains late goods only if they are still wanted.[86] The certainty sought by the draftsman in Article 20.1 is mainly certainty for the consignee and, it seems, once the case is one of total loss under Article 20.1, that does not change. This the view taken by most of the commentators.[87]

57. Damage

Damage concerns the state or condition of the goods, and must be distinguished from partial loss,[88] which affects the quantity, weight or volume of goods, and perhaps also from damage so great that the goods have in effect been destroyed and thus totally lost.[89] In the CMR, however, "damage" is not defined. In the French version, damage is generally "avarie",[90] and the ordinary meaning of that word is "physical harm, or injury to an object".[91] However, the precise meaning depends on the context in which the word is used. In Article 17.1 of the CMR, damage means any change in the physical state of the goods which reduces their value.

---

[83] In this sense *O.L.G. Frankfurt 20.1.81*, VersR 1981.1131, as reported by Haak, p. 202, who also supports that view, as does Pesce, p. 197. *Contra*: Helm, Art. 20 Anm 1; Herber/Piper, Art. 20, 3; Hill and Messent, p. 164; Koller, Art. 20, 1; Thume, Art. 20, 4.

[84] Loewe, para. 177.

[85] Below, para. 59a.

[86] Below, para. 94b.

[87] See above, n. 83.

[88] Above, para. 55. "No doubt in an English context loss is one thing, damage another"—*Fothergill v. Monarch Airlines Ltd* [1981] A.C. 251, 273, *per* Lord Wilberforce; *idem*, 290, *per* Lord Scarman and 301, *per* Lord Roskill. In the context of the Warsaw Convention it was held in that case that "damage" included loss of some of the contents of a case. However, the text of the Warsaw Convention does not distinguish damage from both total loss and partial loss, as does the CMR in Article 17; and whereas in the former "damage" is translated variously as "avarie" and "dommage", in the CMR it is translated as "avarie", except in the special case of "damage" from delay ("*préjudice*": Art. 23.5). Although Art. 30 CMR, a provision of the kind in issue in *Fothergill*, refers only to "loss or damage", the entire context, including Art. 17, suggests that in the CMR "loss" embraces both total and partial loss, so that in the CMR "damage" has a narrower meaning than in the Warsaw Convention.

[89] In so far as this amounts to constructive total loss, this is doubtful: see above, para. 56a.

[90] See above, n. 88.

[91] *Fothergill*, above, n. 88 at 290, *per* Lord Scarman. No doubt he had followed the advice of his brethren in that case and looked at the dictionary.

It even includes wear and tear, although at the end of the day in court this is a kind of damage for which the carrier may be exonerated.[92] It also includes damage which results from delay.[93]

In *O.L.G. Celle 13.1.75*[94] deep frozen beans were sent from Italy by refrigerated transport to a place in Germany, where it was found that a partial thaw had occurred. Although perfectly edible, the beans could no longer be retailed in the way originally intended, that is, divided into small frozen packets for purchase by consumers. The O.L.G. had to decide on the appropriate date for the commencement of the limitation period, which, according to Article 32, depends on whether it is a case of damage, of total loss or of something else.[95] The court noted[96] that damage is not defined in the CMR, except that certain types of damage are enumerated in Article 17.4(d)[97]; also that expert evidence showed that the fitness of the beans for consumption had not been prejudiced, and that no objection could be taken to either their bacteriological state or to their taste or smell. Nonetheless, the court held that the goods had suffered damage: since the beans could now be sold only in a more limited market, they were less valuable than on consignment and thus were damaged.

The principle, said the court in that case,[98] is that "damage is characterised by external or internal physical deterioration, which results in diminution of value".[99] Diminution of the value of goods without physical deterioration, however, is not damage; were it otherwise it would be too difficult to distinguish damage from loss of market, for which the carrier is not liable under the CMR.[1] So, in the case of damage to goods, the carrier is liable for the amount by which the goods have diminished in value,[2] and it is this

---

[92] In the case of sensitive goods: below, para. 89.
[93] Below, para. 59b.
[94] (1975) 10 E.T.L. 410. Also in this sense: *O.L.G. Hamburg 30.8.89*, VersR 1989.1214.
[95] See above, para. 44.
[96] At 415.
[97] See below, para. 89.
[98] At 415. *idem* in Denmark: *Erik v. Borge Landhoff Ufr* 1971.183, as reported by Sevon 1971 U.L.C. 291, 303 (discoloured turkeys, edible, but not saleable at the full price). Austria: *OGH 31.3.82*, TranspR 1984.196, Greiter 137, 141; *O.L.G. Vienna 23.2.89*, TranspR 1990.156. Herber/Piper, Art. 17, 5; Pesce p. 197; Thume, Art. 17, 73 *et seq. cf.* Koller, Art. 17, 2, who assumes that the meaning of damage, like that of loss, is to be sought in national law. However, others, too (*e.g.* Herber/Piper, *loc.cit.*), agree.
[99] Thume, TranspR 1992.1.
[1] See below, para. 94. See also De la Motte, VersR. 1988.317. If, however, something has been contaminated but can be decontaminated, it is damaged even though, in the end, the only loss to the owner is the cost of decontamination: *The Orjula* [1995] 2 Lloyd's Rep. 395. Also in this sense: Herber/Piper, Art. 17, 6; Thume, Art. 17, 78.
[2] Art. 25.1, discussed below, para. 94a.

diminution which in turn characterises damage. However, compensation for damage may include not only the actual diminution in value but also, it has been said,[3] any expense necessarily incurred to mitigate the diminution in value which the goods would have suffered, if that expense had not been incurred.

58. Delay not amounting to total loss: Article 19

Article 17.1 says that the carrier is liable not simply for delay but for "any delay in delivery". Distinguish therefore, first, the case of the carrier who fails to take over the goods at all[4]; and, secondly, the carrier who delays take over but, having once taken the goods over, catches up on lost time, so that the "actual duration of carriage", mentioned by Article 19, does not exceed "the time it would be reasonable to allow a diligent carrier".[5] Although these two cases may give rise to the liability of the carrier under rules of national law,[6] they are not cases of "delay" in the sense of Article 17.1 of the CMR.

Cases of delay under the CMR are, first, delay in delivery treated as total loss, and governed by Article 20,[7] as well as two further cases of delay governed by Article 19: delivery later than the time agreed and delivery after a reasonable time for delivery has elapsed.

58a. The agreed time-limit

By Article 19, delay arises when "the goods have not been delivered within the agreed time-limit". It has been held that the agreed time-limit can be proved by any appropriate means and does not have to be stated in the consignment note[8]; it may be found, for example, in the carrier's advertising.[9] If a note has been issued,

---

[3] *O.L.G. Vienna 23.2.89*, TranspR 1990.156.

[4] *Milan 11.7.75*, 1977 1 U.L.R. 336. This conclusion can be inferred from Art. 19 and the reference, in the absence of an agreed time-limit, to the "actual duration of the carriage".

[5] *cf. O.L.G. Hamm 14.11.85*, below, para. 58a.

[6] See below, para. 65.

[7] Above, para. 56b.

[8] *O.L.G. Hamm 14.11.85*, TranspR 1986.77; *O.L.G. Köln 7.12.93*, TranspR 1994.197. Also in this sense decisions reported by Haak, p. 201; Herber/Piper, Art. 19, 4; Koller, Art. 19, 4; Putzeys, para. 72; Thume, Art. 19, 11, noting also some decisions to the contrary.

[9] *Paris 25.3.94*, B.T.L. 1994.389: an "express" consignment of fashion wear, which took several weeks, was treated as such.

omission of the limit from the note is no more than an "irregularity" in the note, which does not affect "the existence or validity of the contract of carriage",[9a] nor by implication the existence or validity of the limit. This is likely to be the view taken in England, where it is not essential that contractual terms be recorded in the consignment note.[10]

There is an agreed time-limit when, by a certain date or within a certain time of taking over the goods, a carrier is required by the contract of carriage to deliver those goods.[11] This is the clear inference of Article 19 and Article 20. A German court has stated[12] that under Article 17.1, just as the carrier might be liable for lateness in delivery, the carrier might also be liable for failure to meet a date for loading. However, it seems that that is correct, if at all, if the date for loading was stipulated with a view to the time of delivery; and then only for the purpose of identifying "delay" in Article 19. If the same ruling were applied to Article 20, the effect would be that Article 20.1, a provision generally regarded as favourable to the claimant, would become yet more so, as the date of the presumption of total loss would be brought forward; such a decision would be doubtful.[13] Easier to support is the decision in *Aix 20.12.77*,[14] which did not concern Article 20 and in which the contract stipulated that a consignment of potatoes from Mauguio to London should reach Dieppe in time to catch a ferry of specified time and date, and this was treated as an agreed time-limit.

The usual case is that of goods delivered too late. Recent trends to just-in-time delivery (JIT) of, for example, goods of which the consignee wishes to limit stocks and thus storage and handling costs, raise and question whether the carriage may be liable under the CMR for tendering delivery too soon. If the agreed time-limit is not simply by date "y" but between dates "x" and "y", "x" appears to be just as much a time-limit as "y". Accordingly, delivery too soon is not delivery "within the agreed time-limit", as required by Article 19.

If the carrier is outside the time-limit agreed, the carrier is liable, whether aware of the importance of punctuality or not[15]; and, it is submitted, even if there was never any serious possibility that the carrier would be able to deliver on time: the assumption of such a

---

[9a] Art. 4: above, para. 22.

[10] Below, para. 202. Also in this sense: Hardingham (above, n. 78).

[11] Clearly, "prompt" delivery or delivery "as soon as possible" are not of this kind: Thume, Art. 19, 12.

[12] *O.L.G. Hamm 14.11.85*, TranspR 1986.77, 79. The court was influenced by national law.

[13] Also in this sense: Hardingham (above, n. 78), p. 195; and Hill and Messent, p. 161.

[14] B.T. 1978.245, 1979 U.L.R. I 299.

[15] A defence, that the carrier had not been told that timeous delivery was important, was rejected in *Bordeaux 9.2.72*, B.T. 1972.114, 1974 U.L.R. I 341.

(strict) duty is, like the condition of the vehicle,[16] within the carrier's sphere of risk.[17]

The meaning of what has been agreed is a matter of construction of the contract, but this may be difficult if the parties have agreed not a date but a period, such as seven days.[18]

58b. A reasonable time

By Article 19, delay also arises when, in the absence of an agreed time-limit,[19] the actual duration of the carriage "exceeds the time it would be reasonable to allow a diligent carrier". A reasonable time is not defined, and the English court is likely to fall back on English common law.[20] The only guidance from the CMR is that the court is directed by Article 19 to have regard to "the circumstances of the case, and in particular, in the case of partial loads, the time required for making up a complete load in the normal way". In practice, a court will have regard to a number of other factors, including the nature of the goods,[21] the type of vehicle,[22] any instructions given to the carrier by the sender,[23] the permitted driving hours, and the road conditions. Essentially, the duty seems to be a duty to exercise reasonable endeavours to get the goods to destination promptly.[24]

For example, the court will take into account a ban on the movement of heavy goods vehicles in certain areas on Sundays, but the carrier must do all that can reasonably be done within the law to overcome obstacles of this kind.[25] In a case like that, the

---

[16] Below, para. 75f.

[17] *Semble* also in this general sense: Koller, Art. 19, 4; and Thume, RIW 1992. 966, 967 and Thume, Art. 19, 14. *cf.* the view (Thume, Art. 19, 14) that this issue is not governed by the CMR but by national law. If so, national law may treat the carrier's impossible promise as a nullity. This may be the result under German law: Mutz/Glockner, Art. 19, 9; and also under English law: see *The Fanti* [1987] 2 Lloyd's Rep. 299, 306 *per* Staughton J., citing Halsbury's *Laws of England* (4th ed., London, 1980), Vol. 25, para. 437.

[18] At common law in other contexts the tendency is to construe such periods literally, for example: *Adamson & Sons v. Liverpool & London & Globe Insurance Co.* [1953] 2 Lloyd's Rep. 355 (insurance); and as regards lay-days, see Scrutton (20th ed.), pp. 302 *et seq. cf.* Putzeys, para. 704, who suggests an allowance for impediments.

[19] Above, para. 58a.

[20] Below, para. 225c.

[21] Evidently more speed is required in the case of perishable goods. Herber/Piper, Art. 19, 15. Concerning whether the carrier must employ two drivers to enable transit without periods of rest, and thus observe regulations on drivers' hours, see Thume, Art. 19, 18.

[22] Assuming that the type used is appropriate. On this see above, para. 30.

[23] Putzeys, para. 706.

[24] The German translation suggests to commentators that the duty is that of *ein vernünftiger, sorgfältiger Frachtfuhrer*: Herber/Piper, Art. 19, 14; Koller, Art. 19, 5; Thume, Art. 19, 15. They also conclude (*e.g.* Thume, Art. 19, 17), *inter alia* from the use of the present tense in Article 19, that what is reasonable is to be assessed *ex ante* on the basis of information available at the time that the contract is concluded: *sed quaere.*

[25] *Venice 31.10.74* (1975) 10 E.T.L. 242. Herber/Piper, Art. 19, 16.

court might hold that the carrier was not guilty of delay, because, considering the actual road conditions, the carrier had delivered the goods within a reasonable time. Alternatively, the court might find that the carrier was prima facie liable but exonerated on the ground that the delay was unavoidable, a defence under Article 17.2.[26] The correct analysis depends on how the question of delay arises in such a case. If the issue arises under Article 19, until the issue has been resolved against the carrier, *ex hypothesi*, there has been no breach of contract by the carrier: it is the claimant who seeks to establish the liability of the carrier for delay under Article 17.1, and it is the claimant who must prove that the goods have not been delivered within a reasonable time. If, however, the issue arises under Article 20, because the goods have not arrived 60 days after having been taken over, prima facie the carrier is liable under Article 17.1, and must plead that the delay was unavoidable under Article 17.2. Whether the issue arises under Article 19 or Article 20 is important, not only because of the different onus of proof, but also because the strict nature of the defence under Article 17.2 is such that the carrier may find it easier to mount a defence under Article 19 than under Article 20.[27]

59. The consequences of delay

In providing that the "carrier shall be liable for . . . any delay in delivery", Article 17.1 makes the carrier liable for the consequences of delay. The consequences may be "purely" economic, for example, loss of market, or economic in the less direct form of deterioration in or damage to the goods themselves.

59a. Economic loss

"In case of damage", compensation for "damage" is limited by Article 25.[28] In case of delay", compensation for "damage" is limited by Article 23.5.[29] The obvious meaning of "damage" is physical damage to the goods, damage of the kind referred to in Article 17.1.[30] However, if the "damage" in Article 23.5 were limited to physical damage to goods, Article 23.5 would be unnecessary in view of Article 25. Article 23.5, it appears, contemplates

---

[26] On the ground of "delay . . . through circumstances which the carrier could not avoid and the consequences of which he was uanble to prevent." On this defence, see below, para. 78.
[27] Hardingham (above, n. 78), p. 194.
[28] Below, para. 93.
[29] Below, para. 96.
[30] Above, para. 57.

a different kind of "damage", namely damage to the claimant's pocket: "purely" economic loss,[31] and nothing else.[32]

The equivalent word in Article 23.5 of the French text, *préjudice*, is treated in French law as synonymous with *dommage*.[33] *Dommage*, a better-known term which is used elsewhere in the CMR, normally includes both reliance loss and expectation loss,[34] including, therefore, loss of profit, and loss of market. Decisions to that effect can be found under the CIM[35] and under the Hague Rules,[36] as well as the CMR. Under the CMR damage has included a loss of market at the place of destination,[37] the sender's liability to his consignee for late delivery,[38] and even the costs associated with the cancellation of a theatrical performance.[39]

59b. Physical damage associated with delay

If damage in case of delay includes consequential economic loss, does it include consequential physical damage or deterioration in the goods as well? This appears to have been the intention of the authors of the CMR,[40] who considered that, whereas loss or damage was something the carrier could be expected to prevent, delay was often difficult to prevent and they provided therefore in Article 23.5 a lower limit on the compensation recoverable for delay than for loss or damage.[41] This suggests that, if delay leads to damage, the case should be one of delay, but this had not been the general view since 1956. That view has been that, if damage to

---

[31] Also in this sense: Haak, p. 229; Putzeys, para. 885*bis*.
[32] Below, para. 59b.
[33] Marty et Raynaud, *Droit Civil*, Vol. II, para. 375; Carbonnier, *Droit Civil*, Vol. IV, para. 71.
[34] French civil code, art. 1149.
[35] *B.G.H. 14.4.76* (1976) 11 E.T.L. 787.
[36] *G.H. Renton & Co. v. Palmyra Trading Corp. of Panama* [1975] A.C. 149; *Adamastos Shipping Co. v. Anglo-Saxon Petroleum Co.* [1959] A.C. 133 (concerning loss of commercial opportunity) where their Lordships approved the decision at first instance of Devlin J. who said ([1975] 1 Lloyd's Rep. 79, 87–88): "The Act is dealing with responsibilities and liabilities under contracts of carriage of goods by sea, and clearly such contractual liabilities are not limited to physical damage." Also *Marifortuna Nav. S.A. v. Government of Ceylon* [1970] 1 Lloyd's Rep. 247, 252, *per* Mocatta J. (concerning expenses resulting from delay), Tetley, p. 309.
[37] For example, *Paris 2.4.71*, B.T. 1971.155, 1971 U.L.C. 154; *Paris 29.10.80*, B.T. 1981.256, 1981 U.L.R. I 267; *OGH 31.3.82*, TranspR 1984.196, Greiter 137; and *O.L.G. Hamm 14.11.85*, TranspR 1986.77.
[38] For example, *Cass. 26.6.84*, B.T. 1984.610.
[39] As a result of delay in the carriage of theatrical properties: *Paris 18.10.73*, B.T. 1973.488, 1976 U.L.R. I 242.
[40] Nickel-Lanz, paras. 112 and 167, by reference to the legislative history. Also in this sense: Putzeys, para. 700.
[41] Nickel-Lanz, para. 111.

goods leads to delay, the case is one of damage[42] to be compensated under Article 25[43]; and that, if delay leads to damage, that is also a case of damage to be compensated under Article 25,[44] and not a case of delay for Article 23.5.

In *Cass. 5.12.89*[45] conifer saplings were delayed and during the delay the wind rose and the temperature fell with consequent damage to the goods, damage which would have been avoided, if the vehicle (and goods) had not been left standing outside the depot. It was held that this damage was not a case of damage "in case of delay" under Article 23.5 but of ordinary damage under Article 25.

In France it has been argued[46] that, if as a result of delay the claimant has suffered depreciation in the quality of the goods, the claim will be treated as a damage claim in respect of the damage, but if the claimant has also lost market (purely economic loss) there is also a (distinct) delay claim subject to Article 23.5. The two can be kept apart, in theory, because while the damage claim is based on the value of the goods at the place of taking over,[47] the delay claim is based on their market value at the place of delivery.

59c. Causation and remoteness

In general, the CMR rules out liability for consequential loss, except in certain cases.[48] One of the cases is delay and, as the damage may include loss of bargain[49] and as the carriage charges may be high, the question arises, whether a rule of remoteness of damage can be read in to Article 23.5. An English court could, it is submitted, imply a doctrine of remoteness or a requirement of

---

[42] *OGH 15.2.79*, SZ 52/19, 1979 U.L.R. II 229, 231, Greiter 76, 78, refusing a counterclaim in respect of loss of trading profits that would have been made if the machine carried had not been damaged. *idem* as regards consequential expense: *Vienna 23.2.89*, TranspR 1990.156.

[43] Below, para. 93.

[44] For an outline of doctrinal differences, see Haak, p. 229.

[45] B.T. 1990.310. Also in this sense *OGH 31.3.82*, TranspR 1984.196, Greiter 137, 141–142; *Aix 14.1.92*, B.T.L. 1992.809; *B.G.H. 15.10.92*, TranspR 1993.137. Glöckner, Theunis, p. 103; Helm, Art. 23 Anm. 9; Herber/Piper, Art. 23, 38; Hill and Messent, p. 142; Koller, Art. 23, 17; Putzeys, para. 885; Thume, Art. 23, 45 *et seq.*

cf. Aix 20.12.77, B.T. 1978.245, 1979 U.L.R. I 299: apples were sent from Mauguio (France) to London, the lorry broke down, the apples arrived late and had deteriorated. The court held that, as the only cause of the damage was delay, compensation should be governed by Art. 23.5 of the CMR.

[46] With reference to *Cass. 17.4.80*, B.T. 1980.284 on the CIM.

[47] Below, para. 94a.

[48] The other cases are set out below, para. 94.

[49] Above, para. 59a.

causation, if that is an essential question on which the CMR is silent.[50]

No requirement of causation is expressed in Article 17.1: the carrier is liable for loss, damage and delay "occurring between" the time of taking over and of delivery. The German view of Article 17.1 (*Gefährdungshaftung*) implies risk[51] rather than attribution and fault.[52] Moreover, to the English lawyer the language of Article 17.1 is in this respect reminiscent of insurance policies that speak of loss "occasioned by" a stated event or operation. The effect of such drafting is that, if there is a mere coincidence in time and space of the loss or damage claimed and the exonerating event, that changes the nature of the risk and is enough to excuse the insurer from the inconvenience of payment.[53] Likewise, it might be said of Article 17.1, that the coincidence of loss, damage or delay with carriage, when the carrier has control of the goods, is enough to place it in the carrier's sphere of risk, and to raise a presumption that the carrier must pay compensation, without imposing on the claimant the inconvenience of proving a link of causation between the carrier and the loss or damage in question.

In a sense this is true, for if loss or damage occurs during carriage or there is delay in delivery, a causal connection is presumed.[54] But, at the same time, a causal link is still required.[55] To defend an action, the carrier must defeat that very presumption. To establish a defence under Article 17.2 the carrier must prove that the loss, damage or delay was "caused" by something for which he was not responsible, such as inherent vice or unavoidable circumstances.[56] Alternatively, to establish a defence under Article 17.4 the carrier alleges loss or damage which "arises from" the special risks there set out. This, too, might be read as the language of risk rather than of causation,[57] but Article 17.4 must be read with Article 18.2, whereby responsibility ultimately depends on whether the loss, damage or delay was "attributable" to the special

---

[50] Loewe, para. 203. In other statutory contexts the word damage has been understood to be limited to direct and non-consequential loss: *R. v. Whiteman* (1854) 23 L.J.M.C. 120; *Vernon v. St James, Westminster* (1881) 50 L.J.Ch. 81.

[51] See above, para. 54.

[52] However, German law does require a causal connection of a kind. Loss, etc. must be caused "through the operation of carriage by road", *i.e.* that it was caused or contributed to by some aspect of the operation: Zweigert & Kötz, p. 347. *idem*: Thume, Art. 19, 27. Hence there is a causal requirement, albeit a tenuous one and one not with the carrier's fault but with his transport operation.

[53] For example, riot or civil commotion: *Cooper v. General Accident Fire & Life Assurance Co.* (1923) 128 L.T. 481, H.L. Clarke, *Insurance*, para. 25–9C1.

[54] Buyl, Theunis, p. 276.

[55] See also below, n. 61.

[56] See below, para. 69b.

[57] However, in English law "arising from" has been treated as more or less synonymous with "caused by": For example, *Lambert v. Lewis* [1981] 1 All E.R. 1185, 1191, *per* Lord Diplock, H.L., *Oei v. Foster* [1982] 2 Lloyd's Rep. 170, 175, *per* Glidewell J. *Aliter* in the context of Art. 17.4: see below, para. 76.

risk.[58] Finally, if the loss, damage or delay was partly caused by exonerating events, the carrier is liable only to the extent that those factors for which he is liable "have contributed to" the loss, damage or delay.[59]

If, as appears, some kind of causal connection is required for liability under Article 17, it must be conceded that the CMR does not indicate the rule of causation that applies, perhaps because the domestic concepts in contracting states are so different that a uniform rule would be hard to agree. In these circumstances, the courts will fall back on rules of national law,[60] both as regards the causal connection between the carrier's performance and the delay and between the delay and its consequences.[61]

In England, Article 17.1 is seen as part of a contractual framework of liability,[62] whereby to establish that a case falls within Article 17.1 is to establish a prima facie breach of the carrier's contractual obligation to deliver the goods in the same condition and quantity in which they were taken over. Moreover, the common law instinct is to require a causal connection between the breach of contract and the loss, in respect of which the claim is made, and, in particular, to bar recovery, if the loss claimed was one that the claimant should have mitigated.[63] Hence it appears that in cases of delay the CMR carrier will be liable for loss of market at destination, unless the carrier can prove that it was unavoidable (or excused on some other ground) and unless the claimant could have mitigated that loss by obtaining such goods in time elsewhere.

60. Proof of loss or damage: Article 30

To make a claim based in contract, the claimant must prove that the carrier has broken the contract of carriage. The claimant must

[58] Below, para. 78.

[59] On this provision see below, para. 72.

[60] For a survey see Honoré, *Encyclopedia of Comparative Law*, vol. XI, Chap. 7, paras. 44 *et seq.*

For example, the German courts apply to CMR cases the theory of the "adequate" cause: *B.G.H. 27.6.85* (1986) 21 E.T.L. 102, 108. On this theory, see Honoré (above), paras. 80 *et seq.* In France, the carrier is liable under art. 1151 c.civ. for damage which is *une suite immédiate et directe* of non-performance of the contract of carriage, and this would normally include loss of market at the place of delivery: Brunat B.T. 1982.202. On this theory, see Honoré (above), paras. 71 *et seq.*; and Marty et Raynaud (above, n. 33), para. 37.

[61] For example, in *Cass. 26.6.84.*, B.T. 1984.610 the Court of Cassation censured the court below because it had not established a causal connection between the carrier's *faute* (delay) and the loss (liability of the consignee) suffered by the claimant. *idem* in Germany: *B.G.H. 27.6.85* (1986) 21 E.T.L. 102; *B.G.H. 14.7.93*, TranspR 1993.426.

[62] Above, para. 54.

[63] Thus, for example, Hill and Messent, p. 168 argue that the claimant must mitigate his loss in accordance with the common law principles, which, arguably, are but an aspect of the rule of remoteness, or, at least, rules that are closely linked: see below, para. 246.

rebut a presumption under Article 30.1 that the carrier did not break the contract: that the goods were delivered by the carrier in the same quantity and condition in which they had been taken over,[64] even if there is no consignment note,[65] against which the presumption might be tested.[66] To rebut the presumption and to establish a claim for loss or damage, the claimant must prove that loss or damage occurred between the time of taking over and the time of delivery.[67] To do this, the claimant brings evidence of the quantity or condition of the goods at the time of delivery (below, paragraph 61), and contrasts it[68] with the quantity or condition at the time of take over (above, paragraph 25). Unless rebutted by the carrier, the inference, that any difference (loss or damage) occurred between the two points in time,[69] leads to the conclusion that the carrier is liable under Article 17.[70]

In Belgium, Putzeys,[71] writing under the heading "Présomption de faute à l'égard de l'état de la marchandise", put it neatly thus: "L'objet du déplacement, c'est la marchandise, confiée au transporteur dans un état déterminé, qui a été 'cliché' à la prise en charge par les indications portées sur la lettre de voiture, et qu'il s'est obligé à restituer dans le même état à la livraison . . . Si cet état lors de la livraison ne correspond plus à l'état lors de la prise en charge, il y a présomption de faute." In one case, for example, the claimant had to prove, first, that the tomatoes were wet on delivery and, secondly, that they were not wet when they were taken over. The second turned on the evidential force of the consignment note,[72] the first turned on compliance with Article 30.

In France, however, the course of a claim is different, because reservations are given an importance not found elsewhere. If loss or damage is established at the time of delivery, French courts have seen that alone as sufficient to make a case against the carrier, and without requiring evidence of the quantity or condition of the goods at the time that the goods were taken over. Moreover, the

---

[64] *TC Brussels 19.3.74* (1974) 9 E.T.L. 773, 775; *Brussels 19.10.72* (1974) 9 E.T.L. 608, 614.

[65] *Limoges 2.6.67*, B.T. 1967.273.

[66] In so far as Art. 30 benefits the carrier, it is a benefit which the carrier does not lose by wilful misconduct or equivalent default: Helm, Art. 30 Anm. 10. This penalty is found in Art. 32 for that provision alone, and in Art. 29 for "the provisions of this chapter", hence Arts. 17 to 29. By clear implication Art. 30 is unaffected.

[67] *B.G.H. 8.6.88* (1988) 23 E.T.L. 705.

[68] Rodière, para. 503.

[69] *City Vintages v. SCAC Transport International* (High Court, 1.12.87). Buyl, Theunis, p. 277.

[70] Above, para. 54.

[71] Paras. 658–659.

[72] Thus, if the packing is such that wetness, if present when the tomatoes were taken over, would have been apparent to the carrier, a lack of reservations in the note about wetness, means that it can be inferred that they were not wet at that time. Otherwise, the carrier is entitled to say that they might have been wet before they were taken over, and the claimant has yet to make a case under Art. 17.

loss or damage on delivery is established merely by making reservations. In *Cass. 15.6.86*[73] the court rejected the view of the court below, that in addition to sending reservations to "establish" the existence of the damage the consignee had to prove the *amount* of the damage: the reservations alone were enough to establish a claim against the carrier, and to require the carrier to set up a defence, or to prove that the loss or damage did not occur between taking over and delivery. If the consignee sends reservations in accordance with Article 30.1, the loss or damage "is deemed to have occurred during the transport".[74]

Although describing such decisions as anomalous, French commentators[75] justify them as a consequence of a difference in wording between Article 30 of the CMR and the corresponding provision of the CIM. Whatever the merits of that argument, in the past French courts have needed little encouragement to favour the consignee against the carrier. Just as the French courts, faced with a defect in a product, have been ready to assume that the producer knew or should have known of the defect, so also if goods arrive short or damaged, they have been willing to assume that the carrier knew or should have known the reason and, unless the carrier has included appropriate reservations in the transport document, the carrier is presumed responsible. However, to the English lawyer, as well as those in Belgium[76] and Holland,[77] it appears that, whatever the apparent differences between the CIM and the CMR, the same requirement—proof by the claimant that the loss or damage occurred after take over and before delivery —follows from Article 17.1 and the general onus of proof.

61. To rebut the presumption of conforming delivery: proof of loss or damage

To rebut the presumption,[78] that the goods have been delivered as required by the contract of carriage, the claimant must establish loss or damage to the goods at the time of delivery. If the claimant does nothing of the kind, but takes delivery of the goods without demur, Article 30.1 states that that is "prima facie evidence that he has received the goods in the condition described in the consignment note" or, in the absence of a consignment note, in the

---

[73] B.T. 1986.542.

[74] Nossovitch B.T. 1982.544, citing, *inter alia*, *Cass. 2.2.82*, B.T. 1982.152, (1983) 18 E.T.L. 47. See also *Paris 2.12.81*, B.T. 1982.73; *Cass. 15.2.82*, (1983) 18 E.T.L. 24; *Lyon 3.8.86*, B.T. 1987.256; and *Cass. 9.1.90*, B.T. 1990.492. But now *cf. Cass. 13.12.94*, (1995) 30 E.T.L. 541.

[75] Brunat B.T. 1982.146. This position appears to have the support of Loewe, Theunis, p. 146.

[76] Putzeys, para. 658 (quoted above).

[77] Haak, p. 194.

[78] See above, para. 60.

condition in which the goods were received, and therefore that no loss or damage has occurred between take over and delivery, for which the carrier can be held liable under Article 17. In particular, to rebut the presumption, Article 30.1 stipulates that the consignee (as claimant or on behalf of the claimant) must either check the goods with the carrier (and by implication, thus establish loss or damage) "or" must send the carrier reservations. The claimant is not required to do both. This appears from the text of Article 30.1 and has been confirmed in Belgium,[79] as well as in France.[80] However, we shall see that, in English eyes, reservations alone do not prove anything at all but that proof of loss or damage must be made, whether reservations have been sent or not. As proof, appropriate evidence may include checking the goods with the carrier but, whereas other evidence may be rebutted by the carrier, if the consignee checks the goods with the carrier no rebuttal is allowed; by Article 30.2, the result of the check is conclusive. Hence, the first question to ask in a particular case is whether, as Article 30.1 puts it, the "condition" of the goods has been "duly" checked by the consignee with the carrier.

61a. Checking the goods

Checking the goods in the presence of an impartial and unimpeachable witness is just one way of proving the existence of loss or damage,[81] but it is checking with the carrier, a legacy from the CIM assumption that railwaymen were disinterested parties, that is prescribed by Article 30.1 to rebut the presumption of delivery in conformity with the contract. Unlike the case of carriage by rail, however, at the end of the road journey the carrier must usually be represented by his driver[82] who, quite naturally, may be more interested in food and rest than in checking goods.[83] Nonetheless, Article 30.5 provides:

> "The carrier and the consignee shall give each other every reasonable facility for making the requisite investigations and checks."

A carrier who, for example, has been told that the meat is deteriorating, and that the consignee has appointed an expert to examine the meat with a view to its being sold promptly, cannot drag his

---

[79] *Liège 6.5.70* (1970) 5 E.T.L. 717, 722.

[80] Above, para. 60.

[81] In the idiom of the French courts, evidence is admitted *par tous les moyens* (*Cass. 15.5.84*, B.T. 1984.526) notably *une constatation contradictoire*. If loss or damage is disputed, the *constatation* is *judicaire*, if undisputed, it is *aimable*.

[82] The driver is considered to have authority to represent the carrier in this regard: Haak, p. 193; Rodière B.T. 1978.73.

[83] As, for example, in *Paris 23.3.79*, J.C.P. 1980.19372.

feet and then complain that he was not given a reasonable opportunity to have the meat examined by his own expert,[84] or that, in the absence of due checking, the consignee has failed to send a reservation.[85] However, although he also spoke of the "psychological and economical preponderance" of the consignee, the claims manager for one insurance company has stated that this rule, which "should be an expression of good faith from the general law of contracts, seems to be for many no more than a virtuous wish, and Article 30.5 remains a dead letter for lack of sanctions".[86] Perhaps the readiness of the French courts to find a prima facie case against the carrier on the basis of reservations alone[87] is intended to encourage the carrier to co-operate in checking the goods with the consignee.

If checking takes place, Article 30.1 indicates that it must occur at the time of delivery.[88] As the time that ends the carrier's liability under Article 17.1, the time of delivery is a point that must be minutely defined and respected. However, as the time not by which but *at* which checking must be done, the time is less a point in time than a period of time. Were it otherwise, the time of delivery (and thus the chance to do these things) would cease at the moment when, for example, the trailer is simply unhitched at the consignee's depot, and the consignee might have little or no opportunity to examine the goods. For the purpose of Article 30.1, a flexible view must be taken of the time of delivery, and this approach has collateral support in Article 30.4, whereby the date of delivery and the date of checking do not count in the time in which reservations must be sent. Nonetheless, the checking must occur soon after the point in time at which control has passed to the consignee, lest the carrier contend that the loss or damage occurred in between.[89]

If the goods are checked and any damage or discrepancy agreed, that check is conclusive of apparent[90] loss or damage against both carrier and consignee. This is the effect of Article 30.2:

> "When the condition of the goods has been duly checked by the consignee and the carrier, evidence contradicting the result of this checking shall only be admissible in the case of loss or damage which is not apparent . . . "

---

[84] *Antwerp 21.6.78* (1978) 13 E.T.L. 601.

[85] Helm, Art. 30 Anm. 9.

[86] Buyl, Theunis, p. 284. In England there is, of course, no general principle of good faith of the kind found, for example, in Germany. However, a similar result might be achieved in the present case by robust application of an implied term of the kind upheld in *Southern Foundries in Shirlaw* [1940] A.C. 701. See Clarke [1993] H.K.L.R. 318.

[87] Above, para. 60.

[88] Above, para. 37.

[89] For example, *O.L.G. Vienna 22.6.89*, TranspR 1990.158, in which, however, the carrier's contention failed.

[90] As to "apparent", see above para. 25a and below para. 61b. In the case of loss or damage which was not apparent in the check but is discovered later, the consignee is expected to send written reservations within seven days of delivery: see below, para. 61b.

If that check does not take place, the consignee must find other proof of the discrepancy by obtaining, for example, evidence from an official or recognised expert at the place of delivery.[91] If it is the carrier who wants evidence, it should be recalled that the IRU form of consignment note contains a space for the consignee's signature, acknowledging receipt of the goods as described in the note, and that, while a signed receipt is not essential to a successful defence, it reinforces the presumption[92] of delivery in conformity with the contract.[93]

61b. Reservations

To defeat the presumption[94] that the goods have been delivered in accordance with the contract of carriage, the consignee is required to check the goods with the carrier[95] or to send the carrier "reservations giving a general indication of the loss or damage". The English text of the CMR suggests that general reservations, such as "in poor condition", will suffice.[96] However, the French text, "réserves . . . indiquant la nature générale de la perte ou de l'avarie", suggests that something more informative is required.[97] If the consignee sends reservations which specify damage type A, they do not cover damage type B which, although apparent in the sense of Article 30.2,[98] the consignee did not initially observe and specify[99]: the consignee's interests are better served by generality. However, the carrier wants reservations which contain enough information for the preparation of a defence to any claim that might be made. The carrier's position was preferred in *O.L.G. Vienna 22.6.89*,[1] in which a stamp "taken over subject to reservation" was held insufficient, as it did not indicate the approximate

---

[91] *Toulouse 26.3.69* (1971) 4 E.T.L. 131, 136; *Brussels 17.6.71* (1971) 6 E.T.L. 825: in these cases such evidence was accepted to establish the carrier's breach of contract (and rebut the presumption that the carrier had performed the contract properly), even though neither the reservations nor the joint checking, suggested by Art. 30.1, had occurred. *cf. Brussels 19.10.72* (1974) 9 E.T.L. 608, 614.

[92] Above, para. 60.

[93] As no particular form is required for reservations under Art. 30.1, however, signature of the receipt by the consignee does not deprive oral reservations about damage of their effect: *Liège 6.5.70* (1970) 6 E.T.L. 716, 722. Moreover, it is not unknown for the consignee's signature to have been forged.

[94] Above, para. 60.

[95] Above, para. 61a.

[96] Glass and Cashmore, para. 3.69; Hill and Messent, p. 220. See also above, para. 45b(*i*), as regards claims, for which a "general intimation of intention to hold the carrier liable" is sufficient.

[97] *Antwerp 15.11.78* (1979) 14 E.T.L. 660; Loewe, Theunis, p. 146.

[98] See above at n. 90.

[99] Putzeys, para. 571. In England, see *Thorman v. NHIC* [1988] 1 Lloyd's Rep. 7, 11–12, C.A., *per* Sir John Donaldson M.R.

[1] TranspR 1990.158.

circumstances and nature of the damage.[2] In contrast, the French Court of Cassation has upheld a reservation "goods received in poor condition".[3] If the purpose of reservations is to alert the carrier to the necessity of investigation before the trail becomes cold or muddied, perhaps a general indication of that kind is sufficient.

The reservations must be sent. Information is sent when it is put into the post or other means of transmission, so as to be out of the power of the sender to withdraw it,[4] regardless of whether the information reaches the addressee. As for the person who sends reservations, it matters not whether it is the sender of the goods or the consignee.[5] They must be sent, however, to the carrier and not, for example, to the sender of the goods[6] or to the forwarding agent[7] or to the main carrier in respect of a claim against the sub-carrier.[8] The question has been posed whether the driver is authorised to receive such reservations as the carrier's agent. As the requirement of the CMR is not that the reservations be accepted as such or even that they be received, but that they be sent to the carrier,[9] giving reservations to the driver would be enough,[10] if the driver can be said to be an authorised channel of communication to his employer.

61b(*i*). The form of reservations

As regards apparent[11] loss or damage, the French text ("*adresser*") indicates that the reservations may be "sent", not only by letter or telex, but also by word of mouth.[12] This is confirmed as regards apparent loss or damage but denied as regards non-apparent loss or damage by Article 30.1 *in fine*, which requires in the latter case but not in the former, that "the reservations referred to shall be

---

[2] Adopting Helm, Art. 30 Anm. 3.1.(b). Also in this sense: Nickel-Lanz, para. 117; Putzeys, paras. 553–555; Rodière (1971) 6 E.T.L. 306, 322.

[3] *Cass. 29.4.75*, 1977 U.L.R. I 334. Also, "all the tomatoes wet and rotting" was a sufficient reservation in *Cass. 15.7.86*, B.T. 1986.542. But *cf. Douai 16.1.97*, TranspR 1997.103.

[4] *Re London and Northern Bank, ex p. Jones* [1900] 1 Ch. 220. A similar rule is found in Belgium: Putzeys, para. 549. The CMR does not define "sending".

[5] *Limoges 7.11.77*, B.T. 1977.537, 538.

[6] *Ghent 17.11.67* (1969) 4 E.T.L. 145.

[7] Loewe, Theunis, p. 148.

[8] Loewe, *loc. cit.*

[9] Putzeys, para. 552.

[10] Also in this sense: Herber/Piper, Art. 30, 11–12; Koller, Art. 30, 5; Thume, Art. 30, 18.

[11] As to "apparent," see above, para. 25a.

[12] Loewe, Theunis, p. 146; Putzeys, paras. 547 and 551. So held in *TC Verviers 18.5.68* (1968) 3 E.T.L. 1240 (oral notice to the driver and a telephone call to the carrier); *Liège 6.5.70* (1970) 5 E.T.L. 717, 721–722 (telephone to the carrier); *Antwerp 21.6.78* (1978) 13 E.T.L. 601 (telephone to the carrier, followed by letter confirming the call, to which no objection was raised by the carrier).

made in writing". Subject to this, no particular form or formula is required for reservations, as long as the import is clear.[13] For example, reservations may be scribbled on the copy of the consignment retained by the carrier,[14] although it is not essential that reserves be entered on the consignment note: any other written form will suffice.[15]

As regards "writing", required for reservations about non-apparent loss or damage, the CMR does not define it. In England,[16] therefore, the court will seek the meaning of "writing" in the Interpretation Act 1978, Schedule 1: "'Writing' includes typing, printing, lithography, photography, and other methods of representing or reproducing words in visible form." The essential features are visual display and some kind of note or record. A receiving instrument must have a memory store or a print-out facility.[17] In Belgium, writing has been held to include a telex message,[18] and hence will also include any electronic means of communication with print-out facilities, including telefax and electronic mail.

61b(*ii*). The time of reservations

The time for reservations depends on whether the loss or damage is apparent. Apparent loss or damage is not defined in the CMR, but there is case law on the loss or damage that may be apparent to the carrier when taking over the goods, which applies also to loss or damage at the time of delivery.[19] For example, the common case of missing, contents, the absence of which cannot be established without opening the parcel or packing, has been treated as a case of non-apparent loss.[20] Although generally what is apparent when the goods are taken over is the same as what is apparent on delivery, it is arguable that, as the consignee has a "right" to have the goods checked, apparent loss or damage includes that which

[13] *City Vintages v. SCAC Transport International* (High Court, Queen's Bench Division, December 1, 1987).

[14] *Cass. 29.4.75*, 1977 U.L.R. I 334.

[15] Reservations need not be entered on the consignment note: *Antwerp 21.6.78* (1978) 13 E.T.L. 601, 604; *Rennes 19.3.87*, B.T. 1988.89; but it will be enough to do so: *Cass. 29.4.75*, B.T. 1975.298, 1977 U.L.R. I 334.

[16] See above, para. 5.

[17] *cf.* the view of Loewe, para. 228, that it would be enough to give oral reservations immediately on delivery, because such notice is more onerous. This seems to be correct only if in such circumstances the loss or damage was apparent and oral reservations thus allowed by Art. 30.1.

[18] *Antwerp 30.5.79* (1979) 14 E.T.L. 924.

[19] See above, para. 25a.

[20] For example, *Lyon 22.4.88*, B.T. 1989.176. *cf.* Nossovitch, B.T. 1982.544.

would have been discovered, if the packaging had been opened. Consignees are unlikely to receive this suggestion with enthusiasm in view of the practical difficulties of insisting on checking at the time of delivery.[21]

In the case of apparent loss or damage, the consignee must act "not later than the time of delivery".[22] In the case of non-apparent loss or damage, the consignee must act "within seven days of delivery, Sundays and public holidays excepted".[23] In both cases, Article 30.4 provides that "the date of delivery, or the date of checking, or the date when the goods were placed at the disposal of the consignee shall not be included".

61b(*iii*). The absence of reservations

Failure to send reservations or to send them in time does not debar a claim.[24] Indeed, to the English lawyer the requirement of reservations has little importance at all.[25] By sending reservations the consignee has done no more than assert the liability of the carrier and rebut the "prima facie evidence that he has received the goods in the condition described in the consignment note".[26] Whether the consignee has sent reservations or not, the consignee still has to prove that there has been "total or partial loss of the goods [or] damage thereto occurring between the time when [the carrier] takes over the goods and the time of delivery", and, in particular, that the assertion contained in any reservations sent is true[27]: the consignee must prove by whatever means available the reality of loss or damage at the relevant time.[28]

---

[21] See above, para. 61a.

[22] For the meaning of delivery, see above, para. 37. For this purpose delivery does not occur until the entirety of the consignment has been handed over to the consignee: Putzeys, para. 564. For the meaning of the time of delivery, see above, para. 61a.

[23] This probably means days that are public holidays at the place of delivery: Loewe, para. 225.

[24] *O.L.G. Zweibrücken 23.9.66*, N.J.W. 1967.1717; *Cass. 19.6.68*. B.T. 1968.315; *Toulouse 26.3.69* (1971) 6 E.T.L. 131; *Cass. Belge 7.6.74* (1975) 10 E.T.L. 68, 1976 U.L.R. I 370; *Paris 26.10.82*, B.T. 1982.593; *Brussels 21.1.87* (1987) 22 E.T.L. 741; *Brussels 7.2.92* (1993) 28 E.T.L. 286. In this respect the CMR is unlike comparable regimes such as the CIM, KVO and, indeed, an earlier draft of Art. 30: Haak, p. 191; Helm, Art. 30 Anm. 1; Nickel-Lanz, paras. 116 *et seq. cf. Poitiers 20.1.82*, B.T. 1982.233.

[25] Hill and Messent, p. 218. Likewise, the Dutch lawyer: Haak, p. 192. But *cf.* Rodière, paras. 457 and 590. In the same sense as the text on the parallel provision of the Hague-Visby Rules, Article III.6 see Clarke, HR, pp. 133–134.

[26] Art. 30.1.

[27] This view was rejected in *Cass. 15.7.86*, B.T. 1986.542: the court below had required of the claimant not only proof of reservations but also proof of the existence and extent of the damage mentioned in the reservations. On appeal this decision was censured: it sufficed that the claimant had sent reservations. See above, para. 61.

[28] *Brussels 21.1.87* (1987) 22 E.T.L. 741.

62. Proof of delay

In a case of delay, the consignee must establish and contrast the date on which the goods should have been delivered,[29] and the date of actual delivery, if it has occurred, by whatever evidence is available.[30] In addition, a reservation is required by Article 30.3. If delay causes damage to the goods, the more general view[31] is that the case is not one of delay regulated by Article 30.3 but one of damage regulated by Article 30.1. In any event, the consignee should be warned that Article 30.3 says that:

> "No compensation shall be payable for delay in delivery unless a reservation has been sent in writing[32] to the carrier, within twenty-one days from the time that the goods were placed at the disposal of the consignee.

As in the case of damage or loss, there is excluded from this time period the date on which the goods were in fact placed at the consignee's disposal. However, in the case of delay, time runs through Sundays and public holidays; and the reservation does not have to contain a "general indication of loss or damage": this is because, even after 21 days, the nature of the loss or damage, for example suit by third parties, may still be unknown to the consignee.[33] Moreover, failure to send the reservation results in more than a presumption in favour of the carrier: it bars the recovery of compensation.[34] If the consignee is unaware of the name and address of the carrier, because, for example, there is no consignment note, it has been suggested[35] that this requirement will be relaxed; however, the text of Article 30.3 appears to be uncompromising and, faced with unambiguous notice periods, English courts tend to apply the words to the letter.[36]

63. The carrier's liability in connection with documents

Apart from loss, damage or delay to goods, the CMR states the liability of the carrier on two further grounds, which are more or less self-explanatory and which have given rise to little reported litigation.

Article 11.3 provides that:

---

[29] Above, para. 58.
[30] Any mode of proof will do: Libouton, para. 65.
[31] See above, para. 59b.
[32] The meaning of "writing" is discussed above, para. 61b.
[33] Helm, Art. 30 Anm. 7.
[34] *B.G.H. 14.11.91*, TranspR 1992.135; (1993) 28 E.T.L. 265; Nickel-Lanz, para. 120.
[35] Putzeys, para. 578.
[36] Clarke, *Insurance*, para. 26–2E.

> "The liability of the carrier for the consequences arising from the loss or incorrect use of the document specified in and accompanying the consignment note or deposited with the carrier shall be that of an agent provided that the compensation payable by the carrier shall not exceed that payable in the event of loss of goods."

The basis of the carrier's liability will thus be the English law of agency with its requirement that the agent exercise reasonable care. The principal will be the person for whom the carrier holds the documents, *i.e.* the person entitled to dispose of the goods at the relevant time.[37]

Article 12.7 provides that:

> "A carrier who has not carried out the instructions (of the sender or consignee with regard to the disposal of the goods) or who has carried them out without requiring the first copy of the consignment note to be produced, shall be liable to the person entitled to make a claim for any loss or damage caused thereby."

Again, the basis of liability referred to in this provision appears to lie in national law, the obvious though not the only such liability in English law being conversion.[38]

64. Common law and the CMR

No clear line can be drawn between liability at common law and liability under the CMR. The CMR applies to the international contract of carriage, as defined in Article 1. This contract contains a number of promises express or implied. The central liability regime of the CMR is found in Article 17,[39] and that regime is the corollary of some but not all of the promises contained in the contract. It is the corollary chiefly of the promise to carry the goods to the agreed destination on time and deliver them there in the same order and condition, in which they were taken over. So, the CMR regime is best seen as the central but not the sole component of liability under the contract of carriage, the binding force of which is ultimately derived from the contract in common law as national law.

The CMR regime is mainly concerned with liability for loss or damage, mostly loss or damage to the goods, sustained during carriage, as well as liability for delay. When the CMR alone regulates a question, common law is out of sight but even then, on some matters, the coverage of the CMR is so thin that it will take its colour from the substratum of common law beneath, especially

---

[37] Donald, para. 40.
[38] See below, para. 231.
[39] Above, para. 54.

on the meaning of certain words.[40] On some other matters, courts have found gaps[41] in the CMR regime and these matters are governed by the express or implied terms of the contract and by common law. Indeed, the CMR Convention was never intended by those who drafted it to contain "an exhaustive system of regulations for the transport contracts within its scope" and it was always "presumed that national laws and regulations are to apply whenever there are no relevant provisions in the Convention".[42]

In other CMR states, a line of that kind is also drawn but not always in the same place. Clear, but restrictive of the CMR, is the view taken in Germany that the CMR is limited to a (strict) duty of care (*Obhutschaftung*)[43] between taking over and delivery of the goods. Everything else is contractual and a matter for the substratum of national law governing breach of contract. This is *die positive Vertragshaftung*, a device developed in German law for breaches of contract falling outside specially regulated areas[44] such as the CMR, and applied also in CMR cases in Austria.[45]

Matters to which national law have been applied are as follows:

(a) The allocation of essential duties, such as the duty of loading (above, paragraph 28) and unloading (paragraph 36).
(b) The meaning of key words or phrases: "goods" (paragraph 11), "takes over" goods (paragraph 27), "delivery" of goods (paragraph 37), "apparent condition" of goods (paragraph 25a), "inherent vice" in goods (paragraph 72), a "reasonable time" for their delivery (paragraph 60b), "reservations" "in writing" (paragraph 61b), "payment" of C.O.D. charges (paragraph 38), "ordinary residence" and other connecting factors for the purpose of jurisdiction (paragraph 46b), and the "date on which legal proceedings were instituted" (paragraph 99).
(c) The meaning of key concepts: title to sue the carrier (paragraphs 40 *et seq.*), the appropriate vehicle (paragraph 30)

[40] See (b), below.
[41] On the identification of gaps in the CMR, see above, para. 5.
[42] W/TRANS/212, p. 2.
[43] For example, *Düsseldorf 26.10.78*, VersR 1979.405; B.G.H. 27.10.78, N.J.W. 1979.2473, 2474. Helm, Art. 17 Anm. 31; Schmid/Kehl. TranspR 1996.89. However, although liability may be based on national law, Art. 32 has been applied as the limitation period for that liability: *O.L.G. Hamburg 9.2.89*, TranspR 1990.191.
[44] *Leges speciales* or *Sonderfälle*: Helm, Art. 17 Anm. 31. Generally, see Horn, Kötz and Leser, *German Private and Commercial Law: An Introduction* (Oxford, 1982, trans. Weir). Chap. 6.
Even to the extent of a monograph devoted to the resulting gaps in the CMR: B. Lieser, *Die Ergänzung der CMR durch verein-heitliches deutsches Recht*, (Berlin, 1991). For such issues in other countries, see Haak and Swart, part I.
[45] *OGH 14.11.84*, Greiter 245, 248; *OGH 13.6.85* SZ 58/102, Stra GüV 1985/12 p. 10.

and route (paragraph 31) for the journey, causation in connection with consequential loss (paragraph 59c), the court within a state which has jurisdiction under the CMR (paragraph 46), and the law governing the interpretation of arbitration clauses (paragraph 47).

(d) Matters on which the CMR makes express reference to national law, such as extension of the limitation period (Article 32.3), the procedure for dealing with late but unclaimed goods (Article 20.4), and the notion of equivalent default (Article 29). In some cases the CMR indicates the applicable national law: law of the place (Article 20.4), *lex fori* (Article 29, Article 32.3).

(e) Undertakings stipulated by the CMR itself, for which resort is to national law on the question of remedies for breach of duty by the carrier, such as[46] the duty to ensure that the consignment note states that the carriage is subject to the CMR,[47] the duty to deal with the goods when the contract cannot be carried out,[48] or when delivery becomes impossible[49] and the duty to obey instructions about the disposal of goods.[50] Again, the carrier's liability for loss of or incorrect use of documents,[51] and the carrier's failure to collect cash on delivery[52] are matters to be taken, as far as possible,[53] outside the CMR.

(f) Liability for the expense, not being the loss of, damage or delay to goods covered by the CMR and Article 17, incurred in consequence of the breach of implied duties, including, notably, expense incurred by the carrier to prevent or minimise loss or damage resulting from inadequate loading or stowage by the sender (paragraph 87).

(g) Liability for loss of, damage or delay to goods at any stage while in the custody or control of the carrier, if the CMR does not have obligatory force but has been adopted voluntarily in part or in combination with terms proffered by the carrier, to the extent that the latter override the former and govern the question in issue.

(h) Loss of or damage to goods occurring outside the time/space frame of Article 17 (paragraph 54b), *i.e.* before the goods

[46] Some instances are listed in *OGH 14.11.84*, Greiter 245, 248.

[47] The duty is imposed by Art. 7.3; see above, para. 24.

[48] Art. 14: see above, para. 33a.

[49] Art. 15: see above, para. 33b.

[50] The duty is imposed by Art. 12, see above, paras. 32 *et seq*. Liability for breach of this duty is regulated partly by the CMR and partly by national law: see above, para. 33d.

[51] The duty is imposed by Art. 11.3; see above, para. 63.

[52] The duty is imposed by Art. 21; see above, para. 38.

[53] The latter duty is something of a hybrid, for it is affected by some provisions of the CMR, such as Art. 29: see above, para. 38b.

have been taken over (paragraph 65) or after delivery (paragraphs 33d(i) and 66, or caused before delivery but materialising after delivery (paragraph 54b). This includes loss or damage to goods as the result of the condition of the carrier's vehicle or trailer left with the sender for loading and hence occurring before the goods have been taken over by the carrier; and loss or damage occurring during a preloading stage in which the carrier has custody of the goods, if contrary to the submission above (paragraph 27), this phase is not governed by the CMR.

If the carrier arrives to take over the goods so late that the sender, perhaps having arranged substitute carriage, repudiates the contract of carriage and refuses to hand over the goods to the carrier, again, taking over has not occurred, and here too the rights and remedies of the parties *inter se* will be governed by national law.[54] However, although liability is based in national law, it has been held[55] that the period of limitation for an action to enforce that liability is the period set by Article 32.1 of the CMR.

What has been said about non-performance when the carrier fails to collect the goods at all can also be said about the case in which the carrier collects the goods but the wrong goods: consignment A instead of consignment B. Less easy is the case of collection of the right consignment when those goods turn out to be of the wrong quality.

> In *O.L.G. Munich 3.5.89*[56] the carrier promised the consignee, with whom the carriage was contracted, to check the temperature of the goods (plums) on take over, and if they were about five degrees celsius to cease loading and obtain instructions from the consignee. In breach of this promise the carrier loaded plums at a much higher temperature which on delivery were totally spoiled. For this the carrier was held liable, not under the CMR but under (German) national law.

On the basis that the plums were already spoiled and mouldy when taken over, the court concluded that the damage did not occur between take over and delivery and was therefore outside the scope of the CMR. This is doubtful. However, the court also took the view that the contract was a contract for the carriage of suitable goods received by the carrier were not the contract goods but unsuitable goods "rubbish". As the contract goods had not been taken over, the case was not subject to the CMR but a case of *die Vertragsverletzung* for (German) national law.

---

[54] See below, paras. 220 *et seq.*
[55] *O.L.G. Hamburg 9.2.89*, TranspR 1990.191.
[56] TranspR 1991.61.

Finally, fundamentals of the law of contract: the courts apply national law,[57] to the conclusion of the contract of carriage (paragraph 202), and attendant matters such as rescission for misrepresentation (paragraph 241) or duress (paragraph 242) as well as non-enforceability on grounds of the public policy of the *lex fori* (paragraph 243).

65. Non-performance

The liability of the carrier under Article 17 of the CMR arises only in respect of loss or damage to the goods after the carrier has taken them over.[58] If the carrier takes the goods over late, the carrier takes them over nonetheless, and a consequent claim may be governed by the CMR.[59] But if the carrier fails to collect the goods at all, the goods have not been taken over and the carrier is liable not under the CMR but under national law.[60]

In *Lg Bremen 6.5.65*[61] the defendant agreed two contracts of transport from Italy, one to France and one to Germany, but did not begin to carry out either contract. The court noted[62] that "the taking over of the goods or the issue of the consignment note were not necessary for the realisation of the contract of transport", which had indeed been concluded in each instance. These contracts were within the scope of the CMR, but it did not govern the carrier's liability in this case. As the CMR did not "contain provisions which suggested at all conclusively that the carrier could not be liable for other kinds of breach of the contract",[63] the carrier was liable under national law.

This point has not come before the courts in England, but it is likely that the decision would be the same. If so, the carrier could plead exemption clauses going beyond the exoneration permitted by the CMR, although not without limit. The more drastic effects of the carrier's terms can be neutralised by construction.[64]

---

[57] *B.G.H. 9.2.79* (1980) 15 E.T.L. 84, 89.

[58] Above, para. 54.

[59] *O.L.G. Hamm 14.11.85*, TranspR 1986.77. In this case the fruit was rotten on arrival. If, as was not the case, the taking over had been so late that the deterioration was already apparent, the case would have fallen outside Art. 17 and the CMR, as, in its origin as distinct from its development, the damage did not occur between taking over and delivery. *cf.* Nickel-Lanz, para. 110: the case should be governed by national law.

[60] This seems to have been the intention of the authors of the CMR: TRANS/WP.9/11, p. 32.

[61] (1966) 1 E.T.L. 691. See also *Hg Vienna 3.4.84*, TranspR 1984.152 in which the court declined to take jurisdiction under Art. 31.1(b), which refers to "the place where the goods were taken over by the carrier", because, although the carrier had promised to take over the goods in Vienna, he had been unable to do so. But *cf. Besançon 23.6.82*, B.T. 1982.394 in which the CMR was applied to such a case.

[62] At 696.

[63] At 697.

[64] See below, para. 205.

66. Abandonment

If the goods have been taken over by the carrier, the CMR governs his liability for loss or damage occurring between then and delivery. Evidently, loss or damage occurring after delivery is not governed by the CMR. However, delivery of the goods must be distinguished from abandonment of the goods which, in turn, must be distinguished from premature termination of the journey on the instructions of the carrier or as the consequence of circumstances over which the carrier has no control.

If the carrier obeys lawful instructions from the person entitled to dispose of the goods,[65] instructions to deliver at place A rather than place B, delivery at A is delivery under Article 17 and loss or damage occurring to the goods after delivery is not governed by the CMR. Again, if the carrier finds that it is impossible to deliver at place B,[66] the carrier is obliged to seek instructions and may be instructed to deliver at place A; if the carrier does so, the effect is the same. Again, if the carrier finds that it is impossible to deliver at place B, and before obtaining instructions, the carrier decides in accordance with the CMR to "unload the goods for account of the person entitled to dispose of them", Article 16.2 states that "thereupon carriage shall be deemed to be at an end". Here too, the goods have been "delivered"[67] and liability for loss or damage occurring after unloading is governed not by the CMR but by national law. By contrast, if the transport is delayed, for example by bad weather or a strike of customs men, and the carrier puts the goods into temporary storage, the goods are in law if not in fact in movement under the contract of the carriage and the CMR, and the CMR governs liability for loss or damage.

> *cf. Düsseldorf 26.10.78*[68] in which the carrier took over the goods, began to move them, then realised that he had failed to obtain final instructions from the sender, as required by the contract, and so put the goods into storage. The (open) storage was inappropriate and the goods were destroyed. This, said the court, was a breach of duty (*Vertragsverletzung*), but one closely related to the carrier's duty of care under the CMR. Whether the carrier's liability in respect of temporary storage should be based on the CMR had to be decided from case to case. In the view of the court this case fell outside the CMR.

---

[65] See above, para. 32a.
[66] See above, para. 33a.
[67] See above, para. 33c(*ii*).
[68] VersR 1979.405. The court saw failure to obtain instructions and the poor choice of storage as *Vertragsverletzung* (above, para. 64) and hence outside the CMR.

In so far as each case must be considered on its merits, an English court would probably agree. However, in its reasoning[69] this is one of a number of decisions in Germany unduly restrictive of the scope of the CMR.

> In *B.G.H. 9.2.79*[70] the defendant carrier contracted with the claimant to carry machines from Hemer (Holland) to Isfahan (Iran). The carrier sub-contracted the journey but the sub-contractor, having taken over the goods, went into liquidation and the machines got no further than a trailer park in Rotterdam. The question arose whether the carrier's standard clauses were nullified by Article 41.[71] The B.G.H. noted that Article 41 applies only when the CMR applies and concluded that[72] "that is not the case when it is a question of the sender's claim for damages for *non-fulfilment*".[73] The CMR governs liability for delay arising out of performance of the contract, but not a case of non-performance of the contract such as this,[74] to which (German) national law applied.

In so far as this decision turns on the scope of the CMR, it is difficult to support.[75] The CMR applies to loss or damage occurring between the time of taking over the goods and the time of delivery: Article 17.1. The goods in that case had been taken over but not delivered. Abandonment is not delivery[76] if it occurs on the road outside the consignee's warehouse and still less if it occurs in the carrier's back yard. If total loss of goods occurs between taking over and delivery, the CMR (Article 23.1) applies, without regard to whether the cause of loss was that goods were mislaid, destroyed,[77] stolen or, it is submitted, abandoned. Why should the CMR apply when goods cannot be delivered because the goods have been destroyed, but not when goods cannot be delivered because the sub-carrier or his vehicle has been "destroyed"? Little logic is apparent in a line of demarcation like this, which creates

---

69 At least one of the factors which influenced the Düsseldorf court might not influence a court in England. The storage arose out of a duty which the carrier had undertaken to perform prior to the actual movement of the goods. If, as appears, the carrier had control of the goods with a view to their carriage, an English court would see this pre-carriage phase as one occurring after the goods had been taken over and hence as a part of the carriage governed by the CMR: see above, para. 27.

70 (1980) 15 E.T.L. 84. See also *Milan 11.7.75*, 1977 U.L.R. I 336.

71 Below, para. 92.

72 At 89.

73 Emphasis added.

74 At 90.

75 See also above, para. 33d(*i*).

76 Even in Germany, delivery to the wrong person is not delivery under the contract of carriage: *O.L.G. Munich 27.3.81*, VersR 1982.264: see above, para. 37. See also *The Hague 27.5.83*, S. & S. 1984 no. 68: the driver "delivered" to the wrong tank at the consignee's premises, and the CMR was applied to damage (leakage) that subsequently occurred; and in England *Shell Chemicals U.K. Ltd v. P & O Roadways* [1993] 1 Lloyd's Rep. 114; affirmed [1995] 1 Lloyd's Rep. 297, C.A. Clarke [1993] L.M.C.L.Q. 156.

77 For example, *TC Paris 14.3.78* (1978) 13 E.T.L. 742, 746: the cases assimilate total loss and non-delivery.

more problems than it solves. The CMR applies to delay but, if the B.G.H. is right, there is the further question, as difficult as it should be superfluous, of finding the point at which delay, which is governed by the CMR, becomes "nonfulfilment", which is not. It would defeat the purposes of the CMR, both as to uniformity and as to a reasonable level of liability, if the carrier in difficulties could abandon the goods and with them ("non-fulfil") his contract under the CMR, and run for cover behind his own exemption clauses.

67. Tort

Although the CMR was not intended to be entirely self-contained or self-sufficient, it was intended to unify the law, at least as regards what has been described[78] as the central component of the contract of carriage, the liability of the carrier for loss or damage to the goods during carriage, or for delay in delivery. Other conventions such as the CIM have expressly ruled out extra-contractual liability under national law, but the CMR does not.[79] Nonetheless, it was not the intention to encourage extra-contractual actions, hereafter referred to in the English idiom as actions in tort, when the CMR applied, so, actions in tort are discouraged by Article 28.

68. Article 28

Article 28 provides:

> "1. In cases where, under the law applicable loss, damage or delay arising out of carriage under this Convention gives rise to an extra-contractual claim, the carrier may avail himself of the provisions of this Convention which exclude his liability or which fix or limit the compensation due.
>
> 2. In cases where the extra-contractual liability for loss, damage or delay of one of the persons for whom the carrier is responsible under the terms of article 3 is in issue, such person may also avail himself of the provisions of this Convention which exclude the liability of the carrier or which fix or limit the compensation due."

[78] Above, para. 64.

[79] This is of importance in some countries, including England, Germany, Holland, Italy, and Switzerland, where parallel actions in contract and tort are allowed, but not in other countries, such as Belgium and France, in which parallel actions are not allowed: Haak, p. 238; Pesce, p. 299; Putzeys, para. 985.

The purpose of Article 28 is to preserve the allocation of responsibility and risk under the CMR.[80] A carrier who is exonerated by the CMR should not have any greater liability on the same facts in tort. As regards "loss, damage or delay arising out of carriage under this Convention", a claimant should not be better served in tort than under the CMR.[81] On a literal construction of these words, Article 28 would apply CMR exclusions to every aspect of the carrier's liability, including the carrier's contractual liability outside the scope of the CMR, for example, for failure to take over the goods; with one exception that is not its effect. Literal construction would give to Article 28 an effect that goes beyond its purpose. The result would be that, whereas a contractual action for breach outside the scope of the CMR, being outside it, would be unimpeded by the carrier's CMR defences, a tortious action on the same facts would be subject to those defences. To avoid this anomaly, "loss, damage or delay arising out of carriage under this Convention" should be read as loss, damage or delay for which the carrier is liable under the CMR. Hence, it is submitted, an action against the carrier outside the scope of the CMR, whether based in contract, tort, or statute,[82] is not affected by Article 28.[83]

This submission is subject to one exception: courts, particularly in Austria and Germany, have subjected actions based outside the CMR to the limitation period in Article 32, not, however, as a consequence of Article 28 but to give effect to their interpretation of Article 32.[84]

As regards the carrier's liability within the scope of the CMR, notably Article 17, it has been suggested[85] that, as Article 28 refers only to provisions of the CMR, which "exclude his liability or which fix or limit the compensation due", it does not extend to a defence based on the special risks in Article 17.4 and the associated shift in the burden of proof in Article 18.2.[86] This suggestion finds some support in the reference, to "provisions . . . which shift the burden of proof", found in Article 29 but not in Article 28. Prima facie the suggestion is correct, for Article 17.4 and Article 18.2 do not exclude liability but make liability harder to

---

[80] Haak, p. 237; Helm, Art. 28 Anm. 1.

[81] *OGH 14.11.84*, Greiter 245, 248, a view repeated verbatim in *OGH 12.12.84*, Stra GüV 1985/5 p. 12, 13, Greiter 263, 265.

[82] Notably, the Misrepresentation Act 1967, s.2(1): below, para. 241.

[83] *OGH 14.11.84*, Greiter 245, 248, a view repeated in *OGH 12.12.84*, Stra GüV 1985/5 p. 12, 13, Greiter 263, 265. Also in this sense: Haak, p. 238 (but *cf.* p. 241); Helm, Art. 28 Anm. 4 *et seq.*; Herber/Piper, Art. 28, 3; Hill and Messent, pp. 206–207; Koller, Art. 28, 2; Muth/Glöckner, p. 168; Nickel-Lanz, para. 183; Thume, Art. 28, 5. *Contra*: Loewe, para. 212.

[84] *O.L.G. Hamburg 9.2.89*, TranspR 1990.191. Herber/Piper, Art. 28, 6; Koller, Art. 28, 4; Muth/Glöckner, p. 168; Thume, Art. 28, 14. See above, para. 43a.

[85] Hill and Messent, pp. 206–207. A similar suggestion is made about reservations under Art. 30 and the jurisdiction provisions in Art. 31.

[86] Art. 18.2. See below, Chap. 7.

establish, although in practice the effect may be the same.[87] However, even on a strict construction of Article 28, there is some common law authority for treating clauses about the onus of proof as exclusionary. For example, an exclusion clause has been described[88] as one which "restricts the rights of a party by limiting the situations in which a right can be relied upon or the extent to which it can be enforced". Moreover, the purpose of Article 28, that the CMR regime of liability should not be bypassed by an action framed in tort, would be seriously undermined[89] by the suggestion that it does not apply to special risks. Thus, it is submitted, Article 17.4 may be pleaded to defend an action in tort in accordance with Article 28.[90]

If this is correct, the effect of Article 28 is that a claimant with an action under the CMR has little to gain by framing an action in tort. But, a claimant may wish nonetheless to sue the carrier in tort, first, because the complaint concerns a breach of contractual duty outside the scope of the CMR, and the chance of success or the extent of damages recoverable is greater in tort than in contract.[91] Secondly, a claimant may wish to sue the carrier in tort because the claimant has suffered loss as a result of the carrier's act or omission, but has no contract with the carrier or any other basis for a title to sue under the CMR.[92] For example "if a shipper has employed a forwarder to arrange the contract in such circumstances that the forwarder is the sender for the purposes of CMR, the shipper will have no right of action under the Convention unless the forwarder assigns his rights to him. Where such an assignment has not taken place or is not legally possible in the country in question, the only direct right of action which the

[87] In section 13 of the Unfair Contract Terms Act 1977 (below, para. 239) the legislator thought it both desirable and necessary to single out, and, by implication, to distinguish from other exclusions a clause "excluding or restricting rules of evidence or procedure", which is also to be treated as an exclusion under the Act. However, the section also singles out a clause "excluding or restricting any right or remedy", which by most definitions would be regarded as an exclusion or, which is generally treated as meaning the same, an exemption. *Semble* the special treatment given by the Act to these clauses is purely precautionary.

[88] Carter, *Breach of Contract* (Sydney, 1984), para. 248. *Semble* terms affecting the onus of proof come within Lord Devlin's category of "exceptions and the like": [1966] C.L.J. 192, 208–209. See also to this effect: Yates and Hawkins, *Standard Business Contracts* (London, 1986), para. 1(C)2. But *cf.* Coote, *Exception Clauses* (London, 1962), Chap. 1; and Lewison, *Interpretation of Contracts* (London, 1988), Chap. 11.

[89] *OGH 10.11.81*, SZ 54 no. 165, TranspR 1982.111, Greiter 108. Helm, Art. 28 Anm. 7.

[90] Also in this sense: Haak, p. 239; Helm, Art. 28 Anm. 7; Herber/Piper, Art. 28, 5; Koller, Art. 28, 4; Nickel-Lanz, para. 181; Thume, Art. 28, 9 *et seq.* It appears, however, that Art. 28 is not aptly worded to preserve the jurisdictional provisions of the CMR (Art. 31, above, paras. 46 *et seq.*)

[91] In the case of the tort of negligence, however, the duty of care may be limited by the contractual setting, so that the claimant is no better off framing his action in tort than he would have been, if he had framed it in contract. See below, para. 229a.

[92] See above, paras. 41 and 42.

shipper will have against the carrier will be in tort or delict. . . ."[93]

The governing law depends on the conflict rules of the forum. Most CMR states look in some degree to the *lex loci delicti commissi*.[94] The relevant rules of the English law of tort are discussed below, paragraphs 229 *et seq*.

[93] Hill and Messent, p. 205. Note: in some countries he may have title to sue on some ground other than contract, such as the right of disposal: above, paras. 41 and 42.

[94] Generally, see *International Encyclopedia of Comparative Law*, Vol. III, Chap. 32 (Ehrenzweig) and Chap. 33 (Stromholm); Batiffol & Lagarde, *Droit International Privé* (7th ed., Paris, 1983), paras. 554 *et seq*.; Dicey, Chap. 35; Helm, Art. 28 Anm. 3; *cf.* De Boer, *Beyond Lex Loci Delicti* (Deventer, 1987); Patocchi, *Règles de Rattachement Localisatrices* (Geneva, 1985), paras. 317 *et seq*.

Chapter 6

DEFENCES AVAILABLE TO THE CARRIER

69. The defences

Apart from a defence with respect to dangerous goods, which is a defence resembling the common law defence of necessity and found in Article 22,[1] the carrier's defences are stated in Article 17.2. The defences are the wrongful act or neglect of the claimant,[2] the instructions of the claimant,[3] inherent vice,[4] and unavoidable circumstances.[5] If the carrier establishes[6] that the cause[7] of the loss, damage or delay lay wholly or in part in facts constituting one of these defences, the carrier is exonerated wholly or in part,[8] as appropriate. Alternatively, the carrier may resort to a provisional defence by reference to the special risks[9] stated in Article 17.4. The main difference with the defences in Article 17.2 is that, if the carrier establishes the operation of a special risk, it is presumed that that was the cause of the loss, damage or delay and that the carrier is not liable; however, this double presumption may be rebutted by the claimant. As the onus of proof is easier for the carrier, in practice the carrier tries first to make a defence under Article 17.4 and, if that fails, falls back on Article 17.2. This chapter is concerned with the defences stated in Article 17.2. The special risks are considered in Chapter 7.

69a. The burden of proof

> "The proof or admission of certain facts may . . . give rise to inferences of fault or absence of fault which then need to be rebutted by other evidence. The facts which give rise to such an inference, as for

---

[1] Below, para. 73.
[2] Below, para. 70.
[3] Below, para. 71.
[4] Below, para. 72.
[5] Below, para. 74.
[6] On the burden of proof, see below, para. 69a.
[7] On the causal connection between loss, damage or delay and exonerating events, see below, para. 69b.
[8] On apportionment, see below, para. 69c.
[9] Below, paras. 76 *et seq.*

example the occurrence of damage to goods while in the care of the defendant, which raises an inference of want of care by such defendant, are the subject-matter of the evidential burden of proof. The legal burden of proof arises from the principle: He who alleges must prove. The incidence of the legal burden of proof can therefore be tested by answering the question: What does each party need to allege?"[10]

As to the evidential burden of proof of exonerating events under Article 17.2, in England it is the usual burden in civil cases, the balance of probability.[11] As regards the legal burden of proof of defences in Article 17.2, Article 18.1 prescribes the rule that one would expect: "The burden of proving that loss, damage or delay was due to one of the causes specified in article 17, paragraph 2, shall rest upon the carrier." The carrier must prove that the exonerating event occurred, and that it caused the loss, damage or delay, in respect of which the carrier seeks to be excused. The formal allocation of onus, the legal burden of proof, matters little in most cases; the court hears all the evidence and only if there are gaps in the story is the formal or legal burden of proof decisive. "Such burden of proof, when, as here, all the evidence which either party wishes to produce has been heard, usually as a practical matter is of importance only in the, fortunately, rare cases where, after considering all the evidence, the Court is unable to come to a conclusion as to the balance of probability."[12]

69b. Exonerating events: causation

If the carrier is to be held liable for loss, damage or delay, it must have been caused by the carrier.[13] Similarly, if the carrier is to be excused by one of the exonerating events, defences in Article 17.2, that event must have caused the loss, damage or delay in respect of which suit is brought although, as in other parts of the CMR, the exact nature of the causal connection has been left or "abandoned", one might say to national law.[14] Nations agree, at least,

---

[10] *The Torenia* [1983] 2 Lloyd's Rep. 210, 215, *per* Hobhouse J.

[11] This burden may be lighter than found in some countries, such as France, where it has been said of Article 17.2 that "the proof brought by the carrier must allow no doubt to remain". "La preuve que rapporte le voiturier ne doit laisser subsister aucun doute . . . de simples conjonctures ne suffisent pas, la loi exigeant une preuve complète et précise": *Aix 9.2.63*, B.T. 1963.234, quoted in this connection by Rodière, para. 543.

[12] *Ulster Swift v. Taunton Meat Haulage* [1977] 1 Lloyd's Rep. 346, 361, *per* Megaw L.J., C.A.

[13] Above, para. 59c.

[14] For example, in *O.L.G. Zweibrücken 23.9.66*, N.J.W. 1967.1717, 1718 inherent vice was regarded as a cause of loss according to the theory of "adequacy", applied in Germany; on this theory, see Hart and Honoré, *Causation in the Law* (2nd ed., Oxford, 1985), Chap. XVII. See also *Paris 17.3.93*, B.T.L. 1993.488. *cf. O.L.G. Hamm 15.3.90*, VersR 1991.360 in which the court took account of concurrent independent causes. See further above, para. 59c.

that a cause must be a *conditio sine qua non*[15] of the loss, damage or delay, but that that connection alone is not enough.

> In *Cass. Belge 12.12.80*[16] a load of cigarettes was stolen from a vehicle left by the driver at the customs post at Chiasso. Having lost the argument that the loss was unavoidable, the carrier argued that he should not be held entirely responsible, for the vehicle would not have been there at all if the sender had provided the right documents. While not disputing the truth of, the latter proposition, the court held that this was not a relevant cause of the loss.

In practice, the court is likely to ask, not whether a particular event had a sufficient causal connection with the loss, damage or delay, but whether, in the circumstances, the latter could or should have been avoided by the defendant carrier.

For the defence of unavoidable circumstances,[17] as the name suggests, the evidence must disclose a cause that was the unavoidable cause of the loss, damage or delay. At first sight, the description of the defence suggests loss, damage or delay which *could* not have been avoided by the carrier; something, quite literally, inevitable. However, in England, the defence of unavoidable circumstances is not read literally. It does not require absurd or extravagant measures of the carrier, but that the circumstances causing loss, damage or delay could not be avoided by the exercise of "utmost care" on the part of the carrier.[18]

For the defence of inherent vice,[19] Donaldson J. said[20] that it would "cover a situation in which the meat was shipped at a temperature, such that the deterioration was *inevitable*, despite the taking of all reasonable and proper precautions". Here too, the court may not take this absolutely literally.[21]

---

[15] Sometimes called the "but for" test: Hart and Honoré (above, n. 14), Chap. V.

[16] (1981) 16 E.T.L. 250, 257–258.

[17] Below, para. 74.

[18] Below, para. 74e.

[19] Below, para. 72.

[20] *Ulster-Swift v. Taunton Meat Haulage* [1975] 2 Lloyd's Rep. 502, 506 (emphasis added), affirmed [1977] 1 Lloyd's Rep. 346, C.A. *idem* in relation to carriage by sea: *Albacora S.R.L. v. Westcott & Laurance Line* [1966] 2 Lloyd's Rep. 53, 59, *per* Lord Reid, 62, *per* Lord Pearce, H.L. *cf.* in relation to inherent vice in insurance contracts: *Soya GmbH v. White* [1983] 1 Lloyd's Rep. 122, 124, *per* Lord Diplock, H.L.

[21] In *Noten BV v. Harding* [1990] 2 Lloyd's Rep. 283 (below, para. 236h), it was argued that, as the consignment was one of a number of similar consignments in which the damage had occurred sometimes but not other times, the damage was not inevitable and hence not a case of inherent vice. This argument was rejected by Bingham L.J. (at 289), saying that damage "may be caused by inherent vice without being inevitable". It is submitted that this statement should be seen in the context of the argument that the judge thus sought to reject; that there may be inherent vice in a particular case, although damge was not inevitable in consignments of that kind; and that it does not necessarily contradict, therefore, the argument that, for inherent vice in the circumstances of a particular case tested at the commencement of the period of cover, damage from the inherent vice must be inevitable for that consignment at that time.

The remaining defences in Article 17.2—the wrongful act or neglect of the claimant[22] and the instructions of the claimant[23]—are pleaded less often, and questions of causation have not arisen for decision. Looking at the CMR as a whole, it is submitted that the key to the level of duty expected of the carrier is the residual duty of care. In principle, that duty is neither strict nor one or reasonable care but, as with the defence of unavoidable circumstances, a duty of "utmost care"[24] with, however, two qualifications when the matter is in the sender's area of risk, *i.e.* as regards packing and loading undertaken by the sender.

First, the reaction or response of the carrier is assessed at a lower level of duty, usually reasonable care.[25] Secondly, the court is more likely to find that the loss, damage or delay is caused both, for example, by the claimant's neglect and the carrier's failure to deal with the problem, and to apportion loss between them. This is clearly true when the sender has packed the goods defectively and, it is submitted, it is also the case when there is evidence of a causal link with some other wrongful act or neglect on the part of the sender, or with the sender's instructions. The instinct of the judge will be to approach these defences as if they raised a question of intervening or contributory negligence on the part of the carrier. If the claimant provides defective documents or instructions, defects which the carrier could not be expected to discover or do anything about, and which in other words, could not be dealt with by "utmost care" on the part of the carrier, the carrier is not liable: the sole cause lies with the claimant. If, however, the carrier should have discovered the defect and could then have done something, something neither absurd nor extravagant, to avoid the loss, damage or delay, liability will be apportioned under Article 17.5. If, however, defective documents are provided by the sender and consequently the vehicle is held up at a customs post, where the goods are stolen while the vehicle is not properly secured against thieves, the carrier is fully liable for the loss, because the carrier's failure has broken the chain of causation between the sender's fault and the loss: the sender's act is not a (significant) cause.[26]

In *Cass. 19.4.82*[27] the carrier obeyed the instructions of the sender as to the temperature at which nectarines should be carried, with the result that the fruit was damaged, in circumstances in which the court considered that the carrier should have known better. The

[22] Below, para. 70.
[23] Below, para. 71.
[24] Below, para. 77.
[25] *ibid.*
[26] *Cass. Belge 12.12.80* (1981) 16 E.T.L. 250.
[27] B.T. 1982.309 (1983) 18 E.T.L. 13. At common law *cf. Caledonian Ry v. Hunter* (1858) 20 Sess. Cas. 2nd Ser. 1097 below, para. 228.

court censured the decision of the court below, that the damage was exclusively caused by the sender's instructions.

69c. Apportionment: Article 17.5

When loss, damage or delay is caused partly by an event for which the carrier is exonerated, such as the wrongful act or neglect of the claimant, and partly by a factor for which the carrier is liable, the liability may be apportioned by the court.[28] This is the effect of Article 17.5:

> "Where under this article the carrier is not under any liability in respect of some of the factors causing loss, damage or delay he shall only be liable to the extent that those factors for which he is liable under this article have contributed to the loss, damage or delay."

The carrier must prove one or more of the exonerating events set out in Article 17.2, but is also obliged to prove the "extent" to which the event "contributed" to the loss, damage or delay before getting the partial exoneration provided for in Article 17.5? With regard to carriage by sea, the common law courts have seen partial exoneration as an exception like any other and have required the carrier to prove the extent of contribution; failing this, with one reservation,[29] the sea carrier is liable in full.[30] The analogy is appropriate[31] in so far as the maritime rule is based on (a) construction *contra proferentem* and (b) the widespread premise that the defendant carrier must prove that the loss, damage or delay, for which the carrier is otherwise presumed responsible, was caused by the exonerating event: not just some loss but all that for which the carrier seeks exoneration.[32] However, the common law

[28] A common case is that in which some loss, etc., could not have been avoided and is thus excused under Art. 17.2 (below, para. 74) but the full extent of the actual loss of that kind could have mitigated by the carrier. For example, the vehicle could not have avoided hitting the road obstruction, but the damage would have been less severe if the driver had been more alert and applied the brakes sooner than he did: *Cass. 22.7.86*, B.T. 1986.591.

[29] An exception arises when the only other cause, apart from the exonerating event, is the claimant's breach of contract; in that case the claimant must prove the extent of loss apart from the claimant's own breach: *Govt of Ceylon v. Chandris* [1965] 2 Lloyd's Rep. 204.

[30] In England see *Gosse Millerd v. Canadian Government Merchant Marine* [1929] A.C. 223, 241, *per* Viscount Sumner; and *The Torenia* [1983] 2 Lloyd's Rep. 210, 218–219, *per* Hobhouse J. See also Tetley, *Marine Cargo Claims* (3rd ed., Montreal, 1988), p. 365. In the United States see *Schnell & Co. v. Vallescura* 293 US 296 (1934), where the rule is known as the *Vallescura* rule: Tetley, p. 314.

[31] *cf.* Mance (1984) 100 L.Q.R. 501, 504.

[32] *The Hobsons Bay* (1933) 47 Ll.L.Rep. 207, 213, *per* Langton J.; *Heskell v. Continental Express* (1950) 83 Ll.L.Rep. 438, 458, *per* Devlin J. In the USA too this rule is seen as a logical consequence of the proposition that the carrier must prove that the loss in respect of which he seeks exoneration was caused by or attributable to the exonerating event: *Vallescura* (above, n. 30), at 303–304; *Golodetz v. S.S. Lake Anja* (1985) 20 E.T.L. 234 (5 Cir., 1985).

approach to this problem is alien to some of the other countries[33] party to the CMR, where such an approach is unlikely to be adopted.[34] Better, perhaps, for the common law court to see Article 17.5 as an instruction to apportion. Once it has been proved, for example, that the claimant was partly responsible, the initiative lies with the court to apportion. This is the view of Article 17.5 taken in other CMR states, such as France,[35] Italy[36] and Germany.

> In *O.L.G. Saarbrücken 21.11.74*[37] rolls of metal were improperly loaded by the sender. One roll fell off the vehicle and was reloaded. Then, while the lorry was travelling too fast on a bend, four rolls of metal fell off and were badly damaged. Clearly, the fault of the sender was one cause of the damage, but the court also found that the carrier, through the driver, was in breach of a general duty of care: it was apparent when the first roll fell off that the loading was defective and the driver should not have proceeded without taking certain precautions, such as contacting the sender or taking better steps to secure the load.[38] The court then proceeded to apportion liability itself and, noting that it had not been shown that one cause was more preponderant then the other, the court divided responsibility equally between the sender and the carrier.

70. The wrongful act or neglect of the claimant

Article 17.2 provides that

> "the carrier shall however be relieved of liability if the loss, damage or delay was caused by the wrongful act or neglect of the claimant . . . "

The most obvious example of a wrongful act or neglect of the claimant occurs when the claimant is the sender and it is the sender's duty to load, stow or unload the goods, and this is done in a defective manner, causing loss, damage or delay. If the carrier can prove this, the case falls within Article 17.2,[39] but it is likely that the carrier will invoke not Article 17.2 but, more simply, the fact that loading was by the sender and thus a special risk under

[33] As regards carriage by sea, see Ripert, *Droit Maritime*, para. 1719. *Aix 4.11.65*, D.M.F. 1966.417.

[34] It is specifically rejected by Rodière as regards the CMR: (1971) 6 E.T.L. 6, 15. See also Loewe, para. 168; Libouton, para. 56 and Rodière, para. 562 and cases cited, notably *Req. 31.3.43*, S. 1943. 1.96; *Comm. 12.4.48*, S. 1948. 1.115.

[35] For example, *Paris 7.4.86*, B.T. 1987.9.

[36] For example, *Venice 31.10.74* (1975) 10 E.T.L. 242.

[37] (1976) 11 E.T.L. 261; see also *O.L.G. Nuremburg 14.6.65* (1971) 6 E.T.L. 247; and *O.L.G. Hamm 15.3.90*, VersR 1991.360.

[38] At 265.

[39] Rodière (1971) 6 E.T.L. 2, 15.

Article 17.4, as that is easier to prove.[40] The same is true of defective packing.[41] If the sender gives inaccurate or inadequate instructions relating to the goods, that gives rise to a separate defence.[42] There remains only a cluster of cases in which the defence, act or neglect of the claimant has been invoked.

A carrier was excused for delay caused when a consignment was minutely examined by customs officials after it had been found to contain contraband.[43] A carrier was excused when the vehicle turned over as a result of a false declaration of weight by the sender.[44] A carrier was excused when the vehicle was held up by German customs officials, who were unable or unwilling to read documents, documents provided by the sender, which related to the goods and which were written in French but not in German.[45] Although a carrier was not excused when, the sender (brewery) having rinsed the tanker as usual, the beer was contaminated by a previous load, it has also been held that the carrier is excused if the sender has assumed responsibility for the cleanliness of the tank.[46]

The act or neglect must be that of the "claimant". A literal interpretation of that word would mean that the carrier sued by the consignee could not plead the act or neglect of the sender. To refuse the defence to the carrier in such a case "would be a ridiculous solution because it would depend on the sender ridding himself of the consequences of his negligence by means of a quick despatch of the second consignment note, and such a solution would be unfair to the carrier. Nobody therefore interprets this phrase too strictly and it is admitted that it covers negligence by the sender as well as by the consignee, without distinction."[47]

The act or neglect must also be "wrongful", at least in the sense that it is the cause of loss, damage or delay. For Rodière,[48] this is sufficient, on the doubtful assumption that the "wrongful act" of

---

[40] See below, para. 77. However, in such a case the carrier has sometimes pleaded not Art. 17.4 but Art. 17.2: for example, *Paris 2.12.81*, B.T. 1982.73.

[41] See below, para. 83.

[42] Below, para. 71.

[43] *Cass. 14.2.94*, D. 1894, 1.163 (carriage by rail).

[44] *Pau 3.6.65*, B.T. 1965. 255 and *Rouen 18.2.66*, B.T. 1966. 273.

[45] *Paris 27.1.71*, 1971 U.L.C. 151. Likewise, if the sender has failed to provide the required documents: *TC Delft 13.5.65*, 1966 U.L.C. 104, 108; or if they are produced late: *Paris 2.12.81*, B.T. 1982.73; *Cass. 15.5.57*, B.T. 1957.255 (CIM).

It should be recalled that by Art. 11.2 "the carrier shall not be under any duty to enquire into either the accuracy or the adequacy" of documents to be provided by the sender: see above, paras. 26 and 63.

[46] *TC Brussels 14.2.69*, JCB 1972.548 and *Brussels 15.4.71*, JCB 1972.552, as reported by Libouton, Theunis, pp. 80–81.

[47] Rodière (1971) 6 E.T.L. 2, 15; in the same Glass and Cashmore, para. 3.44; Haak, p. 140; Helm, Art. 17 Anm. 9; Herber/Piper, Art. 17, 57; Koller, Art. 17, 31; Loewe, para. 151; Nichel-Lanz, para. 13; Thume, Art. 17, 81. So, for example, in *Paris 2.12.81*, B.T. 1982.73 the carrier was allowed to plead, as a defence to an action brought by the consignee, the failure of the sender to provide a document.

[48] Rodière, paras. 538 and 542.

the CMR is the same as *le fait de l'expéditeur* in French law. But, in view of the language of Article 17.1 and Article 17.2 and the normal strictness of contractual obligations in English law, it seems that an English court would prefer the view of Loewe[49] that the defence works only if it can be said that the claimant's act was such as to indicate that he was at fault. Moreover, delay damage caused to goods because the consignee refused to accept them is not a fault attributable to the consignor[50] nor, at least where there is some substance in the allegation, a fault of the consignee.[51]

71. The instructions of the claimant

Article 17.2 provides that

> "the carrier shall . . . be relieved of liability of the loss, damage or delay was caused by . . . the instructions of the claimant given otherwise than as the result of a wrongful act or neglect on the part of the carrier".

Although this defence refers to the instructions of the "claimant", it is likely to be interpreted as the instructions of the person entitled to give instructions of the kind in question.[52] As to the kind of instructions, the B.G.H.[53] has rejected the view of a lower court that the only instructions in question are instructions about disposal of the goods under Article 12. The instructions might also concern the care of the goods during transit,[54] the disposition of the vehicle at the place of loading or unloading,[55] as well as instructions about disposal. Even the commission to carry specified goods from Y to Z is an instruction by the sender, but one that is unlikely to give rise to this defence for, if he agrees to do it, the carrier assumes a large measure of responsibility for how it is

---

[49] Loewe, para. 151. See also in this sense: Helm, Art. 17 Anm. 9; Nickel-Lanz, para. 123.

[50] *O.L.G. Hamburg 31.3.94*, TranspR 1995.245.

[51] *ibid.* The judgment also suggests *in fine* that liability in such cases is governed exclusively by Art. 15 and Art. 16: above, paras. 33 *et seq.*

[52] Also in this sense: Nickel-Lanz, para. 124; Putzeys, para. 756.

[53] *B.G.H. 27.10.78*, VersR 1979.419.

[54] For example, as to the temperature of fruit: *Cass. 23.2.82* (1983) 18 E.T.L. 13; and *Cass. 19.4.82* (above, para. 69b). Failure to give any instructions, when instructions were necessary, is likely to be an instance of the associated defence "wrongful . . . neglect": above, para. 70.

[55] In *Paris 25.11.77*, B.T. 1978.66, 1979 U.L.R. II 233, affirmed *Cass. 9.10.79*, B.T. 1979, 545: the goods had arrived in Belgium and were ready to be unloaded. The consignee ordered the vehicle forward, the driver complied with the order and the vehicle struck a cable which the driver could not see with the result that part of the goods were knocked off the vehicle and damaged. The courts held that the carrier should be exonerated because the cause of the accident was the consignee's order.

done.[56] In many cases responsibility for loss, damage or delay consequent on instructions will be apportioned.[57]

Whether this defence offers any refuge to the carrier, in addition to that provided by "wrongful act or neglect of the claimant", depends on what is meant by "wrongful". If, as suggested above,[58] "wrongful" connotes actual fault, such as negligence, the defence of "instructions" will be available to the carrier when the claimant is not at fault,[59] when, for example, the sender has provided information derived from a source normally impeccable but erroneous on this occasion.

The defence is not available to the carrier in respect of an instruction given "as the result of a wrongful act or neglect on the part of the carrier".[60] Hence, if the goods are damaged in a road accident, the carrier at fault may be obliged to seek instructions on what to do with the goods from the sender, but cannot plead the instructions then received as an excuse for any new or aggravated damage unless, it has been suggested,[61] the instructions are the main cause of later damage. This suggestion is in line with general principle, but is not supported by the unqualified wording of Article 17.2: once the carrier has been guilty of "wrongful act or neglect", it appears that any instructions given by the claimant in response are part of the situation created by the carrier and do not provide a ground for exoneration or for apportionment under Article 17.5.

72. Inherent vice

Article 17.2 provides that

> "The carrier shall . . . be relieved of liability if the loss damage or delay was caused by . . . inherent vice of the goods . . . "

The CMR does not contain a definition of inherent vice; however, the concept is found in the CIM[62] and in the law relating to

---

[56] *Cass. 5.7.76*, B.T. 1976, 377, 1977 U.L.R. II 204: the carrier could not blame the sender for ordering the carriage of a quantity of apples to England, the weight of which was greater than allowed on the carrier's vehicle by English law, with consequent delay and expense in transhipment of the excess. See also above, para. 30, concerning the information on the basis of which the carrier is obliged to select a vehicle suitable for the goods.

[57] For example, *Cass. 19.4.82* (above, para. 69b).

[58] Para. 70.

[59] Glass and Cashmore, para. 3.45, adopting Loewe, para. 151. In *Paris 25.11.77* (above, n. 55) the consignee appears to have been at fault but this is not emphasised by the courts; therein lies the advantage of this defence to the carrier.

[60] According to Nickel-Lanz (para. 124), the absence of "wrongful act or neglect" must be proved by the carrier.

[61] Putzeys, para. 757.

[62] However, the CMR version differs from that expressed in the CIM in ways which, it has been argued by Haak (p. 142), are significant.

carriage by sea, and is thought to be the same in all branches of transport law.[63] English courts will refer to English law.[64]

The vice must be an inherent vice.[65] In *Rb Antwerp 7.1.77*[66] chemicals carried under a contract governed by the CMR were proved to have been contaminated when taken over, and the carrier was able to establish successfully the defence of inherent vice. If, however, the source of contamination was external to the chemicals, the law would see a vice but not an inherent vice.

Inherent vice is relative. Most things carry within them the seeds of their own destruction or decay which will develop sooner or later, according to the circumstances. The notion of vice is relative, therefore, to the circumstances of the case: relative to what is expected of the goods. Goods fall below expectations when they are unfit to survive the journey and be fit for use or consumption at destination.[67]

As regards the journey, goods are expected to be fit to withstand the ordinary incidents of the journey in question, assuming that they receive the amount of care which the carrier is required by the contract and by the CMR to give them. If, for example, the carrier fails to provide proper conditions of carriage, such as a waterproof cover, and if the goods would have arrived safely if there had been a cover,[68] their inability to survive the (defective) conditions is not itself inherent vice, as the latter is assessed not in relation to the conditions of the journey as they were in fact, but in relation to the conditions as the sender was entitled to expect them to be.[69] If rust develops in metal carried in uncovered vehicles, that is a vice, but whether it is an inherent vice that the carrier can plead as a defence depends on whether the use of uncovered vehicles was authorised by the contract of carriage.[70]

---

[63] Rodière, paras. 539 and 542; Rodière (1971) 6 E.T.L. 2, 16. This was the intention of the authors of the CMR: TRANS/WP.9/11, p. 44.

[64] Below, para. 236h.

[65] In France the defect must be "*inhérente à leur constitution*": *Nîmes 29.10.80*, 1981 U.L.R. I 267, 269. However, in Belgium, Libouton (Theunis, p. 81) distinguishes inherent defects (Art. 17.2) from the inherent nature of the goods, with the latter referring to sensitivity (Art. 17.4(d)). The French view of inherent vice in all branches of transport law is that the vice in the thing must be one which is "in its very nature"—Rodière (1971) 6 E.T.L. 2, 17. Referred to as *vice propre*, it means *toute cause d'avarie dérivant de la nature propre de la marchandise: TC Dunkirk 5.6.78* (1978) 13 E.T.L. 697, 701.

[66] (1977) 12 E.T.L. 420.

[67] Also in this sense: Nickel-Lanz, para. 125. A distinction is sometimes drawn between fitness for use or consumption and fitness to travel: Rodière (1971) 6 E.T.L. 2, 17. However, what counts is fitness for use or consumption at destination after travel.

[68] *TC Dunkirk 5.6.78* (1978) 13 E.T.L. 697. Muth/Glöckner, p. 135.

[69] As regards the kind of vehicle that the carrier must provide, see above, para. 30.

[70] *TC Brussels 4.2.72* (1972) 7 E.T.L. 573, 583. In *TC Brussels 3.10.70*, JPA 1970.487, as reported by Libouton, para. 38, it was held that chemicals which reacted to the ferrous metal of the tanks in which they were contained suffered from inherent vice. *cf.* Putzeys, para. 761. In *O.L.G. Köln 30.8.90*, TranspR 1990.425, when covered transport was expected, metal goods were stored outside in rain. The consequent corrosion, it was held, was not a case of inherent vice but of damage for which the carrier was liable.

In *Ulster-Swift v. Taunton Meat Haulage*[71] the defendants carried 300 pig carcasses belonging to the plaintiffs to Basle in a refrigerated trailer belonging to a third party. On arrival in Basle the carcasses were found to be decaying. The defendants pleaded inherent vice, contending *inter alia* that prior to loading the carcasses had been kept at too high a temperature. Donaldson J. thought that this might have been a telling argument if a lower temperature could not have been expected in the refrigerated trailer. He said[72] that the "plaintiffs were entitled to expect that the interior of the trailer would reach (32 degrees Fahrenheit) within a short time of leaving their premises". Speaking of inherent vice, he concluded[73] that "in the context of refrigerated carriage, the deterioration of the meat cannot, of itself, be so described. It would, however, cover a situation in which the meat was shipped at a temperature, such that the deterioration was inevitable, despite the taking of all reasonable and proper precautions for its carriage." The defence on the ground of inherent vice failed.

The argument in this case provides a common illustration of inherent vice: the natural process of decay in perishable goods, which becomes a vice when it reaches such a stage of development that the goods are unfit. This case also illustrates a common bone of contention between a claimant who says that the goods deteriorated because the temperature in the vehicle's refrigeration was too high, and a carrier who says that the goods deteriorated because the temperature of the goods was not low enough on shipment.[74] Another common dispute is between the claimant who contends that the goods have deteriorated because they were delivered late, and the carrier, who does not deny that delivery was late but contends that the goods suffered from inherent vice and would have deteriorated anyway.[75] Although the carrier in such a case may be unaffected by statements in the consignment note about the apparent condition of the goods,[76] as the vice is not apparent, the carrier's contention that the goods were unfit on consignment may be hard to prove.[77]

Other illustrations of inherent vice include goods packed in a way that will not enable them to survive the journey in question, goods which have not been properly stored or shored inside a

---

[71] [1975] 2 Lloyd's Rep. 502; affirmed [1977] 1 Lloyd's Rep. 346.
[72] [1975] 2 Lloyd's Rep. 502, 505.
[73] At 506.
[74] See also *Rb Arnhem 28.1.71*, S. & S. 1973 para. 218, 1977 U.L.R. II 207; *Paris 10.11.81*, B.T. 1982.183.
[75] For example, *Paris 29.10.80*, B.T. 1981.256, 1981 U.L.R. I 267, in which the carrier's contention failed; and *Cass. 24.2.81*, DMF 1982.74, in which the claimant's contention failed.
[76] See above, para. 25a.
[77] The court will infer what it can from the evidence available; see *e.g. Lyon 25.11.94*, B.T.L. 1995.287.

container,[78] and goods so moist on shipment that there is spontaneous combustion.[79] Again, if perishable goods, say soft fruit, are damaged by their own weight and the inevitable shaking of the moving vehicle, they are injured through their own intrinsic qualities.

The last example comes from the common law of carriage by rail and, although it could also be an example of inherent vice under the CMR, it is one of those cases that is more likely to be seen as a case of sensitive goods[80]: goods of a nature "which particularly exposes them to total or partial loss or to damage".[81] Certainly, the inherent vice in a particular case may also be a condition of the goods which makes them sensitive goods, as well, incidentally, as a latent defect.[82] However, sensitivity is a permanent feature of all goods of that kind, whereas an inherent vice is not one that is found in all goods of that type all of the time.[83] The distinction is developed further, below.[84]

73. Dangerous goods: Article 22[85]

Article 22 contains a special provision for dangerous goods, modelled on Article IV, rule 6 of the Hague Rules,[86] and including what amounts to a defence of necessity for the carrier who has been forced to take action which causes loss or damage to such goods.

Dangerous goods are not defined in the CMR. From the *travaux préparatoires*, a working definition has been provided by Loewe,[87]

---

[78] *Paris 6.11.79* (1980) 15 E.T.L. 399, 427–428.

[79] *Agen 26.11.85*, B.T. 1986.235.

[80] In *Centrocoop Export-Import SA v. Brit European Transport* [1984] 2 Lloyd's Rep. 618, 625, Bingham J. held that a case of meat consigned at too high a temperature was one of unavoidable circumstances, and of sensitivity, but made no mention of inherent vice.

[81] Art. 17.4(d). For example, a tendency of goods to rust may be seen as both sensitivity and inherent vice: *Paris 10.12.71*, B.T. 1972.35, 1973 U.L.C. 274. *cf. Agen 26.11.85*, B.T. 1986.235, in which these concepts were confused by the court. As the commentator says (*ibid.*), the potatoes in that case were sensitive, as they were new, and also had an inherent vice, as they were wet.

[82] The notion of latent defect, found for example in the Hague Rules, is not found in the CMR.

[83] Helm, Art. 17 Anm. 11. Thus, for example, a finding that the apricots were fragile, which would be enough for a defence under Art. 17.4(d), does not establish inherent vice: *Cass. 27.11.73* (1974) 9 E.T.L. 455.

[84] Para. 89a.

[85] Generally see Wijffels (1969) 4 E.T.L. 870; *Transports de Matières Dangereuses, Numéro Spécial du Bulletin des Transports*, B.T. 1986.697 *et seq.*; Gottrau, Theunis, pp. 197 *et seq.*, which is published in French in B.T. 1986.706 *et seq.*; Lamy, *Transports de Marchandises Dangereuses* (16th ed., Paris, 1990); various authors (1991) 26 E.T.L. 1.

[86] Gottrau, Theunis, p. 197 and B.T. 1986.706; Helm, Art. 22 Anm. 3.

[87] Para. 186.

and widely adopted by other commentators[88]: goods are dangerous goods if, in the context of normal carriage by road, those goods are a source of immediate danger to people and property. On this basis, the reference is to "goods which are dangerous *in themselves*, rather than goods which only become dangerous, for example, as result of the way in which they are carried".[89] The reference is not, however, primarily one to goods that are dangerous *to themselves* but to goods that are dangerous to other goods, property and persons.[90] Another suggestion[91] is that dangerous goods are "les marchandises qui par la composition et l'état de leurs matières inhérentes présentent de façon générale un risque pour la sécurité et/ou l'intégrité des personnes et des biens". Dangerous substances are listed in the ADR; however, this convention, concluded subsequently to the CMR, does not purport to contain an exhaustive list and a substance may be regarded as dangerous under the CMR although not listed in ADR.[92] In these circumstances, parties are free to adopt their own definition in their standard terms of contract.[93]

Examples from CMR cases include cigarette lighters, from which, it was alleged, gas had leaked,[94] and varnish which leaked on to a motorway.[95] At common law, it has been held that goods may be dangerous, though not physically dangerous in the normal sense, if the goods might leak or render the carriage illegal.[96] Most recently, however, as concerns the Hague Rules on carriage by sea, it has been held that dangerous goods means goods that are physically dangerous and not "goods which are legally dangerous in that if they are likely to involve detention or delay".[97] The same appears to be true under the CMR.

If the goods are dangerous, the carrier's liability to the goods interest depends on whether, as stated in Article 22.1, the carrier

---

[88] Glass and Cashmore, para. 3.28; Gottrau, Theunis, p. 198 and B.T. 1986.706; Herber/Piper, Art. 22, 5; Hill and Messent, p. 175; Koller, Art. 22, 2; Putzeys, para. 824; and Thume, Art. 22, 24.

[89] Hill and Messent, p. 175.

[90] *O.L.G. Düsseldorf 23.1.92*, TranspR 1992.218.

[91] Wijffels (1969) 4 E.T.L. 870, paras. 10 *et seq*. Also in this sense; Muth/Glöckner, p. 156.

[92] Also in this sense: Helm, Art. 22 Anm. 2. An amended and updated list of dangerous substances came into force on January 1, 1990. The ADR is concerned not with liability between parties to the contract of carriage but with the regulation of the mode of carriage and its documentation, reinforced by the criminal law.

[93] Thus, for example, Condition 1 of the RHA Conditions of Carriage 1991 states: "'*Dangerous Goods*' means dangerous substances listed by the Health and Safety Commission in Part I of the Authorised and Approved List of Dangerous Substances, explosives, radioactive substances and any other substance presenting a similar hazard."

[94] *Lyon 1.7.75*, B.T. 1975.395; also *Lyon 7.10.76*, B.T. 1977.84, 1979 U.L.R. I 289, affirmed *Cass. 20.6.78*, B.T. 1978.468.

[95] *Douai 11.3.82*, B.T. 1982.199; below, para. 73a.

[96] *Ministry of Food v. Lamport & Holt Line* [1952] 2 Lloyd's Rep. 371, 382, *per* Sellers J.; *Mitchell, Cotts & Co. v. Steel* [1916] 2 K.B. 610, 614, *per* Atkin J.

[97] *The Giannis NK* [1996] 1 Lloyd's Rep. 577, 585, *per* Hirst L.J., C.A.

has been informed "of the exact nature of the danger and . . . if necessary, of the precautions to be taken".[98] If, or to the extent that, the information has not been entered in the consignment note,[99] Article 22.1 continues: "the burden of proving, by some other means, that the carrier knew the exact nature of the danger constituted by the carriage of such goods shall rest upon the sender or the consignee". The carrier will probably be taken to know the danger of things notoriously dangerous,[1] but by inference is not obliged to make inquiries in other cases, as the carrier is entitled to expect to be warned by the sender.[2] This expectation is reinforced when the transport is governed by ADR, as this convention indicates in some detail the information with which the sender is obliged to provided the carrier.

If the carrier has been given the information required by Article 22.1, and the goods are damaged, the carrier has no obligation under the CMR or under common law[3] to inspect the goods to ensure, for example, that the chemicals are in a state for safe carriage, unless perhaps there is a trade custom to the contrary, or the transport is such that loading and stowage by the sender needs to be checked to ensure the safety of the vehicle.[4] Subject to this, the carrier may be liable for damage to the goods in the same way that the carrier is liable for damage to non-dangerous goods.[5] The carrier may also, for example, plead the sensitivity of the goods as a special risk under Article 17.4(d).[6] The carrier's care of such goods will be assessed by reference to the ADR: although the purpose of ADR is the welfare of the public rather than the regulation of private contract, the ADR sets standards for the mode of carriage to which a court is likely to turn.

If the carrier has not been given the information required by Article 22.1, the carrier may plead that any loss, damage or delay

---

[98] This phrase, too literally translated from the French, appears to mean that Art. 22.2 operates if the carrier did not know from the sender the exact nature of the danger.

[99] Entry in the consignment note is required in part by Art. 6.1: "The consignment note shall contain . . . (f) the description in common use of the nature of the goods and the method of packing, and, in the case of dangerous goods, their generally recognized description." Failure to include this information does not invalidate the contract: see above, para. 24. The "generally recognized description" was understood to mean "the description given in the regulations of the country of despatch": TRANS/WP9/35, p. 7.

[1] *Shaw, Savill & Albion Co. v. Electric Reduction Sales* [1955] 3 D.L.R. 617. *Lyon 7.10.76*, B.T. 1977.84, 1979 U.L.R. I 289, affirmed *Cass. 20.6.78*, B.T. 1978.468 (gas cigarette lighters). *cf. Rb Antwerp 25.11.74*, JPA 1975–6.70, reported by Gottrau, Theunis, p. 199 and B.T. 1986.706, 707, that to mention a chemical by its technical or scientific name may be insufficient to alert the carrier. On the level of knowledge to be expected of terms and abbreviations associated with dangerous goods, see also *B.G.H. 16.10.86*, VersR 1987.304.

[2] Gottrau, Theunis, p. 199 and B.T. 1986.706, 707. Pesce, p. 267.

[3] *Polskie Line v. Hooker Chemical* 1980 AMC 1748 (S.D. N.Y.).

[4] Below, para. 87b.

[5] *Cass. 16.10.90*, B.T. 1990.797.

[6] As in *Lyon 7.10.76* (above, n. 1). See generally, below, para. 89.

was caused by the wrongful neglect of the claimant,[7] or by the instructions of the claimant,[8] defences under Article 17.2. In addition, the carrier may have a defence under Article 22.2:

> "Goods of a dangerous nature which, . . . in the circumstances referred to in paragraph 1 of this article, the carrier did not know were dangerous, may, at any time or place, be unloaded, destroyed or rendered harmless by the carrier without compensation."

The extent to which the carrier must consider the sender's interests on discovering that the goods are dangerous goods is unclear. The power given to the carrier by Article 22.2, to unload, destroy or render harmless the goods "at any time or place", suggests a greater concern with the interests of the public than of the goods owner. However, the perspective of principle is that the carrier's action, in the face of a serious breach of an implied obligation not to ship dangerous goods,[9] can be construed in one of two ways. First, the carrier has accepted the sender's repudiation of the contract and now holds the goods as an involuntary bailee[10] or, in the event of destruction of the goods, has no obligations to the goods interest other than those under Article 22.2. Secondly, if the carrier does not treat the contract as repudiated but, for example, renders the goods harmless and continues the carriage, the contract remains in force and with it the carrier's duty of care,[11] as well as the duty under Article 14.1 to seek instructions[12] from the person entitled to dispose of the goods, while obeying the overriding imperative to protect others from the danger posed by the goods. In any event, a court will be slow to condemn a carrier who was too quick or too thorough in eliminating the danger.[13]

73a. The liability of the sender

Article 22.2, the first sentence of which is set out above, continues: "the sender shall be liable for all expenses, loss or damage arising out of their handing over for carriage or of their carriage".[14]

---

[7] Nickel-Lanz, para. 123. Above, para. 70.
[8] Above, para. 71.
[9] *Brass v. Maitland* (1856) 6 E. & B. 470. Kahn-Freund, p. 378.
[10] For the duties of an involuntary bailee, see Palmer, Chap. 12.
[11] See below, para. 79.
[12] Above, para. 33.
[13] Putzeys (para. 832) states that the carrier may plead Art. 22.2 unless his action is mistaken and his mistake "*grossière*". See also *ibid.*, para. 1048. *cf.* Gottrau, Theunis, p. 201 and B.T. 1986.706, 708, who contends that in any event the carrier must prove that his response to the situation was "beyond reproach".
[14] Alternatively, it will be recalled, the sender is liable under Art. 7.1(a) "for all expenses, loss and damage sustained by the carrier by reason of the inaccuracy or inadequacy of (a) the particulars specified in article 6", including paragraph (f), which requires an appropriate description of dangerous goods; see above, para. 26.

Liability, it appears, is without limit in amount.[15] The sender is the person who contracted for the carriage of the goods in question.

> In *Douai 11.3.82*[16] a consignee ordered the claimant carrier to transport varnish from the defendants' factory in Béthune to Graz. While the vehicle was parked near Munich, the varnish leaked on to the adjacent motorway, the police and fire services had to be called in, the vehicle towed away, and the remaining goods transferred. The carrier's claim to recover the expense of the episode from the defendants failed. Although the defendants were named as senders in the consignment note, were familiar with the hazards of their product, and were the party from whom the goods had been taken over, the court held that the sender was the one who concluded the contract. In this case that was the consignee who had ordered the carriage and who, moreover, must have been aware of the dangerous nature of the goods, which they had bought from the defendants over a period of nearly two years.

The sender's liability arises only for failure to inform the carrier, as required by Article 22.1, of the dangerous nature of the goods and, as stated in Article 22.2, if "the carrier did not know they were dangerous."[17] The carrier, who having received the requisite information nonetheless agrees to carry the goods, assumes the risk of carriage and cannot complain under Article 22. Of course, the carrier may have an action against the sender on another basis, such as defective packing.[18]

The damage for which the sender may be liable includes damage to other goods in the same consignment but in different ownership.[19] As to the sender's liability under Article 22.2 for damage to the vehicle, however, opinions conflict.[20] The natural and ordinary meaning of the words, "the sender shall be liable for all expenses, loss or damage arising out of" the carriage, might suggest a broad risk liability, including liability for damage to the vehicle and without regard to whether there was fault on the part of the sender.[21] However, indications[22] are that courts will award damages against the sender only if the sender was at fault.

---

[15] Putzeys, para. 1050.

[16] B.T. 1982.199. See also *B.G.H. 16.10.86*, VersR 1987.304, in which it was held that the sender liable under Art. 22.2 was not the person named in the note as sender, but who had not signed it or stamped it, but the person had who actually contracted with the carrier for the carriage on behalf of the person named. The latter was not a party to that contract.

[17] Above, para. 73.

[18] Below, para. 83.

[19] For example, *Brussels 25.1.78*, B.T. 1978.429, note Brunat, at 424.

[20] Against liability: *Brussels 9.6.70*, B.T. 1970.343; *Antwerp 13.12.89* (1990) 25 E.T.L. 319. But *cf. B.G.H. 16.10.86*, VersR 1987.304 in which a claim of this kind was successful, the point not apparently having been disputed.

[21] Helm, Art. 22 Anm. 4; Herber/Piper, Art. 22, 15; Koller, Art. 22, 5; Muth/Glöckner, p. 156; Thume, Art. 22, 45.

[22] *Lyon 7.10.76*, B.T. 1977.84 1979 U.L.R. I 289, affirmed *Cass. 20.6.78*, B.T. 1978.468. Hill and Messent, p. 179; Putzeys, para. 829.

The person to whom the sender is liable under Article 22.2 is not specified, but the assumption is that it is the carrier, and that any third party affected must sue the sender under national law[23] or sue the carrier, leaving the carrier to seek indemnity from the sender. A further possibility in due course may be an action by third parties against the carrier under the Convention on Civil Liability for Damage caused during the Carriage of Dangerous Goods by Road, Rail and Inland Navigation Vessels (CRTD) 1989, which became open for signature on February 1, 1990.[24]

74. Unavoidable circumstances

The most important defence in Article 17.2, a key concept in the CMR, is that

> "the carrier shall . . . be relieved of liability of the loss, damage or delay was caused . . . through circumstances which the carrier could not avoid and the consequences of which he was unable to prevent".

As to what is required of the carrier to avoid loss, damage or delay, and the consequent level of obligation on the carrier, the leading case in England is *Silber v. Islander Trucking*,[25] a decision of Mustill J., in which the judge considered the following possibilities.

74a. Absolute liability

The first possibility is "a liability which is absolute, or nearly so", whereby the "carrier is liable as an insurer, for all loss and damage occurring in transit, otherwise than in the cases specifically referred to", the other cases of exoneration under Article 17.2: the wrongful act or neglect of the claimant,[26] the instructions of the claimant,[27] and inherent vice.[28] This level of liability would be no novelty in the English law of carriage, but it was evidently not the intention of the authors of the CMR, and was rejected in *Silber*.[29]

---

[23] Helm, Art. 22 Anm. 4. Herber/Piper, Art. 22, 16; Koller Art. 22, 5.

[24] Herber, TranspR 950.51. CRTD does not apply to "claims arising out of any contract for the carriage of goods" (Art. 3.1). Dangerous goods are defined (Art. 1.9) by reference to ADR.

[25] [1985] 2 Lloyd's Rep. 243, 245. The facts of the case are described below, para. 75a.

[26] Above, para. 70.

[27] Above, para. 71.

[28] Above, para. 72.

[29] [1985] 2 Lloyd's Rep. 243, 246.

74b. *Conditio sine qua non*

The second possibility is that the "carrier is liable in any case where, if the carrier had done something different from what he actually did, the loss would not have occurred". In *Silber* the judge thought[30] that this interpretation of the defence "best fits the literal meaning of the words. If there is something which the carrier could have done which would have led to the result that the loss did not occur, the loss was one which the carrier 'could have' avoided. Nevertheless, this reading can also be rejected with confidence, for it leads to an absurdity. Imagine a vehicle destroyed by lightning-stroke, or by an unforeseeable explosion at the roadside, or by an unprecedented major road accident, brought about entirely by the actions of third parties. In these and similar cases, the carrier 'could have' avoided the loss by the chance of starting the journey 15 minutes earlier or later." The absurdity lies in the significance that would attach to the decision, a purely fortuitous decision, to set out at 12.15 instead of 12.30.

A second version of this possibility concerns any active steps which the carrier could have taken "precisely *with the object* of forestalling the peril in question".[31] However, even this qualified version of the rule could be pushed to a point of absurdity, as there are "many perils which a carrier could avoid, if endowed with unlimited foresight and resources. An armed robbery can be prevented, if the carrier employs an armoured vehicle, surrounded by scores of armed guards. Yet the parties to the [CMR] can scarcely have intended to force the carrier to such extreme measures, in order to avoid liability for events not of his own making."[32]

74c. Force majeure

A third possibility, that the carrier is liable for all loss, damage or delay unless it arose from events amounting to force majeure, was

---

[30] At 246.

[31] *ibid.* (emphasis added). Also in this sense *Galley Footwear v. Iaboni* [1982] 2 All E.R. 200, 203, *per* Hodgson J.

[32] *Silber v. Islander Trucking* [1985] 2 Lloyd's Rep. 243, 246, *per* Mustill J. Also against an absolute test of what the carrier must do to avoid the loss: *O.G.H. 16.3.77*, SZ 50 no. 40, TranspR 1979.46, 47, 1978 U.L.R. I 370, Greiter 46. Putzeys para. 742.

A similar view has been taken of the requirement of "all necessary measures" in Art. 20 of the Warsaw Convention, for example, in a case of armed robbery: *Manufacturers Hanover Trust Co. v. Alitalia Airlines* 429 F. Supp. 964, 967 (S.D. N.Y. 1977), affirmed 573 F. 2d (2 Cir., 1977), cert. den. 435 US 971 (1978): if the phrase were taken literally, "there could scarcely be a loss of goods—and consequently no call for the operation of Article 20—were a carrier to have taken every precaution literally necessary to the prevention of loss". However, the court went on to apply a criterion of "reasonable measures", a test that has been rejected for Art. 17.2 of the CMR: below, para. 74d. For English cases on the Warsaw Convention, see Shawcross & Beaumont, *Air Law* (4th ed., London, 1989), para. VII.116.

also rejected in *Silber.*[33] Force majeure is a well-known concept and, if the draftsman had intended force majeure, there is no apparent reason why he should not have said so.[34] The same is true of the corresponding defence of *die höhere Gewalt.*[35] The CMR defence is taken from Article 27.2 of the CIM (1952),[36] which replaced the previous reference in CIM to force majeure with a formula like that now found in the CMR, and moved to a formula which has been described[37] as a step halfway between accidental loss and force majeure. Clearly, the draftsman set out to avoid concepts established in national law.[38] The result is a rule for the CMR, which differs from the classic version of force majeure in two important respects.

First, whereas Article 17.2 focuses attention on the acts or omissions of the carrier, force majeure must stem from events external to the carrier's sphere of operation. Moreover, if force

---

[33] [1985] 2 Lloyd's Rep. 243, 245, *per* Mustill J.

[34] At 246–247. This text was also rejected by Hodgson J. in *Michael Galley Footwear v. Iaboni* [1982] 2 All E.R. 200, 206.

[35] *B.G.H. 28.2.75*, N.J.W. 1975.1597, 1975 U.L.R. II 370; *O.L.J. Düsseldorf 27.3.80* (1983) 18 E.T.L. 89, 93. *Die höhere Gewalt* excuses the defendant only in respect of extraordinary events, and the theft of goods and vehicles is not extraordinary: *O.G.H. 16.3.77*, SZ 50 no. 40, TranspR 1979.46, 1978 U.L.R. I 370, Greiter 46. Also in this sense: *B.G.H. 28.2.75* (above). Helm, Art. 17 Anm. 4; Herber/Piper, Art. 17, 40; Koller, Art. 17, 16; Loewe, para. 153; Ramberg (1974) 9 E.T.L. 3, 16; Thume, Art. 17, 96.

[36] Nickel-Lanz, paras. 126 *et seq. B.G.H. 28.2.75* (above). *cf.* Hill and Messent, p. 113.

[37] Nanassy-Wick, reported by Ramberg (1974) 9 E.T.L. 3, 14: "eine Mittelstufe zwischen dem gewöhnlichen Zufall and her höheren Gewalt".

[38] *O.G.H. 16.3.77* (above, n. 35); *O.L.G. Düsseldorf 27.3.80* (1983) 18 E.T.L. 89, 93. Glass and Cashmore, para. 3.47; Haak, p. 147; Muth/Glöckner, pp. 130 and 132; Ramberg (1974) 9 E.T.L. 3, 16. Also in this sense: Loewe, para. 153, *inter alia* because the concept of force majeure is different in each country; yet, he observes that the CMR concept is "very close to the concept of force majeure".

cf. Courts in both Belgium and France, which have sometimes (erroneously) equated the CMR defence with force majeure: *Brussels 25.5.72*, JPA 1972.219, (1972) 7 E.T.L. 219, 1974 U.L.R. I 338; *TC Brussels 22.6.73* (1974) 9 E.T.L. 330, B.T. 1974.252, 1975 U.L.R. I 265; *Brussels 30.10.75* (1976) 11 E.T.L. 238, 243; *Brussels 12.12.77* (1977) 12 E.T.L. 1013, 1020, 1978 U.L.R. I 376, 379, B.T. 1978.39, 40. Also: *Paris 18.10.73*, B.T. 1973.488, 1976 U.L.R. I 242; *Toulouse 16.4.81*, B.T. 1981.318, 1981 U.L.R. II 232; *Montpellier 28.2.85*, B.T. 1985.600. Thus Libouton, Theunis, p. 92: "Article 17.2 is, essentially, hardly any different from [the modern] conception of force majeure." In *Colmar 11.1.72*, B.T. 1972.90, 1973 U.L.C. 276 the defence was equated with *cas fortuit*.

The CMR defence has also been equated (by Muth/Glöckner, pp. 130–131, citing *O.L.G. Düsseldorf 27.3.80*, VersR 1980.826 (1983) 18 E.T.L. 89, and by Thume, Art. 17, 96) with *das unabwendbares Ereignis*, a concept found *inter alia* in Art. 7.2 of the German *Strassenverkehrsgesetz* (StVG), which provides for exoneration if an accident "is due to an unavoidable event that is caused neither by a defect in the condition of the vehicle nor by failure of its mechanism"; and that "An event is particularly considered unavoidable when it is caused by the behaviour of the injured party, or of a third person who is not engaged in the operation, or by the behaviour of an animal, and both the holder and the driver of the vehicle conducted themselves with all the care required by the circumstances." A similar rule is found in Austria; and in Italy where the driver is liable "unless he can prove that he has done everything possible in order to avoid the damage" (CC Art. 2054): Tunc, *Encyclopedia of Comparative Law*, Vol. 11, Chap. 14, para. 22. *cf. O.G.H. 27.8.81*, Greiter 97: in the CMR defence not only the event but also the consequences must be unavoidable.

majeure were the rule for the CMR, Article 17.3, stating that the carrier is not exonerated by reason of the defective condition of the vehicle,[39] would be superfluous.[40] Accordingly, other events within the carrier's sphere, such as strikes, which could not be classified as force majeure, may yet be causes of unavoidable loss under Article 17.2.[41] Herein lies an important difference between force majeure and unavoidable loss,[42] although, in practice, if the events were within the carrier's sphere, the carrier will find it difficult to prove that their consequences were unavoidable.

Secondly, for force majeure the event must be both *inévitable* and *imprévisible*.[43] While Article 17.2 does not require the event to be *imprévisible*,[44] the intention was to remain close to force majeure as regards the *inévitable*. This position is echoed in some of the cases.[45] However, although foreseeability may be irrelevant as such, it remains relevant to what can be avoided.

If a hazard is foreseeable, whether as a general possibility or as an imminent event, more can be expected of the carrier by way of measures to avoid it. Of course, an event, of a *kind* which is foreseeable as a general possibility, may yet be unavoidable in the circumstances in which it occurs. For example, although erratic and dangerous manoeuvres by other vehicles may be foreseeable features of a journey across Europe, in a particular case the collision may be unavoidable. In such cases the carrier not at fault may be exonerated.[46] In other cases, foresight of the general possibility could have led to effective measures to prevent the loss. For example, driver A could not prevent the robbery at the time it happened, but he should have foreseen that, if he spent the night in a layby near Bari, an armed robbery might well occur.[47] A court cannot decide whether an event was avoidable without considering whether it was foreseeable,[48] so, the likelihood (or foreseeability) of loss is one of the factors that influence a court in

---

[39] Below, para. 75f.

[40] *B.G.H. 28.2.75*, N.J.W. 1975.1597, 1975 U.L.R. II 370; *O.G.H. 16.3.77*, SZ 50 no. 40, TranspR 1979.46, 1978 U.L.R. 370, Greiter 46. Loewe, para. 153; Muth/Glöckner, p. 130; Pesce, p. 211; Putzeys, para. 742; Ramberg (1974) 9 E.T.L. 3, 14. A proposal to confine the defence to "circumstances not connected with the operation of the transport service" was rejected: W/TRANS/WP.9/38 no. 12.

[41] Helm, Art. 17 Anm. 4; Putzeys, para. 742, citing Loewe, para. 153.

[42] *O.L.G. Munich 16.1.74* (1974) 9 E.T.L. 615, 618; *B.G.H. 28.2.75*, N.J.W. 1975.1597, 1975 U.L.R. II 370.

[43] Putzeys, para. 738; Sériaux D.1982.I.111.

[44] E/ECE/TRANS/SC 1/130 Annexe 3 no. 9. Also in this sense: Brunat, B.T. 1983.327; Nickel-Lanz, para. 130. *cf.* Putzeys, para. 742, that Art. 17.2 is less strict on both points.

[45] For example, *TC Paris 9.6.83*, B.T. 1983.457.

[46] Below, para. 75b.

[47] Rodière B.T. 1974.279; Brunat B.T. 1984.132. For example, *TC Paris 9.6.83*, B.T. 1983.457; and the numerous cases of armed robbery in Italy, discussed below, para. 75a in which the defence failed. But *cf. Cass. 27.1.81*, B.T. 1981.219, D.1982.I.110 note Sériaux.

[48] Pesce, p. 206; Sériaux *loc. cit.*

assessing whether, the carrier has done what is required for exoneration under Article 17.2.[49]

74d. Reasonable care

The fourth possibility considered in *Silber*[50] is that the carrier is required to exercise no more than reasonable care in accordance with current practice in the transport industry. This level of duty was rejected[51] in that case because reasonable care is a well-known concept and, as with force majeure,[52] if the draftsman had intended a duty of reasonable care, there is no apparent reason why he could not have said so. He could, said the judge, "have borrowed 'due diligence' from the Hague Rules, or could have used words such as 'care' or 'neglect' ",[53] as he did earlier in Article 17.2, by speaking of the act or "neglect" of the claimant and of the carrier.

> In *Iaboni*[54] the two drivers parked the vehicle in Milan, locked it, activated its alarm, and went for a meal in a restaurant only 35 yards away but out of sight of the vehicle. The vehicle was stolen. Hodgson J. found that the drivers had behaved in accordance with current trade practice and that they had not been negligent,[55] but held, nonetheless, that the carrier's defence under Article 17.2 failed.

74e. Utmost care

Having rejected some interpretation as too strict and others as too lenient, Mustill J. in *Silber* found a middle way. He concluded that Article 17.2 "sets a standard which is somewhere between, on the

---

[49] Below, para. 75.
[50] [1985] 2 Lloyd's Rep. 243, 247.
[51] *ibid.* This possibility was also rejected by Neill J. in *Thermo Engineers Ltd v. Ferrymasters Ltd* [1981] 1 Lloyd's Rep. 200, 206; and by Hodgson J. in *Michael Galley Footwear v. Iaboni* [1982] 2 All E.R. 200, 206–207, as interpreted in *Silber*, at 246, by Mustill J. A similar standard was rejected in *B.G.H. 21.12.66*, N.J.W. 1967.499, 500; and *TC Liège 13.12.77*, JPA 1977/8.268, 1980 U.L.R. I 270, 273. However, this standard has been advocated in France: Brunat B.T. 1983.327.
[52] Above, para. 74c.
[53] In this sense as regards "reasonable care": *Thermo Engineers* (above, n. 51).
As regards "due diligence", this argument is less convincing: French commentators found the "due diligence" of the Hague Rules vague and unclear (Clarke, HR, pp. 205–206), and whatever the intention of the draftsman, this form of words would not have commanded support in some quarters. An early draft of the CMR allowed the carrier to be exonerated if the carrier could prove that the negligence did not contribute to the loss, damage or delay, but this provision was discarded: TRANS/WP.9/11, p. 42.
[54] *Michael Galley Footwear v. Iaboni* [1982] 2 All E.R. 200.
[55] At 207.

one hand, a requirement to take every conceivable precaution, however extreme, within the limits of the law, and on the other hand a duty to do no more than act reasonably in accordance with prudent current practice".[56] In Article 17.2 the expression "could not avoid", he concluded, means "could not avoid even with the utmost care".[57] Utmost care is not, in any literal sense, extreme care but imports some notion of what is "practical" and "short of the absurd".[58]

On this last point, at least, the English judge echoed[59] the view of the OGH,[60] that Article 17.2 requires "die äußerste, vernünftigerweise zumutbarer Sorgfalt": the utmost reasonable care compatible with good sense. In other words used by the OGH in the same case, the rule requires "die äußerste, nach den Umständen des Falles möglicher und vernünftigerweise zumutbarer Sorgfalt". Statements like this have been made in Austria both before and since that case,[61] and also by some courts in Germany.

In Germany the first major decision[62] on the point required, as in the law of carriage by rail, the utmost care possible: "die äußerste nach den Umständen mögliche Sorgfalt." Again,[63] "an dem Merkmal der Unabwendbarkeit fehlt es schon dann, wenn die Beobachtung jeder nach den Umständen möglichen Sorgfalt eine auch an sich nicht voraussehbare Schadenursache unwirksam gemacht haben würde". The formula has been used in later cases but softened to include some reference to what is reasonable: "die äußerste, zumutbare Sorgfalt",[64] or "die äußerste wirtschaftliche zumutbare Sorgfalt".[65] This being so, the outline of the concept as perceived in Germany, as well as in Austria, is close to that in England.

---

[56] [1985] 2 Lloyd's Rep. 243, 247.

[57] *ibid.*

[58] *ibid.*

[59] At 247. The English report omits the word "äußerste", but this may well be an error, as this adjective is almost invariably found in this standard form of words, and is found in the judgment of the O.G.H. to which Mustill J. referred: *O.G.H. 29.6.83*, Stra GüV 1985/1 p. 8, (1984) 19 E.T.L. 526, 1986 U.L.R. II 602, Greiter 192, 194.

[60] *O.G.H. 29.6.83* (above).

[61] *O.G.H. 16.3.77*, SZ 50 no. 40, TranspR 1979.46, 1978 U.L.R. I 370, Greiter 46; *O.G.H. 18.3.86*, Stra GüV 1986/7 pp. 8, 9; *O.G.H. 8.4.87*, Stra GüV 1987/11 pp. 23, 26; *O.G.H. 19.1.94*, TranspR 1994.282; and TranspR 1995.65.

[62] *B.G.H. 21.12.66*, N.J.W. 1967.499, 500. See also: *O.L.G. Frankfurt 25.10.77*, VersR 1978.535; *B.G.H. 5.6.81* (1982) 17 E.T.L. 301, 309; *O.L.G. Hamburg 1.4.82*, VersR 1982.1171; *O.L.G. Hamburg 30.11.95*, TranspR 1996.280 and *O.L.G. Hamburg 14.5.96*, TranspR 1997.101. *idem* in Austria: *O.G.H. 27.8.81*, Greiter 97. However, the latter judgment also used the "softer" formula, so perhaps no difference was intended.

[63] *B.G.H. 21.12.66* (above) *loc. cit.*

[64] *O.L.G. Düsseldorf 27.3.80*, (1983) 18 E.T.L. 89, 93; *B.G.H. 5.6.81* (above, n. 62); *O.L.G. Düsseldorf 25.6.81*, VersR 1982.606; *B.G.H. 16.2.84*, VersR 1984.551; *O.L.G. Düsseldorf 11.5.89*, TranspR 1990.60, 63, Herber/Piper, Art. 17, 41; Muth/Glöckner, p. 132; Thume, Art. 17, 96. *cf.* Koller, Art. 17, 20 *et seq.*

[65] *O.L.G. Munich 27.3.81*, VersR 1982.264, 265.

In these countries the defence may be hard to establish in practice. In Germany, the liability of the carrier is seen as an instance of *Gefährdungshaftung*,[66] to which an exception, if utmost care has been exercised, is the natural complement. Speaking of the liability (also *Gefährdungshaftung*) of persons who deal in dangerous substances, Zweigert and Kötz observed, not only as regards Germany but also England[67]:

> "The degree of 'care' demanded of the defendant is often so extreme as to be barely distinguishable from liability without fault. In general, whenever it seems necessary in order to achieve a socially acceptable distribution of the accident risks peculiar to modern life, the courts tend to insist on precautions which it is virtually impossible to satisfy, and they can do this because, judging a case *ex post facto*, they can always discover some precaution or other which, had the defendant adopted it at the time, would have prevented the occurrence of the harm."

Although Mustill J. in *Silber* set the level of the carrier's duty below the absolute level, and although the CMR is not concerned with people living in the shadow of factories making chemicals, it is striking how rare it is to find a successful defence in an action in England, Austria or Germany on the ground of utmost care and unavoidable loss in circumstances which did not also exonerate the carrier on other grounds.[68] Moreover, the warranties in respect of precautions against theft written in the carrier's liability insurance are now so severe that, unless the level of the carrier's liability for the goods is pushed higher still, as regards theft, there is no layer of liability to insure.

75. Unavoidable circumstances: utmost care in practice

To apply the test of utmost care, the court takes the template of a carrier with the standard of knowledge and skill of a competent professional carrier.[69] Against this model carrier, the conduct of the actual carrier is measured and judged, in the light of the following factors.

---

[66] Above, para. 54a.

[67] *Introduction to Comparative Law*, Vol. I, p. 344 (trans. Weir, Oxford, 1982).

[68] Such as inherent vice, the more appropriate ground of exoneration in *Centocoop Export-Import SA v. Brit European Transport* [1984] 2 Lloyd's Rep. 618. The exception is a successful defence, usually in respect of delay, caused by third parties: officials or strikers: below, para. 75e.

[69] Sériaux, *loc. cit.*, above, n. 43.

The first factor is the likelihood of loss, damage or delay. In the theft cases,[70] the high likelihood of theft and robbery in Italy, well publicised by insurers and by trade associations, has been a factor that has influenced courts all over Europe,[71] especially when the load was one popular with thieves,[72] to require strict precautions of the carrier.

A second factor is the practicality of the measures which, in the contention of the claimant, the carrier should have taken to avoid the loss, damage or delay in question. For example, in *Silber*,[73] one precaution, the formation of convoys of vehicles, was rejected because the claimant had not shown it to be possible in practice. Practicality also depends on the knowledge and information available to the carrier, the fourth factor (below).

A third factor is legality: carriers will not be required to break the law, notably regulations governing driving hours,[74] in order to reach a place in which the goods can be salvaged or made secure.

Finally, the standard of care is affected by a fourth factor, the state of knowledge in the industry.[75] Insurers, directly or indirectly through trade associations, have offered information to carriers, for example, on security devices for vehicles and the location of secure parks.[76] This process of "education" has been reinforced here as in other contexts by insurance warranties, whereby the

---

70 Below, para. 75a.

71 *O.L.G. Düsseldorf 56.6.81*, VersR 1982.606; *O.G.H. 29.6.83*, Stra GüV 1985/1 p. 8, (1984) 19 E.T.L. 526, 1986 U.L.R. II 602, Greiter 192; *B.G.H. 16.2.84*, VersR 1984.551; *O.L.G. Düsseldorf 11.5.89*, TranspR 1990.60, 63; *Cass. 20.1.90*, B.T. 1990.778; *O.L.G. Munich 12.5.90*, TranspR 1989.427. *cf. Cass. com. 16.11.93*, B.T.L. 1993.874.

Similarly, in *TC Liège 13.12.77*, JPA 1977/8.268, 1980 U.L.R. I 270, 274, rejecting the defence, the court was influenced by the location of the loss: the port area of Rotterdam. Likewise, *Texas Instruments v. Nason (Europe) Ltd* [1991] 1 Lloyd's Rep. 146: a public car park in the East End of London.

72 For example, cigarettes: *Antwerp 30.5.79* (1979) 14 E.T.L. 924, *O.L.G. Hamburg 14.5.96*, TranspR 1997.101; jeans: *B.G.H. 16.2.84*, VersR 1984.551; stereo equipment and clothing: *Silber Ltd v. Islander Trucking* [1985] 2 Lloyd's Rep. 243; tin: *TC Liège 13.12.77*, JPA 1977/8.268, 1980 U.L.R. I 270; cassette players: *Longmill Corp. plc v. Andrea Merzario Ltd* (Central London County Court, unreported) and, at any rate in France, foodstuffs: Fourcade B.T. 1982.398. By contrast, theft of some goods is less likely and such goods require fewer precautions: *Caen 15.11.83*, B.T. 1984.131 (large boilers); *Cicatiello (G.L.) S.R.L. v. Anglo-European Shipping Services Ltd* [1994] 1 Lloyd's Rep. 678, 684 *per* Marr-Johnson J. (pickled pelts). "Utmost care" forbids drivers to mention in public not only their route or their destination but also the nature of their load: Fourcade, *loc. cit.* Of course, in some cases such as containers loaded by the sender, the driver may have little or no idea of the nature of the goods in his charge.

73 *Silber v. Islander Trucking* [1985] 2 Lloyd's Rep. 243, 249, *per* Mustill J.

74 *Michael Galley Footwear v. Iaboni* [1982] 2 All E.R. 200, 207, *per* Hodgson J.; *Silber* (above), *loc. cit.*

75 *O.L.G. Hamburg 1.4.82*, VersR 1982.1172; *Cass. 20.1.90*, B.T. 990.778.

76 For example, the location of secure parks in France and the nature of the security offered by each park has been published and subsequently updated by the Syndicat des stés. françaises maritimes et de transport (B.T. 1983.279, 290); and by the Italian insurers for Italy (B.T. 1983.451, 522, 534).

carrier loses liability cover, unless certain procedures are observed.[77] Knowledge has been a mixed blessing for carriers, because their liability has risen with the tide of information. A like reputation has now been acquired by parts of the former Soviet Union.[78] Although insurers are loath to lose the high premium that can be charged for commercial vehicle cover and are afraid that they will lose business, many insurers are convinced that the vehicle manufacturers could do more to improve the security of their products and the attitude of insurers is hardening. Moreover, effective retro-fitting of tracker devices is now an option for carriers, and insurers would like to see more of that.[79] Insurers have also published details of the nature and location of secure parks.[80]

By contrast, another factor,[81] common practice in the transport industry, has been rejected.[82] Rejection of that factor, however, must be seen in the context of rising crime in Italy which had rendered previous but still common security practice inadequate. In other cases, in which common practice is in line with the time and place, evidence of that practice may yet influence the court.

In *Iaboni*[83] factors of this kind, in particular the first and second factors discussed above, were dismissed as irrelevant, because they are also associated with the standard of reasonable care. However, while it is accepted that the standard of reasonable care is lower than the "utmost care" of Article 17.2 once it is also accepted that the carrier's level of duty is less than absolute, the duty becomes a relative duty, and it is difficult to see how utmost care can be distinguished from absolute care without considering factors of this kind; the difference will be in the weighting. Utmost care cannot be assessed in the abstract and in practice these factors have been considered by the courts.

---

[77] For example, *Paris 14.10.81*, B.T. 1982.158; *Chambéry 27.6.84*, B.T. 1985.159. In recent times, for consignments destined for Italy, French insurers have required use of the vehicle manufacturer's anti-theft "system", locking the vehicle, a watchman of some kind and/or an enclosed area: B.T.L. 1993.278.

[78] See, *e.g. O.L.G. Hamburg 30.11.95*, TranspR 1996.280, 282.

[79] See *Post Magazine*, January 26, 1995, p. 21, and *Post Magazine*, February 29, 1996, pp. 18–19.

[80] For example, B.T.L. 1993.279.

[81] This factor is influential in cases in which the level of duty is that of reasonable care or due diligence. The rejection of this factor for Article 17.2 is an important point of difference between those levels and that of utmost care.

[82] *Michael Galley Footwear v. Iaboni* [1982] 2 All E.R. 200, 207, *per* Hodgson J. Reference to a practice common in 1962 in (West) Germany of leaving vehicles unattended in a service station overnight was rejected as evidence of utmost care in *B.G.H. 21.12.66*, N.J.W. 1967.499, 500. Such strictness has been criticised by Libouton, Theunis, p. 82.

[83] *Michael Galley Footwear v. Iaboni* [1982] 2 All E.R. 200, 206, *per* Hodgson J.: factors which he referred to as "the negligence equations": "the magnitude and likelihood of the risk, the gravity of the consequences and the cost and practicality of overcoming the risk".

If it appears that there were no measures that would have avoided the loss, the carrier is exonerated,[84] even though in fact the carrier had not taken the measures.[85] In other cases the approach advocated by Mustill J. in *Silber*[86] is that, although the legal onus of proof is on the carrier, the first move should come from the claimant; that it is for the claimant to suggest what the carrier could and should have done to avoid the loss, damage or delay (an exercise in reasonable speculation[87] rather than proof) and that it is then for the carrier to rebut the suggestion, to prove that the suggested measure would not have avoided the loss, damage or delay. Consequently, the carrier is not required to list all the steps which could conceivably have been thought appropriate, and then methodically demonstrate, one by one, that they were not called for in order to perform the duty, or that, if they had been taken, they would not have prevented or reduced the loss or damage. If this appears to reverse the onus of proof established by Article 18.1, that the carrier must prove that the loss, damage or delay was due to one of the exonerating causes, it is not to be supposed that this was the judge's intention: not only is the claimant's role one of speculation rather than of proof, but the carrier must first give "evidence of facts sufficient to bring the defence into play".[88] In any event, as has been said[89] in Belgium, the circumstances must be considered "in concreto" and, indeed, the test of utmost care can best be understood through the cases.

75a. Theft and robbery

The utmost care required to avoid theft or robbery of the goods depends *inter alia* on the likelihood that theft will be attempted. Having been well publicised in transport journals since at least

---

[84] *Cicatiello (G.L.) S.R.L. v. Anglo-European Shipping Services Ltd* [1994] 1 Lloyd's Rep. 678 (a case of theft).

[85] *O.G.H. 19.1.94*, TranspR 1994. 282; and TranspR 1995.65.

[86] [1985] 2 Lloyd's Rep. 243, 247. Support for this approach can also be found from Hodgson J. in *Michael Galley Footwear v. Iaboni* [1982] 2 All E.R. 200, 207; and His Honour Judge Diamond Q.C., in *Longmill Corp. plc v. Andrea Merzario Ltd* (Central London County Court, unreported).

Similarly in France, the defence of force majeure is considered in the light of concrete measures which might have avoided the loss, and this is also regarded as the proper approach to defences such as that of unavoidable loss in the CMR: Sériaux D.1982.I.111.

[87] One suggestion from the claimant in that case was that the vehicle should have travelled in convoy. Observing (at 249) that there was no evidence before the court on whether this was practicable, the judge rejected the suggestion: "While giving full weight to the burden of proof, I think that something rather more solid is required of the plaintiffs than merely throwing out the suggestion, with nothing to back it up."

[88] Glass and Cashmore, para. 3.47.

[89] *Brussels 12.12.77* (1977) 12 E.T.L. 1013, 1020, 1978 U.L.R. I 376, 379, B.T. 1978.39, 40; *TC Liège 13.12.77*, JPA 1977/8.268, 1980 U.L.R. I 270, 273.

1978,[90] it is notorious that there has been a high level of theft in "the Bermuda Triangle" between Rome, Naples and Bari, and, indeed, in Italy as a whole, which has been described as "top of the hit parade".[91]

To be forewarned is not always to be forearmed, as knowledge may be poor protection against machine guns, yet there have been very few cases indeed in which a carrier's defence has succeeded on the ground that the theft or robbery was unavoidable. Perhaps a lingering suspicion remains[92] that theft may be the fruit of collusion between the carrier or his employees and the thieves. To counter the threat of robbery and theft, various measures have been suggested.

First, in *Silber*[93] the claimant argued[94] that the vehicle should have had various security devices[95]; however, this argument was rejected in that case, as these would not have prevented the particular robbery.[96] Generally, however, the use of an anti-theft device appears to be a *conditio sine qua non* of exoneration of the carrier.[97] It also appears that in situations in which theft and robbery are rife the use of anti-theft devices without more is not enough.[98]

Secondly, the claimant in *Silber*[99] argued that the vehicle should have travelled in convoy with other vehicles. This argument was also rejected in that case, as there was no evidence "to indicate whether in practice road hauliers in Italy find it possible to constitute convoys and, if so, whether it has any appreciable effect on the incidence of armed robbery".[1]

---

[90] *Paris 19.10.87*, B.T. 1988.73, 74; *Poitiers 4.11.87*, B.T. 1988.426. And by warnings from insurers from at least 1975: *Poitiers 7.2.83*, B.T. 1983.455.

[91] Fourcade, B.T. 1982.398. Point taken, *e.g.* by Diamond J. Q.C., in *Longmill Corp. plc v. Andrea Merzario Ltd* (Central London County Court, unreported). Generally, see also Humphreys (1992) 27 E.T.L. 735, 742.

[92] Haak, p. 144. For the general position on theft in Germany, see Herber/Piper, Art. 17, 44; Koller, Art. 17, 29; Thume, Art. 17, 100; and for the position in Austria, see Thume, Art. 17, A100. In the common law tradition the possibility of collusion was one of the reasons given for the strict liability of the common carrier: *Coggs v. Bernard* (1703) 2 Ld. Raym. 909, 918, *per* Hold C.J. Today, the carrier's liability insurer may require the carrier to retain a certain percentage of the risk and to take certain precautions.

[93] *Silber v. Islander Trucking* [1985] 2 Lloyd's Rep. 243.

[94] In accordance with the approach suggested by the judge: above, para. 75.

[95] The devices suggested were an internal lock, a manually operated alarm, and a time delay fuel cutout.

[96] At 248–249. See also *Cicatiello (G.L.) S.R.L. v. Anglo-European Shipping Services Ltd* [1994] 1 Lloyd's Rep. 678, 684.

[97] For example, *Limoges 1.3.83*, B.T. 1983.330; *O.L.G. Munich 12.5.89*, TranspR 1990.427; *O.L.G. Innsbruck 26.1.90*, 1991.12. Muth/Glöckner, p. 131. Equally, it may be a continuing warranty of the insurance contract: *Cass. 31.3.87*, B.T. 1987.280.

[98] For example, *Toulouse 16.4.81*, B.T. 1981.318, 1981 U.L.R. II 232; *B.G.H. 16.2.84*, VersR 1984.551.

[99] *Silber v. Islander Trucking* [1985] 2 Lloyd's Rep. 243.

[1] At 249, *per* Mustill J.

Thirdly, it has been successfully argued in various cases[2] that in the circumstances utmost care required the employment of extra men, a watchman or a second driver.

> In *Silber*[3] the driver and unit arrived at Reggio Calabria from the United Kingdom at 2 a.m. The driver had six hours' sleep in the cab and was then required to set off alone to Paris with a load of stereo equipment and clothes worth £100,000 (in 1980). After 250 km he stopped for coffee and a snack. After a further 68 km he stopped for two hours and attempted, unsuccessfully, to repair another vehicle owned by his employer. The driver proceeded for a further 124 km and at 10.30 p.m. parked at the tollgate at Salerno in a well-lit area. The judge observed[4] that "He says that by then he was tired, and it is hard not to believe him." After about an hour, another lorry pulled up, a man smashed his cab window, and two armed and masked men made off with the load. The carrier's defence, that this loss could not have been avoided, was rejected.

As the carrier cannot be expected or encouraged to break EEC regulations governing the permitted maximum of hours that a driver may drive, the decisive argument against the carrier in *Silber* was that the carrier should have employed an extra driver and that, if he had done so, the vehicle could have been brought to a secure park, without breach of the regulations, and the robbery could have been avoided.[5] Although the employment of a second driver was an expensive measure, there was no evidence before the court in *Silber* that "the extra expense would have been so absurdly disproportionate as to put it outside the confines of 'the utmost care' ".[6] In later cases, however, evidence has suggested that this is unrealistic—that the cost of an extra driver could be covered only by freight charges that most customers would be unwilling to pay.[7]

Be that as it may, the existence of a secure park, which the carrier did not use, is a common feature of cases in which the carrier's defence on this ground fails.[8] If he is unable to reach a

---

[2] Or there is a strong hint to this effect from the court: for example, *B.G.H. 16.2.84*, VersR 1984.551.

[3] *Silber v. Islander Trucking* [1985] 2 Lloyd's Rep. 243, 250.

[4] At 245.

[5] At 250.

[6] *ibid.* For Italy the same suggestion is made by *O.L.G. Hamburg 1.4.82*, VersR 1982.1172; *TC Paris 9.6.83*, B.T. 1983.457, 459; *B.G.H. 16.2.84*, VersR 1984.551. Muth/Glöckner, p. 131.

[7] See *Cicatiello (G.L.) S.R.L. v. Anglo-European Shipping Services Ltd* [1994] 1 Lloyd's Rep. 678, 682–683.

[8] For example, *Aix 11.3.69*, B.T. 1969.389, 1970 U.L.C. 122; *O.L.G. Hamburg 1.4.82*, VersR 1982.1172; *Cass. 20.1.90* B.T. 1990.778; *Texas Instruments v. Nason (Europe) Ltd* [1991] 1 Lloyd's Rep. 146; *O.L.G. Innsbruck 26.1.90*, TranspR 1991.12; *Cass com. 15.5.91*, B.T.L. 1992.11; 27 E.T.L. 124; *Longmill Corp. plc v. Andrea Merzario Ltd* (Central London County Court, unreported); *O.L.G. Hamburg 14.5.96*, TranspR 1997.101. For Dutch cases in which the use of secure parking was required, see Haak, p. 146. *cf. O.L.G. Hamburg 7.12.95*, TranspR 1996.283.

secure park, the carrier must pay[9] for some kind of watchman: a dog in the vehicle will not do.[10]

Leaving a loaded vehicle unattended at night in a public place,[11] even though the driver was asleep in the vehicle,[12] or even leaving it on private premises if the vehicle is visible from a busy road,[13] is usually a lack of the utmost care required by Article 17.2. Locking the vehicle during a short absence, for example to take a meal, may be sufficient in many places but not in places where there is a high risk of theft: to drive the driver must eat, but if he does not have a co-driver, he must eat in the cab.[14] Leaving goods unguarded by the roadside after an accident is failure to exercise utmost care, even if the accident was not the fault of the carrier's driver and the driver was in a state of shock or concussion.[15]

---

[9] In *B.G.H. 21.12.66*, N.J.W. 1967.499, 1967 U.L.C. 283, (1969) 4 E.T.L. 516 a loaded lorry was left in the precincts of a petrol station on the German side of the border with Holland, without being guarded and without any check on the part of the driver whether the petrol station would remain open for the whole of the time that the lorry would be there. While the station was shut overnight the lorry was driven off and its load of cobalt removed. The carrier was held liable. The court was unimpressed by the argument that there was no safer overnight parking place in the area. The argument that it was too expensive to employ a watchman for a vehicle with a valuable load was rejected. The court declined to answer the carrier's contention that with a load of material important to the nuclear industry, both valuable and politically sensitive, theft could only be prevented altogether by "a cordon of policemen armed to the teeth and with machine guns at the ready". *cf. O.L.G. Munich 5.7.96*, TranspR 1997.147.

[10] *Paris 14.6.77* (below, n. 20).

[11] For example, *B.G.H. 21.12.66* (above, n. 9); *Aix 11.3.69* B.T. 1969.389, 1970 U.L.C. 122; *Brussels 30.10.75* (1976) 11 E.T.L. 238; *Antwerp 30.5.79* (1979) 14 E.T.L. 924, 1981 U.L.R. 237; *Cass. Belge 12.12.80* (1981) 16 E.T.L. 250, 256–257; *O.L.G. Düsseldorf 25.6.81*, VersR 1982.606; *O.G.H. 15.12.81*, Greiter 119; *The Hague 22.3.85*, S. & S. 1985 no. 122; *O.L.G. Munich 17.7.91*, TranspR 1991. 427.

[12] *Cass. 27.1.81*, B.T. 1981.219, D.1982.I.110; *O.L.G. Hamburg 1.4.82*, VersR 1982.1172; *Poitiers 7.2.83*, B.T. 1983.455; *O.G.H. 8.3.83*, TranspR 1983.138, Greiter 181; *Cass. 18.3.86*, B.T. 1986.251, 1986 U.L.R. II 639; *Paris 19.10.87*, B.T. 1988.73; *Poitiers 4.11.87*, B.T. 1988.426; *Cass. com. 15.5.91*, B.T.L. 1992.11; 27 E.T.L. 124. In earlier times and perhaps still in places of low risk it would have been sufficient for the driver to lock the vehicle and sleep in it, unless perhaps the load was particularly attractive to thieves. Contrary decisions are still regarded as hard by some writers in France and Holland, for example Haak, p. 146.

[13] *TC Liège 13.12.77*, JPA 1977/8.2.68, 1980 U.L.R. I 270: behind a padlocked gate 2.5 m. high in the port area of Rotterdam. Or in a locked garage in Turin, where some kind of anti-theft device, as well as a watchman was required: *Limoges 1.3.83*, B.T. 1983.330, regarded by Brunat (B.T. 1983.327) as a hard decision. However, in the same sense: *'s Hertogenbosch 4.2.86*, S. & S. 1987 no. 25.

[14] For example, *O.G.H. 16.3.77*, SZ 50 no. 40, TranspR 1979.46, 1978 U.L.R. I 370, Greiter 46: parked in a side street in Milan around the corner from the restaurant where the (sole) driver had lunch while waiting for a telephone connection to Austria to obtain instructions from his employer; the call was not a matter of urgency, and he could have stayed with his vehicle and had a cold meal. Also: parked for thirty minutes with other goods vehicles near a restaurant on the outskirts of Milan: *O.G.H. 29.6.83*, Stra GüV 1985/1 p. 8, (1984) 19 E.T.L. 526, 1986 U.L.R. II 602, Greiter 192. In similar vein: *O.L.G. Munich 27.3.81*, VersR 1982.264; *Supreme Court Finland 18.5.84*, 1986 U.L.R. II 634; *Cass. 31.3.87*, B.T. 1987.280; *O.L.G. Düsseldorf 11.5.89*, TranspR 1990.60. *Paris 26.2.97*, B.T.L. 1997.335. *cf.* the relatively lenient decision in favour of the carrier in *Amsterdam 25.3.82*, S. & S. 1983 no. 9.

[15] *Chambéry 27.6.84*, B.T. 1985.159: the driver left the goods by the side of the road in Italy, and returned to France with his daughter who had been injured in the accident.

Equally, leaving a vehicle in need of repair at the roadside in order to seek assistance is not justified unless no other course is open to the driver.[16] In all these cases, utmost care requires that the carrier shall pay for extra security of the kind that suits the situation.

All this suggests that a successful defence in respect of theft will be rare.[17] However, in the French courts the defence has sometimes succeeded in respect of theft or robbery involving an element of deception. Here too, however, particular kinds of deception, such as the diversion of drivers who do not know the location of the place of delivery, have been well publicised, and the carrier deceived may have no defence.[18] *Aliter*, perhaps, when deception and violence come together.

> In *Paris 17.6.86*[19] the vehicle was flagged down by a man with a red light, a circumstance suggesting an emergency which could not be ignored by the driver, who was then overpowered. This has been held to amount to force majeure under French domestic law. By contrast, in *Paris 14.6.77*[20] parcels of clothes were to be sent from Paris and the driver went to collect them from an upstairs workroom. He was about to drive away in the belief that he had collected all the parcels, when a person unknown to him came and told him that there were more to be taken, which was untrue. The driver went back upstairs, leaving his dog in the vehicle, and on his return found no vehicle. The vehicle was found empty the next day. The court rejected a plea of unavoidable loss.

Further, armed robbery may be a defence if an attack occurs while the vehicle is on the move. Most cases have concerned sitting ducks: vehicles stationary and unattended where and when they should not have been left unattended, and so the defence has failed. However, just as the merchantman in open sea is vulnerable to a more mobile enemy, so it has been held,[21] there is little that the driver of a goods vehicle can do to avoid the armed occupants of a saloon car or of another lorry that rams his own.

> In *Cass. 21.6.88*[22] the driver was signalled to stop by the armed occupants of a car, and the court considered that he had little choice but to obey, as he could not outdistance the car, nor defend himself against the weapons of the occupants. The loss was unavoidable. By contrast, in *Poitiers 23.4.86*[23] the defence did not succeed, although

---

[16] *Cass. com. 25.10.94*, B.T.L. 1994.827: in Italy.
[17] In this sense: *O.G.H. 29.6.83*, Stra GüV 1985/1 p. 8, (1984) 19 E.T.L. 526, 1986 U.L.R. II 602, Greiter 192.
[18] *e.g. O.L.G. Hamburg 30.11.95*, TranspR 1996.280.
[19] B.T. 1987.174. A similar decision was reached in *Rouen 30.5.84*, B.T. 1984.598: the driver was stopped and then overpowered by robbers disguised as policemen.
[20] B.T. 1977.354.
[21] *TC Paris 31.5.83*, reported by Brunat, B.T. 1984.132.
[22] B.T. 1988.437; see also *Cass. com. 10.12.91*, B.T.L. 1992.176; *O.L.G. Munich 5.7.96*, TranspR 1997.147.
[23] B.T. 1987.362.

the carrier's vehicle was in motion and the attacker was mobile, because the attack occurred in Italy after dark, and might have been avoided if the vehicle had travelled by day.

75b. Collision

If the driver falls asleep at the wheel, the carrier is liable for the consequent damage.[24] Moreover, if the vehicle hits a permanent object, like a bridge, the carrier will be liable, unless perhaps the sign stating the height of the bridge was inaccurate.[25] A high degree of skill and alertness is expected of drivers to avoid impact damage in collision with other objects, whether mobile or stationary. An unexpected obstacle confronting the driver in the road is avoidable unless the carrier can produce "proper proof that violent braking really was necessary and in circumstances which, in the heavy traffic of the present day, were altogether abnormal and unforeseeable".[26] The defence has succeeded sometimes in cases of erratic and unexpected manoeuvres by other vehicles[27]; and in cases in which the carrier's vehicle was properly parked[28] or in a statutory line of traffic held up by fog[29] when it was hit by another vehicle. In many cases, when the driver finds the way blocked by an obstacle which he is unable to avoid altogether, the carrier may nonetheless be liable in part under Article 17.5, if a quicker response by the driver would have reduced the force of impact and thus the degree of damage.[30]

If the effect of violent evasive action, which successfully prevents damage by collision, is that the goods shift and are damaged in other ways, that is not a case of unavoidable damage under Article 17.2. If loading stowage were the duty of the carrier,[31] the carrier is in breach of duty, as the operations should have been done with this possibility in mind.[32] If loading and stowage were the responsibility of the sender, the same is true: loading and stowage are defective unless carried out in such a way that the

---

[24] *Rb Dordrecht 18.5.66*, 1968 U.L.C. 155, (1968) 3 E.T.L. 416.

[25] Pestel-Debord, B.T. 1988.33, with reference to *TC Marseille 23.10.87*, B.T. 1988.43.

[26] *JP Antwerp 26.10.71* (1972) E.T.L. 1058, 1061. Libouton, Theunis p. 82. Generally, see Herber/Piper, Art. 17, 48; Koller, Art. 17, 24; and Thume, Art. 17, 107.

[27] *O.L.G. Munich 16.1.74* (1974) 9 E.T.L. 615, 620: the defendant's vehicle was being driven carefully at an appropriate speed, when a goods vehicle proceeding in the opposite direction skidded and crossed the centre line of the road. The same decision was reached in *Antwerp 13.10.86* (1987) 22 E.T.L. 443: the other vehicle braked and changed lanes without warning.

[28] *Paris 13.12.76*, B.T. 1977.37.

[29] *TC Brussels 31.5.96* (1996) 31 E.T.L. 586.

[30] For example: *Agen 15.10.84*, B.T. 1985.558; *Cass. 22.7.86*, B.T. 1986.591. But *cf. The Hague 3.6.76*, S. & S. 1977 no. 3: the fault of other road users is not a ground for reducing the amount of damages awarded against a carrier who was driving too fast.

[31] Above, para. 28.

[32] *Rouen 11.4.91*, B.T.L. 1992.11. A defence of unavoidable loss in bad weather at sea will fail for the same reasons: *Paris 23.3.88*, B.T. 1988.265.

goods will not be harmed in the course of evasive action by the driver.[33] However, in the latter case the carrier will plead not Article 17.2 (unavoidable circumstances) but Article 17.4(c) (loading by the sender), although the same issue (avoidable damage) may arise on the counter allegation of the sender that the loss was attributable not to the manner of loading or stowage but to the manner of driving.

If the effect of a collision is not impact damage but delay, the carrier is generally liable. A degree of delay, for example while other vehicles are moved, is one of the normal incidents of modern driving, and a risk which the carrier must bear.[34]

75c. Vandalism

Fire loss, which is a distinct ground of exoneration under regimes such as the Hague Rules, has no such importance under the CMR. Liability depends on how the fire broke out. A fire which starts in the vehicle or its equipment is a defect in the vehicle and thus no defence, whether it could have been avoided by the carrier or not.[35] Arson is another matter, but courts have been unwilling to assume that, if fire broke out in a stationary vehicle, it was the result of arson.

> In *O.L.G. Düsseldorf 18.11.71*[36] yarn was being carried from Turkey to Germany when the vehicle made a halt after a downhill stretch of road and fire broke out destroying 15 tonnes of the load. There was evidence that the fire started in the tyres. The court said[37] that the onus was on the defendant carrier to show the absence of any defect in the vehicle. The carrier showed that the vehicle was new and in good condition and argued that therefore the origin of the fire must have been external to the vehicle, probably arson by some person or persons unknown. The court was not satisfied with this explanation, stating[38] that the carrier must prove that the cause "could not" lie with the vehicle: in particular, that the driver had

---

[33] *O.L.G. Munich 27.11.68*, (1971) 6 E.T.L. 115; *Brussels 6.4.77* (1977) 13 E.T.L. 881; *O.G.H. 18.12.84*, Greiter 270.

[34] On delay as an unavoidable circumstance, see below, para. 75e.

[35] Article 17.3: below, para. 75f.

[36] (1973) 8 E.T.L. 510. See also *Walek & Co. v. Chapman & Ball*, below, n. 82.

[37] At 514.

[38] At 515. In *Rb Alkmaar 5.6.67* (1967) 2 E.T.L. 1013, goods were damaged on the vehicle by a fire that broke out overnight while the vehicle was unattended. The defendant carrier said that the cause was a lighted cigarette carelessly dropped on the tarpaulin cover or arson, contending that, although he was unable to prove the exact cause of the fire, it sufficed to make "indirect proof" (at 1020) by showing that he had taken reasonable care of the goods in all the circumstances, thereby establishing a defence of unavoidable circumstances. The court rejected this contention, and the carrier was held liable. Also in this sense: *Antwerp 24.11.82*, JPA 1981/2. 257.

checked the temperature of the tyres and the brakes as soon as he made the halt. The carrier was held liable.

Even if the court is satisfied that the case is one of arson or other vandalism, the next question concerns the precautions that can be expected of the carrier against it. In this regard, theft and vandalism are regarded as closely analogous.[39] Thus, if someone sets fire to an unattended vehicle parked overnight in a public place, the carrier's defence under Article 17.2 will fail,[40] just as it would in a case of theft.[41]

Official vandalism is another matter. If customs or other officials, in the purported exercise of their powers of search and inspection, mishandle goods and cause loss, damage or delay, there may be nothing that the carrier can do to prevent this; in that case, the carrier will be exonerated under Article 17.2,[42] unless, perhaps, the carrier has invited such treatment by, for example, smuggling.

75d. Bad weather

In Wales people say that there is no such thing as bad weather, only unsuitable clothing. In the CMR, it might also be said, there is no such thing as bad weather, only unsuitable equipment. Change in the temperature outside the vehicle is something for which the carrier must allow.[43] Even if delay and cold (or heat) combine, a plea of unavoidable circumstances will generally fail,[44] although in many such cases the carrier will defend under Article 17.4 by pointing an accusing finger at the sender; for example, by alleging insufficient chilling of sensitive goods such as meat,[45] or defective packing.[46]

---

[39] For example, *Brussels 12.12.77* (1977) 12 E.T.L. 1013, 1020; 1978 U.L.R. I 376, 379; B.T. 1978.39, 40; *B.G.H. 5.6.81* (1982) 17 E.T.L. 301, 309.

[40] *ibid.*

[41] Above, para. 75a. *cf. O.L.G. Hamburg 7.12.95*, TranspR 1996.283.

[42] For example, a customs inspection at the border crossing into Saudi Arabia, the goods being unloaded and reloaded by local labour: *Paris 7.4.86*, B.T. 1987.9.

[43] *Montpellier 28.2.85*, B.T. 1985.600.

[44] *Paris 30.9.87*, B.T. 1988.59. Generally see Herber/Piper, Art. 7, 50; Koller, Art. 7, 25; and Thume, Art. 17, 110.

[45] Below, para. 89.

cf. Centrocoop Export-Import SA v. Brit European Transport Ltd [1984] 2 Lloyd's Rep. 618, 625 in which deterioration in meat, tending to decay as a result of having been insufficiently chilled at the centre by the sender, was treated by Bingham J. as a case not only of sensitive goods but also of unavoidable loss; but usually this kind of case is seen as one of sensitive goods (below, para. 89) or inherent vice (above, para. 72).

[46] For example, *Montpellier 28.2.85* (above, n. 43). Chao B.T. 1985.117. On responsibility for packing, see below, para. 82.

Rain, hail and snow are matters which the carrier must anticipate and allow for. For example, storms in August between Antwerp and Basle are foreseeable and storm damage, therefore,[47] is avoidable.[48] If the storm is truly exceptional, the driver usually has time and opportunity to stop and take measures to protect the goods.[49] Impact damage in conditions of ice and snow is treated like any other damage due to collision.[50]

75e. Delay

The possibility of delay at certain stages of the transport is something, which the carrier must allow for in contracting and planning carriage by a stipulated date. If delay occurs, although it may be unavoidable at the point of occurrence, in many if not most cases it is a risk that the carrier must bear.[51]

If the vehicle or the goods have been detained unlawfully by public authorities, that may be a case of unavoidable delay.[52] If the vehicle or the goods have been detained lawfully by public authorities for a period in excess of the delay commonly incidental to the movements of that kind, liability depends on the reason for the delay and the allocation of risk. If customs clearance is unusually and unexpectedly long, the carrier has been excused the delay.[53] If, however, delay arises on account of difficulty in obtaining documents such as a visa for the driver,[54] that is a matter within the area of risk assumed by the carrier and for which the carrier is responsible.[55] Equally, if the roads are icy, that alone does not normally excuse delay by the carrier.[56] If, however, the carrier has good reason to believe a route open but finds that it is not and that the vehicle must wait or detour, the consequent delay has been held to be unavoidable.[57] Again, the carrier may be unable to

---

[47] On the relationship between what can be foreseen and what can be avoided, see above, para. 74c.

[48] *Brussels 25.5.72*, JPA 1972.219, (1972) 7 E.T.L. 219, 1974 U.L.R. I 338. *idem*, snowstorms in December in Turkey: *Bordeaux 13.7.82*, B.T. 1983.542.

[49] *Rb Amsterdam 11.3.64*, 1966 U.L.C. 93. Except in *Antwerp 15.3.89* (1989) 24 E.T.L. 574 in which Art. 17.2 applied to a maritime stage, the goods were damaged by an exceptional storm and the carrier was exonerated.

[50] Above, para. 75b.

[51] *Paris 30.9.87*, B.T. 1988.59. Generally, see Herber/Piper, Art. 17, *55 et seq.*

[52] *O.G.H. 25.4.84*, Stra GüV 1984/11 p. 12, Greiter 223, 231.

[53] *Agen 21.9.83* (unpublished).

[54] For example, a visa to enter Saudi Arabia: *O.G.H. 8.4.87*, Stra GüV 1987/11 p. 23, 26.

[55] English law takes a similar view of the risk attached to the obtaining of essential permits and other such documents: Yates and Carter [1988] J.C.L. 57.

[56] *Bordeaux 9.2.72*, B.T. 1972.114, 1974 U.L.R. I 341; *Amiens 28.10.92*, B.T.L. 1992.766.

[57] *Rb Amsterdam 20.4.77*, S. & S. 1978 no. 194, cited by Hill and Messent, p. 120.

avoid delay caused by a strike by dockers[58] or by customs personnel[59] or even by the carrier's own employees.[60]

75f. Defects in the vehicle: Article 17.3

Article 17.3 provides that

> "The carrier shall not be relieved of liability by reason of the defective condition of the vehicle used by him in order to perform the carriage, or by reason of the wrongful act or neglect of the person from whom he may have hired the vehicle or of the agents or servants of the latter."

The first and main part[61] of Article 17.3 qualifies defences otherwise available to the carrier, but which? If Article 17.3 had provided that the carrier should not be relieved of liability *in the case of* a defective condition of the vehicle,[62] it might qualify all defences in Article 17, including cases within Article 17.4, but it does not. In *O.L.G. Hamburg 27.10.88*[63] it was held that Article 17.3 only affects Article 17.2 and does not affect Article 17.4.[64] This follows, in the view of the court, because Article 17.3 is placed immediately after Article 17.2 and before Article 17.4; and because, whereas Article 17.4 is expressed to be subject to Article 18, there is no such reference in Article 17.4 to Article 17.3. Moreover, if Article 17.3 were applied to Article 17.4, Article 18.4 would be redundant.

Worded as it is, however, Article 17.3 must refer to a case in which, but for Article 17.3, the carrier would be "relieved of liability by reason of the defective condition of the vehicle". That

---

[58] *Cass. 9.10.7*, below, para. 75g.

[59] But, evidently, if there is a strike at the customs post on the intended route, the carrier must detour to another post which has not joined the strike: *Paris 27.5.80*, B.T. 1981.435; *Amiens 28.10.92*, B.T.L. 1992.766.

[60] This would not have been an instance of force majeure but is thought to be possible under the CMR: Putzeys, para. 742, citing Loewe, para. 153.

[61] The second part of Art. 17.3 reiterates in this context the general rule found in Art. 3: *Thermo Engineers v. Ferrymasters* [1981] 1 Lloyd's Rep. 200, 206, *per* Neill J.

[62] It was interpreted like this, erroneously it is submitted, in *Paris 2.12.81*, B.T. 1982.73: the carrier pleaded the defective state of the packing not, it appears, under Art. 17.4(c) but under Art. 17.2. However, the court held that the damage had been caused by the dirty state of the vehicle and that therefore the carrier *could* not be exonerated. However, the decision would have been more satisfactory on the basis of the second sentence of Art. 18.2, that, although the packing may have been defective, the damage was attributable not to the packing but to the state of the vehicle.

[63] VersR 1989.719,720. Herber/Piper, Art. 17, 79. *Contra*: Nickel-Lanz, para. 139; Thume, Art. 17, 112. The *travaux préparatoires* are silent on the point, Art. 17.3 having been adopted at a late stage, with very little comment.

[64] Presumably, if a defect in the vehicle was created by the sender in the course of loading, a defect which could not then be discovered by the carrier, the carrier could defend in respect of consequent damage by reference to Art. 17.4(c): below, para. 85.

case, perhaps the only case,[65] is the case of loss, damage or delay through unavoidable circumstances: if damage is caused by a latent defect in the vehicle, the carrier is not excused under Article 17.2. If, therefore, damage is partly caused by the condition of the vehicle and partly by inherent vice in the goods, the carrier is partly excused, and the courts will apportion liability, not because the condition of the vehicle has made the vice any the less an inherent vice, but because there is more than one cause of damage (inherent vice) for which he is excused and one (defective vehicle) for which he is not. The partial exoneration is not "by reason of the defective condition of the vehicle" but by reason of the inherent vice in the goods. In spite of the prominent and separate position given in Article 17.3 to the strict liability of the carrier for the condition of the vehicle, the only defence that is qualified, qualified in the sense that the scope of the defence is thereby significantly reduced, is the defence of unavoidable circumstances.

As Article 17.3 qualifies a defence in Article 17.2, the allegation that the vehicle is defective is an exception to an exception and the burden of proof, a matter on which the CMR is silent and which has caused controversy,[66] should be on the claimant. In practice, the degree of proof required varies.[67] In most cases, if the carrier has met the normal onus of proving the defence of unavoidable circumstances, it will be apparent that the cause was not a defect in the vehicle and, effectively, the onus as regards the vehicle is on the carrier. The onus is heavy,[68] perhaps because courts are aware that defects may appear in the vehicle as a result of misuse by the driver: tyres may burst because the driver has hit the curb and may catch fire because of overheating in the brakes.[69]

> In *Brussels 17.6.71*[70] a tyre on the vehicle burst and the resulting fire damaged part of the load. The carrier proved that the tyre in question was in good condition at the beginning of the journey and argued that therefore the damage had occurred in circumstances which he could not avoid. The court held the carrier liable, saying[71] that the evidence produced by the carrier "does not exclude the possibility that the damage was caused by error, carelessness or

---

[65] *cf.* Nickel-Lanz (para. 131), who suggests that it also rules out any claim by the carrier to have loss apportioned on the ground that the sender was aware of the defect in the vehicle.

[66] Helm, Art. 17 Anm. 6.

[67] Hill and Messent, pp. 118–119. See also Haak, p. 148.

[68] The onus has been described as herculean: Haak, *loc. cit.*

[69] *O.L.G. Düsseldorf* 18.11.71 (1973) 8 E.T.L. 510, 514.

[70] (1971) 6 E.T.L. 825; see also in this sense *O.L.G. Zweibrücken 23.9.66*, N.J.W. 67. 1717, 1718; *Rb Alkmaar 5.6.67* (above, para. 75c); *O.L.G. Düsseldorf 18.11.71* (above para. 75c); *Brussels 31.12.79*, JT 1980.388; *Antwerp 4.4.84*, RW 1985/6.184; *O.G.H. 10.7.91*, TranspR 1991.422. Further Belgian decisions to this effect are cited by Libouton, Theunis, p. 83. See also Herber/Piper, Art. 17, 82; and Thume, Art. 17, 120.

[71] (1971) 6 E.T.L. 825, 829.

negligence on the part of the driver . . . and does not at all imply that it was impossible for the carrier to avoid the circumstances causing the damage or to prevent their consequences". Likewise, in *Rb Amsterdam 28.10.64*[72] tyres deflated and caught fire, tyres that were relatively new and which had been regularly checked, and in which any latent defect would most probably have shown itself earlier in their life. Nonetheless, the carrier's defence under Article 17.2 failed, because the carrier had been unable to prove what the cause of the deflation and fire had been.

The condition of the vehicle refers not only to the state of the vehicle as a vehicle but also to its fitness to receive and to contain goods of the type in question. Fitness to receive goods concerns not only exterior protection against rain and snow[73] but also internal cleanliness: unfitness is a defective condition of the vehicle. This is true both under the CMR and under the common law.[74]

In *Amiens 28.11.74*[75] fibres carried from Saint-Quentin (France) to Greven (Germany) were damaged because the sub-contractor's lorry had traces of chemicals from a previous load. The carrier was unable to raise any of the defences in Article 17.2 because the court treated the case as one of a defective condition of the vehicle within the meaning of Article 17.3. More recently, in *Cass.com. 22.2.94*,[76] canvasses by Magritte carried from Spain to France were damaged because they were carried in a large trailer more suitable for the carriage of window frame than works of art. Again, this was treated as a case of a defective vehicle under Article 17.3.

An unsuitable vehicle is a defective vehicle only if its unsuitability is a breach of contract by the carrier.[77] If the vehicle turns out to be unsuitable for the particular goods but the carrier has not broken his contract in this respect, because, for example, the carrier neither knew nor should have known that the vehicle would be unsuitable, the case is not one of vehicle unsuitable for

[72] S. & S. 1965, no. 5, 1966 U.L.C. 96.

[73] In *Paris 26.5.82*, B.T. 1982.503 a torn tarpaulin was treated as a defect in the vehicle. In *Walek & Co. v. Chapman & Ball* (below, para. 75f(*i*)) a defective tilt cover was held to be a defect in the vehicle.

[74] *John Carter (Fine Worsteds) v. Hanson Haulage (Leeds)* [1965] 2 Q.B. 495, 514, *per* Sellers L.J., C.A. On this question generally, see above para. 30; and Thume, RIW 1994.357, 358. Some writers are critical of the extension of Art. 17.3 to the suitability of the vehicle: Haak, p. 151.

[75] B.T. 1975.23. It might be otherwise if the sender had undertaken responsibility for the cleanliness of the vehicle, but generally this responsibility falls on the carrier: for example, *Colmar 11.1.72*, B.T. 1972.90, 1973 U.L.C. 276.

[76] B.T.L. 1994.263; (1994) 29 E.T.L. 669; see also *O.G.H. 21.2.96*. TranspR 1996.422.

[77] Above, para. 30. Also in this sense: Helm, Art. 17 Anm. 6; Herber/Piper, Art. 17, 85; Koller, Art. 17, 34.

goods, but of goods unsuitable for the carriage contracted, *i.e.* of sensitive goods[78] or of goods suffering from inherent vice.[79]

Equally, the carrier is not liable for defects in a container supplied by the sender. Nor is a successive carrier or a sub-carrier liable for a trailer, which that carrier was obliged to accept from the principal carrier, in a recourse action by the latter.[80] "Clearly, to hold a sub-contractor liable to the principal carrier for loss or damage resulting from a defect in the vehicle supplied by the principal carrier, which defect could not have been discovered by reasonable examination, would seem somewhat grotesque."[81] Grotesque, perhaps, but equally clearly this was the effect of Article 17.3 in the view of Mocatta J. in *Walek v. Chapman & Ball (International)*.[82] His decision against the sub-carrier can be supported, however, not on that ground but on the failure of the sub-carrier to notice the defects in the trailer at crucial points in the operation, thus, it might be said, taking responsibility for the risks posed by the defects. In other words, the sub-carrier was unable to raise a successful defence under Article 17.2 based on unavoidable circumstances as, *ex hypothesi*, the damage was not unavoidable.[83] There remains, however, the possibility of a defence in such cases based on the wrongful act of the sender (principal carrier), with apportionment under Article 17.5 in view of the sub-carrier's own negligence.[84]

The result is that exoneration is possible only when the defect in the vehicle was not there when the journey began but arises out of something that befalls the vehicle en route, something which has its cause outside the vehicle and which could not have been avoided.[85]

75f(*i*). Special equipment distinguished: Article 18.4

The carrier may defend an action by pleading the sensitivity of the goods.[86] If the carriage was performed in a vehicle "specially

---

[78] Below, para. 89.

[79] Above, para. 72.

[80] Helm, Art. 17 Anm. 6 and Libouton, p. 85, citing *Rb Antwerp 20.6.75* (1975) 10 E.T.L. 540.

[81] Glass, "CMR and Hired Trailers—A Tilt Too Far?" [1981] L.M.C.L.Q. 384, 386.

[82] [1980] 2 Lloyd's Rep. 279.

[83] Glass (above, n. 81), p. 387.

[84] See above, para. 30 concerning responsibility for the suitability or characteristics of the vehicle. The allocation of responsibility between principal carrier and sub-carrier may be the same as that between sender and carrier: for exemple, *TC Brussels 26.10.72* (1973) 8 E.T.L. 516, 526, where the principal carrier was treated as a sender at fault (presumably under Art. 17.2) for providing a vehicle that was too small for the load, and liability was apportioned (presumably under Art. 17.5). However, as that allocation depends on what the relevant parties knew or should have known, this will not always be the same.

[85] Muth/Glöckner, pp. 131–132. See also Loewe, para. 155.

[86] A special risk under Art. 17.4(d): below, para. 89.

equipped to protect the goods from the effects of heat, cold" and the like, the carrier must prove not that the equipment had no defects but that, in the language of Article 18.4, "all steps incumbent on him . . . with respect to the choice, maintenance and use of such equipment were taken". Clearly, the strict liability under Article 17.3 with respect to the condition of the vehicle does not extend to the condition of the vehicle's special equipment.[87] It is important therefore to distinguish the special equipment from the rest of the vehicle. Article 18.4 is *lex specialis*, which qualifies Article 17.3.[88] Equipment is special, not because it is uncommon or because it is supplementary[89] but if, in the terms of Article 18.4, it is "to protect the goods from the effects of heat, cold variations in temperature or the humidity of the air". It concerns any equipment or fitting for "carriage at controlled temperatures". This includes "vehicles equipped with a device that generates heat or cold (refrigerated or heated vehicles) as well as isothermic vehicles (with no independent source of heat or cold but equipped with insulating material) and refrigeration equipment (which has a source of cold but does not generate it)".[90]

As regards equipment "to protect the goods from the effects . . . of humidity in the air", neither a tarpaulin nor a tilt cover, useful as they may be to keep out humidity heavy to the point of precipitation, are either special or equipment. However, in *Paris 10.12.71*[91] it was held that tarpaulins are special equipment to protect goods from the atmosphere. If so, any cover on the vehicle is special equipment, and this inference was later drawn in *TGI Paris 11.12.73*.[92] Undoubtedly, these covers were to protect the goods, in the last case paintings, from rain and snow, but the real question is whether they were special, not in the sense of uncommon, but something to which the strict regime of Article 17.3 for the vehicle itself is inappropriate. Given the existence of a distinction between a strict liability for the vehicle and a less strict duty

---

[87] *cf.* the equipment on board ship; the warranty of seaworthiness extends as much to the ship's equipment as to the ship's structure.

[88] *O.L.G. Hamburg 27.10.88*, VersR 1989.719, 720. Herber/Piper, Art. 18, 26; Koller, Art. 17, 51.

[89] *ibid.*

[90] Chao, Theunis, pp. 114–115. See also in this sense Herber/Piper, Art. 18, 29; Koller, Art. 17, 51. For example, a refrigerated trailer: *Ulster-Swift v. Taunton Meat Haulage* [1975] 2 Lloyd's Rep. 502, 506 *per* Donaldson J.; *Cass. 15.2.82*, B.T. 1982.182; *O.L.G. Hamburg 27.10.88*, VersR 1989.719.

cf. Montpellier 28.2.85, B.T. 1985.600 in which a vehicle insulated by means of a lining of cardboard and straw was not treated as a specially equipped vehicle. *cf.* also *Rb Rotterdam 27.4.71*, S. & S. 1971, no. 73, 1974 U.L.R. II 224: grapes were carried in a refrigerated vehicle sealed by the customs authority and lacking any kind of external temperature gauge to enable the driver to check whether the temperature inside was too cold. The court held that this was a defect in the vehicle in the sense of Article 17.3, and that the carrier was liable for the damage to the grapes.

[91] B.T. 1972.35, a case approved by Brunat: B.T. 1975.510, 511.

[92] B.T. 1974.68.

for its equipment, the decision in *Paris 26.5.82*,[93] that a plastic cover was a defect in the vehicle, is to be preferred.[94] Covers and tarpaulins, like tyres, are squarely in the carrier's sphere of expertise and risk.

> In *Walek & Co. v. Chapman & Ball*[95] the defendants owned a trailer which was leased to the third party for a journey to Jeddah. On the return journey the defendants obtained a contract to carry yarn from Wiener Neustadt (Austria) to Blackburn, a contract to which the CMR applied, and which was performed by the third party sub-carrier. While the trailer was parked at Dover, rain entered and damaged the yarn. The defendants were liable to the plaintiff consignees and brought a recourse action against the third party sub-carrier. The third party pleaded Article 17.2 and circumstances which they could not avoid. This defence failed in view of evidence that, when the tilt cover of the trailer arrived at Blackburn, it was so defective that it had to be patched in 73 places and in view of the inference that some of the holes must have been detectable at Wiener Neustadt. The judge also decided[96] that, in any event, this was a defective condition of the vehicle in respect of which the defences in Article 17.2 did not apply.

Prima facie, the same is true of an ordinary metal or wooden container supplied by the carrier. If a dirty trailer is a defect in the vehicle, for which the carrier is strictly liable under Article 17.3, why not also a dirty container? Is not a box a box, whether it has wheels of its own or not?[97] The clear but unsatisfactory answer lies in the definition of vehicle in Article 1.2: that definition, a definition framed when the modern container was virtually unknown, is clearly confined to the tractor and trailer and excludes things placed upon them,[98] unless the thing is superstructure which will not normally be detached. The common container is not part of the vehicle but nor is it special equipment; it is *sui generis*.

The result is that, as regards liability for loss, damage or delay to goods occurring between the time of taking over and delivery and in which other property, over which he has control, is instrumental, the carrier has four categories of property to consider. First, as regards the vehicle, which includes the motor vehicle and

[93] B.T. 1982.503. This was also the view taken of a tarpaulin in *TC Brussels 4.2.72* (1972) 7 E.T.L. 573.

[94] Also in this sense: Chao, Theunis, p. 115; and Herber/Piper, Art. 18, 29.

[95] [1980] 2 Lloyd's Rep. 279.

[96] At 283. On this see Glass [1981] L.M.C.L.Q. 384.

[97] In *Hawkins v. Russett* [1983] 1 All E.R. 215 it was held that a container which clipped to the bed of the lorry was part of the vehicle for the purpose of an offence (excessive overhang) under reg. 58 of the Motor Vehicle (Construction and Use) Regulations 1978.

[98] Also in this sense; Herber/Piper, Art. 18, 29. See above, para. 16.

any trailer, the carrier is strictly liable by reason of Article 17.3.[99] Secondly, as regards special equipment, the carrier may utilise the defence in Article 17.4(d), if the carrier has taken "all steps incumbent on him in the circumstances with respect to the choice, maintenance and use" of that equipment.[1] Thirdly, as regards containers and any other things which are neither vehicle nor special equipment but are provided by the carrier for the purpose of carriage, there is no special regime. If loss, damage or delay is caused to the goods by a defect in such things between the time of taking over and delivery, the carrier will be liable under Article 17.1, unless the carrier can prove a defence under Article 17.2, such as claimant's fault[2] in respect of a container supplied by the sender, or that the loss, damage or delay was unavoidable. On this last point, the carrier's liability differs from liability for the vehicle itself and for special equipment. Finally, the carrier may be liable for damage to goods caused by other goods, if the carrier has broken the general and implied duty of care in respect of the latter.[3]

75g. Damage limitation

The carrier will be liable, unless unable by the exercise of utmost care to avoid not only the event causing loss, damage or delay but also the consequences which have flowed from that event. In this regard, there is a difference of emphasis between the CMR rule and certain provisions of national law,[4] otherwise considered to be close to the CMR rule, in which attention is focused largely or exclusively on the event. The emphasis of the CMR on both the event and its consequences follows both from the wording of Article 17.2 itself and also from the general duty of the carrier to take care of the goods.[5]

In *Cass. 9.10.74*[6] peaches being carried from France to England were held up by a strike by English dockers, which the carrier could not avoid. On arrival at destination the driver obeyed an instruction

---

[99] Above, para. 75f.
[1] Below, para. 89b.
[2] Above, para. 70.
[3] Below, paras. 79 and 82a. As regards dangerous goods, see above, para. 73.
[4] *O.G.H. 27.8.81*, Greiter 97, with reference to Art. 7 StVG and the equivalent provision in Austria. Pesce, p. 212. *cf.* Sériaux D.1982.I.111, 112, suggesting that in effect the CMR rule is also true of force majeure.
[5] Below, para. 79.
[6] B.T. 1974.491. Also in this sense: *Paris 7.4.86*, B.T. 1987.9, 10: the goods having been badly reloaded by agents of the customs authority, the carrier made no attempt to improve the loading before proceeding to final destination, and was hence partly responsible for the damage.

to continue to London, without inspecting the state of the fruit. The court said[7] that "by acting in this way the carrier made it impossible for himself to establish that he could not avoid the consequences of the docker's strike, itself an unavoidable event".

[7] At 492.

CHAPTER 7

THE SPECIAL RISKS

A. THE ONUS OF PROOF

76. The presumption of non-responsibility

The carrier who seeks to set up a defence under Article 17.2 must satisfy the usual burden of proof in civil cases[1] that the event occurred and that it caused the loss, damage or delay. By contrast, if the carrier seeks to defend the claim by reference to one of the special risks set out in Article 17.4, the onus of proof divides into two parts and on the second, the burden is unusually light.

First, the carrier must prove on the balance of probabilities that the risk occurred, for example that loading was in fact carried out by the sender. But then, as to causation, the carrier is required to prove not that the risk did cause the loss or damage[2] but that it *could* have caused it.[3] Having proved this, the carrier benefits from a presumption that the risk *did* cause the loss or damage, a presumption of non-responsibility. This is the effect of Article 18.2:

> "When the carrier establishes that in the circumstances of the case, the loss or damage could be attributed to one or more of the special risks referred to in Article 17, paragraph 4, it shall be presumed that it was so caused. The claimant shall, however, be entitled to prove that the loss or damage was not, in fact, attributable either wholly or partly to one of these risks."

---

[1] Above, paras. 69 *et seq.* In England that is the balance of probabilities. The appropriate burden of proof in civil cases is applied in other contracting states. For example, Belgium: *Antwerp 26.10.71* (1971) 7 E.T.L. 1058, 1061; *Brussels 13.1.72* (1972) 7 E.T.L. 11. France: *Cass. 9.10.74*, B.T. 1974.491; *Paris 25.1.82*, B.T. 1982.123. Germany: *O.L.G. Hamm 4.11.71* (1974) 9 E.T.L. 499: "Beweis erbringen", words appropriate to the normal burden of proof in German law in civil cases, the precise burden not being fixed but left to the discretion of the court. The *lex fori* also governs the admissibility or evaluation of evidence: *B.G.H. 4.10.84* (1985) 20 E.T.L. 154, 157.

[2] Art. 17.4 makes no reference to delay.

[3] Libouton, Theunis, p. 92, and cases cited. Proof of the risk is quite distinct from "proof" that the risk could have caused loss: Helm, Art. 17 Anm. 13.

To benefit from the presumption the carrier has to establish no more than a plausible hypothesis[4]: that the special risk was a possible cause.[5] There may well be other possible causes, for which the carrier would be liable, but the carrier is not required to rule them out.[6] It is enough that the loss or damage is consistent with what might be expected to arise from the risk in question.[7] A similar rule is found in the CIM.[8]

In *O.L.G. Munich 27.11.68*[9] crates being carried from Naoussa (Greece) to Munich shifted and the contents, peaches, were squashed. "To 'establish' something in the sense of Article 18.2 of the CMR," said the court,[10] "the mere suggestion of facts inferring a case of Article 17.4 does not suffice. The carrier must prove that one of the exonerating circumstances did occur." Thus the carrier had to prove that loading was indeed by the sender, and did so. The court went on to accept various aspects of the stowage not as the actual cause of loss but as "possible" causes and held the carrier not liable.

The presumption in favour of the carrier has been justified as follows. First, when there is a special risk, such as loading by the sender, it will be particularly difficult for the carrier to prove on the balance of probabilities that some act or omission on the part of the sender did cause the loss or damage so as to establish a defence of the normal kind under Article 17.2.[11] Secondly, it is said that the special risks concern matters more within the sphere of the sender or consignee than of the carrier, in particular, the sphere of the sender[12]; prima facie, the sender or consignee should bear the loss or damage associated with these risks[13] unless it can be shown that the loss or damage was caused by the carrier.

The defence by reference to special risks applies to cases of loss and damage but not to cases of delay.[14] Given the traditional reluctance of carriers to bear any liability at all for delay, it is curious that the carrier should be better placed to defend damage claims than claims for delay. However, it should be recalled that,

---

[4] *Lyon 7.10.76*, 1977 U.L.R. I 289.

[5] Helm, Art. 17 Anm. 13.

[6] *The Hague 19.12.73*, S. & S. 1974 no. 71.

[7] Glass and Cashmore, para. 3.48.

[8] Art. 37.2. See Yates, paras. 4.1.2.37.1 *et seq.*

[9] (1971) 6 E.T.L. 115.

[10] At 129.

[11] *Brussels 12.3.69* (1969) 4 E.T.L. 931, 935; Loewe, para. 170 for similar reasoning in English law, see below, para. 77 *in fine*.

[12] *Cass. 17.6.69* (1970) 5 E.T.L. 57, 59; *O.L.G. Munich 27.11.68* (1971) 6 E.T.L. 115, 123; *O.L.G. Hamm 4.11.71* (1974) 9 E.T.L. 499, 503; *O.G.H. 2.9.87*, 1988 U.L.R. II 724, 727.

[13] *O.L.G. Munich 27.11.68* (1971) 6 E.T.L. 115, 123; *O.L.G. Saarbrücken 21.11.74* (1976) 9 E.T.L. 261, 263.

[14] Pesce, p. 218. *cf.* Putzeys, para. 771: there is no good reason for distinguishing delay from loss or damage, and the distinction should be ignored.

in a case of serious delay, the case is treated as one of loss[15] and that, in less serious cases, the amount of the carrier's liability for delay is less than the amount for damage.[16] Moreover, the nature of the special risks is such that they are more likely to cause loss or damage than to cause delay[17]; and, if damage gives rise to delay or delay gives rise to damage, the case is treated as one of damage.[18]

77. A possible cause: the plausibility of the carrier's case

The carrier must establish that the special risk could have caused the loss. People do not always agree about what might have been. There has been considerable litigation under the CMR over whether proof brought by a defendant carrier was sufficient to show that "the loss or damage could be attributed to one or more of the special risks", within the meaning of Article 18.2. A typical early case is this:

> In *TC Namur 22.7.65*,[19] 13 cases of plate-glass were carried between France and Italy, via Munich, where the driver had to swerve the vehicle with the result that the load shifted, the vehicle overturned and the glass was damaged. Noting[20] the manner in which wood had been wedged between the sheets of glass by the sender, and that it had not been proved (by the claimant) that the damage was not caused by the manner of wedging, the tribunal concluded this could have been a cause of the damage, and that the carrier benefited from the presumption arising from the special risk (loading by sender) in Article 17.4(c).

At first, the English judges reacted to the special risks with some surprise,[21] as is evident from some of the bemused observations in the leading English decision on Article 18.2.

> In *Ulster-Swift v. Taunton Meat Haulage*,[22] meat, carried from Northern Ireland to Basle by refrigerated trailer, arrived in unmerchantable condition, suffering from bacteriological damage. The carrier appealed to Article 18.2 and the special risk in Article 17.4(d)

---

[15] Above, para. 56b.
[16] Hill and Messent, p. 163. The damages are limited to the amount of the carriage charges: below, para. 97c.
[17] This is the explanation of the distinction, according to Nickel-Lanz, para. 152.
[18] Above, para. 59b.
[19] (1966) 1 E.T.L. 133.
[20] At 136.
[21] In *Ulster-Swift v. Taunton Meat Haulage* [1975] 2 Lloyd's Rep. 502, 506, Donaldson J. described Art. 18.2 as "curious". See also Megaw L.J. in the same case: [1977] 1 Lloyd's Rep. 346, 354, C.A.
[22] [1975] 2 Lloyd's Rep. 502; affirmed [1977] 1 Lloyd's Rep. 346. *cf. Arnhem 10.4.73*, 1977 U.L.R. II 212.

(the sensitivity of the goods). On the one hand, there was insufficient evidence to prove that on shipment the meat was at too high a temperature for the intended journey. On the other hand, Donaldson J. accepted evidence that the driver had acted properly, that the temperature gauge for the trailer showed a sufficiently low temperature at all relevant times, and that within two days of arrival at Basle the trailer had been tested and found to be in good working order. The judge observed[23]: "Looking at each piece of evidence individually, it is clear that the meat was always at an appropriate temperature and that the loss of the meat could not have occurred. But it did."

This is precisely the situation in which the burden of proof in Article 18.2 is intended to operate in favour of the carrier. Although it could not be proved that the temperature of the meat was too high when consigned, it could have been, and that was the conclusion reached by the judge.

Turning to Article 18.2 the judge said[24]: "Plainly para. 4 of art. 17 covers uncovenanted heating of the cargo in transit—this could be the cause of the loss. Indeed, I have already said that on a fine balance of probabilities, I think that it was. But the defendants do not need this. The defendants have established that the loss could have happened in this way and the paragraph therefore introduces a presumption that it did." The defendant carriers had established a plausible hypothesis, that the cause of loss was the inability of the goods (sensitivity) to travel to Basle under those conditions. In the end, however, the decision went against the defendants, because they were unable to satisfy Article 18.4, that is, to show that all steps incumbent on them in the circumstances with respect to the choice, maintenance and use of the refrigeration equipment had been taken.[25] The decision was affirmed on appeal.

In *Ulster-Swift*,[26] Megaw L.J. said of Article 18.2 that, " 'Could be attributed to' presumably connotes something less than a balance of probabilities. But how much less than that will do? Presumably it has to be something more than a remote possibility? And, of course, it has to be 'in the circumstances of the case'." The circumstances of the case are, of course, the background, the conditions in which all causes must operate: for example, "considering the circumstances of the case (very warm weather, the cauliflowers being in the lorry, some of them from the Friday, some

[23] [1975] 2 Lloyd's Rep. 502, 505. He went on to say "I have to decide this matter on the balance of probabilities." The context is an examination of the evidence prior to any discussion of the CMR and, in view of what the learned judge then said, it is clear that he did not have Art. 18.2 in mind when he referred to the normal English burden of proof.

[24] [1975] 2 Lloyd's Rep. 502, 506.

[25] On this point see below, para. 89b.

[26] [1977] 1 Lloyd's Rep. 346, 354.

of them the Saturday until the Monday) the damage could have been a result of normal loss of quality".[27] No cause can operate in a vacuum.

However, the reference to "circumstances of the case" in Article 18.2 has acquired more importance than this, perhaps more importance than intended by the draftsman. As the carrier must establish that the risk could have caused loss in the circumstances of the case, the effect has been that a court inclined to hold against the carrier is able to reach that result by finding that, although the carrier has proved the existence of the risk, not enough is known about the circumstances of the case (for example, the accident on the road in which goods loaded by the sender were displaced)[28] for the court to be able to hold that the risk could have caused damage. This gives a court room to manoeuvre but gives the writer or adviser a problem in predicting future decisions, and encourages litigation which does little to make the law more predictable. So, in 1976 in *Ulster-Swift*, Megaw L.J.[29] dismissed the case law as too diverse to be useful. Indeed, must of it is concerned only with issues of fact.

Given, however, the variety of jurisdictions concerned and the lack of a European tribunal to draw together the national strands, the pattern formed by the cases is surprisingly clear.[30] The essential idea is simple. By showing the operation of a special risk, and that it could have caused loss, the carrier shows that "in the circumstances of the case" what occurred was in the claimant's area of risk,[31] and that it is not for the carrier but for the claimant to prove that the loss was not in fact attributable wholly or partly to the risk. To show the operation of a special risk, the carrier proves (on the balance of probabilities) that the risk occurred (for example, stowage by sender) and that the damage is consistent with improper stowage (for example, that it is damage by shifting rather than damage by fire). That is enough to invoke Article 17.4(c) and to suggest that the damage is of a kind that could have

---

[27] *Rb Roermond 18.11.71* (1972) 7 E.T.L. 416, 420. Similarly, in *Arnhem 11.5.76*, S. & S. 1976 no. 89, having accepted evidence that the meat was kept at the required temperature during the journey, the court concluded that the cause of damage could have been that the meat was too warm when loaded.

[28] See, for example, cases discussed below, para. 85.

[29] *Ulster-Swift v. Taunton Meat Haulage* [1977] 1 Lloyd's Rep. 346, 350. His scepticism was prompted by Wijffels (1976) 11 E.T.L. 209, who discerns 13 different, but not necessarily conflicting, approaches to the distribution of proof in reference to Art. 17.4(c). Some of the categories are barely different from the next, and some rest on decisions that are clearly wrong: see n. 38 below, on deviant cases. Other commentators have been less pessimistic (or less perceptive).

[30] In addition to the cases discussed here, see also *Rb Antwerp 28.3.66* (1966) 1 E.T.L. 712; *Brussels 19.12.68* (1969) 4 E.T.L. 953; *Paris 3.11.70* (1971) 6 E.T.L. 264, 271; *Rb Antwerp 26.5.71* (1971) 6 E.T.L. 547; *Cass. 5.6.72*, B.T. 1972.484; *T. Milan 22.3.73* (1974) 9 E.T.L. 490; *O.L.G. Hamm 4.11.71* (1974) 9 E.T.L. 499; *Rb Antwerp 6.9.74* (1975) 10 E.T.L. 253; *Venice 31.10.74* (1975) 10 E.T.L. 242; *Paris 23.12.75*, B.T. 1976.48, 50; *Rb Roermond 4.11.76* (1977) 11 E.T.L. 432.

[31] See above, para. 76.

been caused by the sender's stowage without, at this stage of the debate, considering whether there is other evidence that the sender's stowage was perfect or whether other causes come into play.

The essential simplicity of the scheme is not apparent, in many cases, because of the way in which the evidence and argument are summarised in the judgment. In some cases, it appears that the claimant is allowed from the beginning to contest the special risk that the carrier's evidence might otherwise have suggested—to contest that it could have been the cause—by evidence which, of course, Article 18.2 *in fine* allows to be brought. In other cases, the court may conclude rightly that the carrier is liable, without indicating clearly whether that is because the carrier has been unable to show that the damage could have been caused by a special risk, or because the carrier has shown it but the claimant has been able to bring counter-proof "that the loss or damage was not, in fact, attributable" to the risk.[32] In such cases, common in England,[33] the court accumulates all the evidence first and then seeks the relevant cause. However, with the benefit not only of hindsight but of all the evidence, the court's perception of what "could" have been the cause has changed; in most cases it knows (on the balance of probabilities) what the cause was. Cases like this, in which in the end the cause was clear, should not be allowed to obscure the presumption in Article 18.2, which is aimed at cases of doubt.

To summarise what Megaw L.J. called[34] the "artificial or conventional burden of proof" on the carrier under Article 18.2, the carrier must establish that the loss or damage *could* have been caused by the special risk. The risk need not appear to have been the probable cause but must have been a possible cause.[35] People sometimes say that "anything is possible", but whimsical speculation[36] of this kind will not suffice: the carrier must show that the

---

[32] See, for example, *Cass. 17.6.69*, below, para. 78. See also *Tetroc v. Cross-Con (International)* [1981] 1 Lloyd's Rep. 192, discussed below, para. 82.

[33] For example in *Ulster-Swift v. Taunton Meat Haulage* [1977] 1 Lloyd's Rep. 346, 351 Megaw L.J. said this about a defence under Article 17.2 of the CMR: "Such burden of proof, when, as here, all the evidence which either party wishes to produce has been heard, usually as a practical matter is of importance only in the, fortunately, rare cases where, after considering all the evidence, the Court is unable to come to a conclusion as to the balance of probability."

[34] *ibid.*

[35] *Brussels 19.12.68* (1969) 4 E.T.L. 953; *Brussels 28.6.69* (1969) 4 E.T.L. 925, 929; *B.G.H. 20.10.83* (1985) 20 E.T.L. 160, 164. Putzeys, para. 682, who equates possibility with *vraisemblance*. In the latter sense also: *Liège 20.1.71* (1971) 6 E.T.L. 541, 544.

[36] Speculation or allegation alone are not enough: Muth/Glöckner, p. 149; Putzeys, para. 682. For example in *The Hague 19.12.73* (1974) 9 E.T.L. 319, 325, the court said that if the carrier "wants to appeal to the presumption about causation (Art. 18.2), it will not be enough to make vague statements which suggest that one of the special risks in Article 17.4 has occurred, but he must present acceptable evidence that the presumption is justified that—although other causes may come into consideration—that risk may have been the cause of the damage".

risk is a plausible explanation[37] of the loss or damage. If he can do this, it matters not that there are other equally plausible explanations.[38] What exactly is plausible cannot be stated with mathematical precision in the abstract; it is a matter for judicial assessment in the particular circumstances of the case, but it is an exercise of a kind with which English courts are familiar.[39]

78. Rebuttal by the claimant

When the defendant carrier has shown that the loss or damage could have been caused by one of the special risks, it is open to the claimant to counter that suggestion by proving, in the words of Article 18.2, "that the loss or damage was not, in fact, attributable either wholly or partly to one of these risks". The mode of proof, on which the CMR is silent, is that of the *lex fori*[40] in civil cases.[41] The same is true of the onus of proof: thus in an English court, the claimant must prove his point on the balance of probabilities.[42]

What Article 18.2 requires of the claimant, to rebut the presumption that loss or damage was caused by a special risk, is proof that it was not caused by the risk involved. He is not obliged to prove what did cause the loss. To rebut the presumption, to undermine the carrier's hypothesis, it may suffice to provide evidence merely to suggest (but not prove) another hypothesis, itself sufficiently plausible to reduce the plausibility of that advanced by

---

[37] *Brussels 19.12.68* (1969) 4 E.T.L. 953, 957. Rodière, para. 543; Rodière (1971) 6 E.T.L. 306, 307; Herber/Piper, Art. 18, 11; Koller, Art. 18, 5; Libouton, paras. 44, 58–59. But *cf*. Thume, Art. 18, 46 and 65.

[38] *Liège 20.1.71* (1971) 6 E.T.L. 541, 544; *Besançon 15.12.82*, B.T. 1983.96, 97; *Cass. 4.2.86*, B.T. 1986.197.

There are some deviant cases: for example, *Liège 20.7.71* (1971) 6 E.T.L. 541, 544–545; *O.L.G. Düsseldorf 13.1.73* (1973) 8 E.T.L. 620; also *T. Civ. Charleroi 1.10.68*, 1969, U.L.C. 327, 330; and *Rb Roermond 24.1.69* (1969) 4 E.T.L. 1005, 1010. There is a more orthodox statement by the same tribunal in *Rb Roermond 24.10.68* (1969) 4 E.T.L. 1012, 1016. These and other decisions requiring, for example, a "distinct possibility", or "probability" of causal connection, or a "genuine causal link" are rightly attacked by Libouton, Theunis, pp. 92–93.

[39] For example, *res ipsa loquitur* in the law of tort. Also cases that, once there is a suggestion of negligence on the part of a bailee, the onus is cast upon the latter to disprove it: *H.C. Smith v. G.W. Ry* [1922] 1 A.C. 173, 183, *per* Lord Buckmaster; *Woolmer v. Delmer Price* [1955] 1 Q.B. 291; *Spurling v. Bradshaw* [1956] 1 W.L.R. 461, 470, *per* Parker L.J., C.A.; *Levison v. Patent Steam Carpet Cleaning Co.* [1978] Q.B. 69, C.A. Wedderburn: "Fundamental Breach of Contract" [1962] C.L.J. 17, 19. Another example is found in the Hague-Visby Rules whereby proof that damage was caused by unseaworthiness of the ship, not itself a breach of contract, is enough to cast the onus on the defendant shipowner to prove that he has performed his contractual duty and exercised his due diligence: Clarke, HR, pp. 159 *et seq.*

[40] *Arnhem 27.11.73* (1974) 9 E.T.L. 748, 752.

[41] *O.G.H. 21.3.77*, SZ 50 no. 43, TranspR 1982.111, 1978 U.L.R. II 292.

[42] In *Ulster-Swift v. Taunton Meat Haulage* [1975] 2 Lloyd's Rep. 502, 505, *per* Donaldson J.; [1977] 1 Lloyd's Rep. 346, 352, *per* Megaw L.J., C.A. For the facts of the case see above, para. 77.

the carrier,[43] so that the court is persuaded no longer that the loss or damage could have been caused by the special risk. In other cases, the claimant can go one better and prove that it was physically impossible for the special risk to have caused the particular loss, for example, that it was impossible for a shift in this load to have overturned this vehicle on this stretch of road. In practice, however, the claimant usually tries to prove not what the cause of loss was *not* (the special risk) but what the cause *was*. That cause is frequently, but not of necessity,[44] something involving fault or negligence on the part of the carrier.

In *Cass. 17.6.69*[45] part of an electric motor fell from the vehicle and was damaged. The carrier pleaded stowage by the sender, a special risk under Article 17.4(c) and, in the circumstances, it was clear that that could have been the cause of damage. However, the lower court[46] accepted evidence that stowage had been carried out in a normal and orthodox manner and, given that the motor fell outwards on a bend, inferred that the cause of damage was that the vehicle was travelling too fast at the time. The Court of Cassation declined to annul this decision.[47]

78a. Apportionment

If the claimant cannot defeat the presumption, cannot prove that something else was the sole cause of the loss or damage, the court may apportion responsibility between the parties. This is commonly the case when, for example, the primary cause is a special risk, such as defective loading or packing, but the carrier fails to mitigate its effects or the loss is aggravated by the impact of other factors.

In *O.L.G. Saarbrücken 21.11.74*[48] damage to the rolls of lead being transported was due partly to improper loading, a special risk under Article 17.4(b), and partly to lack of due care by the driver when he became aware that the load might fall off. The court said

---

[43] *Paris 8.6.67* (1969) 4 E.T.L. 907, 909. Nickel-Lanz, para. 148. To English eyes, the claimant seeks to traverse the points made by the carrier's defence: *The Dias* [1972] 2 Q.B. 625, 647, *per* Cairns L.J., C.A.

[44] *B.G.H. 28.3.85* (1986) 21 E.T.L. 174, 181–182. *cf.* Muth/Glöckner, p. 149. The carrier may be liable without negligence: see below, para. 79.

[45] (1970) 5 E.T.L. 57.

[46] *Paris 8.6.67.*

[47] The court stated (at 59) that the carrier had failed "to establish that the damage could have materially resulted from the improper stowage". However, with respect, the carrier had established the point but his case had been defeated by other evidence adduced by the claimant.

[48] (1976) 11 E.T.L. 261, 265; see also *O.G.H. 21.3.77*, SZ 50 no. 43, TranspR 1982.111, 1978 U.L.R. II 292, Greiter 50; *Rb Roermond 2.1.69* (1969) 4 E.T.L. 1005; *Paris 7.4.86*, B.T. 1987.9; *Metz 28.10.87*, B.T. 1988.168.

> that there was no doubt that his conduct materially contributed to the damage; that as neither cause of damage was obviously more significant than the other, liability should be apportioned equally.[49]

79. The carrier's residual duty of care

Whereas the Hague Rules contain an express duty of care imposed on the carrier by Article III, no such provision is found in the CMR; but that does not rule it out. Like the Hague Rules in other respects, the CMR is silent on important duties. There is no statement, for example, of the carrier's undisputed duty to carry the goods to destination and deliver the goods in the same order and condition in which they were received. Nonetheless, both a duty to deliver and duty of care exist. To rebut the suggestion that a special risk could have been the cause of the loss or damage in question, the claimant is not formally required to prove a lack of care on the part of the driver, the carrier or anyone else.[50] Nonetheless, as a means of rebutting the presumption that the special risk could have caused the loss or damage, the claimant may choose to establish that the carrier showed insufficient care in the circumstances, and that this was the cause of what has occurred.[51]

> For example, in *Metz 28.10.87*,[52] shortly after commencing the journey the driver discovered that his fragile load of glass, loaded by the sender, had moved. The court held that the driver was at fault in attempting to stabilise the load himself, and continuing the journey, rather than returning and having the task done properly. Liability was apportioned: sender 2/3, carrier 1/3.

---

[49] Similarly, in *'s Hertogenbosch 21.12.65* (1966) 1 E.T.L. 684 goods were improperly stowed by the sender and the carrier was able to show with ease that the damage could have been caused by this. However, the claimant sender was able to prove that the loss was partly due to the lorry being driven too fast, so the court apportioned loss between them.

Also: *B.G.H. 20.10.83* (1985) 20 E.T.L. 160 where it appeared that damage could have been caused by both defective packing and external impact, loss was apportioned; and *Supreme Court of Denmark 16.10.86*, 1987 U.L.R. II 734 where damage to meat was caused by its having been kept at too high a temperature both before loading and during refrigerated transport.

[50] See above, para. 78. *cf. Rb Roermond 18.11.71* (1972) 7 E.T.L. 416, 420 where the tribunal said that in order to rebut the presumption in favour of the carrier contained in Art. 17.4, the claimant must show that the carrier had been negligent; this statement goes too far.

[51] For example, *O.G.H. 21.3.77*, SZ 50 no. 43, 1978 U.L.R. II 292, TranspR 1982 S.111, Greiter 50, 53. See further below, para. 84, in relation to defective packing.

[52] B.T. 1988.168.

The implication of such cases is that the CMR carrier is under a general or residual duty of care of some kind in respect of the goods; this sets a standard for the carrier's conduct and hence for the identification of causes of loss or damage, whenever the carrier defends by reference to a special risk under Article 17.4 and Article 18.2. Again, it is clear that the corollary of the most important defence under Article 17.2—unavoidable circumstances—is that there is a duty of care: that the carrier must exercise what has been called the utmost care in the circumstances of the case.[53] With the exception of situations remaining within the sender's area of risk,[54] it is submitted that, whether the carrier's conduct is assessed under Article 17.2 or Article 18.2, the level of duty is the same: he is required to exercise the utmost care.[55]

To take the example of a driver whose load has worked loose during the journey, it would surely be odd and impractical that the level of care expected of him should differ according to whether the cause, unknown to the driver at the time, was the sender's stowage, a special risk under Article 17.4(c), or vandalism, a case of unavoidable circumstances under Article 17.2. If the load shifts and this becomes apparent to the driver en route, it is natural and, it is submitted, correct for a court to ask in the terms of Article 17.2 whether the occurrence amounted to "circumstances which the carrier could not avoid and the consequences of which he was unable to prevent". Thus, in *O.L.G. Saarbrücken 21.11.74*,[56] although a case of defective loading by the sender and a special risk under Article 17.4(c), the court, holding the carrier liable, used the language of Article 17.2: "Out of the contract of transport there arises, in the interests of the sender, the consignee and perhaps the owner, a duty on the carrier to handle the goods entrusted to him carefully and to avoid damage. If special circumstances occur in which loss or damage cannot in the end be prevented, the carrier is required to carry out his contractual duty of protection, to minimise the damage."[57]

---

[53] See above, para. 74c.

[54] Below, at n. 58.

[55] *cf.* the view expressed in France that the carrier has no more than a general duty to show the goods *les soins d'un bon père de famille*: note to *Cass. 10.6.86*, B.T. 1986.608. Also in this sense, Glass and Cashmore, para. 3.48, who suggest that proof of the carrier's (ordinary) negligence will defeat the presumption in all cases. It is true that in some cases, in which the claimant was able to show breach of the residual duty of care, the claimant was able to establish ordinary negligence by the carrier, and that was enough, in the present submission more than enough, for the court to give a decision against the carrier. It does not follow that negligence was essential to the decision or that conduct less negligent, breach of the more severe duty of utmost care here proposed, would not have justified the same decision. Such cases are *Toulouse 26.3.69* (1971) 6 E.T.L. 131; *Liège 6.5.70* (1970) 5 E.T.L. 716, 724; *Paris 10.2.84*, B.T. 1984.588; *Cass. 10.6.86*, B.T. 1986.608; *Metz 28.10.87*, B.T. 1988.168.

[56] (1976) 11 E.T.L. 261, 264; for this case, see above, para. 78a.

[57] Also in this sense: *B.G.H. 24.9.87*, 1988 U.L.R. II 713, 714.

The exception to the requirement of utmost care arises in cases in which the carrier was aware that loading or stowage *might* have been such as to threaten not the safety of the vehicle but the condition of the goods, but was excused the damage which arose: while a duty of utmost care would have required the carrier to check the loading and stowage, or to insist that extra precautions be taken, the courts applied a lesser duty, whether it is called a duty of reasonable care or not, which did not require the further action by the carrier. That situation, for obvious reasons, remained within the sender's area of risk.[58]

In conclusion, the carrier has a residual duty of care in respect of the goods. The level of care is that of the corollary to the defence in Article 17.2 of unavoidable circumstances, that the carrier must exercise not just reasonable care but the utmost care to avoid or minimise loss or damage or delay,[59] except in those cases where the fate of the goods remains primarily within the sender's area of risk. In the latter cases, notably when the carrier is aware of the possibility that there may be defective packing[60] or loading by the sender,[61] and perhaps also when the carriage involves livestock,[62] the level of care expected of the carrier is less stringent, being one of no more than reasonable care.[63]

B. THE RISKS

80. Open unsheeted vehicles

Article 17.4 provides that, subject to Article 18, the carrier shall be relieved of liability in case of:

> "(a) Use of open unsheeted vehicles, when their use has been expressly agreed and specified in the consignment note."

[58] See below, para. 87a. For example, the risk of non-verification: *O.G.H. 8.10.84*, Stra GüV 1985/6 p. 28, Greiter 239; *Paris 22.9.86*, B.T. 1987.139, and of non-insistence on extra precautions in cases of doubt: *Paris 3.11.70*, B.T. 1971.268 (1971) 6 E.T.L. 264, 1971 U.L.C. 144.

[59] See also below, para. 89b(*i*) where it is argued that the level of duty under Art. 18.5 in respect of special equipment is similar to that of utmost care under Art. 17.2.

[60] Below, paras. 81 *et seq.*

[61] Below, paras. 85 *et seq.*

[62] Below, para. 91.

[63] *idem* at common law: *L.N.W. Ry v. Hudson* [1920] A.C. 324, 330, *per* Lord Atkinson as regards defective packing.

This defence, which comes from the CIM and seems to have had no previous counterpart in domestic law governing carriage by road,[64] has given rise to little litigation under the CMR.[65] The elements of the defence are as follows.

(a) The carrier must prove that the goods were carried on an open unsheeted vehicle. The intention of the draftsman appears to have been that this refers to a vehicle open at the top.[66] However, in the view of some writers,[67] a vehicle that has a top but is open at the back and sides is also an open unsheeted vehicle. This seems right, as the essence of the special risk is exposure to weather and to wastage[68]: that rain, wind and snow can get in and that goods can get out. This was the thinking behind the borderline decision[69] that, although a tarpaulin cover, in position over a hood or frame under which goods were stowed, would put the vehicle outside the scope of Article 17.4(a), if the goods were placed on a flat trailer, and then a tarpaulin put over the goods, that was a case of an unsheeted vehicle.

(b) The carrier must prove that the sender had agreed to carriage in an open unsheeted vehicle. The agreement must have been express.

In *O.L.G. Düsseldorf 8.5.69*[70] motor cars, carried from Bochum to Antwerp on open transporters, were damaged on arrival. The carrier was not allowed to rely upon Article 17.4(a) because, although it was admittedly customary to carry motor cars in this manner, express agreement was lacking.[71]

(c) The existence of agreement is not enough: it must have been recorded in the consignment note in question.[72] If there was no such record or no consignment note in which to record the agreement, it appears that this special risk cannot be

64 Muth/Glöckner, p. 138.

65 For an example under CIM see *Cass. 19.1.70*, D.70.241: goods being carried by steam train from Italy to France in the first wagon were ignited by sparks from the engine. The carrier was allowed to plead equivalent provisions of the CIM: Art. 27.3 subject to Art. 28.2; these provisions are now found respectively in Art. 36.3 and Art. 37.2: Yates, para. 4.1.2.36.9.

66 TRANS/WP.9/ p. 11, p. 44 and p. 55.

67 Haak, p.154; Herber/Piper, Art. 17, 91; Koller, Art. 17, 36; Nickel-Lanz, para. 136; Putzeys, para. 777.

68 See below, (d).

69 *The Hague 24.6.87*, S. & S. 1988 no. 73.

70 (1970) 5 E.T.L. 446. See also below, para. 81. For other decisions in this sense see Haak, p. 155.

71 At 468.

72 *O.L.G. Düsseldorf 8.5.69* (above, n. 70); *O.L.G. Frankfurt 25.10.77*, VersR 1978.535. Helm, Art. 17 Anm. 14.

pleaded.[73] The only reason for the requirement was to harmonise the CMR with the CIM.[74] It has been argued[75] that entry in the note is just one way of proving that the sender agreed to that mode of carriage, and that other kinds of proof will be accepted instead. In any event, the terms required of the record are not clear. In particular, it is not clear whether the note must specify that an open unsheeted vehicle would be used or whether it is enough to state agreement that such use is permitted.[76]

(d) Article 18.3 provides that the presumption in favour of the carrier in the case of an unsheeted vehicle shall not apply, "if there has been an abnormal shortage, or a loss of any package", a limitation drawn from German law. Article 17.4(a) is concerned not only with the effect of weather or atmosphere[77] but also with wastage in bulk or weight, *freinte de route*,[78] as a degree of wastage is to be expected if an open unsheeted vehicle is used. *A contrario*, anything more than ordinary wastage will be "abnormal" and outside the special risk.

In a case falling within Article 18.3, the carrier must defend a claim on some other ground, and this will be difficult. "Experience shows that damage of this kind is more often the result of theft, a circumstance for which the carrier, even if an open unsheeted vehicle has been used, cannot claim relief from liability except in very exceptional circumstances."[79] Article 17.4(a) is concerned with things that fall off the back of a lorry—literally, not metaphorically. If an abnormal shortage or the loss of a package is

---

[73] *O.L.G. Düsseldorf* (above) at 466–467. Loewe, para. 159. Notwithstanding Art. 4: see above, para. 22.

[74] TRANS/WP.9/22 p. 8.

[75] Hill and Messent, p. 129; Putzeys, para. 774. *idem*, Libouton, Theunis, p. 86, as regards relations between carrier and sender, but not between carrier and consignee. But *cf.* Herber/Piper, Art. 17, 95.

[76] *cf.* the Hague-Visby Rules, Art. 1(c): the Rules do not apply in the case of carriage of goods on deck except in the case of "cargo which by the contract of carriage is stated as being carried on deck and is so carried". In this context it has been held that to insert in the bill of lading a liberty to carry on deck is insufficient to satisfy (Art. 1(c) (*Svenska Traktor v. Maritime Agencies (Southampton)* [1953] 2 Q.B. 295) for it is important that the consignee should be warned about the actual mode of shipment. It does not appear that the record serves this purpose in the case of carriage by road governed by the CMR.

[77] *O.L.G. Frankfurt 25.10.77*, VersR 1978.535. *idem*, Glass and Cashmore, para. 3.49, accepting, however, that a line may have to be drawn between cases where the risk remains on the sender and cases in which in spite of the agreed use of open vehicles, the carrier must take steps to protect the goods, for example, from the rain, as part of the residual duty of care: above, para. 79.

[78] Putzeys, para. 781.

[79] Loewe, para. 171. *cf.* Haak, p. 154, that Art. 17.4(a) does apply to theft: presumably, this means to cases of minor theft, cases which do not come within Art. 18.3. Otherwise, his view is hard to support.

due to theft, the carrier must plead that the loss was unavoidable under Article 17.2, and this plea is only rarely successful.[80]

81. Lack of packing

Article 17.4(b) provides that, subject to Article 18, the carrier shall be relieved of liability when there is

> "lack of . . . packing in the case of goods which, by their nature, are liable to wastage or to be damaged when not packed".

The lack of packing, the special risk, must be proved by the carrier on the balance of probabilities.[81]

In *Lg Offenburg 21.1.69*[82] grain was carried—in bulk at the request of the sender—from France to various destinations in southern Germany. It was held that the carrier, who pleaded Article 17.4(b) and (c), was not liable for wastage, for, in view of the tendency of grain when in bulk to be lost by leakage or by being scattered, it should be carried in bags or in silo trucks.[83]

There are few goods which are not better protected when packed than when unpacked. A literal application of the words of Article 17.4(b) would lead to easy exoneration for the carrier or uneconomic activity for the sender. Consequently, the question whether there *is* a lack of packing, is answered by whether the goods *should* be packed, according to current trade practice.[84]

In *O.L.G. Düsseldorf 8.5.69*[85] 225 Opel Kadett motor cars were sent from Bochum to Newark (USA) via Antwerp, the first road stage being by means of car transporters. On arrival at Antwerp several motor cars were found to be damaged. One of the defences raised by the carrier was the lack of packing, the special risk under Article 17.4(b), but this defence was rejected by the court[86]: "Goods are not by their nature liable to be damaged when they are so constituted that they can withstand the dangers to be expected during transportation carried out with care by a methodical carrier."

---

[80] Above, para. 75a.
[81] Above, para. 76.
[82] (1971) 6 E.T.L. 283.
[83] At 290–291.
[84] *Orléans 18.1.95*, B.T.L. 1995.129. Herber/Piper, Art. 17, 99; Koller, Art. 17, 37; Rodière, para. 545; Thume, Art. 17, 132.
[85] (1970) 5 E.T.L. 446. See also in this sense: *Lg Duisberg 10.5.68* (1969) 4 E.T.L. 979.985 (motor cars); *Colmar 17.10.70*, B.T. 1970.712 (rolls of aluminium foil); *O.L.G. Frankfurt 25.10.77*, VersR 1978.535 (sheet metal); *Orléans 18.1.95*, B.T.L. 1995.129 (a large machine 6 metres long and weighing 9 tons).
[86] At 468.

> Moreover, the court continued, motor cars were designed to move around in the open air and, provided that they were driven on and off the transporter carefully, they were in no greater danger on the transporter than in normal use. Hence there is a lack of packing only if the goods should have been packed, and in a case like this the carrier must find, if he can, exoneration on some other basis, such as Article 17.2.

82. Defective packing of the claimant's goods

If the goods are packed, but it is done by the sender and done defectively, that is a special risk under Article 17.4(b). To plead the risk, the carrier must prove

> "the . . . defective condition of packing in the case of goods which, by their nature, are liable to wastage or to be damaged . . . when not properly packed".

The defective condition on the packing, the special risk, must be proved by the carrier on the balance of probabilities.[87] In *B.G.H. 4.10.84*[88] the court declined to infer that packing was defective simply and solely from evidence (i) that the goods were damaged at the time of delivery and (ii) that, according to the driver, the journey was uneventful.

Packing is defective if it does not enable the particular goods to withstand the dangers of normal transit of the kind contemplated by the particular contract of carriage. When packing the goods, the sender must take into consideration the nature of the goods,[89] the length of the journey,[90] and the road[91] and weather[92] conditions to be expected. Further, perhaps, the sender must ensure that the mode of packing enables the goods to be properly stowed or secured,[93] considering not only whether the goods are sufficiently

---

[87] Above, para. 76.

[88] (1985) 20 E.T.L. 154.

[89] *Paris 12.7.78*, B.T. 1979.159: carpets sent from Teheran to Paris arrived damaged by water. The court held that this was partly due to the sender's packing which was defective, having regard to the great value and relative fragility of the goods and to the length of the journey.

[90] *Paris 12.7.78, ibid.*

[91] The loading and packing must take account of poor road surfaces to be expected on a journey from Austria to Baghdad: *O.G.H. 18.12.84*, Stra GüV 1985/4.34, Greiter 270; and likely chafing in contact with other goods: *Paris 23.6.75*, B.T. 1975.360; *O.G.H. 17.11.81*, Greiter 115.

[92] For example, pineapples in cardboard boxes for four days in July in an unrefrigerated vehicle are defectively packed: *Versailles 29.2.84*, B.T. 1984.249. Likewise, fruit and vegetables without insulation from Perpignan to Delft in late December: *Montpellier 28.2.85*, B.T. 1985.600.

[93] The court appeared willing to consider this contention in *'s Hertogenbosch 21.12.65*, 1966 U.L.C. 119, 126–127; however, the carrier failed to prove that the packing was defective in this respect. *idem: Lyon 7.10.76*, 1979 U.L.R. I 289.

protected or cushioned from external dangers by other goods[94] but also whether the goods will damage other property. On many of these points, the carrier may be better informed than the sender, and may be obliged, therefore, to advise the sender about what can be expected[95] or, at least, to respond to the sender's inquiries. If, for example, the carrier has a choice of route, notably whether to route the goods entirely by land or partly by sea, the carrier should advise the sender of his choice, especially if he chooses the latter. Subject to these considerations, packing is not defective if it is done in the usual way,[96] or in the way which has proved sufficient in the past.[97]

In *Tetroc v. Cross-Con (International)*[98] machines were sent from Copenhagen to various parts of the United Kingdom. For transport, each machine was bolted to a wooden base, protected by an anti-corrosive oil and covered by polythene sheeting, which was attached to each side of the base. The machines crossed the North Sea on the closed deck of a "ro-ro" ferry, arrived at Immingham on December 17, and disappeared. They were found in Sweden and returned to Immingham, where they arrived on January 10, damaged mainly by rusting. The carrier defended the action by reference to Article 17.4(b), alleging that the packing was defective. Martin J. said[99]: "I think that these goods when they left Denmark were packed in the usual way . . . and I find that this method of packing was adequate for the intended journey, that is, for one crossing of the North Sea . . . I think that all these goods had been tampered with in some way, and that that, coupled with the long delay in delivery brought about by two extra sea voyages and the fact the machines had been lying around in Sweden, was the probable cause of the damage." Whether or not the latter was true, it was enough for the carrier's defence under Article 17.4 to fail,[1] that the packing had not been shown to be defective.[2]

In *T. Civ. Milan 22.3.73*[3] the court held that when "handling dangerous materials (matches, cellulose, acetone, plastic materials) it was necessary to adopt special precautions".[4] The goods may be of such a nature as to be not only a danger to themselves but also a

---

94 *O.G.H. 17.11.81*, Greiter 115: but in the case of groupage the sender cannot assume that other goods next to his own at the time the latter are taken over will be there throughout the journey.

95 *O.G.H. 17.11.81*, Greiter 115.

96 *Tetroc* (below, at n. 98), at 199, *per* Judge Martin. See also *O.G.H. 17.11.81*, Greiter 115. Haak, p. 156; Putzeys, para. 784; Rodière, para. 545. *cf.* Muth/Glöckner, p. 139 who puts more emphasis on the perceived needs of the particular case; also in the latter sense: *O.L.G. Nuremburg 12.4.91*, TranspR 1991.63.

97 *Colmar 10.7.70*, 1971 U.L.C. 137, 139. *idem* in respect of carriage by sea: *The Lucky Wave* [1985] 1 Lloyd's Rep. 80, 86, *per* Sheen J.

98 [1981] 1 Lloyd's Rep. 192; see also *Rb Dordrecht 18.5.66* (1968) 3 E.T.L. 416.

99 At 199.

1 *ibid.*

2 On the impact of delay, see above, para. 59b.

3 1975 U.L.R. I 267.

4 At 269.

source of danger to other goods, and must be packed accordingly. When the consignment caught fire, the carrier relied successfully on defective loading and packing: "the loading was effective without taking account of the toughness of the packaging or of the different shape or weight of the goods". However, in *Cass. 20.6.78*[5] it was held that packing does not have to be crash proof, even if the contents are combustible. What counts is current practice, and as regards dangerous goods standards are set by the ADR.[6]

One of the most important elements to be taken into consideration when packing goods is the vehicle. Packing may be defective or not, according to what can be expected of the vehicle.[7] Is it the function of the packing to protect the goods from buffeting, condensation,[8] heat, cold,[9] rain, wastage,[10] and so on? Or is that the function of the vehicle? Or is it the function of both and, if so, in what respect? The answers turn on trade custom in general and the contract of carriage in particular.[11]

Packing must be sufficient for the normal hazards of the journey contracted for, and these do not include unexpected delay.[12] Nor do they include negligent handling[13] or carelessness by the driver, for example the driver falling asleep at the wheel.

In *'s Hertogenbosch 21.12.65*[14] a machine, which was crated for carriage from Salzgitter (Germany) to Maastricht, was taken first to

---

[5] 1979 U.L.R. I 296.

[6] Above, para. 73.

[7] Helm, Art. 17 Anm. 15. In *O.L.G. Köln 30.8.90*, TranspR 1990.425, as the sender was entitled to expect a covered vehicle, the sender could not be required to utilise waterproof packing. Also in this sense: *O.L.G. Nuremburg 12.4.91*, TranspR 1992.63.

[8] Libouton, Theunis, p. 86 argues that, as it is difficult for the driver to deal with condensation inside the vehicle during the journey, in general, the sender should make allowance for condensation when packing the goods.

[9] In *Montpellier 28.2.85*, B.T. 1985.600, as regards fruit and vegetables being sent from Perpignan to Delft in late December, whereas there was some insulation in the vehicle, the court simply said that packing is a matter for the sender and exonerated the carrier entirely in respect of cold damage. Chao (B.T. 1985.117, 118 and 601) contends that this is generally correct and, indeed, this is the inference of Article 17.4(b) itself.

Compare, however, a tendency in some courts to place responsibility on the carrier, unless the carrier is unaware of the nature of the goods: for example, as regards wine in low temperatures: *Nîmes 18.5.88*, B.T. 1988.472. See also *Paris 10.2.84*, B.T. 1984.558, discussed below, para. 84. This position is reinforced by the general obligation of the carrier to provide a vehicle suitable for the carriage: above, para. 30.

[10] The sender may accept wastage of bulk cereals sent in ordinary vehicles in order to save the higher transport cost of special vehicles: *Lg Offenburg 21.1.69* (1971) 6 E.T.L. 283.

[11] As regards the obligation to ensure that the vehicle is suitable, see above, para. 30. Also Thume. TranspR 1992.1, 2.

[12] *Tetroc* (above, n. 98).

[13] *Rb Antwerp 23.6.66* (1966) 1 E.T.L. 712. *cf.* common law below, para. 236k. By contrast, the defence under Art. IV, rule 2(n) of the Hague-Visby Rules, "insufficiency of packing", means that packing is insufficient, with consequent exoneration of the carrier, only if it is insufficient to "withstand such handling as the goods will be *likely* to undergo in the course of the contract of carriage"—Scrutton (20th ed.), p. 445 (emphasis added).

[14] 1966 U.L.C. 119.

Venlo and there reloaded on the vehicle of a sub-contractor for carriage to Maastricht. During carriage to Maastricht, the crate turned over on the lorry and the machine was damaged. The defendant carrier argued, *inter alia*, that the packing was defective because, if the machine had been fully boxed in, there would have been less damage. The court rejected this plea,[15] for it could not be said to have been the duty of the sender when packing the machine to anticipate the possibility that the carrier would let it turn over.

82a. Defects in the packing of other goods

In *T. Civ. Milan 22.3.73*[16] the carrier was not liable for damage caused to parcel A by parcel B in the same consignment. Likewise, under the Hague-Visby Rules[17] it is clear that, if parcel A and parcel B are in the same ownership, the exception "insuccifiency of packing" exonerates the carrier.[18] It has been suggested[19] that the carrier should also be free of liability under the Rules if the two parcels are in different ownership. This is a doubtful suggestion. When parcel A is damaged as a result of the defective packing of parcel A, this is clearly a matter within the sphere of risk of sender A, who packed it, rather than of the carrier, who received it from A. When parcel B is damaged as a result of the defective packing of parcel A, between the carrier and sender B, if this is the sphere of risk of anyone at all, it is that of the carrier: the carrier owes B a duty to take care of B's goods,[20] and the hazards against which care is required should include defects or, at least, apparent defects in the packing of other goods.[21] Moreover, the immediate risk should be borne by the one in the better position to exercise

---

[15] At 126. Also in this sense: *Rb Dordrecht 18.5.66*, 1968 U.L.C. 155, (1968) 3 E.T.L. 416.

[16] Above, para. 82.

[17] Art. IV, rule 2(n).

[18] *Silver & Layton v. Ocean SS. Co.* (1929) 34 Ll.L.Rep. 149 (reversed by the C.A. on a different ground: [1930] 1 K.B. 416): when points or sharp edges on tins punctured other adjacent tins, Roche J. held that there was insufficiency of packing, which exonerated the carrier.

[19] *Goodwin, Ferreira & Co. v. Lamport & Holt* (1929) 34 Ll.L.Rep. 192, 196, *per* Roche J. the argument concerned a machine which fell out of its case during unloading and holed a lighter, so that other goods already in the lighter were damaged by sea water.

[20] Above, para. 79.

[21] Harrington (1982) 17 E.T.L. 3, 14–15. In *The Grumant* [1972] 2 Lloyd's Rep. 531 containers of A's apple concentrate split and the contents damaged B's cargo. B's action against the carrier on a bill of lading incorporating the Hague Rules succeeded before the Canadian Federal Court, on the basis that the defect in A's packing was apparent to the carrier, who should have refused it or put it where there was no danger of the containers' splitting. A defence under an exemption clause, "damage arising from defects, slightness or insufficiency of packages" was rejected, as contrary to Art. III, rule 8 of the Rules. Significantly, perhaps, Art. IV, rule 2(n) was not pleaded. Also in this sense: *The Bernd Wesch II* [1971] E.C. 273. *cf.*, however, *HR 15.4.94*, 1994 S. & S. no. 72: acid in a tank was adulterated (damaged) by contaminated acid, for which the carrier was responsible, when the latter was delivered by discharge into the tank. The court held that the CMR did not apply.

recourse against the person ultimately responsible, sender A. Recourse is best exercised by the carrier, not only because the carrier possesses the relevant information about sender A, but also because Article 10 of the CMR gives the carrier an action in such circumstances.[22] These points come together to suggest that the carrier may be liable to sender B for damage to parcel B caused by the defective packing of parcel A.

83. The liability of the sender for defective packing

Article 10 provides:

> "The sender shall be liable to the carrier for damage to persons, equipment or other goods, and for any expenses due to defective packing of the goods, unless the defect was apparent or known to the carrier at the time when he took over the goods and he made no reservations concerning it."

83a. Types of loss or damage

The type of damage for which the sender is liable to the carrier is limited to damage to persons, equipment and other goods.

> In *O.G.H. 2.4.82*[23] the defendant sender's casks of varnish leaked and, in consequence, the claimant carrier incurred expense cleaning the vehicle. The carrier recovered this but not the cost of a damage survey; nor the cost of replacing mudguards on the vehicle, as these were not mentioned in Article 10: mudguards are not equipment.

In that case it was held that the decision on the CMR did not rule out the possibility of liability under Austrian domestic law. As to an alternative claim in England based in tort, see below, paragraph 83c.

83b. The claiming carrier

Article 10 states that the sender shall be liable to the carrier. Given that the provisions of the CMR become terms of the contract of carriage between sender and carrier, it is clear that an action may be brought by the carrier against the sender responsible, and that action may be based on Article 10 as part of the contract. However, when the claimant is a sub-carrier, the court may infer that

---

[22] Below, para. 83.

[23] SZ *55* no. 48, TranspR 1984.151, Greiter 144. See also *Lyon 21.2.91*, B.T.L. 1992.166.

the sub-carrier is a carrier but has no contract with the sender containing Article 10 and, in some cases, the court has fallen back on domestic law to base liability of the sender to the sub-carrier for damage to equipment,[24] rather than base the action on Article 10. In any event, the sender's liability is not limited by Article 23 of the CMR, as Article 23 is expressly confined (paragraph 1) to cases of the liability of the *carrier*.[25]

83c. Apparent defects in packing: actions in tort

By Article 10 the sender is not liable when the defect was "apparent or known to the carrier at the time when he took over the goods and he made no reservation concerning it". In the face of this clear limit on his right of action under Article 10, the carrier may seek another basis for action against the sender, but will fare no better with a parallel action against the sender for breach of implied contractual duty or with an action in tort. The implied contractual duty is subject to the express contractual limit in Article 10. An action in tort is likely to be based in negligence, and the question whether a duty of care is owed by sender A to the carrier "can only be answered in the context of the factual matrix including especially the contractual structure against which such a duty is said to arise".[26] From this perspective, whether the action was brought by the carrier or sub-carrier, an English court is likely to hold that the sender's duty of care is limited by the terms of the contract of carriage,[27] including Article 10.

Moreover, in terms of Article 10 the sender is liable only for damage "due" to the defective packing. Negligent acts or omissions by the carrier (or sub-carrier), whether as regards inspection[28] of A's goods or steps taken to save B's goods from defects in the goods and packing of A, may break the causal connection between A's defective packing and the damage or expense in respect of which the carrier claims. Where a person (carrier) has been held liable to a third party (sender B) for negligent failure to take a certain precaution, and seeks to recover from the defendant with whom that person had a contract (sender A) on the ground that the liability to the third party was caused by a breach of contract by the defendant, that person can recover only if the

---

[24] *O.G.H. 18.12.84*, Stra GüV 1985/4.34, Greiter 270.

[25] See below, para. 97.

[26] *Pacific Associates v. Baxter* [1989] 2 All E.R. 159, 171, *per* Purchas L.J., C.A. See also *Norwich* C.C. *v. Harvey* [1989] 1 All E.R. 1180, 1187, *per* May L.J., C.A. and below, para. 229a.

[27] *idem* if the claimant were a sub-contractor with no contract with the defendant: *Harvey* (above).

[28] See below, para. 84.

defendant (sender A) had contracted that that person need not take the very precaution (inspection and/or cure) for the failure to take which the person was held liable to the third party.[29] The position is the same if the property damaged belongs not to sender B but to the carrier.

> In *Liège 18.12.67*[30] strip-iron, being carried from France to Germany, shifted. The carrier used a crane to rearrange the load and continued, without consulting the sender as required by Article 14.1. Almost at once part of the load fell off and seriously damaged the tractor. The carrier brought an action against the sender based on defective packing of the iron. But the court said[31] that the carrier was wrong to plead that what occurred en route was the consequence of defective packing, for it "was in no way compelled by the defective packing; on the contrary, once the trouble with the goods was apparent, the carrier, having reckoned that it was impossible to carry out the contract, should have referred the matter to the sender. The fault of the [carrier's] servant thus has the effect of removing any causal connection between the [sender's packing] and the accident." Moreover, the action of the carrier against the sender failed because the carrier had not made the reservations required by Article 10.[32]

If, however, at the time of taking over the carrier observes the defective packing and makes appropriate reservations in the consignment note, the inference of Article 10, a term of the contract of carriage between the carrier and the sender A, is that the consequences are a risk assumed by A, and the chain of causation between A's packing and loss or damage to the carrier or sender B is not broken by any act or omission by the carrier.

84. The response of the carrier to defective packing

If the carrier is aware of defective packing when the carrier takes over the goods, the carrier's first response should be to make reservations about the defect, preferably in the consignment note. This serves a double purpose. First, it helps to prevent the possibility of an action against the sender.[33] Secondly, given the duty

---

[29] See below, para. 227.
[30] (1969) 4 E.T.L. 965; see also *Liège 6.5.70* (1970) 5 E.T.L. 716, 724.
[31] At 973.
[32] At 972: "suivant l'article 10, *a contrario*, ce n'est donc pas [l'expéditrice], mais [le transporteur] qui est responsable du dommage au matériel ainsi que des frais qui ont pour origine la défectuosité de l'emballage de la marchandise."
[33] Above, para. 83c.

imposed on the carrier by Article 8.1 to check the condition of packaging,[34] a carrier who makes no such reservation will have some difficulty in proving that the packing was defective at all.[35] In France, the courts have gone further: the carrier is not allowed to rely on defective packing, apparent when the goods were taken over, if the carrier failed to enter reservations in the consignment note[36]; this, however, is an error, based on a misunderstanding of Article 8.[37]

If the carrier does enter reservations in the consignment note, that is not the end of the matter. The carrier may thereby establish that there were defects in packing at the time of taking over the goods and for which the carrier was not responsible, but the carrier may still become responsible for the consequent damage to the goods, if nothing is done to put them right. This is the next question.

One answer starts from the premise that the CMR is silent, and proceeds to apply common law, which, it seems, is carte blanche for the carrier to take the goods as they are with the promise of exoneration for any loss, damage or delay that ensues. That cannot be true of the CMR in view of the residual duty of care,[38] nor was it true of the common law as it later developed, although the duty of the carrier at common law may have been less onerous in some respects than the duty of the carrier under the CMR.[39]

A second, simpler and, perhaps, better answer to the question is that the CMR is not entirely silent and that the excursion into common law is unnecessary, for the matter is governed under the CMR by the residual duty of care.[40] The result is broadly similar to that concerning goods loaded by the sender,[41] as follows:

---

[34] Above, para. 25b.

[35] *Aliter*, of course, if the defect was not one that the carrier should have noticed at that time: Loewe, para. 159.

[36] For example, *Cass. 12.10.81*, B.T. 1981.576 (1982) 17 E.T.L. 294: in such circumstances, if the carrier proceeds with the carriage, it is the carrier who is deemed to have assumed the risk that the packing will be sufficient. See also in this sense *Agen 19.3.80*, B.T. 1980.502; and *Aix 9.4.91*, B.T.L. 1991.767.

There is a suggestion in the head note to *'s Hertogenbosch 21.12.65*, 1966 U.L.C. 119, that absence of reservations may bar the defence, but that is not confirmed by the report of the judgment (at 126–127).

In the case of carriage by sea at common law the carrier who has issued a clean bill of lading may be estopped from defending an action by the consignee by reference to the state of the goods at the time of shipment, including apparent defects in packing: *Silver v. Ocean SS. Co.* [1930] 1 K.B. 416, C.A. However, this rule appears inappropriate to CMR carriage, as the consignee does not normally act in reliance on what the carrier does or does not say in the consignment note about the condition of the goods.

[37] See below, para. 87a.

[38] Above, para. 79.

[39] See below, para. 236k.

[40] Above, para. 79.

[41] Below, paras. 87 *et seq.*

(a) The carrier is not obliged to check the sender's packing.[42] In many cases the carrier will lack the experience and knowledge of the goods to do so.[43] Subject to the terms of the particular contract of carriage, in general packing is a responsibility of the sender.

(b) If the carrier observes a defect at the time of taking over the goods, the carrier should draw the sender's attention to the defect.[44]

(c) If there is a defect, of which the carrier is aware, and the sender indicates that the goods should go as they are, of if the state of packing is such that the carrier is unsure whether it will adversely affect the goods,[45] the carrier is entitled to assume that the sender is willing to take the risk and to commence the journey with the goods as they are.

(d) If, however, at the time of taking over there can be no reasonable doubt in the mind of the carrier that the goods, packed as they are, will be damaged, and that this is not a consequence which the sender has accepted, the carrier must refuse to take them or must take steps to put the packing in a state in which the goods can be carried in safety.

In *Paris 10.2.84*[46] three large computers, on wheels and uncovered by any packing, were carried from Coventry to Orly by carrier A, and there taken over by carrier B, without reservations in the consignment note, for delivery at Argenteuil. There they were rejected in view of bad condition brought about by buffeting on the journey, and action was brought against carrier B. The court accepted evidence that it was customary to send such goods unpacked, and stated that when goods are presented to a carrier unpacked, if the carrier considered that they could not travel safely like that, he must either refuse to accept them in that condition or (as was possible with computers like this) use a vehicle specially equipped to take them.

(e) If a defect becomes apparent after taking over, the carrier must fulfil his residual duty of "utmost" care[47] and take steps to safeguard the goods.[48]

---

[42] Nickel-Lanz, para. 151; Putzeys, para. 787. *cf.* French cases (for example, *Cass. 12.10.81*, B.T. 1981.576 (1982) 17 E.T.L. 294) and a minority of writers (for example, Nossowitch, B.T. 1982.463, 464) who base a duty to check packing on Art. 8. This is an error: see below, para. 87a.

[43] See, for example, *Lyon 21.2.91*, B.T.L. 1992.166, in which the court made allowance (in favour of the carrier) for the driver's inexperience of goods of the kind (gas bottles) in question; and *Antwerp 23.6.92* (1993) 28 E.T.L. 293, in which, it was held, the carrier was entitled to assume that a trailer, which had been supplied by the sender, was of suitable dimensions (to go under a bridge).

[44] *Aix 9.12.80*, B.T. 1981.143. Nickel-Lanz, para. 151; Putzeys, para. 788.

[45] *Antwerp 8.10.86*, B.R.H. 1987.65.

[46] B.T. 1984.558.

[47] Above, para. 79.

[48] See, for example, *Liège 18.12.67* (1969) 4 E.T.L. 965, above, para. 83c.

(f) In the case of goods, the escape of which would affect the roadworthiness of the vehicle or the safety of the public, the carrier must check the packing to ensure that it is not defective.[49]

(g) If the carrier is in breach of duty in any of these situations, he may be liable in full or in part, as the court considers appropriate.[50]

85. Loading and stowage by the sender

Article 17.4(c) provides that, subject to Article 18.2, the carrier shall be relieved of liability when the loss or damage arises from the special risks inherent in the

> "handling, loading, stowage or unloading of the goods by the sender, the consignee or persons acting on behalf of the sender or the consignee".

This defence is usually raised in respect of loss or damage arising out of loading by the sender. For ease of reference in the discussion of this defence, loading by the sender refers to all the risks specified in Article 17.4(c) and thus, for example, to stowage by the sender and to unloading by the consignee, unless the context otherwise requires. However, it should be underlined that the carrier may plead any one of those risks for example, loading by the sender, even if another operation such as stowage is undertaken by the carrier.[51]

Read with Article 18.2, the effect of Article 17.4(c) is that the carrier has a defence if it can be established that the loss or damage could have been caused by the sender's loading. The carrier is not required to prove that loss or damage occurred *during* loading[52]; indeed, as such loss or damage would usually be obvious, the defence is usually raised in respect of loss or damage manifesting itself later. Nor is the carrier required to prove that the loading was defective but simply that loading was carried out by the sender.[53]

---

[49] By analogy with the more likely case of sender's loading, below, para. 87b.

[50] Art. 17.5. See above, para. 69c.

[51] *Brussels 19.12.68* (1969) 4 E.T.L. 953, 957.

[52] *Lg Berlin 12.11.70* (1970) 9 E.T.L. 764, 765–766; *O.L.G. Munich 27.11.68* (1971) 6 E.T.L. 115, 122; *O.L.G. Düsseldorf 13.1.73* (1973) 8 E.T.L. 620, 624–625; *O.G.H. 8.10.84*, Stra GüV 1985/6.28, Greiter 239, 243; *O.G.H. 2.9.87*, 1988 U.L.R. II 724, 728. Haak, pp. 158–159.

[53] *HR 18.5.79*, S. & S. 1979 no. 574; *Lyon 5.2.82*, B.T. 1982.154; *Cass. 24.10.89*, B.T. 1990.99. Pesce, p. 225; Putzeys, para. 796, who is most emphatic. See also above, para. 28.

cf. Muth/Glöckner, p. 149. It is a common error to state that the carrier *must* prove *defective* loading, found even at the highest level, for example, *O.G.H. 27.9.83*, TranspR 1984.191, VersR 1984.548, Greiter 205; *O.L.G. Munich 27.11.68* (1971) 6 E.T.L. 115, 129.

If the carrier proves loading by the sender, it is presumed that the sender took responsibility for the operation, and the carrier does not have to prove that the sender accepted the responsibility, for example, by inserting a clause to that effect in the consignment note.[54] What counts is not so much who is obliged to load but who actually loads the goods,[55] unless one party loads as agent for the other.[56] However, as it must also be established that the sender's loading could have caused the loss,[57] the carrier has an interest in bringing what evidence there is that loading was indeed defective, usually by inference from subsequent events; but that is a different and lighter burden than proof that loading *was* defective and *did* cause loss.

Evidence, for example, that the vehicle overturned may not be enough, even though the load has shifted, as the shift may have been a result of the accident rather than its cause.[58] Evidence of overloading, without evidence of the accident,[59] may not be enough, as the presumption appears to be that, if a vehicle overturns, the cause is to be sought first at the time of the accident. However, much depends on the evidence of cargo movement, of the way it was secured and of the nature and extent of the damage: in some cases the accident itself does not offer a satisfactory (counter) explanation of the shift.[60] Still, the result is that, although in theory the special risk arises merely in the event of loading by the sender, in practice, if the carrier is to show that the sender's loading could have caused the loss, the carrier is advised to try to show that loading was defective[61] in circumstances for which the carrier was not responsible.[62]

---

[54] *Amsterdam 4.9.73*, S. & S. 1974 no. 16.

[55] *O.L.G. Düsseldorf 25.3.93*, TranspR 1994.439.

[56] See below, para. 85a.

[57] Loading would not be a "cause" of loss, as distinguished from a (background) circumstance or condition of loss, unless it was defective.

[58] *Paris 25.1.82*, B.T. 1982.123. In this case there was also evidence that the accident occurred on an uneven stretch of road with an adverse camber, where accidents frequently happened.

[59] *Amiens 6.5.81*, B.T. 1982.271; pourvoi rejeté: *Cass. 26.10.83*, B.T. 1984.360. This tendency is reinforced in this kind of case by the existence of a duty of surveillance by the carrier of aspects of loading affecting safety, which, if broken, severs the chain of causation between (over)loading and loss. See below, para. 87b.

[60] *Rb Roermond 4.10.73*, 1975 U.L.R. II 375: as only the damaged part of the load shifted, while the rest was unmoved and undamaged, the court inferred that the damage could have been caused by the sender's loading and stowage.

The Hague 19.12.73 (1974) 9 E.T.L. 319, 325: as it was obvious, at first sight anyway, that, as the machine being carried had broken away from the blocks, it had been insufficiently secured, in these circumstances the court accepted the carrier's argument that the damage could have been caused by the loading and stowage of the sender.

[61] See *Besançon 15.12.82*, B.T. 1983.96. It is unlikely to suffice to prove loading by the sender and evidence from the driver that the road conditions were normal: *Milan 26.2.88*, Riv.Dir.Int.Proc. 1989.681.

[62] Because for example the defect was not apparent. *Besançon 15.12.82*, B.T. 1983.96. See further below, para. 87.

If the sender is responsible for loading, what may not be entirely clear is the scope of the responsibility assumed by the sender. For example, is the sender responsible for the quality of products made and supplied by third parties, such as ropes? If they come with the vehicle, the assumption appears to be that, whether or not the defect can be said to be part of the vehicle and hence covered by Article 17.3,[63] they are things within the carrier's sphere of risk.[64]

85a. The sender's agents

Article 17.4(c) confirms that, if the sender employs another person to load on the sender's behalf, loading is regarded as undertaken by the sender.

(a) A transport operator who groups goods is prima facie the agent of the sender in dealings with the carrier: groupage is not part of the carrier's area of risk, whether or not it could be truly said to be that of the sender.

In *Brussels 23.12.71*[65] the sender admitted that he had loaded the goods and that there was a presumption in favour of the sub-carrier under Article 17.4(c), but argued that the presumption did not arise in the case of groupage, as this was not loading by the sender but by the transport operator. But the court held that the special risk had arisen, as the risk concerned loading by the sender or his agent, and the transport operator was the sender's agent.[66]

(b) Customs authorities who intervened en route and left the goods poorly stowed are not, it has been held,[67] the agents of the claimant consignee, still less the agents of the carrier, but a third party inflicting loss or damage between taking over and delivery for which the carrier would therefore be liable, unless the carrier proved that it was unavoidable,[68] a defence under Article 17.2.[69]

(c) The carrier may have a dual role. When the loading is to be carried out by the carrier on the instructions and at the risk

---

[63] Above, para. 75f.

[64] This appears to be the assumption in respect of an accident in which the immediate cause of damage to six crates of glass was the rupture of a steel rope securing the goods: *Brussels 28.6.69* (1969) 4 E.T.L. 925. This case is also discussed below, para. 86.

[65] (1972) 7 E.T.L. 865.

[66] At 869–870.

[67] *Paris 7.4.86*, B.T. 1987.9.

[68] In that case the carrier remained liable in part for failure to remedy the effects.

[69] Above, para. 74.

of the sender,[70] the carrier loads as agent of the sender and this does not preclude a plea as carrier under Article 17.4(c). The same is true at destination if the driver unloads under the instructions of the consignee.[71] If the (un)loading causes damage, the carrier who has carried out instructions carefully and to the letter may be able, both as agent and as carrier, to resist an action by the sender in respect of that damage.[72] If the carrier has not been careful, the carrier may be excused as carrier but liable as agent.

86. Counter-proof by the claimant

The claimant commonly responds by bringing evidence that loading was properly carried out. Loading and, particularly, stowage must be designed to protect the goods during normal transit,[73] which must be expected to include violent movement by the vehicle: "the jolting of goods as a result of bad road surfaces and of sudden braking which is often unavoidable in today's traffic is one of the hazards of road transport which the sender has to take into account when loading the goods."[74] In addition, the claimant commonly seeks to show driver error in dealing with road conditions, a risk which is assumed by the carrier.[75] Alternatively, the claimant may admit the defect, but argue that the carrier bears some responsibility for it, in which case liability may be apportioned.

In *Brussels 28.6.69*[76] goods stowed by the sender fell off the vehicle, raising a presumption in this case that the cause could have been the sender's loading. It was enough to defeat the presumption of the claimant to show (a) that a rope had broken,[77] and (b) that the

---

70 *O.G.H. 15.10.69*, Greiter 26. Equally, if the carrier is responsible for loading, it makes no difference that employees of the sender lend a hand: *O.G.H. 25.9.68* (1973) 8 E.T.L. 309, 314, Greiter 19.

71 *Ag Hamburg 21.6.77*, VersR 1977.1048.

72 *cf.* Putzeys, para. 794 *et seq.* that what matters is less the person responsible for loading than the person who actually did it.

73 *B.G.H. 28.3.85* (1986) 21 E.T.L. 174, 177–178. Nickel-Lanz, para. 53 and references cited.

74 *O.L.G. Munich 27.11.68* (1971) E.T.L. 115, 130. Also in the sense *Brussels 6.4.77* (1977) 12 E.T.L. 881; *O.G.H. 18.12.84*, Stra GüV 1985/4.34, Greiter 270. Willenberg N.J.W. 1968.1020, 1023.

75 For example, *Paris 25.1.82*, B.T. 1982.123: in deciding against the carrier, the court found that the vehicle had taken a bend too fast, but also noted that the sender, who had loaded and stowed the vehicle, was well accustomed to the task. See also *'s Hertogenbosch 21.12.65* (1966) 1 E.T.L. 684 (vehicle driven too fast); *B.G.H. 28.3.85* (1986) 21 E.T.L. 174 (vehicle left road on to soft verge).

76 (1969) 4 E.T.L. 925.

77 On this aspect of the case, see above, para. 85a.

driver had made no mention of the sender's loading when questioned after the incident by the police.

This decision makes two important assumptions: that the driver had a duty to inspect the sender's loading, and that a reasonable inspection would have revealed the defect. Certainly, the driver must deal with defects that become apparent en route,[78] but it is another matter to make the driver responsible at an earlier stage, when the sender is still in charge of the operation. A summary of the position, which is broadly similar to that as regards defective packing,[79] is as follows:

(a) The carrier is not obliged to check loading for defects affecting goods only.[80]
(b) If, however, the carrier observes a defect affecting the goods, he must draw it to the sender's attention.
(c) If there is a defect affecting goods only, of which both the carrier and the sender are aware, and the sender nonetheless indicates that the goods should go loaded as they are,[81] or if the state of loading is such that the carrier is unsure whether it will adversely affect the goods,[82] the carrier is entitled to assume that the sender knows what he is doing and to commence the journey with the goods loaded as they are.[83]
(d) If there can be no reasonable doubt in the mind of the carrier that the goods, loaded as they are, will be damaged, and this is not a consequence which the sender has accepted, or if the danger to the goods becomes apparent after taking over, the carrier must fulfil his residual duty of "utmost" care[84] and take steps to safeguard the goods or, if the carrier becomes aware of the situation before movement of the goods has begun, he may refuse to transport the goods.[85]

---

[78] For example, *Metz 28.10.87*, B.T. 1988.168: shortly after commencing the journey the driver discovered that glass, loaded by the sender, had moved. The court held that the driver was at fault in attempting to stabilise the load himself, and continuing the journey, rather than returning and having the task done properly. Liability was apportioned: sender 2/3, carrier 1/3.

[79] Above, para. 84.

[80] *O.G.H. 8.10.84*, below, para. 87a.

[81] By analogy with cases on defective packing, above, para. 84.

[82] *Lg Berlin 12.11.70*, below, para. 87a.

[83] *O.L.G. Saarbrücken 21.11.74*, below, para. 88. See also *Antwerp 8.10.86*, B.R.H. 1987.65. In each case the objective strength of the doubts must be measured against the cost, feasibility and inconvenience of action to still those doubts.

[84] Above, para. 79 and below, para. 88.

[85] *cf. O.L.G. Vienna 8.11.90*, TranspR 1991.100, 103: it may not be reasonable to expect the driver to take this stance. *cf.* also *Cass. com 1.12.92*, (1993) E.T.L. 618, which simply decided that, if the carrier is or should be aware of the defective loading, the carrier cannot plead the defence. French courts are hard on carriers: Tilche, B.T.L. 1996.411.

(e) The carrier must check loading for defects that might affect roadworthiness and public safety.[86]

(f) If the carrier is in breach of duty in any of these situations, he may be liable in full or in part, as the court considers appropriate.[87]

87. The carrier's duty to check loading by the sender

When the carrier contends that damage could have been caused by the sender's loading, a common reply from the claimant is that the carrier had a duty to check the loading and that, ultimately, the responsibility for the quality of loading belongs to the carrier. Is this true? Certainly, the carrier has a residual care of duty in respect of the goods while they are in the carrier's charge.[88] Thus, if goods are loaded by the sender in such a manner that they fall off the lorry during the journey, the carrier must minimise the damage.[89] Moreover, if further goods are loaded during the journey, the carrier must ensure that there is no damage to goods previously loaded by their sender.[90] From this it can be inferred that some concern is required from the carrier about the manner of loading at the beginning of the journey. Indeed, in the view of some French courts, Article 8.1 requires it: the French view is that the carrier must state the apparent condition of the goods in the consignment note, that this implies a statement about their chances of getting to their destination in the same condition, and that this, in turn, implies something about the way they have been loaded by the sender.[91] Moreover, "it amounts to a serious fault (*faute lourde*) on the part of the carrier to take a passive stance and to undertake the transport, after having become aware that the handling, loading or stowage of the load by the sender is patently defective and of a kind to cause damage and loss . . . ".[92]

General statements of this kind must be regarded with some caution. If the checking required of the carrier were sufficiently thorough to cover all aspects of loading and stowage by the sender

---

[86] Below, para. 87b.

[87] *O.L.G. Saarbrücken 21.11.74*, below, para. 88. *Paris 18.5.89*, B.T. 1989.577.

[88] See above, para. 79.

[89] *Liège 18.12.67*, above, para. 83c. Below, para. 88.

[90] *O.L.G. Düsseldorf 13.1.73* (1973) 8 E.T.L. 620; *Lg Salzburg 29.6.90*, TranspR 1991.62.

[91] Above, para. 25a; Rodière, CMR, para. 29. As understood outside France, however, it does not follow from Art. 8.1, which concerns proof that loss or damage occurred during transit, that the carrier is liable; see below, para. 87a.

[92] *Liège 6.5.70* (1970) 5 E.T.L. 716, 723. In that case the poor stowage by the sender affected cargo only and, as will be seen below (para. 87a), most courts would regard the statement as too severe in a case of that kind.

within the carrier's professional expertise, the carrier's defence in Article 17.4(c) would be largely nullified,[93] and valuable time would be lost to both parties. The cases suggest that a distinction must be drawn,[94] a distinction between matters affecting the condition of the goods alone[95] and matters affecting the condition or safety of the vehicle, goods and third parties.[96]

87a. Defects affecting only goods

The carrier's duty is to draw the attention of the sender to any aspect of the sender's loading which might adversely affect the goods during the journey and of which the carrier is aware. However, the carrier is not obliged to check for defects of this kind.

In *Lg Berlin 12.11.70*[97] eggs to be transported from Belgium to Berlin were improperly loaded by the sender with the result that on delivery 4,000 (out of 25,000) were broken. The defect was that the cartons containing the eggs were not bound together so that en route the upper cartons slid to the rear of the trailer, where they bounced about with consequent damage to the contents. The carrier pleaded Article 17.4(c); the claimant consignee countered with the contention that safe stowage was the responsibility of the carrier; and that, although loading had been carried out by the sender, the carrier's knowledge about loading overrode the sender's knowledge about the quality of the goods. Noting that the lorry's crew had expressed doubts about the loading to the sender, the court held that loading and stowage remained the responsibility of the sender, and that the carrier was not liable for the damage.

In *O.L.G. Hamm 19.2.73*[98] meat was loaded by the sender in Germany with insufficient space for air to circulate; the doors at the rear had to be closed by reversing the vehicle against a piece of timber held against a wall. On arrival in France the meat was beginning to decay. The court said[99] that "For having loaded the vehicle too tightly and improperly the defendant [carrier] is not . . .

93 Rodière, para. 545.

94 A similar line, but leading to the opposite allocation of responsibility, is found in the maritime distinction between negligence in the management of the ship and negligence in the management of cargo on the ship: *Gosse Millerd v. Canadian Government Merchant Marine* [1929] A.C. 223. Generally, see Tetley, Chap. 16.

95 Below, para. 87a.

96 Below, para. 87b.

97 (1974) 9 E.T.L. 762; see also *'s Hertogenbosch 12.12.65* (1966) 1 E.T.L. 684.

98 (1974) 9 E.T.L. 753.

99 At 758. Also in this sense: *O.L.G. Düsseldorf 1.7.95*, TranspR 1996.109; Koller, Art. 17, 42.

responsible, the loading of the refrigerated vehicle being the concern of the sender or his assistants, so the defendant only had to see that in a general way the vehicle was safe to be driven. This was not prejudiced by the pork having been loaded too tightly, particularly as the lorry did not exceed its weight limit." The carrier was held not liable on this ground.

In *O.G.H. 8.10.84*[1] deep-frozen fish for Austria was loaded and stowed by the sender in Denmark. The driver offered advice to the sender's men concerning stowage, but did not check whether it had been followed. The men told him later that they had followed his advice, but this proved not to be the case, and as a result the load slid during transit and split the side of the vehicle, letting in air which raised the temperature to a point which damaged the fish. The court held that in the absence of agreement that the carrier should be responsible for checking the sender's loading and stowage, the carrier was not liable for what had occurred.

In cases like these, if the carrier (usually through his driver) brings the defect to the attention of the sender, then, if the sender ignores the warning, unless the roadworthiness of the lorry is threatened, responsibility remains with the sender. This appears to be the common law rule,[2] as well as that most commonly applied to CMR contracts in other countries.[3] However, if it is obvious that the manner of loading will damage the goods, the effect of the carrier's general duty of care[4] under the CMR is that the carrier must take immediate action to rectify the situation.[5]

There are decisions that take a stricter view. In particular, some French courts have imposed a condition, an extra condition for the defence in Article 17.4(c), that the defect, whether it concerned the safety of the goods or the safety of the vehicle, was one that was

---

[1] Stra GüV 1985/6.28, Greiter 239. See also to the same effect: *Amsterdam 9.11.79*, S. & S. 1980 no. 69; and *O.G.H. 21.2.85*, Stra GüV 1985/10.18, Greiter 285.

But *cf. O.L.G. Munich 27.11.68* (1971) 6 E.T.L. 115, 125: when the driver pointed out to the sender's employees, who were loading the vehicle, that it was desirable to load the consignment of peaches so that there was a gap between the boxes of peaches and the cab, the court said that it was gross negligence by the driver not to make (an easily made) check to see if they had followed his advice.

[2] By analogy with cases on defective packing, such as *Gould v. S.E. & Chatham Ry. Co.* [1920] 2 K.B. 186, below, para. 236k.

[3] Costanzo, pp. 27–28; Nickel-Lanz, para. 151; Willenberg N.J.W. 1968.1020, 1021.

According to Chao (B.T. 1987.140), French courts are generally reluctant to allow carriers to escape on this ground, and so it seems: see the "deviant" French decisions discussed in the next paragraph of text. However, in *Cass. 10.10.89*, B.T. 1989.673 the court did not contradict the opinion of the court below that the carrier had a duty to check the loading, but held that, if the carrier failed to check it and there was damage, the court was wrong to put the entire responsibility on the carrier; the implication, of course, is that there should be apportionment under Art. 17.5.

[4] Above, para. 79.

[5] For example, *B.G.H. 24.9.87*, 1988 U.L.R. II 713; *O.L.G. Düsseldorf 25.3.93*, TranspR 1994.439. Below, para. 88.

not apparent to the carrier at the time of loading.[6] This is an error, which stems from a misunderstanding of Article 8. Whereas Article 8 requires the carrier to check the apparent condition of the goods and this check must involve some appraisal of the way they have been loaded and stowed,[7] "breach" of Article 8 has only one consequence: failure to check and consequent failure to enter reservations in the consignment note gives rise to an evidential presumption against the carrier that he received the goods in good condition. The presumption facilitates proof by the claimant that loss or damage occurred during the journey and that therefore, at a first stage of debate, there is a prima facie case against the carrier. However, Article 8 creates a presumption and not an estoppel. Nor does it impose a condition of the defence to that prima facie case which, at a second and distinct stage of debate, the carrier may choose to make under Article 17.4(c). French[8] and Belgian[9] writers have criticised this *jurisprudence* of the French courts as being without basis in the text of the CMR, and the present writer respectfully agrees.

87b. Defects affecting roadworthiness

Whether or not the carrier has grounds for suspicion about the sender's loading, the carrier must check the loading to ensure the roadworthiness of the vehicle: the means of reaching destination remain the responsibility of the carrier. Drivers are expected to have the necessary level of knowledge and skill.[10] The carrier also has a duty to ensure that the unit is not a danger to the public, but this is distinct from the duty to supply a vehicle fit to receive and carry the goods[11] and is not in any respect a contractual duty owed to the sender or consignee.[12]

---

[6] The decisions include *Toulouse 14.1.81*, B.T. 1981.158; *Cass. 23.2.82* (1983) 18 E.T.L. 19; *Cass. 3.3.82*, B.T. 1982.285; *Paris 26.5.82*, B.T. 1982.503; *Besançon 15.12.82*, B.T. 1983.96; *Cass. 22.7.86* (*2 arrêts*), B.T. 1986.516; *Aix 5.7.89*, B.T. 1990.398; *Limoges 18.3.91*, B.T.L. 1991.573; *Paris 24.5.91*, B.T.L. 1991.573; *Aix 12.5.92*, B.T.L. 1993.328. However, in some instances the carrier was not liable in full but only in part: in *Cass. 10.10.89*, B.T. 1989.673 the court suggested apportionment, while maintaining the principle that the carrier had a duty to check loading, in respect of a defect that did not apparently affect the safety of the vehicle. See also *Cass. 20.12.83*, B.T. 1984.430.

[7] Above, para. 25a.

[8] Brunat, B.T. 1984.132; Chao, B.T. 1984.422; B.T. 1986.509; B.T. 1988.158; Nossovitch B.T. 1982, 102, 103; Rodière, CMR, para. 545.

[9] Libouton, Theunis, p. 87; Putzeys, para. 787.

[10] However, in a particular case, the court may also ask whether the carrier was given sufficient information about the goods: *Antwerp 13.12.89* (1990) 25 E.T.L. 319.

[11] Above, para. 30.

[12] Loewe, para. 161.

In *Cass. 3.5.76*[13] a machine in transit from the United Kingdom to France fell off its trailer in Dieppe. The defendant carrier pleaded the sender's loading, but the court affirmed[14] that Article 17.4(c) "does not relieve the carrier from the duty . . . to check the stowage carried out by other people and to remain responsible for damage which arises when he commences transport in spite of *patent* defects in the stowage."

The carrier's duty has been qualified when it was clear that the sender's expertise was significantly greater than that of the carrier.

In *Antwerp 27.4.83*[15] a load of 475 pieces of fibreboard shifted and caused an accident, in which the driver was injured. Although the accident could have been caused by the sender's loading in a manner which affected the safety of the vehicle, and the driver had not checked the loading for safety, the defence was successful, as the

---

[13] (1978) 13 E.T.L. 106.

In France there are other cases which are consistent with the distinction suggested here between the safety of the goods and the safety of the vehicle, although the distinction is not recognised in principle. In these cases the defect affected roadworthiness and the carrier was held liable, wholly or in part, for failure to discover (and remedy) the defect. The carrier must check for defects in the loading that affect roadworthiness: *Cass. 3.5.76* (1978) 13 E.T.L. 106 (vehicle with heavy load overturned); *Paris 22.6.82*, B.T. 1982.432 (unstable load of vegetables); *Cass. 26.10.83*, B.T. 1984.360 (overloading); and *Cass. 20.12.83*, B.T. 1984.430 (vehicle with heavy load overturned) which can be interpreted in this sense if (as is possible but not clear—Chao, B.T. 1984.422) liability was apportioned between the parties; likewise *Paris 18.5.89*, B.T. 1989.577. See also *Cass. 30.11.82*, B.T. 1983.129 (goods broke loose and damaged property of third party: carrier not liable as the defective stowage was not apparent).

In Austria: *O.G.H. 25.9.68* (1973) 8 E.T.L. 309, Greiter 19; machinery fell off the vehicle on the Brenner pass, because it had been inadequately lashed down, something which, the court held, should have been checked and noticed by the driver. The carrier must check for defects in the loading that affect roadworthiness: Thume, Art. 17, A168.

In Belgium: *Brussels 12.3.69* (1969) 4 E.T.L. 931: sheets of glass, loaded on the vehicle, were too high and were consequently destroyed when they struck a bridge during the journey. The court held (at 935–936) that the origin of the damage lay, not in the loading by the sender, but in the negligence of the carrier's personnel in not checking the gauge of this load in the light of their experience of similar loads on the same route. *Liège 23.2.72*, reported by Liboutin, Theunis, p. 94; carrier liable as the driver, but not the sender, knew that the sender had overloaded the vehicle, and nonetheless proceeded with carriage; the trailer coupling broke and this could have been caused by the overloading. *Rb Antwerp 7.3.80* (1981) 16 E.T.L. 466: the carrier was responsible for checking the loading and lashing by the sender of heavy goods, the movement of which might affect the stability of the vehicle. Also in this sense: *Antwerp 13.12.89* (1990) 25 E.T.L. 319.

In Denmark: *Supreme Court 2.3.79* (1980) 15 E.T.L. 208: steel pipes shifted and broke through the side of the vehicle. The carrier was held liable.

In Germany: *O.L.G. Hamm 19.2.73* (1974) 9 E.T.L. 753, 758, above, para. 87a; *O.L.G. Düsseldorf 25.3.93*, TranspR 1994.439, 440; *O.L.G. Munich 28.7.95*, TranspR 1996.240. Herber/Piper, Art. 17, 124; Koller, Art. 17, 42; Thume, Art. 17, 168.

In Holland the principle was recognised in *Arnhem 27.11.73* (1974) 9 E.T.L. 748.

[14] (1978) 13 E.T.L. 106, 108–109 (emphasis added).

[15] RW 1983/4.1814. Also, in *'s Hertogenbosch 19.3.86*, S. & S. 1987 no. 23 it was held that, if in real doubt, the carrier may be entitled to trust the expertise of the sender in such matters, even though in that case the heavy load fell off on the first bend.

sender knew so much more than the driver about the safe loading of this kind of consignment.

The carrier's duty may also be qualified by the contract of carriage. As the contractual duty owed by the carrier to the sender—to check the roadworthiness of the vehicle after loading by the sender—is not explicit in the CMR, it is arguable that the parties to the contract can agree otherwise without infringing Article 41.[16]

> In *B.G.H. 27.10.78*[17] the load by the sender was slightly too high and struck the roof of a tunnel with consequent damage to both load and vehicle. Initially, the driver had refused to take the load, but had accepted it under commercial pressure from the sender and under protest, after having obtained from the sender a signed declaration in the consignment note that the sender was to be responsible for the consequences of the excessive height. Given the slight character of the excess, the improper nature[18] of the pressure from the sender, the improbability that it would hit anything, and that the driver had gone so far in his resistance as to obtain the declaration, the court held that the carrier was not liable at all for the damage to the goods. An argument based on Article 41 was rejected.

The difficulty about this argument is that it could lead to exoneration which the draftsman did not intend. Clearly, a clause that the carrier shall not be liable for theft which the carrier could have avoided is a provision that directly derogates from Article 17.1 and Article 17.2, and hence null and void under Article 41. Equally, a clause that the carrier shall not be liable for the failure of the driver to activate anti-theft devices is null and void under Article 41. There is no provision of the CMR that drivers shall activate anti-theft devices, but failure to do so is a breach of the duty of care,[19] a duty which, although residual and not expressed in the CMR, is the corollary of express provisions of the CMR, notably the defence of "unavoidable circumstances"[20] in Article 17.2. Such a clause would "indirectly" derogate from the CMR. The decision in *B.G.H. 27.10.78* (above) may be supported, however, because the allocation of risk concerned loading and stowage, a grey area on which the CMR is largely silent, and a matter that the draftsman left to the parties.

---

[16] Below, para. 92.
[17] VersR 1979.417.
[18] *Eine treuwidrige schuldhafte Vertragsletzung.*
[19] Above, para. 79.
[20] Above, para. 74.

88. Defects becoming apparent during the journey

If during the journey the carrier observes a defect in loading which is likely to damage the goods or has begun to do so, whether a defect affecting the safety of the goods or of the vehicle, the carrier must take steps to safeguard the goods or to minimise damage. In many cases performance of this duty will require instructions from the sender in accordance with Article 14.[21] The carrier's duty to safeguard the goods has the twin base of Article 17.1 and the residual duty of care.[22]

> In *O.L.G. Saarbrücken 21.11.74*[23] rolls of lead, being sent from France to Germany, were improperly loaded by the sender with the result that a roll fell off after 40 kilometres of the journey. Without consulting the sender, the carrier reloaded the roll and continued the journey, but four rolls of lead fell through the side of the lorry into a village street and were seriously damaged. The court referred to the general duty of care imposed by implication on the carrier,[24] which had been breached in this case, and held the carrier to be jointly responsible with the sender.

Equally, if the stowage of goods is disturbed en route by customs authorities, although the carrier is not directly responsible for the actions of the authorities, the carrier is obliged to mitigate the effects of their action on the stowage.[25] Again, if two consignments on the same vehicle are for consecutive destinations, on delivery of the first the carrier must ensure that the stowage of the second is satisfactory for the remaining leg of the journey.[26]

89. Sensitive goods: "difficult travellers"[27]

Article 17.4(d) provides that, subject to Article 18, the carrier shall be relieved of liability in case of

---

[21] See above, para. 33.
[22] See above, para. 79.
[23] (1976) 11 E.T.L. 261.
[24] On this aspect of the case, see above, para. 79. *cf. Metz 28.10.87*, B.T. 1988.168; note Chao, B.T. 1988.157: a defect in stowage of 10 cases of glassware, not apparent to the driver at the time of loading, became apparent 20 kilometres down the road when five cases were thrown off the vehicle and smashed. Having sought to secure the remaining load, the driver continued, whereas the court considered that he should have returned to have the sender check the stowage. Although there was no further damage which suggests (Chao, *loc. cit.*) that the carrier should have been entirely exonerated, the court apportioned liability between sender (2/3) and carrier (1/3).
[25] *Paris 7.4.86*, B.T. 1987.9: the carrier was liable in part for failure to remedy the effects.
[26] *Cass. 10.6.86*, B.T. 1986.608 (without load A, which had been delivered, load B was unstable).
[27] Glass (1979) 14 E.T.L. 687, 709.

> "the nature of certain kinds of goods which particularly exposes them to total or partial loss or to damage, especially through breakage, rust, decay, desiccation, leakage, normal wastage, or the action of moth or vermin".

For convenience of description, these goods are referred to in this book as sensitive goods. If the carrier can establish that the goods were sensitive and that the loss or damage could have arisen from their sensitivity, the carrier is not liable, unless the claimant can prove that the loss or damage was not, in fact, attributable to their sensitivity.[28]

All goods, like mortal flesh and grass, are liable to decay, but not all goods are sensitive.[29] To be sensitive, the nature of the goods must "particularly" expose them to loss or to damage in transit, such as breakage or decay. They include fruit,[30] flowers,[31] flower bulbs,[32] hothouse plants,[33] vegetables,[34] chocolate biscuits,[35] cheese,[36] meat[37] and fish,[38] as well as combustible goods,[39] steel strip[40] and glass,[41] but not machinery,[42] paving-stones,[43] or rolls of aluminium foil.[44]

Goods that are sensitive in one context may not be sensitive in another. Fruit, while still on the bough, is not particularly exposed to damage, but becomes so when carried by road. Article 17.4(d)

---

[28] Art. 18.2. See *Donald & Son (Wholesale Meat Contractors) Ltd v. Continental Freeze Ltd* 1984 S.L.T. 182.

[29] Rodière, para. 543.

[30] *O.L.G. Zweibrücken 23.9.66*, N.J.W. 1967, 1717 (peaches); *O.L.G. Stuttgart 24.1.67*, N.J.W. 1968.1054 (grape juice); *Venice 31.10.74* (1975) 10 E.T.L. 242 (bananas); *Versailles 29.2.84*, B.T. 1984.249 (pineapples); *O.G.H. 22.11.84*, Greiter 253 (figs); *O.L.G. Hamm 14.11.85*, TranspR 1986.77 (grapes).

[31] *The Hague 15.6.79* (1980) 15 E.T.L. 871.

[32] *The Hague 21.5.87*, S. & S. 1988 no. 24 (tulip bulbs from Hungary to Holland).

[33] *Toulouse 17.2.71* (1971) 6 E.T.L. 412.

[34] *O.L.G. Nuremberg 14.6.65* (1971) 6 E.T.L. 247 (mushrooms); *Rb Roermond 24.10.68* (1969) 4 E.T.L. 1012 (cauliflowers); *O.G.H. 31.3.82*, TranspR 1984.196, Greiter 137 (potatoes); *Brussels 17.12.84* (1985) 20 E.T.L. 354 (artichokes and French beans); *Agen 26.11.85*, B.T. 1986.235 (new potatoes); *The Hague 9.1.87*, S. & S. 1987 no. 141 (gherkins).

[35] In summer: *Cass. 4.2.86* (1986) 21 E.T.L. 263.

[36] *Aix 10.11.76*, B.T. 1977.248, 249.

[37] *Kg Delft 13.5.65*, 1966 U.L.C. 104; *Donald & Son (Wholesale Meat Contractors) Ltd v. Continental Freeze Ltd* 1984 S.L.T. 182; *Centrocoop Export-Import SA v. Brit European Transport* [1984] 2 Lloyd's Rep. 618.

[38] *Paris 10.11.81*, B.T. 1982.183.

[39] For example, cigarette lighters: *Lyon 7.10.76*, 1979 U.L.R. I 289.

[40] *O.L.G. Hamm 2.11.95*, TranspR 1996.335.

[41] In view of the wording of Art. 17.(b): particular exposure to "damage, especially through breakage".

[42] *'s Hertogenbosch 21.12.65*, 1966 U.L.C. 119; *Tetroc v. Cross-Con (International)* [1981] 1 Lloyd's Rep. 192, 200, *per* Judge Martin as regards machinery constructed of heavy gauge steel; *O.L.G. Munich 5.7.89*, TranspR 1990.16. *Aliter* if the machinery is vulnerable to rust.

[43] *Colmar 7.11.73*, B.T. 1974.144.

[44] *Colmar 10.7.70*, 1971 U.L.C. 137, B.T. 1970.358.

is concerned with sensitivity in the context of carriage by road at the time of year in question.[45] If goods are sensitive in that sense, they are classified as goods subject to Article 17.4(d), even though they may cease to be particularly exposed to damage if carried carefully. The essence of Article 17.4(d) is that the senders know their goods and that, if they choose to expose them to conditions to which they are sensitive, that is prima facie a risk that is theirs and not the carrier's. Senders may transfer part of that risk to the carrier by contracting for special precautions, but if they do, the case remains within Article 17.4(d) and it is not for the carrier to prove that the goods were "particularly exposed" to loss or to damage in spite of the precautions, but for the claimant to prove, in accordance with Article 18.2, that "the loss or damage was not, in fact, attributable" to the sensitivity of the goods, but to something else, such as the carrier's failure to take the special precautions contracted for.

Errors abound; for example, in *Colmar 10.7.70*[46]: "It is, in effect, obvious that the transport of rolls of aluminium foil hardly involves any more risks than the transport of many other manufactured objects; that the large number of movements of the same kind of goods in identical or analogous conditions, without having given rise to any damage, demonstrates that this risk is not abnormal, if sufficient precautions are taken." The conclusion, that aluminium foil is not sensitive, is sound, but the suggestion that this is because aluminium foil can be carried without damage, if carried in accordance with good practice and with sufficient precautions, is mistaken.[47] If it were correct, the carrier would be deprived of the full benefit of the presumption in Article 17.4(d). Indeed, the *Colmar* view is contradicted by the examples of sensitivity given by Article 17.4(d) itself. Goods are classified, as sensitive or not, without reference to any precautions that might be taken by either the sender or the carrier.

The same error underlies one writer's surprise[48] that ferrous metal should be described as sensitive; it also explains the decision

[45] Glass and Cashmore, para. 3.52 contend that the nature of the goods "must be considered in the light of actual circumstances, *e.g.* fresh vegetables may be expected to arrive in perfect condition when carried for a short distance in winter, but it should not be surprising if they suffer some deterioration when carried for long periods in mid-summer", and by implication are sensitive only in the summer case. This is supported by *Cass. 4.2.86*, (1986) 21 E.T.L. 263: chocolate biscuits in summer. However, the relevant circumstances are those external to the vehicle.

[46] 1971 U.L.C. 137, 139.

[47] If goods cannot be carried safely in accordance with good practice and with sufficient precautions, they may suffer from inherent vice, but that alone does not make them sensitive goods. On the meaning of inherent vice, see above, para. 72. On the distinction between inherent vice and sensitivity, see below, para. 89c.

[48] Putzeys, para. 817.

in *O.L.G. Frankfurt 25.10.77*,[49] rejecting the argument that sheet metal was sensitive because of a tendency to rust, on the basis that the goods were sensitive only if the tendency to rust still occurred when, as the contract of carriage in that case required, the metal was carried in a vehicle with a cover to protect the metal from the wet.[50] The reasoning proves too much. The same might be said of fruit, vegetables and meat, which will deteriorate unless carried under controlled temperatures, but are clearly cases of sensitive goods. Moreover, rust is one of the consequences of particular exposure listed in Article 17.4(d) itself. Hence it is clear from both the terms of Article 17.4(d) and from the intention behind it, that sensitive goods must be identified without regard to the precautions that may be required under the contract of carriage. Goods which are sensitive do not cease to be subject to Article 17.4(d) because, if they are packed or carried in a way which protects them, they cease to be sensitive.[51] Conversely, goods which are not sensitive do not come under Article 17.4(d) because they are packed or carried (badly) in a way which particularly exposes them to loss or damage.[52]

The special risks in Article 17.4 are not mutually exclusive. Metal without sufficient protection against rusting[53] or fruit without sufficient insulation[54] may be both sensitive goods under Article 17.4(d) and goods defectively packed under Article 17.4(b). A case of "normal wastage" in sensitive goods, referred to in Article 17.4(d), may also be a case of wastage from unsheeted vehicles, a

---

[49] VersR 1978.535, 536. A similar error is found in *Paris 10.11.81*, B.T. 1982.183, in which the court declined to treat frozen shrimps as a case of sensitive goods because, if the shrimps had been carried at a sufficiently low temperature, they would not have been damaged; and in *Gent 20.6.86* (1986) 21 E.T.L. 371, holding that sensitive goods do not include glass, unless damage cannot be prevented by adequate packing. See also *O.L.G. Köln 30.8.90*, TranspR 1990.425. *cf.* however, *O.L.G. Hamm 2.11.95*, TranspR 1996.335, in which the court (correctly) treated a load of steel strip as sensitive.

[50] In other words, that was not a case of sensitive goods under Art. 17.4(d) but of defective packing under Art. 17.4(b): above, para. 82. The truth is that a case may fall under both provisions.

[51] In *Versailles 29.2.84*, B.T. 1984.249, the carrier was exonerated under Art. 17.4(d) in respect of damage to pineapples carried in an unrefrigerated vehicle in July, as he had not been instructed by the sender to use a refrigerated vehicle and the usual carriage charge for refrigerated carriage would have been appreciably higher than that contracted for. In *Paris 10.12.71*, 1973 U.L.C. 274, B.T. 1972.35, galvanised steel arrived in a state of rust, and the carrier's defence under Art. 17.4(d) failed. However, the main reason for the decision was the failure of the carrier to carry out, as required by Art. 18.4, the sender's instructions that, the goods being vulnerable to humidity, a watertight tilt cover or awning should be used. Art. 18.4 is concerned only with the case of sensitive goods; it is clear that the court accepted the premise of the carrier's defence, that naked steel is a case of sensitive goods.

[52] *cf.* the suggestion (Libouton, Theunis, p. 90, citing *Rb Antwerp 6.9.74* (1975) 10 E.T.L. 253) that wool bobbins packed in plastic bags were sensitive because of the danger of condensation: this appears to be a case of defective packing rather than of sensitive goods.

[53] As in *Tetroc v. Cross-Con (International)* [1981] 1 Lloyd's Rep. 192, 199–200, *per* Judge Martin.

[54] *Versailles 29.2.84* (above, n. 51).

special risk in its own right under Article 17.4(a).[55] Again, "breakage" has not been a common case under Article 17.4(d), but arises as a case of defective packing under Article 17.4(b)[56] or of sender's loading under Article 17.4(c).

The list of consequences in Article 17.4(d) is not exhaustive.[57] The most common reported case of loss or damage under Article 17.4(d) is "decay" in perishable goods. In the French translation decay is "détérioration interne et spontanée", but decay is not the same as "détérioration" and does not cover every instance of deterioration.[58] As appears from the next case, decay does not occur without the *normal* effects of the earth's atmosphere, notably warmth and moisture.

> In *Donald & Son (Wholesale Meat Contractors) Ltd v. Continental Freeze*[59] meat sent from Scotland to France was carried at too low a temperature and arrived damaged. The carrier appealed to Article 17.4(d), arguing that "decay" includes deterioration and that this was what had occurred. However, the court accepted the claimant's argument that there was no "decay" in the meat, since decay involved a natural process of deterioration and what had happened here was that the meat had been excessively (and unnaturally) preserved.

A further argument in *Donald* was that, as meat was sensitive in the sense of susceptible to decay, any loss related to that attribute of the meat was within Article 17.4(d), even if the actual damage could not be described as "decay". But Lord Murray adopted the claimant's emphasis on the words of the first paragraph of Article 17.4, that the loss or damage must "arise from" the special risk. The loss in *Donald*, he held, occurred to sensitive goods and was related to their sensitivity, but did not arise from their sensitivity, the special risk. The loss arose not from the risk itself but from the measure (overcooling) taken by the carrier to avert the operation of the risk (overheating). This assumes, however, that the special risk is not simply sensitivity to temperature of any kind anywhere, but, more narrowly, sensitivity to the "normal" temperature outside the controlled environment of a refrigerated vehicle. If, instead of being too cool, the unit temperature had been lower than the temperature in the air outside but not low enough,

---

[55] *Lg Offenburg 21.1.69* (1971) 6 E.T.L. 283.

[56] For example, *Cass. 12.10.81*, B.T. 1981.576 (1982) 17 E.T.L. 294 (works of art); *Paris 10.2.84*, B.T. 1984.558 (computers).

[57] Herber/Piper, Art. 17, 128.

[58] Lord Murray, in the Outer House of the Court of Session in *Donald* (below), observed that decay is not a synonym for deterioration but a form of deterioration; and that if all kinds of deterioration were special risks, the list in sub-paragraph (d) would have been unnecessary.

[59] 1984 S.L.T. 182. For a detailed study of cases concerning the movement of goods in isothermic or refrigerated vehicles, see Thume, TranspR 1992.1; and Thume (*op. cit.*), Art. 17, 192 *et seq.*

presumably there would have been a case of damage due to sensitivity. The assumption is not beyond dispute.[60] In any event, Article 17.4(d) includes sensitivity to cold in the climate at large,[61] as can be inferred from the reference in Article 18.4 to "vehicles specially equipped to protect the goods from the effects of . . . cold".[62]

89a. Sensitivity and inherent vice distinguished

Whereas most instances of sensitive goods are obvious, the concept itself is hard to define. Professor Rodière[63] likened sensitivity to the tendency to self-destruction found in the notion of inherent vice. However, the concepts are not exactly alike.[64] Nor are they mutually exclusive: in a particular case goods may be sensitive under Article 17.4(d) as well as suffering from an inherent vice under Article 17.2.[65] Damage resulting from sensitivity is a notion peculiar to Article 17.4(d), which provides a defence additional to and not exclusive of the concept of inherent vice as a defence under Article 17.2, while offering the defending carrier a lighter onus of proof.[66] Differences between them are as follows:

(a) As regards the journey in question, inherent vice applies to some goods of that type but not to all goods of that type[67]: for example, the particular apples may be overripe for the journey, but not all apples. Sensitivity is a feature of all goods of that type: for

---

[60] In *The Hague 9.1.87*, S. & S. 1987 no. 141 the goods were damaged as a result of having been carried at too low a temperature, and the court allowed the carrier to defend under Art. 17.4(d), rejecting the defence not as in *Donald* because the damage did not arise from the special risk but because the carrier failed to bring the proof required by Art. 18.4.

[61] *Toulouse 26.3.69*, discussed below, para. 89b. In *Nîmes 18.5.88*, B.T. 1988.472, wine was damaged by exposure to the cold; the defence was not Art. 17.4(d) but that the sender had failed to provide sufficient insulation. However, special risks overlap, and reliance on one does not preclude another. Similarly, defective packing was the successful defence of the carrier in *Montpellier 28.2.85*, B.T. 1985.600, as regards fruit and vegetables sent from Perpignan to Delft in early January, and damaged by cold. Sub-paragraph (d) was not pleaded.

[62] If goods are overcooled by exposure to the outside air, it cannot be described as "decay", but the list of damage in Art. 17.4(d) does not purport to be exhaustive: there are other kinds of loss which, without being *ejusdem generis* those listed, are nonetheless within the provision. The risks narrated do not constitute a genus: *Donald & Son (Wholesale Meat Contractors) Ltd v. Continental Freeze* 1984 S.L.T. 182, 183 *per* Lord Murray.

[63] Rodière, para. 544, citing cases decided under the CIM. Also in this sense, Van Ryn (1966) 1 E.T.L. 638, 658. *Contra: Ulster-Swift v. Taunton Meat Haulage* [1977] 1 Lloyd's Rep. 346, 354, *per* Megaw L.J., C.A. Also *contra*: Chao, Theunis, p. 133; Hill and Messent, p. 112; Herber/Piper, Art. 17, 128; Loewe, para. 152; Putzeys, para. 760; Thume, Art. 17, 173.

[64] *Agen 26.11.85*, B.T. 1986.235, 236; *O.L.G. Hamm 11.6.90*, TranspR 1990.375, 376.

[65] For example, *Agen 26.11.85* (above): the new potatoes were sensitive goods, and also suffering from an inherent vice.

[66] Above, paras. 76 *et seq.*

[67] *O.L.G. Hamm 11.6.90* (above, n. 64). Also in this sense: Glass and Cashmore, para. 3.52; Libouton, para. 38; Loewe, para. 152; Putzeys, paras. 813–814.

example, apples, in general, are susceptible to bruising, but paving-stones are not.

An important but difficult case is that of meat insufficiently cooled when it is taken over. Meat is an established example of goods sensitive to the temperature of the air during transport, but in the case of meat insufficiently cool on being taken over the damage that has developed by the time of delivery can be seen as arising out of the inherent vice (insufficient cooling immediately prior to the transport) rather than the special risk (effect of ambient temperature during the transport on goods more sensitive than they should be). However, it could also be said that the state of the meat on being taken over would not have led to damage or to as much damage but for the effect of the ambient temperature during the transport.[68] Although that can be seen as a case for Article 17.4(d),[69] it is more often seen as a case of inherent vice.[70] The carrier must prove the existence of the vice, but does not have to prove the precise nature of the vice[71] and therefore does not have to prove its origin, such as insufficient cooling.[72]

(b) For inherent vice, the vice must indeed be inherent in the sense that it arises mainly from characteristics of the goods themselves, as distinguished from external factors associated with transportation, such as exposure to bruising and breakage. By contrast, some but not all of the hazards to which sensitive goods are susceptible, such as breakage, involve external factors.[73] Climatological factors, however, play a part in both concepts.

(c) Inherent vice relates to the particular journey to be undertaken: goods fit for immediate use or consumption at the time they are taken over nonetheless suffer from inherent vice if, in spite of the exercise of care required of the carrier, they cannot withstand the normal incidents of that journey, including the time that it can be expected to take, and remain fit for use or consumption on

---

[68] But *cf. Donald* (above, para. 89) which suggests that the special risk is sensitivity not to the temperature in the controlled environment of the vehicle but to the general temperature outside.

[69] In *Centrocoop Export-Import SA v. Brit European Transport* [1984] 2 Lloyd's Rep. 618, the court was mainly concerned with the factual question of identifying the cause of the damage, and was able to find by a process of elimination (at 625) that the cause of damage was indeed that the meat was at too high a temperature when taken over by the carrier. The court concluded that the carrier was exonerated on the ground of unavoidable circumstances, reflecting perhaps the way the case had been argued, Art. 17.4(d).

[70] Chao, Theunis, pp. 133–134. Thus in *Ulster-Swift v. Taunton Meat Haulage* [1975] 2 Lloyd's Rep. 502, 506, *per* Donaldson J., affirmed [1977] 1 Lloyd's Rep. 346, a similar allegation was treated as raising an issue of inherent vice rather than of sensitivity, whereas an allegation of deterioration due to excessive temperature *during* transit raised a question of Art. 17.4(d). See also Thume, TranspR 1992.1.

[71] Above, para. 72.

[72] *O.L.G. Hamm 11.6.90*, TranspR 1990.375.

[73] *cf. O.L.G. Nuremberg 14.6.65* (1971) 6 E.T.L. 247, 260, which appears to be wrong on this point.

delivery. Inherent vice (such as cracks) may occur in both sensitive goods (glass) and non-sensitive goods (paving-stones).

Although sensitive goods are categorised as sensitive because of the possible effect of hazards associated with transportation, the sensitivity of goods is assessed without reference to the particular journey[74] or to the care required of the carrier,[75] except in so far as failure by the carrier to use or to use properly a specially equipped vehicle, in which the journey is to be performed, takes the case (but not the categorisation of the goods as sensitive goods) outside Article 17.4(d).[76]

Whereas an inherent vice is present as a less than perfect state of the goods when the goods are taken over, sensitivity damage is the realisation of something no more than *possible* when the goods are taken over, the actual loss or damage usually occurring later during the journey.

(d) Most things are liable to decay, but goods are sensitive only if their nature "particularly" exposes them to the kinds of damage listed in Article 17.4(d). No such limit is found in the concept of inherent vice, when can include all kinds of defect and deterioration of an ordinary kind. As Lord Murray observed,[77] "had the concept of sub-para. (d) been to relieve the carrier of liability, where loss arose through the inherent nature of certain goods to deteriorate, then there would have been no need to list the specific risks narrated. For all of them, and a great deal more besides, would have been covered by deterioration."

(e) Finally, both sensitivity and inherent vice can be distinguished from latent defect.[78] A latent defect may be any kind of defect, whether arising from the sensitivity of the goods or from the inherent characteristics of the goods or from something else altogether. The defect must, however, be latent: undiscoverable by the exercise of reasonable care at the relevant time.[79] Latency has no bearing on whether there is sensitivity damage or inherent vice, although of course it may affect the carrier's response and thus whether the carrier can appeal to Article 17.4(d) or Article 17.2 as a defence.

---

[74] Except perhaps in broad terms: goods may be sensitive in summer but not in winter or vice versa: *Cass. 4.2.86* (1986) 21 E.T.L. 263 (chocolate biscuits in summer).

[75] If the claimant proves that the carrier failed to take the care required, and this is a cause of loss or damage, the carrier will be liable: Art. 18.2 *in fine*.

[76] See below, para. 89b.

[77] *Donald & Son (Wholesale Meat Contractors) Ltd v. Continental Freeze* 1984 S.L.T. 182, 183. It is doubtful, however, whether wastage can be described as deterioration: Putzeys, para. 818.

[78] Not found in the CMR, but found in kindred regimes such as the Hague-Visby Rules Art. IV, rule 2(p).

[79] The time at which latency is tested depends on the context in which the notion of latent vice is employed.

89b. Specially equipped vehicles

The duty, if any, to use specially equipped vehicles is discussed in Chapter 3.[80] The meaning of special equipment is discussed in Chapter 6.[81] The way in which the carrier deals with such equipment is the subject of Article 18.4:

> "If the carriage is performed in vehicles specially equipped to protect the goods from the effects of heat, cold, variations in temperature or the humidity of the air, the carrier shall not be entitled to claim the benefit of Article 17, paragraph 4(d), unless he proves that all steps incumbent on him in the circumstances with respect to the choice, maintenance and use of such equipment were taken and that he complied with any special instructions issued to him."

If the carrier pleads the sensitivity of the goods under Article 17.4(d), it is for the carrier to prove[82] fulfilment of Article 18.4; and if, after all the evidence has been considered, the cause of the damage cannot be established on the balance of probabilities, the carrier's defence based on the sensitivity of the goods fails.[83] However, the issue of special equipment may arise in another way. If the carrier pleads not Article 17.4(d) but one of the other special risks, the claimant's reply under Article 18.2 *in fine* may be that the real cause is a failure in the special equipment: in that case, the onus of proof with respect to the equipment lies not on the carrier but on the claimant.[84]

89b(*i*). The level of duty

As to the level of duty, the words "all steps incumbent on him in the circumstances" tell us little (except that a duty of some kind exists) as they could refer to virtually any level of duty.

One answer[85] is that the words refer to a duty of due diligence, a duty like that under Article III, rule 1 of the Hague-Visby Rules to make the ship seaworthy. Unlike Article III, rule 1, however,

---

[80] Above, para. 30.

[81] Above, para. 75f(*i*).

[82] *O.G.H. 22.11.84*, Greiter 253, 259. Chao, Theunis, p. 152; Loewe, para. 172.

[83] *e.g. Aix 14.1.92*, B.T.L. 1992.809.

[84] *O.L.G. Hamm 19.2.73* (1974) 9 E.T.L. 753; 760: meat, evidently a sensitive commodity, was placed too tightly by the sender and hence insufficiently cooled during the journey. The carrier pleaded (successfully) not para. (d) (sensitivity) but para. (c) (sender's loading).

The same should be true if the carrier decides to plead not sensitivity but inherent vice (Art. 17.2); but in *Arnhem 10.4.73*, S. & S. 1973 no. 82, 1977 U.L.R. II 212, the court insisted that, notwithstanding the carrier's plea of inherent vice, it was a case of sensitivity, so the carrier was required to prove compliance with Art. 18.4. This decision has been criticised: see Haak, p. 169.

[85] Loewe, para. 172; Pesce, p. 233; Putzeys, para. 820.

Article 18.4 imposes the duty as regards use of the equipment during the journey, and the language, "all steps incumbent", is quite different. Further, due diligence is a well-known concept and, as with Article 17.2,[86] one must ask why, if due diligence was the level of duty intended for the CMR, those words or words like them were not used?

A second answer is that the carrier's duty with regard to special equipment is strict; this answer has some support in cases both in France[87] and in England. In France, where there appears to have been more litigation on this question than anywhere else, an analysis[88] of 32 decisions on Article 18.4 down to 1986 revealed that the carrier's defence had failed in 30 and that in the two remaining cases liability had been apportioned. In some cases, there had been no apparent attempt to judge the carrier's conduct, and the carrier was held liable, it appears, simply because a defect in the equipment existed,[89] thus aligning liability for equipment with the strict liability for the vehicle under Article 17.3.[90] That is generally agreed to be an error,[91] as the existence of a distinct provision for equipment implies a distinct duty.

In England in *Ulster-Swift*,[92] Donaldson J., having found that the meat did not suffer from inherent vice, said that, if the defendant carriers could bring themselves within the defence in Article 17.4(d) and Article 18.4, "the logical conclusion would be that the loss never occurred". But this conclusion was logical only from the premise that the duty with regard to the equipment was strict and that, if the duty had been performed, failure in the equipment could not occur and be a cause of the unexplained damage. If, however, that duty were less than absolute, there could be sensitive cargo delivered damaged because of some failure in the equipment which the carrier had been unable to detect or prevent, in spite of having chosen, maintained and used the equipment with the level of care required. Nonetheless, the judge went on to find that the carrier had not fulfilled the steps incumbent even though, as he said, "I am quite unable to identify what that step was".[93] His decision on this point was affirmed by the Court of Appeal.[94]

By contrast, in *Centrocoop*[95] the tenor of the judgment of Bingham J. is quite different: "With reference to art. 18.4, the

---

86 See above, para. 74d.
87 Brunat B.T. 1982.174: "La jurisprudence se montre très rigoureuse."
88 Chao, Theunis, pp. 113 *et seq.*
89 *ibid.*, p. 127 and p. 129.
90 Above, para. 75f.
91 Except by Nickel-Lanz (para. 139), whose position is examined critically by Haak, p. 172.
92 *Ulster-Swift v. Taunton Meat Haulage* [1975] 2 Lloyd's Rep. 502, 507.
93 *ibid.*
94 [1977] 1 Lloyd's Rep. 346, C.A. See at 350 and 353, *per* Megaw L.J.
95 *Centrocoop Export-Import SA v. Brit European Transport* [1984] 2 Lloyd's Rep. 618, 626.

carrier has shown to my satisfaction that he took all steps incumbent. . . . He hired the unit from an apparently reputable hirer with whom he regularly dealt; the unit was inspected by a driver before delivery, and in all probability by the yard on arrival; it was the subject of regular maintenance . . . and there was no suggestion of any previous mishap which had not been attended to." This is the language appropriate to a duty of care, although it does not indicate very clearly what level of care is required.

If the duty is strict, as the *Ulster-Swift* case suggests, it is not obvious why the CMR expresses it twice, both with regard to the vehicle in Article 17.3 and with regard to special equipment in Article 18.4. The inference is that a similar level of duty was not intended. The negative inference of the existence and wording of Article 18.4 is that the level of duty is neither one of due diligence nor one of strict liability but a level between. Beyond this, Article 18.4 itself is unhelpful, but construed in the context of the entire CMR Convention, the answer is, it is submitted, that the level of care required of the carrier under Article 18.4 is that of the residual duty[96] of "utmost care".[97] Many of the cases are consistent with this conclusion, and one decision of the OGH[98] explicitly equates the level of duty under Article 18.4 with the more general level of the carrier's duty under Article 17. Moreover, the contention is supported by a leading German commentary,[99] in so far as that too asserts that the level of duty under Article 18.4 is the same as that under the CMR in general. Were it otherwise, the pattern of liability in the CMR as a whole would be anomalous and uneven.[1]

89b(*ii*). Steps incumbent: performance of the duty

With respect to special equipment, the "steps incumbent" on the carrier concern the choice of equipment, its maintenance and its

[96] Above, para. 79.

[97] Above, para. 74e.

[98] *O.G.H. 22.11.84*, Greiter 253, 260.

[99] Helm (Art. 17 Anm. 4 and Anm. 18) describes the carrier's liability for equipment under Art. 18.4 in the same terms as the carrier's general liability for goods under Art. 17.1: *eine Haftung für vermutetes Verschulden. idem*: Herber/Piper, Art. 18, 27. The latter does not necessarily indicate any particular level of duty, as the level may vary according to context. It should, however, be said that as regards the particular level for Art. 18.4 Helm concludes (Art. 17 Anm. 18): "Der Verschuldenmaßstab in art. 18 Abs. 4 CMR ist wohl der normale, also nach deutschem Recht para. 347 HGB: Sorgfalt eines ordentlichen Kaufmanns." In the opinion of the present writer that puts the level too low, but what counts for the purpose of the present argument is that Helm considers the level in Art. 18.4 and the general or residual level for the CMR to be the same.

[1] If there is an accident for which the carrier is excused under Art. 17.2, the carrier is nonetheless required to exercise utmost care to prevent or minimise harm (above, para. 75g) to the goods through, for example, exposure to excessive temperature as a consequence of the accident. It would be odd if in the aftermath of the same accident the level of duty to minimise the damage were different as regards the use of any special equipment affecting temperature.

use.[2] To a degree, the steps are taken in three stages, but evidently the stages are interrelated, as, for example, the ability of the driver to use the equipment may be affected by the features of the equipment.

As to the choice of special equipment, the preliminary question is whether the contract requires special equipment at all.[3] If the carrier is required to provide a refrigerated vehicle, fails to do so with consequent damage to the goods, and yet pleads the sensitivity of the goods, the carrier will be liable for failure to provide and hence to use the special equipment required. If, although the carriage in question is normally performed with special equipment, the court finds that in the particular case the carrier was not obliged to provide it, the carrier will not be liable for having employed a vehicle without it.[4] If, however, it should be obvious to the carrier that the state of the goods is such that the vehicle provided is incapable of preserving them for the journey in question but the carrier nonetheless takes the goods in that vehicle, the carrier will bear some responsibility at least for any consequent loss or damage.[5] If special equipment is required and the equipment chosen by the carrier works perfectly but is ill-designed for the task in hand, the carrier is liable for consequent loss or damage.

As to the maintenance of special equipment, in most cases some evidence of routine maintenance and checking is required. Although some cases focus attention almost entirely on the choice and maintenance of equipment prior to the journey,[6] that is only a facet of the particular case, and it is quite clear that "steps incumbent", including, perhaps, steps intended to check the wording of the equipment, must be taken during the carriage as well. It has been rightly held that the carrier must provide maintenance support in case of malfunction—not only during normal working hours but also, for example, during the weekend.[7]

As to the use of equipment, if, although the carriage in question is normally performed with special equipment, the court finds that in the particular case the carrier was not obliged to provide it, it

---

[2] Note that the International Carriage of Perishable Foodstuffs Act 1976 gives effect to the United Nations Agreement on the International Carriage of Perishable Foodstuffs (APT), and is concerned with the technical features of vehicles employed for this kind of transport. Helm, Art. 17 Anm. 18; Herber/Piper, Art. 18, 26; Thume, Art. 17, 189.

[3] See above, para. 30.

[4] *Versailles 29.4.84*, B.T. 1984.249 (pineapples in an ordinary vehicle in July met unexpectedly an unavoidable delay at the frontier).

[5] *Cass. 15.2.82*, B.T. 1982.182, note Brunat B.T. 1982.174. Especially, if it is apparent to the driver at the time of loading that there is a breakdown in the equipment: *O.L.G. Nuremberg 14.6.65* (1971) 6 E.T.L. 247, 260.

[6] For example, *O.L.G. Nuremberg 14.6.65* (1971) 6 E.T.L. 247, 260; *O.L.G. Hamm 6.12.93*, TranspR 1994.195. *Centrocoop Export-Import SA v. Brit European Transport* [1984] 2 Lloyd's Rep. 618, 626, *per* Bingham J.

[7] Herber/Piper, Art. 18, 34, and Koller, Art. 17, 51, citing *O.L.G. Hamburg 2.5.85*, VersR 1986.865.

has been held[8] that the carrier cannot be liable for failure to use it. But in that case the vehicle did not have the equipment, whereas, if in such a case it had had the equipment and it became apparent to the driver that the goods were suffering without the use of the equipment, he would be obliged to use it to fulfil the carrier's general duty of care.[9] Similarly, as to the mode of use, if refrigeration is required and used, but the carrier obeys the sender's instructions as to temperature, which, as the carrier should be aware, will lead to damage, the carrier bears partial responsibility for consequential damage.[10]

Evidently, it is not enough to put perfect machinery in the hands of a driver who is too careless or too incompetent to use it as the circumstances require.

> In *Riom 28.10.82*[11] it was not enough for the carrier to show that the refrigeration system had been checked the day before the damage, as it was also established that the driver had left the doors of the vehicle open for six hours while waiting to load. The driver deserved more sympathy in *Nancy 20.2.81*[12]: the vehicle broke down close to private dwellings and remained there for four days, during which time the driver was "obliged" to turn off the refrigeration, as it disturbed the occupants of the dwellings. Given that the source of the delay was a breakdown in the vehicle, for which the carrier is strictly liable under Article 17.3, and that "utmost care" would not spare the expense of having the vehicle towed to a spot where people would not be disturbed by use of the special equipment, it is not surprising that the carrier was held liable for deterioration in the goods.

Even a competent driver may make an occasional mistake and it is this possibility that the carrier will find it hard to rule out.[13] Indeed, one inference from the strictness of most of the decisions on Article 18.4 is that, to take the example of the refrigerated transport of meat,[14] if the carrier succeeds in proving steps incumbent as regards the choice and maintenance of the equipment, the carrier will be liable on the supposition that the equipment was not used properly, unless it can be established that there was some other explanation of the damage to the meat,[15] such as inherent vice or unavoidable delay to a degree that goes beyond the normal risks of transportation.

---

[8] *Versailles 29.4.84* (above, n. 4).
[9] Above, para. 79.
[10] *Cass. 19.4.82*, B.T. 1982.309. Herber/Piper, Art. 18, 36; Koller, Art. 17, 51.
[11] Unpublished, but reported by Chao, Theunis, p. 126.
[12] B.T. 1981.330.
[13] See further decisions in France reported by Chao, *loc. cit.*
[14] See discussion of *Ulster-Swift* by Glass and Cashmore, para. 3.53.
[15] This appears to have been the position in *Ulster-Swift*: see above, para. 89b(*i*).

In particular, the carrier will be liable to the extent that damage to goods is caused by the driver not having checked the temperature inside a refrigerated vehicle during the journey, even if he lacks the means of doing so, such as a gauge.[16] Moreover, if there is a gauge, unless there is also a device to record the temperature maintained, a court may still conclude that the carrier has failed to prove that the equipment was used properly throughout.[17] Worse still for the carrier is the contention[18] that, even though it may be impossible to check the interior of the vehicle because it has been sealed, it is not enough to rely on the readings of an external temperature gauge or on a thermostat setting. If that were correct, the carrier would have to bring evidence of the state of the goods when the seals are broken at destination to establish that any damage could not have occurred during transit[19]; this might be difficult. However, decisions in Holland are against the contention[20] and cases in which the carrier has been sanctioned for failure of this kind appear to have concerned gauges that did not work or did not provide the relevant information.[21]

In practice, carriers, apprehensive of the court's response to the evidence of the driver, may well seek to defend themselves by bringing evidence to show that the equipment did work properly or to demonstrate the actual cause of loss, such as defective stowage by the sender,[22] although in principle that evidence is not required by Article 18.4.

In many cases, the steps incumbent on the carrier must be assessed in conjunction with the carrier's other duties: use of the equipment is part of a wider web of responsibility. If, for example, the goods are loaded and stowed by the sender, the carrier may nonetheless be obliged to check that the manner of loading and stowage[23] does not reduce the effectiveness of the special equipment during the journey. In one case a carrier failed under Article 18.4 because, although all the normal steps in respect of the use of refrigeration had been taken, the carrier had allowed the goods to be packed so tightly that the refrigeration would be inadequate.[24]

---

[16] *O.L.G. Koblenz 2.7.76*, VersR 1976.1153; *Paris 20.11.80*, B.T. 1980.615; *Toulouse 14.1.81*, B.T. 1981.158. Herber/Piper, Art. 18, 33; Koller, Art. 17, 51.

[17] Chao, Theunis, p. 128 and p. 141.

[18] Hill and Messent, p. 149; but the contention is supported by some of the decisions such as *Aix 14.1.92*, B.T.L. 1992.809.

[19] For example, *Centrocoop Export-Import SA v. Brit European Transport* [1984] 2 Lloyd's Rep. 618, 624–625, *per* Bingham J.

[20] In *Arnhem 11.5.76*, S. & S. 1976 no. 89, the court was satisfied with evidence from external gauges; and in *The Hague 21.5.87*, S. & S. 1988 no. 24 the (Hill and Messent) contention was put, but rejected by the court (at 85).

[21] For example, *Rb Rotterdam 27.4.71* (1971) 6 E.T.L. 830; *O.L.G. Koblenz 2.7.76* (1979) E.L.D. 41. *Semble* the report of the Danish case cited by Hill and Messent *loc. cit.*, n. 18 does not support the proposition: 1971 U.L.C. 292, 301.

[22] For example, *Brussels 17.12.84* (1985) 20 E.T.L. 354.

[23] Above, para. 87.

[24] *The Hague 15.6.79* (1980) 15 E.T.L. 871, 894.

Again, if the sender has given instructions concerning the temperature of the goods in transit, the carrier's use of the equipment will be judged in the light of the sender's instructions, which may include not only matters directly affecting the equipment, such as temperature, but also other related matters such as the time for delivery[25]: instructions about temperature may have been framed in the light of the expected duration of the journey. Thirdly, in any case, if it becomes apparent that in spite or because of obedience to the instructions the goods are at risk, the carrier's use of equipment will be judged as part of the residual duty of "utmost" care.[26]

89b(*iii*). Causation

Article 18.4 is not itself a ground of liability but a condition of the defence in Article 17.4(d). If the carrier fails to prove fulfilment of Article 18.4, the carrier cannot rely on Article 17.4(d), whether or not the failure has a causal connection with the loss or damage.[27] In practice in such a case, however, if the goods are sensitive, a causal connection is likely.

> In *O.L.G. Nuremburg 14.6.65*[28] mushrooms were loaded on to a refrigerated vehicle and it was apparent at the time to the driver that the refrigeration was failing to keep the mushrooms to the temperature of –2°C specified. The driver telephoned his employer, who instructed him to make the journey to the border where a repair team would be waiting. This was done but the mushrooms were damaged. The court held the carrier liable in breach of Article 18.4, as the refrigeration unit had broken down, and the sender's instructions had not been carried out.[29]

In that case, the court observed that it was not obvious that the damage had any cause other than the breakdown of the equipment and the failure to follow instructions. The court listened to evidence brought by the carrier that the damage would have occurred in any event; however, if the carrier had been successful in this line of argument, the result would have been a successful defence not under Article 17.4(d) but on the basis of inherent vice under Article 17.2.

---

[25] *Paris 4.3.85*, B.T. 1985.396.
[26] Above, para. 79.
[27] *cf.* Pesce, p. 235.
[28] (1971) 6 E.T.L. 247.
[29] At 260–261.

89c. Counter-proof by the claimant

When the loss or damage could have been caused by sensitivity (Article 17.4(d)) and the carrier has proved steps incumbent (Article 18.4), it is still open to the claimant to defeat the defence by proving "that the loss or damage was not, in fact, attributable either wholly or partly to" the sensitivity of the goods (Article 18.2).

> In *Kg Delft 13.5.65*[30] meat was carried from Holland to Spain, a journey which normally took six days. The refrigerated vehicle was delayed for a further eight days at the Spanish border because the vehicle lacked an import permit for the load. The carrier relied on Article 17.4(d). If the carrier could show that all steps incumbent had been taken with respect to the use of the refrigeration, in accordance with Article 18.4, it was then for the claimants to prove, if they could, that the delay at the border into Spain had occurred because, although supplied with proper documents, the carrier had not used them properly.

If the carrier has proved both the sensitivity of the goods and that steps incumbent have been taken and, after all the evidence has been considered, the cause of loss in such a case is still uncertain, it is presumed to lie in the sensitivity of the goods and in theory the carrier's defence succeeds.[31] The claimant has failed to prove otherwise. In practice, however, the strictness of the obligation[32] to prove steps incumbent is such that only rarely does a carrier make that proof in circumstances in which the actual cause of the loss or damage is not apparent.

90. Marks

Article 17.4(e) provides that, subject to Article 18, the carrier shall be relieved of liability when the loss or damage arises from "insufficiency of marks or numbers on the packages". This cause of exoneration overlaps to a large degree with the broader exception of "wrongful act or neglect of the claimant" in Article 17.2,[33] but with the crucial differences that, in the case of Article 17.4(e), the

---

[30] 1966 U.L.C. 104. Similarly, in *Toulouse 26.3.69* (1971) 6 E.T.L. 131 hothouse plants, being transported in January, were damaged by frost. The carrier pleaded Art. 17.4(d). The claimant argued in reply that the real cause was that the lorry broke down for 48 hours in Ghent and that during this time the driver took no precautions to protect the plants from the cold. This kind of argument was clearly acceptable to the court; but as the facts alleged by the claimant, though not their significance in law, were denied by the carrier, the court ordered an *expertise*.

[31] For example, *Agen 26.11.85*, B.T. 1986.235: the claimant failed to prove that the damage was caused by delay during the journey.

[32] Above, para. 89b(*i*).

[33] Above, para. 70.

carrier is not required to prove the claimant's fault[34] or to prove that the insufficiency or inadequacy did in fact cause the loss: as with all special risks, it is enough that it could have caused the loss.[35]

This defence has provoked little litigation or comment.[36] As in the other cases of special risk, the carrier will be liable[37] to the extent that the claimant can prove[38] that the loss or damage was not attributable to the risk. In this instance, the claimant may seek to prove that it was attributable, at least in part,[39] to the failure of the carrier to comply with Article 8.1: failure to check "the accuracy of the statements in the consignment note as to the number of packages and their marks and numbers."[40] However, non-compliance with Article 8.1 is not a breach of duty as such,[41] although a failure to warn the sender that the marks are insufficient or inadequate may be a breach of duty of a more general kind.[42]

91. Livestock

Article 17.4(f) provides that, subject to Article 18, the carrier shall be relieved of liability when the loss or damage arises from "the carriage of livestock". However, it must be read with Article 18.5: "The carrier shall not be entitled to claim the benefit of Article 17, paragraph 4(f), unless he proves that all steps normally incumbent on him in the circumstances were taken and that he complied with any special instructions issued to him."

The carriage of livestock is a particular case of sensitive goods, the special risk in Article 17.4(d).[43] Livestock are the subject of a special provision because the CMR derives from the CIM and, when the CIM was being agreed, some states did not regard livestock as goods.[44] The defence in Article 17.4(f) is conditional on fulfilment of Article 18.5 in the same way as that in Article 17.4(d) is conditional on fulfilment of Article 18.4.[45] Both the context, as well as the similarity of the wording in Article 18.4 and

---

[34] Helm, Art. 17 Anm. 19.
[35] Above, para. 76.
[36] Loewe, para. 166; Rodière (1971) 6 E.T.L. 306, 313.
[37] Under Art. 17.1.
[38] By virtue of Art. 18.2 *in fine*: above, para. 78.
[39] Apportionment is possible: above, para. 78a.
[40] Above, para. 25b.
[41] See above, para. 87a.
[42] By analogy with his responsibility for defective packing by the sender: above, para. 84.
[43] See above, para. 89.
[44] Nickel-Lanz, para. 147.
[45] See above, para. 89b.

Article 18.5, suggest a similar level of duty. If so, the carrier would be required to perform the condition in Article 18.5 with "utmost care". However, there are also differences between Article 18.4 and Article 18.5, differences which suggest that the level of duty may be no higher than that of reasonable care.

First, the duty of utmost care applies to special equipment because, like the vehicle itself, the equipment is seen as essentially part of the carrier's sphere of risk. In contrast, although *ex hypothesi* the carrier has agreed to transport the animals in question, it is less obvious why the carrier should assume the risk on the basis of a relatively strict duty, such as utmost care.

Secondly, the responsibility for special equipment does not apply to all cases of sensitive goods but only to those cases, admittedly common, in which such equipment is required by the contract. In contrast, the duty in Article 18.5 applies to each and every carriage of livestock and, if the carrier must prove the exercise of utmost care as a precondition of a defence based on Article 17.4(f), there is little advantage for the carrier in Article 17.4(f). The result is that the special risk associated with livestock is not retained by the sender but largely transferred to the carrier, whether the carrier wills it or not.

Thirdly, whereas the duty of utmost care in respect of equipment is to take "all steps incumbent", the duty in respect of livestock is to take "all steps normally incumbent", suggesting a benchmark of current practice which is below the level of duty imposed on a carrier by the duty of utmost care.[46] Article 17.4(f) has provoked little or no reported litigation.

92. Public policy: Article 41

Article 41.1 provides that:

> "any stipulations which would directly or indirectly derogate from the provisions of this Convention shall be null and void. The nullity

[46] Above, para. 75. For Art. 18.5 Glass (1979) 14 E.T.L. 687, 710 suggests a duty of reasonable care. *idem*, Putzeys, para. 840. Koller (Art. 17, 53) suggests *eine Verschuldenshaftung*, which also seems to be the view of Thume: Art. 17, 209. Nickel-Lanz, para. 147 suggests a level of duty slightly below that required under Art. 18.4. *cf.* Haak, p. 174 who contends that in this context "normally" "has scarcely any meaning"; and Loewe, para. 173, who thought that the word "does not seem to make any difference as to the substance".

For some states, such as Germany (Thume, Art. 17, 210), the standard of current practice is set by the European Convention on the Protection of Animals in International Transport, Paris (December 13, 1968) and the European Convention (of May 10, 1979) on the Protection of Animals for Slaughter.

of such a stipulation shall not involve the nullity of other provisions of the contract."

The effect is that, as regards matters regulated by the CMR, the terms of the contract of carriage are fixed, except for a few changes allowed by the CMR itself concerning contribution[47] and suit.[48] For example, a clause limiting the range of courts in which the claimant can bring proceedings is void[49]; and for obvious reasons an arbitration clause allowed by Article 33 will not be enforced unless, as stipulated by Article 33, the arbitrators are required to apply the CMR.[50] Most importantly, the carrier's liability under the CMR may not be reduced or limited, for example to the amount of the carrier's liability cover.[51] Nor, unlike regimes such as that of the Hague-Visby Rules, may the carrier's liability be increased,[52] for example by a penalty clause for late delivery.[53] Moreover, although Article 41 is mainly aimed at preventing a derogation from the duties of the carrier, it also ensures that the carrier does not lose any of his rights against the sender or consignee.[54] Whether, in states with developed rules of good faith in the conclusion and performance of contracts, those rules apply to a CMR contract is a matter of debate.[55] In view of the importance of these rules and the differences in their impact from one

[47] Article 41 is expressed to be subject to the provisions of Article 40, which allows carriers to agree between themselves contribution provisions other than those contained in Article 37 and Article 38. On this, see above, para. 51.

[48] Few changes are allowed: changes allowed include a limited choice of forum: Art. 31.1, above, para. 46c; and arbitration: Art. 33, above, para. 47. Other matters concerning suit, notably the rules of prescription, cannot be changed: *O.G.H. 22.5.78*, TranspR 1980.143, Greiter 66.

[49] *Dresser U.K. Ltd v. Falcongate Freight Management Ltd, The Duke of Yare* (1991) 26 E.T.L. 798, affirmed on other points: [1992] Q.B. 502, C.A.

[50] *A.B. Bofors-UVA v. A.B. Skandia Transport* [1982] 1 Lloyd's Rep. 410.

[51] *Cass. 17.5.83*, B.T. 1983.445. See also *Brussels 12.2.77* (1978) 13 E.T.L. 285; *Antwerp 4.5.77* (1978) 13 E.T.L. 478.

[52] *Paris 27.1.71*, B.T. 1971.115, 1971 U.L.C. 151. Loewe, para. 292: "The reasons for this are first, that there was no way of knowing which party to a contract for the carriage of goods would be the strongest economically and therefore in a position to exercise pressure on the person with whom he has contracted and, secondly, that it seemed advisable to avoid competition between individual transport enterprises which might wish to attract clients by offering them terms which were actually or allegedly better." These reasons are unconvincing: first, market forces, including competition and economic inequality, make themselves felt in any case in other ways. Secondly, experience under the Hague-Visby Rules, where it is possible to increase but not decrease the liability of the carrier, suggests that few consignors are willing to pay the higher freight rates inevitably required by the carrier for higher responsibility. The same has been true of the declaration of special interest permitted by the CMR: Hill, "Carriage of Goods by Road to the Continent" (1976) 11 E.T.L. 182, 205.

[53] *O.L.G. Munich 26.7.85*, TranspR 1985.395, reported by Glöckner, Theunis, p. 104.

[54] For example, *O.G.H. 5.7.77*, Greiter 54, as regards the carrier's right to enforce the consignee's duty under Art. 13.2 to pay charges.

[55] Herber/Piper, Art. 41, 3; Koller, Art. 41, 1. Another more particular matter of debate is whether the carrier can be made liable for failure to check customs documents; Thume, Art. 41, 16.

state to another, their application is not in the interest of uniformity of law.[56]

Article 41 invalidates stipulations which derogate from the provisions of the CMR and not, therefore, stipulations which are included in a contract of carriage governed by the CMR but which regulate matters on which the CMR itself is silent.[57] These may include not only matters clearly collateral to the CMR, for example an agreement between sender and carrier relating to security for performance,[58] but also matters relating to how the carrier is to perform his CMR duty to carry. Evidently, a promise to carry to A rather than to B does not infringe Article 41 because A is harder to reach than B, but nor does a promise to carry the goods at a temperature selected not by the carrier but stipulated by the sender.[59] Again, a clause which excludes rights of set-off between sender and carrier is not invalidated by Article 41[60]: whereas Article 32.4 contemplates the possibility of set-off between the carrier and the sender or consignee,[61] it does not require it. The existence and enforcement of rights of set-off, together with many other matters,[62] are left to national law and to the agreement of the parties.

If the carrier wishes to avoid CMR liability altogether, the carrier must ensure that the contract does not fall within the scope of the CMR.[63] In practice, this means that the carrier will have to divide a single international movement into a series of stages, each of which lacks the international character required for the application of the CMR,[64] each governed by a single and separate contract of transport subject only to local domestic law. Apart from the obvious inconvenience of cutting up a single operation and then stringing it together again, the carrier will be faced with a succession of domestic laws, which will not only differ from each other with resultant uncertainty but which may well be less advantageous to the carrier than the CMR.[65]

---

[56] Koller, *loc. cit.*

[57] Such as disputes over personal injuries suffered by the driver when the load shifted or events after the goods had been delivered; *Noble v. R.H. Group Ltd*, C.A. (February 5, 1993). See also *B.G.H. 9.2.79*, N.J.W. 1979.2470, (1980) 15 E.T.L. 84. More illustrations from cases can be found in Thume, Art. 41, 6 *et seq.* In English law *cf. Shell Chemicals U.K. Ltd v. P & O Roadways Ltd* [1993] 1 Lloyd's Rep. 114, affirmed on other points [1995] 1 Lloyd's Rep. 297, C.A.; Clarke [1993] L.M.C.L.Q. 156.

[58] *O.G.H. 20.1.81*, Greiter 82; and *O.G.H. 18.5.82*, TranspR 1983.48, Greiter 154. *Sed quaere* in view of decisions concerning stipulations in contracts, other than the contract of carriage, notably contracts of insurance: below, para. 92a.

[59] *O.G.H. 22.11.84*, Greiter 253.

[60] *O.G.H. 18.5.82*, TranspR 1983.48, Greiter 154; *B.G.H. 7.3.85* (1985) 20 E.T.L. 343; *O.L.G. Munich 5.7.89*, TranspR 1990.16.

[61] See above, para. 45g.

[62] See above, para. 64.

[63] Art. 1: above, paras. 12 *et seq.*

[64] Above, para. 18. See, for example, *Cass. 25.3.1997*, B.T.L. 1997.276.

[65] Rodière, para. 258.

If the carrier wishes to remain within the CMR regime but to reduce the CMR liability, this can be done by limiting the range of operations which the carrier contracts to perform. If the carrier undertakes to load or unload the goods, these operations are subject to the CMR and any clause reducing the level or amount of the carrier's liability for those operations would be invalid under Article 41. However, the CMR does not require the carrier to assume responsibility for loading or unloading the goods[66] and, if a term of the contract of carriage requires these operations to be carried out by the sender, the carrier will not be liable for loss or damage attributable to the way in which these operations are carried out[67]: such a term is not invalidated by Article 41.[68] Similarly, although it is generally inferred that the carrier is required to check the sender's loading as regards the safety of the vehicle, it has been held[69] that responsibility may be transferred to the sender without infringing Article 41. But a clause which attributes to the carrier the role and the liability of a forwarder, in place of that of a carrier, is invalid under Article 41, if in reality his role is that of a carrier and the operation is within the scope of the CMR.[70]

92a. The benefit of insurance: Article 41.2

Article 41.2 singles out two kinds of stipulation for special mention as null and void under Article 41.2:

> "In particular, a benefit of insurance in favour of the carrier or any other similar clause shifting the burden of proof shall be null and void."

A clause shifting the burden of proof is mentioned to avoid any doubt about the function of such clauses.[71] A clause giving the

---

[66] See above, paras. 28 and 36.

[67] Unless the carrier is in breach of the duty to check the sender's loading: above, para. 87.

[68] *O.G.H. 14.9.82*, TranspR 1984.195, Greiter 174; *O.G.H. 8.10.84*, Stra GüV 1985/6 p. 28, Greiter 239; *O.G.H. 18.12.84*, Stra GüV 1985/4 p. 34, Greiter 270; *O.G.H. 21.2.85*, Stra GüV 1985/10 p. 18, Greiter 285. Thume, Art. 41, A17.

[69] See *B.G.H. 27.10.78* and *Antwerp 27.4.83*, discussed above, para. 87b.

[70] For example, *Rb Rotterdam 12.4.72*, S. & S. 1972 no. 103, 1976 U.L.R. I 253 in which the defendant sought, unsuccessfully, to rely on the standard conditions of Dutch forwarders (FENEX). A similar decision in Austria is *O.G.H. 4.11.81*, TranspR 1982.80, Greiter 103; and in Belgium: *Brussels 25.2.72*, J.P.A. 1972.219, 1974 U.L.R. I. 338; and in Germany: *B.G.H. 18.2.72* (1972) 7 E.T.L. 860. Helm, Art. 41 Anm. 2; Muth/Glöckner, p. 189. On the distinction between a carrier and a forwarder, see above, para. 10a.

[71] Loewe, para. 296.

carrier the benefit of insurance[72] is a device well tried by carriers and its mention in the CMR, which Rodière found inappropriate,[73] reflects experience,[74] originally in the United States, in maritime law.[75] The benefit of insurance, invalidated by Article 41.2, refers not to any insurance at all, but to goods insurance taken out and paid for by the sender[76]; it does not refer to liability insurance taken out by the carrier[77] or by a sub-carrier and assigned to the carrier,[78] unless the contract of carriage provides that the liability insurance premium is to be paid by the sender.

In Belgium[79] and in Germany,[80] it has been held that a clause in goods insurance contracted by the sender, whereby the insurer agrees not to exercise rights, in subrogation against the carrier, would have an effect similar to that of a benefit of insurance clause and that therefore the clause is null and void under Article 41. Indeed, the prohibition in Article 41 does not refer specifically to terms in the contract of carriage and might extend to terms in other contracts, such as the contract of insurance itself, if the carrier seeks to defend a claim under the contract of carriage by reference to a term in the insurance contract.[81] In England, also, the courts are likely to deny the carrier a defence of this kind, however, for reasons unconnected with the CMR.[82] As for the CMR, the purpose of Article 41 is said[83] to be the establishment of a uniform and fixed allocation of responsibility between the parties to the contract of carriage. If this purpose is to be carried through, the defence should fail if it results in an increase in the share of the risk being placed on the sender or consignee through

---

[72] A clause giving the "benefit of insurance" has been construed as a clause exempting the beneficiary from any liability for loss or damage covered by the insurance: Clarke, *Insurance*, para. 31–5A1. Thus a clause, whereby the sender undertook to indemnify the carrier against any liability that the carrier incurred to the consignee in respect of the sender's consignment, is null and void under Art. 41: *Shell Chemicals U.K. Ltd v. P & O Roadways Ltd* [1993] 1 Lloyd's Rep. 114, affirmed on other points [1995] 1 Lloyd's Rep. 297, C.A.; Clarke [1993] L.M.C.L.Q. 156. See also Herber/Piper, Art. 41, 1.

[73] (1971) 6 E.T.L. 574, 589.

[74] Putzeys, para. 978.

[75] The clause is expressly outlawed by the Hague-Visby Rules (Art. III, r. 8).

[76] *O.G.H. 15.12.77*, VersR 1978.980, Greiter 62; *O.G.H. 26.4.84*, Greiter 233.

[77] *O.G.H. 15.12.77* (above). Herber/Piper, Art. 41, 6; Koller, Art. 41, 2; Thume, Art. 41, 31.

[78] *O.G.H. 26.4.84* (above).

[79] *Brussels 31.12.79*, J.T. 1980.388, adopting the view of Loewe, para. 295.

[80] *Lg Duisberg 18.3.75* (1975) 10 E.T.L. 527. Herber/Piper, Art. 41, 6; Koller, Art. 41, 2. *cf.* Thume, Art. 41.

[81] *cf. O.G.H. 20.1.81*, Greiter 82, and *O.G.H. 18.5.82*, TranspR 1983.48, Greiter 154, upholding a collateral contract between sender and carrier relating to security for performance.

[82] In England, quite apart from any considerations of public policy as are thought to defeat the defence in Belgium (Putzeys, para. 980*bis*), the defence would be defeated by the rule of privity of contract: *Scruttons v. Midland Silicones* [1962] A.C. 446. The privity rule is applied to any attempt by a wrongdoer to defeat an insurer's exercise of rights in subrogation by reference to the insurer's contract with the victim: Clarke, *Insurance*, 31–3B2.

[83] *Stuttgart 24.1.67*, N.J.W. 1968.1054. Muth/Glöckner, p. 188.

higher insurance premiums or in a decrease in the share of the risk on the carrier because the carrier's liability for the loss or damage is not enforced.[84] In so far as the indemnity, for which the carrier is liable, is paid for by the sender or consignee, this offends the spirit of Article 41.[85]

In France, however, the courts are out of sympathy with Article 41.2. It has been held[86] that a clause in the contract of carriage whereby the sender was obliged to insure the carrier's liability as carrier, and which is valid in French domestic law, is also valid under the CMR. Given the frequency with which the carrier is held liable by French courts for *faute lourde*[87] and hence for the full value of the goods, but cannot get adequate liability cover, such clauses are said to be desirable, as they ensure adequate indemnity. In essence, this is one of the arguments in the wider debate[88] on the relative merits of first-party and third-party insurance, a debate, however, that is not open to courts required to apply transport conventions such as the CMR: the premise is that the carrier shall bear a certain level of liability for loss or damage to the goods in

---

[84] The underlying assumption appears to have been that, if the carrier is without liability, *de jure* or *de facto*, he will be less careful: Buyl, Theunis, p. 287; Basedow, *Der Transportvertrag* (1987, Tübingen), Chap. 18. This view is found in the *travaux préparatoires* of the CMR: for example, E/ECE/TRANS/SC1/116 p. 12. However, there is little evidence that fear of liability makes people more careful or that the existence of liability insurance makes people less careful: Hanson and Logue (1990) 76 Cornell L.Rev. 129; *cf.* Schwartz, "The Ethics and Economics of Tort Liability Insurance" (1990) 75 Cornell L.Rev. 313.

As regards carriage by sea, in Comité Maritime International (CMI), "Apportionment of Risk in Maritime Law", pp. 28–29, Lord Diplock concluded that "fear of liability, whether strict or fault, is not a major factor in making shipowners take precautions to limit the loss or the risk of loss or damage to cargo"; but that "premium rating based on records, since they reflect over two or three years the actual loss and damage which has been caused, [does] provide the shipowner and the cargo owner with material which enables them to judge whether precautions which are possible in order to prevent or reduce these losses are economically justified by the amount of loss which they will prevent". Moreover, "a deterrent effect no less closely related to the amount of the losses could still be produced by the cargo insurers charging differential premiums as they do already according to the method of transportation used. The cargo insurer can distinguish, and does, between one shipowner and another if he finds that the loss record on any particular shipments by a particular line is above the average."

[85] Loewe, para. 295; Putzeys, para. 980; Rodière, para. 754.

[86] *Poitiers 7.12.83*, B.T. 1985.425.

[87] See below, para. 102c.

[88] There is considerable opinion in common law countries too in favour of first-party (rather than third-party) cover: for example, *Iligan Integrated Steel Mills Inc. v. SS. John Weyerhaeuser* 507F. 2d 68, 73 (2 Cir., 1974), with reference to Diplock (1970) 1 JMLC 525, 528–529. See also Calabresi (1984) 69 Iowa L.Rev. 833; Rea (1987) 12 Can. Bus.L.J. 444; O'Connell and Guinivan (1988) 49 Ohio State L.J. 757; Fleming (1990) 24 UBCL Rev. 1, *5 et seq. Atiyah's Accidents, Compensation and the Law* (5th ed., Oxford, 1993), p. 193. In Germany, see Basedow, *Der Transportvertrag* (1987, Tübingen), Chap. 18. A more sympathetic view of liability insurance in the case of the carrier is taken by the CMI report (above, n. 84); also by Gilles (1992) 78 Va.L.Rev. 1291; and by Clarke, *Policies and Perceptions of Insurance* (Oxford, 1997) Chap. 8–F2. *cf.* also the view that discussion of (and preference) for first party insurance has been skewed by emphasis on motor cover, for which the classification of risk is relatively precise: Hanson, above, n. 84.

order to promote care and loss prevention.[89] The French decisions are difficult to reconcile with Article 41.2.

92b. The Unfair Contract Terms Act 1977

This Act applies to business liability[90] in certain cases. The cases include that of a sender who contracts with a carrier on the carrier's written standard terms of business such as a consignment note.[91] Clearly, subject to what is said in the next paragraph, most contracts for the carriage of goods fall into this category.[92] When the Act applies to a contract, certain clauses, notably ones which "exclude" the carrier's liability, will not apply except to the extent that a court finds them reasonable.[93]

By way of exception, the Act does not apply, first, to "any contractual provision which (a) is authorised or required by the express terms or necessary implication of an enactment; or (b) being made with a view to compliance with an international agreement to which the United Kingdom is a party, does not operate more restrictively than is contemplated by the agreement".[94] Thus, obligations imposed or defences available under the CMR cannot be challenged under the Act, except in those cases in which the CMR does not apply *proprio vigore* but has been adopted voluntarily by the parties.[95] The Act also applies *a contrario* to provisions which are *not* "required by the express terms or necessary implication of an enactment", *i.e.* to other terms of the contract not derived from the CMR but drafted by the parties, notably by the carrier.[96]

Secondly, a partial exemption from the Act, and thus from the requirement of reasonableness, occurs when "goods are carried by *ship* or hovercraft in pursuance of a contract which . . . specifies that as the means of carriage over *part* of the journey to be covered",[97] in so far as the contract "operates for and in relation to the carriage of goods by that means". Thus the carrier from Manchester to Venice, who specifies[98] in the consignment note that the load will cross the English Channel by sea, need fear no interference under the Act for the sea stage.

---

[89] The truth of this premise is disputed: see, for example, Rea, *op. cit.*, as well as references above, nn. 84 and 88.
[90] s.1(3).
[91] s.3.
[92] *cf.* s.7.
[93] See below, para. 239a.
[94] s.29(1).
[95] Hill and Messent, p. 37.
[96] See below, para. 239.
[97] Sched. 1, para. 3 (emphasis added).
[98] *Quaere* how specific must be the specification.

Thirdly, the relevant part[99] of the Act does not apply to international supply contracts. These include contracts "under or in pursuance of which the possession . . . of goods passes"[1] and under which "the goods in question . . . will be carried from the territory of one State to the territory of another".[2] If this were the only requirement of a supply contract, all contracts under the CMR would be outside that part of the Act. However, to be an international supply contract (outside the grip of the Act) the contract must also be "made by parties whose places of business (or, if they have none, habitual residences) are in the territories of different states".[3]

Thus, while the contract of carriage between a sender based in Manchester and a carrier in Venice for carriage from Manchester to Venice will be largely unaffected by the Act, the contract for the same journey between the same sender and a carrier based in Manchester will be subject to the Act: the carrier's liability "cannot be excluded or restricted . . . except in so far as the term satisfies the requirement of reasonableness".[4] Prima facie, therefore, the carrier based in Venice and the carrier based in Manchester do not compete for the contract on the same footing, a position that Parliament intended to avoid. Although the English court will not use its power under the Act to interfere with terms imposed by or taken from the CMR itself, it may well interfere with other terms agreed by the parties for aspects of their contract not governed by the CMR,[5] with the curious result that the English court can protect the English sender from any unreasonable terms used by the English carrier but not from those used by the carrier based in Italy.

---

[99] *i.e.* according to s.26: "(1) The limits imposed by this Act on the extent to which a person may exclude or restrict liability by reference to a contract term . . . [Moreover] (2) The terms of such a contract are not subject to any requirement of reasonableness under section 3 or 4; and nothing in Part II of this Act [concerning Scotland] shall require the incorporation of the terms of such a contract to be fair and reasonable for them to have effect."

[1] s.26(3)(a).

[2] s.26(4).

[3] s.26(3)(b).

[4] s.7(3). See also s.3(2).

[5] See above, para. 64.

CHAPTER 8

REMEDIES

A. COMPENSATION

93. Compensation for damage

The amount of compensation when goods are damaged[1] is the subject of Article 25.1:

> "In case of damage, the carrier shall be liable for the amount by which the goods have diminished in value, calculated by reference to the value of the goods fixed in accordance with Article 23, paragraphs 1, 2 and 4."

Some courts have quantified compensation for damage on the basis of the cost repair,[2] but this has been held to be an error, as Article 25.1 refers only to the amount by which the goods have diminished in value.[3] Nevertheless, the court may take account of the cost of mitigation: the value is fixed not only in accordance with Article 23.1 and Article 23.2, the market value, but also Article 23.4, which allows the recovery of "charges incurred in respect of the carriage of the goods".[4] The inference is that the cost of mitigation should be, not a separate item of loss recoverable under Article 23.4, but an element in an award under Article 25.1: effective salvage mitigates loss in market value which would otherwise occur[5] and it is "part of the cost of realising the damaged value of the goods".[6]

As Article 25.1 provides that the amount of compensation for damage shall not exceed that payable in case of total loss, the

---

[1] For the meaning of damage, see above, para. 57. Although in general terms the scheme of compensation under the CMR is based on that of the CIM, Art. 25 differs in that the corresponding provision of the CIM was thought by the authors of the CMR to be too complicated: Nickel-Lanz, para. 163.

[2] For example, *Arr Rotterdam 12.4.72*, 1976 U.L.R. I 253.

[3] *B.G.H. 13.2.80*, N.J.W. 1980.2021, 1981 U.L.R. I 260.

[4] Below, para. 98.

[5] *O.G.H. 21.2.85*, Stra GüV 1985/10 p. 18, Greiter 285; *O.L.G. Vienna 23.2.89*, TranspR 1990.157. Also in this sense: *O.L.G. Hamburg 11.9.86*, VersR 1987.375; and Haak, pp. 206–207, citing decisions to this effect in Holland.

[6] *ICI Fibres v. MAT Transport* [1987] 1 Lloyd's Rep. 354, 362, *per* Staughton J., with regard to survey fees.

amount of compensation for damage, with mitigation costs *included*, appears to be limited to the amount for total loss fixed by Article 23.3. However, in a case of actual total loss, the limit recoverable does not include an element for (unsuccessful) mitigation,[7] which may be recovered "in addition" as an "other charge" under Article 23.4. The reason for this difference between a case of damage and a case of total loss is not obvious and, as Haak has observed,[8] the "independent treatment of loss and damage is scarcely justified".

Article 25.1 refers to the value of goods fixed in accordance with Article 23.1 and Article 23.2, and thus to market value at the place and time of acceptance for carriage.[9] Ambiguity arises from the adjacent reference to the amount by which the goods *have* diminished in value as a result of the damage, *ex hypothesi*, since the time of acceptance. The interpretation might be that depreciation is measured by the difference between the value of the goods undamaged at the time and place of acceptance and, unless they were damaged there and then, their post-damage value at a subsequent time and place.[10] If the movement of goods normally increases their value, this measure might understate the real effect of the damage.[11] However, as the intention appears to have been against the recovery of consequential loss,[12] and the cost of moving the goods to the place where their value has increased is recoverable under Article 23.4,[13] this interpretation, although perhaps the natural one,[14] is probably not what the authors of the CMR intended.[15] It appears that the correct comparison is between value, measured at the time and place of acceptance, damaged and undamaged.[16]

94. Compensation for loss

Article 23.1 provides that in respect of total[17] or partial[18] loss of goods,

[7] Also in this sense: Haak, p. 226.
[8] At 203.
[9] Below, para. 94.
[10] In this sense for the CMR: Lamy, para. 937.
[11] Haak, p. 227.
[12] Below, para. 94.
[13] Below, para. 98.
[14] Above, para. 3.
[15] *cf.* Haak, p. 227 who proposes a comparison of the value of such goods damaged and undamaged at the place of destination, and an award of that difference expressed as a proportion applied to the value of the goods at the place and time of acceptance of carriage. He cites doctrinal authority for this approach, called the "damage allowance method", under the CIM.
[16] In this sense: *O.L.G. Düsseldorf 14.7.83*, TranspR 1984.16, reported by Glöckner, Theunis, p. 99. Also Helm, Art. 25 Anm. 2.
[17] For the meaning of total loss, see above, para. 56.
[18] For the meaning of partial loss, see above, para. 55.

"compensation shall be calculated by reference to the value of goods at the place and time at which they were accepted for carriage".

Measure by reference to the place and time of acceptance for carriage[19] is quite unlike the corresponding rule at common law, which refers to the market value at destination.[20] In the opinion of the authors of the CMR, "knowledge that part of a consignment of goods will not be arriving on account of loss may in itself raise the price of similar goods at the place of destination. Such increase should not be taken into account."[21] As a matter of the construction of the words used, in some contexts loss may refer to purely pecuniary or economic loss,[22] but its meaning depends on the context, and Article 23.1 refers to "loss of goods". The general conclusion is that the claimant cannot recover consequential loss,[23] such as loss of market at the place of destination,[24] or the loss caused by having capital tied up in goods which, as a result of damage during carriage, could not be used,[25] or the rise in the cost of replacing lost goods between the time of acceptance and the time of compensation. Still, consequential loss is recoverable by way of exception under the CMR in the following cases:

(a) a declaration of special interest under Article 26[26]; or
(b) a claim based on delay[27]; or

---

[19] Acceptance for carriage refers to the moment of taking over (above, para. 27) rather than the time when the carrier agreed to perform the carriage.

[20] *James Buchanan & Co. v. Babco Forwarding & Shipping (U.K.)* [1977] 1 Lloyd's Rep. 234, 240–241, *per* Roskill L.J., C.A. The reference in Art. 23.1 is taken from (what is now) CIM Art. 40.1 and contrasts both with the Hague-Visby Rules Art. IV.5 (b) under which compensation is calculated "by reference to the value of such goods at the place and time at which the goods are discharged from the ship"; and with the rule of French domestic law, which looks to value at destination: Brunat, B.T. 1982.202, by reference to c. civ. Art. 1149 and Art. 1150.

[21] TRANS/WP.9/11, p. 46.

[22] *cf. Adamastos Shipping Co. v. Anglo-Saxon Petroleum Co.* [1959] A.C. 133, in which it was held that in the context of the Hague Rules "loss or damage" was not limited to physical loss of or damage to the goods.

[23] *e.g. O.L.G. 22.3.94*, TranspR 1994.439; Evans, para. 189; Glöckner Theunis, pp. 98–99: "in parallel with the CIM"; Haak, p. 204; Helm, Art. 23 Anm. 2; Herber/Piper, Art. 23, 4; Koller, Art. 23, 5; Muth/Glöckner, p. 158; Putzeys, para. 890; Thume, Art. 23, 5.

Reference will be to the market price at the place of acceptance, even if that price is not lower but higher than that obtainable at destination: *Supreme Court, Denmark 11.11.68*, 1969 U.L.C. 305.

[24] *O.G.H. 15.2.79*, SZ 52 no. 19, Greiter 76, 1979 U.L.R. II 229; *Paris 30.5.84*, B.T. 1985.75.

[25] *Cass. 3.2.87*, B.T. 1987.270.

[26] Brunat B.T. 1982.146, 147; and B.T. 1982.202; Loewe, para. 204. On Art. 26, see below, para. 100.

[27] *O.G.H. 15.2.79*, SZ 52 no. 19, Greiter 76; 1979 U.L.R. II 229. See above, para. 59a. According to *O.G.H. 21.2.85*, Stra GüV 1985/10 p. 18, Greiter 285, apart from Art. 26, consequential loss is only recoverable in cases of delay under Art. 23.5.

(c) a case of wilful misconduct or default under Article 29[28]; or

(d) in some countries, notably England and France, the recovery of some kinds of consequential loss as "charges" under Article 23.4[29]; or

(e) in Germany, the recovery of consequential loss under residual national law, if it flows not from the loss, damage or delay, which are governed by the CMR and hence limited by Article 23, but from some other breach of the contract of carriage.[30]

The reason for the emphasis on dispatch value and the bias against making the carrier liable for economic loss is said[31] to be, like that behind the similar regime for the CIM, a desire to keep the cost of transport low.

94a. The value of the goods: Article 23.2

The value to be placed on the goods is the subject of Article 23.2:

> "The value of the goods shall be fixed according to the commodity exchange price or if there is no such price, according to the current market price or, if there is no commodity exchange price or current market price, by reference to the normal value of goods of the same kind and quality."

Although this provision refers to objective, external indications of value, if the parties agree the value of the goods, the court is likely to accept that value, in particular, a value stated in the invoice.[32] The court will look beyond the invoice price, however, if there is evidence that it does not represent the true value of the

---

[28] See below, para. 101. It has been held that the carrier loses the benefit of any limits on his liability, including those in Art. 23, and must compensate the claimant for all loss directly caused: *Nancy 21.1.87*, B.T. 1987.344, in which the claimant recovered the cost of buying (expensively) replacement goods for his customer, as well as damages payable to the latter for late delivery.

[29] Below, para. 98.

[30] For example in *B.G.H. 27.10.78*, NJW 1979.2473, the claimant recovered loss of market caused not by late delivery but by delivery to the wrong person. On the role of residual national law, see above, para. 64.

[31] Koller, "Die Erstattungspflicht von Frachten, Zollen and sonstigen Kosten gem. Art. 23 Abs. 4 CMR" VersR 1989.2.

[32] *William Tatton & Co. v. Ferrymasters* [1974] 1 Lloyd's Rep. 203. Also in this sense: *O.L.G. Nuremberg 14.6.65* (1971) 6 E.T.L. 247, 262; *Chambéry 27.6.84*, B.T. 1985.159; *O.L.G. Hamburg 11.9.86*, VersR 1987.373; *O.L.G. Hamm 25.5.92*, TranspR 1992.410. Brunat B.T. 1982.146, 147, Hill and Messent, pp. 183–184; Nickel-Lanz, para. 156.

goods,[33] for example, in the case of a change in value between the time of the invoice and the time that the goods were accepted for carriage,[34] or the case of a deliberate understatement of value,[35] including the case of transfer pricing between associated companies,[36] or the case of a sale in which the invoice price contains an element for the cost of consignment: Article 23 appears to distinguish between the value of the goods at the place of acceptance, which can be claimed under Article 23.1, and the carriage charges from that place, the possible subject of a distinct claim under Article 23.4.[37] Thus, in *James Buchanan & Co. v. Babco Forwarding & Shipping (U.K.)*[38] Lord Wilberforce stated: "The price stated in the invoices being a price F.O.B. Felixstowe, it is appropriate, in order to arrive at the price 'at the place . . . at which [the goods] were accepted for carriage' (article 23, paragraph 1) to make a small deduction, representing the cost of carriage from Glasgow to Felixstowe."

Nevertheless, the value of the goods at the place where they are accepted for carriage is not their intrinsic value[39] but their value on the market there: the price at which they can be sold, including therefore a margin for profit.[40]

Market is not defined in the CMR and is therefore a matter for national law. In English law, the existence of a market depends on the "availability of buyers and sellers and their ready capacity to supply or absorb such goods".[41] The existence of a market and of a market price depends on the category of goods. Even though the CMR rule requires reference to the market at the place of acceptance for carriage, the categorisation of goods may depend not

---

[33] *Cass. 8.2.82*, B.T. 1982.152 (1983) 18 E.T.L. 43. In this case Michelin (Italy) sold tyres to Michelin (France) at a price equivalent to the cost of manufacture. *Sur renvoi* in the same sense: *Chambéry 23.1.84*, B.T. 1984.574. See also *B.G.H. 15.10.92*, TranspR 1993.137; and *O.G.H. 13.7.94*, TranspR 1995.285 in which the court ignored an invoice for computer equipment, which reflected the high price of such goods in Hungary, and looked to the lower market price in western Europe.

[34] *Amiens 18.5.81*, B.T. 1982.208; *Cass. 7.12.83*, B.T. 1984.538.

[35] That is contrary to Art. 41: *Cass. 17.5.83*, B.T. 1983.445. *cf.* Putzeys, para. 902: a collateral agreement, that the (actual) value of the goods shall not exceed a stated value, is valid.

[36] This can be inferred from *Cass. 10.1.83*, B.T. 1983.154, (1983) 18 E.T.L. 43, in which the sale price was not taken as the measure of value, because the "buyer" had a special relationship with the seller which led to a discount.

[37] *cf.* carriage charges *to* the place of acceptance, which may be an element in the value of the goods at that place: *Paris 30.5.84*, B.T. 1985.75.

[38] [1978] A.C. 141, 151. *cf. B.G.H. 13.2.80*, N.J.W. 1980.2021, 1981 U.L.R. I 260, which arrived at the value of undamaged goods by adding the transport costs, and citing the decision of the Court of Appeal in *Buchanan* [1977] 1 Q.B. 208. The B.G.H. may have got this impression from 217, *per* Roskill L.J.; but *cf.* 222, *per* Lawton L.J.

[39] *Cass. 8.2.82*, B.T. 1982.152 (1983) 18 E.T.L. 43, censuring *Grenoble 19.11.1980*, B.T. 1981.23 which had adopted the intrinsic value; and *sur renvoi: Chambéry 23.1.84*, B.T. 1984.574.

[40] Brunat B.T. 1982.146, 147; Putzeys, para. 866.

[41] Benjamin, para. 16–056. *W.L. Thompson v. Robinson (Gunmakers)* [1955] Ch. 177, 187, *per* Upjohn J. *cf.* the position in Germany: De La Motte, VersR 1988.317.

only on physical features of the goods themselves but also on other attributes such as their destination. The value of wombles on and for the home market may differ from the value of wombles on the home market but earmarked for export.

In *James Buchanan & Co. v. Babco Forwarding & Shipping (U.K.)*[42] defendant carriers agreed to carry 1,000 cases of whisky from Glasgow to Teheran, via Felixstowe. Before export from the United Kingdom, the whisky was left unattended over a weekend and disappeared. The value of such whisky in bond destined for export was £7,000, but the value of such whisky intended for the home market, and on which, therefore, excise duty had been paid, was about £37,000. Having had to pay the duty on the whisky to the Inland Revenue, because the whisky could not be shown to have left the United Kingdom, the plaintiff senders sought to recover that sum from the carriers as part of the market value of the whisky in the United Kingdom. On this point[43] the claim failed. Lord Wilberforce said[44]: "I think that the market price, or the normal value of this whisky intended for export, was its value ex duty. . . . What is the 'current market price' of any commodity must depend in the first place upon what is the relevant market, for it is obvious that there may well be more than one market for a commodity, or for goods."[45]

94b. Repayment of compensation if goods are recovered

When delay is treated as total loss in accordance with Article 20.1,[46] the rule about compensation in Article 23.1 applies subject to the provisions of Article 20.2–4. The latter concern goods, which, having been treated as lost, are subsequently recovered. The provisions apply, if the person entitled to make a claim, "on receipt of compensation for the missing goods, requests in writing

---

[42] [1978] A.C. 141. *cf. Paris 8.6.82*, B.T. 1982.564.

[43] The claim succeeded on the ground that the duty was an "other charge" under Art. 23.4: see below, para. 98.

[44] At 150–151; see also 156, *per* Viscount Dilhorne; 159, *per* Lord Salmon; 164, *per* Lord Edmund-Davies; and 170, *per* Lord Fraser.

[45] Lord Wilberforce and Viscount Dilhorne applied the decision of the House of Lords in *Charrington & Co. v. Wooder* [1914] A.C. 71, which concerned the interpretation of an agreement made between a brewery and the tenant of a tied public house. The question was, in the words of Viscount Haldane L.C. (at 77), "whether the language of the covenant means that the fair market price was the price to be paid by a tenant of a tied house, as distinguished from the price at which beer could be bought in an altogether open market". One must look at the circumstances of the particular trade. The House found that there was more than one market price, hence more than one market, according to the person to whom the beer was being sold. Lord Wilberforce seemed concerned to avoid the (unlikely) anomaly (suggested by Lord Denning in the Court of Appeal) whereby whisky ran down a drain on the way to Felixstowe and, being demonstrably lost, was not subject to duty yet compensation was claimed from the carrier, as if duty had been paid.

[46] See above, para. 56b.

that he shall be notified immediately should the goods be recovered in the course of the year following the payment of compensation".[47]

If the claimant makes no such request, although the goods are later recovered, the claimant, retains the compensation. If the claimant does make such a request, there are two consequences. First, on receipt of the request, the carrier must give the claimant "a written acknowledgment of such request".[48] Secondly, if the goods are recovered within the year, the carrier must advise the claimant of the recovery and within "the thirty days following receipt of such notification, the [claimant] may require the goods to be delivered to him against payment of the charges shown to be due on the consignment note and also against refund of the compensation he received less any charges included therein".

If the claimant does require delivery of the goods, the claimant does so without prejudice to any claims to compensation for delay in delivery, whether the claim is under Article 23[49] or, where there has been a declaration of special interest in delivery, under Article 26.[50] Why does the CMR not preserve also claims in respect of damage to the goods caused independently of the delay? No answer is apparent.

If any of the conditions for delivery—request, recovery within a year, and requirement of delivery—fail, Article 20.4 provides that "the carrier shall be entitled to deal with [the goods] in accordance with the law of the place where the goods are situated". In England the goods are in the position of abandoned or uncollected goods and the relevant law is uncertain.[51]

95. Compensation for partial loss or damage

In the case of partial loss of goods, the amount recoverable is calculated by reference to the value of the part lost: Article 23.1. In the case of damage to part of the goods, the amount recoverable is based on "the amount by which the goods have diminished in value": Article 25.1, in which the "goods" which "have diminished in value" is a reference not to the damaged part but to the whole of the goods.[52] Whether the case is one of loss or of damage, the calculation of the upper limit on recovery is based not on the value

---

[47] Art. 20.2.
[48] Art. 20.2 *in fine*. On the meaning of writing, see above, para. 45b.
[49] Below, para. 96.
[50] Below, para. 100.
[51] See Palmer, pp. 705 *et seq.*; Goff and Jones, *The Law of Restitution* (4th ed., London 1993), pp. 614 *et seq.*
[52] Helm, Art. 25 Anm. 2.

of the goods but on their weight: Article 23.3, but that, it should be underlined, is not a measure of loss but a limit on recoverable loss.

In the case of partial loss of goods, lost charges may be refunded "in proportion to the loss sustained": Article 23.4. Hence the proportion of charges refunded in a case of partial loss (or, presumably, partial damage) appears to be calculated, as in the case of compensation for partial loss of goods (or damage to goods), according to the proportion of lost value rather than, for example, lost weight. However, opinion is divided.[53] Loewe, for example, has argued[54] for a double rule, whereby in the case of "partial damage, the portion of the charges refunded under [Article 23.4] should be calculated in the light of the method initially adopted for calculating the charges concerned. With regard to carriage charges, the amount will generally have been calculated according to weight. . . . On the other hand, the refunding of Customs duties, value-added tax or other charges call for a different method of calculation", presumably by reference to value.

96. Compensation for delay

As to the amount of compensation in a case of delay,[55] Article 23.5 provides:

> "In the case of delay, if the claimant proves that damage has resulted therefrom the carrier shall pay compensation for such damage not exceeding the carriage charges."

In the case of delay, compensation is recoverable for economic loss, such as loss of market at the place of delivery.[56] Whether it also includes physical damage to the goods caused by delay, such as deterioration due to prolonged exposure to the conditions of transit, is controversial, but the view of the majority is that it does not.[57] In any event, the amount of compensation for delay is limited, as stated by Article 23.5, to the amount of the carriage charges.[58]

---

[53] *Contra* the view here expressed: Evans, para. 193; Haak, p. 226. However, other writers cited by Haak (*ibid.*) take a different view. Others state that the appropriate basis of calculation is unclear: Helm, Art. 23 Anm. 6.

[54] Loewe, para. 193.

[55] For the meaning of delay, see above, para. 58.

[56] See above, para. 59a.

[57] See above, para. 59b.

[58] See below, para. 97a.

97. Limits on compensation

In all cases, the claimant must prove actual loss to the extent of the compensation claimed. Whatever the claimant's actual loss and subject to exceptions described below,[59] there are limits on the amount of compensation recoverable under the CMR, whether action is brought in contract or in tort.[60] These limits apply only when, in the words of Article 23.1, "under the provisions of this Convention, a carrier is liable", and not, therefore, when the carrier's liability rests on residual national law[61] or when the CMR liability in question is that of the sender or consignee.

The CMR limits vary. The authors of the CMR considered that, in general, delay was more difficult for the carrier to avoid than loss of or damage to the goods and that therefore the limit on compensation should be lower in the case of delay.[62] In respect of the recovery of charges under Article 23.4, there is no limit at all.

97a. Loss or damage

In the case of damage to the goods the amount of compensation, for which the carrier is liable under Article 25.1, is limited by Article 25.2. The compensation may not exceed:

> "(a) If the whole consignment has been damaged, the amount payable in the case of total loss;
> (b) If part only of the consignment has been damaged, the amount payable in the case of loss of the part affected."

In case of total loss, the amount payable according to Article 23.1 is the value of the goods at the place and time of acceptance for carriage,[63] subject to a limit by reference to weight. In many cases there is a rough correlation between value and weight but, of course, in some there is not; such a case was that of a consignment of canvasses by Magritte.[64] For the consignor who is not content with that, the CMR offers the possibility of a special declaration of value under Article 24.[65] The ceiling based on weight is stated in Article 23:

---

[59] Para. 100.

[60] Art. 28: above, para. 67a. Further, any attempt to recover the limited amount twice or more in different jurisdictions will be frustrated by Art. 31.2 of the CMR (above, para. 46d) and s.3 of the Carriage of Goods by Road Act 1965.

[61] Such as *die positive Vertragshaftung* (see above, para. 64): *O.G.H. 14.11.84*, Greiter 245, 248; *O.G.H. 13.6.85*, SZ 58/102, Stra GüV 1985/12, p. 10.

[62] Nickel-Lanz, para. 111.

[63] Above, para. 94.

[64] *Paris 24.10.91*, B.T.L. 1991.783.

[65] Below, para. 100.

"3. Compensation shall not, however, exceed 8.33 units of account per kilogram of gross weight short.[66] ... 7. The unit of account mentioned in this Convention is the Special Drawing Right as defined by the International Monetary Fund. The amount mentioned in paragraph 3 of this Article shall be converted into the national currency of the state of the court seised of the case on the basis of the value of that currency on the date of the judgment or the date agreed upon by the parties."[67]

Under section 5(2) of the Carriage by Road and Air Act 1979:

"A certificate given by or on behalf of the Treasury stating—

(a) that a particular sum in sterling has been fixed ... for a particular day; or

(b) that no sum has been fixed for a particular day and that a particular sum in sterling has been ... fixed for a day which is the last day for which a sum has been ... fixed before the particular day,

shall be conclusive evidence of these matters ..."[68]

The gross weight of the goods, which is referred to in Article 23.3 (above), was intended to include packing.[69] This is entirely consistent with a limit like this, which is fixed not according to the value of goods but according to weight so that the carrier is aware of the potential liability[70]: the carrier knows the maximum weight

---

[66] Art. 23.3, as originally in force in its 1956 version, read: "Compensation shall not, however, exceed 25 francs per kilogram of gross weight short. 'Franc' meant the gold franc weighing 10/31 of a gramme and being of millesimal fineness 900." This franc, known as the germinal franc and tied to the price of gold, fluctuated greatly. In terms of national currency there was a difference between the official rate of conversion and the market rate. In these circumstances the E.C.E. (see para. 2) produced in 1978 a Protocol to the CMR, which came into force in the countries that had ratified it on December 28, 1980. According to the Secretary-General of the United Nations, depositary for ratifications, countries having ratified it on December 31, 1989 were Austria, Belgium, Denmark, Finland, Germany, Greece, Holland, Italy, Luxembourg, Norway, Portugal, Romania, Spain, Sweden, Switzerland and the United Kingdom. The Protocol replaced the original Art. 23.3 with the provision here quoted, and added Art. 23.7. As regards English domestic law, these provisions were made part of the Carriage by Air and Road Act 1979, which came into force on December 28, 1980: see Appendix C. On the history of Art. 23.3, see Haak, pp. 207 *et seq.*

[67] In anticipation of the entry into force of Art. 23.7, the court in *B.G.H. 5.6.81*, VersR 1981.1030 (1982) 17 E.T.L. 301, 1981 U.L.R. II 220, selected the date of the judgment as the appropriate date for conversion, because this was the nearest practicable date to that on which the duty to compensate the claimant arose. See further, Haak, pp. 213–214.

[68] The rate of "exchange" between sterling and SDRs is published in the daily financial press.

[69] Helm, Art. 23 Anm. 5; Nickel-Lanz, para. 108 and para. 158; Putzeys, para. 891.

[70] *B.G.H. 30.1.81* (1981) 16 E.T.L. 455, 458.

the vehicle can take and knows, therefore, the maximum exposure in respect of that vehicle.[71]

The CMR rate of units of account per kilogram is in contrast with the rates for other modes of international carriage. These differences, it is said,[72]

> "... reflect to some extent the realities of the mode of transport used. Thus, in carriage by sea, a fairly low limit operates in comparison with other forms of transport. This is because ships carry large quantities of goods, and a high level of liability would require an uneconomic level of insurance which would result in higher freight rates.[73] The limit in carriage by air is relatively high and thus reflects the high value of goods normally carried by air and appropriately high freight levels.[74] CMR has intermediate limits of liability, higher than those in sea carriage but lower than those in carriage by air and by rail."

Or, as Lord Diplock put it[75]:

> "The greater magnitude of the loss of the goods transported in the event of a disaster to the carrying vessel, as compared with a disaster to an aircraft or road or rail truck, and the greater expense of insuring and reinsuring the risk falling upon the shipowner, as compared with spreading it among a large number of cargo insurers, would indicate that a considerably lower figure is appropriate for carriage by sea than for carriage by air, road or rail."

However, the relativity has also been influenced by policy factors, such as the desire in some states that the rail carrier should not be at a disadvantage in competition with the carrier by road.[76]

---

[71] TRANS/WP.9/11, p. 58.

[72] Glass and Cashmore, para. 3.59. The arbitrary nature of this scheme is suggested by a survey (reported by Putzeys, para. 888) showing that in 1964 in 99 per cent of cases the value of the goods did not pass the ceiling in Art. 23.3.

[73] Also in this sense: Diplock (1970) 1 JMLC 525, 530.

[74] *cf.* Diplock, *ibid.*: "the relationship between the limitation figure and the actual value of the goods is unimportant from the commercial point of view so long as it is high enough to act as an inducement to the carrier to take proper precautions to reduce the risk. The relevant relationship is between the limitation figure and the cost of the precautions. Subject to this, it is probably more economical to keep the limitation figure low so as to spread the risk of a disaster to the whole cargo among a large number of cargo insurers, instead of letting it fall upon a single P. and I. insurer and his reinsurers, which is a more expensive way of insuring the risk." It should be recalled that Lord Diplock was speaking mainly of carriage by sea, and that this argument is part of the debate over the relative merits of the goods insurance and liability insurance: above, para. 92a.

[75] At 530–531.

[76] Haak, p. 209.

97b. Partial loss or damage

If part of a single consignment is damaged, but damage to the part renders the rest less useful and hence less valuable, although only temporarily until the damaged part is repaired or replaced, the appropriate limit is that for total loss: Article 25.2(a).[77] Otherwise, the limit is that for partial loss: Article 25.2(b).[78] There is no concept of constructive total loss in the CMR.[79]

If parts of a single consignment, the subject of a single contract,[80] are damaged but in differing degrees, some parts to an amount below the limit per kilogram for those parts and others to an amount above the limit, the carrier may wish to have his liability assessed as an aggregate of liability for the parts, as if they were separate consignments. On that basis, the carrier's total liability would be less than that for the accumulated damage to the whole, when subject to the limit per kilogram for the whole,[81] but the rule is that assessment must be for the whole.[82] This relatively simple rule is said to promote speed and sureness in international transactions.[83] Moreover, it is appropriate when, as is common, the carriage charges are based on the weight of the whole and when, as is required by Article 12.5(c), the exercise of the right of disposal is restricted to the whole consignment.[84] The rule by reference to the whole weight may lead to the anomaly of different levels of liability between essentially similar loads,[85] but the contrary rule would lead to the anomaly of levels of compensation which depended on circumstances considered irrelevant, such as the way in which the goods were packaged and labelled.[86]

---

[77] *B.G.H. 3.7.74*, VersR 1974.1013, 1974 U.L.R. II 216; *Paris 31.1.84*, B.T. 1984.543. Haak, p. 217; Loewe, para. 201. *cf.* Evans, para. 201.

[78] Loewe, para. 201.

[79] See above, para. 56a.

[80] Although there may be more than one consignment note, as when one consignment under one contract is spread over more than one vehicle: Haak, p. 217.

[81] If x = the number (8.33) of units of account per kilogram stated in Art. 23.3, a consignment, made up of five parts each weighing 5 kg, would give rise to a maximum global liability of $5 \times 5x:25x$. If, however, each part were damaged and taken separately, three parts being damaged to an amount (8x) in excess of 5x, but to two parts only damaged to the tune of 3x, the carrier's maximum liability will be, not 25x, but $(3 \times 5) + (2 \times 3)x = 21x$.

[82] *B.G.H. 30.1.81*, VersR 1981.473, (1981) 16 E.T.L. 455; *Paris 15.6.84*, B.T. 1984.545; *O.G.H. 18.3.86*, Stra GüV 1986/7 p. 8; *O.L.G. Stuttgart 15.9.93*, TranspR 1994.156. Loewe, para. 202. *cf. Cass. 26.6.84*, B.T. 1984.610, above, para. 97a.

A similar problem has arisen with respect to containers and bills of lading under the Hague Rules, notably in the USA. Tetley, p. 642. A similar rule prevails in England by statute enacting Art. IV.5(c) of the Hague-Visby Rules.

[83] *B.G.H. 30.1.81*, VersR 1981.473, (1981) 16 E.T.L. 455, 458, 459; *O.G.H. 18.3.86*, Stra GüV 1986/7 p. 8. Also in this sense: Haak, pp. 215–216.

[84] *B.G.H. 30.1.81* (above), at 459.

[85] *O.G.H. 18.3.86* (above), at 10; *B.G.H. 30.1.81* (above), at 460.

[86] *B.G.H. 30.1.81* (above), at 457, 459.

In contrast, if a single load comprises different consignments travelling under different consignment notes, evidently the consignments are treated separately. Less evidently, in the case of groupage, in which a load comprises different consignments travelling under a single consignment note, a note silent as to the nature or value of the goods and addressed to a single consignee, the court will look to the reality of the situation, namely that there is more than one sender and more than one consignee, and will not lose sight of what is really several contracts of carriage under one consignment note: in that situation liability is assessed and limited by reference to the weight of the relevant part.[87] This rule may leave the carrier in some uncertainty about the potential liability, but the feeling is that in this case justice to and between the different goods owners comes first.

97c. Delay[88]

Article 23.5 provides that, in the case of delay,

> "the carrier shall pay compensation for such damage not exceeding the carriage charges".

The carriage charges in question are the charges for the entire journey contracted for and will not be limited to those relating to any particular stage of the journey,[89] or to any particular part of one consignment.[90] For the consignee, lateness of part may well amount to lateness of the whole, as the part that arrives on time may be useless without the part that is late.

Since 1956 both the cost of carriage in general and the length of the longer journeys subject to the CMR, notably journeys to the Middle East, have increased, so that in real terms the ceiling for delay claims has risen. Moreover, like the other limits in Article 23, the limit in the case of delay may be lifted altogether in the case of

---

[87] *Cass. Belgium 3.6.76*, 1977 U.L.R. II 220, 224; *Brussels 16.11.77* (1980) 15 E.T.L. 319; 329; *Paris 23.2.82*, B.T. 1982.550. Haak, p. 216; Putzeys, para. 891*bis*.

[88] On the meaning of delay see above, paras. 58–59. Hardingham, "Delay Provisions of the CMR" [1979] L.M.C.L.Q. 193.

[89] *Paris 18.10.73*, B.T. 1973.488, 1978 U.L.R. I 242, 244. Putzeys, para. 901*ter*.

[90] *Cass. 26.6.84*, B.T. 1984.60: the consignment was divided between several vehicles, only two of which were late. Rejecting the carrier's argument that the limit should be the carriage charges relating to the two vehicles that were late, the court took the limit as the charges relating to the entire consignment. *cf.* also *B.G.H. 30.1.81* (1981) 16 E.T.L. 455.

special interest,[91] for example, an important deadline for delivery.

98. Charges

As compensation for loss of or damage to the goods is quantified under Article 23.1 by reference to their value at the place and time of acceptance for carriage, it is evident that breach of contract by the carrier may leave the claimant with other kinds of loss, which have not been compensated under Article 23.1, notably wasted expense.[92] As this leaves the claimant less than completely compensated, a right to recover some such expense was said[93] to follow, as a matter of logic but not necessarily as a matter of CMR law, from Article 23.1. The fact that in some cases the claimant would have lost that expense in any event, because, for example, the claimant consignor had made a bad bargain with the buyer at destination, would be overlooked in the interests of simplicity of calculation.[94] In the CMR, however, the recovery of expenses is centred on Article 23.4:

> "In addition, the carriage charges, customs duties and other charges incurred in respect of the carriage of the goods shall be refunded in full in case of total loss and in proportion to the loss sustained in case of partial loss, but no further damages shall be payable."

The "carriage charges" refer to freight agreed for the carriage in question. They do not refer to charges for carriage to the place at which they were taken over for the carriage in question, as that element should be reflected in the market value of the goods at that place, recoverable under Article 23.1.[95] Nor do they refer to the cost of returning damaged goods; or to charges for the carriage of goods which, having been returned to the sender for repair, are consigned again to the original destination.[96] These expenses, to

---

[91] Below, para. 100.

[92] Certain kinds of lost expense, such as the cost of mitigating damage, may be recoverable as part of the value at the place and time of acceptance: see above, para. 93.

[93] Koller, "Die Erstattungspflicht von Frachten, Zollen und sonstigen Kosten gem. Art. 23 Abs. 4 CMR". VersR 1989.2, 6. He also suggests that it follows that "other charges" in Art. 23.4 refers to those costs which contribute to the enhancement of the value of the goods at the place of delivery, thus excluding all costs flowing from the way the carriage is actually carried out, such as salvage. As a matter of logic, this suggestion is less easy to follow.

[94] Koller, *ibid.* English law might not allow a claimant to recover the expense in such a case, if the defendant can meet the difficult onus of proving that the expense is of that kind: *CCC Films (London) Ltd v. Impact Quadrant Films Ltd* [1985] Q.B. 16.

[95] Glöckner, Theunis, p. 102; Nickel-Lanz, para. 159 and para. 165. Also Koller (above, n. 93), p. 5.

[96] *O.L.G. Munich 5.7.89*, TranspR 1990.16, in which the court held that these charges were not recoverable as "other charges".

be recoverable at all, must be claimed under Article 23.4 not as "carriage charges" but as "other charges". The amount recoverable is reduced proportionately in the case of partial loss.[97]

The "customs duties" do not include excise duties[98]; however, excise duties may be recoverable as "other charges".

The "other charges" do not include "carriage charges" or "customs duties", from which they are distinguished by Article 23.4 itself. In *James Buchanan & Co. v. Babco Forwarding & Shipping (U.K.)*[99] a majority of the members of the House of Lords[1] held that the excise duty which had become payable by the claimant on whisky, because it had been lost before it could be exported free of duty, was an instance of "other charges incurred in respect of the carriage".

In *James Buchanan* the narrow view, taken by the dissenting minority,[2] was that "other charges" referred to items such as the cost of packing, obtaining insurance and certificates of quality, because these were incurred "in respect of carriage", *i.e.* "with a view to or for the purpose of carriage", Here, carriage means the carriage contracted for[3] and, unlike the view of the majority, rules out charges consequential on the way it was actually performed by the carrier in breach which, *ex hypothesi*, was not the way contracted for. On the narrow view, for example, it has been held in Austria[4] that the cost of a survey on damaged goods does not arise

---

[97] For example, *B.G.H. 14.12.88*, VersR 1989.309.

[98] *James Buchanan & Co. v. Babco Forwarding & Shipping (U.K.)* [1978] A.C. 141. *Semble* they do include an import tax: *O.L.G. Munich 17.7.91*, TranspR 1991.427.

[99] [1978] A.C. 141, affirming [1977] Q.B. 208, C.A. The facts of this case are set out above, para. 94. See also *O.G.H. 25.1.90*, TranspR 1990.235, 239: recovery of *Einführ-Umsatzsteuer.*

[1] Lord Wilberforce, Viscount Dilhorne and Lord Salmon. Lord Edmund-Davies and Lord Fraser dissented on this point.

[2] Their Lordships relied in particular on *Amsterdam 30.3.77*, 1978 U.L.R. II 299 in which, on facts very similar to those before the House, the Dutch court rejected such a claim because the obligation to pay tax had not been based on carriage as such, it was not (at 305) "in direct connexion with the carriage such as it should have been performed." For an account of this case, see Haak, p. 223. The same line seems to have been taken in subsequent decisions in Holland: *'s Hertogenbosch 4.2.86*, S. & S. 1987 no. 25; *The Hague 14.8.86*, S. & S. 1987 no. 24; *HR 6.4.90*, S. & S. 1990 no. 74. Also cases cited by Haak, *loc. cit.*

[3] Haak, p. 219; Nickel-Lanz, para. 165; Rodière (1971) 6 E.T.L. 306, 315.

[4] *O.L.G. Vienna 23.2.89*, TranspR 1990.157. The same emphasis is found in *O.L.G. Munich 5.7.89*, TranspR 1990.16, 17, in which the court refused to award the cost of getting the damaged goods back to the sender. Also in favour of the narrow view: Herber/Piper, Art. 23, 27 *et seq.*; Koller, Art. 23, 10; Thume, Art. 23, 32 *et seq.* For more German literature in this sense, see Thume, Art. 23, 35. In this sense in France: *Cass. 14.3.95*, (1996) 31 E.T.L. 413 in which the court ruled out recovery of costs incurred as a result of the loss or damage.

The Vienna court also indicated that, if the survey were necessary to minimise damage to the goods, the cost would be an element in the amount recoverable in respect of damage under Art. 25. *cf. Poitiers 31.3.71*, B.T. 1971.168 (below, n. 15).

out of the carriage but out of the damage, and is thus not recoverable under Article 23.4. Indeed, given the apparent intention to promote commercial certainty, by ruling out recovery of consequential loss of bargain in most cases,[5] while also allowing recovery of consequential loss generally if declared as a special interest under Article 26, it is not obvious why the claimant should have been intended to recover consequential loss of expense under Article 23.4. On the contrary, given that the scheme of compensation in the CMR is modelled on that of the CIM, the *travaux préparatoires* suggest[6] that it was intended to limit to a foreseeable level the normal level[7] of the carrier's liability.[8]

In *James Buchanan* the broad view, taken by the majority,[9] was that the excise duty "became chargeable having regard to the way in which the goods were carried by the defendants. 'In respect of' is wide enough to include the way in which the goods were carried, miscarried or lost." Moreover, "the right meaning to give (the words) is that in the context in which they appear they mean 'in consequence of' or 'arising out of' ".[10]

The broad view is broad in three different places. First, instead of construing "charge" narrowly as "payment for goods or services rendered", the majority in *James Buchanan* construed it broadly as "pecuniary burden". Secondly, instead of construing "in respect of" narrowly and, some would say, normally, as "with a view to" or "in relation to", the majority construed it broadly as "in consequence of".[11] In particular, the judges who mentioned it thought the French equivalent, "à l'occasion de", could be translated as "on the occasion of", whereas, it is submitted, a better rendering is the narrower phrase "with a view to"[12]; this emerges more

---

[5] See further, above, para. 94.

[6] TRANS/WP.9/11, p. 58.

[7] That is, the level apart from any declaration under Art. 24 or Art. 26.

[8] Koller, "Die Erstattungspflicht von Frachten, Zollen und sonstigen Kosten gem. Art. 23 Abs. 4 CMR", VersR 1989.2, 6.

[9] [1978] A.C. 141, 154, *per* Lord Wilberforce, adopting the words of Master Jacob; *idem* Lord Salmon at 160.

[10] At 158, *per* Viscount Dilhorne. He reinforced his view by reference to the intentions of the draftsmen (at 157–158): "I find it difficult to believe that those who were engaged in drafting the Convention were not alive to the possibility that in a number of countries loss of goods in transit might expose the consignor to liability to pay large sums in duty or prevent him from recovering sums paid in tax on importation . . . I can see no reason for concluding that it was their intention that the carrier should be exonerated from liability to refund the consignor charges incurred as a result of his negligence." His first sentence is not supported by the *travaux*: for example, TRANS/WP.9/11, p. 58. His second sentence seems to contain the fallacy of *argumentum ad ignorantiam*.

[11] [1978] A.C. 141, 154, 158, *per* Viscount Dilhorne, 160, *per* Lord Salmon. In the Court of Appeal [1977] 1 Q.B. 208, 224 Lawton L.J. construed Art. 23.4 as meaning "any other expenses which the owner of the goods has to pay as a result of the carriage".

[12] Harrap's French Dictionary. Also in this sense: Munday (1978) 27 I.C.L.Q. 453.

clearly from the German translation.[13] Thirdly, instead of construing "carriage" narrowly as "the kind of carriage contemplated by the contract", the majority construed it broadly as "carriage in the manner in which it was actually carried out".[14] A similar view in France, for example, has enabled the claimant to recover the cost of sending experts to survey the damage,[15] although, as the court said,[16] "the costs . . . are the direct consequence of the accident and have nothing to do with the normal performance of the contract".

The trouble with the broad view is that it makes it difficult for the carrier to estimate exposure to liability. Whereas there is a monetary limit on the amount of liability for loss, damage or delay to the goods, there is no limit in the CMR on the amount of compensation that can be awarded for "other charges".[17] Inevitably, some kind of rule is required to identify those charges which are "in consequence of" the carriage and those which are not. In the CMR the question was not anticipated and has not been answered. An answer must be found in national law,[18] and found, it appears, in rules of causation and remoteness.[19] In terms of causation, charges will be recoverable under English law if they were incurred as part of a reasonable response to the threat posed by the carrier's breach of the contract of carriage.[20] In terms of remoteness, charges will be recoverable if they are losses of a type which the carrier should reasonably have contemplated would be incurred in the event of his breach of the contract of carriage.[21] By contrast, under German law it appears that such costs may be recovered under Article 23.4, but only, it seems, if it was *necessary* to incur them in order to mitigate loss, damage or delay.[22]

---

[13] *O.L.G. Vienna 23.2.89*, TranspR 1990.157; *O.L.G. Munich 5.7.89*, TranspR 1990.16. The equivalent German words are "*aus Anlaß der Beförderung des Gutes*", which, in the view of Koller (above, n. 8), are nearer to the English than the French.

[14] In substance the view of Master Jacob, as reported in *James Buchanan & Co. v. Babco Forwarding & Shipping (U.K.)* [1978] A.C. 141, 165 by Lord Edmund-Davies; and approved at 154, *per* Lord Wilberforce and 162, *per* Lord Salmon.

[15] *Poitiers 31.3.71*, B.T. 1971.168, in respect of a machine damaged when it struck a bridge on a route between points in Germany and France, the claimant was awarded the cost of sending experts to investigate and report, although not in order to minimise damage: after repairs, trials over several days were necessary to make sure the appliance was working well, and for this the presence of experts was necessary. *cf. O.L.G. Vienna 23.2.89*, TranspR 1990.157.

[16] At 169–170.

[17] Above, para. 97.

[18] Loewe, para. 204. *cf.* Lord Denning, M.R., in *James Buchanan* [1977] 1 Q.B. 208, 214, C.A., who would have allowed recovery of "expense incurred directly by reason of the loss", thus dealing with the question without reference to English law.

[19] Glass and Cashmore, para. 3.63; Hill and Messent, p. 192. *cf.* Hardingham, "Damages under the CMR" [1978] L.M.C.L.Q. 51, 53–54.

[20] See below, para. 227.

[21] *The Heron II* [1969] 1 A.C. 350. See below, para. 246.

[22] *B.G.H. 3.7.74*, VersR 1974.1013, 1974 U.L.R. II 216, 220. Also in this sense in Belgium: Putzeys, para. 870.

The range of charges that have been recovered includes not only excise duty,[23] VAT[24] and legal costs,[25] but also operational costs: the cost of packing,[26] return carriage,[27] lost insurance premium,[28] warehousing,[29] reconditioning and salvage,[30] and survey fees

---

[23] *James Buchanan & Co. v. Babco Forwarding & Shipping (U.K.)* [1978] A.C. 141; *JP Antwerp 26.10.71* (1972) 7 E.T.L. 1058; *B.G.H. 13.2.80*, N.J.W. 1980.2021, 1981 U.L.R. I 260; *Paris 25.3.82*, B.T. 1982.434; *Paris 30.5.84*, B.T. 1985.75; *Supreme Court of Denmark 4.5.87* (1994) 29 E.T.L. 360. *Contra*, *Douai 19.6.81*, B.T. 1981.512, discussed by Haak, p. 223; and criticised by Brunat, B.T. 1982.202, 203. But *cf.* also *Cass. 14.3.95* (1996) 31 E.T.L. 413.

[24] *Cass. 28.1.75*, B.T. 1975.442, affirming the decision of *Paris 30.3.73*, B.T. 1973.195 (while annulling it on other grounds), that when VAT which had been paid on goods when they were imported, could not be recovered because the goods had been too damaged by the carrier to be delivered, this sum could be recovered from the carrier. In the words of the lower court: "it is the carrier's doing, that (the claimant) is unable in effect to ask for reimbursement from anyone". See also *O.G.H. 25.1.90*, TranspR 1990.235, 239; *Poitiers 23.8.90*, B.T. 1990.586. *Contra* in Holland, where a narrow view of Art. 23.4 is taken: *'s Hertogenbosch 4.2.86*, S. & S. 1987 no. 25; *The Hague 14.8.86*, S. & S. 1987 no. 24.

[25] In *Paris 9.6.67*, (1969) 4 E.T.L. 911, there was a total loss of a load of blocks of stone. The court noted (at 916) that the senders "have incurred expenses, suffered anxiety and had to pursue a lawsuit to appeal; thus they have suffered loss which will be indemnified as hereafter set out . . . ". The court then awarded, in addition to the sum for the total loss of the load, 2,000 francs (of which 859.13 francs were carriage charges).

[26] *William Tatton & Co. v. Ferrymasters* [1974] 1 Lloyd's Rep. 203. The contrary view has been expressed by Loewe, para. 192, Rodière (1971) 6 E.T.L. 306, 315, and, surprisingly, in *James Buchanan & Co. v. Babco Forwarding & Shipping (U.K.)* [1978] A.C. 141, 157–158 by Viscount Dilhorne. This overlooks the clear rule of English law that reliance loss, such as preparatory expenses, may be recovered as damages within a remoteness rule, if those expenses are "such as would reasonably be within the contemplation of the parties as likely to be wasted if the contract was broken": *Anglia Television v. Read* [1972] 1 Q.B. 60, C.A. Such expenses are not a consequence of carriage but their utility or value is lost in consequence of the carriage, as it is actually performed, *i.e.* in breach of contract.

[27] *Thermo Engineers v. Ferrymasters* [1981] 1 Lloyd's Rep. 200, 207, *per* Neill J. *cf. William Tatton & Co. v. Ferrymasters* [1974] 1 Lloyd's Rep. 203 in which Browne J. refused recovery of the costs of returning the goods. However, this was on the basis that "other charges in respect of the carriage" referred to "the carriage covered by the contract", a basis similar to that rejected by the majority of the House of Lords in *James Buchanan*. Moreover, in the Court of Appeal in *James Buchanan* [1977] 1 Lloyd's Rep. 234, the decision of Browne J. on this point was singled out for criticism: recovery should have been allowed, because it was (238, *per* Lord Denning M.R., 241, *per* Roskill L.J.) "an expense reasonably incurred in consequence of the negligent carriage". Unreported French decisions awarding such costs as charges are mentioned by Lamy, para. 943.

cf. O.L.G. Munich 5.7.89, TranspR 1990.16, in which the court, taking the narrow view of Art. 23.4, declined to award compensation for this kind of expense. But in the earlier decision, *B.G.H. 3.7.74*, VersR 1974.1013, 1974 U.L.R. II 216, this expense was recovered under Art. 23.4 without explanation. Conflicting German case law on the "other charges" recoverable under Art. 23.4 is summarised by Koller, "Die Erstattungspflicht von Frachten, Zollen und sonstigen Kosten gem. Art. 23 Abs. 4 CMR", VersR 1989.2.

[28] *B.G.H. 13.2.80*, N.J.W. 1980.2021, 1981 U.L.R. I 260. This seems to have been accepted in *James Buchanan & Co. v. Babco Forwarding & Shipping (U.K.)* [1977] 1 Q.B. 208, see, for example, 217, *per* Roskill L.J., C.A.

[29] In *Kg Delft 13.5.65* (1966) 1 E.T.L. 722, meat arrived at destination having an abnormal colour. The claimant was awarded the cost of unloading the meat and of cold storage until a buyer could be found, on the basis of Art. 23.4, for (at 725) such costs would not have been incurred if the meat had been delivered in a normal condition. Putzeys (para. 870) places this kind of case on the edge of Art. 23.4, contending that warehousing costs are recoverable under Art. 23.4 only if they are a necessary consequence of the loss or damage.

[30] Nickel-Lanz, para. 159 and para. 165. *cf. Rb Antwerp 7.1.77* (1977) E.T.L. 420, 427–428 refusing to award the cost of cleaning out contaminated tanks belonging to the sender as a charge under Art. 23.4.

expended with a view to the latter.[31] Moreover, in the view of Lawton L.J. in *James Buchanan*,[32] charges include toll charges and, in the view of Professor Rodière,[33] they include the cost of loading and stowage if these operations have been performed by the sender in accordance with the contract but to no purpose. All these costs are losses which should have been in the contemplation of the carrier, when he concluded the contract, as consequences of his breach and are hence not too remote.

Lost charges of these kinds, described by the common lawyer as reliance loss or consequential loss, are recoverable on the broad view of Article 23.4. They are distinguished by the common law, and, it appears by the CMR, from expectation loss. Article 23.4 limits the right of recovery to compensation for *charges* and continues *in fine* that "no further damages shall be payable". Although not too remote to be recovered in English law for breach of the contract of carriage,[34] under the CMR compensation for expectation loss, loss of market or bargain is ruled out by the wording of Article 23.4.[35] For the same reason, it is submitted, the claimant cannot recover as "charges" the damages he may have had to pay his buyer for breach of a contract to sell the goods.[36]

99. Interest

The claimant is entitled to interest on compensation payable at the rate of 5 per cent per annum: Article 27.1,[37] which also provides that interest

> "shall accrue from the date on which the claim was sent in writing to the carrier or, if no such claim has been made, from the date on which legal proceedings were instituted".

---

[31] *ICI Fibres v. MAT Transport* [1987] 1 Lloyd's Rep. 354, 362 *per* Staughton J. In so far as any of these charges are incurred to mitigate damage to the goods, it can be argued that they are not a proper item of loss under Art. 23.4, but should be taken into consideration when assessing the value of the goods for a claim regulated by Art. 23.1: Haak, p. 220. See also in this sense: *O.L.G. Vienna 23.2.89*, TranspR 1990.157. More generally on this point, see above, para. 93.

[32] [1977] Q.B. 208, 223, C.A.

[33] (1971) 6 E.T.L. 306, 315.

[34] *The Heron II* [1969] 1 A.C. 350.

[35] "That would not be an expense at all"—*James Buchanan & Co. v. Babco Forwarding & Shipping (U.K.)* [1977] 1 Q.B. 214, 211, *per* Lord Denning M.R., C.A. Also in this sense: *Nancy 21.1.87*, B.T. 1987.344, in which the claimant sought to recover the cost of buying (expensively) replacement goods for his customer, as well as damages payable to the latter for late delivery. In principle, these were not recoverable under Art. 23.4, but were awarded by the court on the ground that limits on compensation in Art. 23 were not available to the defendant carrier, because he had committed *une faute lourde* (Art. 29). As regards expectation loss see further, above, para. 94.

[36] He might, however, recover damages payable under a liquidated damages clause: Hardingham, "Damages under the CMR", [1978] L.M.C.L.Q. 51, 54.

[37] Generally, see Fischer, TranspR 1991.321; and Thume, TranspR 1993.365.

That date is determined by the procedural law of the forum.[38] The written claim is probably the written claim referred to in Article 32.2 and has been held to mean a general intimation that the claimant considers the carrier liable, without any specific quantification of the complaint.[39]

The amount of interest is fixed by Article 27.1 at 5 per cent, so the claimant against the carrier will look for any opportunity to claim the higher rate that is likely to be awarded under national law, while the carrier as claimant will not be slow to point out that Article 27.1 applies only to claims against carriers.[40]

Under Article 27.1 no interest can be recovered for the period prior to a written claim or to the institution of legal proceedings. Is this a gap in the CMR, which may be filled by national law, or is the question answered, *a contrario* by Article 27.1, in the negative? The question has not been answered by the courts.[41] Nor has the associated question of the amount recoverable between the time of judgment and the time of payment by the defendant. Although the prospect of a higher rate of interest than the 5 per cent of the CMR must be attractive to the claimant, here the argument *a contrario* must be strong.[42]

Article 27.2 provides:

> "When the amounts on which the calculation of the compensation is based are not expressed in the currency of the country in which payment is claimed, conversion shall be at the rate of exchange applicable on the day and at the place of compensation."

This provision anticipates the possibility that compensation claimed will be calculated mainly in accordance with Article 23.1 and Article 23.2 and hence in the currency of the place of acceptance of the goods, but that the claim may be brought and an award made in another jurisdiction and in another currency.[43]

---

[38] Evans, para. 206; Loewe, para. 206.

[39] *William Tatton & Co. v. Ferrymasters* [1974] 1 Lloyd's Rep. 203, 207, *per* Browne J. See above, para. 45b.

[40] For decisions in Holland to this effect, see Haak, p. 235.

[41] In favour of an interim award under national law: Hill and Messent, p. 204.

[42] Herber/Piper, Art. 27, 7; Koller, Art. 27, 3; Thume, Art. 27, 21. *Contra*: Hill and Messent, p. 204. That Art. 27 is in general exhaustive: *B.G.H. 10.10.91*, TranspR 1992.100. Herber/Piper, Art. 27, 6. Thume, Art. 27, 26 *et seq.* That Art. 27 is not exhaustive and that courts may resort to rules of national law, in particular, a rule allowing interest on unpaid interest: *Anvers 30.5.90*, B.T.L. 1991.134; *Cass. 17.3.92*, B.T.L. 1992.253. This is accepted *e.g.* by Koller, Art. 27, 4. However, the rate of 5 per cent is a ceiling that (unlike other ceilings—below, para. 101) cannot be lifted because the carrier has committed wilful misconduct: *Cass. com. 19.12.95*, B.T.L. 1996.463. *cf.*, however, Thume, Art. 27, 38 and cases cited.

[43] Putzeys, para. 881.

Although today many courts are empowered to make awards in foreign currency,[44] Article 27.2 is for those courts that are not.

Professor Loewe has suggested[45] that, if between the date of the award and the date of payment currency rates of exchange have moved against the claimant, the defendant should pay an additional sum sufficient to bring payment to the level of the award at the date of the award; if, on the other hand, rates have moved against the defendant, this is the product of the defendant's own delay and no adjustment is required.

100. Raising the limits on compensation: selection of higher limits

The limits on liability imposed by Article 23 may[46] be raised by contract[47] in two cases, and only if both parties agree.[48] The carrier is not obliged, however, to alert the sender to the possibility of raising the limits[49] and in practice they are rarely raised.

The first case, regulated by Article 24, is that of a declaration that the value of the particular cargo exceeds the limit which would otherwise apply. The value referred to is the actual value of the goods fixed in accordance with Article 23.2.[50]

The second case, regulated by Article 26, envisages a sender with a special interest in the arrival of the goods in accordance with the contract. If the sender declares a special interest,[51] there can be a claim[52] for consequential loss, loss of a kind for which the carrier would not otherwise be liable,[53] such as loss of value at destination, a case to which neither Article 23[54] nor Article 24 applies.

---

[44] For the power of the English court to do so, see Dicey (12th ed., London, 1993), p. 1573. For the powers of the court in Belgium: Putzeys, *loc. cit.*

[45] Para. 210.

[46] Art. 23.6.

[47] They may also be raised after the event by the operation of Art. 29: see below, para. 101.

[48] W/TRANS/SC 1/438 no. 65. If the carrier is asked by the sender to accept a higher limit, the carrier may be reluctant to agree, as the carrier's liability insurance may not cover the extra layer: Glöckner, Theunis, p. 104 and p. 106.

[49] *Cass. 12.10.81*, B.T. 1981.476, (1982) 17 E.T.L. 294. The sender's agent, however, may be in breach of duty to the sender if the agent does not mention the possibility in an appropriate case: *Paris 6.1.82*, B.T. 1982.84.

[50] Nossovitch, B.T. 1982.521, 522.

[51] Presumably, the declaration must be made to the carrier, but Art. 26 does not state this expressly.

[52] Presumably, but again the CMR is silent, the claimant may not only claim but, *ceteris paribus*, also recover the amount of his loss. *cf.* the more positive wording of Arts. 23, 24 and 25.

[53] One suggestion is that it is only under Art. 26 that the carrier was intended by the authors of the CMR to incur liability for consequential loss. See above, para. 94.

[54] See above, para. 94.

Article 24 provides:

> "The sender may, against payment of a surcharge to be agreed upon, declare in the consignment note a value for the goods exceeding the limit laid down in Article 23.3, and in that case the amount of the declared value shall be substituted for that limit."

Article 26 provides:

> "1. The sender may, against payment of a surcharge to be agreed upon, fix the amount of a special interest in delivery in the case of loss or damage or of the agreed time-limit being exceeded, by entering such amount in the consignment note.
> 2. If a declaration of a special interest in delivery has been made, compensation for the additional loss or damage proved may be claimed, up to the total amount of the interest declared, independently[55] of the compensation provided for in articles 23, 24 and 25."

In each case the claimant must prove actual loss of the amount claimed. The main difference between Article 24 and Article 26 is that Article 24 concerns goods of particular value, while Article 26 enables the sender to prepare the ground for a claim for consequential loss, including any loss of market at destination[56] and any other consequential loss which is not in the nature of a "charge" and is thus not recoverable under Article 23.4.[57] Consequential loss is not defined in the CMR and reference must be made to national law.[58] However, certainly in the case of a declaration of special interest, *ex hypothesi*, the carrier will have enough knowledge of the claimant's likely loss to be liable notwithstanding the English rule of remoteness of damage.[59]

Both Article 24 and Article 26 state that the higher limit must be entered by the sender in the consignment note.[60] It is not stated when this must be done. Nor is it clear whether the carrier is obliged to carry the goods on these terms, but courts are unlikely

---

[55] Art. 26.2 might be understood to enable the claimant to recover compensation twice, once under Arts. 23, 24 and 25 and again under Art. 26; however, the intention is simply that these articles should not limit the amount that he may recover under Art. 26.

[56] *James Buchanan & Co. v. Babco Forwarding & Shipping (U.K.)* [1977] Q.B. 208, 215, *per* Lord Denning M.R., C.A. Brunat B.T. 1982.146, 147; Nickel-Lanz, para. 177.

[57] *James Buchanan, loc. cit.* On Art. 23.4, see above, para. 98.

[58] Haak, p. 232; Loewe, para. 204; Rodière, (1971) 6 E.T.L. 317.

[59] On remoteness, see below, para. 246.

[60] Entry in the note was intended to be a condition of the operation of these provisions: TRANS/WP.9/11, p. 63. *O.G.H. 30.8.90*, TranspR 1992.406; *O.L.G. Düsseldorf 29.5.91*, TranspR 1992.291. *idem:* Helm, Art. 24 Anm. 2; Putzeys, para. 904. It is essential to alert sub-carriers or successive carriers.

to impose a higher limit against the will of the carrier,[61] or against a carrier with insufficient notice of the entry in the note. Presumably, the sender should make the necessary entry when he fills out other parts of the note and, in any case, in time to enable the carrier to consider a surcharge or to make any other response that he considers appropriate, including refusal to carry on those terms.[62] Once an entry has been made in the relevant consignment note for the goods and journey in question and agreed by the carrier, that entry is effective even though the goods are later grouped and become the subject of another consignment note which lacks any such entry.[63]

The reference to a surcharge, found in both Article 24 and Article 26, indicates that the carrier is entitled to make a surcharge, but does not make it a condition of higher limits under Article 24 or under Article 26.[64] Hence, the absence of evidence of agreement on a surcharge does not invalidate the entry of a higher limit. The carrier's fear that he will be bound by a note with an entry which was not noticed by his driver on receipt[65] is unfounded: the driver has no authority to bind the carrier to higher limits of liability and thus vary the terms of the contract of carriage concluded by his employer.[66] The sender who wishes to raise the limit must not only make the entry in the note but also contact the appropriate representative of the carrier and obtain agreement.

If it appears that the carrier wants a surcharge, until the amount has been agreed or the sender has withdrawn the request for higher limits, the contract of carriage has not been finally concluded. Agreement on the payment to be made for services is usually regarded as an essential element of the contract in question, without which such a contract is incomplete, uncertain and "void": courts will not write contracts and can only uphold what parties have themselves agreed.[67] In England, however, courts are

---

[61] Also in this sense Glöckner, Theunis, p. 105; Haak, p. 233; Putzeys, para. 905. This appears to have been the wish of the authors of the CMR: W/TRANS/SC 1/438 no. 65.

[62] Helm, *loc.cit.*, in this sense, but only if no contract of carriage has been concluded. If a contract has been concluded, he states that the carrier must accept the higher limit; *sed quaere*.

[63] *Brussels 16.11.77* (1980) 15 E.T.L. 319.

[64] Most writers conclude that a surcharge is not essential: Evans, para. 198; Glass and Cashmore, para. 3.66; Glöckner, Theunis, p. 104; Haak, pp. 233–234, citing *O.L.G. Düsseldorf 28.10.82*, VersR 1983. 749; Herber/Piper, Art. 24, 9; Koller, Art. 24, 2; Helm, Art. 24 Anm. 2; Hill and Messent, p. 200; Loewe, para. 198 and para. 203; Nickel-Lanz, para. 173; Putzeys, para. 905. This conclusion is confirmed by TRANS/WP.9/11, p. 50 and p. 63. *Contra*, however: *Cass. 10.7.89*, B.T. 1989.591; *Versailles 4.11.93*, B.T.L. 1994, 19, and German writers referred to by Haak, p. 233.

[65] Putzeys, para. 906.

[66] Putzeys, *loc. cit.*

[67] *Loftus v. Roberts* (1902) 18 T.L.R. 532.

now unsympathetic to a plea of uncertainty, especially if the parties have begun to perform the contract[68] or if the defendant will profit from the success of the plea. Thus, if before any agreement on the amount of the surcharge has been reached the goods arrive safely and timeously at destination, a plea of uncertainty by the sender will be rejected. The surcharge will be what is (later) agreed or, failing agreement, what is decided by a court or arbitrator to be a reasonable surcharge.

In practice, loss in excess of that recoverable under Article 23 is rarely the subject of an entry under Article 24 or under Article 26, the excess being insured by the goods insurer.[69] The same observation has been made of higher limits under the Hague Rules, and the reason, too, appears to be the same.

> "Experience has shown that the economic advantages to cargo-owner and carrier of accepting the limitation outweigh the economic advantages of declaring a higher value and so imposing a higher liability upon the shipowner. . . . [T]he increase over the standard freight rates which the carrier requires for accepting the higher liability is greater than the reduction in the insurance premium which the cargo insurer is prepared to offer for the prospect of recovering a higher amount from the carrier. . . . And this is not surprising. There are so many risks covered by the cargo insurance policy that the prospect of recovery in respect of one of them has little influence in fixing the premium, whereas the risk of liability to the cargo-owner is one of the principal risks insured under the carrier's P. and I. policy, and his maximum liability is a significant factor in the rates of premiums."[70]

A second and simpler reason is the unwillingness of insurers to cover the carrier's extra liability.[71]

101. Wilful misconduct

If wilful misconduct occurs, first, by virtue of Article 29 none of the defences in Chapter IV (Articles 17–29), notably the limits on liability in Article 23,[72] is available to the defendant. Moreover, if the application of Article 27(2) concerning the rate of exchange would be unfavourable to the claimant, that provision, too, will be

---

[68] *Foley v. Classique Coaches* [1934] 2 K.B. 1, C.A.; *British Bank for Foreign Trade v. Novinex* [1949] 1 K.B. 623, 629–630, *per* Cohen L.J., C.A.
[69] Haak, p. 231; Putzeys, para. 907.
[70] Diplock (1970) 1 JMLC 525, 529.
[71] *Post Magazine*, September 19, 1993, p. 14.
[72] Except Art. 23.1: *Paris 22.4.92*, B.T.L. 1992.362.

disregarded.[73] Secondly, the limitation period, although not removed altogether, is increased from one year to three years: Article 32.1. Article 29.1 reads:

> "The carrier shall not be entitled to avail himself of the provisions of this chapter which exclude or limit his liability or which shift the burden of proof if the damage was caused by his wilful misconduct or by such default on his part as, in accordance with the law of the court or tribunal seised of the case, is considered as equivalent to wilful misconduct."[74]

Article 29.2 contains a similar provision for the case of wilful misconduct by the carrier's agents, servants or "persons of whose services he makes use for the performance of the carriage" acting within the scope of their employment or agency. Even theft of the goods, evidently an instance of wilful misconduct, is in the course of servants' employment if it is part of their employment to take care of the goods.[75]

Wilful misconduct or equivalent default may be committed not only by the carrier but also by the sender, for example the sender who consigns highly dangerous goods without alerting the carrier to their nature: the carrier would have longer to sue under Article 32.1.[76]

Wilful misconduct or equivalent default must be proved by the party alleging it, usually the claimant.[77] The supposition is that the burden of proof is the usual burden in such cases in the *lex fori* and that in England, therefore, wilful misconduct has to be proved on the balance of probabilities. The significance of the *lex fori* is reinforced, as regards equivalent default, by the express reference in Article 29.1 to "the law of the court or tribunal seised". In some countries this has led to a modified burden of proof, for example when the sender alleged equivalent default in respect of missing goods. Because the evidence was very much in the carrier's sphere of activity the Supreme Court held that the underlying duty of good faith in Austrian law indicated that the carrier owed a duty of explanation—to give an account of the security measures,

---

[73] *Lacey's Footwear (Wholesale) Ltd v. Bowler Int. Freight Ltd* (High Court, March 13, 1995).

[74] Generally, see Haak and Swart, part 2, Chap. 1; Tuma (1993) 28 E.T.L. 649; Zapp, TranspR 1994.142.

[75] *Rustenburg Platinum Mines v. SAA* [1977] 1 Lloyd's Rep. 564; affirmed [1979] 1 Lloyd's Rep. 19, C.A. *Cass. 21.7.87*, B.T. 1987.529. *idem*, the smuggling of alcohol into Saudi Arabia, in spite of an express prohibition by the employer: by smuggling alcohol in the same vehicle as the goods, the drivers put the goods at risk: *B.G.H. 27.6.85* (1986) 21 E.T.L. 102, 107. See further above, para. 49.

[76] Costanzo, p. 46.

[77] *Paris 4.7.84*, B.T. 1985.158; *O.L.G. Düsseldorf 14.7.87*, VersR 1987.932; *O.L.G. Hamburg 7.2.91*, TranspR 1991.294; *O.L.G. Düsseldorf 29.5.91*, TranspR 1991.291; *O.L.G. Nuremburg 22.3.95*, TranspR 1996.381.

which the carrier had in place, both in general and as affected the facts of the particular case.[78] This should be no surprise to the English lawyer in view of the common law response to an allegation that a bailee, such as a carrier, is guilty of fundamental breach. An explanation is required of the bailee and, if the bailee leaves the cause of loss or damage undiscovered and unexplained, the bailee is liable.[79] If this is sound reasoning and good law for equivalent default, it might also be thought good for wilful misconduct.

Article 29 was modelled[80] on Article 25 of the Warsaw Convention on Air Transport 1929. This seems a curious choice of model for a draftsman at a time when the model itself was under review, a review which soon led to change by a Protocol of 1955,[81] as Article 25 in its original form was thought to produce an unacceptable divergence between the decisions of different jurisdictions, in particular between decisions in civil law countries and decisions in countries of common law.[82] However, agreement on a new formula for the CMR was thought to be unobtainable and the 1929 model was preferred precisely to permit imprecision[83] and to accommodate certain civil law countries which wanted to treat *faute lourde* and *faute grave*[84] as equivalent default.

In the three languages most relevant to the present inquiry, Article 25.1 of the Warsaw Convention 1929 reads:

> "The carrier shall not be entitled to avail himself of the provisions of this Convention which exclude or limit his liability, if the damage caused by his wilful misconduct or by such default on his part as, in

[78] *O.G.H. 14.7.1993*, TranspR 1994.189. See also *O.L.G. Munich 12.4.90* TranspR 1990.280, 286 a case of unexplained delay, in which the court said that when the claimant had established facts which (merely) *suggested* that the defendant carrier might have been guilty of equivalent default, and when the carrier alone was in a position to explain the cause of loss or damage occurring in his sphere of operation, the onus was on the carrier to explain what had happened; and that, as the carrier had failed to offer any sufficient explanation, equivalent default was regarded as proven. Also in this sense, *O.L.G. Munich 10.10.90* TranspR 1991.138 and *O.L.G. Nuremburg 10.12.92*, TranspR 1993.138. Piper, VersR 1988.201, 208.

[79] See below, para. 240.

[80] *O.L.G. Munich 29.11.68* (1971) 6 E.T.L. 115, 126; *B.G.H. 14.7.83*, 1986 U.L.R. II 596; *O.G.H. 10.10.74*, Greiter 37, 39, by reference to the legislative history of the CMR. Loewe, para. 217.

[81] The amended version of Art. 25 of the Warsaw Convention, found in the Protocol of 1955, purported to restate wilful misconduct in different words but the same sense: "an act or omission . . . done with intent to create damage or recklessly and with the knowledge that damage would probably result". This is believed to be close to the common law concept of wilful misconduct.

[82] Rodière (1978) 13 E.T.L. 24, 25.

[83] Nickel-Lanz, para. 187. It is also her opinion that the intention was to adopt the wording of Art. 25, without the substance; however, the English court has referred to precedent on Art. 25. Certainly, any attempt to define wilful misconduct was abandoned by the draftsman: TRANS/WP/9/35 no. 73, pp. 19–20.

[84] TRANS/WP/9/35 no. 73, p. 19.

accordance with the law seised of the case, is considered to be equivalent to wilful misconduct."

"Le transporteur n'aura pas le droit de se prévaloir des dispositions de la présente Convention qui excluent ou limitent sa responsabilité, si le dommage provient de son dol ou d'une faute qui, d'après, la loi du tribunal saisi, est considéré comme èquivalente."

"Hat der Luftfrachtführer den Schaden vorsätzlich oder durch eine Fahrlässigkeit herbeigeführt, die nach dem Recht des angerufenen Gerichts dem Vorsatz gleichsteht, so kann er sich nicht di Bestimmungen diese Abkommens berufen, die seine Haftung ausschliessen oder beschränken."

"Wilful misconduct" is an inaccurate translation[85] of the narrower French concept, *dol.*[86] The primary meaning of *dol* is *un acte illicite intentionnel* but it has been extended to include a deliberate breach of duty, by which damage is caused: although the infliction of damage may not have been the principal intention behind the breach of duty,[87] awareness that damage will result or probably result from breach amounts to *dol.*[88] *Dol* is therefore very similar to the German notion of *Vorsatz.*[89]

Dol has also been described as conduct outside the terms of the contract[90] or, as the common lawyer might say,[91] outside the four corners of the contract. Any suggestion of an analogy with common law doctrines of deviation or fundamental breach as applied to bailment and carriage of goods, however, would be misleading. Not only are the doctrines of deviation and fundamental breach inapplicable to CMR contracts[92] but also the concept of wilful misconduct has developed differently: it has developed subjectively by reference to the mind of the actor, rather than objectively

---

[85] McGilchrist, "Wilful Misconduct and the Warsaw Convention" [1977] L.M.C.L.Q. 539, 542. Wilful misconduct, as applied under the Warsaw Convention, is closer to the French notion of *faute inexcusable.* "... un acte ou une omission du transporteur commis témérairement et avec conscience qu'un dommage en résulterait probablement": Sériaux, *La Faute du Transporteur* (Paris, 1984), para. 318. While this is true of wilful misconduct under the Warsaw Convention, as applied in the United States, it is not true of the Convention, as applied in England: below, para. 101b.

[86] Also referred to as *la faute dolosive.* Generally, see Sériaux, paras. 265 *et seq.*

[87] *Cass. 4.2.69,* DS 1969. J. 601, note Mazeaud.

[88] Sériaux, para. 316.

[89] Sériaux, para. 318. The carrier is guilty of *Vorsatz* "wenn er die Möglichkeit des Schadenseintritt kennt und den Schaden bewusst bezweckt (direkter Vorsatz, *dolus directus*) oder billigend in Kauf nimmt (bedingter Vorsatz, *dolus eventualis*)": Herber/Piper, Art. 29, 2. *O.L.G. Nuremberg 22.3.95,* TranspR 1996.381. See also Koller, Art. 29, 2; Thume, Art. 29, 6.

[90] Putzeys, para. 917.

[91] For example Lord Greene, M.R., in *Alderslade v. Hendon Laundry* [1945] 1 K.B. 189, 192, C.A.

[92] Above, paras. 30a and 31.

by reference to the purpose of the contract or the consequences of breach.[93] Nonetheless, the idea that the actor has put himself beyond the pale prose of the contract points to conduct to which normal defences should not or were not intended to apply.

The meaning of wilful misconduct, as understood in the CMR, came before the English court for the first time in *Jones v. Bencher*[94] and the judge turned to cases on the meaning of the expression, first, in contracts for carriage by rail and, secondly, in contracts for carriage by air governed by the Warsaw Convention.[95]

101a. Carriage by rail: common law

From cases at common law on carriage by rail, it appears that there is wilful misconduct if the person intends the loss or damage[96] or "acts with recklessness, not caring what the results of his carelessness may be".[97] This suggests something worse than negligence[98] or even gross negligence. As Kahn-Freund observed,[99] wilful misconduct "includes the doing of an act with reckless indifference, not caring what the result of that indifference might be. This attitude is something beyond negligence even of a gross kind. . . . At its worst negligence may be defined as an 'it will be all right' attitude. Wilful misconduct is an 'I don't care' attitude."

---

[93] The argument, that misconduct might become wilful misconduct in the sense of Art. 29 by reason of the gravity of the consequences, was rejected in *B.G.H. 27.6.85* (1986) 21 E.T.L. 102, 109, thus distinguishing Art. 826 BGB.

[94] [1986] 1 Lloyd's Rep. 54.

[95] Art. 25, set out above. The expression has also been discussed in the context of s.419(2) of the Merchant Shipping Act 1894 and an infringement of the Collision Regulations. In *Taylor v. O'Keefe, the Nordic Clansman* [1984] 1 Lloyd's Rep. 31, 35, C.A., Webster J., with whom Robert Goff L.J. concurred, concluded, without reference to cases under the CMR or the Warsaw Convention, that wilful misconduct meant either (1) that the act or omission was deliberate and that it was a conscious act in the sense that the actor was aware of all relevant facts giving rise to the infringement, or (2) that he did not care whether his act or omission would cause an infringement or not.

[96] Kahn-Freund, p. 258. Wilful misconduct arises when "the person guilty of it [knows] that mischief will result": Bramwell L.J. in *Lewis v. GWR* (1877) 3 Q.B.D. 195, 206, C.A., applied to the CMR by Popplewell J. in *Jones v. Bencher* [1986] 1 Lloyd's Rep. 54. It includes action taken as part of an industrial dispute, such as a refusal to handle and move perishable goods: *Young & Son (Wholesale Fish Merchants) v. British Transport Commission* [1955] 2 Q.B. 177.

[97] *Forder v. GWR* [1905] 2 K.B. 532, 535, *per* Lord Alverstoke C.J., relied upon in *Jones v. Bencher* (at 59) by Popplewell J. See also *Glenister v. GWR* (1873) 29 L.T. 423; for other such decisions, see Shawcross & Beaumont, *Air Law* (4th ed., London, 1989), VII.210, n. 12. Also Andrews, "Wilfulness, a lesson in ambiguity", (1981) 1 L.S. 303.

[98] *Lewis v. GWR* (1877) 3 Q.B.D. 195, 206, *per* Bramwell L.J., C.A.

[99] At 257, speaking of carriage by rail at common law.

In *Jones v. Bencher*[1] the judge relied on a statement by Bramwell L.J. in *Lewis v. GWR*,[2] that wilful misconduct

> "means misconduct to which the will is a party, something opposed to accident or negligence; the *mis*conduct, not the conduct must be wilful. It has been said, and, I think, correctly, that, perhaps, one condition of 'wilful misconduct' must be that the person guilty of it should know that mischief will result from it. But to my mind there might be other 'wilful misconduct'. I think it would be wilful misconduct if a man did an act not knowing whether mischief would or would not result from it. . . . He might say, 'Well, I do not know which is right, and I do not care; I will do this.' I am much inclined to think that that would be 'wilful misconduct', because he acted under the supposition that it might be mischievous, and with an indifference to his duty to ascertain whether it would be mischievous or not. I think that would be wilful misconduct."

> In *Lewis v. GWR*[3] Cheshire cheeses sent by rail from London to Shrewsbury were stowed on their rims and in two layers in an open truck. Stowed like this in hot weather the cheeses suffered damage. Under the contract of carriage the carrier was liable for the damage if it had been caused by wilful misconduct, but given the finding that the carrier's packers in London, unlike perhaps his packers in Cheshire, were not aware that Cheshire cheeses had to be stowed differently from other smaller cheeses, the Court of Appeal held that the damage had not been caused by wilful misconduct.

101b. Carriage by air: the Warsaw Convention

From the cases of carriage by air governed by Article 25 of the Warsaw Convention it appears, rather as it does from the cases of carriage by rail at common law, that a person commits wilful misconduct if that person intends the loss or damage or acts with recklessness, not caring what the results may be. In *Horobin v. BOAC*[4] Barry J. said: "To be guilty of wilful misconduct the person concerned must appreciate that he is acting wrongfully, or

---

[1] [1986] 1 Lloyd's Rep. 54, 59.

[2] Above, (n. 98), *loc. cit.* In the same case Brett L.J. said (210–211): "if it is brought to his notice that what he is doing or omitting to do, may seriously endanger the things which are to be sent, and he wilfully persists in doing that against which he is warned, careless whether he may be doing damage or not . . . he is guilty of wilful misconduct." See also 213, *per* Cotton L.J.

[3] Above, n. 98.

[4] [1952] 2 All E.R. 1016, 1022. In this case a Dakota aircraft crashed while on a flight from London to Lagos. It was argued that there was wilful misconduct, within the meaning of Art. 25 of the Warsaw Convention, in that the company had selected a crew which did not know the route and had failed to provide the crew with adequate maps. The jury was unable to agree a verdict and, before the issue was resolved, the action was settled.

is wrongfully omitting to act, and yet persists in so acting or omitting to act regardless of the consequences . . . or with reckless indifference to what the results may be." This points to something worse than negligence or even gross negligence.[5]

In the United States, however, wilful misconduct has been "defined as the wilful performance of an act that is likely to result in damage or wilful action with a reckless disregard of the *probable consequences*".[6] An "act may be characterised as wilful misconduct when there is an intent to do an act or to omit doing an act with knowledge that the act or omission will *probably result* in damage or injury".[7] The "obvious foreseeability of the resulting damage to plaintiffs requires the inference that those damages were intentionally inflicted".[8]

In England, not to care about the consequences makes a person reckless, whether the loss or damage is likely to result or not, whereas these influential statements[9] by courts in the United States make it clear that, for wilful misconduct there, the loss or damage must be a probable result.[10] In England, the emphasis is not on the objective probability of the loss or damage but on the state of mind of the actor and the wrongful character of the conduct: that is what makes the misconduct wilful. Consequently, whereas in the United States the state of mind of the carrier may be inferred from objective facts,[11] and wilful misconduct "may be based upon the

---

[5] *ibid.*, at 1019. *idem*, *Rustenburg Platinum Mines v. SAA* [1977] 1 Lloyd's Rep. 564, 569, *per* Ackner J.; affirmed [1979] 1 Lloyd's Rep. 19, C.A.

[6] *Wing Hang Bk Ltd v. JAL Co.* 357 F Supp 94, 96–97 (S.D. N.Y., 1973), with emphasis added, applying *Pekelis v. Transcontinental & Western Air Inc.* 187 F. 2d 122, 124 (2 Cir., 1951): "Wilful misconduct is the intentional performance of an act with knowledge that the performance of that act will probably result in injury or damage, or it may be the intentional performance of an act in such a manner as to imply reckless disregard of the probable consequences of the act. Likewise, the intentional omission of some act, with knowledge that such omission will probably result in damage or injury, or the intentional omission of some act in a manner from which could be implied reckless disregard of the probable consequences of the omission, would also be wilful misconduct." *Pekelis* has been applied on this point in a number of decisions, including *Republic National Bank v. Eastern Airlines* 815 F. 2d 232, 239 (2 Cir., 1987).

[7] *Cohen v. Varig Airlines* 495 NYS 2d 44, 47 (1978), quoting from *Berner v. British Commonwealth Pacific Airlines* 346 F. 2d 532, 537 (2 Cir., 1965), with emphasis added.

[8] *Cohen* (above).

[9] The influence appears in the United Nations Convention on International Multimodal Transport of Goods 1980, Art. 21.1: "The multimodal transport operator is not entitled to the benefit of the limitation of liability provided for in this Convention if it is proved that the loss, damage or delay in delivery resulted from an act or omission of the multimodal transport operator done with the intent to cause such loss, damage or delay or recklessly and with the knowledge that such loss, damage or delay would probably result." The Convention is not in force.

[10] A similar test for the Warsaw Convention, by reference to probability, can be found in France: *Cass. 16.4.75* (1976) 30 RFDA 105.

[11] A "subtle but immensely significant shift of emphasis", which thus broadened the scope of wilful misconduct: McGilchrist, "Wilful Misconduct and the Warsaw Convention" [1977] 1 L.M.C.L.Q. 539, 540.

cumulative effect of numerous departures from required standards",[12] this is not true in England.[13] Moreover, a result is probable if it is likely to happen.[14] In England, if misconduct is wilful, it is enough that the risk of loss or damage has been increased, whether it has become probable or not:

> "You may think that what was actually done matters less than the intention or state of mind of the person who did it. The same act may amount on one occasion to mere negligence, and on another to wilful misconduct. Two men driving motor cars may both pass traffic lights after they have changed from yellow to red. In both cases there are the same act, the same traffic lights, the same cross-roads and the same motor cars. In the first case the man may have been driving a little too fast. He may not have been keeping a proper look-out, and he may not have seen the lights (although he ought to have seen them) until he was too close to them and was unable to stop, and therefore, crossed the roads when the lights were against him. He was not intending to do anything wrong, to disregard the provisions of the Road Traffic Act or to endanger the lives of anyone using the road, but he was careless in not keeping a proper look-out and in going too fast, and as a result, without intending to do anything wrong, he committed an act which was clearly an act of misconduct. The second driver is in a hurry. He knows all about the lights, and he sees in plenty of time that they are changing from yellow to red, but he says to himself: 'Hardly any traffic comes out of this side road which I am about to cross. I will go on. I am not going to bother to stop.' He does not expect an accident to happen, but he knows that he is doing something wrong. He knows that he should stop, and he is able to stop, but he does not, and he commits exactly the same act as the other driver. But in that frame of mind no jury would have very much difficulty in coming to the conclusion that he had committed an act of wilful misconduct. Of course, he did not intend to kill anyone or to injure anyone coming out of the side road. He thought that in all probability nobody would be coming out of the side road. None the less, he took a risk which he knew he ought not to take, and in those circumstances he could be rightly found to have committed an act of wilful misconduct."

In this passage in *Horobin v. BOAC*,[15] the judge came down to earth to provide a touchstone of wilful misconduct for the jury. It

---

[12] *Reiner v. Alitalia Airlines* 9 Avi.Cas. 18,228 (N.Y., 1966). The same is true of *faute lourde* in France under the CMR: *Paris 25.2.54* (1954) 8 RFDA 45; Gouilloud B.T. 1985.337, citing *Cass.29.1.85*, B.T. 1985.345. However, *faute lourde* is distinguishable from wilful misconduct: below, para. 102c.

[13] *Horobin v. BOAC* [1952] 1 All E.R. 1016, 1032, *per* Barry J.

[14] *Goldman v. Thai Airways International* [1983] 3 All E.R. 693, 700, *per* Eveleigh L.J., C.A. However, this decision establishes that under the 1955 version of Art. 25 the English courts require subjective awareness of the *probability* of loss or damage; and this view has been adopted in New South Wales: *Qantas Airways v. S.S. Pharmaceuticals* [1991] 1 Lloyd's Rep. 288; McQueen [1991] L.M.C.L.Q. 165.

[15] [1952] 2 All E.R. 1016, 1020.

has been set out here because the "red light" case has been influential on other judges, not least in *Jones v. Bencher*,[16] where the passage was also quoted.

101c. Carriage by road: the CMR

The carrier of goods by road under the CMR commits wilful misconduct, by conduct intended to cause loss or damage to the goods. This much is obvious, except that the carrier will be considered to have intended any loss or damage that is the inevitable consequence of an intentional act or omission. Thus, if a carrier agrees to deliver goods by a certain date but then arranges matters in such a way that the goods cannot be delivered on time, the carrier can be considered to have intended any consequent loss or damage[17] consequent[18] on late delivery. Difficulty, however, arises in the area of recklessness located, as it is, between intention and gross negligence.

> In *Jones v. Bencher*[19] Popplewell J. held that a driver, who, in the hope of being able to spend the night at home, exceeded the length of time permitted for continuous driving[20] and fell asleep at the wheel, committed wilful misconduct. He accepted[21] the argument of counsel for the defendant carrier that the driver "must have appreciated that, by reason of his conduct, he increased the risk either to himself, or his load, or other drivers"; that "it is not enough simply to say that he acted contrary to the regulations even though they were there to prevent this particular danger"; and that the "driver must be shown to have adverted to the increased risk". On the facts of the case, however, the judge concluded[22] that "the driver was well aware of the regulations. . . . He chose to ignore them and did so deliberately. He knew that, by ignoring them, he exposed the load that he was carrying, the vehicle he was driving, himself, and other road users, to a greater risk than if he had complied with the regulations. . . . In my judgment he appreciated that he was acting wrongfully, persisted in so acting and was wholly indifferent to the consequences."

From this case it does not appear, any more than it did in the "red light" case,[23] that the accident was the probable result of the

---

[16] [1986] 1 Lloyd's Rep. 54, 59, *per* Popplewell J.
[17] *TC Paris 12.10.71*, Gaz. Pal. 1972.I.133, 1973 U.L.C. 268. This would be *une faute dolosive* in French law: *Cass. 4.2.69*, DS 1969. J. 601, note Mazeaud.
[18] Problems of causation are discussed below, para. 101d.
[19] [1986] 1 Lloyd's Rep. 54.
[20] EEC Reg. 543/69. Under Art. 7 no period of continuous driving could exceed four hours, and for this purpose a period was continuous notwithstanding a break, unless the break was one of 30 minutes or more. Also under Art. 7 the total period of driving time was not to exceed eight hours.
[21] At 59.
[22] At 60. See also *Lacey's Footwear Ltd v. Bowler* (C.A., April 18, 1997, unreported).
[23] Quoted by Barry J. in *Horobin* (above, n. 13 and para. 101b).

driver's misconduct. It was enough that the driver's conduct was deliberate and was known to increase the risk of loss or damage. The judge was evidently influenced by the "red light" case and by the railway cases, in which it was said[24] of a man that there "would be 'wilful misconduct', because he acted under the supposition that his act or omission *might be* mischievous". Popplewell J. accepted[25] the argument of counsel for the claimant that the driver "must have appreciated that, by reason of his conduct, he increased the risk either to himself, or his load or other drivers" and that the "driver must be shown to have adverted to the increased risk". The judge concluded[26] that there was wilful misconduct because the driver knew that, by ignoring the regulations, he exposed all concerned to a greater risk than if he had complied with the regulations. Similarly, in a subsequent case,[27] there was wilful misconduct when the carrier had the trailer left unguarded, "appreciating that it was risky and wrong to do so or being recklessly indifferent".

An outline of the law is as follows:

(a) The objective probability of loss or damage is not decisive.
(b) There is wilful misconduct if (i) the misconduct increases the risk, and (ii) the carrier was aware of this.[28]
(c) One corollary of (b) is that in the case of the carrier in an emergency, a carrier on the horns of a dilemma in which damage is probable whatever the carrier chooses to do, the course chosen will not be wilful misconduct[29] unless the

---

[24] *Lewis v. GWR* (1877) 3 Q.B.D. 195, *per* Bramwell L.J. (emphasis added). On the railways cases see above, para. 101a.

[25] [1986] 1 Lloyd's Rep. 59.

[26] At 60. *cf. O.L.G. Karlsruhe 17.2.1995*, TranspR 1995.439: evidence that the driver fell asleep at the wheel (and had an accident) is not without more evidence of *grosse Fahrlässigkeit*.

[27] *Texas Instruments Ltd v. Nasan (Europe) Ltd* [1991] 1 Lloyd's Rep. 146, 154 *per* Tudor Evans J. See also *Longmill Corp. plc v. A. Merzario Ltd* (Central London County Ct, June 6, 1995). *cf. National Semiconductors (UK) Ltd v. UPS Ltd* [1996] 2 Lloyd's Rep. 212 in which the court reached a different decision because the driver was not conscious that in leaving the vehicle locked but attended in a Milan street in daytime he was taking a risk.

[28] The test is subjective rather than objective. Certainly, this is the impression left by *Horobin v. BOAC* (above, para. 101b) and by *Jones v. Bencher* (above, n. 19). In this sense as regards the Warsaw Convention: *Goldman* (above, n. 14); and as regards "wilful misconduct" in standard railway conditions: Glass and Cashmore, para. 1.60.

[29] *Jones v. Bencher* [1986] 1 Lloyd's Rep. 54, 59 with reference to this statement by Barry J. in *Horobin v. BOAC* [1952] 2 Lloyd's Rep. 450, 487: "the mere fact that [an act was done contrary to a flight plan or to some instructions, or even to the standards of safe flying, to the knowledge of the person who did it], does not necessarily establish wilful misconduct on his part, because in the exigencies of the flight it is always possible that a pilot may consciously depart from instructions, taking the view that, in the best interest of the safety of his aircraft, it is wiser and safer for him to depart from that instruction than to adhere to it".

carrier deliberately chooses the course that is most likely to lead to damage or to the greatest amount of damage.

(d) A second corollary of (b) is that negligence or even gross negligence does not amount to wilful misconduct. Loss caused by negligence, even gross negligence, is best spread and borne at least in part by cargo interests: "loss due to an allegedly exceptional degree of negligence . . . falls into Lord Diplock's category of risks concerning which 'it is more practical and economical from the point of view of insurance to spread the risk to the cargo in excess of a fixed limit among a number of cargo insurers rather than to concentrate it in the carrier's . . . insurer' ".[30] But when the carrier embarks on deliberate misconduct, which the carrier knows will increase the risk, a line is crossed: the carrier must bear the risk in full.

101d. Cause and effect

Article 29 operates if damage was "caused by" wilful misconduct or equivalent default.[31] However, Article 32.1 operates to extend the limitation period "in the case of" wilful misconduct or equivalent default. The use of different wording in Article 32.1 might suggest a looser connection with the misconduct or default,[32] but no obvious reason for any difference has been advanced. Article 32.1 should be construed neither literally[33] nor in isolation. The apparent difference largely disappears, if "the case" of wilful misconduct or equivalent default mentioned in Article 32.1 is the case mentioned just above in Article 29, that is, the case of wilful misconduct or equivalent which has *caused* damage. Further support for this view lies in the fact that the CMR is modelled on

---

[30] *Iligan Integrated Steel Mills Inc. v. SS. John Weyerhaeuser* 507 F. 2d 68, 73 (2 Cir., 1974), with reference to Diplock, 1 JMLC 525, 528–529 (1970), quoted above, para. 100 *in fine*. The *Iligan* case concerned the Hague Rules and the provision of an unseaworthy ship.

[31] The causal link is essential: *Longmill Corp. plc v. A. Merzario Ltd* (Central London County Ct, June 6, 1995); *O.L.G. Munich 27.11.68* (1971) E.T.L. 115, 125; *B.G.H. 27.6.85* (1986) 21 E.T.L. 102, 107, 109; *Paris 25.3.88*, B.T. 1989.46 (discussed above, para. 43a). Haak, p. 244.

[32] As in the case of the doctrine of deviation at common law: *Thorley v. Orchis SS. Co.* [1907] 1 K.B. 660, C.A.

[33] A further difficulty is that Art. 29 mentions only a causal connection with damage, which in other parts of the CMR, for example Arts. 23 and 25, is clearly distinguished from loss and delay. The inference might be drawn, therefore, that when wilful misconduct causes loss or delay, it has no effect on the carrier's rights. This point has not been taken in the cases: *Brussels 30.10.75* (1976) 10 E.T.L. 238; *Rb Antwerp 3.3.76* (1977) 11 E.T.L. 437.

provisions of the Warsaw Convention in which a causal connection was clearly required.[34] The nature of the causal connection required is a matter for national law.[35]

The effect of wilful misconduct or equivalent default is that under Article 32.1 the period of limitation is extended from one year to three; and that under Article 29.1 the carrier is deprived of "provisions of this chapter which exclude or limit his liability or which shift the burden of proof", notably those in Articles 17 and 18, which expressly "relieve" the carrier of liability or speak of presumptions, as well as those in Article 23, which limit the amount of the carrier's liability. In the latter case, however, the liability will still be limited by rules of national law relating to remoteness of damage and causation.[36]

As regards apportionment under Article 17.5, it has been decided in Germany[37] that Article 29.1 applies. Given the background of a common law rule, whereby the carrier is liable in full unless the carrier proves the extent to which loss or damage was caused by an exonerating event,[38] the English court is likely to agree.

English law is sometimes uncertain about whether it is faced with an exclusion clause, which assumes a breach of duty, or a clause which defines the basic duty of the party whose liability is in question.[39] All that can be said with any confidence of the CMR is that the English court is likely to give a purposive rather than a literal interpretation of the provisions of Chapter 4, when identifying "provisions of this chapter which exclude or limit" the liability of the carrier.[40]

102. Equivalent default

Articles 29 and 32 refer not only to wilful misconduct[41] but also to "such default . . . as, in accordance with the law of the court to tribunal seised of the case, is considered as equivalent to wilful

[34] *Froman v. PanAm* 1953 U.S.Av. R. 1, 6: the damage must "come about because" of the wilful misconduct. *idem: Wing Hang Bk Ltd v. JAL Co.* 357 F. Supp. 94 S.D. N.Y., 1973).

[35] *B.G.H. 27.6.85* (1986) 21 E.T.L. 102, 107, 109.

[36] *O.L.G. Munich 12.4.90*, TranspR 1990.280, 287.

[37] *B.G.H. 27.6.85* (1986) 21 E.T.L. 102, 107, 108. Also in this sense: Haak, p. 244; Helm, Art. 29 Anm. 3; Loewe, para. 216.

[38] See above, para. 69c.

[39] *Photo Production v. Securicor Transport* [1980] A.C. 827, 851, *per* Lord Diplock. Clarke, *Insurance*, para. 19–1A.

[40] The court will look at the substance rather than the form: *Phillips Products v. Hyland* [1987] 2 All E.R. 620, 626, *per* Slade L.J., C.A.; *Smith v. Bush* [1990] A.C. 831.

[41] Above, para. 101.

misconduct". In English law, there is no default equivalent to wilful misconduct under the CMR[42] and therefore the words are of no relevance,[43] but in other countries equivalent default can be found with various shades of meaning.

102a. Equivalence in fault

The first and narrowest kind of equivalent default is modelled on rules of national law which, although labelled differently, apply a concept which is equivalent in substance to wilful misconduct —equivalent as regards the nature and quality of the defendant's conduct. This position is taken by the courts of Belgium. In consequence, *faute lourde*, being conduct less serious than wilful misconduct, is not regarded as equivalent default.[44] In this the Belgian position resembles that taken in England, but it differs in that in Belgium the person must be aware that damage will *probably* result.[45]

In *Brussels 30.10.75*[46] the court refused to apply Article 29 to the conduct of the driver who left his vehicle parked unattended overnight on the public highway, with resulting theft of a consignment of electronic flashguns. The court said[47] that "Belgian law has no notion of default equivalent to wilful misconduct (*dol*) and both the writers and the cases condemn the assimilation of gross negligence (*faute lourde*) to wilful misconduct; article 29 should be interpreted as having introduced default equivalent to wilful misconduct under the *lex fori*, less to add to wilful misconduct equivalent grounds of

---

[42] In general, an equivalent might be found in the rule relating to deviation; however, it has been argued above (paras. 30a and 31) that that rule is inapplicable to contracts governed by the CMR.

[43] Also in this sense: Hill and Messent, p. 205. Nor is any such default known to the law in Greece: TranspR 1992.175.

[44] *Ghent 26.3.92* (1992) 27 E.T.L. 847; *Cass. Belge 27.1.95* (1996) 31 E.T.L. 694. Putzeys, para. 932. See also Libouton, para. 76. However, the intention of the draftsman appears to have been to include *faute lourde*: TRANS/WP.9/11, p. 63–64.

[45] Putzeys, para. 934: "les auteurs de la CMR . . . ont entendu que celui qui avait agi avec la *conscience effective de la survenance probable du dommage*, avec temérité donc, soit sanctionné par le retrait du bénéfice . . . ".

[46] (1976) 11 E.T.L. 238. Belgian courts have taken a similar position with regard to Art. 25 of the Warsaw Convention and it is on the premise that the CMR was modelled on Art. 25 that a narrow view is taken of the CMR: see Putzeys, paras. 923 *et seq.* He also argues (para. 932) that the narrow view is typical of the Dutch courts. However it appears that Art. 29 has only rarely come before the Dutch courts: Haak, p. 249. Austria: see *Lg Salzburg 12.10.95*, TranspR 1996.340 and argument for the Belgian rule (at 343) in a note to the decision by Tuma. Norway: the Supreme Court appears to have required something greater than *die grosse Fahrlässigkeit: Norges Høyesterett 16.3.95* (1995) 30 E.T.L. 563, 571.

[47] At 244.

exclusion in legal systems which recognise wilful misconduct, than to authorise the courts to give effect to wilful misconduct in systems which have no such notion."[48]

102b. Equivalence in effect: *die grosse Fahrlässigkeit*

The second and broadest kind of equivalent default is shaped by rules of national law which reflect such a degree of social disapproval of the defendant's conduct that they have an equivalent effect on defences: to eliminate them or, in the case of time limitation, to extend the time in which action may be brought. The best example is *die grosse Fahrlässigkeit*[49] in the law of Austria and of Germany, a concept which corresponds roughly to gross negligence.[50] This is the meaning of equivalent default given to the expression in the CMR by Loewe[51] and by Rodière,[52] in accordance with the maxim, found in some countries but not others, *culpa lata dolo aequiparatur.*

According to the B.G.H. in 1983,[53] while only the courts in Belgium took a narrower view,[54] the broad view was taken by

---

[48] See also *Rb Antwerp 3.3.75* (1977) 12 E.T.L. 437: leaving a lorry locked but unattended in the customs (unofficial) park, with the result that a consignment of cigarettes was stolen was negligence but not wilful misconduct.

cf. Liége 6.5.70 (1970) 5 E.T.L. 718: goods on pallets, placed on the lorry by the sender, were then secured on the lorry by the driver who saw that some of the pallets and some of the packing were defective. Holding the carrier liable under the CMR, the court found that the damage that resulted was primarily due to the wedging of the pallets and their load by the driver; the court said (at 723), however, that in any event "it is undoubtedly gross negligence (*faute lourde*) when a carrier, having ascertained that the handling, loading or stowage of his freight by the sender is manifestly defective and likely to cause damage or loss, adopts a passive attitude and undertakes the transport without taking the measures necessary to bring it to a satisfactory conclusion". This decision has been criticised by Putzeys (para. 936), who regards it as atypical. Even in France (below, para. 102c) this kind of conduct does not amount to equivalent default: *Paris 3.11.70*, B.T. 1971.213, (1971) 6 E.T.L. 264, 1971 U.L.C. 144.

[49] *B.G.H. 16.2.84*, VersR 1984.551, 552: "Grosse Fahrlässigkeit liegt vor, wenn die im Verkehr erforderliche Sorgfalt in besonders schwerem Masse verletzt worden und unbeachtet geblieben ist, was im gegebenen Fall jedem einleuchten mußte." *B.G.H. 27.6.85* (1986) 21 E.T.L. 102, 108–109: "Bei der Fahrlässigkeit genügt die allgemeine Vorhersehbarkeit eines schädigenden Erfolges, der konkrete Ablauf braucht in seinen Einzelheiten nicht vorhersehbar gewesen zu sein." See also *O.L.G. Düsseldorf 23.11.89*, TranspR 1990.63, 65.

In Austria in *O.G.H. 25.1.90*, TranspR 1990.235, 239 the concept was described as "eine auffällige Vernachlässigung ihrer Sorgfalspflicht, die den Eintritt des Schadens geradezu als wahrscheinlich erscheinen läßt." See also *O.G.H. 11.7.1990*, TranspR 1992.322, 323.

[50] Shawcross and Beaumont (above, n. 97), p. 207.

[51] Para. 218.

[52] (1971) 6 E.T.L. 306, 318.

[53] *B.G.H. 14.7.83*, VersR 1984.134 (1985) 20 E.T.L. 95, 1986 U.L.R. II 596. *cf.* Muth/Glöckner, p. 169.

[54] Above, para. 102a.

courts in Austria,[55] France, Germany[56] and Switzerland. Belgium, however, may be joined by Holland,[57] and to the second group we can add Italy.[58] But in France it now appears that, whereas gross negligence in the form of *faute lourde* is still regarded as equivalent default, a stricter definition of *faute lourde* has been applied since 1985.[59]

> In *O.L.G. Munich 27.11.68*[60] damage was caused to peaches by the movement of the vehicle because a space had been left between the peaches and the rear door of the vehicle. Having pointed this out to an employee of the sender responsible for loading, the driver did nothing further about it when the employee simply shrugged his shoulders. The court held[61] that this was gross negligence (*grosse Fahrlässigkeit*) which, by virtue of Article 29, disentitled the carrier to rely on the defence in Article 17.4(c).

In Germany, the equation of gross negligence with equivalent default has been maintained,[62] on the grounds that the text of the CMR is ambiguous; that no uniform interpretation has been reached in decisions and commentaries; and that in these circumstances it is permissible to resort to the legislative history of the CMR.[63] The history shows that the draftsman had before him the CIM (1952) and the Warsaw Convention (1929), especially thc

---

[55] For example, *O.G.H. 10.10.74*, Greiter 37; *O.G.H. 25.4.84*, Stra GüV 1984/11, p. 12, Greiter 223; *O.G.H. 25.1.90*, TranspR 1990.235; *O.G.H. 11.7.1990*, TranspR 1992.322.

[56] *B.G.H. 14.7.83* (above, n. 53); *B.G.H. 16.2.84* (above, n. 49); *B.G.H. 27.6.85* (1986) 21 E.T.L. 102; *O.L.G. Hamburg 7.2.91*, TranspR 1991.294; *O.L.G. Düsseldorf 29.5.91*, TranspR 1991.291; *O.L.G. Nuremburg 22.3.95*, TranspR 1996.381. However, the writers are divided. Some writers, such as Helm, Art. 29 Anm. 2, who stress the relevance of national (German) law, being in favour and others, such as Muth/Glöckner, p. 169 and writers cited by Haak (pp. 248–249), who stress the importance of the legislative history of the CMR, being against the case law. For more recent surveys of the German literature, see Herber/Piper, Art. 29, 4; Koller, Art. 29, 3; and Thume, Art. 29, 10 *et seq.* However, the legislative history has been used by the courts to justify the broad view: for example, *B.G.H. 14.7.83* (1985) 20 E.T.L. 95, 1986 U.L.R. II 596.

[57] Haak, p. 245; Putzeys, para. 932.

[58] *Cass. It. 16.9.80*, 1980 U.L.R. II 341; *Cass. It. 29.3.85*, 1986 U.L.R. II 640. Pesce, pp. 236 *et seq.*

[59] Below, para. 102c.

[60] (1971) 6 E.T.L. 115. Another case of *die grosse Fahrlässigkeit* is the use of forged documents relating to the vehicle: *O.L.G. Munich 12.4.90*, TranspR 1990.280.

[61] At 125. *cf. O.L.G. Hamm 19.2.73* (1974) 9 E.T.L. 753, discussed below, para. 103b. Putzeys (para. 932) cites this decision to support the (narrow) Belgian position, *sed quaere.*

[62] *B.G.H. 14.7.83* (1985) 20 E.T.L. 95, 1986 U.L.R. II 596; *B.G.H. 16.2.84*, VersR 1984.551; *O.L.G. Düsseldorf 14.7.87*, VersR 1987.932; *O.L.G. Hamm 10.12.87*, 1987 U.L.R. II 713; *O.L.G. Düsseldorf 23.11.89*, TranspR 1990.63, 65. The equation is not without critics; see Koller, Art. 29, 3; Thume, Art. 29, 10 *et seq.*; Tuma (1993) 29 E.T.L. 649; Zapp, TranspR 1994.142.

[63] *B.G.H. 14.7.83* (1985) 20 E.T.L. 95, 1986 U.L.R. II 596.

latter, in which the corresponding provision in the German translation spoke of *die grosse Fahrlässigkeit*, and so, concluded the B.G.H.,[64] that must have been contemplated by the draftsman of the CMR as an instance of equivalent default.

102c. Equivalence in effect: *la faute lourde*

In 1983, the position in France was similar to that in Germany. Cases of negligence in the care of the goods[65] or at the wheel of the vehicle[66] could be *faute lourde*, in a sense that gave an extended meaning to default equivalent to wilful misconduct.

> In *Cass. 8.1.74*[67] the lorry turned over after striking the rear of another lorry travelling at 70 km/h in the same direction in the middle lane of a three-lane carriageway; the accident occurred at 23.30 hours with no other vehicle in the lane on either side. The entire cargo was destroyed. The decision of *Poitiers 19.4.72*[68] was that in these circumstances the driver was guilty of equivalent default (*faute lourde*). The carrier contended on appeal that the *lex fori*, French law, regarded wilful misconduct as *fraude* or *infidélité*, whereas what had occurred was not equivalent to this but something different. The Court of Cassation rejected the legal premise of the carrier's contention, holding[69] that the prescription period would be extended under Article 32.1.

---

[64] At 599–600, noting in particular that in the French version of the CMR (Art. 29) and the Warsaw Convention 1929 (Art. 25) the corresponding words (*faute . . . équivalente au dol*) are the same. Although the *travaux préparatoires* are in English as well as French, the CMR was negotiated largely in French.

[65] For example, *Paris 10.2.84*, B.T. 1984.558: computers, taken over without protest by the defendant carrier in a vehicle which, given the way that the computers had been stowed, was evidently unsuitable, were damaged. The court held that, as a professional, the carrier, who should have obtained a suitable vehicle or refused to transport the computers, committed *une faute lourde*. Again, stowage without dunnage was held to be *faute lourde* in *Paris 15.3.83*, B.T. 1983.305. Not all French decisions were so strict: for example, *cf. Paris 3.11.70* (1971) 6 E.T.L. 264. Since 1985, compare, for example, *Cass. 18.3.86*, B.T. 1986.336.

[66] In addition to *Cass. 8.1.74* (below, at n. 67), see *Cass. 22.9.83*, B.T. 1983.566 (driving too fast, so that goods were damaged by vibration, etc.).

[67] (1974) 9 E.T.L. 314. *idem* in another case of bad driving: *Versailles 29.2.96*, B.T.L. 1996.385. Other early examples of *faute lourde* including *Paris 18.12.68*, B.T. 1969.98 (neglecting to give a sub-carrier correct instructions about the destination of the goods); *Paris 21.6.75*, B.T. 1975.380; *Cass. 14.1.75*, B.T. 1975.81 (permitting the load to strike a bridge during the journey); *Paris 17.2.73*, B.T. 1973.134 (loss of customs documents, disappearance of the driver, taking much too long over the journey, leaving the cargo under a defective tarpaulin during snow, refusing to deliver between December 26 and January 3—each treated as *faute lourde*). Other early cases in France have been chronicled by Putzeys, para. 930.

[68] B.T. 1972.183.

[69] (1974) 9 E.T.L. 314.318.

However, in *Cass. 29.1.85*,[70] the court, while retaining the premise that equivalent misconduct included *faute lourde*, turned back to a stricter notion of *faute lourde*[71]: "une negligence d'une extrême gravité, confinant au dol et dénotant l'inaptitude du transporteur, maître de son action, à l'accomplissement de la mission contractuelle qu'il avait acceptée."[72] This formula has been repeated since[73] and, while the issue remains a question of fact, the French courts appear to have taken a step away from Germany in the direction of the position taken by the courts in Belgium.

103. Wilful misconduct in practice

To one degree or another, the courts in different countries require an awareness on the part of the carrier of the wrongfulness of the conduct in question or of the likely consequences to the goods. In this regard the specialist carrier is more severely judged[74] than others: "ce qui n'est qu'une erreur pour le profane peut devenir une faute pour le professionnel et faute lourde pour le spécialiste."[75] In assessing the attitude of the carrier and the carrier's awareness of the likely consequences of the acts or omissions, the court expects and assumes a professional level of knowledge and competence on the part of the carrier.[76]

103a. Prevention of theft

Disregard of the risk of theft may amount to wilful misconduct. In France, for example, it has been held to be *faute lourde* to

[70] B.T. 1985.345. *idem* in respect of carriage by sea: *Cass. 18.3.86*, B.T. 1986.336.
[71] Gouilloud, B.T. 1985.337. Whereas at one time almost any theft of a vehicle was treated as *faute lourde*, this has changed: note to *Cass. 5.1.88*, B.T. 1988.102, 103.
[72] *Cass. 17.12.51*, B.T. 1952.234.
[73] *Cass. 26.2.85*, B.T. 1985.270; *Cass. 5.1.88*, B.T. 1988.102; *Cass. 30.10.89*, DMF 1990.245: pending shipment, two valuable parcels were placed by the defendant *commissionnaire de transport* in an open spot near his office without surveillance, and were stolen. The court censured the decision of the Besançon court, that this was a case of *faute lourde*, by reaffirming the strict definition of the latter. A similar case is *Aix 15.11.95*, B.T.L. 1996.133. *Paris 28.6.91*, B.T.L. 1991.688: vehicle left unlocked at night at the side of the main road. This too was *faute lourde*. *idem* when the driver slept in the vehicle, when the goods (alcoholic drinks) were only covered by a tarpaulin: *Paris 8.4.94*, B.T.L. 1994.424. For a catalogue of such cases up to 1992, see Tilche, B.T.L. 1993.88.
[74] *Cass. 29.1.85*, B.T. 1985.345.
[75] Gouilloud, B.T. 1985.337. Of course, the same rising level of care is required by a common law court assessing an allegation of negligence: for example, *Whitehouse v. Jordan* [1981] 1 All E.R. 267, 277, *per* Lord Edmund-Davies H.L.
[76] *TC Paris 12.10.71*, Gaz. Pal. 1972.I.133, 1973 U.L.C. 268.

"deliver" goods by dumping them on the highway near the premises of the consignee[77]; and, when an enclosed and guarded parking place was available, to leave the vehicle and the goods without surveillance overnight in an exposed and public place, from which they were stolen.[78] Although these two decisions were reached in France prior to the emergence of a stricter test of *faute lourde*,[79] it appears that these cases would not be decided differently today. Indeed, a decision similar to the second French decision has been reached recently in England.[80] In Germany, it has been held[81] that a lone driver with a load of photographic equipment, who, at a time when the high risk of theft in Italy had been well publicised in the transport industry, spent the night in an unguarded park adjacent to an Italian motorway, committed equivalent default. It has also been held in Germany to be wilful misconduct to leave a load in an open unguarded place over the weekend, during which the load was vandalised.[82] The more attractive the goods, the more likely the court is to find against the carrier.[83]

By contrast, it is not a case of *faute lourde* to park a vehicle even without anti-theft devices in a *gare routière*, to which access is limited and which is generally thought to be safe, while the driver has lunch,[84] or, still less, to leave a vehicle, albeit unlocked with the keys inside, in the sender's yard for a few moments while the

---

[77] *Cambrai 12.9.78*, B.T. 1978.445. See also *Aix 15.11.95*, B.T.L. 1996.133.

[78] *Cass. 13.1.81* (1981) 16 E.T.L. 686: a locked but unguarded lorry with valuable goods was left in a Paris street overnight; *Cass. 14.12.81* (1983) 18 E.T.L. 51; goods of considerable value were left in the vehicle for three nights in the courtyard of a busy railway station, where, as the carrier knew or should have known, thefts had occurred in the past. *cf. Paris 3.7.92*, B.T.L. 1992.559: to park outside the driver's house, where theft was unlikely, while he ate supper was not *faute lourde*. If vehicles have been safe in a place in the past, courts are unlikely to decide against the carrier when theft occurs: *O.L.G. Cologne 4.7.95*, TranspR 1996.284.

[79] Above, para. 102c.

[80] *Texas Instruments Ltd v. Nasan (Europe) Ltd* [1991] 1 Lloyd's Rep. 146.

[81] *B.G.H. 14.7.83* (1985) 20 E.T.L. 95, 1986 U.L.R. II 596. See also *O.L.G. Düsseldorf 22.11.90*, TranspR 1991.59; and *B.G.H. 16.2.84*, VersR 1984.551: in 1979 a lone driver left his route to call on a friend in Milan and to have a meal. Within seven minutes of having been parked without surveillance after dark near the friend's house, the vehicle and its load of jeans was stolen. This was held to be a case of equivalent default. And in *O.G.H. 25.1.90*, TranspR 1990.235, when the vehicle and load, left in a street in Milan in the evening without surveillance or anti-theft device for 30 minutes, were stolen, this was held to be *grosse Fahrlässigkeit*. Yet another case of this kind is *O.L.G. Munich 12.5.89*, TranspR 1990.427. For more such cases in Germany see Thume, Art. 29, 29 *et seq. cf. O.L.G. Nuremburg 22.3.95*, TranspR 1996.381, in which the court found for the carrier *inter alia* because the claimant had failed to prove that there was a secure parking place which the (sole) driver could reach in time.

[82] *O.L.G. Munich 12.5.89*, TranspR 1990.427. FOr more cases in Germany see Thume, Art. 29, 29 *et seq. cf. O.L.G. Nuremberg 22.3.95*, TranspR 1996.381, in which the court found for the carrier *inter alia* because the claimant had failed to prove that there was a secured parking place which the (sole) driver could reach in time.

[83] For example, *Paris 8.4.94*, B.T.L. 1994.424 (alcoholic drinks); *O.L.G. Hamm 12.7.95*, TranspR 1996.237 (computers). *O.L.G. Hamm 10.12.87*, 1987 U.L.R. II 713 (arson).

[84] *Cass. 26.2.85*, B.T. 1985.270. See also *Cass. 5.1.88*, B.T. 1988.102; and *Paris 3.7.92*, B.T.L. 1992.559.

driver goes to the sender's office to collect some essential documents.[85] Careless supervision without more is neither wilful misconduct[86] nor equivalent default.[87] Much depends on the neighbourhood.[88]

103b. Defective packing, loading or stowage

Overloading in a manner both unsafe and contrary to law is a case of equivalent default, even in Belgium.[89] However, failure to check stowage or to prevent defective stowage by the sender, even if goods subsequently break loose and render the vehicle unstable, is not a case of equivalent default, even in Austria.[90] Equally, defective stowage adversely affecting the goods but not the safety of the vehicle, such as placing goods sensitive to heat in an unrefrigerated unit, will not be equivalent default, even in France as an instance of *faute lourde*,[91] unless the likelihood of damage is high. This is also true in Germany, where equivalent default has an extended meaning.[92]

> In *O.L.G. Hamm 19.2.73*[93] overloading and insufficient refrigeration led to damage to meat. The driver had closed the door on the meat by reversing the vehicle against a wall. Without mention of *die grosse Fahrlässigkeit* as such, the court said[94] that Article 29 did not apply because the driver was not aware that the damage was a possible consequence of his action and, given that the sender had the expertise and responsibility to ensure that the meat was loaded properly, the driver was entitled to assume that all was well.

103c. Road accidents

Under the Warsaw Convention there is wilful misconduct if there is a knowing violation of safety regulations, which is likely to

---

[85] *Cass. 25.6.85*, B.T. 1985.436. *cf. O.L.G. Düsseldorf 22.11.90*, TranspR 1991.59.
[86] *National Semiconductors (UK) Ltd v. UPS Ltd* [1996] 2 Lloyd's Rep. 212.
[87] *O.L.G. Stuttgart 15.9.1993*, TranspR. 1994.156, 158.
[88] *cf. O.L.G. Hamm. 12.7.95*, TranspR 1996.237. *O.L.G. Koblenz 13.2.96*. TranspR 1996.378.
[89] *Brussels 21.1.87* (1987) 22 E.T.L. 741. On the relatively narrow scope given to Art. 29 in Belgium, see above, para. 102a.
[90] *O.G.H. 21.3.77*, TranspR 1982.111, 1978 U.L.R. II 292, Greiter 50. See also *O.G.H. 17.2.82*, Greiter 127. On the relatively broad scope of equivalent default in Austria, see above, para. 102b.
[91] *Cass. 18.3.86*, B.T. 1986.336 (carriage by sea—film); see also *Cass. 13.10.81* (1982) 17 E.T.L. 288. *cf. Paris 27.5.86*, B.T. 1986.676: to place something large and heavy on top of something fragile is *une faute lourde*: see above, para. 102c.
[92] Above, para. 102b.
[93] (1974) 9 E.T.L. 753. See also *O.L.G. Munich 28.7.95*, TranspR 1996.240; but *cf. O.L.G. Munich 16.1.91*, TranspR 1992.181. For more such cases in Germany, see Thume, Art. 29, 28. See also in France: *Paris 3.11.70*, B.T. 1971.213, (1971) 6 E.T.L. 264, 1971 U.L.C. 144.
[94] At 759.

cause damage[95]; the same appears to be true of the CMR. For example, if a driver deliberately ignored a red traffic light in the belief that there would be no vehicles on the lateral road with priority, "he took a risk which he knew he ought not to take, and in those circumstances he could be rightly found to have committed an act of wilful misconduct".[96] The driver who has had too much (alcohol) to drink is guilty of equivalent default in Austria,[97] but it is not clear that an English court would regard this as wilful misconduct.[98] Although the point cannot be proven, many insurers believe that fatigue is a bigger "killer" on the roads than alcohol. In Germany, the driver who "nods off" at the wheel commits *die grosse Fahrlässigkeit*, if he knew or should have known that he was in need of sleep[99]; and in England the driver who has had too little rest and is responsible for an accident, when has driven in excess of the permitted period,[1] is guilty of wilful misconduct. Drunk or sober, tired or fresh, the driver who takes a bend much too fast commits *une faute particulièrement lourde* under French law.[2]

103d. Misdelivery

If the carrier delivers goods to the wrong person without making any inquiry to establish the true identity of the person to whom he delivers, this is likely to be characterised as wilful misconduct.[3]

---

[95] *American Airlines v. Ulen* 186 F. 2d 529 (D Col., 1949).

[96] This is the "red light" case cited in *Jones v. Bencher*, above, para. 101c.

[97] *O.G.H. 10.10.74*, Greiter 37.

[98] See *Beller v. Hayden* [1978] Q.B. 694, an insurance case in which a driver, with three times the permitted amount of alcohol in his bloodstream, was killed by accident, with the corollary that his conduct was not reckless: Clarke, *Insurance*, para. 17–5C and para. 17–5E3.

[99] *O.L.G. Karlsruhe 17.2.95*, TranspR 1995.439. For more such cases in Germany see Thume, Art. 29, 34.

[1] *Jones v. Bencher*, above, para. 101c.

[2] *Nancy 21.1.87*, B.T. 1987.344. So does the carrier whose vehicle hits the underside of a bridge: *Cass. com. 16.4.96*, B.T.L. 1996.334; and of the carrier who maintained too high an average speed on a route considered to be difficult, between Moscow and the Paris region: *Cass. 22.9.83*, B.T. 1983.566, criticised in a note by Brunat (*ibid.*) as being too strict. That the vehicle left the road on a bend is not without more sufficient evidence of *grosse Fahrlässigkeit: O.L.G. 15.9.93*. TranspR 1994.156.

[3] *Cass. 12.12.89* (1991) 26 E.T.L. 359. So held in *Hoare v. GWR* (1877) 37 L.T. 186, in which the contract for carriage by rail excluded the liability of the carrier, except for "wilful misconduct". The decision that the carrier had committed wilful misconduct is weakened by the view of Lord Coleridge C.J. (187) that wilful misconduct might include gross negligence. However, in *Hoare* the station master made no inquiry whatever of the person to whom he delivered the goods and it is submitted that such conduct would be wilful misconduct under the CMR. Although the doctrine of fundamental breach does not apply to CMR contracts (above, paras. 30a and 31), it is worth recalling that misdelivery, in the sense of delivery to a person who did not present the required documents, may be fundamental breach (*Sze Hai Tong Bank v. Rambler Cycle Co.* [1959] A.C. 576, P.C.), see below, para. 240. *Hoare* was applied to a CMR case in *Lacey's Footwear (Wholesale) Ltd v. Bowler Int. Freight Ltd* (1995, unreported).

The decision is likely to be the same if, in order to divert the vehicle to another job, the carrier dumps the goods in an exposed position.[3a] Delivery of valuable goods to the right consignee, but without obtaining the payment C.O.D. which the carrier knew he was required to obtain from the consignee, with consequent loss of lien on the goods, has been held to be a case of *faute lourde* in France,[4] and is likely to be held to be wilful misconduct in England.

B. OTHER REMEDIES

104. Termination of obligations in the case of breach

In the event of repudiation or serious breach of a contract of carriage governed by English common law, the innocent party may terminate the contract. More exactly, that party may terminate the primary obligations under the contract, while leaving in force secondary obligations relating, for example, to arbitration and compensation. Termination of contract is not mentioned by the CMR, but there is nothing to suggest that termination under national law was ruled out.[5]

105. Termination of obligations in the case of impossibility of performance

If the carrier has failed to complete performance of the contract of carriage as a result of "unavoidable circumstances", the carrier is "relieved of liability" by Article 17.2.[6] Equally, at common law, if the carrier is unable to perform the contract through causes beyond his control, impossibility of performance is a defence to an action on the contract.[7]

In most cases impossibility of performance has been provided for by Articles 14–16 of the CMR.[8] In particular, Article 15 deals with circumstances which "prevent delivery after their arrival at the place designated for delivery", and Article 14 deals with other cases in which it "becomes impossible to carry out the contract in

---

[3a] *Versailles 14.11.96*, B.T.L. 1997.198.

[4] *Aix 6.11.81*, B.T. 1982.258. The payment C.O.D. concerned carriage charges owed by the consignee to the sender/forwarder for that and previous transports. *cf.* also *O.G.H. 11.7.90*, TranspR 1992.322.

[5] See below, para. 249.

[6] Above, paras. 64 *et seq.*

[7] See below, para. 250.

[8] Above, paras. 33 *et seq.*

accordance with the terms laid down in the consignment note before the goods reach the place designated for delivery". The common law is left to deal with remaining cases, notably that in which the carrier is unable to take over the goods at all.[9]

106. The carrier's lien

Article 13.2 provides that, if the consignee requires delivery of the goods, he "shall pay the charges shown to be due on the consignment note, but in the event of dispute on this matter the carrier shall not be required to deliver the goods unless security has been furnished by the carrier". Subject to this,[10] the CMR is silent on rights of retention available to the carrier and any such rights under national law will remain effective.[11] The appropriate national law may be the law governing the contract of carriage[12] or the *lex rei sitae*.[13]

The existence of any lien depends on the carrier's retention of possession of the goods. Further, in the case of charges due in respect of CMR carriage, it has been argued[14] that the lien is effective only in respect of the charges stated in the consignment note.

107. Action for carriage charges

An action in debt lies at the suit of the carrier in respect of carriage charges against the person with whom the contract of carriage was concluded.[15] Action lies only in respect of charges due, so, in the case of charges due on delivery, the carrier must have carried out the carriage and delivered the goods or, at least, have been ready and willing to deliver them.[16] Unless stipulated by the contract of carriage, the carrier is not entitled to carriage charges *pro rata*

---

[9] Above, para. 64.

[10] *cf.* Loewe, para. 140 *à propos* Art. 16.2: "CMR does not purport to regulate any right the carrier may have as creditor to detain the goods carried."

[11] For a survey of the relevant law in England, Belgium, Denmark, France, Germany, Holland, Norway, Spain and Sweden, see Claringbould, Theunis, Chap. 14.

[12] If the question is characterised as one of bailment, this is the rule in England: *Kahler v. Midland Bank* [1950] A.C. 24. But it has been widely criticised, for example, as the decision of a court "mesmerised by the presence of some contractual relationship into disregarding the special quality of a concurrent . . . bailment": Palmer, p. 59.

[13] This is the rule, for example, in Holland: Claringbould (above, n. 11), para. 1.1. And in practice it is the rule under the Restatement, Conflict of Laws 2d, section 251. For English law, see below, para. 251.

[14] Claringbould (above, n. 11), para. 2.2, with reference to Art. 13.

[15] *Paris 8.11.95*, B.T.L. 1996.132.

[16] *Paris 21.12.82*, B.T. 1983.233.

itineris.[17] If the consignee repudiates the contract before the carrier has completed performance, the carrier may nonetheless have a legitimate interest in completing the carriage, if that is a condition of a lien or other security on the goods and on completion the carrier may tender the goods and become entitled to the full amount of the carriage charges.

108. Restitution of goods delayed

Article 20.1 provides that after a certain delay, "the person entitled to make a claim" may treat the goods as lost,[18] an election which generally increases the amount of compensation recoverable from the carrier. In many cases, that person would still like to have the goods if they should eventually arrive in satisfactory condition. The provision is intended to resolve uncertainty,[19] but certainty is not promoted by a rule which encourages the claimant to wait and see, so the claimant who would like the goods can revoke his election and the carrier is warned that this may become a serious possibility by the claimant's request for notification, required by Article 20.2, without which the claimant has no right to restitution[20]:

> "The person so entitled may, on receipt of compensation for the missing goods, request in writing that he shall be notified immediately should the goods be recovered in the course of the year following the payment of compensation. He shall be given a written acknowledgment of such request."

If the carrier fails to give notification, the consequences are not covered by the CMR but left to national law.[21] English law is likely to see the carrier's failure as a breach of a secondary obligation of the contract of carriage, an obligation imposed by Article 20.[22] Alternatively, and subject to the effect of the *lex situs* on property rights in the goods, the claimant might bring an action against the carrier for the tort of conversion.[23]

Article 20.3 provides:

> "Within 30 days following receipt of such notification, the person entitled as aforesaid may require the goods to be delivered to him

[17] A similar decision has been reached in France as regards CMR carriage, at least when the part performance of the contract by the carrier was of no use to the sender, from whom the carrier sought unsuccessfully to recover carriage charges: *Grenoble 4.2.88*, B.T. 1988.700.
[18] Above, para. 56b.
[19] Helm, Art. 20 Anm. 1.
[20] Helm, Art. 20 Anm. 3.
[21] Loewe, para. 180.
[22] See Art. 20.4, set out in the text below.
[23] See below, para. 231.

> against payment of charges shown to be due on the consignment note and also against refund of the compensation he received less any charges included therein but without prejudice to any claims to compensation for delay in delivery under article 23 and, where applicable, article 26."

Refund of compensation "less any charges included therein" refers to an element in compensation, payable under Article 23.4, for carriage charges and customs duties incurred by a claimant. To the extent that this loss to the claimant is not wiped out by restitution of the goods, the claimant retains this element of the compensation. The corollary is also found in paragraph 3, that on restitution the claimant must pay "the charges shown to be due on the consignment note".

Restitution "without prejudice" to certain claims accommodates the claimant, who may desire to have the dates but is still left with loss, loss of business claimed under Article 23 or special interest loss claimed under Article 26, sustained because the goods were not delivered on time according to the contract.

Finally, Article 20.4 provides:

> "In the absence of the request mentioned in paragraph 2 or of any instructions given within the period of thirty days specified in paragraph 3, or if the goods are not recovered until more than one year after the payment of compensation, the carrier shall be entitled to deal with them in accordance with the law of the place where the goods are situated."

[THE NEXT PARAGRAPH IS PARAGRAPH 201.]

PART II

ENGLISH DOMESTIC LAW

CHAPTER 9

THE CONTRACT OF CARRIAGE

201. Prologue

A contract for the carriage of goods by road entirely within the United Kingdom is governed by national law, *i.e.* the common law of England or Scotland, as the case may be. There appears to be no significant difference in the law as it applies to contracts for the carriage of goods by road and in this book any reference to English law is also a reference to the law of Scotland.

202. Formation of the contract

In English law, contracts are based on the agreement of the parties.[1] A point is reached in the dealings between the parties when each is ready to commit himself contractually to the other, the one to carry the goods and the other to pay. It is the customary view that the moment an acceptance is made by one party of an offer of contract made by the other party, a contract is formed; if negotiations have been protracted, it may be quite arbitrary which party is seen as the offeror and which party is seen as the offeree.

Most contracts to carry goods are formed quite simply. For example, a customer who may be either the sender or the consignee of the goods, having learned of the service advertised by a particular carrier, approaches that carrier and requests a copy of the carrier's consignment note.

(a) Neither the advertisement nor the issue of the note amounts to an offer of contract by the carrier: it makes no sense that the carrier should wish to be bound contractually to every customer who "accepts the offer" by requesting a consignment note. It would take the carrier too long to withdraw the "offer" in the advertisement, should the carrier wish to do so in the light of changed trading conditions, so that the carrier would be bound by unwanted trade; in particular,

---

[1] Generally, see Treitel, Chap. 2; Walker, Chap. 7.

the carrier could not ensure that the number of customers who "accepted the offer" and concluded contracts matched the carrier's capacity to carry the goods.[2]

(b) When the customer completes the consignment note and brings or sends it to the carrier, this action usually amounts to an offer to contract, an offer which the carrier may accept or reject. It is not an offer, however, if it is incomplete: such an "offer" lacks the certainty necessary for it to be the basis of a contract. The offer must contain, expressly or by implication, the essential components of the kind of contract in question. There must, for example, be a reference to the kind and quantity of goods and to the destination: it makes no sense that a carrier should agree to carry "something somewhere". However, certain important questions may be taken to have been settled implicitly, for example, freight by reference to standard rates.[3]

(c) The carrier may accept the customer's offer expressly by letter or other form of communication or by some other act indicating acceptance, for example, by collecting or receiving the goods in question. A contract will have been formed when the letter has been put in the course of transmission, so as to be beyond the control of the acceptor[4]: or when the telex or fax is sent and received[5]; or when the carrier's other act of acceptance comes to the attention of the offeror customer.[6] If the goods and the consignment note are sent together to the carrier, this action remains an offer requiring acceptance by the carrier; however, as communication of acceptance is usually required for the benefit of the offeror customer, the customer, being more interested in action than words, may be taken to have waived the requirement of formal acceptance; in such circumstances any unequivocal act of acceptance, such as loading the goods on a trailer going to the required destination, would suffice to conclude a contract, even though the offeror customer were unaware of the carrier's act.

(d) The customer may revoke the offer at any time before it has been accepted by the carrier, but revocation is not effective until it has been received by the carrier.[7]

(e) For the purposes of acceptance by telex or by fax (above, (c)), or revocation of offer (above, (d)), receipt occurs when the communication reaches the appropriate (business) address. What happens beyond the recipient's machine is, as

---

[2] *Grainger & Sons v. Gough* [1896] A.C. 325.
[3] *Foley v. Classique Coaches* [1934] 2 K.B. 1, C.A.
[4] *Henthorn v. Fraser* [1892] Ch. 27, C.A.
[5] *Entores v. Miles Far East Corp.* [1955] 2 Q.B. 327, C.A.
[6] *Brinkibon v. Stahag Stahl* [1983] 2 A.C. 34.
[7] *Byrne v. Van Tienhoven* (1880) 5 C.P.D. 344.

> a matter of risk allocation[8] and risk avoidance, the responsibility of the recipient. The corollary is that receipt has occurred although it may not have come to the attention of the relevant executive.[9] By leaving a machine on to receive messages, the recipient represents that any message transmitted to the machine during business hours will be dealt with properly.[10] However, receipt in law will occur later than receipt on the machine, if to the knowledge of the sender of the message it cannot be dealt with immediately on arrival, for example, because it is outside business hours: receipt in law does not occur until business opens in the normal way.[11]

In the case of groupage the customer usually contacts the carrier by telex, fax, email or telephone and follows this with written confirmation. The customer's instructions are then recorded on a shipping instruction form and, if there is one, on the computer for the carrier's internal use. A regular customer may have a stock of shipping instruction forms, one of which is completed in respect of a given consignment and sent to the carrier. If the instructions appear acceptable, they are acknowledged, thus accepting the customer's offer to contract, and this is often done by the carrier's transport manager who knows, for example, the available capacity and whether any particular time stipulation required by the customer can be met. The goods are either brought to the carrier's groupage point by a feeder service or collected at the sender's place of business by the trailer on which they will make the journey contracted for. Meanwhile, the details about goods on any trailer with goods belonging to a number of different customers are recorded on a manifest, the contents of which are telexed or faxed to the carrier's agent at the place of destination. The customer receives a certificate of shipment in respect of his part of the load. When the goods arrive, the carrier's agent sends a delivery note to the consignee named on the manifest who collects the goods against production of the note.

---

[8] *Brinkibon*, above, n. 6 at 42, *per* Lord Wilberforce.

[9] *cf. Henthorn*, above, n. 4 at 32, *per* Herschell L.J.

[10] *The Brimnes* [1975] Q.B. 929, at 966–967, *per* Megaw L.J., C.A.; *The Pamela* [1995] 2 Lloyd's Rep. 249. Haslam (1996) 146 N.L.J. 549. *The Brimnes* concerned a charterparty, Megaw L.J. accepted the argument that, by leaving a telex machine on in his office, the recipient "in effect represented that any message so transmitted to them during business hours would be dealt with properly". Or, as Russell L.J. put it in *Holwell Securities v. Hughes* [1974] 1 All E.R. 161, 164, C.A., the recipient "had impliedly invited communication by use of an orifice in his front door designed to receive communications". See also *Nissho Iwai Petroleum Co. Inc. v. Cargill Int. S.A.* [1993] 1 Lloyd's Rep. 80. The reasons are: (a) the recipient controls lines of communication and can better avoid risks within his own office; and (b) this rule avoids a paper trail inside that office, with attendant uncertainty and, perhaps, an impossible burden of proof for the sender.

[11] *The Brimnes* (above).

203. The terms of the contract: notice

The terms of the contract of carriage are those agreed by the parties. Usually the terms are those of the carrier, such as the Securicor Conditions, or those adopted by the carrier, such as the Road Haulage Association Ltd's Conditions of Carriage (RHA terms).[12] The terms are nonetheless part of the contract of carriage in two situations.

First, the terms are part of the contract if the customer has signed a document containing the terms,[13] unless at the time the customer had no reason to believe that the document had contractual significance.[14] Normally, however, people can be expected to read what they sign and the exception only arises when there was something about the document or the circumstances of signature to mislead the signatory about the nature of the document.

Secondly, the terms are part of the contract of carriage, if the customer has sufficient notice of the terms. The customer has sufficient notice or, as is generally thought to be the same, reasonable notice of the terms[15] given before or at the time that the contract of carriage was concluded.[16] Sufficient notice means not that the customer has read the terms or knows what they say[17] but that the customer is or should be aware that the terms exist and that the carrier intends those terms to apply to the contract of carriage.[18]

> In the *Poseidon* case[19] the parties to the litigation had done business with each other before the occasion in dispute, but business of more than one kind. When, in the course of the disputed transaction, one party received a document referring to the other's standard terms for carriage and forwarding the goods of customers,[20] that party was entitled to assume that, because the transaction in question was not of that kind at all (but one of agency for the other in the other's business with customers), the terms referred to were not intended to apply in that particular transaction.

Sufficient notice of the existence of terms that the other intends to apply may be actual or constructive. Whether or not they have

[12] See Appendix E.
[13] *Harris v. GWR* (1876) 1 Q.B.D. 515.
[14] *Grogan v. Robin Meredith Plant Hire*, *The Times*, February 20, 1996, C.A., discussed by MacMillan [1996] C.L.J. 427.
[15] *Circle Freight*, below, n. 17 at 430, *per* Taylor L.J. Clarke [1976] C.L.J. 51. Treitel, pp. 198 *et seq*. Walker, Chap. 21.
[16] *Olley v. Marlborough Court Hotel* [1949] 1 K.B. 532, C.A. See also *Grogan* (above).
[17] *Circle Freight International v. Medeast Gulf Exports* [1988] 2 Lloyd's Rep. 427, C.A.
[18] *Parker v. S.E. Ry* (1877) 2 C.P.D. 416, C.A.
[19] *Poseidon Freight Forwarding Co. Ltd v. Davies Turner Southern Ltd* [1996] 2 Lloyd's Rep. 388.
[20] These were the well-known British International Freight Association Standard Trading Conditions (BIFA terms) (reproduced in Appendix D).

actual knowledge that such terms exist, those who contract with carriers by road will be held to have constructive notice of the existence of the terms, either as a matter of general commercial knowledge[21] or, in appropriate cases, as a result of past dealings with the carrier concerned.[22] If, however, terms are to apply on the basis of past dealings, those dealings must have been consistent.[23] It would not be enough to show that a reference to the terms had been made on some occasions if no such reference has been made on other similar occasions.[24]

> In *Circle Freight International v. Medeast Gulf Exports*[25] freight forwarders claimed monies due, and the defendant pleaded the theft of their goods (dresses) from a van left unattended by the claimants' driver in central London. In reply, the claimants, while conceding that the driver had been negligent, pleaded a clause in their contract taken from well-known standard conditions. Under the clause the forwarders were not liable for loss caused by negligence, unless due to wilful default. The parties had contracted on at least 11 occasions in the past, and had done so by telephone. After each contract had been performed by the claimants, an invoice was sent by them to the defendants. In small print at the bottom of the invoice was a reference to the standard conditions. In addition, the defendants had been told by letter that the claimants traded under those conditions, but had not requested a copy of the conditions or been sent one. The court of first instance ruled that the conditions were not part of the contract with the defendants, but this decision was reversed by the Court of Appeal.

As Taylor L.J. observed in that case,[26] "It is sufficient if adequate notice is given identifying and relying upon the conditions and they are available on request. Other considerations apply if the conditions or any of them are particularly onerous or unusual." So, it is submitted, that persons in business, who contract with carriers by road, will be taken to know that carriers have terms in

---

[21] *British Crane Hire Corp. v. Ipswich Plant Hire* [1975] Q.B. 303, C.A., a case concerning the standard terms of plant hire, which was applied to a CMR contract in *Eastern Kayam Carpets v. Eastern United Freight* (High Court, December 6, 1983, unreported). See also *Keeton & Sons Ltd v. Carl Prior Ltd* [1985] B.T.L.C. 30, C.A. *cf.*, however, the *Grogan* case (above n. 14).

[22] *Henry Kendall & Sons v. William Lillico & Sons* [1969] 2 A.C. 31. Swanton (1989) 1 J.C.L. 223. See also *Eastman Chemical International AG v. NMT Trading* [1972] 2 Lloyd's Rep. 25; and *William Teacher & Sons Ltd v. Bell Lines Ltd* 1991 S.L.T. 876. A similar rule was applied by the Supreme Court of Denmark to carriage by road and rail from Struer (Denmark) to Gloucester (U.K.) in its decision of April 28, 1989, (1989) 24 E.T.L. 345.

[23] *McCutcheon v. David MacBrayne Ltd* [1964] 1 W.L.R. 125, H.L.; *SIAT di del Ferro v. Tradex Overseas S.A.* [1978] 2 Lloyd's Rep. 470.

[24] *Poseidon Freight Forwarding Co. Ltd v. Davies Turner Southern Ltd* [1996] 2 Lloyd's Rep. 388, 392 *per* Leggatt L.J., C.A.

[25] [1988] 2 Lloyd's Rep. 427, C.A. See also *Keeton & Sons Ltd v. Carl Prior Ltd* [1985] B.T.L.C. 30, C.A.

[26] At 433; quoted with approval by Leggatt L.J. in *Poseidon* (above) at 392.

their contracts, and will be bound by them subject, however, to the following exceptions.

First, the terms will not be binding if they are not accessible: available on request[27] and in time for the customer to decide how to respond to the terms, for example, whether to seek an alternative carrier or to take precautions, such as extra insurance.[28]

> In the *Poseidon* case[29] one party sent to the other a document stating: "NOTE: The only conditions on which we transact business are shown on the back." However, the document had been faxed so that there was nothing on the back; nor were conditions sent subsequently and before contract. These circumstances were enough to confirm the conclusion drawn by the Court of Appeal from other features of the case that the terms were not intended to apply.[30] Even if the sender of the document had intended the conditions to apply, the notice of them would have been insufficient—in the absence of previous dealings on those conditions or some other way in which the recipient could reasonably be expected to discover what the conditions actually contained. This was in contrast with the earlier case of *Keeton*[31] in which the other party's attention was drawn to the conditions of which a copy could be obtained from the carrier on request. In *Keeton* that was notice enough.

If, indeed, copies of the terms are accessible, the copy must be legible[32] and, although at common law the conditions do not have to be intelligible to a person untrained in the law,[33] there is some suggestion that, if "the draughtsmanship is so convoluted and prolix that one almost needs an LL.B. to understand them",[34] the conditions will be unreasonable under the Unfair Contract Terms Act 1977.[35] However, if the contract is concluded in England, the carrier is entitled to assume that the customer understands English,[36] and it will suffice that the available copy of the terms is in English, unless perhaps the carrier is aware that the customer is unable to read English and it is reasonably practicable to make a translation available.[37]

---

[27] *Circle Freight*, above, n. 17 and *William Teacher & Sons Ltd v. Bell Lines Ltd* 1991 S.L.T. 876.

[28] *Mertens v. Flying Tiger Lines* 1965 US Av.R. 1.

[29] Above.

[30] At 394 *per* Leggatt L.J.

[31] *Keeton & Sons Ltd v. Carl Prior Ltd* [1985] B.T.L.C. 30, C.A.

[32] *Chellaram & Co. v. China Ocean Shipping Co.* [1989] 1 Lloyd's Rep. 413, S.C. N.S.W.

[33] *Derby Cables v. Frederick Oldridge* [1959] 2 Lloyd's Rep. 140, 149, *per* Winn J.

[34] *The Zinnia* [1984] 2 Lloyd's Rep. 211, 222, *per* Staughton J.

[35] *ibid.* On the Act, see below, para. 239a.

[36] *Geier v. Kujawa* [1970] 1 Lloyd's Rep. 364.

[37] Treitel, p. 199. Certainly, if a translation of some conditions is tendered, there is a presumption that those are the only conditions of the contract: *H. Glynn (Covent Garden) v. Wittleder* [1959] 2 Lloyd's Rep. 409, 420, *per* Pearson J.: this is an illustration of the third exception, misleading presentation, discussed below.

Secondly, a term will not be binding if the content of the term is unusual, unless it has been specifically drawn to the attention of the customer.[38]

Thirdly, a term will not be binding in the sense in which it is actually written if the carrier misrepresents the nature or content of the term. In these circumstances, the term will be taken to be or to mean what the customer reasonably understood it to be or to mean.[39]

204. Documentation

No particular form is required of the contract of carriage by English law—not even writing. In practice, parties commonly contract with reference to written standard forms of condition such as the Road Haulage Association Ltd's Conditions of Carriage 1991[40] or the Securicor Conditions.[41]

205. Interpretation of the contract

When interpreting a contract, the court's overriding objective is said to be to find the intention of the parties. To this end, the courts apply the same rules to all kinds of commercial contract which, in summary, are applied to contracts for the carriage of goods as follows.

First and foremost, words are to be understood in their ordinary sense. To establish the ordinary sense the court starts with the dictionary meaning of the word. For example, a "deficiency of manpower" is likely to be interpreted in the (normal) numerical sense rather than a qualitative sense, and thus refer to a staff shortage.[42] However, words are not to be understood in isolation but in context—the context of the contract. For example, what "inherent vice" might mean in a tabloid newspaper is likely to be rather different from its meaning in a contract of carriage.[43] Again, "premises" "is an ordinary word of the English language which takes colour and content from the context in which it is

---

[38] *Thornton v. Shoe Lane Parking* [1971] 2 Q.B. 163, C.A.; *Interfoto Picture Library v. Stiletto Visual Programmes* [1989] Q.B. 433, C.A. For the Act, see below, para. 239a.

[39] *Glynn v. Wittleder*, above, n. 37; *Curtis v. Chemical Cleaning & Dyeing Co.* [1951] 1 K.B. 805, C.A. Clarke, "The Reasonable Expectations of the Insured—In England?", [1989] J.B.L. 389; Carter, *Unequal Bargaining* (Oxford, 1991), p. 44.

[40] See Appendix E. For commentary on these conditions, see Palmer, pp. 1094 *et seq.*; and Yates, para. 3.2.1.

[41] See Palmer, *loc. cit.*

[42] *Royal Greek Govt v. Min. of Transport* [1949] 1 K.B. 7. See also *Barnett & Block v. National Parcels Ins. Co. Ltd* (1942) 73 Ll.L.Rep. 17, C.A. ("garage").

[43] See below, para. 236h.

used".[44] To read words in context the court has aids to interpretation, aids of such long tradition that they have Latin labels:

(a) If particular words have a generic character, more general following words are construed as having the same character (*ejusdem generis*). For example, in the words "strikes, lock-outs, civil commotions, or any other causes or accidents beyond the control of the carrier", the other causes would include intentionally obstructive human conduct but not the situation in which there was a shortage of labour caused by an epidemic.[45]

(b) The express mention of one thing may imply the exclusion of another related thing (*expressio unius est exclusio alterius*). For example, if one clause of a contract is described as a "condition" and another clause is not, the legal effect generally given to conditions by the law of contract will be given to the first clause but not the second.

Secondly, in the event of inconsistency in the ordinary meaning of words in different parts of the contract, respect for the likely intention of the parties gives primacy to that part to which the partics gave actual attention.

Thirdly, if it appears that the words have been used in a special sense, either (a) as previously defined by the courts or (b) the sense used in a particular commercial context, the words will be interpreted in that special sense. An example of (a) is the curious definition of "riot".[46] An example of (b) might be a local custom concerning the manner or place of delivery.[47]

Fourthly, if the court is unable to find the meaning with the first three rules and the words still appear to be ambiguous, (a) the words will be read with reference to any evidence of the purpose of the contract extrinsic to the contract itself; and (b) the words will be construed *contra proferentem*, that is, against the carrier and liberally in favour of the customer. An example of (a) is the construction of "locked" in the light of contractual concern that

---

[44] *Maunsell v. Olins* [1975] A.C. 373, 383 *per* Viscount Dilhorne, applied in *Mint Security Ltd v. Blair* [1982] 1 Lloyd's Rep. 188. See also *Laurence v. Davies* [1972] 2 Lloyd's Rep. 231 that in the context of the Road Traffic Acts "motor car" includes a van.

[45] See *Mudie v. Strick* (1909) 14 Com. Cas. 135.

[46] Below, para. 236f.

[47] See *Aktieselkab Helios v. Ekman & Co.* [1897] 2 Q.B. 83, C.A. Also there is a presumption that words such as "theft" are used in the sense established by the criminal law: *Grundy (Teddington) Ltd v. Fulton* [1981] 2 Lloyd's Rep. 266, affirmed [1983] 1 Lloyd's Rep. 16, C.A. But the presumption is weaker in respect of the terminology of the civil law: *De Maurier (Jewels) Ltd v. Bastion Ins. Co. Ltd* [1967] 2 Lloyd's Rep. 550 that goods "owned" included goods held on hire-purchase.

the security of valuable goods be enhanced.[48] An example of (b) is a printed exclusion of the carrier's liability for the consequences of "unavoidable delay"; this will be limited to delay in the course of the carriage contracted for but not apply to the knock-on effect of delay on availability of the vehicle arising out of something that occurred during a previous carriage.[49]

Fifthly, if the court is able to find a meaning with the first three rules but one that is so very unreasonable or inconvenient as to be absurd, that meaning will be disregarded and another more sensible meaning will be sought. For example, a clause will not be construed in such a way as to require the carrier to commit a breach of the law.[50]

---

[48] *De Maurier* (above). See also *Leo. Rapp Ltd v. McClure* [1955] 1 Lloyd's Rep. 292 ("warehouse"); and *Lowenstein & Co. Ltd v. Poplar Motor Transport (Lymm) Ltd* [1968] 2 Lloyd's Rep. 233 in which, to decide whether a contractual duty "could not be complied with", the court took into account the practices of the road haulage industry.

[49] See, *e.g. The Helvetia-S* [1960] 1 Lloyd's Rep. 540.

[50] *J. Lowenstein & Co. Ltd v. Poplar Motor Transport (Lymm) Ltd* [1968] 2 Lloyd's Rep. 233. Generally, see *Wickman Machine Tool Sales Ltd v. Schuler A.G.* [1974] A.C. 235, 251, *per* Lord Reid.

Chapter 10

THE JOURNEY

206. Taking over the goods

The carriers' obligations as carrier have to be performed mainly during the journey; in other words, they begin and end with transit. Courts generally infer that transit begins when carriers get the custody and control of the goods[1]; it is at this point that the nature of the operation and the nature of the risk affecting goods change[2]; hence, it is submitted, there is a conscious alignment of transit in the sense of the carrier's period of responsibility as carrier and transit in the sense understood in transit insurance cover. Moreover, the inference drawn by the courts appears also to be that intended by RHA Condition 6(1) which provides that transit shall commence when the carrier "takes possession" of the goods. Thus goods which have been loaded on the vehicle, but remain in the control of the sender, have not commenced transit[3]; but goods which have yet to be loaded (probably by the carrier) but have been handed over to the carrier pending loading, have commenced transit. An exception arises when, although custody and control have passed to a carrier, the goods have been sent on the wrong journey[4] or on the wrong vehicle[5]: the cover contracted for has not commenced. Equally, the journey contracted for has not commenced and, although the carrier is responsible for the goods *qua* carrier, a court will be slow to hold that the carrier's terms and conditions apply.[6]

207. Loading

The party obliged to load (or unload) the goods is a matter for agreement between the parties to the contract of carriage. Carriers

---

[1] *Crow's Transport Ltd v. Phoenix Assurance Co. Ltd* [1965] 1 Lloyd's Rep. 139, 143, *per* Lord Denning M.R., C.A.; *S.C.A. (Freight) Ltd v. Gibson* [1974] 2 Lloyd's Rep. 533, 534, *per* Ackner J.

[2] *Re Traders & General Ins. Assoc. Ltd* (1924) 18 Ll.L.Rep. 450, 451, *per* Eve J.

[3] *e.g.* locked in his warehouse: *Kessler Export Corp. v. Reliance Ins. Co.*, 207 F. Supp. 355 (E.D. N.Y. 1962).

[4] *Israel & Co. v. Sedgwick* [1893] 1 Q.B. 303, C.A.; *Kallis (Manufacturers) Ltd v. Success Ins. Ltd* [1985] 2 Lloyd's Rep. 8, P.C.

[5] *Kallis* (above).

[6] See below, para. 240.

are not obliged to provide any special equipment for loading (or unloading) unless they have agreed to do so, and usually the contract provides that that is the duty of the customer; see, for example, RHA Condition 4(1)(b). If the customer fails to provide it in breach of contract but instructs the carrier to load (or unload) nonetheless, it is commonly provided by the contract that the carrier shall not be liable for any damage howsoever caused[7]; see, for example, RHA Condition 4(1)(c).

208. Sub-contracting

The contract of carriage may contain a term permitting the carrier to sub-contract the whole or part of the journey. If not, permission will usually be implied, unless the terms of the contract forbid it or the nature of the contract suggests otherwise.[8] The nature of the contract suggests otherwise, when the personal care, skill or integrity of the contracting carrier are of the essence of the contract, for example, in the case of difficult or vulnerable goods.

> In *Garnham, Harris & Elton v. Alfred Ellis (Transport)*[9] the contract was to carry copper wire, then worth nearly £4,000, from London to Glasgow. The carrier entrusted the carriage to a third party who made off with the wire; sub-contracting was neither allowed nor forbidden by the express terms of the contract of carriage. Paull J. said[10]: "Normally, undoubtedly, I should hold that a contract of carriage may be sub-contracted." But he went on[10a]: "This load was, to the knowledge of both parties the 'gold of thieves', in other words, the sort of cargo that every gang of lorry thieves . . . will strive with every nerve to steal." In these circumstances he held that the carrier had committed a fundamental breach of the contract of carriage; breach lay, not in sub-contracting to a person about whom too little was known, but in sub-contracting at all.

---

[7] Concerning these words, see below, para. 238a.

[8] See RHA Condition 2. Generally, see Treitel, pp. 671 *et seq*. Walker, para. 31.10.
cf. Edwards v. Newland & Co. [1950] 2 K.B. 534, C.A.: the person who undertakes to store furniture cannot delegate for his personal skill and care are of the essence of the contract.

[9] [1967] 2 All E.R. 940.
cf. John Carter (Fine Worsteds) v. Hanson Haulage (Leeds) [1965], 2 Q.B. 495, C.A., in which it was held that to employ a driver without requiring references or making inquiries, a driver who then stole a load of worsted suiting, was an act of negligence on the part of the employer but did not amount to a fundamental breach, as understood in 1964, prior to the decision of the House of Lords in the *Suisse Atlantique* case [1967] 1 A.C. 361; and see also *Gillette Industries Ltd v. W.H. Martin Ltd* [1966] 1 Lloyd's Rep. 57, C.A.

[10] [1967] 2 All E.R. 940, 944.

[10a] *ibid.*

When sub-contracting is allowed, both common law and the implied duty of reasonable care under section 13 of the Supply of Goods and Services Act 1982 combine to require the carrier to exercise reasonable care in the selection of a competent and trustworthy sub-contractor.[11] Moreover, arguably section 13 requires care in the work itself so that, if the sub-contractor is negligent, the carrier is liable for that negligence; in other words, the carrier can delegate performance but not responsibility.[12]

209. The vehicle

Prima facie, it is for the carrier to choose a vehicle which will get the contract goods to destination in the same good order and condition in which the goods were received. The choice of vehicle and ancillary equipment is influenced by the needs of the particular cargo, a matter of which the sender usually has more knowledge than the carrier, although rarely to a degree that relieves the carrier of all responsibility in the matter. Sensible parties will get together prior to the carriage and agree what is required, but this does not always happen. Disputes about the suitability of vehicle and equipment arise. The questions that may have to be asked are as follows.

First, is there any express term of the contract of carriage governing the type of vehicle or special equipment to be used? Secondly, is there any implied term of the contract of carriage governing the type of vehicle or special equipment to be used? No such term will be implied by an English court, unless it satisfies the strict common law rule about the implication of terms: the implication must be necessary to give business efficacy to the contract[13]; or it can be inferred from the implied duty in section 13 of the Supply of Goods and Services Act 1982 that, to exercise the service of carriage with reasonable care and skill, means that the carrier must use a vehicle which, in the light of what the carrier knows about the goods and the journey, is suitable. If it is clear that sensitive goods (for example, mushrooms) are to be carried at a specified (low) temperature, it can be inferred that the carrier must ensure that the vehicle used by him is capable of the task in hand.[14]

In maritime law there is an implied (and absolute) warranty that the ship is seaworthy, including a warranty that the ship is fit to

---

[11] *Metaalhandel J.A. Magnus B.V. v. Ardfields Transport Ltd* [1988] 1 Lloyd's Rep. 197.

[12] See *Metaalhandel* (above); and Palmer, pp. 902 and 995.

[13] *Liverpool C.C. v. Irwin* [1977] A.C. 239; *Scally v. Southern Health and Social Security Board* [1992] 1 A.C. 294. Phang [1993] J.B.L. 242. Treitel, pp. 185 *et seq. cf.* Walker, para. 22.6.

[14] *O.L.G. Nuremburg 14.6.65* (1971) 6 E.T.L. 247, 262. On this, however, see discussion of the third question (below).

receive the particular cargo. An equivalent warranty will be implied as to roadworthiness in a contract to carry goods by road, but it differs[15] chiefly in that the road warranty is not absolute.[16] "Such a contract at common law requires that a carrier should take reasonable care to provide a vehicle suitable for the carriage in contemplation and that it should be driven by a person, not only fully competent to drive, but also honest and to whom the goods could be properly entrusted."[17]

209a. Transhipment

Transhipment from one road vehicle to another road vehicle for the operational convenience of the carrier is allowed, unless it is prohibited expressly or implicitly by the terms of the contract. Transhipment from vehicle A to similar vehicle B, because vehicle A has broken down, is likely to be allowed. Transhipment from vehicle A to a fleet of rickshaws, because the carrier wants vehicle A for another job, is not.

Cases of unauthorised transhipment include that of perishable goods sent by a slow vehicle when the contract required a fast one[18]; and that of storage in place A when the contract required place B.[19] Transhipment of this kind has been treated as a case of "quasi-deviation" or "fundamental breach". In a case of unauthorised transhipment of goods carried by sea,[20] Brandon J. said that "the shipowners were making a fundamental departure from the method of performing the contract contemplated by the parties at the time it was made" and that the rule of fundamental breach applied "so as to prevent the shipowners from relying on the exception concerned". A similar decision is likely in the case of unauthorised transhipment of goods carried by road: it will be treated as one of "quasi-deviation" and "fundamental breach".[21]

---

[15] A term "corresponding to the absolute warranty of roadworthiness" was rejected by Kahn-Freund, pp. 268–269. The usefulness of the analogy with seaworthiness was rejected in general terms by Lord Alness in *Trickett v. Queensland Insurance Co.* [1936] A.C. 159, 165, P.C.

[16] In *John Carter (Fine Worsteds) v. Hanson Haulage (Leeds)* [1965] 2 Q.B. 495, 517, C.A. Sellers L.J. accepted an analogy with the warranty of seaworthiness, except that the "standard of liability in carriage by road is not that of warranty but of reasonable care". The other judges in *John Carter* also rejected the analogy with carriage by sea in so far as it imposed on the carrier an absolute warranty or a duty which was in any sense fundamental or special, as is true of the warranty of seaworthiness: see 528–529, *per* Davies L.J. and 534–535, *per* Russell L.J.

[17] *John Carter*, above at 514, *per* Sellers L.J. The actual breach of contract in the case was stated quite narrowly by Russell L.J. (at 531): failure to take reasonable care to put the goods in the charge of an honest man.

[18] *Gunyan v. S.E. and Chatham Ry* [1915] 2 K.B. 370.

[19] *Gibaud v. G.E. Ry.* [1921] 2 K.B. 426.

[20] *The Berkshire* [1974] 1 Lloyd's Rep. 185, 191.

[21] See further below, para. 240.

210. The route

210a. Transit and deviation

Transit, the movement of goods from the point of taking over to the point of delivery, includes the ordinary incidents of transit, among them incidental detours, or certain limited departures from the planned route. Any greater detour or departure may amount to deviation and have important legal consequences.[22] Actual movement is a typical but not an essential feature of transit. Transit includes stops while the driver of the vehicle sleeps[23] or takes refreshment.[24] It also includes "normal" delay, such as the period while goods in the custody of the carrier are awaiting loading[25] or, having been unloaded, await delivery to the consignee.[26] It includes delay caused by third parties but does not include delay ordered by the customer for reasons not directly connected with the transport of the goods[27] or perhaps, as regards the carrier's right to rely on contract defences, an unduly lengthy delay for the operational convenience of the carrier.[28] As the court observed in a marine case, transit "may properly be interrupted for efficient and economical loading, transhipment, discharge and storage to await the most convenient carrier and any other necessary steps in transit, but not merely for the commercial convenience of one of the parties, especially that of the consignor or the consignee".[29] In transit "does not necessarily mean in motion or subject to a mere brief suspension of motion. How long a period of suspended movement will be consistent with the [goods] being in transit depends on the circumstances."[30]

As to the chosen route, goods "may be carried by as long and circuitous a route as [the carrier] pleases, provided no delay or injury is caused thereby, unless he has agreed to carry by a certain route",[31] or has agreed to deliver by a certain time and the change of route causes delivery to be late or the contract stipulates a different route. A route may be agreed, however, not only expressly but also implicitly. If there is a usual route, it is normally

---

[22] See below, at n. 36.

[23] *Ries & Sons Inc. v. Automobile Ins. Co.*, 3 A. 2d 610 (N.J. 1939).

[24] *Sadler Bros. Co. v. Meredith* [1963] 2 Lloyd's Rep. 293, 307, *per* Roskill J.

[25] *Symington & Co. v. Union Ins. Sy. of Canton Ltd* (1928) 30 Ll.L.Rep. 280, 283, *per* Roche J.; (1928) 31 Ll.L.Rep. 179, 181, *per* Scrutton L.J., C.A.

[26] *Crow's Transport Ltd v. Phoenix Assurance Co. Ltd* [1965] 1 Lloyd's Rep. 139, 144, *per* Danckwerts L.J., C.A.

[27] *Safadi v. Western Assurance Co.* (1933) 46 Ll.L.Rep. 140.

[28] *cf. Hartford Casualty Ins. Co. v. Banker's Note*, 817 F. Supp. 1567, 1573 (N.D. Ga., 1993).

[29] *Verna Trading Pty Ltd v. New India Assurance Co. Ltd* [1991] 1 V.L.R. 129, 168, *per* Ormiston J. (Vict. Sup. Ct.).

[30] *Commercial Union Assurance Co. v. Niger Co. Ltd* (1922) 13 Ll.L.Rep. 75, 81–82, *per* Lord Sumner, H.L.

[31] Kahn-Freund, p. 285.

that route which is implied. The usual route is normally the shortest route, unless the carrier normally takes a different route and the customer is aware of that.[32]

Clearly the carrier may depart from the agreed route to take account of roadworks and other impediments for which the carrier is not responsible.[33] If, however, the departure from the route is unjustified, by analogy with the law governing carriage by sea,[34] that is a deviation.[35] As such, it is a serious breach of contract akin to a fundamental breach of contract, with the consequences that the carrier is disentitled to rely on contract defences, even though the breach is not a cause of the loss or damage complained of.[36]

210b. Reasonable dispatch

The shipowner, whose ship is chartered for a voyage, must proceed with reasonable dispatch, not only during the charter voyage but also when proceeding to the agreed port of loading. This means that the carrier must have taken all steps to get the ship to the place of loading, all steps that were reasonable in the particular circumstances that actually arose. If this implied term is broken by delay sufficiently serious to frustrate the adventure, the charterer may refuse to load the ship and is free to find another ship.[37] The requirement of reasonable dispatch is less a rule of maritime law than of the general law of contract, and rests on the implied intention of the parties to the contract,[38] an instance of the wider rule in *The Moorcock*,[39] whereby a term may be implied by the court into any contract, on the basis of what the parties are presumed to have intended "with the object of giving efficacy to the transaction and preventing such a failure of consideration as cannot have been within the contemplation of either side".[40] So, it is more than possible that the court would hold that a carrier must send his vehicle to collect the goods with reasonable dispatch, either by analogy with the duty imposed on the carrier by sea or on the basis of an implied term of the contract of carriage necessary to give business efficacy to the contract.

---

[32] *Hales v. L.N.W. Ry Co.* (1863) 4 B. & S. 66, 72, *per* Blackburn J.

[33] *Taylor v. G.N.R. Ry* (1866) L.R. 1 C.P. 385, 388.

[34] *Stag Line v. Foscolo, Mango & Co.* [1932] A.C. 328, 340, *per* Lord Atkin; *Reardon-Smith Line v. Black Sea & Baltic Ins. Co.* [1939] A.C. 562, 584–585, *per* Lord Porter.

[35] *L.N.W. Ry Co. v. Neilson* [1922] A.C. 263.

[36] Palmer, pp. 989 *et seq.* and Chap. 26.

[37] *Freeman v. Taylor* (1831) 8 Bing. 124; *cf. McAndrew v. Chapple* (1866) L.R. 1 C.P. 643.

[38] *McAndrew v. Adams* (1834) 1 Bing. N.C. 29, 43, *per* Park J.

[39] (1889) 14 P.D. 64, 68, *per* Bowen L.J.

[40] See n. 13.

211. Difficulties on the road

If performance of the contract of carriage becomes more difficult or more expensive for the carrier than expected, the carrier is obliged nonetheless to perform the contract and to bear the extra cost.[41] Difficulties on the road are carriers' business, matters within their sphere of risk. If, however, the contract of carriage becomes impossible to perform in accordance with its terms, for example the stipulated route is blocked and there is no viable alternative,[42] the contract is discharged. The only common exception to that is when the contract has also provided a solution (other than discharge) for whatever has made performance as originally intended impossible; for example, if there is a strike preventing delivery at place A, the consignment to be delivered at place B.[43]

These are the black and white rules of classical contract law, mainly relevant to commerce, rules developed by the courts in litigation arising out of the carriage of goods by sea. The courts did not consider the question, which has been asked more recently by writers such as Collins, whether there is a duty to give the other contracting party relevant information that comes in during performance of the contract.[44] As an example, he asks whether a customer should tell the carrier of the customer's goods about a traffic "problem" en route. Collins reminds the reader that a seller of goods may be obliged to give the buyer of those goods the information necessary for the buyer to obtain an import licence. Here, surely, are the seeds of a duty of co-operation that might suggest an affirmative answer to the question. In general, however, apart from developments in employment law, he concludes that there is no duty but that, on the ground of saving cost, there should be one. He points out[45] that in the United States this kind of question is gradually being subsumed under the implied duty of good faith. Eventually English law, which has no general duty of good faith such as is found in the United States but is moving slowly in that direction, may reach the same result but, it is submitted, not yet.

212. Destination

The carrier must deliver the goods at the contractual destination. If goods are brought to the agreed place of delivery, for example a

---

[41] *Tsaskiroglou & Co. v. Noblee & Thorl GmbH* [1962] A.C. 93.
[42] *Fibrosa S.A. v. Fairburn Lawson Combe Barbour* [1942] 1 K.B. 12, C.A., reversed on different grounds: [1943] A.C. 32; Devlin [1966] C.L.J. 192, 206–208.
[43] *The Caspiana* [1957] A.C. 149. Concerning difficulties at the point of delivery, see below, para. 215.
[44] (1992) 55 M.L.R. 556.
[45] At 557.

named city, but the precise point of delivery has not been specified, English law implies a duty to deliver at the consignee's place of business there.[46]

If the destination is the place of business of the carrier, from where the goods are to be collected by the consignee, it can be argued that delivery occurs when the consignee collects the goods or, perhaps the better view, when the goods have arrived at the carrier's place and are at the disposal of the consignee. In such circumstances it has been argued[47] that, if the contract is silent on the point, the carrier has an implied duty to give the consignee notice of arrival. Only when effective notice has been given are the goods at the disposal of the consignee, so that the carrier can proceed on the basis that delivery has occurred: in particular the carrier will cease to be liable as carrier but be liable as warehouseman and, possibly therefore, on different terms and conditions. Here the assumption is that the carrier has tendered delivery of the goods and that this amounts to performance of the contract. Otherwise the contract will be discharged because (complete) performance has become impossible.[48] In each case there remains the question of what is to be done with the goods. Contracts of carriage commonly provide for sale of the goods by the carrier; see, for example, RHA Condition 7.

213. The consignee

The consignee has no document, such as the bill of lading for goods carried by sea, which demonstrates the consignee's right to the goods. It suffices that the consignee can be identified in some other way as the person to whom the carrier has been instructed to deliver the goods, but the question arises, what must the carrier do to check that the person demanding the goods is indeed the consignee?

If the carrier delivers the goods to a person who, to the carrier's actual knowledge, has no right to receive the goods, the carrier commits a fundamental breach of the contract of carriage, which deprives the carrier of contractual defences.[49] If the carrier delivers the goods to a person in circumstances which should arouse the carrier's suspicion, the carrier commits a breach of the contract of

---

[46] Kahn-Freund, p. 301.

[47] Kahn-Freund, p. 303. The argument has some support in *Mitchell v. Lancashire & Yorkshire Ry Co.* (1875) L.R. 10 Q.B. 256, 260, *per* Blackburn J., as well as the general rule about contract terms, that they will be implied when necessary to give business efficacy to the contract: *Liverpool C.C. v. Irwin* [1977] A.C. 239. Phang [1993] J.B.L. 242.

[48] *Fibrosa S.A. v. Fairburn Lawson Combe Barbour* [1942] 1 K.B. 12, C.A., reversed on different grounds: [1943] A.C. 32.

[49] *Sze Hai Tong Bank v. Rambler Cycle Co.* [1959] A.C. 576, P.C. See also below, para. 240.

carriage; and, if it proves that that person was not entitled to receive the goods, the carrier has been negligent and is liable under common law.

> In *Stephenson v. Hart*[50] a person calling himself West ordered a consignment of combs from the plaintiff manufacturer. He paid with a bill of exchange, which had two months to run and which was forged. The defendant carrier brought the combs to the address specified by the plaintiffs, but found the address uninhabited and West unknown to those in the vicinity. The carrier retained the combs until receiving a letter, signed by West, requesting delivery of the combs at the public house known as the Pea Hen in St Albans. The carrier obliged. The plaintiffs said this was negligent and a breach of duty. Park J. agreed,[51] as did Burrough J., who said this[52]: "When it was discovered that no such person as the consignee was to be found in Great Winchester St, that contract (of carriage) was at an end and, the goods remaining in the hands of the carriers as the goods of the consignor, a new implied contract arose between the carrier and the consignor, to take care of the goods for the use of the consignor."

The carrier fulfils the duty by delivery of the goods at the correct address to a person who has apparent authority to receive them[53]: it is enough that the carrier has not been negligent.

214. Unloading

The party obliged to (load or) unload the goods is a matter for agreement between the parties to the contract of carriage. Carriers are not obliged to provide any special equipment for the operation unless they have agreed to do so, and usually the contract provides that that is the duty of the customer; see, for example, RHA Condition 4(1)(b). If the customer fails to provide it in breach of contract but instructs the carrier to load (or unload) nonetheless, it is commonly provided by the contract that the carrier shall not be liable for any damage howsoever caused[54]; see, for example, RHA Condition 4(1)(c).

---

[50] (1828) 4 Bing. 576.
[51] *ibid.*, 484.
[52] *ibid.*, 486. *cf.* Glass and Cashmore para. 1.70, that the plaintiffs, not being the owners, had no right to sue the carrier. On the right of suit, see below, paras. 216–217.
[53] In *M'Kean v. M'Ivor* (1870) L.R. 6 Ex. 30 the carrier delivered the goods at the correct address to a person who was not entitled to them and who made off with them. The carrier was held not liable to the sender on that account. Martin B. said (at 41): "But if the carrier delivers at the place indicated . . . he does all that he is bound to do. . . . To make him liable there must have been some fault; it is a question of fact whether there has been any such negligence as makes him guilty of a conversion. . . . "
[54] Concerning these words, see below, para. 238a.

Loading must be distinguished from the (legally significant) act of taking over the goods and, for similar reasons, unloading must be distinguished from delivery of the goods, the point at which the carrier's liability *qua* carrier usually comes to an end.

215. Delivery

Transit (the journey) ends when custody and control of the goods pass from the carrier to the consignee or to a third person not the agent of the carrier.[55]

If, for example, goods enter the (locked) premises of the consignee but remain on the carrier's (unlocked) vehicle pending unloading the next day, transit has not ended.[56] If, however, goods in transit are delivered to a third party, such as a customs authority, a port authority or a warehouseman, the position depends on whether the third party holds for the consignee or for the carrier.[57] For example, in a case of marine transit insurance cover,[58] goods arrived and for a month were left with a stevedore entirely for the convenience of the consignee and for no purpose related to transportation: transit and transit insurance had ended.

If goods in transit never reach the custody and control of the consignee, at least three situations should be distinguished.

First, if that is because the carrier has delivered to a person other than the consignee in the (mistaken) belief that that person was the consignee, that may nonetheless be delivery ending transit. It will be so, provided that the carrier intended to deliver to that person and that the carrier's belief in the identity of that person as the proper consignee was a reasonable belief.[59]

> Compare *Scothorn v. South Staffordshire Ry Co.*[60] The claimant contracted with the defendant carrier for the transport of goods to Birmingham and on to London, where the goods were to be delivered according to the claimant's instructions, it being understood that the goods would be actually carried by the defendants to Birmingham and by a second carrier, as agent of the defendants, from Birmingham to London. The servants of the second carrier agreed to carry out the claimant's instruction to deliver the goods to an address in London docks, an instruction which countermanded an earlier instruction, but instead followed the earlier instruction

---

[55] *Bartlett & Partners Ltd v. Meller* [1961] 1 Lloyd's Rep. 487, 489, *per* Sachs J.

[56] *A. Tomlinson (Hauliers) Ltd v. Hepburn* [1964] 1 Lloyd's Rep. 416; appeals on other grounds dismissed: [1966] 1 Q.B. 21, C.A.; [1966] A.C. 451.

[57] *Marten v. Nippon Sea & Land Ins. Co. Ltd* (1898) 3 Com. Cas. 164; *A. Gagnière & Co. v. The Eastern Co. Ltd* (1921) 7 Ll.L.Rep. 188, C.A.

[58] *Verna Trading Pty Ltd v. New India Assurance Co. Ltd* [1991] 1 V.L.R. 129 (Sup. Ct., Victoria).

[59] See Palmer, pp. 1005 *et seq.*

[60] (1853) 8 Exch. 341.

and put them on a ship bound for Australia, where they were lost. The defendants were held liable. Platt B. said[61]: "If a carrier undertakes to carry goods from one place to another, it is subject to a countermand at any part of the journey, though the owner may be bound to pay for the whole distance; for the carrier has no right to carry them against the will of the owner."

In *Scothorn* the second carrier held the goods as agent for the defendants, who remained bailees and who were liable for the negligence of their agent.[62] In that case, however, the agent was in possession of the goods in purported performance of the contract.

Secondly, if the carriers, having retained the goods in spite of a reasonable request by the consignee to have delivery at a point on the route short of destination, it seems that the carrier was not only entitled[63] but also obliged to deliver as requested, albeit at the consignee's expense, and is in breach of contract *qua* carrier.

Thirdly, if the carrier does not find or hear from the consignee and retains the goods, then the question may arise whether the carrier holds the goods as carrier under the contract of carriage or in some other capacity and on some other basis. In *Verna*[64] the Supreme Court of Victoria stated that "unduly protracted steps in the cargo's transportation are not within, and may terminate 'ordinary course of transit' ". The Court adopted the words of Ackner J. in an English case: "Goods cease to be in transit when they are on a journey which is not in reasonable furtherance of their carriage to their ultimate destination."[65] For the carrier there is the real problem of having goods but no consignee to deliver them to. Accordingly, transit ends not only on actual delivery to the consignee but also when the goods are appropriately *tendered* to the consignee.[66] This is amplified by RHA Condition 6(2), which provides that at the usual place of delivery at the consignee's address "within the customary cartage hours of the district". If it has been agreed that the carrier shall wait until contacted by the consignee, the carrier holds as carrier until the consignee contacts him and takes over the goods or until a reasonable time has elapsed without take over, after which the carrier holds not as carrier but as bailee for reward[67] because, although the carrier

---

[61] At 345.

[62] At 344, *per* Alderson B.

[63] *L. & N.W. Ry v. Bartlett* (1861) 7 H. & N. 400, 408, *per* Bramwell B.; *Cork Distilleries Ltd v. G.S. & W. Ry* (1874) L.R. 7 H.L. 269.

[64] Above, n. 58.

[65] *SCA (Freight) Ltd v. Gibson* [1974] 2 Lloyd's Rep. 533.

[66] See *Heugh v. L.N.W. Ry* (1870) L.R. 5 Ex. 51; *Startup v. Macdonald* (1843) 6 Man. & G. 593. Glass and Cashmore, para. 1.67.

[67] *Chapman v. G.W. Ry Co.* (1880) 5 Q.B.D. 278. The carrier's duty may be modified (usually reduced) by contract; see RHA Condition 6(2) and Condition 9(3); and *Mitchell v. Lancashire & Yorkshire Ry Co.* (1875) L.R. 10 Q.B. 256.

does not hold as carrier, a role which requires of the carrier to take reasonable care of the goods is justified as it can be said that, in the nature of things, it is ancillary to carriage.[68] Any attempt to exclude liability altogether after transit[69] invites challenge under the Unfair Contract Terms Act 1977.[70]

The other problem that arises is that, although the carrier may have found the consignee and the consignee wants the goods, the access to the consignee's premises or the unloading facilities there are either inadequate or unsafe. For situations like these, or any impediments to delivery, carriers' contracts commonly provide. RHA Condition 6(2), for example, indicates that the carrier is not obliged to attempt delivery in such situations and that, if the carrier gives sufficient notice in writing to the consignee of the arrival of the goods, the transit ends and with it the carriers' liability as carrier.

If, without breach of contract, the carrier is completely unable to deliver the goods to the consignee, the carrier is not entitled to return them to the sender.[71] Subject to the terms of the contract,[72] if it is agreed that the carrier shall wait until contacted by the consignee, the carrier holds as carrier until the consignee collects, thus obtaining control of the goods and ending carriage, or until a reasonable time has passed without collection, after which the carrier holds not as carrier but as involuntary bailee.[73] Further, if there is no such agreement and the carrier is able to contact the consignee, he must do so[74]: once again the carrier holds as carrier until the consignee collects or a reasonable time has passed without collection, after which in the latter case the carrier holds as

---

[68] Palmer, p. 1003, who also suggests that, in the event of exceptionally protracted delay the carrier becomes an involuntary bailee and, as such, does not have any obligation of safekeeping.

[69] See, for example, RHA Condition 9(3).

[70] See below, para. 239a.

[71] *G.W. Ry v. Crouch* (1858) 3 H. & N. 83. In these circumstances, the contract commonly entitles the carrier to sell the goods: see, for example, RHA Condition 7.

[72] *Chapman v. G.W. Ry Co.* (1880) 5 Q.B.D. 278, 282, *per* Cockburn C.J. A case in point is *Mitchell v. Lancashire & Yorkshire Ry Co.* (1875) L.R. 10 Q.B. 256; the common law rule was modified by the contract, which included a clause that the goods "are now held by the company, not as carriers, but as warehousemen, at owner's sole risk".

[73] *Chapman v. G.W. Ry Co.* (1880) 5 Q.B.D. 278, in which Cockburn C.J. said (at 281): "the obligation of the carrier not having been fulfilled by the delivery of the goods, the goods remain in his hands as carrier". Also (at 282), the consignee "should know when the goods may be expected to arrive. If he is not otherwise aware of it, it is the business of the consignor to inform him. His ignorance—at all events where the carrier has no means of communicating with him—which was the case in the present instance—cannot avail him in prolonging the liability of the carrier, as such, beyond a reasonable time."

RHA Conditions of Carriage 1991, Condition 6(2)(b): "when a Consignment is held by the Carrier 'to await order' or 'to be kept till called for' or upon like instructions and such instructions are not given or the Consignment is not called for and removed, within a reasonable time, then transit shall be deemed to end."

[74] A duty to give notice may be implied.

involuntary bailee. In a case of carriage by rail, Blackburn J. stated[75]:

> "The goods are then to be carried at the risk of the carrier to the end of the journey, and when they arrive at the station to which they were forwarded, the carrier has then complied with his duty when he has given notice to the consignee of their arrival. And after this notice, and the consignee does not fetch the goods away, and becomes *in mora*, then I think the carrier ceases to incur any liability as carrier, but is subject to the ordinary liability of bailee."

In each case, the shorter the period of transit the shorter the time in which it is reasonable to require the carrier to hold the goods as carrier.[76]

Exceptionally, the contract may provide for delivery without the immediate presence or co-operation of the consignee. In this case delivery occurs in accordance with the contract. Agreement in the contract may be express or based on a local custom[77] to that effect, this providing a definition of delivery for the particular case.

Delivery without the consignee present in person or through an agent is exceptional. Generally, delivery requires the co-operation of the consignee. Without this there can be no delivery, so prima facie no consignee, no delivery. However, if the carrier brings the goods to the consignee's address and finds it impossible to contact the consignee, the carrier may unload the goods at an appropriate place. At that point the carriage ends, and there is therefore a notional delivery.

> In *Heugh v. L.N.W. Ry*[78] a rogue placed an order with the plaintiff sender, giving a name and address which was not his own. The goods were taken to that address by an agent of the defendant carriers, where they were rejected by the occupier, who said that the consignee named no longer lived there. The goods were taken back to the defendants' station, remaining there until the rogue obtained them by presenting forged papers. The Court of Exchequer considered that the sender's action based on the tort of conversion failed because, as regards delivery, the defendant carriers had performed their side of the contract. Kelly C.B. said[79]: "The defendants, in strict accordance with their duty, sent the goods to the place to which they were addressed. . . . They could not deposit them on the pavement, and they were not permitted to bring them into the house . . . the

---

[75] *Mitchell v. Lancashire & Yorkshire Ry Co.* (1875) L.R. 10 Q.B. 256, 260. See further Kahn-Freund, p. 323.

[76] Glass and Cashmore, para. 1.67.

[77] In *Chapman* (above, n. 73) at 280–281, Cockburn C.J. was ready to consider the effect of "any established practice on the part of the railway company in dealing with goods, addressed to, and to be delivered at the railway station".

[78] (1870) L.R. 5 Ex. 51.

[79] At 56.

defendants' character of carrier had ceased." After that, the defendants held the goods not as carriers but as involuntary bailees: as such, they would have been liable only if, as was not the case, there were negligence on their part.

CHAPTER 11

CLAIMS

A. THE CLAIMANT

216. Title to sue: parties to the contract of carriage

If the claim is in tort, title to sue depends on the tort. If, the most likely example, the allegation is one of negligence, title to sue depends on whether the defendant carrier owes the claimant a duty of care.[1] If the claim against the carrier is in contract, the claimant must be party to contract with the carrier. Generally, the presumption is that it is the owner of the goods at the time of loss of or damage to the goods who has contracted with the carrier.[2] This presumption is said to correspond with commercial reality,[3] for it is the owner who has the commercial interest in the goods. There is a further presumption that the owner is the consignee, although, evidently, in some cases ownership remains with the sender.[4] Presumptions, of course, are rebuttable. If, for example, the contract makes it clear that the "Customer" who contracts with the carrier is a person other than the consignee, so be it.

216a. The consignee as owner

"It is clear that where goods are despatched by a carrier, the contract for payment of carriage is between him and the consignee, even though the goods should have been booked by the consignor; and though the property in these goods turned out afterwards to be in the consignor."[5] The carrier is entitled to assume that the "property", the ownership of the goods, is in the

---

[1] See below, para. 229.
[2] *The Albazero* [1977] A.C. 774, 847, *per* Lord Diplock. Glass and Cashmore, para. 1.05; Palmer, p. 962; Halsbury (4th ed.), Vol. 5, p. 234.
[3] *The Kapetan Markos N.L. (No. 2)* [1987] 2 Lloyd's Rep. 321, 329, *per* Mustill L.J., C.A.
[4] *cf.*, *The Albazero* [1977] A.C. 774, 786, *per* Brandon J.
[5] *Stephenson v. Hart* (1828) 4 Bing. 476, 487, *per* Gaselee J.: see also *Heugh v. L.N.W. Ry* (1870) L.R. 5 Ex. 51, 57–58, *per* Martin B.

consignee, because for many years and in most cases that has been true. Professor Kahn-Freund said back in 1965[6]:

> "the consignor, when delivering the goods to the carrier, is still the owner of the property, but the very act of delivery to the carrier usually makes the consignee the owner of the property. Though the contract in such a case has the appearance of having been made with the consignor, it is in fact made by him on behalf of, and as agent for, the consignee as owner, and it does not matter what arrangements have been made between seller and buyer with regard to the payment of the freight . . . The law regards this as the normal case, and gives the carrier the right to assume that, if goods are entrusted to him for carriage, that is done in performance of a contract of sale. It is not the carrier's duty to inquire into the internal relationship between consignor and consignee."

Brandon J. in 1973[7]: "the consignor, in delivering the goods to the carrier was acting as agent for the consignee, and . . . the property and risk in the goods were either in the consignee before such delivery or passed to him upon its taking place." Finally, Tudor Evans J. in 1990[8]: "when a seller is required to send the goods to the buyer in a foreign country, the goods in transit being at the buyer's risk, business efficacy requires that, when the seller makes a contract with a carrier for the carriage of goods to the buyer, he does so on behalf of the buyer."

This, the most common case, is associated with the sale of goods ex warehouse, ex factory, free on truck (FOT), free on rail (FOR) and free on board (FOB), in which ownership passes from the sender to the consignee on or before consignment. The passing of ownership to the consignee is chiefly the effect of the Sale of Goods Act 1979, section 18, rule 5(2):

> "Where, in pursuance of the contract, the seller delivers the goods to the buyer or to a carrier or other bailee or custodier (whether named by the buyer or not) for the purpose of transmission to the buyer, and does not reserve the right of disposal, he is taken to have unconditionally appropriated the goods to the contract."

The effect of unconditional appropriation, which may occur not only on consignment but also at an earlier stage,[9] is to pass the

---

[6] Kahn-Freund, p. 210; the quotation is part of a passage which has been adopted in Canada: *Magna Electric & Computers v. Speedway Express* (1978) 91 D.L.R. (3d) 310, 314 (Nova Scotia). A presumption that the consignee is the owner is found in Italy: Maccarone, Theunis, p. 65. *cf.* Mance (1984) 100 L.Q.R. 501, 503. This presumption was not questioned by Lord Diplock delivering the judgment of the House of Lords in *The Albazero* [1977] A.C. 774.

[7] *The Albazero* [1977] A.C. 774, 785–786, *per* Brandon J., and cases cited. See also *Heugh v. L.N.W. Ry* (1870) L.R. 5 Ex. 51, 57–58, *per* Martin B. Brandon J.'s review of the cases was referred to with apparent approval in the House of Lords in the same case: [1977] A.C. 774, 842.

[8] *Texas Instruments Ltd v. Nasan (Europe) Ltd* [1991] 1 Lloyd's Rep. 146, 148–149.

[9] *Wardar's (Import & Export) Co. v. Norwood & Sons* [1968] 2 Q.B. 663, C.A.

ownership of the goods from the seller/consignor to the buyer/consignee.[10] As appropriation is governed by the contract of sale and must occur with the express or implicit consent of the buyer, there is no appropriation and no transfer of ownership to the consignee, if the goods delivered to the carrier do not conform to the requirements of the contract of sale.[11] However, unless this is apparent to the carrier, the presumption that the consignee is the owner and hence the person, the customer, contracting with the carrier is not affected.

216b. The sender as owner

"The second category of cases comprise those in which it was held that the consignor rather than the consignee was the proper person to sue. The ground of decision in those cases was that the consignor, in delivering the goods to the carrier, was acting as principal, and that the property and risk remained in them remained in him during the carriage."[12]

216c. The sender's influence on the rights of the consignee

If the sender is acting as the agent of the consignee, the consignee is bound by any concession within the actual or apparent authority of the sender. In English law, the consignee is in the position of a bailor of the goods, whose bailee (the sender) contracts with a sub-bailee (the carrier) with the result that the bailor/consignee is bound by the contract terms, unless they are unusual. This rule stems from a dictum of Lord Denning M.R.[13] that "the owner is bound by the conditions if he has expressly or impliedly consented to the bailee making a sub-bailment containing those conditions . . . So also if the owner of a ship accepts goods for carriage on a bill of lading containing exempting conditions (*i.e.* a 'bailment upon terms') the owner of the goods (although not a party to the contract) is bound by those conditions if he impliedly consented to them as being in 'the known and contemplated form'." Lord Denning's case concerned the repair of goods but his statement was subsequently confirmed for the carriage of goods by sea in *The Pioneer Container*.[14] In the later case the Privy Council held

---

[10] Sale of Goods Act 1979, s.18, r. 5(1).

[11] Goods which do not correspond with the contract description are not contract goods. The status of unmerchantable goods is less certain. See Benjamin, para. 5–085.

[12] *The Albazero* [1977] A.C. 774, 786, *per* Brandon J., and cases cited. See also *Heugh v. L.N.W. Ry* (1870) L.R. 5 Ex. 51, 57–58, *per* Martin B.

[13] *Morris v. Martin & Sons* [1966] 1 Q.B. 716, 729–730, C.A.

[14] [1994] 2 A.C. 324. Devonshire [1996] J.B.L. 329; Wilson [1996] L.M.C.L.Q. 187, 192 *et seq.* For doubts, *e.g.* about the basis for holding that in spite of the rule of privity of contract the sub-bailee owes corresponding duties to the owner, see Swadling [1993] L.M.C.L.Q. 9, 12.

that, if a bailee (carrier) sub-contracted performance to a sub-bailee (sub-carrier), the relationship of the owner and the sub-bailee was that of bailor and bailee and the owner was bound by the terms on which the goods were sub-bailed. The decision was subject, however, to the proviso, first, that the bailee (carrier) had authority to sub-contract[15] and, secondly, that it could be said that the owner of the goods consented to the bailee sub-contracting on the terms in question[16]; such consent might be express or implied. A third proviso appears to be that the sub-bailee is aware of the existence of the principal bailor (the owner of the goods). If not (if, for example, the sub-bailee believes erroneously that the goods are owned by the bailee), the rule that emerges from *The Pioneer Container* does not apply because, according to that case,[17] the (only) legal basis of bailment is lacking: the sub-bailee has not voluntarily taken into possession the goods of the principal bailor. Clearly, rules sanctioned by *The Pioneer Container* for the carriage of goods by sea apply equally to the carriage of goods by road[17a] and, it has been suggested,[18] to all sub-contractors.

The answer is likely to be different if the consignee had been led (whether by the sender or carrier) to expect rights different from those actually agreed between sender and carrier.

> In England in *Leduc v. Ward*[19] an action against the carrier, whose ship had sunk in the Clyde, was brought by an indorsee of the bill of lading, and was met by the defence of perils of the sea. The indorsee contended that the carrier having deviated from the contract route, had lost this defence.[20] The carrier's answer was that, although not mentioned in the bill of lading, a new route taking in the Clyde had been agreed with the shipper. The Court of Appeal held that the indorsee was not bound by this agreement.

What counted in that case was that the consignees had been given bills of lading, the terms of which led them to expect that the ship would proceed by the normal or direct route, and had no prior notice of the deviation[21] or of the shipper's agreement with the carrier. The rule might be different if the consignee is not led to

[15] See above, para. 208. The situation in which the bailee had no authority was left open in *The Pioneer Container* (above), at 338: see Bell [1995] L.M.C.L.Q. 177, 181.

[16] By insisting on consent the Privy Council rejected the view of Donaldson J. (in *Johnson Matthey & Co. Ltd v. Constantine Terminals Ltd* [1976] 2 Lloyd's Rep. 215, 222) that consent was unnecessary. See Bell [1995] L.M.C.L.Q. 177, 179.

[17] At 342. *cf.*, however, *Awad v. Pillai* [1982] R.T.R. 266, C.A.; Bell (above), p. 182.

[17a] See *Spectra Int. plc v. Hayesoak Ltd* [1997] 1 Lloyd's Rep. 153.

[18] Bell (above), p. 182.

[19] (1888) 20 Q.B.D. 475, C.A., approved by Lord Wright in *Tate & Lyle v. Hain SS. Co.* (1936) 55 Ll.L.Rep. 159, 178, H.L.

[20] See above, para. 210a.

[21] *Per* Lord Wright, *loc. cit.*, n. 19. If the consignee has not been led to expect otherwise, it does not matter that the terms are more onerous than those to which the consignee is accustomed, as long as they are not unusual where the sub-bailee operates: See *Spectra* (above).

expect anything in particular because, as commonly occurs, the consignee receives no document of any kind.

Finally, if the consignee has rights under the contract of carriage against the carrier, does the carrier have rights against the consignee? If the legal basis of their relationship is a *Brandt* contract (below), clearly the answer is affirmative: they are bound reciprocally by the terms of the contract. If it is not that but a relationship of bailor and bailee of the kind sanctioned by *The Pioneer Container* (above), the answer is not clear, however, in principle the answer is again affirmative: they are bound reciprocally by the terms of the bailment.

217. The *Brandt* contract

Evidently, if the sender is the customer owning the goods at the time of consignment, it is the sender and not the consignee who has the right of action at common law on that ground.[22] If, for example, the sender sells the goods between the time of taking over and the time of delivery, something that does not happen often, the question may arise whether the consignee has a right of action. The most likely basis of an action[23] at law is an implied contract between carrier and consignee, sometimes known as the *Brandt* contract.

---

[22] Above, para. 216a.

[23] Other possibilities include:

(a) The rule, whereby "an original party to the contract", the sender, "is to be treated in law as having entered into the contract for the benefit of all persons who have or may acquire an interest in the goods . . . and is entitled to recover by way of damages for breach of contract the actual loss sustained by those for whose benefit the contract is entered into". The claimant is accountable to the latter for the damages recovered. See *The Albazero* [1977] A.C. 774, 847, *per* Lord Diplock, explaining *Dunlop v. Lambert* (1839) 6 Cl. & Fin. 600, H.L. This exception has been extended to contracts generally including, therefore, contracts for the carriage of good by land in a decision in a construction case: *Linden Gardens Trust v. Lenesta Sludge Disposals Ltd* [1994] 1 A.C. 85. The rationale of the application of the exception to carriage by road would be that, as the parties to the contract of carriage (sender and carrier) must have contemplated that ownership in the goods might be transferred to third parties after the contract had been made, the sender must be treated in law as having made the contract of carriage for the benefit of all persons who might after the time of contracting acquire interests in the goods: Treitel, p. 546. The utility of the rule for the consignee of goods sent by road is however, limited. In one sense the rationale of the rule proves too much: usually, as we have seen, the consignee is known at the time of the conclusion of the contract of carriage and the strength of the interest of the consignee is such that it is presumed that the contract is made on behalf of the consignee. Moreover, the speed of carriage by road is such that the transfer of ownership between the time of the conclusion of the contract of carriage and delivery of the goods is not common.

(b) Assignment: the sender may assign the benefit of the contract of carriage to the consignee: *Britain & Overseas Trading (Bristles) v. Brooks Wharf & Bull Wharf* [1967] 2 Lloyd's Rep. 51, 60, *per* Widgery J.; *The Aliakmon* [1986] A.C. 785, 818, *per* Lord Brandon. In practice, this does not happen. It is "a defect on our law that we should require businessmen to go through such hoops"—Lloyd [1989] L.M.C.L.Q. 47, 55.

The *Brandt*[24] contract arises from the inference that, when the consignee requests delivery of the goods, the consignee implicitly contracts with the carrier on the terms of the sender's contract. The inference was first drawn in the context of carriage by sea: courts found an implied contract when the consignee presented a bill of lading or (later) a delivery order, which refers to the bill of lading,[25] or a guarantee that the bill of lading will be presented in due course.[26] When a transport document exists, the implied contract is limited to the terms of that document.[27]

In principle, an implied contract might be inferred on the basis of a consignment note, even if the consignee does not present a consignment note, when the consignee is identified as the person entitled to the goods, goods which the consignee knows are being sent under a consignment note.[28] Even when there is no consignment note, a contract might be inferred on the basis of the carrier's standard terms. For many years, a similar approach to the same problem has been taken in France[29] and other countries,[30] although the doctrinal basis given to the consignee's right of suit has varied.[31] In England, however, the courts have recently shown less confidence in the *Brandt* device, and have hesitated in the face of the theoretical difficulties which the *Brandt* contract presents.

The first difficulty lies in the need to find consideration moving from consignee to carrier. Consideration may be a payment of some kind to the carrier.[32] However, in a significant number of cases the carrier gets nothing from the consignee[33] or, at least, nothing obvious and direct.[33]

---

[24] *Brandt v. Liverpool Brazil & River Plate SN Co.* [1924] 1 K.B. 575, C.A. Cases earlier than *Brandt* are reviewed by Bingham L.J. in *The Aramis* [1989] 1 Lloyd's Rep. 213, 218 *et seq.* See also Powles [1989] J.B.L. 157.

[25] *The Dona Mari* [1973] 2 Lloyd's Rep. 366.

[26] *The Elli 2* [1985] 1 Lloyd's Rep. 107, C.A.

[27] *The Athanasia Comninos* [1990] 1 Lloyd's Rep. 277, 281, a decision of Mustill J. in 1979, that the consignee did not assume the consignor's undertaking that the goods were fit for carriage, and not dangerous.

[28] J.F. Wilson, paper presented in Hamburg, October 1987, pp. 3–4 *dubitante. Contra*: Tetley, (1986) 17 J.M.L.C. 153, 164, citing *The Aliakmon* [1983] 1 Lloyd's Rep. 203, 207, *per* Staughton J., but there the absence of any document was not considered.

[29] In cases of carriage by road it has been held that, by accepting delivery and purporting to pay outstanding charges, the consignee accepts the contract of carriage with all the terms and conditions recorded in the document produced at the time of delivery, and cannot plead lack of privity (*défaut de lien de droit*) with the carrier, to whom the consignee became liable: *Paris 14.11.69* (1970) U.L.C. 133, 134; *Paris 19.11.81*, B.T. 1982.62; *Paris 8.12.81*, B.T. 1982.61; *Paris 19.12.82*, B.T. 1983.111. See also *Cass. 10.7.89*, B.T. 1989.619.

[30] Such as Germany and Holland: Haak, pp. 254–255; and the USA: *Waterman S.S. Corp. v. 350 Bundles of Hardboard* 1984 AMC 2709 (D.Mass, 1984).

[31] For example, *stipulation pour autrui*: Haak, pp. 254–255. *cf.* Ripert, *Droit Maritime* (4th ed., Paris, 1950, *mise à jour* 1963), paras. 1585–1586; Rodière, paras. 362 *et seq.*

[32] *Brandt* (above, n. 24). *The Elli 2* [1985] 1 Lloyd's Rep. 107, C.A.

[33] *The Aramis* [1989] 1 Lloyd's Rep. 213, C.A.; this is a typical case: Lloyd [1989] L.M.C.L.Q. 47, 53.

The second difficulty is to find evidence of the implied agreement, on which to infer a contract, when the goods do not arrive and there is no exchange between carrier and consignee.[34] Even if goods do arrive, unless there is an arrangement by which the carrier does something more than simply deliver the goods (a new arrangement), the court may feel unable to find conduct by carrier and consignee which is referable to any new contract concluded at the place of destination.[35]

In the face of these difficulties, Mustill L.J. said in 1987[36] that the "court should . . . recognise that this part of English commercial law is not perfectly harmonious and should not strain established general principles to achieve an apparently acceptable result in the individual case". Since 1987, willingness to find a contract and overcome theoretical objections has varied from court to court and case to case[37]; however, most recently the validity of the *Brandt* rule was accepted in passing by Lord Goff in *The Mahkuhtai.*[38] Sir Anthony Lloyd pronounced in 1988 that "the implied contract, as a device, has reached the end of the road".[39] If this is so, the United Kingdom may be the only state in Europe in which the consignee, who acquires ownership of the goods after consignment, has no independent right of action based in some way or other on the contract of carriage. Perhaps, it is submitted, it is a mistake to see the carrier's relation with the consignee in isolation from the other sides of the transport triangle, sender/carrier and sender/consignee. The reality is a tripartite arrangement with interdependent contractual components,[40] and that it may well be in the commercial interests of the carrier to undertake obligations to the consignee, whether their relations satisfy the criteria of classical contract law or not, and to underwrite an effective legal mechanism for international trade in the interests of those who

---

[34] *The Aramis*, above, n. 33.

[35] *The Aramis*, at 224–225, *per* Bingham L.J., at 231, *per* O'Connor L.J., and at 228–229, *per* Stuart-Smith L.J., citing in this sense *The Elli 2* [1985] 1 Lloyd's Rep. 107, 116, *per* May L.J., C.A., and declining to follow a dictum of Sir John Donaldson M.R. in *The Aliakmon* [1985] Q.B. 350, 364, C.A. This is an unusually subjective approach to the quest for consent in a modern commercial case. *cf.* consent by reliance: Coote (1988) 1 J.C.L. 91, 105 and references cited.

A similar concern about whether there was real consent by the consignee was shown in *The Anna Oden, Paris 13.10.86*, DMF 1988.101. Also in *Cass. 10.9.89*, B.T. 1989.619.

[36] *The Kapetan Markos NL (No. 2)* [1987] 2 Lloyd's Rep. 321, 330, C.A.

[37] *cf. The Captain Gregos (No. 2)* [1990] 2 Lloyd's Rep. 395, C.A. and *The Gudermes* [1993] 1 Lloyd's Rep. 311, C.A.

[38] [1996] 3 All E.R. 502, 512, P.C.

[39] Lloyd [1989] L.M.C.L.Q. 47, 53.

[40] See *The Good Luck* [1989] 2 Lloyd's Rep. 238, C.A.; Clarke [1989] C.L.J. 363. The decision was affirmed by the House of Lords: [1992] 1 A.C. 233. Other possibilities are as follows:

(a) the consignee takes the goods off the carrier's hands, and enables the vehicle to be put back to work: *The Eurymedon* [1975] A.C. 154, 168, *per* Lord Wilberforce, P.C.; and (b) consideration may be unnecessary if there is reliance: Clarke [1991] L.M.C.L.Q. 5.

trade and those who carry. The implied contract is indeed "at the end of the road", but only in the sense that the device is not yet dead, and the contract might still be inferred between consignee and carrier when goods carried by road are delivered today.

B. LIMITATION OF ACTIONS

218. Limitation

The time in which the claimant must institute proceedings, lest the action be out of time, depends on the basis of claim, contract or tort, and on whether the time applicable has been modified by the contract or by conduct.

218a. Contract

By section 5 of the Limitation Act 1980, actions founded on a contract not under seal shall not be brought after the expiration of six years from the date on which the cause of action accrued. If the contract is under seal, by section 8 of the Act the period is 12 years. The effect on contracts is not to prescribe or extinguish the right but to bar the remedy. A cause of action arises upon the existence of every fact necessary to sustain the claim,[41] *i.e.* that the defendant is in breach of a binding contract of carriage with the claimant.

The period of six years may be shortened by clear terms of the contract. The period may also be lengthened by the terms of the contract (unlikely) or by the conduct of the carrier (estoppel) in a particular case. Moreover, when the claim is characterised as a debt, (*i.e.* a claim by the carrier for charges, the effect of section 29(5) of the 1980 Act is (not to extend the original period but) to create a fresh accrual and to initiate a new period: if the insurer "acknowledges the claim or makes any payment in respect of it the right shall be treated as having accrued on and not before the date of the acknowledgement or payment".

The statutory period runs even though the claimant may be unaware of the existence of the cause of action. This was the intention behind the legislation.[42] It is also the implication of those provisions of the Limitation Act 1980, whereby a longer time limit

---

[41] *Coburn v. Colledge* [1897] 1 Q.B. 702, 706–707, *per* Lord Esher M.R., with whom other members of the Court of Appeal agreed. See Mullaney [1993] L.M.C.L.Q. 34, 52 *et seq.*

[42] Law Revision Committee, Fifth Interim Report, 1936 (Cmd. 5334).

is provided for certain cases—negligence actions (section 14A), fraud and concealment (section 32)—in which the facts relevant to the cause of action are not known at the date of accrual; the inference, of course, is that in other cases, such as that of a carriage claim in which there has been no fraud or concealment, time is to run regardless of the claimant's knowledge of the circumstances.[43] When there has been fraud or concealment, however, time does not begin to run against the claimant until the concealed information becomes known to or reasonably discoverable by the claimant: section 32(1)(b). This rule applies even though the fraud or concealment occurs after time would otherwise have started to run.[44] In other words, "the subsequent concealment resets the limitation clock to zero and keeps it at zero until the fact is discoverable".[45]

218b. Tort

If the cause of action is tort, notably the tort of negligence, the limitation period is stated by section 14A of the Limitation Act 1980: not more than "six years from the date on which the cause of action accrued" or "three years from the starting date", whichever period expires later. The starting date (section 14A(5)) is the earliest date on which the claimant, assumed here to be a person with an interest in goods with a claim against the carrier of the goods, "had both the knowledge required for bringing an action for damages in respect of the relevant damage and a right to bring such an action".[46]

The requisite knowledge is of two kinds.[47] The first is knowledge that the claimant has been wronged, *i.e.* according to section 14A(7), knowledge of "such facts about the damage as would lead a reasonable person who had suffered such damage to consider it sufficiently serious to justify his instituting proceedings for damages against a defendant who did not dispute liability and was able to satisfy a judgment".[48] The second kind of knowledge concerns who to sue. In particular, according to section 14A(8), this refers

---

[43] See *Chandris v. Argo Ins. Co.* [1963] 2 Lloyd's Rep. 65, 73, *per* Megaw J., and cases cited; the judgment of Megaw J. was approved in *Castle Ins. v. Hong Kong Shipping* [1984] A.C. 226, P.C.

[44] *Sheldon v. RHM Outhwaite (Underwriting Agencies) Ltd* [1996] 1 A.C. 102.

[45] McGee (1995) 111 L.Q.R. 580, 581.

[46] s.14A(5). By s.14A(10), "a person's knowledge includes knowledge which he might reasonably have been expected to acquire (a) from facts observable or ascertainable by him; or (b) from facts ascertainable by him with the help of appropriate expert advice which it is reasonable for him to seek; but a person shall not be taken by virtue of this subsection to have knowledge of a fact ascertainable only with the help of expert advice so long as he shall have taken all reasonable steps to obtain (and, where appropriate, to act on) that advice".

[47] s.14A(5).

[48] s.14A(6).

to knowledge "(a) that the damage was attributable in whole or in part to the act or omission which is alleged to constitute negligence; and (b) the identity of the defendant . . .".

In many cases, the claimant knows exactly the carrier to sue but, in the event of successive carriage, that may not be so. The meaning of the second kind of knowledge was disputed in *Hallam-Eames v. Merrett Syndicates Ltd.*[49] The reference in section 14A(7) to a defendant who did not dispute liability assumes attributability and focuses attention on wrongful damage. Attributability is another matter and that is the concern of section 14A(8). If the act required full knowledge of attributability in law, it would have been simple to say so. Section 14A(8) does not say that and seems to require something less. In *Hallam-Eames*, Hoffmann L.J. thought it enough that the client knew something of which "he would prima facie seem entitled to complain". He "does not have to know that he has a cause of action or that the defendant's acts can be characterised in law as negligent". However, he "must have known the facts which can fairly be described as constituting the negligence". The claimants in that case would know something of which they were prima facie entitled to complain, if "on the facts known to or ascertainable by them, it would have been reasonable for them to instruct an expert who could have discovered the circumstances" in which the wrong occurred.[50] Thus, goods claimants know something of which they are entitled to complain, when there is sufficient suspicion for it to be reasonable to have the goods examined for the possibility of (latent) damage or for the exact nature and hence the source (in terms of time and wrongdoer) of the damage.

As regards the right to bring such an action, the right accrues when the claimant suffers loss as a result of the carrier's breach of duty. As regards negligence, a distinction can be drawn between acts or omissions, which occur at particular points in time, and conduct, which continues over a period of time. But what counts here is loss or damage to the claimant which also may be pinpointed in time or, if not continuous, recurrent.

218c. Waiver and estoppel

The time-limit will not bar the claimant's action if the carrier has waived the limit or is estopped from pleading it. The distinction between waiver and estoppel is controversial[51] but, arguably, it is

---

[49] C.A., January 13, 1995, *The Times*, January 25, 1995.

[50] *ibid.*, *per* Hoffmann L.J. See also Mullaney, *op. cit.*, above.

[51] References to the literature and a more extensive discussion of the differences can be found in Clarke, *Insurance*, para. 26–4; and Clarke [1990] C.L.J. 206.

drawn as follows.[52] The carrier has waived the limit if, with sufficient knowledge of the right to plead it,[53] the carrier has elected not to do so; such an election is irrevocable.[54] The carrier is estopped from making a plea of limitation if, whatever the intention,[55] the carrier has behaved in such a way that the claimant acts in reliance on the reasonable supposition that the carrier will not do so; the inference must be unequivocal. Estoppel, unlike waiver, is revocable by reasonable notice.[56] With waiver the focus is on the intention of the waivor/defendant. With estoppel the focus is on the response of the other person although, because the response must be reasonable, attention reverts to the *apparent* intention of the person said to be estopped.

In most cases, the legal effect on the question of limitation is clear although it may be that the legal basis, waiver or estoppel, is not. When is the case one for waiver and when is it one for estoppel? The doctrinal answer[57] is that for waiver the party must be faced with an unavoidable election. "It is of the essence of election that the party electing shall be 'confronted' with two mutually exclusive courses of action between which he must, in fairness to the other party, make his choice. In this respect, election is clearly distinguishable from promissory estoppel, in which a party makes a declaration of his intention, similar in many ways to an election, but in circumstances which do not call upon him to make any choice at all." Generally, therefore, waiver arises after the period of limitation has run and the issue of limitation has to be faced, while estoppel arises before the period has expired and the issue is not immediate. In practice, the distinction is often fudged or ignored. The court looks to see whether the claimant has been "lulled to sleep . . . or was induced to act in a particular way

---

[52] The distinction that follows is based on that drawn by the High Court of Australia in *Craine v. Colonial Mutual Fire Insurance Co.* (1920) 28 C.L.R. 305, affirmed [1922] 2 A.C. 541, P.C.

[53] There is controversy here too, according to whether the defendant must not only know the facts supporting the plea of limitation but also be aware of the legal right to do so. It is probably enough that the defendant knows the facts: *Eagle Star Insurance Co. v. National Westminster Finance Australia* (1985) 58 A.L.R. 165, 174, *per* Lord Roskill, P.C.; *The Kanchenjunga* [1990] 1 Lloyd's Rep. 391, 399, *per* Lord Goff, P.C. *cf.*, however, *Peyman v. Lanjani* [1985] Ch. 457, 483, *per* Stephenson L.J., C.A.

[54] This aspect was not discussed in *Craine* (above). See Thompson [1983] C.L.J. 257, 261.

[55] *Toronto Ry Co. v. National British & Irish Millers Insurance Co.* (1914) 111 L.T. 555, 563, *per* Scrutton L.J., C.A.

[56] *The Kanchenjunga, loc. cit. Ajayi v. Briscoe (Nigeria)* [1964] 1 W.L.R. 1326, 1330, *per* Lord Hodson, P.C. *cf. D. & C. Builders v. Rees* [1966] 2 Q.B. 617, 624, *per* Lord Denning M.R., C.A.

[57] Bower and Turner, *The Law Relating to Estoppel by Representation* (3rd ed., London 1977), para. 310. Also in this sense: Lord Goff in *The Kanchenjunga, loc. cit.* A different view can be found in *The Athos* [1981] 2 Lloyd's Rep. 74, 87–88, *per* Neill J., citing *Kammins Ballrooms Co. v. Zenith Investments (Torquay)* [1971] A.C. 850, 882–883, *per* Lord Diplock.

in reliance"[58] on the supposition that the period has been suspended or extended.

219. Counterclaim and set-off

In general contract law, a buyer of goods or services can set up the damages to which the buyer is entitled by reason of a breach of contract on the part of the provider in diminution or extinction of the price payable by the customer.[59] One might have expected the same rule in favour of the customer who has agreed to pay charges for the services of a carrier of goods by road, but it is not so.

In *United Carriers Ltd v. Heritage Food Group (UK) Ltd*,[60] against a claim for freight charges, the defendant customers cross-claimed for short delivery and other breaches of contract by the claimant carriers. The carriers argued that the rule, that a claim in respect of cargo could not be asserted by way of deduction from freight charges for carriage by sea, should also apply to the carriage of goods by land within the United Kingdom. May J., noting "an astonishing lack of reported authority which addresses the question",[61] considered the indistinguishable but unreported case of *A.S. Jones Ltd v. Burtson Gold Medal Biscuits Ltd*,[62] which supported the carriers' argument. He said that the maritime rule had "little if any intrinsic justification but applies to carriage of goods by sea because it is a rule of considerable antiquity which has been applied consistently and on the basis of which owners, charterers and insurers may be taken to have contracted. It is very difficult, in my view, to apply this latter justification to carriage of goods by land, where there is only one reported case (in 1984), and where discussions to be found in textbooks are equivocal."[63] Left to himself, he said, he would not apply the maritime rule to carriage by land; however, with "unconcealed reluctance", he held that as the rule had been consistently applied to the international carriage of goods by road,[64] it should also be applied to carriage by land within the United Kingdom.[65]

---

[58] *Webster v. GAFLAC* [1953] 1 Q.B. 520, 532, *per* Parker J.

[59] Treitel, pp. 703–704; Walker, para. 34.12. The claim for damages must be one that arises out of the same contract or transaction and is "so inseparably connected that the one ought not to be enforced without taking account of the other": *Dole Dried Fruit & Nut Co. v. Trustin Kerwood Ltd* [1990] 2 Lloyd's Rep. 309, 311, *per* Lloyd L.J., C.A.

[60] [1995] 4 All E.R. 95.

[61] At 99.

[62] April 11, 1984, a decision of Nolan J.: see at 100–101.

[63] At 102.

[64] See above, para. 45g.

[65] At 102.

The maritime rule is so well entrenched that a determined attack on it in *Aries*,[66] was repulsed, although "neither the reason nor the justification for this rule of English law has ever been defined".[67] In times past, the justification for the maritime rule appears to have been the liquidity needed to finance carriage by sea, and "the protection of British shipowners who might be faced with insubstantial claims for damages by foreign shippers".[68] In 1864 Willes J.,[69] while admitting that there "would be apparent justice in allowing [culpable damage] to be set off or deducted in an action for freight" affirmed that "our law does not allow deduction in that form; and . . . for the sake perhaps of speedy settlement of freight and other liquidated demands, it affords the injured party a remedy by cross-action only". In 1973 Roskill L.J.,[70] having reviewed the nineteenth-century cases, said that "the reason for the existence of the [rule] does not clearly emerge from the authorities unless it be that it was to encourage prompt payment of freight to British shipowners trading in distant countries in days when communications were scarce to the point of non-existence and money could not be transferred as it can today. Freight was historically 'the mother of wages' and if a master did not get the freight, the crew's wages and repair bills were liable to go unpaid.

---

[66] *Aries Tanker Corp. v. Total Transport* [1977] 1 All E.R. 398 H.L. Tetley, pp. 894 *et seq.* There is support for the English rule in Canada: Tetley, p. 908. However, the rule has not been adopted in the USA, where by the rule of "recoupment" it is a defence to a carrier's action for freight that the carrier has not fulfilled his obligations: Tetley, pp. 899 *et seq. cf.* for example, *Shipping Corp. of India v. Pan American*, 583 F.Supp. 1555 (S.D.N.Y., 1984). Nor is anything like the English rule found in France: Tetley, p. 910. In England, however, "whatever its merits or demerits, [the rule] is not open to challenge" *Bank of Boston Connecticut v. European Grain and Shipping Ltd, The Dominique* [1989] A.C. 1056, 1100, *per* Lord Brandon, H.L. Further, in *The Dominique* the main issue was (at 1101, *per* Lord Brandon) whether "although a claim in respect of non-repudiatory breach of voyage charterparty cannot opeate as a defence by way of set-off to a claim for freight, a claim in respect of a repudiation of such contract, accepted as such, is capable of doing so", when the owner's right to freight has accrued prior to repudiation. The owners had repudiated the charter by failing to make the vessel available to the charterers, and this repudiation had been accepted by the charterers as terminating the contract. The House of Lords held that the owners' right to freight survived the repudiation (*Johnson v. Agnew* [1980] A.C. 367) and that the owners' breach could not operate as a defence to an action for freight. Again, the rule in the USA is different: McMahon (1989) 20 J.M.L.C. 429, 434.

If in such a case the right to freight has not accrued at the time of repudiation by the carrier, the possibility remains that the decision would be different, as there is an "equity sufficient to impeach the legal title": see at 1106, *per* Lord Brandon. However, Lord Brandon also made (at 1107) a convincing case against any distinction in this regard between repudiatory and non-repudiatory breach, so the defendant would still have to overcome *Aries* (above). See also *The Elena* [1986] 1 Lloyd's Rep. 425, 427, *per* Steyn J.

[67] At 409, *per* Lord Salmon. The leading and contrary case in the USA is *Pennsylvania Railroad v. Miller*, 124 F.2d 160 (5 Cir. 1941).

[68] *The Brede* [1974] Q.B. 233, 254; [1973] 2 Lloyd's Rep. 333, 341, *per* Cairns L.J., C.A.

[69] *Dakin v. Oxley* (1864) 15 C.B.N.S. 646, 667, *per* Willes J.

[70] *The Brede* [1973] 2 Lloyd's Rep. 333, 346–347, C.A. This explanation was adopted by Steyn J. in *The Elena* [1986] 1 Lloyd's Rep. 425, 427.

No doubt these considerations do not apply with as much force today." Indeed, the argument based on liquidity has been rejected altogether at the highest level.[71] As for the other arguments, they scarcely justify the extension of the rule, which has been described as anomalous,[72] contrary to principles of the law of contract,[73] unsafe,[74] and a rule that should not be extended[75] from carriage by sea to carriage by road.

The same is true of two further arguments advanced by Roskill L.J.[76] to counter the contention that the rule was out of date and should be abandoned.

> "First, the law has been as we have held it to have been for at least a century and a half. That of itself is good reason not to change it. Secondly (though Counsel through no fault of theirs were unable to help us greatly on this point) to alter the existing law would or at least might disturb the present distribution of risk between the shipowners' freight underwriters and their Protection and Indemnity Association. At present on the footing that there is no defence to a claim for freight, any liability of shipowners to cargo owners falls on the Protection of Indemnity Association. If there were a defence to a claim for freight it is at least arguable that there would then be a loss of freight which would or might fall on the owners' freight underwriters and not on the Protection and Indemnity Association . . . Courts should not lightly alter the law from what it has hitherto been thought to be when to do so would be to disturb existing contractual arrangements."

Whether or not these arguments are convincing in shipping law,[77] they have no apparent relevance to carriage by road to which the rule had not been applied.[78]

---

[71] *Gilbert-Ash (Northern) v. Modern Engineering (Bristol)* [1974] A.C. 689, 707, *per* Viscount Dilhorne, rejecting argument for a similar rule against set-off in a building contract.

[72] *James & Co. v. Chinacrest* [1979] 1 Lloyd's Rep. 126, 129, *per* Stephenson L.J., C.A. The more general rule is that when the contractor sues for the price of work and labour but has himself broken the contract, the defendant can set up the breach as a defence or set his loss in diminution or extinction of the contract price: *The Brede* [1973] 2 Lloyd's Rep. 333, 337–338, *per* Lord Denning, M.R., C.A.

[73] Glass and Cashmore, para. 1.107, citing *Morgan & Son v. Johnson & Co.* [1949] 1 K.B. 107, C.A. Treitel, pp. 703–704.

[74] *The Dominique* [1989] A.C. 1056, 1076 *per* Mustill L.J., C.A. as regards a carrier who has wrongfully repudiated, in a decision, however, which was reversed by the House of Lords: [1989] A.C. 1056. Glass and Cashmore, para. 1.107. *Drew Ameroid International v. M/V Green Star* 1988 A.M.C. 2570, 2578 (S.D.N.Y., 1988). McMahon, 20 J.M.L.C. 429, 438 (1989).

[75] *Seven Seas Transportation v. Atlantic Shipping Co.* [1975] 2 Lloyd's Rep. 188, 191, *per* Donaldson J., with whom Goff L.J. agreed in *Federal Commerce & Navigation Co. v. Molena Alpha Inc.* [1978] 1 Q.B. 927, 982, C.A.

[76] *The Brede* [1973] 2 Lloyd's Rep. 333, 347, C.A.

[77] As regards the first argument, the rule has been described as "time hallowed" by Ackner L.J. in *The Cleon* [1983] 1 Lloyd's Rep. 586, 591, C.A. and as "sacrosanct" by Hirst J. in *The Khian Captain (No. 2)* [1986] 1 Lloyd's Rep. 429, 433.

[78] Cashmore [1985] J.B.L. 68. In *Pennsylvania Railroad v. Miller* 124 F.2d 160 (5 Cir., 1941) argument that such a rule should be applied to cariage by rail was rejected as contrary to English common law as adopted in Texas.

Nonetheless, stripped of its imperial connotation, one argument for the maritime rule, one advanced in 1864 by Willes J. in the passage quoted (above), has survived. The passage was quoted by Lord Denning M.R. in 1973,[79] who then said that "this rule about freight is to be justified in the same way as the like rule about a sum due on a bill of exchange . . . The good conduct of business demands that freight should be paid according to the terms of the contract. Payment should not be held up because the goods are alleged to have been damaged in transit. If that were allowed, it would enable unscrupulous persons to make all sorts of unfounded allegations—so as to avoid payment. In any case, even with the most scrupulous, it would lead to undesirable delay." If true of carriage by sea, it is no less true of carriage by road, in which it is the carrier who may be in the weaker bargaining position and cargo interests need no encouragement to withhold carriage charges.[80] This may explain the extension of the rule to carriage by road in 1984. In a more recent case, argument for a distinction of this kind was rejected but, as we have seen, the maritime rule was applied to carriage by road nonetheless.[81]

If, as now appears, the maritime rule applies to carriage by road, there is some comfort for the consignee in that the rule may be modified or excluded by the contract of carriage[82]; and that, unless the consignee abuses a dominant economic position, the court is unlikely to exercise its discretion to award the carrier interest on unpaid carriage charges, "because the basic reason for an award of interest is to compensate a party for the *wrongful* detention of his money".[83] Moreover, a claim for carriage charges will fail if the carrier has not performed the service contracted for.[84]

---

[79] *The Brede* [1973] 2 Lloyd's Rep. 333, 338, C.A.

[80] Buyl, Theunis 285. Not surprisingly, the FIATA Report (p. 27) on CMR reform maintained: "Freight, demurrage and incidental charges shall be paid without deduction. Counterclaims of any nature may not be exercised by way of set-off."

[81] *United Carriers Ltd v. Heritage Food Group (UK) Ltd* (above, n. 60).

[82] This is certainly true of time charters: *The Kostas Melas* [1981] 1 Lloyd's Rep. 18, 25, *per* Robert Goff J.: and voyage charters: *The Olympic Brilliance* [1982] 2 Lloyd's Rep. 205, C.A.; and is probably true of other contracts for the carriage of goods by sea (Tetley, p. 896) and, presumably, contracts for the carriage of goods by road.

[83] *The Khian Captain (No. 2)* [1986] 1 Lloyd's Rep. 429, 434, *per* Hirst J.

[84] The maritime rule does not apply to time charters, where there will be equitable set-off as regards the payment of hire, if "the charterers have been deprived of the use of the ship by the fault of the owners"—*The Aliakmon Progress* [1978] 2 Lloyd's Rep. 499, 501, *per* Lord Denning M.R., C.A.; *The Leon* [1985] 2 Lloyd's Rep. 470, 475, *per* Hobhouse J.

CHAPTER 12

THE LIABILITY OF THE CARRIER

220. Contract or tort

If goods are lost, damaged or delayed during carriage, action may be brought against the carrier based in contract or in tort. In the present state of English law, although liability is concurrent in tort and contract,[1] the extent of the carrier's liability in tort is unlikely to be greater than the carrier's liability in contract. There is a difference, however, as regards the limitation of actions.[2] In any event, the carrier's primary liability is in contract, so consideration of that comes first in this chapter[3] followed by consideration of the carrier's liability in tort[4] and, after that some issues common to both contract and tort.[5]

221. The pattern of liability

In principle, the carrier is strictly liable for loss of or damage to the goods occurring while in charge of the goods *qua* carrier, as well as for delay in delivery[6]; the liability is to any person entitled to bring an action on those grounds.[7] To resist such an action, the carrier's first line of defence is to dispute the evidence of loss, damage or delay brought by the claimant. The second line of defence is, while not disputing that there was such loss, damage or delay, to prove that it was caused by inherent vice in the goods or by some other cause for which the carrier is excused by a term of the contract of carriage.[8] If unable to establish one of these

---

[1] In *Henderson v. Merrett Syndicates Ltd* [1995] 2 A.C. 145, the argument against concurrent liability was rejected. Lord Goff said (at 193–194) that although the "result may be untidy", in that context at least (negligent underwriting at Lloyd's), "the common law is not antipathetic to concurrent liability, and that there is no sound basis for a rule which automatically restricts the claimant to either a tortious or a contractual liability".

[2] See above, para. 218.

[3] Below, paras. 223 *et seq.*

[4] Below, paras. 229 *et seq.*

[5] Such as remoteness of damage: below, paras. 246 *et seq.*

[6] *e.g. Peek v. North Staffs Ry* (1863) 10 H.L. Cas. 472, 560, *per* Cockburn L.C.J.

[7] See above, paras. 216 *et seq.*

[8] See below, paras. 236 *et seq.*

defences, the carrier may fall back on a third line of defence, that the action is out of time[9] or that the amount in money of the liability is limited.[10] A defence in the second or third line can be dismantled, however, if the claimant can establish that the term is unreasonable under the Unfair Contract Terms Act[11] or that the carrier committed a fundamental breach of the contract of carriage.[12]

222. The basis of liability

To establish a claim against the carrier, the claimant must prove that the carrier was in breach of what the carrier promised in the contract of carriage. Generally, the carrier undertakes a strict obligation to deliver the goods in the quantity and condition, in which they were taken over, at a certain destination and within a certain time.[13] This interpretation of the level of the duty is in line with the presumption found in the general law of contract about the absolute nature of commercial promises.[14] The corollary is that the claimant does not have to prove that the carrier was negligent; but nor is it for the carrier to prove delivery of the goods in accordance with contract: it is for the claimant to prove otherwise.

In the past, this view has been clouded, first, by the possibility that the carrier is a common carrier. Common carriers have a strict liability for loss of or damage (but not delay) to the goods and that strict liability is subject to exceptions: Act of God, Act of the Queen's enemies, inherent vice and fraud on the part of the sender or consignee.[15] Carriers are not common carriers, however, unless they hold themselves out as willing to carry for reward for all and sundry (without reserving the right to refuse the goods tendered for carriage).[16] Not many do[17]; anyway, if there is a contract the contract terms prevail and these can modify and reduce the carrier's liability, although the carrier remains a common carrier in

---

[9] See above, para. 218.
[10] See below, para. 246.
[11] See below, para. 239.
[12] See below, para. 240.
[13] *A. Siohn & Co. Ltd v. R.H. Hagland & Son (Transport) Ltd* [1976] 2 Lloyd's Rep. 482. For a similar interpretation of the contract to carry goods by sea, see *Albacora S.R.L. v. Wescott & Laurance Line* [1966] 2 Lloyd's Rep. 53, H.L.
[14] Treitel, p. 778; Walker, para. 31.39.
[15] See Glass and Cashmore, paras. 1.27 *et seq.* The carrier loses the defence if the claimant shows that the loss or damage was caused by the carrier's negligence.
[16] *Siohn*, above. *cf. Belfast Ropework Co. Ltd v. Bushell* [1918] 1 K.B. 210. Palmer, pp. 969 *et seq.*
[17] See Glass and Cashmore, para. 1.25. See also the Carriers Act 1830: Palmer, pp. 980 *et seq.* Note that the Post Office is not a common carrier; on the contrary, its liability for postal consignments is governed by statute: Post Office Act 1969, ss.29–30.

matters not covered by the contract terms.[18] What counts in practice is the terms.

In the past, the strict and contractual basis of the carrier's liability has also been obscured by associated rules of bailment. In theory, bailees owe a duty that is not strict but one of reasonable care; because a carrier is also a bailee, some authors have suggested that the carrier's level of duty as contracting carrier should be that of a bailee.[19] The better view today, however, is that the question is a smoke-screen for a red herring: the answer is a matter of no more than theoretical interest—like the question. This is because, first, the basic and strict contractual obligation of the carrier *qua* carrier, although strict in theory, is not strict in practice: it is always modified by the terms of the contract. Secondly, if bailees fail to redeliver goods in the quantity and condition received, there is a presumption that they are in breach of duty as bailees; this presumption immediately casts on the carrier, like other bailees, the burden of proving an excuse of some kind recognised by law.[20] Although not a strict duty in theory, in practice the bailees' duty looks and feels like one. Indeed, it is like the contractual duty of the carrier at common law which, in theory, is strict. Under the "historic common-law contract of carriage of goods [by sea] it had long been settled in this country that when goods had been accepted in apparent good order and condition and were delivered in a damaged state, that was enough to provide *prima facie* evidence of breach of contracting, casting on the carrier the burden of bringing himself within one of the recognised and contractual exceptions".[21] So, contract and bailment, coming from different theoretical starting points, converge in practice.

223. Liability: contract terms

In practice most, if not all, contracts of carriage modify the basic liability of the carrier at common law (above, paragraph 222).

---

[18] Palmer, pp. 971–972. Simply to declare in the contract that the carrier is not a common carrier is not conclusive of the carrier's status: Palmer, p. 1094.

[19] *e.g.* Scrutton, p. 200.

[20] *H.C. Smith v. G.W. Ry* [1992] 1 A.C. 173, 183, H.L.; *Woolmer v. Delmer Price* [1955] 1 Q.B. 291. *W.L.R. Traders (London) Ltd v. British & Northern Shipping Agency Ltd* [1955] 1 Lloyd's Rep. 554, 561, *per* Pilcher J.; *Hunt & Winterbotham (West of England) Ltd v. B.R.S. (Parcels) Ltd* [1962] 1 Q.B. 617 *per* Donovan L.J., C.A.; *Pye Ltd v. B.G. Transport Service Ltd* [1966] 2 Lloyd's Rep. 300, 303, *per* Browne J.; *The Sansei Maru, Port Swettenham Authority v. T.W. Wu & Co.* [1979] A.C. 580, 590, *per* Lord Salmon, P.C.; *Victoria Fur Traders Ltd v. Road Line (U.K.) Ltd* [1981] 1 Lloyd's Rep. 570, 578, *per* Mocatta J. Similarly in Australia: *The Antwerpen* [1994] 1 Lloyd's Rep. 213, 238, *per* Sheller J.A. (N.S.W.)

[21] *Albacora SRL v. Westcott & Laurance Line Ltd* [1965] 2 Lloyd's Rep. 37, 46 (Ct. Sess.); affirmed [1966] 2 Lloyd's Rep. 53, H.L. See also *The Theodegmon* [1990] 1 Lloyd's Rep. 52, 53, *per* Phillips J.

A leading example is RHA Condition 9, which provides for three levels of liability, all of which reduce the basic liability of the carrier at common law; the scheme is that the customer chooses the level for which the customer is willing to pay.

The first and lowest level of liability is that whereby (with the customer's agreement in writing) the goods are carried entirely at the customer's risk. This is no liability at all and it is difficult to see how the clause can survive attack under the Unfair Contract Terms Act 1977,[22] unless the rate charged by the carrier is very low indeed.[23] This, at least, was the opinion of Blackburn J. in a case decided under the comparable requirement of the Railway and Canal Traffic Act 1854 that contracts be "just and reasonable": "a condition exempting the carriers wholly from liability for the neglect and default of their servants is *prima facie* unreasonable".[24] However, he continued: "A carrier is bound to carry for a reasonable remuneration, and if he offers to do so, but at the same time offers in the alternative to carry on the terms that he shall have no liability at all, and holds forth as an inducement a reduction of the price below that which would be reasonable remuneration for carrying at carrier's risk, or some additional advantage, which he is not bound to give, [that condition] may be reasonable enough".[25]

The second level of liability is a liability for negligence in respect of the carriage of special items: livestock, bullion, money, securities, stamps, precious metals and precious stones. The third and highest level of liability is residual in that it applies to other cases but, it seems, is the most important in practice. It starts from the strict liability of the carrier at common law but reduces it by a string of specific exemptions, which go well beyond those allowed at common law.[26]

In contrast, the liability of a forwarder under BIFA terms for performing the carriage is much more simply expressed. The fowarder undertakes in clause 26 to "perform its duties with a reasonable degree of care, skill and judgement". The clause confirms the duty implied by section 13 of the Supply of Goods and Services Act 1982.[27] The corollary of the clause is articulated by clause 27B whereby the company is relieved of liability for loss or damage, principally, for loss or damage caused by "any cause or event, which the Company is unable to avoid and the consequences whereof the Company is unable to prevent by the exercise of reasonable diligence". This makes it clear that the forwarder as

---

[22] Also in this sense: Glass and Cashmore, para. 1.55; Palmer, p. 1103. For the Act, see below, para. 239a.

[23] *cf. Coupar Transport (London) Ltd v. Smith's (Acton) Ltd* [1959] 1 Lloyd's Rep. 369.

[24] *Peek v. North Staffs Ry* (1863) 10 H.L. Cas. 472, 511.

[25] At 511–512.

[26] See below, Chap. 14.

[27] See Yates, paras. 7.2.7.1 *et seq.*

carrier does not accept the strict contractual duty of the carrier at common law.[28]

224. The scope of liability in time

In principle, the carrier's liability *qua* carrier beings when the carrier takes the goods over in that role, *i.e.* when the goods come into the carrier's control. That liability continues until, by delivery, control is passed to another person, usually the consignee.[29] The matter is often regulated in the contract of carriage by a "transit clause". For example, the effect of BIFA clause 6 is that when the forwarding company is performing the service of carriage it "accepts liability for loss of or damage to goods taken into its charge occurring between the time when it takes the goods into its charge and the time when the Company is entitled to call upon the Customer, Consignee or Owner to take delivery of the goods".[30]

225. The nature of breach

Breach is a failure of the undertaking to deliver the goods in the quantity and condition in which they were taken over, at a certain destination and within a certain time.[31] Hence it is the incidence of loss or damage to the goods, non-delivery or delay.

225a. Loss or damage

Loss, which may be partial or total, occurs when the goods become less in volume or quantity than they were before. Loss it has been held,[32] includes a case of misdelivery of goods. Damage usually refers to a changed physical state. In "common parlance", it means "mischief done to property".[33] "Damage to", "when used in relation to goods, is a physical alteration or change, not necessarily permanent or irreparable, which impairs the value or usefulness of the things said to be damaged. It follows that not every physical change to goods would amount to damage."[34] The precise definition, however, depends on the context in which the word

---

[28] *cf.* Yates, paras. 7.2.7.10 *et seq.*

[29] The law on this is the same under the CMR; see above, paras. 27 and 40.

[30] This appears to be in line with the common law rules. See Yates, paras. 7.2.6.1 *et seq.* See also, for example, RHA Condition 6 which, largely, confirms the common law rules; for these rules, see above, paras. 206 and 215.

[31] Above, para. 222.

[32] *Shipworth v. G.W. Ry* (1888) 59 L.T. 520.

[33] *Smith v. Brown* (1871) 40 L.J.Q.B. 214, 218, *per* Cockburn C.J.

[34] *Ranicar v. Frigmobile Pty Ltd* (1983) Tas. R. 113, 116.

is used.[35] For example, scallops, which are perfectly fit for immediate consumption but have been raised to a temperature, which has shortened their shelf life, may be damaged scallops for the customer who does not want them for immediate consumption but for sale later in the market.[36] The goods have become less valuable than they were before, however, for there to be damage in the sense of a carriage contract,[37] it will usually also be necessary to produce the report of a food laboratory that a physical change has occurred in the scallops. Moreover, as the carrier is not liable contractually for ordinary wear and tear[38] (or in some cases inherent vice), in practice, to be damage, the change in the goods must be one which was not inevitable in the circumstances or in the speed of its development.

225b. Non-delivery

Non-delivery occurs when the goods are totally lost in transit[39] or delivered to the wrong person or in the wrong place.[40]

225c. Delay

The carrier is liable for the consequences of delay but only, it has been said,[41] if the carrier has been negligent; alternatively, it has been said,[42] lateness raises a presumption of liability which can be defeated by proof that the carrier has not been negligent. However, these propositions are based on early cases of carriage[43] and it is not clear that a rule reflecting the days of horse and cart on rutted roads can stand with more recent developments in the law and practice of carriage.[44] It is submitted that, although what has been said is true of many cases in practice, the theoretical starting point is rather different: if the carrier agrees to deliver by a specific time or date, that is a strict contractual obligation, and if the carrier is late, the carrier will be liable, subject to contract defences, whether negligent or not.

---

[35] *Swansea Corp. v. Harpur* [1912] 3 K.B. 493, 505, *per* Fletcher Moulton L.J., C.A.
[36] *Ranicar* (above).
[37] But *cf.* carriage of goods by sea: *Goulandris Bros. Ltd v. B. Goldman & Sons* [1958] 1 Q.B. 74, 105, *per* Pearson J.
[38] Below, para. 236j.
[39] Above, para. 210a.
[40] Above, paras. 212 *et seq.*
[41] *e.g.* Glass and Cashmore, para. 1.37; Palmer, p. 986.
[42] Palmer, p. 986.
[43] *e.g. Taylor v. G.N. Ry* (1866) L.R. 1 C.P. 385.
[44] As regards the parallel issue in carriage by sea, see the judgment of Diplock L.J. in *The Heron II, Koufos v. C. Czarikow Ltd* [1966] 2 Q.B. 695, 725–726, C.A.; affirmed without consideration of this point: [1969] 1 A.C. 350.

Generally, English courts tend to construe time stipulations strictly[45]: they assume that "time is of the essence of the contract" and hold that, if performance is late, the other party is entitled to terminate the contract.[46] If, in the case of carriage, the goods have arrived late at destination, the right to terminate the contract is of little practical importance. It will matter mostly when the goods have not got there but it has become apparent that they will not be delivered on time by the carrier in breach; in these circumstances it does matter that the customer is entitled to terminate the contract and regain possession of the goods—perhaps to employ another carrier and perhaps for an alternative destination.

In the absence of a time stipulation in the contract of carriage, "there is an implied contract to deliver within a reasonable time . . . a time within which the carrier can deliver, using all reasonable exertions",[47] in the circumstances of the actual carriage; in practice, that duty will be breached only if the carrier has been negligent.[48]

226. Proof of loss or damage

For the claimant to prove loss or damage may be difficult. Under Article 30.1 of the CMR, if the consignee takes delivery of the goods, there is a presumption that the carrier has performed the contract, unless the consignee protests.[49] English common law seems to have no such rule; the common law response to the CMR rule is, if the consignee does protest, what of that? Certainly, protest has a function, namely to alert the carrier that a dispute has arisen: the wise carrier will investigate before it is too late. To get a claim off the ground, however, protest alone is not enough—either under the CMR or at common law. It still remains for the claimant, assumed for discussion here to be the consignee, to prove that the carrier was in breach of the undertaking to get the goods to the agreed destination; the claimant does not, however, have to prove how or why the breach occurred.

---

[45] *Bunge Corp. v. Tradax Export S.A.* [1981] 2 All E.R. 513, 542, *per* Lord Wilberforce, H.L. Treitel pp. 713 *et seq.*; Walker para. 31.6. But *cf. The Naxos* [1991] 1 W.L.R. 1337, H.L.; Clarke [1991] C.L.J. 29. There must be a "commercial necessity" that time be regarded strictly, *i.e.* a matter of "practical importance in the scheme of the contract" (*Torvald Klaveness A/S v. Arni Maritime Corp.* [1994] 4 All E.R. 998, 1009, *per* Lord Templeman, H.L.) and courts are now less ready to presume that this is so than appeared after *Bunge* in 1981.

[46] In this sense for contracts of carriage: *Horne v. Midland Ry* (1873) L.R. 8 C.P. 131 (Exch. Ch.); Palmer, p. 986.

[47] *Taylor v. G.N. Ry Co.* (1866) L.R. 1 C.P. 385, 387, *per* Earle C.J. See also *Raphael v. Pickford* (1843) 5 Man. & G. 551; *Postlethwaite v. Freeland* (1880) 5 App.Cas. 599. Kahn-Freund, pp. 277 *et seq.*; Palmer, p. 986.

[48] Supply of Goods and Services Act 1982, s.14(1).

[49] See above, paras. 60–61.

The claim is established in two parts. One is to prove the state or quantity of the goods on delivery. That alone does not prove a claim, even if they are damaged, because the carrier is a carrier and not a repairer. So, the claimant must establish also, in a damage claim, that the goods were different in condition when the carrier took them in charge on consignment. And in a loss claim the claimant must establish that the goods were different (greater) in quantity when the carrier took them in charge on consignment. The carrier's obligation is not an obligation to deliver the goods in a state of perfection but in the same quantity and condition, whatever that was, in which they were taken over.

As to the first part, condition or quantity on delivery, the claimant must use whatever proof is available—usually the report of a reliable third party—as soon as possible, to avoid the riposte that damage or pilfering occurred between the time of delivery and report.[50] If the carrier's only representative there is the driver, that may pose problems: the driver may be less interested in checking goods than in food and rest.

As to the second part of the claimant's task, to establish the condition and quantity of the goods when the carrier took them in charge, the evidence available depends on the efficacy of the transport document in its role as a receipt: usually the claimant seeks to establish what the carrier received by reference to a document, such as a consignment note, issued by the carrier when the carrier took the goods over.

Unless the carrier has no reasonable means of checking the accuracy of what it states, the transport document is prima facie evidence of the truth of the statements made in it; however, the evidentiary value of consignment notes is commonly affected by contract terms. For example, RHA Condition 5 obliges the carrier, if so required, to sign a document prepared by the sender but provides also that "no such document shall be evidence of the condition or of the correctness of the declared nature, quantity, or weight" of the goods at the time that they are received by the carrier. In such a case, the claimant must produce other evidence of what the carrier received.

If the consignee alleges non-delivery of the entire consignment, *ex hypothesi*, there are no goods at destination to be checked or examined. If the carrier denies having taken the goods in charge at all, attention focuses more heavily then ever on the transport document. In the case of carriage by sea, the claimant makes a case by producing a bill of lading for the goods which would have been surrendered in exchange for the goods if, contrary to the claimant's case, they had been delivered. In the case of carriage by road,

[50] *cf.* Art. 30.2 of CMR (above, para. 61a) whereby, if the consignee checks the goods with the road carrier, whatever they agree is conclusive, except as regards information that was not apparent at the time.

the consignee has no such document and may find it difficult to prove this kind of claim: the claimant must prove not only that the goods were taken in charge by the carrier but also the negative proposition that they were not delivered.[51]

227. Causation

The carrier's breach of contract must have been the "effective or dominant" cause[52] of the loss for which the customer is claiming damages. What does that mean? Until quite recently, the answer would have been along these lines: that it was really "all a matter of remoteness",[53] and that a separate discussion of causation was largely superfluous.[54]

> In *Heskell v. Continental Express*[55] the defendants did not perform their undertakings to the plaintiffs to dispatch goods, and the plaintiffs sought to recover the amount of damages which the plaintiffs had paid to their overseas buyers. The action was defended *inter alia* on the ground of what the law of tort refers to as *novus actus interveniens*: the act of a third party, a loading broker, who issued a bill of lading for the goods, stating inaccurately that the goods had been received by or for a sea carrier, which stifled inquiry about the whereabouts of the goods. But for this, the non-dispatch would have been discovered. The defence failed. The defendants were held liable by Devlin J. for the entire loss claimed.

In *Heskell* the defence was put in two ways. First, in terms of intervening causation, it was argued that the brokers' carelessness was the dominant cause of the loss. On this Devlin J. observed[56] that "the intervening acts, while not destroying the wrong as a causative event, may contribute to the damage that occurs; the damage is then caused both by the wrong and by the intervening act". In *Heskell*, however, the dominant cause remained the defendants' breach of contract. Secondly, in terms of remoteness of damage, it was argued that delay and consequent loss after the date for dispatch was not a foreseeable consequence of the breach of contract: the chances were that the non-dispatch would have been discovered, if the loading broker had not been careless as

---

[51] *cf.* CMR Art. 20, above, para. 56b.

[52] *e.g. Galoo v. Bright Grahame* [1994] 1 All E.R. 16, C.A.

[53] See, *e.g. Monarch S.S. Co. v. Karlhmans Oljefabriker* [1949] A.C. 196, 227–228. Concerning remoteness of damage, see below, para. 246.

[54] Alternatively, problems of causation are addressed with rules of remoteness, for example, Walker, para. 33.25.

[55] [1950] 1 All E.R. 1033.

[56] At 1047. On the possibility of apportionment, see *Tennant Radiant Heat v. Warrington Development Corp.* [1988] 1 E.G.L.R. 41, C.A. and discussion of this possibility by the Law Commission WP no. 114, paras. 3.20, 4.11 and 4.24 *et seq.*

well. The answer to this, said the judge,[57] was that the defendants' breach of contract did not end on the date for dispatch but continued thereafter. However, the argument was sound in principle: an intervening act, which could not have been within the reasonable contemplation as likely to occur, will break the causal link between the conduct of the carrier and the loss, damage or delay in question.[58]

Today a rather different discussion is called for because courts in contract cases have given more thought to questions of causation. The pause for thought arose out of contracts containing duties of care, duties which seemed (rightly) to the court to be like duties owed in tort and which triggered a "tort" response from the court. The law of tort has been much concerned with questions of causation and the response of courts in these contract cases is to show a similar concern and, as some courts have acknowledged, to align contract and tort on questions of causation.[59]

The effect on contract cases is, first, that the loss must have been caused in fact by the breach: the customer must establish that but for the breach the loss would not have occurred.[60]

Secondly, there is a tendency to settle issues of causation at an early stage of analysis, namely at the stage of deciding what the defendant has promised and thus whether the defendant owes a duty of care at all. For example, Lord Hoffmann has said[61]:

> "A duty of care which imposes upon the [defendant] responsibility for losses which would have occurred [anyway] is not in my view fair and reasonable as between the parties. It is therefore inappropriate either as an implied term of a contract or as a tortious duty arising from the relationship between them."

Thirdly, if the breach of contract by the carrier is one of two concurrent causes, "both cooperating and both of equal efficacy . . . [the carrier's breach] is sufficient to carry a judgment for damages".[62]

Fourthly, if the carrier's breach is the first of two consecutive causes, the breach remains the effective and dominant cause as long as it can be said that the later cause probably would have

[57] At 1046.

[58] *Wilson v. The Newport Dock Co.* (1866) L.R. 1 Ex. 177; *Quinn v. Burch Bros.* [1966] 2 Q.B. 370, 390, *per* Sellers L.J., C.A.; *Lambert v. Lewis* [1981] 1 All E.R. 1185, 1191, *per* Lord Diplock, H.L. However, the theorist distinguishes causation and remoteness, for example, Hart and Honoré, *Causation in the Law* (2nd ed., Oxford, 1985) p. xlix. Treitel, p. 880; Walker, para. 33.27.

[59] *South Australia Asset Management Corp. v. York Montagu Ltd* [1996] 3 All E.R. 365, H.L.

[60] *ibid.*, at 372. See also *Beoco Ltd v. Alfa Laval Co. Ltd* [1994] 4 All E.R. 464, C.A. Halson [1996] L.M.C.L.Q. 438, 441.

[61] *South Australia Asset Management Corp. v. York Montagu Ltd*, (above), at 372.

[62] *Heskell v. Continental Express Ltd* [1950] 1 All E.R. 1033, 1048, *per* Devlin J.

occurred anyway[63] or that it consisted of "the very kind of events the terms of engagement were designed to forestall".[64] In other words, it consisted of events which, it might be said, the defendant carrier had assumed responsibility to guard against; for example, as a bailee of the goods entrusted, the carrier has a particular duty to guard against theft and, if careless, the carrier is liable for the lack of care in the event of theft, whether the intervention of the thief was probable or not.[65] If, however, the later cause is neither probable nor something which the carrier is to guard against, it is a *novus actus interveniens* breaking the "chain" of causation between the carrier's breach and the customer's loss or damage.[66]

Finally, just as in the law of tort there comes a point when any subsequent loss is the result of the claimant's failure to respond reasonably to the danger or damage created by the defendant, so also contract law states that the claimant, here the customer, has a "duty" to mitigate loss or damage.[67] Thus, the customer, who finds that the carrier has failed to collect the goods and is unlikely to do so, must look for an alternative carrier.[68] The customer whose goods have been damaged must seek alternative goods[69] or have the damaged goods repaired if that stops the damage getting worse or permits performance of a sub-contract that cannot be performed otherwise. However, if the customer is to reclaim from the carrier the cost of mitigation, that cost, like the cost of "cure" as the main measure of damages,[70] must not have exceeded what is reasonable.

In *The Alecos M*[71] the defendant sellers contracted to sell a ship to the plaintiff buyers, including a spare propellor. They delivered the ship but not the spare propellor and the buyers sought damages. As the value of the (entire) ship was not affected by whether

---

[63] *Allied Maples Group Ltd v. Simmons & Simmons* [1995] 4 All E.R. 907, C.A. For example, the immediate consequence of the carrier's breach is that goods have to be sent back for repacking or reconditioning and, clearly, the carrier is liable for the cost; but the carrier may well also be liable for the loss of market when the consignee buyer rejects the repacked or reconditioned goods as being too late; *Keddie Gordon & Co. v. North British Ry Co.* (1886) 14 R. 233.

[64] *County Ltd v. Girozentrale Securities* [1996] 3 All E.R. 834, 847, *per* Beldam L.J., C.A.

[65] *Stansbie v. Troman* [1948] 2 K.B. 48. See also *Lambert v. Lewis* [1981] 1 All E.R. 1185, 1190, *per* Lord Diplock, H.L.

[66] *Lambert* (above).

[67] It is a "duty" the breach of which does not sound in damages against the party who has failed to mitigate: Treitel, pp. 881 *et seq.*

[68] *Monarch S.S. Co. v. Karlhmans Oljefabriker* [1949] A.C. 196.

[69] *Stroms Bruks A/B v. Hutchison* [1905] A.C. 515.

[70] See *Ruxley Electronics Ltd v. Forsyth* [1995] 3 All E.R. 268, H.L. In a much cited passage from *Radford v. De Froberville* [1978] 1 All E.R. 33, Oliver J. said (at 44) that "the measure of damages and the plaintiff's duty to mitigate are logically distinct concepts. . . . But to some extent, at least, they are mirror images . . . ; for the measure of damages can be, very frequently, arrived at only by postulating and answering the question, what can this particular plaintiff reasonably do to alleviate his loss."

[71] [1991] 1 Lloyd's Rep. 120. See also *The Griparion* [1994] 1 Lloyd's Rep. 533.

the ship had a spare propellor or not, the buyers sought damages by reference to "cost of cure", *i.e.* the cost of somehow getting a propellor. However, reference to the market for spare propellors was not possible: no such market existed. In these circumstances, whereas Steyn J. held that the buyers were entitled to recover the reasonable cost of obtaining a spare propellor by having one specially made, the Court of Appeal preferred the view of the arbitrator that the buyers had failed to meet the burden of showing that it would be reasonable to do so.

In *Darbishire v. Warran*[72] Pearson L.J. stated that "the plaintiff is not entitled to charge the defendant by way of damages with any greater sum than that which he reasonably needs to expend for the purpose of making good the loss. In short, he is fully entitled to be extravagant as he pleases but not at the expense of the defendant." Having referred to this statement, Neill L.J. in *The Alecos M*[73] continued: "It follows, therefore, that the recoverable loss in any case is limited to that which can be said to be 'properly caused by the defendant's breach of duty'." He then referred to a statement by Templeman L.J.: "Whatever principle is invoked—whether it be the principle of causation or mitigation—the acid test . . . must have been reasonableness."[74] The judge concluded by asking: "[w]hat damage did the buyers really suffer as a result of the non-delivery of the spare propellor? . . . this was the question which the arbitrator addressed when he considered whether the buyers were likely to or needed to obtain a replacement for the missing spare propellor and whether it was reasonable to order one to be specially manufactured . . . And he gave the answer: they lost its scrap value which in the circumstances was the only value it had for them."

228. Apportionment: mixed causes

If, for example, the claimant provides defective instructions, defects which the carrier could not be expected to discover or do anything about, the carrier is not liable: the sole cause lies with the claimant. If, however, the carrier should have discovered the defect and could then have done and should then have done something, liability will be apportioned. If, however, defective instructions for the care of the goods are provided by the customer and, as a result, the vehicle is held up somewhere while the goods are attended to but at the same time the goods are stolen because the carrier did

---

[72] [1963] 2 Lloyd's Rep. 187, 193, C.A. The plaintiff had his car repaired at a cost more than twice the value of the car after it had been repaired. See also *Kaines (UK) Ltd v. Osterreichische Waren H.G.* [1993] 2 Lloyd's Rep. 1, 10, *per* Bingham L.J., C.A.

[73] At 124–125 (citations omitted).

[74] *The Borag* [1981] 1 Lloyd's Rep. 483, 491, C.A.

not sufficiently secure the vehicle, the carrier is fully liable for the loss. The carrier's security failure has broken the chain of causation between the customer's fault and the loss.

> Compare *Caledonian Ry v. Hunter*[75]: the plaintiff sold a truss to a person in Sudbury, Suffolk, and consigned it to him from Glasgow by means of the defendant carrier. The goods were addressed to "Mr. R., draper, Sudbury". The carrier took the goods to Sudbury, Derbyshire, which was closer to Glasgow than Sudbury, Suffolk, and only after seeking further information from the plaintiff the carrier delivered it to R, some 31 days after initial dispatch, and R refused to take delivery; the goods were returned to the plaintiff who sued the carrier on account of the delay. The carrier countered that they delay was the fault of the plaintiff. The plaintiff contended in truth, that he did not know that there was more than one place called Sudbury and that the carrier, who did or should have known this, should have sought further guidance from the plaintiffs before sending the goods to Derbyshire. This argument prevailed before the Lord Ordinary but was rejected on appeal in the Court of Session in view of general railway practice to send to the nearest place of the name given and of the difficulty of noticing and resolving the ambiguity before consignment yet without delaying the goods. The court concluded that the carrier was not liable, not on the basis of an exemption clause in the contract relating to parcels improperly directed, but because[75a]: "Where loss arises in a transaction between two parties, he whose negligence in the first instance sets the whole thing wrong is not entitled to damages from the other party, though the conduct of the latter may not be free from observation or blame . . . There is no doubt that, in order to enforce that liability which ought to exist in the case of railway carriers, as well as ordinary carriers, we ought to require a full, distinct and ample address."

At common law apportionment was not possible in cases of breach of contract. In the absence of blame, a court would either conclude that there was no prima facie breach of contract, because the goods had been delivered to the destination contracted for, or that, although there was a prima facie case against the carrier, he was excused by the act or neglect of the claimant.

229. Negligence

To establish in England the tort of negligence, the claimant must prove that the carrier has broken a duty of care owed to the

[75] (1858) 20 Sess. Cas. 2nd Ser. 1097.
[75a] At 1100.

claimant, and that this breach has caused the loss or damage,[76] in respect of which compensation is claimed. For a duty to exist, recent restatements[77] of the law suggest three general "requirements".

(i) Loss of the type in question must be a foreseeable consequence of the carrier's act or omission.
(ii) There must be proximity between carrier and claimant: "such close and direct relations that the act complained of directly affects a person [the claimant] whom the person alleged to be bound to take care [the carrier] would know would be directly affected by his careless act".[78] While recognising the requirement of proximity, some courts[79] regard proximity as part of the third requirement[80]; and others have stated that, if it is clear that the defendant has assumed responsibility to the claimant for particular services, inquiry into whether liability in such a case is "fair and reasonable" is unnecessary.[81]
(iii) The imposition of such a duty on the carrier must be fair and reasonable. The courts will have little hesitation in finding it fair and reasonable that a carrier, in law a bailee, should owe a duty of care to the owner of goods in his charge.[82]

The three requirements do not add up to a general principle that covers all situations.[83] Moreover, the three "separate requirements are, at least in most cases, in fact merely facets of the same thing, for in some cases the degree of foreseeability is such that it is from that alone that the requisite degree of proximity can be deduced,

---

[76] The carrier is not liable for loss or damage caused by third parties, *e.g.* vandals, if their intervention could not have been foreseen: *Topp v. London Country Bus (South West) Ltd* [1993] 1 W.L.R. 976, C.A., discussed by Fleming: (1994) 110 L.Q.R. 191; more generally, see *Smith v. Littlewoods Organisation Ltd* [1987] A.C. 241. Howarth (1994) 14 L.S. 88.

[77] See, for example, *Caparo Industries plc v. Dickman* [1989] Q.B. 653, 678 *et seq.*, *per* Bingham L.J., C.A.; and [1990] 2 A.C. 605, at 618, *per* Lord Bridge, at 633, *per* Lord Oliver, H.L.

[78] *Donoghue v. Stevenson* [1932] A.C. 562, 581, *per* Lord Atkin; *Caparo* (above), *loc. cit.*

[79] See, for example, the dictum of Lord Oliver above, n. 77.

[80] Thus in *Davis v. Radcliffe* [1990] 2 All E.R. 536, 540, P.C. Lord Goff referred to "the label 'proximity', an expression which refers to such a relation between the parties as renders it just and reasonable that liability may be imposed on the defendant".

[81] *Henderson v. Merrett Syndicates* [1995] 2 A.C. 145, 181.

[82] *Morris v. Martin* [1966] 1 Q.B. 716, C.A.; *The Hua Lien* [1991] 1 Lloyd's Rep. 309. As to possible differences between a general duty of care, actionable in tort, and the duty of the carrier as a bailee, see Palmer, pp. 36 *et seq.*

[83] *Caparo* (above, n. 75), at 617, *per* Lord Bridge and at 632, *per* Lord Oliver; *Davis* (above, n. 80), at 540, *per* Lord Goff.

whilst in others the absence of [duty] can most rationally be attributed simply to the court's view that it would not be fair and reasonable to hold the defendant responsible. 'Proximity' is, no doubt, a convenient expression so long as it is realised that it is no more than a label which embraces not a definable concept but merely a description of circumstances from which, pragmatically, the courts conclude that a duty of care exists."[84] Whether as part of what can best be described as principle or as pragmatism, certain of the answers to certain general questions do influence the courts among them these.[85] First, was the defendant in control of the situation? Secondly, which party is best placed to cover the loss in question by insurance? Questions of fair and reasonable proximity are questions to be posed in respect of specific categories of case,[86] categories traditionally defined, and any development in the law will be incremental.

The liability of a carrier as carrier or as bailee is a traditional category of case: the carrier owes a duty of care to the owner of the goods, subject to two qualifications where the category of carrier or bailee is affected by other categories, as follows.

First, if the negligence action against the carrier is for economic loss, it is considered neither fair nor reasonable that a duty should be owed in tort, the action being an action that belongs in the domain of the law of contract, unless the case also falls within one of certain sub-categories, such as negligent misstatement.[87] This was confirmed for the carriage of goods by sea in *The Aliakmon*,[88] in which the House of Lords held that the negligent carrier is liable to the person who is the owner of the goods at the time of loss of or damage to the goods, but not for the economic loss suffered by a person who acquires those goods later.

Secondly, in general there may be liability in the tort of negligence for acts but not for omissions.[89] However, if the driver of a vehicle omits to apply the brakes or to lock the unattended vehicle, that is not omission but careless commission—careless driving of

---

[84] *Per* Lord Oliver, *loc. cit.*

[85] As to the first, see *e.g. Curran v. Northern Ireland Co-ownership Housing Assn. Ltd* [1987] A.C. 718; *Yuen Kun-yeu v. A.-G. for Hong Kong* [1988] A.C. 175, P.C.; *Barrett v. Ministry of Defence* [1995] 3 All E.R. 87, C.A. As to the second, see *e.g. Murphy v. Brentwood D.C.* [1991] 1 A.C. 378; *Caparo Industries plc v. Dickman* [1990] 2 A.C. 605, 643, *per* Lord Oliver. Fleming (1990) 106 L.Q.R. 525, 528. In Canada also: *London Drugs v. Kuehne & Nagel* (1993) 97 D.L.R. (4th) 261, 364, *per* Iacobucci J.

[86] *Caparo* (above, n. 77), at 635 Lord Oliver.

[87] Below, para. 230.

[88] *Leigh & Sillavan Ltd v. Aliakmon Shipping Co. Ltd* [1986] A.C. 786; *The Hua Lien* [1991] 2 Lloyd's Rep. 309, P.C. For the impact of the former case in the general law of tort, see Winfield & Jolowicz, *Tort* (14th ed., London 1994), pp. 96–97. For criticism of its impact on the law of carriage, see Clarke [1986] C.L.J. 382; and on the law of sale, see Goode (1987) 103 L.Q.R. 433.

[89] *Smith v. Littlewoods Organisation Ltd* [1987] A.C. 241, 271, *per* Lord Goff.

the vehicle[90] or careless custody of the vehicle and goods in his charge[91]—for which the carrier is liable.

229a. The contractual setting: networks

If the claimant in tort has a contract with the carrier, the claimant should heed the warning of Lord Scarman that the court should not search "for a liability in tort where the parties are in a contractual relationship. This is particularly so in a commercial relationship . . . it is a relationship in which the parties have, subject to a few exceptions, the right to determine their objections to each other."[92] When the parties to the claim in tort "have come together against a contractual structure which provides for compensation in the event of a failure of one of the parties involved, the court will be slow to superimpose an added duty of care beyond that which was in the contemplation of the parties at the time that they came together".[93] It "should be no part of the law of tort to fill contractual gaps",[94] or to allow the precocious tort of negligence to disturb the allocation of risk made by a commercial contract.[95]

The effect, it is submitted, is that, even if the claimant, A, does not have a contract with the carrier, C, the contract of carriage between the carrier and someone else, such as forwarder B, will be the setting in which the court sees any duty of care owed by carrier C to claimant A. In the language of privity of contract, A is not a party to the contract of carriage between B and C but is still party to and subject to the "carriage situation": the network of contracts

---

[90] *Kelly v. Metropolitan Ry* [1895] 1 Q.B. 944, C.A.

[91] *Stansbie v. Troman* [1948] 2 K.B. 48, C.A., approved in *Smith* (above, n. 89) at 272, *per* Lord Goff.

[92] *Tai Hing Cotton Mill v. Liu Chong Hing Bank* [1986] A.C. 80, 107, *per* Lord Scarman, P.C., cited, for example, in *The Good Luck* [1989] 2 Lloyd's Rep. 238, 266, by May L.J., C.A.

[93] *Pacific Associates Inc. v. Baxter* [1989] 2 All E.R. 159, 170, *per* Purchas L.J., C.A.; also see *Norwich C.C. v. Harvey* [1989] 1 All E.R. 1180, C.A.; *Marc Rich & Co. Ltd v. Bishop Rock Marine Co. Ltd* [1996] 1 A.C. 211. In his influential dissenting judgment in *Junior Books v. Veitchi* [1983] 1 A.C. 520, 552, Lord Brandon said: "If . . . the relevant contracts . . . include provisions excluding or limiting liability for defective products or defective work, or for negligence generally, it seems that the party sued in delict should in justice be entitled to rely on such provisions." *cf.* Glass and Cashmore, para. 1.83.

cf. the defence of *volentia non fit injuria*, which assumes the existence of a duty which is released by the claimant in the particular case: Winfield & Jolowicz, pp. 687–688.

[94] *Keyser Ullmann S.S. v. Skandia (U.K.) Ins. Co. Ltd* [1990] 1 Q.B. 665, 800, *per* Slade L.J., C.A., affirmed *sub. nom. Banque Financière de la Cité S.A. v. Westgate Ins. Co. Ltd* [1991] 2 A.C. 249.

[95] See the cases cited above in n. 93.

of which the contract of carriage is a central part.[96] Hence, if, as seems likely,[97] A knew or should have known that C contracted with B to carry A's goods on the understanding that C would be liable for the safety of the goods only subject to certain terms, C's duty of care to A is modified (or even negated) by those terms.

Although some of the impetus for this view is new, the view itself is old. In decisions at the turn of the century, when A contracted with B for carriage by rail, B performed stage 1 of the carriage but then contracted stage 2 to C, A was bound by the terms agreed between B and C.[98] The surviving explanation of these decisions has been agency—B contracted with C as agent for A.[99] Another explanation was assent by A,[1] the effect of which was described by Blackburn J. in *Hall*[2]: "I think it must be taken that [A] intended the terms on which he travelled to be communicated to [C], and that he must be taken to have assented that the [terms agreed between A and B] should protect [C] just as much as [B]." The "risk throughout the whole journey is assumed by" A.[3] This explanation was obscured but never entirely forgotten or overruled by the prominence given to privity of contract in *Scruttons*.[4]

> In *Mayfair v. Baxter Hoare*[5] A contracted with forwarder B for the carriage of cameras between two points in England. B contracted for actual carriage by C. The cameras were stolen. A's action against B failed, because B's liability was excluded by contract A–B. A's

---

[96] Adams and Brownsword, "Privity and the Concept of a Network Contract" (1990) 10 L.S. 12. These writers describe (p. 12) a network contract as one of "a group of contracts which have collectively as their object the attainment of a common underlying purpose". "Building contracts and carriage contracts are paradigms of network contracts" (p. 28). See also Fleming, "Tort in a Contractual Matrix" (1995) 33 Osgoode Hall L.J. 661. *cf. The Captain Gregos* [1990] 1 Lloyd's Rep. 310, C.A.; Clarke [1990] L.M.C.L.Q. 314.

[97] Persons dealing with carriers are deemed to know that carriers only contract on the basis of (their) standard terms: *Circle Freight International v. Medeast Gulf Exports* [1988] 2 Lloyd's Rep. 427, C.A. Above, para. 203.

[98] Battersby (1975) 25 U. Toronto L.J. 371, 382.

[99] For example, Kahn-Freund, p. 326; and Treitel, p. 568, who describes this analysis as "artificial".

[1] This explanation was ignored in *Scruttons v. Midland Silicones* [1962] A.C. 446, in which almost every judge assumed the decisive relevance of the privity doctrine and did not consider C's position on the defence of assumption of risk by A: Battersby (above), p. 372. The exception in *Scruttons* was Lord Denning (at 485), and later Lord Simon, in *The Eurymedon* [1975] A.C. 154, 182, P.C.

[2] *Hall v. North Eastern Ry Co.* (1875) L.R. 10 Q.B. 437, 442. For further references of this kind, see Battersby (above, n. 98), pp. 383 *et seq.* These cases were not considered by Kahn-Freund. In *Hall* there are also statements than can be used to explain the decision in terms of agency, but these fall short of authority in B to contract for A with C and go no further than an agency to express A's assent to the degree of immunity demanded by C: Battersby, p. 386.

[3] *Bicknell v. Grand Trunk Ry Co.* (1899) 26 OAR 431, 452, *per* Osler J.A., discussing and following *Hall* (above).

[4] *Scruttons v. Midland Silicones* [1962] A.C. 446.

[5] *Mayfair Photographic Supplies (London) v. Baxter Hoare & Co.* [1972] 1 Lloyd's Rep. 410; accepted by Staughton L.J., although with some hesitation, in *The Gudermes* [1993] 1 Lloyd's Rep. 311, 327, C.A.

action in tort against C failed, because A was unable to prove that C had been negligent.[6] However MacKenna J., while recognising[7] that a person such as C "owes an independent duty to the owner [A] which may be enforced in an action in tort", continued: "But that is not to say that the contract of carriage is irrelevant. If the contract [B–C] is within the apparent authority of [B] and [C] obeys [B's] instructions under the contract and commits no breach of its terms, he owes no liability to anyone—none to [B] because he has fulfilled his contract, and none to [A] because he cannot owe him any higher duty than that imposed by the contract. In other words, if [C] does what the contract obliges him or entitles him to do, he cannot be found guilty of negligence against [A]."

More recently in *London Drugs v. Kuehne & Nagel*,[8] A, the owner of a transformer stored with warehouse B under a contract, which extended B's contractual limitation of 40 dollars to B's employee, C, nonetheless sued C in respect of negligent handling of the transformer. The action failed *inter alia* because it "would be absurd in the circumstances of this case to let [A] go around the limitation of liability clause by suing [C] in tort".[9]

Dissatisfaction with *Scruttons* in the context of carriage by sea has led to artificial evasion, agency again.[10] Given current movements in the law of tort, it seems that now is the time to return to the explanation in *Hall*.

229b. Sub-bailment

In the law of bailment, including carriage, there is a rule different from the last[11] but to similar effect. If the claimant is a bailor (for example, sender), whose bailee (for example, forwarder) has contracted with a sub-bailee (for example, carrier) on certain conditions, including exemptions, there is a rule that the bailor "is bound by the conditions if he has expressly or impliedly consented

[6] Having duly performed contract B–C, C "committed no breach of any duty which he owed to" A (at 417).

[7] At 416. A clear statement, that the scope of the duty of care owed to A by C may be limited by the terms of C's contract with B, can be found in the decision of the Supreme Court of Canada in *Cominco v. Bilton* (1970) 15 D.L.R. (3d) 60, 63, *per* Ritchie J.

[8] (1993) 97 D.L.R. (4th) 261; also reported and discussed by Adams and Brownsword (1993) 56 M.L.R. 722; and by MacMillan [1994] L.M.C.L.Q. 22.

[9] At 363, *per* Iacobucci J. MacMillan (above, p. 27) thought that, in view of the English courts are unlikely to take an approach that dents the privity rule. However, Adams and Brownsword conclude (above, p. 731) that the judgments "represent something of a showcase for modern techniques of privity avoidance". The case does indicate that, if the clause is clearly intended to benefit C, the networks view enables the courts, in England as in Canada, to ensure that the benefit ensures to C.

[10] *The Eurymedon* [1975] A.C. 154, P.C.

[11] Above, para. 229a.

to the bailee making a sub-bailment containing those conditions".[12]

230. Negligent misstatement

In general, the claimant owner can succeed against the carrier on the basis of the tort of negligence only if the loss or damage is physical loss or damage to the goods.[13] If loss or damage is purely economic, as when the goods are delivered late, no duty of care is owed by the carrier to the claimant, unless the negligence took the form of a negligent misstatement; examples would be a negligent misstatement about the quality or speed of service, or obstacles likely to be encountered on the proposed journey.[14] For an actionable negligent misstatement, there must be a "special relationship" between claimant and carrier.[15] Unless there is an effective disclaimer of liability,[16] the special relationship arises in the following circumstances.

(a) There must have been a relationship of proximity between claimant and carrier.[17] In words widely quoted in later cases, Lord Oliver said[18] that, typically, there would be a duty of care and hence a special relationship if:

> "(1) the advice is required for a purpose, whether particularly specified or generally described, which is made known, either actually or inferentially, to the adviser at the time when the advice is given,
>
> (2) the adviser knows, either actually or inferentially, that his advice will be communicated to the advisee, either specifically or as a member of an ascertainable class, in order that it should be used by the advisee for that purpose."

---

[12] *Morris v. Martin & Sons* [1966] 1 Q.B. 716, 729, *per* Lord Denning, C.A., applied in *Johnson Matthey & Co. v. Constantine Terminals* [1976] 2 Lloyd's Rep. 215; and *Singer v. Tees & Hartlepool Port Authority* [1988] 2 Lloyd's Rep. 164. See also *The Pioneer Container* [1994] 2 A.C. 324. Swadling [1993] L.M.C.L.Q. 9; Bugden [1997] 4 I.C.C.L.R. 141; Bankes and Rafferty (1997) 28 Can.Bus.L.J. 245. *cf.* Glass and Cashmore, para. 1.84. *cf.* also *Victoria Fur Traders v. Roadline (U.K.)* [1981] 1 Lloyd's Rep. 570 in which the rule might have been argued, albeit *obiter*, but does not appear to have been put to the court (at 578).

[13] Above, para. 229.

[14] For the case of the defendant who has undertaken services but performed them carelessly, see *White v. Jones* [1995] 2 A.C. 207.

[15] The landmark case is *Hedley Byrne & Co. v. Heller & Partners* [1964] A.C. 465. Alternatively in such circumstances, the court may imply a contract between carrier and claimant, a contract collateral to the contract of carriage, to which *ex hypothesi* the claimant is not a party; see *Shanklin Pier v. Detel Products* [1951] 2 K.B. 854. Treitel, pp. 534 *et seq.*; Walker, para. 14.106.

[16] *Hedley Byrne* (above). A disclaimer within the scope of the Unfair Contract Terms Act 1977 will not be enforced to the extent that it is not reasonable: *Smith v. Bush* [1990] 1 A.C. 831.

[17] *Caparo Industries plc v. Dickman* [1990] 2 A.C. 605, 618, *per* Lord Bridge.

[18] At 638.

In other words, used in the earlier cases, the claimant must have been an "identifiable" person, identifiable not necessarily by name but by category of person. The category must be small.[19]

> "(3) [It] is known, either actually or inferentially, that the advice so communicated is likely to be acted on by the advisee for that purpose without independent inquiry."

In other words, again words used in the earlier cases, reliance will be likely only if reliance is reasonable[20] and, for that to be so, the defendant must be a person informed on such matters.[21] Clearly, the claimant acts reasonably in relying on the carrier's advice about transport matters.

(b) It must be fair and reasonable that the defendant carrier should owe such a duty to the claimant. If their relationship is proximate in the sense that the claimant has acted reasonably in relying on the carrier's advice,[22] the claimant has gone much, if not most,[23] of the way to show also that it is fair and reasonable and that in the circumstances the carrier owes a duty. However, in certain cases a separate requirement of fairness allows the court to bring in other considerations[24] to negate the existence of a duty.

---

[19] This requirement is intended to rule out (floodgate) actions by large classes of people, such as map readers or newspaper readers. However, direct contact between the adviser and the advisee is not essential: *Smith v. Bush* [1990] 1 A.C. 831; the relationship, however, must be "akin to contract"—at 846, *per* Lord Templeman.

[20] Compare Lord Devlin in *Hedley Byrne* (above, n. 15 at 528–529), who based the duty on a voluntary assumption of responsibility. However, a basis in reasonable reliance was preferred in *Smith v. Bush* [1990] 1 A.C. 831, 847, *per* Lord Templeman and 864, *per* Lord Griffiths, H.L.

[21] *Hedley Byrne* (above, n. 15) at 503, *per* Lord Morris: a person "in a sphere in which a person is so placed that others could reasonably rely upon his judgment or his skill or upon his ability to make careful inquiry, a person who takes it upon himself to give information or advice to, or allows his information or advice to be passed on to, another person who, as he knows or should know, will place reliance upon it" is an informed person.

In *Mutual Life & Citizens Assurance Co. v. Evatt* [1971] A.C. 794 a majority (3–2) of the Privy Council limited the duty to cases in which the defendant was in the "business" of providing such advice or information, however, this limit has been rejected: *Esso Petroleum Co. v. Mardon* [1976] Q.B. 801, C.A.; *Chaudhry v. Prabhakar* [1988] 3 All E.R. 718, C.A.

[22] Above, (a).

[23] Although many statements of the general duty of care separate (a) and (b), in many cases it is not possible to do so: *Caparo* (above, n. 17) at 585, *per* Lord Oliver; also in *Davis v. Radcliffe* [1990] 2 All E.R. 536, 540, P.C. Lord Goff referred to the "label of 'proximity', an expression which refers to such a relation between the parties as makes it just and reasonable that liability in negligence may be imposed on the defendant". However, in the specific instance of the duty to give careful advice a distinction between (a) and (b) is easier to make.

[24] For example, (a) the purpose of a statement, so that even if reliance is foreseeable and reasonable, that alone is insufficient, if reliance by person such as the claimant is outside the purpose: *Caparo* (above, n. 17); *The Morning Watch* [1990] 1 Lloyd's Rep. 547. (b) The insurability of the defendant's liability: *Caparo* (above, n. 17) at 643, *per* Lord Oliver.

This is unlikely to happen in the case of the claimant's dealings with a carrier.

(c) The claimant must have suffered loss in reliance[25] on that statement. Arguably, this requirement is no more than the general requirement of a causal link between tort and loss.[26]

231. Conversion

The essence of conversion[27] is a dealing with the goods by the carrier which is inconsistent with the rights of the owner. No satisfactory definition of conversion is possible but it is safe to say that the carrier is liable in the tort of conversion in the following circumstances, subject to any qualification of that liability in the terms of the contract of carriage.

(a) The carrier delivers the goods to the wrong person.[28] In this case, prima facie the liability of the carrier is strict: the carrier is liable to the true owner, even though delivery to the wrong person was made in good faith and without negligence,[29] except where the consignor's title to the goods did not exist or was defective: if the carrier delivers to the consignor or the consignor's order without notice of any other claim on the goods, the carrier will not be liable to the true owner.[30]

(b) The carrier does not deliver the goods to the right person,[31] on demand, whether because the carrier believes that person to be the wrong person or because the goods have been lost or destroyed en route, unless

- (i) the carrier declines to deliver in exercise of a valid lien,[32] or
- (ii) the carrier has reasonable doubt as to whether the person demanding delivery is entitled to delivery. This is important in view of a common type of fraud, whereby the thief

---

[25] *JEB Fasteners v. Marks, Bloom & Co.* [1983] 1 All E.R. 583, C.A.; *Caparo* (above, n. 17), at 638, *per* Lord Oliver. Note the convergence of the rules of causation in tort with those applied to breach of contract: above, para. 227.

[26] But *cf.* cases, exceptional perhaps, such as *Ross v. Caunters* [1980] Ch. 297 and *White v. Jones* [1995] 2 A.C. 207.

[27] See Kahn-Freund, Chap. 12; Samuel (1982) 31 I.C.L.Q. 357; Winfield & Jolowicz, pp. 470 *et seq.* I am indebted to Andrew Tettenborn for helpful comments on this subject.

[28] Clerk and Lindsell, paras. 13.01 *et seq.* Action may also lie against the person to whom the goods are delivered by mistake: *Lancashire & Yorkshire Ry v. MacNicoll* (1919) 88 L.J.K.B. 601.

[29] *Marfani & Co. v. Midland Bank* [1968] 1 W.L.R. 956, 970–971, *per* Devlin L.J., C.A.

[30] *Hollins v. Fowler* (1874) L.R. 7 H.L. 757, 766–767, *per* Lord Blackburn; *cf. Willis & Sons v. British Car Auctions* [1978] 1 W.L.R. 438, C.A.

[31] *Perry v. British Railways Board* [1980] 2 All E.R. 579.

[32] *Lord v. Price* (1874) L.R. 9 Ex. 54. The lien must actually exist: it is not enough that the carrier has a bona fide belief that it exists: *Brandeis Goldschmidt & Co. v. Western Transport* [1981] Q.B. 864.

attempts to intercept the goods in the vicinity of the designated point of delivery.[33] Indecision is not a luxury that can be enjoyed for ever, and after a reasonable time the carrier may become liable, unless the carrier interpleads.

(c) The carrier, without lawful excuse destroys the goods.

In *Perry & Co. v. British Railways Board*[34] the plaintiffs were consignees of a quantity of steel which had been transported to the place of delivery by the defendants. The latter, fearing industrial action by railway workers who were supporting industrial action by steelworkers, refused to hand over the steel to the plaintiffs. The defendants admitted that they were liable in damages. The plaintiffs sought an order under section 4(2) of the Torts (Interference with Goods) Act 1977, that the defendants should permit the plaintiffs, with their own men and vehicles, to collect the steel from the defendants' depot. Making the order sought, Megarry V.C. said[35]: "... this is a clear case of conversion. The defendants are denying the plaintiffs most of the rights of ownership, including the right to possession, for a period which plainly is indefinite. There is a detention of the steel which is consciously adverse to the plaintiffs' rights, and this seems to me to be of the essence of at least one form of conversion. ... For the defendants to withhold the steel from the plaintiffs is a wrongful interference with goods within the 1977 Act unless the reason for the withholding provides a justification. I cannot see that it does. This is no brief withholding made merely in order that the defendants may verify the plaintiffs' title to the steel or for some other purpose to confirm that the delivery of the steel would be proper. This is a withholding despite the plain right of the plaintiffs to the ownership and possession of the steel, on the ground the defendants fear unpleasant consequences if they do not deny the plaintiffs what they are entitled to."

Normally damages would have been an adequate remedy, but in view of the strike by steelworkers damages would not have been enough to enable the plaintiffs to buy steel in the market, so the order was granted.

Action may be brought by any person who owns the goods in question or who has an immediate right to possess them,[36] hence by the sender or by the consignee according to the case. If a carrier is sued by a consignee with the immediate right to possession, the carrier may defend the action by pointing to the (better) rights of a third party, the *jus tertii*, notably a third party who owns the goods.[37]

---

[33] *Pillot v. Wilkinson* (1864) 3 H. & C. 345; *Clayton v. Le Roy* [1911] 2 K.B. 1031.
[34] [1980] 2 All E.R. 579.
[35] At 583–584. For criticism of this reasoning, see Samuel (1982) 31 I.C.L.Q. 357, 379 *et seq.*
[36] *Caxton Publishing Co. v. Sutherland Publishing Co.* [1939] A.C. 178, 201–202, *per* Lord Porter, as interpreted by Winfield & Jolowicz, p. 498.
[37] 1977 Act s.8(1), subject to s.7.

232. Other torts

The kind of misstatement discussed above[38] would, if made fraudulently,[39] and relied upon by the claimant with consequent loss, found an action in the tort of deceit. The main disadvantage of this course of action is the difficulty of proving fraud. The main advantage, even to a claimant who has a contract with the carrier, is the possibility of recovering damages for certain types of loss which might not otherwise be recovered.[40]

An action under the rule in *Rylands v. Fletcher*[41] might be brought if, for example, a carrier used his depot to store a dangerous substance, which escaped and caused damage to property outside the depot. That might include the claimant's goods, if on a vehicle parked outside. For this action to succeed, storage of the substance must be a non-natural use of the land in question. Although an early decision[42] held that the storage of petrol in a tank was non-natural, "it is almost inconceivable"[43] that this case would be followed in this respect today. Moreover, although this tort is strict in the sense that the defendant is liable, whether the escape could have been foreseen or not, the defendant is liable only for those kinds of damage which are not too remote—in the ordinary sense of kinds of damage that were foreseeable.[44] However, if in some other way the dam bursts at the defendant's depot, *Rylands v. Fletcher* offers a last line of retaliation to the floundering claimant.

In theory, an action for breach of statutory duty might arise out of the carrier's breach of legislation regulating the construction, condition and use of motor vehicles, but the English courts have shown little inclination to allow an action on this basis.[45]

233. Damages at common law

At common law[46] the type of loss claimed must not be too remote. If the action is based in tort, typically negligence, the type of loss

---

[38] Para. 230.

[39] *Derry v. Peek* (1889) 14 App.Cas. 337: a statement is fraudulent, if it is made (a) with knowledge that it is untrue or (b) without belief that it is true, or (c) recklessly, not caring whether it be true or false.

[40] See below, para. 246.

[41] (1868) L.R. 3 H.L. 330.

[42] *Musgrove v. Pandelis* [1919] 2 K.B. 43.

[43] Winfield & Jolowicz, p. 452. On this issue see *Cambridge Water Co. v. Eastern Counties Leather plc* [1994] 2 A.C. 264.

[44] *Cambridge Water* (above).

[45] See, for example, *Phillips v. Britannia Hygienic Laundry* [1923] 2 K.B. 832, C.A.; and *Tan Chye Choo v. Chong Kew Moi* [1970] 1 W.L.R. 147, P.C.

[46] *cf.* for example, French law: in the case of wilful misconduct under Art. 29 the claimant can recover all immediate and direct consequential loss: code civil Art. 1151. Nicholas, *The French Law of Contract* (2nd ed., London, 1992), p. 229.

claimed must have been one which was reasonably foreseeable by the defendant carrier at the time of the tortious act.[47] If the action is based in contract, the type of loss claimed must be one which should have been within the reasonable contemplation of the defendant carrier at the time of the conclusion of the contract as a likely consequence of a breach of the kind that occurred.[48] The range of loss, that is not too remote and is thus recoverable in tort, is greater than in contract.[49]

If the loss claimed is not too remote, recoverable loss in the case of breach of contract, negligence or negligent misstatement is measured by reference to the actual loss of that type suffered by the claimant, even though the extent of loss was greater than was within the reasonable contemplation or the reasonable foresight of the defendant carrier. Unlike Article 23 of the CMR, whereby compensation is calculated by reference to the value of the goods at the place and time at which they were accepted for carriage,[50] the common law rule calculates loss by reference to the value of the goods at the intended place of delivery. Taking the example of goods lost by the carrier en route, "whether such conduct consists in conversion or negligence, the proper measure of the damages recoverable . . . is the full market value of the goods at the time when and the place where possession of them should have been given" to the claimant.[51]

The tort of deceit is a special case[52] for, although in principle the measure is tortious, the claimant may recover consequential loss that was not reasonably foreseeable[53] and was thus too remote for recovery on the basis of negligence unless, however, the effect of the deceit is that the claimant has been permanently deprived of the goods: in that case the rule is the same as that for the tort of conversion.[54] In the case of conversion, the normal measure, which has been equated with the measure for negligence (above), is the market value of the goods at the time and place of the conversion.[55] If there is a rise in the value of the goods after the act

---

[47] Generally see Clerk & Lindsell, para. 27–01 *et seq.*

[48] McGregor, paras, 231 *et seq.*

[49] *The Heron II* [1969] 1 A.C. 350. McGregor, paras. 247 *et seq.*

[50] Above, para. 94a.

[51] *The Jag Shakti* [1986] A.C. 337, 345, *per* Lord Brandon, P.C.

[52] Clerk & Lindsell, paras. 14–39 *et seq.*

[53] *Doyle v. Olby (Ironmongers)* [1969] 2 Q.B. 158, 167, *per* Lord Denning M.R., C.A.; *Royscott Trust v. Rogerson* [1991] 2 Q.B. 297, C.A.; *Smith New Court Securities Ltd v. Scrimgeour Vickers (Asset Management) Ltd* [1996] 4 All E.R. 767, H.L.; *cf.* Treitel, p. 336.

[54] *Smith Kline & French Laboratories v. Long* [1988] 3 All E.R. 887, C.A.

[55] McGregor, paras. 1298 *et seq.*, especially paras. 1306 *et seq.*; *BBMM Holdings v. Eda Holdings* [1990] 1 W.L.R. 409, P.C. *cf. I.B.L. Ltd v. Coussens* [1991] 2 All E.R. 133, C.A.; and the view that it is not the normal measure (claimant's loss) but a special measure (the value of the goods converted) that is recovered: Tettenborn [1993] C.L.J. 128.

of conversion, the value is measured at the time when the claimant learned of the conversion.[56]

234. Responsibility for the acts and omissions of others

The carrier's responsibility for the acts and omissions of others may be in contract or tort. In tort the carrier's responsibility depends on whether they are the carrier's employees, also referred to in this legal context as servants, or agents, also referred to in this context as independent contractors. The distinction may be difficult to draw. According to *Ready-Mixed Concrete (South-East) v. Minister of Pensions and National Insurance*,[57] the factors to be considered include who controls the manner in which carriage is performed and the way in which remuneration is calculated.[58] The greater the degree of control exercised by the carrier the more likely it is that the relationship is one of master and servant. Again, if the driver is paid by the hour rather than by the job the more likely it is that the relationship is one of master and servant. The name that they give to their relationship is a factor but no more than that.[59]

In the 1990s, however, patterns of employment have changed. For various reasons a driver is more likely to be self-employed than employed. Consequently, earlier cases such as *Ready-Mixed Concrete* are given due consideration but treated with some caution by courts today, which are more likely to look behind the appearance and reach a conclusion based on the purpose or policy of the rule of law in issue.[60]

If the cause of loss or damage is the act or omission of the carrier's servant,[61] the carrier may be liable in tort if the act is within the scope of the servant's employment; but the carrier may be liable in contract, whether the act is within the scope of the servant's employment or not.[62]

If, for example, the carrier's driver is en route and drives carelessly, the carrier is liable for consequent damage to the goods not

---

[56] *Sachs v. Miklos* [1948] 2 K.B. 23, C.A.

[57] [1968] 2 Q.B. 497. The issue in this case was not vicarious liability in tort but whether the drivers were employed under a contract of service for purposes of the National Insurance Act 1965, s.1(2). See also below, para. 235.

[58] See also *Montreal Locomotive Works v. Montreal* [1947] 1 D.L.R. 161, 169, *per* Lord Wright, P.C. The line, between persons for whom the "employer" is vicariously liable and persons for whom he is not, may have to be redrawn in the light of changing conditions and modes of "employment": McKendrick, "Vicarious Liability and Independent Contractors—A Re-Examination," (1990) 53 M.L.R. 770.

[59] *Ferguson v. John Dawson & Partners (Contractors) Ltd* [1976] 3 All E.R. 817, C.A.

[60] *Lane v. Shire Roofing Co. (Oxford) Ltd* [1995] I.R.L.R. 493, C.A.

[61] If the loss is caused not by a servant (employee) but by an agent, subject to certain exceptions, the carrier is not liable in tort at all.

[62] Kahn-Freund, p. 485.

only on the basis of vicarious liability for the negligence of the driver within the scope of his employment but also, primarily, because the damage amounts to a breach of the contract of carriage.[63] If, however, the driver is 20 miles off route with his girlfriend, when he injures another road user, the carrier might defeat an action in tort with the plea that the servant was outside the scope of his employment. But, if the same accident caused loss, damage or delay to the goods, the carrier would be liable under the contract of carriage. Again, if the driver comes back to the carrier's depot at night and steals goods, the theft may be outside the scope of the driver's employment because he was off duty, but the carrier will be liable under the contract of carriage.[64] Finally, generally, when someone is travelling to or from work that person is not acting in the course of employment. However, when someone's work is based in different places, time spent travelling from one base to another may be working time and in the course of employment.[65]

If the cause of loss or damage is the act or omission of an independent contractor employed by the carrier to undertake the whole or part of the performance of a contract of carriage, the carrier is generally not vicariously liable in tort.[66] However, for the same loss or damage the carrier is nonetheless liable under the contract of carriage. By way of exception to immunity in tort, the carrier is also liable vicariously for independent contractors as regards certain categories of tort,[67] and the tort of negligence in the case of certain extra-hazardous activities.[68] These exceptions have little apparent relevance to the carriage of goods, other than dangerous goods: the point has not been taken in reported litigation.

As regards servants, the employer is liable for torts committed by the servant in the scope or course of employment. To decide whether the act or omission is within the scope of the employment, it is necessary to consider the act or omission, not in isolation, but in the context in which it occurred. "The fundamental principle is that an employee is acting in the course of his employment when he is doing what he is employed to do . . . or anything which is reasonably incidental to this employment."[69]

---

[63] *The Coupé Co. v. Maddick* [1891] 2 Q.B. 413, 415, *per* Cave J.

[64] *Sanderson v. Collins* [1904] 1 K.B. 628, 631–632, *per* Lord Collins M.R., C.A.

[65] *Smith v. Stages* [1989] A.C. 928.

[66] *Phillips v. Britannia Hygienic Laundry Co.* [1923] 2 K.B. 832, C.A.—vehicle owner not liable for the negligence of a vehicle repairer.

[67] Such as the strict torts; nuisance, *Rylands v. Fletcher* and breach of statutory duty. See above, para. 232.

[68] *Alcock v. Wraith* [1991] E.G.C.S. 137, C.A.

[69] *Smith v. Stages* [1989] A.C. 928, 936, *per* Lord Goff.

235. The scope of employment

235a. Negligence

Negligence by the servant can be said to be within the scope of employment if the act or omission, although unauthorised as such, is nonetheless a mode of doing what the servant is employed to do.

In *Century Insurance Co. v. Northern Ireland Road Transport Board*,[70] while the respondents' vehicle was being used to deliver petrol to a garage and, in particular, while petrol was being transferred from the vehicle to an underground tank, the driver struck a match to light a cigarette and threw the match on the ground, thus causing a fire and explosion. The House of Lords held that this act was within the scope of the driver's employment. Lord Simon L.C.[71] said: "Admittedly, he was serving his master when he put the nozzle into the tank and turned on the tap. Admittedly, he would be serving his master when he turned off the tap and withdrew the nozzle from the tank. In the interval, spirit was flowing from the tanker to the tank, and this was the very delivery which the respondents were required under their contract to effect." Lord Wright said[72] that the "negligence is to be found by considering the time when and the circumstances in which the match is struck and thrown down". For the driver, smoking while standing by was a more pleasant and convenient way of doing what he was employed to do, to supervise unloading.

The fact that a particular act, practice or manoeuvre has been prohibited by the carrier does not prevent the carrier's being held liable for its consequences[73] if the prohibition "only deal(s) with conduct within sphere of employment" as opposed to limiting the sphere of employment itself.[74] Thus, the driver who drives regularly to Sheffield and breaks an instruction not to drive on to visit his girlfriend in Rotherham is outside the scope of his employment. Again, the driver who, in furtherance of an industrial dispute, drives slowly[75] or who uses the vehicle as part of a blockade,

---

[70] [1942] A.C. 509.
[71] At 514.
[72] At 519.
[73] *Limpus v. London General Omnibus Co.* (1862) 1 H. & C. 526 (prohibition of reckless driving); *Central Motors (Glasgow) v. Cessnock Garage & Motor Co.* 1925 S.C. 796 (prohibition on moving the goods).
[74] *Plumb v. Cobden Flour Mills* [1914] A.C. 62, 67, *per* Lord Dunedin.
[75] If speed is important: *General Engineering Services v. Kingston and Saint Andrew Corp.* [1988] 3 All E.R 867, P.C., in which a fire brigade drove slowly to a fire as part of a dispute with their employer. Lord Ackner (at 870): "Such conduct was the very negation of carrying out some act authorised by the employer, albeit in a wrongful and unauthorised mode."

against the instruction of the employer, is outside the scope of the employment. However, when a driver "exceeds the speed limit, drives on the wrong side of the road, or does anything else by which he violates his duties, he is acting against orders; yet since he is acting in the course of his master's business, the master is liable for the consequences".[76]

> In *Ilkiw v. Samuels*[77] a vehicle loaded sugar at the sender's warehouse and then needed to be moved a short distance away to be sheeted and to make room for other vehicles waiting to load. Without inquiring as to his competence, the driver accepted the offer of a warehouse employee to move the vehicle; the employee proved incompetent and, in the presence of the driver, injured a fellow employee. The driver had been forbidden by the carrier to permit anyone else to drive the vehicle. The Court of Appeal held that the driver's negligence was within the scope of his employment. Willmer L.J. said[78]: "The driver . . . was employed . . . not only to drive, but to be in charge of his vehicle in all circumstances, during any such times as he was on duty." As regards the prohibition, Diplock L.J. said[79]: "the job . . . was to collect a load of sugar at the sugar factory and transport it to its destination, using for that purpose his employers' lorry, of which he was put in charge. The express prohibition was against permitting anyone else to drive the lorry in the course of performing this job. This, it seems to me, was a prohibition upon the mode in which he was to do that which he was employed to do, a prohibition dealing with conduct within the sphere of his employment."

235b. Crime

A driver is authorised to protect the vehicle and its load from theft and other interference, and the carrier will be liable for injury caused to others through any excess of zeal on the part of the driver.[80] If the driver deliberately damages or steals goods being transported, the employer, the carrier, will be liable.[81] However, if the damage or theft is by another servant or agent of the carrier, to whom the goods have not been entrusted, the carrier will not be liable vicariously for the theft or damage.[82]

---

[76] Kahn-Freund, p. 486.
[77] [1963] 1 W.L.R. 991.
[78] At 998.
[79] At 1004.
[80] *Poland v. Parr & Sons* [1927] 1 K.B. 236, C.A.
[81] *Morris v. Martin & Sons* [1966] 1 Q.B. 716, C.A. *idem* fraud: *Armagas v. Mundogas SA* [1986] A.C. 717.
[82] *Sanderson v. Collins* [1904] 1 K.B. 628, 632, *per* Lord Collins M.R., C.A.

235c. Deviation

What is the position if the driver takes an unauthorised route? Distinguish the route prescribed expressly or impliedly by the contract of carriage from that authorised by the carrier/employer. They may coincide, but they may not. We are here concerned only with the second. If the vehicle leaves the route authorised by the carrier in order to obtain spares, repairs or fuel, the driver is acting within the scope of his employment.

> In *Harvey v. O'Dell*[83] workmen were employed to travel from London to Hurley to do work there. After they had commenced the work, they travelled from Hurley to Maidenhead, five miles away, to fetch tools which they needed for the work. On the return journey they were involved in a collision which, it was held by McNair J., occurred while the men were acting within the scope of their employment.

If the vehicle needs fuel and maintenance, so does the driver: "the owner of a lorry has a duty . . . to see that the driver of the lorry is reasonably fit for his work of driving. It must surely be one of the necessary concomitants of the required fitness to see that the driver eats at reasonable intervals",[84] and also sleeps.[85] For this the vehicle may have to leave the direct or customary route, not only to find food and rest but also secure parking.

> In *Stewart's (Edinburgh) Holdings v. Lord Advocate*[86] an army driver, while waiting for a load, decided to go for a meal for which he had been issued with ration money by his employer. The café chosen was not situated on the route which he was authorised to take. On the return journey he negligently collided with a wall. The sheriff court held that this occurred within the scope of his employment.

In that case, the court relied on a statement by Lord Strachan[87] that "when the servant has started his journey on the master's business, the master will not be responsible for the servant's actings if the servant's deviation truly is an entirely new and

---

[83] [1958] 2 Q.B. 78. McNair J. said (at 102): "If the primary purpose was the completion of the work at Hurley, it is clear that the journey into Maidenhead and back to Hurley was as much within the scope of (the men's) employment as was the journey to Hurley from London."

[84] *Stewart's* case, below, n. 86, at 89. Stops for food and drink are generally covered by goods in transit insurance: *Sadler Bros. Co. v. Meredith* [1963] 2 Lloyd's Rep. 293, 307, *per* Roskill J; *SCA (Freight) v. Gibson* [1974] 2 Lloyd's Rep. 533.

[85] Stops for rest are generally covered by goods in transit insurance: *SCA (Freight) Ltd v. Gibson* [1974] 2 Lloyd's Rep. 533, 535, *per* Ackner J.

[86] 1966 S.L.T. (Sh.Ct.) 86.

[87] *Williams v. A. & W. Hemphill*, 1966 S.L.T. 33, 37 (emphasis added). *cf. Crook v. Derbyshire Stone* [1956] 1 W.L.R. 432.

independent journey *not at all* concerned with his master's business, but if the servant is still on the master's business *to any extent*, the master will remain liable". Even when well away from the proper route, the driver is still on his master's business in that he has care of and responsibility for the vehicle,[88] which may have cost his employer as much as £100,000, as well as the goods, which may be worth more. In these circumstances, it can be argued that as regards goods a court is unlikely to find that the act or omission occurred so far away from the authorised route that it was outside the scope of employment. Although not employed to be where he went, he was nonetheless doing carelessly what he was employed to do carefully—to look after the goods.[89]

This argument is underpinned by the insurance position. In general, economic efficiency is best achieved by allocating the loss to goods insurance.[90] But cases of this kind may not be covered by standard goods insurance,[91] and if not, the tendency is to make the employer liable. A century ago it was stated in the Court of Queen's Bench[92]: "Where one of two innocent parties has to suffer a loss arising from the misconduct of a third party, it is for the public advantage that the loss should fall in such a way as to diminish the probability of such a thing happening again, or, in other words, that it should fall on that one of the two who could most easily have prevented the happening or the recurrence of the mischief."

---

[88] *Whatman v. Pearson* (1868) L.R. 3 C.P. 422.

[89] *Sanderson v. Collins* [1904] 1 K.B. 628, 632, *per* Lord Collins M.R., C.A., discussing *The Coupé Co. v. Maddick* [1891] 2 Q.B. 413; *Central Motors (Glasgow) v. Cessnock Garage & Motor Co.* 1925 S.C. 796, at 798, *per* Lord Blackburn, at 803, *per* Lord Cullen, adopted in this respect by Macnaghten J. in *Aitchison v. Page Motors* (1935) 154 L.T. 128, 131. Some of these cases could have been decided in the same way on the basis of breach of contract by the employer through the employee.

[90] *Photo Production v. Securicor Transport* [1980] A.C. 827, 851, *per* Lord Diplock. James (1972) 12 J.S.P.T.L. 105, 113; Tunc, *Encyclopedia of Comparative Law*, Vol. XI, Chap. 1, paras. 91 and 148; MacGrath (1985) 5 O.J.L.S. 350, 376; Rea 12 Can.Bus.L.J. 444 (1987); O'Connell 49 Ohio S.L.J. 757 (1988). See also references above, para. 92a.

[91] In *SCA (Freight) Ltd v. Gibson* [1974] 2 Lloyd's Rep. 533 the driver took the loaded vehicle into Rome for a "joy ride", overturned the vehicle and damaged the goods: Ackner J. held that the damage was not covered by the goods owner's Lloyd's Goods in Transit (CMR) Policy. He said (at 535) that "Goods cease to be in transit when they are on a journey which is not in reasonable furtherance of their carriage to the ultimate destination."

[92] *The Coupé Co. v. Maddick* [1891] 2 Q.B. 413, 417, *per* Cave J.

CHAPTER 13

DEFENCES

A: DEFENCES AVAILABLE TO THE CARRIER

236. Contractual defences

The first line of defence for the carrier is to undermine the credibility of the case made out by the claimant, that the carrier is in breach of contract. The second line of defence consists of one or more of any defences in the contract of carriage. Commonly, the carrier accepts a strict liability in principle[1] but contracts for a string of defences based on specific exonerating events. If the carrier establishes that one of these events caused the loss or damage, the result, with one reservation, is that the carrier is excused.

The reservation is that the claimant can counter the carrier's defence by establishing that the real cause, or one of them, was breach of the carrier's residual or "overriding" duty of care—overriding in the sense that, if the claimant can prove that a breach of the duty is a cause of the loss or damage in issue, the carrier's defence based on an associated exonerating event fails: it is overridden. Moreover, the carrier by *sea* has not one overriding obligation but two. These are due diligence to provide a seaworthy ship and reasonable care of cargo.[2] As to the first, the carrier by land has no such obligation as regards the roadworthiness of the vehicle. If unroadworthiness causes damage or delay, the carrier is in breach not of any duty concerning the vehicle as such but in breach of the central obligation to deliver the goods undamaged and on time. Nor does the nature of the cause (unroadworthiness) override defences. As to the second, however, the carrier by land does have a similar and overriding obligation as regards care of the goods.[3] In a case of the carriage of cattle by rail, for example, the

---

[1] See above, para. 222.

[2] See, *e.g. Notara v. Henderson* (1870) L.R. 5 Q.B. 346; affirmed (1872) L.R. 7 Q.B. 225; *Kopitoff v. Wilson* (1876) 3 Asp. M.L.C. 163, 165; *Steel v. State Line* (1877) 3 App.Cas. 72, 76.

[3] Palmer, p. 1106, with reference to *Taylor v. Liverpool & G.W. Steam Co.* (1874) L.R. 9 Q.B. 546. However, that case does not provide strong support for the proposition which is, perhaps, better supported by analogy with common law rules for other kinds of carriage, above.

carrier pleaded a contract condition as a defence, the excitability of the animal. The judge said:

> "It cannot, I think, be contended that this condition dispenses with the use of reasonable care on the part of the company in the receiving, carrying, and delivering cattle, any more than the exception perils of the sea, in a bill of lading, relieves a shipowner from the obligation to navigate with ordinary skill and care. The exception goes to limit liability, not the duty. It is the duty of the carrier to do what he can, by reasonable skill and care, to avoid all perils, including the excepted perils. If, notwithstanding such skill and care, damage does occur, he is released from liability; but if his negligence has brought on the peril, the damage is attributable to his breach of duty, and the exception does not aid him."[4]

Although not apparent from this judgment, it is for the claimant to establish the carrier's negligence, not for the carrier to establish, as a condition precedent to exoneration, the exercise of skill and care.

Certain exonerating events are commonly specified in the contract as defences available to the carrier. Some of the events specified owe more to tradition and to imitation of standard forms developed for the carriage of goods by sea to distant parts than to a gloomy prognosis of the instability of English society.

236a. Act of God[5]

An Act of God is some elemental force of nature, without human intervention, which was the direct cause of the loss or damage and which could not have been foreseen or, if foreseen, could not have been guarded against by any ordinary or reasonable precaution.[6] Such events, it seems, are not common. Kahn-Freund[7] gives the example of a horse struck by lightning. Another might be that of animals injured by cold weather, when snow blocked the road.[8] Again, a dictum in one decision[9] indicates that, if a driver in apparently good health suffered a sudden heart attack while driving, that would be an Act of God; *sed quare* as modern courts take a less fatalistic view of such illness.

---

[4] *Gill v. Manchester, Sheffield & Lincolnshire Ry Co.* (1873) L.R. 8 Q.B. 186, 196, *per* Lush J. See also *L.N.W. Ry Co. v. Hudson* [1920] A.C. 324, 340, *per* Lord Atkinson as regards the carrier's duty to deal with defects in packing that become apparent during the journey.

[5] *e.g.* RHA Condition 9(2)(b)(i).

[6] *Nugent v. Smith* (1876) 1 C.P.D. 423, 437 concerning carriage by sea.

[7] At 244.

[8] *Briddon v. Great Northern Ry* (1858) 28 L.J.Ex. 51.

[9] *Ryan v. Youngs* [1938] 1 All E.R. 522, 524, *per* Slesser L.J., C.A.

236b. Consequences of war[10]

The consequences of war may come upon the carrier and cause loss, damage or delay, even though no formal declaration of war has taken place.[11] To distinguish private looting, however, war does connote the activity of a government which exists, at least, *de facto*. In that case and, indeed, many cases it is probably also a case of "hostilities".

236c. Hostilities[12]

Hostilities are situations in which, whether or not a state of war exists within the increasingly obscure sense of the matter in international law, there is "armed conflict between competing nations".[13] Once again, a government of some kind must be involved and, therefore, the acts of terrorists do not fall into this category, unless the terrorists can be said to represent or be sponsored by a government.[14]

236d. Civil war[15]

Civil war is a war which is internal to a state[16] rather than war that is external between two states or more; however, if war is mentioned but civil war is not, war includes civil war.[17] When civil war is mentioned together with a string of associated defences such as revolution, rebellion, civil commotion and riot, if they appear in conjunction, one view is that each connotes a disturbance less extensive than the one before,[18] but nonetheless with a degree of overlap so that, for example, the same events may amount to both riot and civil commotion.[19]

---

[10] *e.g.* RHA Condition 9(2)(b)(ii); Securicor Conditions cl. 1(i).

[11] *Kawasaki Kisen Kabushiki Kaisha v. Bantham S.S. Co. (No. 2)* [1939] 2 K.B. 544, 558, *per* Lord Greene M.R., C.A.

[12] *e.g.* RHA Condition 9(2)(b)(ii); Securicor Conditions cl. 1(i).

[13] *Kawasaki Kisen Kabushiki Kaisha v. Bantham S.S. Co. (No. 2)* (1938) 61 Ll.L.Rep. 131, 138, affirmed [1939] 2 K.B. 544, C.A.

[14] *Pan American World Airways Inc. v. Aetna Casualty & Surety Co.* [1975] 1 Lloyd's Rep. 77 (U.S. C.A. 2 Cir., 1974).

[15] *e.g.* RHA Condition 9(2)(b)(ii); Securicor Conditions cl. 1(i).

[16] *Spinney's (1948) Ltd v. Royal Ins. Co. Ltd* [1980] 1 Lloyd's Rep. 406, 429, *per* Mustill J.

[17] *Pesquerias y Secaderos de Bacalao de Espana S.A. v. Beer* (1949) 82 Ll.L.Rep. 501, 514, *per* Lord Morton, H.L.

[18] *Republic of Bolivia v. Indemnity Mutual Marine Assurance Co. Ltd* [1909] 1 K.B. 785, 801, *per* Farwell L.J., C.A. *cf.* the view that this is an over-simplification: *Spinney's* case (above) at 428, *per* Mustill J.; and *Pan American World Airways Inc. v. Aetna Casualty & Surety Co.*, 505 F. 2d 989, 1005 (U.S. C.A. 2 Cir., 1974).

[19] *Motor Union Ins. Co. v. Boggan* (1923) 130 L.T. 588, 591, *per* Lord Birkenhead L.C., H.L. See also *Kuwait Airways Corp. v. Kuwait Ins. Co.* [1996] 1 Lloyd's Rep. 664, 691, *per* Rix J. (aviation).

Recognition by the government of the United Kingdom, that certain events amount to a civil war in the sense of international law, is not decisive.[19a] Although the courts have declined to offer a definition, in a case arising out of events in Beirut in 1976,[20] Mustill J. considered the matter at length and concluded that a civil war had certain characteristics.

First, there must be opposing sides,[21] although the sides need not amount to quasi-states; it must be possible "to say of each fighting man that he owes allegiance to one side or another, and it must also be possible to identify each side by reference to a community of objective, leadership and administration".[22]

Secondly, the objectives of the warring sides must be of a certain scale; (i) to seize or retain the whole or part of the state; or, if not, there may yet be civil war if, for example, (ii) one side sought "to force changes in the way in which power is exercised, without fundamentally changing the existing political structure" or (iii) "if the participants were activated by tribal, racial or ethnic animosities".[23]

Thirdly, as regards the character and scale of the conflict, the judge stated a list of matters to be considered: the number of combatants, the number of casualties, military and civilian, the amount and nature of the armaments involved, the relative size of the territory occupied by the opposing sides, the extent to which it is possible to delineate the territories occupied, the degree to which the populace as a whole is involved in the conflict and, in particular, whether there have been movements of population, the duration and degree of continuity in the conflict, the extent to which public order and the administration of justice have been impaired, the degree of interruption to public services and private life, and the extent to which each side purports to exercise exclusive legislative, administrative and judicial powers.

236e. Rebellion and insurrection[24]

Rebellion and insurrection are closely related. In conjunction with other contract defences such as riot and civil commotion, each connotes an organised attempt to overthrow a government.[25]

[19a] *Spinney's* (above), at 426, *per* Mustill J.
[20] *Spinney's* case (above), at 429–430.
[21] At 430. There may be more than two sides.
[22] *ibid.*: the community of objective may be substantial rather than exactly identical.
[23] *ibid.*
[24] *e.g.* RHA Condition 9(2)(b)(ii); Securicor Conditons cl. 1(i).
[25] *Spinney's (1948) Ltd v. Royal Ins. Co. Ltd* [1980] 1 Lloyd's Rep. 406, 437, *per* Mustill J.; *Home Ins. Co. v. Davila* 121 F. 2d 731, 736 (U.S. C.A. 1 Cir., 1954).

A rebellion (or insurrection), it has been held, is no less a rebellion (or insurrection) because it was originally organised by an outside government (*in casu* Rhodesia) and was subsequently supported or even controlled by an outside government (South Africa), provided that the insurrection is not of outside mercenaries but has a sufficient number of disaffected local inhabitants (between 5,000 and 8,000) and one of its objects was to overthrow the local government:

> In *National Oil Co. of Zimbabwe (Pte) v. Sturge*[26] supporters of the Mozambique National Resistance (Renamo) blew up the pipeline between Beira and Feruka causing losses of gas oil, which were the subject of a subsequent insurance claim. The insurers pleaded an exception of loss caused by "war, civil war, revolution, rebellion, insurrection, or civil strife". Saville J. held[27] that "rebellion" and "insurrection" each meant an organised and violent internal uprising in a country with the main object of trying to overthrow or supplant the government of that country—though "insurrection" denoted a lesser degree of organisation and size than "rebellion". Such was the case before the court: the insurers were not liable.

A rebellion (or insurrection) is no less a rebellion (or insurrection) because the chances of its success are forlorn:

> "At the time of its breaking out, an insurrection may not necessarily look impressive either in numbers, equipment or organization. As the insurrection develops into an affair of greater magnitude, so the insurgents come into *de facto* control of a definite region of the country, the insurrection may be spoken of as a 'rebellion'. If the insurrection or rebellion proceeds to the attainment of its objective, *viz*, the overthrow of the old constituted government and the establishment of a new one in its place, then the movement, retroactively, will be dignified by the characterization of a 'revolution'."[28]

An event on this scale of magnitude in its effects, generally greater therefore than a riot (below) but with participants who are not seeking the overthrow of government, has been characterised as a "civil commotion".[29]

---

[26] [1991] 2 Lloyd's Rep. 281.

[27] At 282, with reference to *Davila* (above, n. 25).

[28] *Davila* (above, n. 25).

[29] See *London & Manchester Plate Glass Co. Ltd v. Heath* [1913] 3 K.B. 411, 416, *per* Vaughan William L.J., C.A.; a civil commotion is "something considerably more serious than a leaderless mob" (*Spinney's* case (above), at 437, *per* Mustill J.), and "is used to indicate a stage between riot and civil war" (*Levy v. Assicurazioni Generali* [1940] A.C. 791, 800, P.C.). It is a "rising of the people . . . for purposes of general mischief" (*Spinney's*, at 438).

236f. Riot[30]

The defence of riot in a contract is interpreted in the technical sense of the criminal law.

> In *Boggan*,[31] a leading insurance case, a vehicle was insured against a number of perils, but riot was excepted. One night in Ireland, the vehicle was commandeered quietly and efficiently by four men with revolvers. The House of Lords held that the case satisfied the legal requirements of the time for a riot.

First, there had then to be three or more rioters. The number required now is twelve. This and the other requirements are now found in section 1(1) of the Public Order Act 1986. Secondly, the rioters must have a common purpose. Thirdly, their purpose must be carried out or at least incepted. Fourthly, they must use or threaten to use unlawful violence. Finally, there must be a display of force or violence such as would cause a person of reasonable firmness present at the scene to fear for his or her personal safety.

What is missing from the English common law notion of riot is any element of tumult. Since the Public Order Act 1986 there is still no requirement of tumult as such; however, the chance of a quiet riot with twelve persons is evidently less than the chance of a quiet riot with three. Nonetheless, the idea of riot without tumult has been rejected in the United States,[32] and the American view is one which in the English courts today "attracts considerable sympathy".[33]

> In *The Andreas Lemos*[34] armed thieves boarded a ship stealthily, and made off with equipment, using force to escape. The court was able to find that the exception of riot did not apply because although a riot did occur, "it was not complete until after the loss". This, said the court, was because the theft was complete before the thieves were discovered and force was used.[35]

This is not entirely convincing; the thieves were apprehended while still on the ship and, although some of the equipment had already been thrown overboard at that time, it is not clear that it was lost at that point and that the theft was complete at that point

---

30 *e.g.* RHA Condition 9(2)(b)(viii).

31 *Motor Union Ins. Co. Ltd v. Boggan* (1923) 130 L.T. 588, H.L.

32 *Pan American World Airways Inc. v. Aetna Casualty & Surety Co.*, 505 F. 2d 989, 1005, 1020–1021 (U.S. C.A. 2 Cir., 1974); *Holiday Inns Inc. v. Aetna Ins. Co.*, 571 F. Supp. 1460, 1467 (S.D. N.Y. 1983).

33 *The Andreas Lemos* [1982] 2 Lloyd's Rep. 483, 492, *per* Staughton J.

34 Above.

35 At 491–492.

and, therefore, complete before all the elements of riot were present. What is clear is that the court was determined not to apply the narrow common law (now statutory) conception of riot.

236g. Act or omission of the sender or consignee

This defence is important and largely self-explanatory. It overlaps with other defences such as insufficient packing (below). Note that the defence does not necessarily require that the act or omission be in any sense wrongful or negligent.[36]

A prime example of this defence is something done or omitted by the sender during loading or by the consignee during unloading. Another is that of failure to give proper instructions about handling and care of the goods. If the carrier does not give sensitive goods the care that they require and that is because the carrier has not been alerted to their needs by the sender, it cannot be said that the carrier is in breach of the residual duty of care or perhaps in breach of contract at all: liability for breach (or the scope of the carrier's duty) is cut back by the complementary impact of the defence—act of omission of the sender. If, however, the carrier should have been aware of the care that the goods required, whether from information from sender or from the carrier's own observation, the carrier will be liable.

236h. Inherent vice[37]

The concept of inherent vice is the same in all branches of transport law[38]; in particular, there is a rich case law on it in the law of carriage by sea.[39] The defence is also found in the CMR[40] but, as the CMR does not define it, reference in CMR cases is likely to be made to national law.

An inherent vice is some defect in the goods which by its development through ordinary processes going on in those goods tends to the injury or destruction of the goods, to such an extent

---

[36] *e.g.* RHA Condition 9(2)(b)(iv). *cf.* CMR Art. 17.2, above, para. 70.

[37] *e.g.* RHA Condition 9(2)(b)(v).

[38] The meaning is also the same in the law of insurance: *Soya GmbH v. White* [1982] 1 Lloyd's Rep. 136, 149, *per* Donaldson L.J., C.A.; [1983] 1 Lloyd's Rep. 122, 126, *per* Lord Diplock, H.L.

[39] Leading maritime cases include *The Barcore* [1896] P. 294 (carrier held not liable when deals, which were shipped wet, become tainted and discoloured by their "own want of power to bear the ordinary transit in a ship"); *Bradley v. Federal S.N. Co.* (1927) 27 Ll.L.Rep. 395, H.L. (carrier not liable for apples found on arrival to be internally damaged, after a normal voyage in properly refrigerated holds); *Albacora S.R.L. v. Westcott & Laurance Line* [1966] 2 Lloyd's Rep. 53 (H.L.: carrier not liable for damage to wet salted fish due to bacteria present in the fish on shipment).

[40] See above, para. 72.

that the goods do not survive the normal rigours of the journey in question or remain fit for their normal commercial purpose for a reasonable time after delivery.[41]

The vice must be an inherent vice, and in English common law that means some defect latent in the thing itself. If, however, the source of the trouble is external to the goods, the result may be a vice in the goods but not an inherent vice.

> In *Noten BV v. Harding*[42] Phillips J. held that goods (leather gloves in cardboard cartons), from which moisture condensed to the walls of the container, and which were then wetted (and became mildewed and mouldy) by drips of condensation from the walls, did not suffer from inherent vice, because "the sweat water has gone, as it were, into the universe on its own, even if it has come from those particular goods . . . and has achieved an identity of its own; and I think it has merited the appellation of an external cause . . . ".[43] On that premise, the decision was, no doubt, correct. However, an appeal from this decision was allowed by the Court of Appeal[44]: the real or dominant cause was not something external to the goods but the excessive moisture in the goods when shipped.

An inherent vice rarely gives rise to loss or damage without any external agency at all. The loss or damage must be produced in the goods by the agency of either, first, the atmosphere (air, moisture and temperature) or, secondly, the conditions of transport contracted for.[45] However, the defendant carrier does not have to prove the precise nature of the vice: it is enough that the loss or damage was caused by some propensity of the goods of the kind described.[46]

Inherent vice is relative. Most things carry within them the seeds of their own destruction or decay which will develop sooner or later, according to the circumstances. The notion of vice is relative, therefore, to the circumstances of the case: relative to what is expected of the goods. Goods fall below expectations when they are unfit to survive the journey and are not fit for use or consumption at destination.

As regards the rigours of the journey itself, goods are expected to be fit to withstand the ordinary incidents of the journey in question,[47] assuming that they receive the amount of care which

---

[41] *Blower v. G.W. Ry* (1872) L.R. 7 C.P. 655, 662, *per* Willes J.

[42] [1989] 2 Lloyd's Rep. 527.

[43] At 531.

[44] [1990] 2 Lloyd's Rep. 283, 288, *per* Bingham L.J.

[45] Evidently, the distinction between these agencies is sometimes unclear, as the conditions of transport include the atmospheric conditions in the vehicle, the temperature and humidity.

[46] *Bradley v. Federal S.N. Co.* (1927) 27 Ll.L.Rep. 395, 399, *per* Viscount Sumner, H.L.

[47] *The Barcore* [1896] P. 294, at 297, *per* Gorell Barnes J.; *Albacora S.R.L. v. Westcott & Laurance Line* [1966] 2 Lloyd's Rep. 53, at 59, *per* Lord Reid, at 62, *per* Lord Pearce, H.L.

the carrier is required by the contract to give them. If rust develops in metal carried in uncovered vehicles, that is a vice, but whether it is an inherent vice that the carrier can plead as a defence depends on whether the use of uncovered vehicles was authorised by the contract of carriage. The same distinction is made by the law of carriage by sea: "It follows that whether there is an inherent defect or vice must depend on the kind of transit required by the contract. If this contract had required refrigeration there would have been no inherent vice. But as it did not there was inherent vice because the goods could not stand the treatment which the contract authorized or required."[48]

A common illustration of inherent vice is the natural process of decay in perishable goods, which becomes a vice when it reaches such a stage of development that the goods are unfit.[49] Other illustrations are goods packed in a way that will not enable them to survive the journey in question,[50] goods which have not been properly stored or shored inside a container, and goods so moist on shipment that there is spontaneous combustion. Again, if "perishable goods, say soft fruit, are damaged by their own weight and the inevitable shaking of the carriage, they are injured through their own intrinsic qualities".[51] Last but not least there is excitability in live animals which injure themselves in transit.[52]

236i. Latent defect[53]

A latent defect is a defect in the goods which is not discoverable by the exercise of reasonable care by the relevant person at the relevant time.[54] The relevant person is the carrier at the time of consignment who, therefore, is not expected to make a thorough survey but only to notice anything suspicious (about the goods) that should be apparent to such a person under the circumstance. Note that, although latent defect has been distinguished[55] from inherent vice the carrier's general and residual duty of care is such that an inherent vice will not usually avail the carrier as a defence unless the vice is also a latent defect, *i.e.* one that the carrier could not be expected to have noticed.

---

[48] *Albacora* (above), at 59, *per* Lord Reid.

[49] *Ulster-Swift v. Taunton Meat Haulage* [1975] 2 Lloyd's Rep. 502, 505, affirmed [1977] 1 Lloyd's Rep. 346, C.A. For discussion of this leading case, see above, para. 72.

[50] *Barbour v. S.E. Ry Co.* (1876) 34 L.T. 67; *Gould v. S.E. & Chatham Ry Co.* [1920] 2 K.B. 191; *L.N.W. Ry Co. v. Hudson* [1920] A.C. 324, 333, *per* Lord Dunedin.

[51] *Kendall v. L.S.W. Ry* (1872) L.R. 7 Ex. 373, 377, *per* Bramwell B.

[52] *e.g. Kendall* (*ibid.*) and *Blower v. G.W. Ry* (1872) L.R. 7 C.P. 655.

[53] *e.g.* RHA Condition 9(2)(b)(v).

[54] Generally see *The Amstelslot* [1963] 2 Lloyd's Rep. 223, H.L.

[55] See above, para. 89a.

236j. Wastage or natural deterioration[56]

These defences are specific instances of inherent vice (above) which is usually a contract defence as well as these.

236k. Insufficient or improper packing[57]

Insufficient packing is packing that falls short of what is required and improper packing connotes inappropriate packing, but the exact difference is not clear. What is clear is that each is also a kind of inherent vice (above, paragraph 236h) and in most cases also an act or omission of the sender (above, paragraph 236g).

Packing is insufficient if it does not enable the particular goods to withstand the normal dangers of the kind contemplated by the particular transit. These include the handling to be expected by the carrier[58] which, in turn, depends on what the carrier can be taken to know abut the contents of the package, bearing in mind that the carrier has neither the right (unless stipulated for in the contract of carriage) nor the obligation to open a package to investigate its contents.[59]

Note that, except as regards goods that might cause loss, damage or injury to the carrier or the carrier's employees and agents, or the owners of other goods in the vicinity,[60] it is incorrect to speak of the sender as having a duty to pack. Generally, the carrier has no claim against the sender for failure to pack; but sufficient and appropriate packing is a measure that the sender must take if the carrier is to be liable for the fate of the goods,[61] unless it can be shown that the loss, etc., would have occurred anyway, *i.e.* that the loss, etc., has not "arisen from" the sender's act or omission.

If the carrier who receives from the sender goods that appear to be insufficiently packed for the journey in question, what, if anything, must the carrier do? If the carrier does nothing and, as a result, goods are lost or damaged in transit, the carrier, it seems, will be wholly or partially liable on the basis of breach of the residual (and overriding) duty of care (above, paragraph 229). Most of the cases on this point are old and concern carriage by

---

[56] Natural deterioration is specified in RHA Condition 9(2)(b)(v).

[57] *e.g.* RHA Condition 9(2)(b)(vi); Securicor Conditions cl. 1(i).

[58] Unless the carrier knows or should know that goods are sensitive, some degree of roughness is to be expected: *Decca Radar Ltd v. Caserite* [1961] 2 Lloyd's Rep. 301, 308, *per* McNair J.

[59] *cf. L.N.W. Ry Co. v. Hudson* [1920] A.C. 324, 341, *per* Lord Atkinson.

[60] See below, para. 237, concerning the warranty of fitness for carriage.

[61] Kahn-Freund, p. 370.

rail. In *Gould*,[62] Atkin L.J. put the issue like this[63]: "does it make any difference that the faulty packing which caused the damage was manifest to the carrier at the time that the goods were delivered to him to be carried?" He gave a negative answer to this question, adopting the view of Cleasby B. in *Barbour*,[64] that the plaintiff sender "took upon himself the risk of anything happening to [the goods]. The real question is, whose duty was it to pack?"

> In *Barbour* a carrier agreed to carry furniture on the basis of no duty to pack or unpack the goods. When the carrier's driver came to collect the goods, packaging materials were at hand, but the goods were not packed. The goods were carried unpacked and were damaged in transit. Stressing the sender's duty to pack, the sender's decision to allow the goods to travel unpacked and that the lack of packing was the sole cause of the damage, Cleasby B. held that the carrier was not liable.

This might be seen as *carte blanche* for the carrier to take the goods as they are, assured of exoneration for any loss, damage or delay that ensues. That might indeed have been so at the time of *Barbour*, but is not today, however, in view of later developments in common law, in particular the residual or overriding duty of care on the part of the carrier. In the later case of *Lister*,[65] Alverstone L.C.J. said that:

> "if there is no evidence of intention by the parties as to how the thing is to be carried, and there are alternative modes of carriage, one of which will give play to an inherent defect in the thing carried and the other of which will not, the carrier will be responsible if he adopts the former mode and damage results therefrom, unless indeed the adoption of the safer mode would involve the taking of precautions which it would be altogether unreasonable to require him to take".

Moreover, in *Hudson*[66] Lord Atkinson said that, if

> "the imperfect nature of the packing be obvious to the carrier when the goods are tendered for his acceptance, and he receives them without objection, he will not be excused for any damage which may

[62] *Gould v. S.E. & Chatham Ry Co.* [1920] 2 K.B. 186, C.A.

[63] At 191. A different emphasis is found in the concurring judgment of Younger L.J. in *Gould* (at 194): on the facts of the case, the plaintiff was saying, in effect, " 'Whether they are well packed or badly packed, take them as they are.' And if that is the effect of what took place between them, the railway company are to my mind in exactly the same position as if they had had no notice of the improper packing."

[64] *Barbour v. S.E. Ry Co.* (1876) 34 L.T. 67.

[65] *Lister v. Lancs. & Yorks. Ry Co.* [1903] 1 K.B. 878, 880. See also *Cox v. L.N.W. Ry Co.* (1862) F. & F. 72, 79, *per* Mellor J.; *Richardson v. N.E. Ry Co.* (1872) L.R. 7 C.P. 75, 82, *per* Willes J.

[66] *L.N.W. Ry Co. v. Hudson* [1920] A.C. 324, 340 (citations omitted).

> subsequently result from the imperfect packing. . . . Again, if the defect in the packing from which damage is likely to occur be discovered on the journey, the carrier should take reasonable means to arrest the loss or deterioration therefrom. And if the defect be discovered in time to prevent the forwarding of the goods, they should not be forwarded till the defect has been remedied."

If the carrier is in breach of duty with regard to insufficient packing, the carrier is liable in full or, on an apportionment of responsibility,[67] liable in part.

Finally, if defective packing in parcel A leads to damage to parcel B, it has been suggested in a case concerning carriage by sea[68] that, *ceteris paribus*, the carrier can raise the defective packing of parcel A as a defence of insufficient packing in an action by the owner of B. This is doubtful. As argued above,[69] insofar as the carrier is or should be aware of the defect, the situation remains in the carrier's sphere of risk and, if there is loss or damage to parcel B, the carrier should be liable.

236l. Strikes[70]

A strike is "a general concerted refusal by workmen to work in consequence of an alleged grievance"[71]; but this "definition" was not intended to be exhaustive and, it seems, a strike can include a "sympathy" strike.[72] A strike "is distinct from a stoppage which is brought about by some external event such as a bomb scare or by apprehension of danger".[73]

A strike of the carrier's employees is, nonetheless, a strike, and a defence available to the carrier, because it occurs in response to something done or not done by the carrier.[74] However, like other defences, the strike does not excuse the carrier unless it is the cause of the loss or damage. Moreover, the carrier may still be liable if the carrier's response to the strike is such that the carrier is in breach of the carrier's residual duty to take reasonable care of the goods.[75]

---

[67] *Higginbotham v. G.N.R. Ry Co.* (1861) 2 F. & F. 796.
[68] Above, para. 82a.
[69] *ibid.*
[70] *e.g.* BIFA cl. 27(A); RHA Condition 9(2)(b)(viii).
[71] *Williams Bros. (Hull) Ltd v. Naamlooze etc.* (1915) 21 Com.Cas. 253, 257, *per* Sankey J.
[72] *Seeburg v. Russian Wood Agency Ltd* (1934) 50 Ll.L.Rep. 146.
[73] *Tramp Shipping Corp. v. Greenwich Marine Inc.* [1975] 2 All E.R. 989, 992, *per* Lord Denning, M.R., C.A.
[74] See, *e.g.* *Channel Island Ferries Ltd v. Sealink U.K. Ltd* [1988] 1 Lloyd's Rep. 323, C.A.
[75] Above, para. 236 *cf.* Yates, para. 7.2.24.3.

236m. Restraints of labour[76]

A restraint of labour is organised interference by employees not amounting to a general withdrawal, and includes, notably, a threat by employees not to move or handle certain goods.[77]

236n. Seizure or forfeiture under legal process[78]

This defence is self-explanatory. Obvious examples are detention of illegal substances by the police or of the goods of a debtor by bailiffs.

236o. Unavoidable events

A defence such as "any cause or event which the Company is unable to avoid and the consequences whereof the Company is unable to prevent by the exercise of reasonable diligence"[79] is a residual defence which replaces many of the more particular defences listed above and reflects the residual duty of care.[80]

237. Dangerous goods

If goods are dangerous, the consequence may be loss of or damage to those goods, as well as other goods, or delay to the entire consignment. As long as the carrier is aware of the danger and the carrier accepts the goods for transit on that basis, the carrier's liability for dangerous goods is much like the carrier's liability for other goods.[81] Dangerous goods are commonly the subject of a special term in the contract of carriage requiring the customer to make the carrier aware of the danger.[82] Some transport documents, such as bills of lading, provide the carrier with an indemnity from the customer against claims, loss, damage or expense arising in consequence of the carriage of such goods.[83] Anyway, common law has long known an implied undertaking by the

---

[76] *e.g.* BIFA clause 27(A); RHA Condition 9(2)(b)(viii).

[77] *Young & Son (Wholesale Fish Merchants) Ltd v. British Transport Commission* [1955] 2 Q.B. 177; Kahn-Freund, p. 249.

[78] *e.g.* RHA Condition 9(2)(b)(iii).

[79] See BIFA clause 27(B). Yates, para. 7.2.24.

[80] Above. *cf.* CMR Article 17.2, above, para. 74.

[81] Above, paras. 236h and 236k.

[82] See, *e.g.* RHA Condition 3. Such goods are defined in Condition 1. For the definition at common law, see Girvin [1996] L.M.C.L.Q. 487, 494 *et seq. cf.* CMR Art. 22 (above para. 73) which goes further and provides for the carrier what amounts to a defence of "necessity" in the carrier's response to dangers posed by the goods.

[83] See Yates, para. 1.6.16.4.

customer that the goods are not dangerous when carried in the ordinary way.[84] Customers have a duty to communicate to the carrier such information as they have about the goods as might affect safe carriage[85]; however, the carrier has no right to expect any communication respecting the nature of the goods when he himself may easily discover it.[86] What if the customer is unaware of the danger? Although controversial, the balance of authority is that the customer's duty is strict.[87]

238. Defences: construction *contra proferentem*

The court will scrutinise any exclusion clause pleaded by the carrier as a defence to ensure that the clause really does cover what has occurred. If the clause is ambiguous,[88] the clause will be construed restrictively against the carrier[89]; however, less so between commercial entities of roughly equal bargaining strength than between carrier and consumer,[90] and less so if the clause is one that admits liability but limits the amount rather than one purporting to exclude liability altogether.[91]

In *Alexander v. Railway Executive*[92] the plaintiff deposited trunks containing theatrical properties at Launceston station. Later a person, who had been with the plaintiff at the time of the deposit, persuaded the station employee in charge of the trunks to let him remove certain items without having produced a ticket showing his entitlement to do so; for this the person was later convicted of larceny. The plaintiff brought an action against the Executive, the

---

[84] *Bamfield v. Goole and Sheffield Transport Co. Ltd* [1910] 2 K.B. 94, C.A. Yates, *loc. cit.*.

[85] *Bamfield* (above), at 105, *per* Vaughan Williams L.J.

[86] *Brass v. Maitland* (1856) 6 El. & Bl. 470, 482, *per* Campbell C.J.

[87] See Girvin [1996] L.M.C.L.Q. 487, 491 *et seq.*

[88] A clause is not ambiguous merely because it is unclear to one party. Ambiguity is assessed objectively by the court: *Higgins v. Dawson* [1902] A.C. 1. See further Lewison, *The Interpretation of Contracts* (London, 1989), Chap. 7.

[89] In accordance with the maxim *verba chartarum fortius accipiuntur contra proferentem*, more usually and more simply known as construction *contra proferentem*. It rests on the assumption that the carrier as the party drafting the words will look to his own interests, and that no greater benefit to himself (or burden to the sender or consignee) can have been intended than the carrier has made clear.

[90] *Photo Production v. Securicor Transport* [1980] A.C. 827.

[91] *Ailsa Craig Fishing Co. v. Malvern Fishing Co.* [1983] 1 All E.R. 101, H.L.; *George Mitchell (Chesterhall) v. Finney Lock Seeds* [1983] 2 A.C. 803, 814, *per* Lord Bridge. According to Yates and Hawkins, *Standard Business Contracts: Exclusions and Related Devices* (London, 1986), para. 2G(6) the suggestion appears to derive from *Tessler Bros. v. Italpacific Line* [1975] 1 Lloyd's Rep. 210, 213, *per* Wright C.J., speaking of the Hague Rules: "This distinction between a limitation on liability and an exemption from liability is crucial. A limitation, unlike an exemption, does not induce negligence." However, as Yates and Hawkins (*loc. cit.*) point out, in practical terms a low limitation might not be significantly different from a total exemption.

[92] [1951] 2 K.B. 882.

body responsible for the station. The Executive relied upon the contract of deposit, which exempted liability for "misdelivery" in Clause 2 and read in Clause 3: "The Company may deliver... to any person who fails to produce a ticket, upon such evidence of the loss of the ticket and of ownership or authority to receive such articles, as the Company's servants may consider satisfactory", on receipt of an indemnity from the person concerned. Devlin J. gave three reasons for his decision that the defence based on these clauses did not succeed. One reason was that there were two possible meanings of "misdelivery", a broad one including deliberate delivery to the wrong person and a narrower one which was confined to delivery in genuine error, and it was the narrower construction that applied.

In particular, the court is reluctant to allow the carrier to exclude liability for breach of contract brought about by the carrier's own negligence.[93]

238a. Negligence clauses

Construction *contra proferentem* has led to particular and important rules of construction[94] for negligence clauses.[95]

(a) If the clause contains language which expressly exempts the person, assumed for discussion to be the carrier, from the consequences of negligence, that effect must be given to the clause. For express exemption, the clause must "contain the word 'negligence' or some synonym for it".[96]

(b) If there is no express reference to negligence, the court asks whether the words used are wide enough, in their ordinary meaning, to cover negligence.

---

[93] Including so-called contractual negligence, *i.e.* negligence that would not be actionable as the tort of negligence: Swanton (1989) 15 U. of Queensland L.J. 157, 179.

[94] The "exercise upon which the Court is engaged ... is one of construction, ... one of deciding what the parties meant or must be deemed to have meant by the words they used; the guidelines or tests which are referred to in the many authorities are only to be used by the Courts as aids to the successful and correct solution of such exercise"—*The Raphael* [1982] 2 Lloyd's Rep. 42, 49, *per* May L.J., C.A., in a passage adopted by Purchas L.J. in *Sonat Offshore S.A. v. Amerada Hess Development Ltd* [1988] 1 Lloyd's Rep. 145, 156, C.A.

[95] *Canada SS Lines Ltd v. R.* [1952] A.C. 192, 208, *per* Lord Morton, P.C., as considered and applied in *The Raphael* [1982] 2 Lloyd's Rep. 42, C.A. These aids apply also to an indemnity clause, "the obverse" of the exclusion: *Smith v. South Wales Switchgear Ltd* [1978] 1 All E.R. 18, 25, *per* Lord Fraser, H.L. See further, Yates and Hawkins (above, n. 91), paras. 4F *et seq.*; Carter (1995) 9 J.C.L. 69.

[96] *Smith* (above) at 26, *per* Lord Fraser, H.L. For example, *Spriggs v. Sotheby Parke Bernet & Co.* [1986] 1 Lloyd's Rep. 487, C.A.: no responsibility for loss or damage of any kind "whether caused by negligence or otherwise".

(c) If the answer to (b) is affirmative,[97] the court asks whether the clause might apply to something other than negligence, for parties "are unlikely to contract to pay something for nothing, particularly if the failure to perform by the payee is due to his own negligence".[98] "When parties make an agreement governing their future relationship, human nature being on balance more inclined to optimism than pessimism, the parties are more likely to be thinking in terms of non-negligent rather than negligent performance of the contract. The law reflects the facts of life by assuming that if there are two potential grounds of liability, both of them real and foreseeable, but one involves negligence, prima facie any words of exemption will be directed to the non-negligent ground of liability."[99] On this basis the clause will be confined in its operation to the strict liability of carriers[1] to carry the goods from the point of takeover to the place of delivery. The effect is that the clause excludes liability, *except* when the carrier has been negligent. However, rule (c) is not generally applied to restrict limitation clauses, whether the limit concerns the amount of liability[2] or the time within which action must be instituted.[3]

(d) If, however, the contractor has not undertaken strict liability but only liability for negligence, the words must be applied to a breach of the contract, for otherwise the words would lack subject-matter.[4] Even then, courts have been ingenious to find

---

[97] For example, "any act or omission"—*The Raphael* [1982] 2 Lloyd's Rep. 42, 45, *per* Donaldson L.J., C.A.; "any liability whatsoever", unless the meaning of the phrase is restricted by the context—*Smith* (above) at 25–26, *per* Lord Fraser, H.L.; "all liability whatsoever"—Treitel, p. 203 and cases cited. *cf.* the words "at charterer's risk", which do not cover negligence: *The Fantasy* [1991] 2 Lloyd's Rep. 391. For further illustrations, see Swanton (above, n. 93), p. 161.

[98] *Sonat* (below, n. 99), at 157, *per* Purchas L.J.

[99] *The Raphael* [1982] 2 Lloyd's Rep. 42, 45, *per* Donaldson L.J., C.A., passage adopted by Purchas L.J. in *Sonat Offshore S.A. v. Amerada Hess Development Ltd* [1988] 1 Lloyd's Rep. 145, 156, C.A. See also *The Fiona* [1994] 2 Lloyd's Rep. 506, C.A.; *Shell Chemicals (U.K.) Ltd v. P & O Roadtanks Ltd* [1995] 1 Lloyd's Rep. 297, C.A.; and *EE Caledonia Ltd v. Orbit Valve plc* [1995] 1 All E.R. 174, C.A. This is the current interpretation of the statement of the rules most commonly cited, that of Lord Morton in *Canada S.S. Lines Ltd v. R.* [1952] A.C. 192, 208, P.C.: "the existence of a possible head of damage other than that of negligence is fatal to the proferens even if the words used are prima facie wide enough to cover negligence on the part of his servants".

The other head of damage "must not be fanciful or remote", *ibid.*, a point stressed in *The Raphael* [1982] 2 Lloyd's Rep. 42, 45 by Donaldson L.J., C.A.

[1] *Alderslade v. Hendon Laundry Ltd* [1945] 1 K.B. 189, 192, *per* Lord Greene M.R., C.A. In a case of carriage by sea Bingham J. observed that "it is inherently improbable that one party to a contract should intend to absolve the other party from the consequences of the latter's own negligence"—*The Emmanuel C* [1983] 1 All E.R. 686, 689. In substance this rule was applied to carriage by rail in *Mitchell v. Lancs. & Yorks. Ry Co.* (1875) L.R. 10 Q.B. 256.

[2] *George Mitchell (Chesterhall) Ltd v. Finney Lock Seeds Ltd* [1983] 2 A.C. 803, 814, *per* Lord Bridge. *Contra: Darlington Futures v. Delco Australia Pty* (1986) 161 C.L.R. 500, 510, H.C.A. For criticism of the English position see Swanton, above n. 93, p. 171.

[3] *The New York Star* [1980] 3 All E.R. 257, P.C.

[4] *Alderslade v. Hendon Laundry Ltd* [1945] 1 K.B. 189, 192, *per* Lord Greene M.R., C.A. See also *Beaumont-Thomas v. Blue Star Line* [1939] 3 All E.R. 127, C.A., concerning the carriage of passengers.

against the clause,[5] and it may be safer to say with Scrutton L.J.[6] that "if the only liability of the [carrier] is a liability for negligence, the clause will more readily operate to exempt him". This is the situation if the contractor has promised, not to achieve a result (for example, to repair the machine), but to exercise reasonable care, skill and endeavour to achieve that end. In the absence of clear words to the contrary, the carrier's undertaking is not of this kind but is strict.

> In *Gillespie Bros. & Co. Ltd v. Roy Bowles Transport Ltd*[7] gold watches belonging to the plaintiffs were stolen from a van left unattended at London airport. The plaintiffs, who had no contract with the defendant carriers, brought an action based on the latter's duty as a bailee to take reasonable care of the goods. The defendants in third-party proceedings sought indemnity; they pleaded clause 3(4) of the RHA's Conditions of Carriage (1967): "The Trader shall save harmless and keep the Carrier indemnified against all claims or demands whatsoever made in excess of the liability of the Carrier under these Conditions." The third parties unsuccessfully argued that this clause was not wide enough to apply when the carrier's servant had been negligent. Lord Denning said[8]: "The judges . . . have repeatedly held that words do not exempt a man from negligence unless it is clear beyond doubt; nor entitle a man to indemnity from the consequences of his own negligence. . . . [But, these] words are too clear."[9]

239. The Unfair Contract Terms Act 1977

This Act applies to business liability[10] in certain cases. The cases include that of a customer who contracts with a carrier on the carrier's written standard terms of business such as a consignment note.[11] A contract remains standard even though the parties have agreed some alterations in the standard terms unless the alteration is the product of real negotiation between them.[12] When the Act

---

[5] See Treitel, p. 205: Swanton, above n. 93, p. 166; Walker, para. 20.61. In particular, clauses have been construed not as excluding liability but as warnings to a bailor that the common law does not impose strict liability on a bailee; however, this is an unlikely construction of a contract between businessmen. Moreover, in considering this issue the court may be influenced by whether the loss is one against which the goods owner is insured: *Rutter v. Palmer* [1922] 2 K.B. 87, 90, *per* Bankes L.J., C.A.; Swanton, above n. 93, p. 175.

[6] *Rutter v. Palmer* [1922] 2 K.B. 87, 92, C.A.

[7] [1973] Q.B. 400.

[8] *ibid.*, at 415.

[9] See also Buckley L.J., at 420. These members of the court considered that this was an instance of case (a), but in *Smith v. South Wales Switchgear Ltd* [1978] 1 All E.R. 18, 26, *per* Lord Fraser, H.L., while the decision in *Gillespie* was approved, it was seen as a case of (b) and this is the better view: Swanton (above, n. 93), p. 160.

[10] s.1(3).

[11] s.3.

[12] *The Flamar Pride* [1990] 1 Lloyd's Rep. 434, 438, *per* Potter J.

applies to a contract, certain clauses, notably ones which "exclude"[13] the carrier's liability, will not apply except to the extent that a court finds them reasonable. Whether or not a clause is an exclusion clause depends not on the form of the clause but on its substance.[14] Generally, however, it is a clause *but for which* the defendant would have been liable.[15]

239a. Reasonableness

The requirement of reasonableness[16] applies mainly to terms excluding or restricting liability.[17] If the term is an exclusion,[18] the onus is on the person seeking to rely on the term[19] to show that it "was fair and reasonable . . . having regard to the circumstances which were, or ought to have been, known to or in the contemplation of the parties when the contract was made".[20] Moreover, the entire term must be shown to be fair and reasonable—not just the part relied on.[21] It has been suggested[22] that English courts will be slow to interfere with such terms in commercial contracts, such as the contract of carriage, but some writers[23] are sceptical about the courts' self-restraint. Subject to this, reasonableness is a matter of impression[24] built up by reference to certain factors[25] as they affect the particular contract of carriage. The factors have no

---

[13] On the types of exclusion clause, among them clauses limiting the amount of damages payable by one party to the contract or the time within which acts, such as the commencement of suit, must be performed, see Yates and Hawkins, *Standard Business Contracts: Exclusion Clauses and Related Devices* (London, 1986), paras. 1A(4) *et seq*: Macdonald (1992) 12 L.S. 277.

[14] *Phillips Products Ltd v. Hyland* [1987] 2 All E.R. 620, C.A.; *Johnstone v. Bloomsbury Health Authority* [1991] 2 All E.R. 293, C.A.

[15] *Smith v. Eric S. Bush* [1990] 1 A.C. 831, 857, *per* Lord Griffiths.

[16] Generally see the Law Commission Report (No. 69), Second Report on Exemption Clauses, 1975, paras. 169 *et seq*. Sched. 2 to the Act offers guidelines on reasonableness in the case of sales of goods, which the courts have applied freely to other kinds of contract: for example, *The Flamar Pride* [1990] 1 Lloyd's Rep. 434, 439, *per* Potter J.; *Stewart Gill Ltd v. Horatio Myer & Co. Ltd* [1992] Q.B. 600, C.A. Generally, see Adams and Brownsword (1988) 104 L.Q.R. 94, 113; Treitel, pp. 237 *et seq*.; Yates, *Exclusion Clauses in Contracts* (2nd ed., London, 1982), pp. 95 *et seq*.

[17] See above, para. 239.

[18] Above, para. 239.

[19] Unfair Contract Terms Act 1977, s.11(5).

[20] s.11(1).

[21] *Stewart Gill* (above).

[22] By reference, for example, to the judgment of Lord Wilberforce in *Photo Production Ltd v. Securicor Transport Ltd* [1980] A.C. 827, 843. See also *Singer & Co. (U.K.) Ltd v. Tees & Hartlepool Port Authority* [1988] 2 Lloyd's Rep. 164, 169, *per* Steyn J.

[23] For example, Adams and Brownsword, (n. 16) *loc. cit.*

[24] *ibid.*, at 103.

[25] *Smith v. Bush* [1990] 1 A.C. 831, at 858, *per* Lord Griffiths, at 874, *per* Lord Jauncey, H.L.

order of precedence, and the court may not indicate which factors were most important in the particular case; however, it is submitted that, of those listed below, the most important in contracts of carriage are factors (a), (b) and (f).

(a) The relative bargaining strength of the parties[26]: the more of a match they are for each other, the less the inclination of the court to interfere. When assessing their relative strength, the courts have been invited[27] to have regard to whether the customer:

(i) knew or should have known that it was possible to enter into a similar contract with another carrier without having to agree to the exemption clause[28];
(ii) was experienced in transactions of that kind; and
(iii) had relied on the advice of the other party (the carrier).

(b) The party best able to insure against the loss or damage in question.[29] The estimate is made in general terms with regard to the availability and cost of insurance in situations of the relevant kind, and without regard to whether one or other of the particular parties were insured in fact.[30] Some courts have been influenced, for example, by the view that indemnity insurance is a more efficient way of covering loss than liability insurance,[31] a point therefore that may work in favour of the carrier.

(c) The party best able to avoid the loss or damage in question[32]; this factor is likely to work against the carrier.

(d) Any inducement offered by the carrier, such as a reduced carrier charge, in return for the reduced level of liability sought by the exclusion.[33]

---

[26] Unfair Contract Terms Act 1977, Sched. 2(a). *Photo Production, loc cit.*; *Smith v. Bush*, (n. 25), *loc cit.*

[27] Law Commission Report (No. 69) Second Report on Exemption Clauses, 1975, para. 189.

[28] *Smith v. Bush* above, n. 25.

[29] Unfair Contract Terms Act 1977, s.11(4). *George Mitchell (Chesterhall) Ltd v. Finney Lock Seeds Ltd* [1983] 2 A.C. 803; *Smith v. Bush* (n. 25), *loc. cit.*

[30] *The Flamar Pride* [1990] 1 Lloyd's Rep. 434, in which Potter J. refused an order for discovery of the defendant's insurance position.

[31] *Rutter v. Palmer* [1922] 2 K.B. 87, 90, *per* Bankes L.J., C.A.; *Photo Production Ltd v. Securicor Transport Ltd* [1980] A.C. 827, 851, *per* Lord Diplock; *Singer & Co. (U.K.) Ltd v. Tees & Hartlepool Port Authority* [1988] 2 Lloyd's Rep. 164, 169, *per* Steyn J. Swanton, above, n. 93, at 174–175. See also above, para. 92a.

[32] Law Commission Report (No. 69) Second Report on Exemption Clauses, 1975, para. 188. *Phillips Products Ltd v. Hyland* [1987] 2 All E.R. 620, 629–630, C.A., where Slade L.J. took account of the party best placed to exercise control over the driver of an excavator, who did the damage. Similarly, in the law of tort this is a major factor influencing whether it is "fair and reasonable" that a person should owe a duty of care: see, for example, *Davis v. Radcliffe* [1990] 2 All E.R. 536, P.C.

[33] Unfair Contract Terms Act 1977, Sched. 2(b).

(e) Whether and to what extent the customer had notice of term[34]: the less the notice, for example because it was in small print or difficult to understand,[35] the less likely it is to be held to be reasonable.

(f) Whether the term is in established and widespread use in the trade context[36]: standard terms of the RHA or BIFA are likely to be respected.[37]

(g) Proportionality[38]: if the loss claimed against the carrier is large in relation to the remuneration received by the carrier under the contract of carriage, the term will receive favourable consideration.

(h) Any special difficulty or danger in performing the work in respect of which liability is excluded.[39]

(i) In the case of a limit on the amount of liability, the court will consider, in the words of section 11(4) of the Act, "(a) the resources he could expect to be available to him for the purpose of meeting the liability that should arise; and (b) how far it was open to him to cover himself by insurance"; and, in the opinion of the House of Lords,[40] (c) the "estoppel factor": any evidence of past practice or evidence in the instant case of settlement of or offers to settle claims at a level significantly above the amount of the limit will suggest that the limit is not fair and reasonable.

(j) In the case of a limit on the time within which suit may be brought, whether it is necessary to enable the carrier to provide efficiently for outstanding claims.[41]

---

[34] Unfair Contract Terms Act 1977, Sched. 2(c). *Phillips Products Ltd v. Hyland* [1987] 2 All E.R. 620, C.A.: if the contract is made at short notice and the profferee is unaware of the terms, he may have insufficient opportunity to take the appropriate action in response, such as obtaining insurance cover.

[35] *The Zinnia* [1984] 2 Lloyd's Rep. 211, 222, *per* Staughton J. Further, the court will be influenced by whether the term was agreed on legal advice: *Walker v. Boyle* [1982] 1 All E.R. 634, 644, *per* Dillon L.J., C.A.

[36] Unfair Contract Terms Act 1977, Sched. 2(c). *George Mitchell (Chesterhall) Ltd v. Finney Lock Seeds Ltd* [1983] 2 A.C. 803.

[37] As was the case of the established terms of the National Association of Seed Potato Merchants in *R.W. Green Ltd v. Cade Bros. Farm* [1978] 1 Lloyd's Rep. 602, 606–607, *per* Griffiths J.

[38] *George Mitchell (Chesterhall) Ltd v. Finney Lock Seeds Ltd* [1983] 2 A.C. 803; see discussion of the case by Adams and Brownsword, above, n. 16, p. 101. Also in this sense: *Smith v. Bush* [1990] 1 A.C. 831, at 859, *per* Lord Griffiths at 874, *per* Lord Jauncey.

[39] *Smith v. Bush*, *per* Lord Griffiths; at 874, *per* Lord Jauncey.

[40] *George Mitchell (Chesterhall) Ltd v. Finney Lock Seeds Ltd* [1983] 2 A.C. 803, 817, *per* Lord Bridge. Adams and Brownsword, above, n. 2, pp. 100, 106 *et seq.* Of course, evidence of recent practice does not demonstrate that a term contracted prior to that practice was reasonable, as required by the Act, at the time of contract. Nor does non-reliance in the past preclude reliance in the present or the future: *The Scaptrade* [1983] Q.B. 529, C.A., affirmed [1983] A.C. 694.

[41] Law Commission Report (No. 69) Second Report on Exemption Clauses, 1975, para. 188.

240. Fundamental breach

English courts construe[42] a clause narrowly, not only when there is ambiguity,[43] but also when there is no apparent ambiguity and, on an ordinary or literal interpretation of the words used, they cover what has occurred, but that interpretation is too wide to make commercial sense.

> "As to the question of 'fundamental breach', I think there is a rule of construction that normally an exception or exclusion clause or similar provision in a contract should be construed as not applying to a situation created by a fundamental breach of the contract. This is not an independent rule of law imposed by the Court on the parties willy-nilly in disregard of their contractual intention. On the contrary it is a rule of construction based on the presumed intention of the contracting parties. It involves the implication of a term to give to the contract that business efficacy which the parties as reasonable men must have intended it to have. This rule of construction is not new in principle but it has become prominent in recent years in consequence of the tendency to have standard forms of contract containing exception clauses drawn in extravagantly wide terms, which would produce absurd results if applied literally."[44]

The absurdity in question would result if exclusions were applied to certain kinds of breach, usually, although it is not a term of art, those called fundamental breach. There is fundamental breach, first, if, having agreed to carry goods from A to B, the carrier fails to carry them at all.[45]

> In *The Cap Palos*[46] the defendant contracted to tow a schooner but did so only intermittently. One day the tug left the schooner in Robin Hood's bay in a position of danger and effectively ceased to carry out the contract. In attempting to escape the danger the schooner was damaged. When sued, the defendant pleaded a clause in the contract which excluded all liability for omission or default. The Court of Appeal held that this clause could not be construed so as to apply to the consequences of omission to perform the contract

---

[42] It is now clear that whether the contract has been terminated or not, this doctrine is not a rule of law but a rule of construction: *Photo Production Ltd v. Securicor Transport Ltd* [1980] A.C. 827. Sealy [1980] C.L.J. 252; Treitel, pp. 205 *et seq.*; Walker, para. 20.62.

[43] Above, para. 238.

[44] *U.G.S. Finance Ltd v. National Mortgage Bank of Greece* [1964] 1 Lloyd's Rep. 446, 453, *per* Pearson L.J., C.A. See also the *Suisse Atlantique* case [1967] 1 A.C. 361, 398, *per* Lord Reid, that the words of a clause will not be given literal effect, if that "would lead to an absurdity, or because it would defeat the main object of the contract".

[45] *Firestone Tyre & Rubber Co. Ltd v. Vokins Co. Ltd* [1951] 1 Lloyd's Rep. 32, 39, *per* Devlin J. "It is illusory to say—'we promise to do a thing but we are not liable if we do not do it.' "See also the *Suisse Atlantique* case [1967] 1 A.C. 361, 432, *per* Lord Wilberforce; and *The Glacier Bay* [1995] 1 Lloyd's Rep. 560, 565–566, *per* Waller J.

[46] [1921] P. 458.

altogether. In the words of Lord Sterndale M.R.[47]: "I think the (clause) extends to cover a default during the actual performance of the duties of the contract, and not to an unjustified handing over of those obligations to someone else for performance."

Similar reasoning could be applied to carriage by land, not only when the carrier abandons the goods but also when the carrier fails to take them over at all. As a rule of construction, the doctrine is designed to avoid the apparent contradiction and absurdity of a contract whereby the carrier says in clause 1, "I promise to carry"; but then says in clause 2, "But I shall not be liable if I do not carry at all".

Secondly, there is a fundamental breach if the carrier does collect the goods but carries them in a way essentially different from that contemplated by the contract, for example to the wrong destination or in an open vehicle when the goods were foodstuffs for which refrigerated transport was contracted.[48] Moreover, at common law, although in general vicarious performance of contracts is allowed, it has been doubted whether a carrier is allowed to sub-contract performance of the work of carriage[49]; and it has been held that to sub-contract the carriage of goods especially attractive to thieves (cigarettes) is a fundamental breach of contract.[50]

Thirdly, there may be a fundamental breach if a breach, which is not of the first two types, is done deliberately and if, in the circumstances, this is sufficiently outrageous to displace the exemptions.[51] Fourthly, there may be a breach which does not fall into any of the first three categories but is nonetheless regarded as fundamental because in the particular case it leads to particularly disastrous consequences.[52]

Normally an allegation of breach has to be proved on the balance of probabilities by the person alleging it, here the claimant. However, the common law response to an allegation that a bailee, such as a carrier, is guilty of fundamental breach is different: "because it is quite likely that the goods were stolen by one of

---

[47] At 468.

[48] *United Fresh Meat Co. Ltd v. Charterhouse Cold Storage Ltd* [1974] 2 Lloyd's Rep. 286, 291, *per* Wien J. (storage of meat in a temperature significanctly higher than contemplated by the contract); *The Berkshire* [1974] 1 Lloyd's Rep. 185, 190–191, *per* Brandon J. (unauthorised transhipment); *Doreb v. Eastern SS. Co.* (1978) 13 E.T.L. 651 (leaving goods outside uncovered during transhipment).

[49] Glass, para. 1.77.

[50] *Garnham, Harris & Elton Ltd v. Alfred W. Ellis (Transport) Ltd* [1967] 1 W.L.R. 940.

[51] Lord Wilberforce in the *Suisse Atlantique* case [1967] 1 A.C. 361, 435. For example, delivery of goods to a person who, to the knowledge of the carrier, is not entitled to take delivery: *Sze Hai Tong Bank Ltd v. Rambler Cycle Co. Ltd* [1959] A.C. 576. *cf. Photo Production Ltd v. Securicor Transport Ltd* [1980] A.C. 827, in which a security guard in a factory deliberately started a fire in some cartons there, not intending to destroy the entire factory, as occurred; but the clause applied to the breach.

[52] *Pollock & Co. v. Macrae* [1922] S.C. 192.

his servants; or delivered by a servant to the wrong address; or damaged by his reckless or wilful misconduct", if in these circumstances the bailee "leaves the cause of damage undiscovered and unexplained", the bailee is liable.[53] This is seen as a "proper extension of the bailee's burden of proof".[54]

The importance of fundamental breach to contracts of carriage is limited, because they are commercial contracts and, as Lord Wilberforce said[55]:

> "in commercial matters generally, when the parties are not of unequal bargaining power, and when risks are normally borne by insurance, not only is the case for judicial intervention undemonstrated, but there is everything to be said, and this seems to have been Parliament's intention, for leaving the parties free to apportion the risks as they think fit and for respecting their decisions.
>
> At the stage of negotiation as to the consequences of a breach, there is everything to be said for allowing the parties to estimate their respective claims according to the contractual provisions they have themselves made, rather than for facing them with a legal complex so uncertain as the doctrine of fundamental breach must be."

Moreover, for contracts governed by the Unfair Contract Terms Act 1977, it is hard to imagine that, having found the operation of a clause reasonable under the Act, the same court would then find that it "would produce absurd results if applied literally" and must be construed inapplicable to fundamental breach. Finally, as regards the case of sub-contracting, the matter is likely to be settled by contract terms. Condition 2(2) of the RHA Conditions, for example, authorises the carrier to employ the services of any other carrier for the purpose of fulfilling the contract of carriage, but obliges the carrier to give the customer the name of that other carrier on request.

B: DEFENCES AVAILABLE TO BOTH PARTIES

241. Avoidance: misrepresentation[56]

The statements by which the carrier brings the service to the attention of customers, although not an offer to contract, are not

---

[53] *Levison v. Patent Steam Carpet Cleaning Co. Ltd* [1978] Q.B. 69, 82, *per* Lord Denning M.R., C.A.; *The Sansei Maru* [1979] 1 Lloyd's Rep. 11, P.C. Treitel, pp. 221–222. *cf. Hunt & Winterbotham Ltd v. BRS (Parcels) Ltd* [1962] 1 Q.B. 617, C.A.: Palmer, pp. 1553 *et seq.*

[54] Palmer, p. 1552. *cf.* the shipping cases, where the onus is different: *ibid.*, p. 1553.

[55] *Photo Production Ltd v. Securicor Transport Ltd* [1980] A.C. 827, 843.

[56] Generally, see Treitel, Chap. 9.

without legal effect. First, a subsequent offer by a customer may incorporate, expressly or implicitly, all or part of the carrier's statements, so that they subsequently become part of the concluded contract of carriage. Secondly, the statements may contain a misrepresentation, in respect of which the law affords the customer a remedy. Equally, it may arise that the carrier is induced to contract the carriage by a misrepresentation made by the customer, for example, about the fitness of the goods for carriage.

A misrepresentation is a misstatement of fact which induces the recipient to make a contract. A statement of fact is any statement which is not a statement of intention,[57] a statement of law[58] or a statement of opinion.[59] A statement may induce a contract of carriage, even though the statement was only one of several factors which induced the recipient customer, assumed for the purposes of discussion to be the sender, to make the contract of carriage.[60] If the statement was of a kind which would influence most (reasonable) customers, inducement will be presumed unless the carrier can prove otherwise. In other cases the customers must prove that they were influenced by the statement in question, even though, *ex hypothesi*, most customers would not have been influenced by it.

The remedies available to the customer depend on what the carrier knew or should have known when the carrier made the misrepresentation. If the customer can prove that the carrier was fraudulent,[61] the remedies available to the customer will be rescission of the contract and damages. If the carrier made the misrepresentation negligently—and the onus is on the carrier to prove that it was not made negligently[62]—the remedies are rescission of the contract and damages. If the carrier made the misrepresentation innocently, that is to say, the case is one in which the carrier

---

[57] A statement is a promise, if it states that an event will occur or a state of affairs will exist after the promise has been made.

[58] A statement of law is notoriously hard to define. A misstatement of law is a statement which contains a mistake as to the content or meaning of the law of England, including statements about the interpretation of documents; see *Solle v. Butcher* [1950] 1 K.B. 671, C.A. Distinguish a misstatement based on an accurate view of the law but a mistaken view of the facts or circumstances to which the law applies: that is a misstatement of fact.

[59] Including exaggerated opinion, sometimes called puff. A statement is an opinion when, to the knowledge of the person to whom it is made, the person making the statement is not in a position to establish its truth or accuracy on reasonable grounds: *Bisset v. Wilkinson* [1927] A.C. 177, P.C.

[60] *Edgington v. Fitzmaurice* (1885) 29 Ch.D. 459, C.A.

[61] There is fraudulent statement when the person making the statement (i) knew that the statement was false, or (ii) made the statement without believing it to be true, or (iii) was reckless as to whether the statement was true or false: *Derry v. Peek* (1889) 14 App.Cas. 337.

[62] In other words, that he had reasonable grounds to believe that his statement was true: Misrepresentation Act 1967, s.2(1).

is able to prove that the statement was not made negligently, the remedies are rescission of the contract or damages at the discretion of the court.[63] In all three cases the misrepresentation will provide the customer with a defence to an action for freight charges.

As the remedies appear to be the same whether the carrier has been fraudulent or negligent, what does the customer gain by attempting the difficult task of proving fraud? First, in the absence of fraud the court has a discretion to refuse the remedy of rescission[64]; however, this matters little as the court is unlikely to refuse rescission to a customer induced to contract by the carrier's misrepresentation. Secondly, whereas it is agreed that the measure of damages in cases of fraud is the tortious measure for deceit,[65] the measure of damages in a case of negligent misstatement actionable under the 1967 Act might have been different but, in recent cases,[66] it has been held that the measure is also the measure for deceit. So the customer gains little more than personal satisfaction by proving fraud. In most cases the customer is best advised not to attempt it but to let the carrier bear the burden of attempting to disprove negligence.

When carriage is governed by the CMR, a further question arises, whether an action based on fraudulent or negligent misrepresentation is a case for Article 28. Article 28 applies when "loss, damage or delay arising out of carriage under this Convention gives rise to an extra-contractual claim". If so, the amount of damages recoverable by the claimant is limited by Article 23.[67] Whether the action is based on the tort of deceit (in the case of fraudulent misrepresentation) or on statute[68] (in the case of negligent misrepresentation), the action is certainly "extra-contractual". But although "loss, damage or delay . . . gives rise to" the action in the sense of motivating the sender to bring the claim, what gives rise to the action, in the sense of justifying the claim in law, is not the loss, damage or delay which may have occurred but the misrepresentation. Hence, it is submitted that Article 28 does not apply.

---

[63] Misrepresentation Act 1967, s.2(2).

[64] *ibid.*

[65] All consequential loss, except that caused by the unreasonable behaviour of the claimant, or by a *nova causa interveniens: Doyle v. Olby (Ironmongers) Ltd* [1969] 2 Q.B. 158, C.A.; *Smith Kline & French Laboratories Ltd v. Long* [1988] 3 All E.R. 887, C.A.; *Smith New Court Securities Ltd v. Scrimgeour Vickers (Asset Management) Ltd* [1996] 4 All E.R. 769, H.L. 12 *Halsbury's Laws* (4th ed.), para. 1173.

[66] *Royscott Trust Ltd v. Rogerson* [1991] 2 Q.B. 297, C.A. For criticism of the decision in *Royscott*, see Brown and Chandler [1992] L.M.C.L.Q. 40; and Chandler (1994) 110 L.Q.R. 35. *cf. André v. Michel Blanc* [1977] 2 Lloyd's Rep. 166, 180, *per* Ackner J.; *Naughton v. O'Callaghan* [1990] 3 All E.R. 191, 198, *per* Waller J. Treitel, pp. 333 *et seq.*

[67] Above, paras. 93 *et seq.*

[68] Misrepresentation Act 1967, s.2(1).

242. Avoidance: economic duress

A contract may be set aside if concluded under economic duress.[69] Economic duress occurs when, first, the person seeking relief has no reasonable or realistic alternative to concluding the contract.[69a] But this alone is not enough to justify relief. "Economic duress must be distinguished from commercial pressure, which on any view is not sufficient to vitiate consent."[70] So, secondly, the pressure must have been illegitimate,[71] that is, a "threat of unlawful damage to his economic interest".[72]

> "In determining whether there was a coercion of the will such that there was no true consent, it is material to enquire whether the person alleged to have been coerced did or did not protest; whether, at the time he was allegedly coerced into making the contract, he did or did not have an alternative course open to him such as an adequate legal remedy; whether he was independently advised; and whether after entering the contract he took steps to avoid it."[73]
>
> In *Atlas Express v. Kafco*[74] the plaintiff carrier agreed to carry the defendants' goods at a stated rate of carriage charge, calculated by the carrier after inspecting the goods on the assumption that each load would be made up of x numbers of cartons. Having found that he was able to take far fewer cartons per load than expected, and knowing that the commercial survival of the defendants depended on their getting the goods to the consignee, the carrier informed the defendants that he would carry no more unless the defendants agreed to pay twice the agreed rate. The defendants, being unable to find another carrier in time, "agreed", in the view of the court,[75] "unwillingly and under compulsion". Their protests were ignored. Later, they refused to pay the difference between the old and the new rate. The plaintiff's action to recover the difference failed, as the new "agreement" had been made under duress. The defendants' apparent consent had been induced by illegitimate pressure, and the agreement had not been approbated by them.[76]

Commonly, as in the *Atlas* case, the issue arises, when one party to a binding contract refuses to perform that contract, unless the

[69] *Pau On v. Lau Yiu Long* [1980] A.C. 614, 635–636, *per* Lord Scarman, P.C.

[69a] *Pau On* (above). MacDonald [1989] J.B.L. 460; Halson (1991) 107 L.Q.R. 649.

[70] *Atlas Express Ltd v. Kafco (Importers and Distributors) Ltd* [1989] Q.B. 833, 839.

[71] *Universe Tankships Inc. v. ITWF* [1983] 1 A.C. 366, 384, *per* Lord Diplock; *CTN Cash and Carry Ltd v. Gallaher Ltd* [1994] 4 All E.R. 714, C.A.

[72] *B. & S. Contracts v. Victor Green Publications* [1984] I.C.R. 419, 423, *per* Eveleigh L.J., C.A.

[73] *Pau On* (above), *loc. cit.*

[74] Above, n. 70. See also *Parker v. GWR* (1844) 135 E.R. 107.

[75] At 838, *per* Tucker J.

[76] See also *The Alev* [1989] 1 Lloyd's Rep. 138, in which, the (sea) carrier refused to deliver the goods to the consignees, unless the consignees paid expenses, which should have been paid by the sender (charterer, financially unsound). The carrier's action to enforce the agreement against the consignee was successfully defended on the ground of duress.

other agrees to new terms advantageous to the first party. But it does not follow that *any* threat to break a contract amounts to duress.[77] The line may be fine between an agreement to compromise a dispute over the terms or performance of an existing contract, which is enforceable, and a threat to break a contract, which is illegitimate, and may give rise to economic duress. Moreover, if "economic duress could be successfully claimed after any illegitimate threat then it would undermine the security of any transaction caused by [the carrier's] announcement of his intention to breach his contract and . . . the law has an interest in ensuring that many such transactions are regarded as binding".[78] If the courts are too responsive to complaints of economic duress, they reduce the role of the economically "efficient" breach, and the economically "efficient" compromise to avert that breach. Operative economic duress is a question of degree, and hence a source of some uncertainty. However, it seems that the line is crossed and pressure becomes illegitimate when it amounts to the deliberate exploitation of the difficulties of the other party,[79] when, as in *Atlas* (above), one party seeks to take advantage of vulnerability brought about by the other's reliance on due performance of the contract.[80]

243. Non-enforcement: illegality[81]

A contract of carriage once formed may be void or unenforceable (the English courts have not finally decided which) because the making or the performance of the contract is against the law or against public policy. The theoretical possibilities are almost infinite; in practice there are at least two types of illegality which concern the contract of carriage by road.

243a. Illegal performance of the contract

The first situation is that in which a contract of carriage, lawful as to its terms and its purpose, is unlawful in the way it is formed by the parties or, more common, unlawful in the way it is performed by the carrier. The carrier may well incur penalties of the criminal law, but there remains the question whether the contract of carriage can be enforced, although some legal prohibition has been infringed. Unfortunately there is no clear rule to separate those

---

[77] *The Siboen* [1976] 1 Lloyd's Rep. 293, 335, *per* Kerr J.; *Williams v. Roffey Bros. & Nicholls (Contractors) Ltd* [1991] 1 Q.B. 1, C.A. Treitel, p. 375.
[78] MacDonald [1989] J.B.L. 460, 466.
[79] Birks [1990] L.M.C.L.Q. 342.
[80] Halson, *op. cit.*
[81] Generally see Treitel, Chap. 11 and Chap. 12, Pt 1; Walker, Chap. 11.

contracts of carriage which are affected and those which are not. The effect of prohibition on contracts varies; there are three possibilities.

The first is an express statutory prohibition of enforcement.[82] The second is that the court implies from an express prohibition, whether of the making of the contract or of the particular mode of performance, a prohibition of enforcement of the contract.[83] However, the court is not obliged to draw that implication in every case,[84] and there is a third possibility: that, if the purpose of the statute is sufficiently protected by other means, such as fines, the contract will be enforced in spite of the infringement of the prohibition.[85] "Whether or not the statute has this effect depends upon considerations of public policy in the light of the mischief which the statute is designed to prevent, its language scope and purpose, the consequences for the innocent party, and any other relevant considerations."[86] Public policy "may at times be better served by refusing to nullify a bargain save on serious and sufficient grounds".[87]

> In *Archbolds (Freightage) v. S. Spanglett*[88] the plaintiff's whisky, sent from Leeds to London on the defendant's lorry, was lost as a result of the driver's negligence. The carrier met the action based on the contract of carriage with the plea that the contract was illegal and hence unenforceable because the lorry used was not properly licensed, as required by the Road and Rail Traffic Act 1933, for the carriage of the goods of others for reward. The carrier's plea was rejected and the appeal was dismissed. In that case Pearce L.J. said[89]:
>
> "The carriage of the plaintiff's whisky was not as such prohibited; the statute merely regulated the means by which carriers should carry goods. Therefore this contract was not expressly forbidden by the statute.
>
> Was it then forbidden by implication? . . .

---

82 An express prohibition is recognised by characteristic phrases, such as "No action shall lie . . . ".

83 *Phoenix General Insurance Co. of Greece S.A. v. ADAS* [1988] Q.B. 216, 271–272, *per* Kerr L.J., C.A., citing *Archbolds (Freightage) Ltd v. S. Spanglett Ltd* [1961] 1 Q.B. 374, C.A. *cf. Fuji Finance Inc. v. Aetna Life Ins. Co. Ltd* [1996] 4 All E.R. 608, C.A. Clarke, *Insurance*, para. 24–3A2.

84 *Archbolds* above, n. 83 at 389, *per* Devlin J.; cited with apparent approval in *Phoenix* above, n. 83 at 569 by Kerr L.J.

85 *Archbolds*, above, n. 83 at 390, *per* Devlin L.J., *St John Shipping Corp. v. Joseph Rank Ltd* [1957] 1 Q.B. 267, C.A.: contract of carriage by sea enforced, although the carrier infringed loadline regulations. This principle was confirmed in *Howard v. Shirlstar Container Transport* [1990] 3 All E.R. 366, C.A.; *Tinsley v. Milligan* [1994] 1 A.C. 340, 360, *per* Lord Goff. Treitel, p. 439.

86 *Phoenix*, above, n. 83, *loc. cit.*

87 *Vita Food Products Inc. v. Unus Shipping Co. Ltd* [1939] A.C. 277, 293, *per* Lord Wright, P.C. See also *Shiloh Spinners Ltd v. Harding* [1973] A.C. 691, 727, *per* Lord Simon.

88 [1961] 1 Q.B. 374.

89 At 385–386.

> The object of the Road and Rail Traffic Act, 1933, was not (in this connection) to interfere with the owner of goods or his facilities for transport, but to control those who provided the transport, with a view to promoting its efficiency. . . . Thus a contract of carriage was, in the sense used by Devlin J., 'collateral', and it was not impliedly forbidden by the statute.
>
> This view is supported by common sense and convenience. If the other view were held it would have far-reaching effects. For instance, if a carrier induces me (who am in fact ignorant of any illegality) to entrust goods to him and negligently destroys them, he would only have to show that (though unknown to me) his licence had expired, or did not properly cover the transportation, or that he was uninsured, and I should then be without remedy against him."
>
> Compare *Ashmore, Benson, Pease & Co. v. A.V. Dawson*,[90] in which the defendants agreed to carry the plaintiffs' tube banks from Stockton-on-Tees to Hull. The defendants used a lorry which, when laden with the goods, exceeded the maximum weight permitted by the law. The lorry overturned en route and the goods were damaged. The plaintiffs sought damages under the contract; the defendants argued that the contract was illegal and unenforceable. The Court of Appeal decided for the defendant carriers.

The difference between *Archbolds* and *Ashmore* appears to be that in *Ashmore* the third possibility, mentioned above (see earlier in this paragraph), was not considered by the court. However, it may also be that the court took such a serious view of the carriage of heavy loads on unsuitable vehicles that, given that the senders knew or should have known this,[91] they failed to protest, and that they were being charged a rate lower than that usual for the low loading vehicles that should have been used, the balance of public policy was clearly against enforcement of the contract of carriage.

243b. Illegal purpose

The second situation is that in which, although the contract may be lawful in its mode of formation and performance, the purpose of the contract of carriage is illegal; for example, smuggling.

Smuggling has always been seen by the courts as a serious matter. If the smuggling is by the carrier or his employees, for example the illegal importation of drugs using the customer's lawful goods as cover, that is a breach of contract actionable by

[90] [1973] 1 W.L.R. 828.

[91] In *Ashmore* the contract might have been enforced by the customers, if they had not been implicated in the illegality: if it had not been that they knew or should have known that the load would be carried in an unsuitable vehicle, in contravention of statute: at 833, *per* Lord Denning M.R.; at 836, *per* Scarman L.J. For cogent criticism of the decision on this point, see Hamson [1973] C.L.J. 199.

the customer. If the smuggling is by the customer, the customer will be unable to enforce the contract of carriage against the carrier,[92] and the carrier, if implicated in the illegal venture, will be unable to enforce the contract against the customer. The carrier will be implicated if the carrier knew or should have known that the customer was smuggling.[93]

243c. Consequences

In both situations discussed above (paragraphs 243a and 243b), we have seen that the court may refuse to enforce the contract. This means that no action may be based, wholly or in part, on the contract.[94] The carrier will be unable to recover the carriage charges. The customer will be unable to recover damages from the carrier for loss of or damage to the goods or for delay. Moreover, the customer will be unable to recover the goods themselves or damages for their detention, if to do so the customer must rely on the terms of the contract or on the fact that it is illegal. Although the contract is illegal, it is still open to the carrier to meet the customer's action with defences provided by the contract,[95] or property rights obtained under the illegal contract.[96]

Exceptionally, the customer will be allowed to recover the goods (or damages instead), first, if the customer is not *in pari delicto* with the carrier.[97] Secondly, the customer may recover, if the case can be based on a cause of action independent of the contract of carriage, an action based, for example, in the tort of conversion. However, if the illegality is so offensive to public policy that the court will have nothing to do with the situation or disputes arising out of it, the action will fail nonetheless,[98] whether the action is based on the contract or not. Thus, while an action based in tort may succeed in respect of a load that included lesser contraband, success is unlikely if the goods include illegal drugs or the proceeds of dealing in such drugs.

---

[92] *Foster v. Driscoll* [1929] 1 K.B. 470, C.A.; *Regazzoni v. K. C. Sethia (1944) Ltd* [1958] A.C. 301; *Mackender v. Feldia A.G.* [1967] 2 Q.B. 590, C.A.

[93] *Pearce v. Brooks* (1866) L.R. 1 Exch. 213.

[94] Exceptionally, if the illegality can be localised in part of the contract, it may be possible to enforce the rest of the contract: *Fielding & Platt Ltd v. Najjar* [1969] 1 W.L.R. 357, 362, *per* Lord Denning M.R., C.A.; *Clifford (Frank W.) Ltd v. Garth* [1956] 1 W.L.R. 570; *Ailion v. Spiekermann* [1976] 1 All E.R. 497.

[95] *Bowmakers Ltd v. Barnet Instruments Ltd* [1945] K.B. 65, C.A.

[96] *Taylor v. Chester* (1869) L.R. 4 Q.B. 309.

[97] Treitel, pp. 454 *et seq.*

[98] This proposition is based on the "public conscience" test. Since the decision of the House of Lords in *Tinsley v. Milligan* [1994] 1 A.C. 340, the correctness of the proposition has been in doubt.

CHAPTER 14

REMEDIES

244. Compensation: damages for breach of contract

If none of the services promised by the carrier have been performed, the money paid for them by the customer (freight charges) can be recovered from the carrier. Beyond that, any money recoverable for breach of the contract of carriage is recovered as damages—usually, as this discussion hereafter assumes, damages recovered by the customer from the carrier.

The object of any award of damages for breach of contract is compensation: to put the claimant customer in a position "as if" the contract of carriage had been performed[1]; but no more than that. If the carrier's breach has caused the customer no loss, the customer can recover no damages.[2] Moreover, if the carrier has breached the contract with the claimant customer in order to make a killing on another more lucrative contract, that does not increase the claimant's loss nor, therefore, the amount of damages recoverable: contract law is not concerned with whether the defendant contract breaker has been unjustly enriched.[3]

245. Assessment of damages

When speaking of the measure or assessment of damages in a particular case, lawyers commonly divide the kinds of loss for which damages are recoverable and have to be assessed into three categories.

First, damages are recoverable for expectation loss, *i.e.* for loss of bargain or loss of profit. Thus, the customer whose goods are lost, damaged or delayed may recover the profit that would have

---

[1] *Robinson v. Harman* (1848) 1 Ex. 850, 855, applied and reaffirmed by H.L. in *Ruxley Electronics and Construction Ltd v. Forsyth* [1995] 3 All E.R. 268, 282, *per* Lord Lloyd.

[2] *e.g. Dennis v. Campbell* [1978] Q.B. 365, C.A. However, concerning the possibility of damages for non-fulfilment of a "premium" carriage service, see *White Arrow Express Ltd v. Lamey's Distribution Ltd* (1995) 15 Tr.L. 69; (1995) 145 N.L.I. 1504, C.A.; and generally, see *Ruxley v. Forsyth* (above).

[3] *Surrey C.C. v. Bredero Homes Ltd* [1993] 1 W.L.R. 1361, C.A.

been made with those goods—perhaps, if that had been the customer's plan, by selling the goods in the market at the place of delivery.[4]

Secondly, damages are recoverable for loss incurred by the customer's acting in reliance on the carrier's promise of performance, for example forwarding expenses, the cost of arrangements for storage or handling at the place of delivery.[5] Usually such damages are sought as an alternative to the first category when the amount of expectation loss is speculative and too hard to prove or simply because the customer wants to maintain good relations with the carrier. Another such occasion is when, in the end, the customer is better off after the breach; for example the customer's search for an alternative carrier or another market finds a cheaper carrier or a more profitable market.

The third category is consequential loss: damages are recoverable for loss resulting not from the promise of performance (the second category) but from the breach of that promise. An instance is the cost of arranging alternative performance of what the customer contracted for: the cost of obtaining alternative means of transporting goods consequential on the defendant carriers' failure to perform.[6]

246. Remoteness of damage

The claimant customer is entitled to recover the full amount of actual loss suffered, provided that that kind of loss is not too remote. The court's approach to remoteness is to ask whether, assuming actual foresight of the breach that occurred, the loss that flowed from it was of a kind which should have been within the contemplation of the carrier as not unlikely to result from the breach.[7] This question can be answered only by making certain assumptions about the actual and imputed knowledge of the carrier at the time of contracting the carriage.

Imputed knowledge is that which can be expected of a carrier of goods of the kind in question. Actual knowledge is any extra knowledge which the particular carrier has of circumstances affecting the customer which might occasion extra loss in the event of breach. With the benefit of such knowledge, the likelihood of loss must be somewhere on a scale between what is likely in "the

[4] Assuming of course that the likelihood of such loss is sufficiently known to the carrier for the possibility not to be too remote: below, para. 246.

[5] Generally, see *Anglia Television Ltd v. Reed* [1972] 1 Q.B. 60, C.A.

[6] Generally, see *Calabar Properties Ltd v. Stitcher* [1983] 3 All E.R 759, C.A.

[7] *The Yanxilas (No. 2)* [1984] 1 Lloyd's Rep. 676, 680, *per* Bingham J. The rule of remoteness thus stated is based on *Hadley v. Baxendale* (1859) 9 Ex. 341, as interpreted in *The Heron II* [1969] 1 A.C. 350.

great multitude of cases"[8] and a point somewhat short of what is reasonably foreseeable to the reasonable man of the law of tort.[9] Understandably, the courts are reluctant to specify the odds with precision.

Words, said Lord Morris, "which are but servants to convey and express meanings—cannot always be servants of precision and may sometimes be given a dominance which is above their status. If 'Language is the dress of thought', it is the thought that must be understood."[10] That is true, but there is another factor at work: a greater precision would tie the hands of the court in future cases. Take a case such as *Hadley v. Baxendale*[11] in which the safe delivery of the goods is crucial because the goods are spare parts without which the customer's factory will grind to a halt. Suppose also, unlike the actual facts of the case, the defendant carrier is informed when concluding the contract about the need for the parts. In such a case, clearly it would be within the contemplation of the carrier that it is (more than) likely that the customer will suffer great loss if the parts do not arrive in time or are damaged in transit. On a mechanical application of a rule of remoteness based only on "odds", the probability of loss, the carrier would be liable for much if not all of the customer's trading loss. That, surely, is a decision that the court will be hesitant to reach. One way out of the dilemma is to fudge the issue of remoteness and, like Lord Morris, eschew any commitment to a particular numerical probability factor.[12] Today, however, there is another way out which avoids fudge and allows a relatively precise probability factor for the rule of remoteness. The solution, which comes from recent decisions in tort, lies in the interpretation of the defendant carrier's duty.

The solution is described here in the words of Lord Hoffmann[13] which, transposed into the context of carriage, run like this.

> "A plaintiff who sues for breach of a duty imposed by the law (whether in contract or tort or under statute) must do more than

---

[8] The phrase was used in *Hadley v. Baxendale* and adopted in *The Heron II* [1969] 1 A.C. 350, 411, *per* Lord Hodson. It is understood to mean in the "great majority of cases", see *e.g. ibid.*, *per* Lord Reid (at 384).

[9] The range recoverable for breach of contract is more restricted in contract than in tort: *The Heron II* [1969] 1 A.C. 350, at 386, *per* Lord Reid, at 411, *per* Lord Hodson, at 413, *per* Lord Pearce and at 422, *per* Lord Upjohn.

[10] At 393, *per* Lord Morris.

[11] (1859) 9 Ex. 341.

[12] *e.g.* to treat the issue as one of "the application of common sense in the particular circumstances of the case": *Parsons (H.) (Livestock) Ltd v. Uttley Ingham & Co. Ltd* [1978] Q.B. 791, 907, *per* Scarman L.J., speaking of the discussion of the issue in *The Heron II* (above).

[13] *South Australia Asset Management Corp. v. York Montagu Ltd* [1996] 3 All E.R. 365, 372, *per* Lord Hoffmann, H.L. See also Cartwright [1996] C.L.J. 488. The duty to pay for loss (at the secondary level) depends *inter alia* on the scope of the duty at the primary level: to that extent questions of remoteness of damage become less important; see Cartwright *inter alia* at 499 and 501.

> prove that the defendant has failed to comply. He must show that a duty was owed to him and that it was a duty in respect of the kind of loss that he has suffered. . . . In the case of an implied contractual duty, the nature and extent of the liability is defined by the term which the law implies. . . . The scope of the duty, in the sense of the consequences for which the [carrier] is responsible, is that which the law regards as best giving effect to the express obligations assumed by the [carrier]."

In other words, used more than once in recent times by Lord Goff,[14] the question whether the loss of production at the customer's factory is a loss for which the carrier is liable, depends on whether that loss is one for which, in all the circumstances, it can be inferred that the carrier has "assumed responsibility". In most instances, unless there has been an appreciable elevation of the normal freight rate, the answer in a case of non-delivery of spare parts such as the one above, surely, will be negative.

Compare, however, the drama conjured up by Lord Pearce in 1967.[15] A faulty repair to the court results in the collapse of the ceiling on those in court. Given the relatively short time during which there were people in court in 1967, the odds against this were no more than 10 to 1. Nonetheless, Lord Pearce thought that the contractor would be liable. It is submitted that a court today would probably agree: responsibility for such loss is one that a professional repairer of ceilings can be taken to have assumed; and this result, and the thinking leading to it, is entirely consistent with the current orthodoxy of contract law that the duty to pay damages for breach of contract is itself a contractual duty at a secondary level based on inferred consent.[16]

247. Common cases

247a. Damage to property

A common case is that in which the customer's goods have been damaged. Generally, in such a case compensation "is achieved by the application of one or other of two quite different measures of damage, or, occasionally a combination of the two. The first is to take the capital value of the property in an undamaged state and to compare it with its value in a damaged state. The second is to take the cost of repair or reinstatement. Which is appropriate will depend on a number of factors, such as the plaintiff's future intentions as to the use of the property and the reasonableness of

[14] *e.g. Henderson v. Merrett* [1995] 2 A.C. 145, 181.

[15] In *The Heron II* [1969] 1 A.C. 350, 417.

[16] *Horne v. Midland Ry* (1873) L.R. 8 C.P. 131, 141, *per* Blackburn J.; *Photoproduction Ltd v. Securicor Transport Ltd* [1980] A.C. 827.

those intentions."[17] In other words[18] the usual choice is between value difference and cost of cure or repair.

In the case of goods or things "commonly available"[19] the usual measure is value difference: the presumption is that the customer with defective goods will sell them (at less than the price of undamaged goods) and recover the "difference in value" as damages from the carrier. If the goods are not commonly available but have some unique quality, and so cannot be replaced on the market, compensation may be the cost of repair, unless the cost of that is so great as to be unreasonable.[20]

247b. Loss of market

If the carrier knows or should know that the goods are intended for a market and that delivery late will cause the goods to miss that market, for example a Christmas market[21] or a regular but periodic cattle market,[22] the carrier will be liable for the customer's loss of market. Even if the market is continuous and the customer can show that the delay caused the goods to miss a peak in the market, the carrier may be liable.[23]

247c. Loss of production

Whether the loss of production at the customer's factory is a loss, for which the carrier is liable, depends on whether that loss is one which, in all the circumstances, the carrier should have had in contemplation as not unlikely to result from the breach (*e.g.* delay) of the contract of carriage. In most cases the carrier will be entitled to believe that the customer has spare parts to ensure continued production.[24] If the carrier has been informed that the customer

---

[17] *Dodd Properties (Kent) Ltd v. Canterbury C.C.* [1980] 1 All E.R. 928, 938, *per* Donaldson L.J., C.A.

[18] Treitel, p. 852. See also Walker, para. 33.32.

[19] *Ruxley Electronics and Construction Ltd v. Forsyth* [1994] 3 All E.R. 801, 806, *per* Staughton L.J., C.A.

[20] *Ruxley Electronics Ltd v. Forsyth* [1995] 3 All E.R. 268, H.L. See also *East Ham Corp. v. Bernard Sunley & Sons Ltd* [1966] A.C. 406. Treitel, p. 853. The view is that from the other side of the duty to mitigate: *Ruxley* (above) [1994] 3 All E.R. 801, 810, *per* Staughton L.J., C.A., quoting Oliver J. in *Radford v. De Froberville* [1978] 1 All E.R. 33, 44. In the language of current contract law, both failure to mitigate and exorbitant repairs are not loss contemplated or losses for which it can be inferred that the defendant has assumed responsibility.

[21] *Panalpina Int. Transport Ltd v. Densil Underwear Ltd* [1981] 1 Lloyd's Rep. 187.

[22] *Simpson v. L.N.W. Ry Co.* (1876) 1 Q.B.D. 274. *cf.* cases in which the carrier did not have enough knowledge to incur such liability, *e.g. Horne v. Midland Ry Co.* (1873) L.R. 8 C.P. 131.

[23] *The Heron II* [1969] 1 A.C. 350, in which the carrier was liable even though, as the carrier should have appreciated, there was (no more than) an even chance that the market (for sugar at Basrah) would move down rather than up: at 382, *per* Lord Reid.

[24] *Hadley v. Baxendale* (1859) 9 Ex. 341.

does not have spare parts and that, therefore, in all probability late delivery of parts will result in lost production, the carrier is still unlikely to be held liable because that is not the kind of risk or responsibility the carrier can be taken to have assumed.[25]

248. Compensation: damages in tort

If the action is based on breach of contract, the claimant customer is to be put in a position "as if" the contract had been performed,[26] but the object of an award of damages based in tort is to put the victim in a position "as if" the tort, usually negligence, had not been committed.[27] Moreover, as regards remoteness of damage, the contract rule is that the loss must have been within the reasonable contemplation of the defendant[28] but the tort rule is that it must have been reasonably foreseeable by the defendant,[29] the understanding being that the latter connotes a wider range of recoverable loss.[30]

In most cases, however, the amounts of damages that the customer will recover from the carrier are the same, whether the basis of the action is contract or tort. However, if the tort in question is not negligence but deceit, it is established that the claimant can recover all consequential loss, whether that kind of loss was reasonably foreseeable and hence not too remote or not, unless the chain of causation between the tort and the loss was broken by a *novus actus interveniens*.[31] The same rule applies in an action based on section 2(1) of the Misrepresentation Act 1967.[32] If, however, the case is one of the tort of conversion, the loss recoverable is the "normal" amount, that is the amount recoverable in a case of negligence.[33]

249. Termination of contractual obligations in the case of breach

In the event of repudiation or serious breach of a contract of carriage governed by English law, the innocent party may terminate the contract, that is may terminate the primary obligations

---

[25] Above, para. 246.
[26] Above, para. 244.
[27] *The Albazero* [1977] A.C. 774, 841, *per* Lord Diplock; *Dews v. National Coal Board* [1988] A.C. 1, 12, *per* Lord Griffiths.
[28] Above, para. 246.
[29] *The Wagon Mound* [1961] A.C. 388.
[30] *The Heron II* [1969] 1 A.C. 390.
[31] *Doyle v. Olby (Ironmongers) Ltd* [1969] 2 Q.B. 158, C.A.; *Smith New Court Securities Ltd v. Scrimgeour Vickers (Asset Management) Ltd* [1996] 4 All E.R. 769, H.L.
[32] *Royscott Trust Ltd v. Rogerson* [1991] 2 Q.B. 297, C.A.
[33] *Sachs v. Miklos* [1948] 2 K.B. 23, C.A.; *BBMM Finance (Hong Kong) Ltd v. E.D.A. Holdings Ltd* [1991] 2 All E.R. 129, P.C. *cf. I.B.L. Ltd v. Coussens* [1991] 2 All E.R. 133, C.A.; Tettenborn (1991) 141 N.L.J. 452.

under the contract, while leaving in force secondary obligations relating, for example, to arbitration and compensation.[34]

Termination is not retrospective but prospective.[35] The obligations of the party in breach which have already fallen due at the time of termination remain due.[36] The primary obligations which have not fallen due are no longer due, but the party in breach remains under a secondary obligation to pay compensation in respect of non-fulfilment: the termination of the contract turns the primary obligation to perform into a secondary obligation to pay damages. As for the obligations of the innocent party, in so far as they were due, these will have been substantially performed or their performance tendered; were it otherwise, that party would not be innocent and, in general,[37] would not be able to enforce the contract against the party in breach.[38] However, the fruits of this performance may be recoverable: for example, the innocent customer may be able to recover prepaid carriage charges.[39] As for those obligations which have not fallen due, from these the innocent party is released.[40]

The innocent party is entitled to terminate the contract if the party in breach has repudiated the contract by failure to perform it at all or by committing a breach of the contract which the law recognises as serious or which the contract itself specifies as a breach that entitles the innocent party to terminate the contract.[41]

Although contract terms about the payment of money are not in general of the essence of the contract, so that their breach is not in general regarded as serious, a flat refusal to pay carriage charges due in advance would justify the carrier in terminating the contract, and thus release the carrier from the duty to take over and carry the goods. Refusal to pay carriage charges due on delivery would also justify termination by the carrier but, in most cases, termination would serve little purpose at that stage and the car-

---

[34] *Photo Production Ltd v. Securicor Transport Ltd* [1980] A.C. 827, 848–849, *per* Lord Diplock. See also Treitel, p. 762 and Walker, para. 33.42, who refer to termination as rescission for breach. The election to terminate must be unequivocal, however, if the innocent party stops performing the contract, that may well be a sufficient indication: *The Santa Clara* [1996] 3 All E.R. 193, H.L.

[35] *Johnson v. Agnew* [1980] A.C. 367.

[36] *Photo Production* (above, n. 34), at 844, *per* Lord Wilberforce, at 849, *per* Lord Diplock.

[37] The situation differs in the case of independent obligations.

[38] *The Simona* [1989] A.C. 788. Unless the breach is not serious, in which case this (relatively) innocent party's performance although incomplete remains "substantial", but for this breach that party remains liable in damages to the other party in breach.

[39] In general: *Photo Production* (above, n. 34) at 844, *per* Lord Wilberforce and at 849, *per* Lord Diplock.

[40] *Photo Production* (above, n. 34), at 849, *per* Lord Diplock.

[41] Treitel, pp. 685 *et seq.*

rier's effective remedy is not termination of the contract but the enforcement of a lien on the goods.[42]

Refusal by the carrier to take over the goods entitles the sender to terminate the contract, and to seek another carrier. Termination may be problematic, however, when the carrier indicates an intention to perform but is late. Late performance will be a serious breach of the contract, which thus justifies termination of the contract whenever "the nature of its subject-matter or the surrounding circumstances make it inequitable" or, in other words, whenever the failure to perform on time deprives the claimant of "substantially the whole benefit which it was intended that he should obtain from the contract".[43] In general, any lateness in commercial contracts will be treated as serious[44]; however, the "treatment of time limits as conditions in mercantile contracts does not appear . . . to be justifiable by any presumption of fact or rule of law,[45] but rather to be a practical expedient founded on and dictated by the experience of businessmen".[46] The experience of businessmen may have been reflected in past decisions of the courts; these will be followed. Thus, there is a tradition of the law relating to carriage by sea that ascribes importance to promises made by the carrier about when the ship will be available to the hirer or consignor[47] and here, at least, an analogy might be drawn with carriage by road. "At the end of the day", however, "if there is no other more specific guide to the correct solution to a particular dispute, the court may have no alternative but to follow the general statement of Bowen L.J. in *Bentsen v. Taylor*[48] . . . by making what is in effect a value judgment about the commercial significance of the term in question."[49] To find the commercial significance of the term, therefore, the court must look "at the contract in the light of the surrounding circumstances", and then make up its mind about "the intention of the parties, as gathered from the instrument itself".[50] Alternatively, if the exercise has already been gone through by arbitrators, their finding about the commercial significance of the term will, as in *The Naxos*,[51] be adopted by the court. At the end of the day, therefore, time

---

[42] Below, para. 251.

[43] *United Scientific Holdings Ltd v. Burnley Borough Council* [1978] A.C. 904, 927, *per* Lord Diplock.

[44] At 928.

[45] See *Bunge v. Tradax* [1981] 2 All E.R. 513, 542, *per* Lord Wilberforce.

[46] *ibid.* at 545 *per* Lord Lowry, cited with approval by Lord Brandon in *Cie. Commerciale Sucres et Denrées v. Czarnikow, The Naxos* [1990] 1 W.L.R. 1337, 1347, H.L.

[47] *The Mihalis Angelos* [1971] 1 Q.B. 164, C.A.

[48] *Bentsen v. Taylor, Sons & Co. (No. 2)* [1893] 2 Q.B. 274, 281, C.A.

[49] *State Trading Corp. of India v. Golodetz* [1989] 2 Lloyd's Rep. 277, 283, *per* Kerr L.J., C.A., cited with approval by Lord Ackner in *The Naxos* (above, n. 46).

[50] Bowen L.J. in *Bentsen* (above, n. 48).

[51] Above, n. 46.

stipulations in commercial contracts are little different from other stipulations in commercial contracts.

The innocent party is not compelled to terminate the contract in the event of serious breach by the other. The innocent customer, having no other carrier to turn to, may think "better late than never" and allow the carrier to take the goods over late. Equally, the innocent carrier who has not been paid may find it wise to continue carriage. Indeed, although, for example, the consignee may repudiate the contract by declaring an intention not to pay the carriage charges due on delivery, the carrier is entitled to ignore that repudiation, to perform the contract and to sue for the carriage charges as an outstanding debt.[52] Only a party with a legitimate interest in taking this course may do so[53]; however, an unpaid carrier will usually have such an interest if continued performance converts a claim against a defendant, which would otherwise be unsecured, into a secured claim.

> In *George Barker (Transport) v. Eynon*[54] an importer commissioned the plaintiff carriers to collect certain cartons of meat in London and deliver them at Gravesend. Prior to delivery the defendant was appointed as receiver of the importer and the plaintiffs, who were owed large sums by the importer in respect of previous contracts of carriage, retained the cartons in their warehouse. The plaintiffs acted in exercise of a lien granted by a term of the contract of carriage. The Court of Appeal held that the receiver's right to have the goods delivered was subject to the right of the carrier to withhold the goods, in accordance with the term of the contract. Edmund-Davies L.J. said[55] that "the defendant sought to repudiate the transport contract of Aug. 23, it is nevertheless clear that the plaintiffs refused to accept that repudiation and insisted on fulfilling their part of the contract. This they were entitled to do . . . and it was greatly to their advantage, for thereby they stood to recompense themselves in full, as opposed to becoming merely one of the general body of unsecured creditors."

250. Termination of obligations in the case of impossibility of performance

If the carrier is unable to perform the contract through causes beyond the carrier's control,[56] impossibility of performance is a

---

[52] *White & Carter (Councils) Ltd v. McGregor* [1962] A.C. 413. Treitel, pp. 914 *et seq.*

[53] *Attica Sea Carriers Corp. v. Ferrostaal Poseidon Bulk Reederei GmbH* [1976] 1 Lloyd's Rep. 250, 255, *per* Lord Denning M.R., C.A.

[54] [1974] 1 Lloyd's Rep. 65.

[55] At 75, with reference to the decision in *White & Carter* (above, n. 52).

[56] *The Hannah Blumenthal* [1983] 1 A.C. 854, 882, *per* Griffiths L.J., C.A.; *The Super Servant Two* [1990] 1 Lloyd's Rep. 1, 10, *per* Bingham L.J., C.A. The fact that performance has become more difficult or more expensive for the carrier is not a defence: *Tsakiroglou & Co. Ltd v. Noblee Thorl GmbH* [1962] A.C. 93.

defence to an action on the contract. Common law, however, goes further and provides that the contract shall be discharged from the time that it has become impossible to perform; and there are further consequences enacted by statute, unless the parties themselves have provided otherwise in their contract. The primacy of the contract is confirmed by the statute.[57] By section 2(3) of the Law Reform (Frustrated Contracts) Act 1943, which applies to contracts to carry goods by land, if any provision of the contract,[58] "is intended to have effect in the event of circumstances which operate, or would but for the said provisions operate, to frustrate the contract, or is intended to have effect whether such circumstances arise or not, the court shall give effect to the said provision and shall only give effect to . . . the Act to such extent, if any, as appears to the court to be consistent with the said provision". Subject to any such contract provision, the law is as follows.

First, the impossibility "brings the contract to an end forthwith, without more and automatically".[59] Thus the carrier is no longer required to carry the goods and the sender, who has yet to load the goods, is not obliged to load them.

Secondly, by section 1(2) of the 1943 Act, any sum such as carriage charges paid before the termination of the contract shall be recoverable and any such sum so payable shall cease to be payable subject, however, to any deduction which a court may consider it just to award to the carrier in respect of any expense incurred by the carrier in and for the performance of the contract of carriage. If any such expenditure, for example money spent servicing the vehicle, can be turned to account on a new venture, as will usually be the case except in times of recession, the carrier will not be allowed the deduction.[60]

Thirdly, by virtue of section 1(3) of the 1943 Act,[61] if, although the contract has been terminated, the sender or consignee obtains a valuable benefit from such part of the carriage as has been performed by the carrier, a court may award the carrier such sum, not exceeding the value of the benefit conferred, as it considers just, having regard to the circumstances of the case. Thus, if the carrier gets the goods most of the way to the place of delivery but has to store them where they are on behalf of the consignee because further carriage has become impossible, the consignee may well have received a benefit which will mature later and the

---

[57] Generally, see Treitel, pp. 821 *et seq.*; Walker, paras. 31.45 *et seq.*; Glanville Williams, *The Law Reform (Frustrated Contracts) Act 1943* (London, 1944).

[58] This includes the case of a contract governed by the CMR and thus incorporating the provisions of Arts. 14 and 15.

[59] *Hirji Mulji v. Cheong Yue SS. Co. Ltd* [1926] A.C. 497, 505, *per* Lord Sumner.

[60] See *Gamerco S.A. v. I.C.M. Ltd* [1995] 1 W.L.R. 1226; Clark [1996] L.M.C.L.Q. 170.

[61] Considered in a reported case for the first time in *B.P. Exploration Co. (Libya) v. Hunt* [1982] 2 A.C. 350.

carrier would appear to be entitled to an award under section 1(3). However, if the goods are destroyed en route, it is difficult to see what benefit has accrued to the consignee: loss will lie where it has fallen. The loss of the goods will fall on the consignee and the cost of carriage will fall on the carrier unless the carrier is entitled to make a deduction from any advance freight by virtue of section 1(2).

In considering whether any sum ought to be recovered under section 1(2) or section 1(3), the court "shall not take into account any sums which have, by reason of the circumstances giving rise to the frustration of the contract, become payable to that party under any contract of insurance unless there was an obligation to insure imposed by an express term of the frustrated contract or by or under any enactment": section 1(5).

251. The carrier's lien

In English common law, the carrier has a "particular" lien for freight and charges relating to goods tendered for delivery or at least brought to destination. The carrier has no "general" lien on the goods in respect of debts due under previous contracts of carriage,[62] nor does the carrier have any right to sell the goods[63] unless these rights have been acquired by the contract of carriage or by trade custom.[64] However, such rights are commonly given by the contract of carriage; see, for example, as regards both the general lien and the right of sale, Condition 15 of the RHA Conditions of Carriage 1991.[65] A contractual lien of this kind is effective only between parties to the contract that creates it, and is subject to the general law of contract. It has been suggested[66] that any contractual lien, such as Condition 15, which purports to entitle the carrier to sell the goods without giving notice to the customer will be held to be unreasonable under the Unfair Contract Terms Act 1977. Finally, it should not be forgotten that the existence of any lien, whatever the legal basis of the lien, is dependent on the carrier's retention of possession of the goods.

252. Action for carriage charges

An action in debt lies at the suit of the carrier in respect of carriage charges against the person with whom the contract of carriage was

---

[62] Glass and Cashmore, para. 1.111; Palmer, p. 1014.
[63] Except perhaps as agent of necessity in the case of perishable goods.
[64] See further Kahn-Freund, pp. 402 *et seq.*; Palmer, pp. 1013 *et seq.*
[65] See *George Barker v. Eynon* (above, para. 251).
[66] Yates, para. 3.2.1.17.

concluded. Action lies only in respect of charges due, so, in the case of charges due on delivery, the carrier must have carried out the carriage and delivered the goods or, at least, have been ready and willing to deliver them. Unless stipulated by the contract of carriage, the carrier is not entitled to carriage charges *pro rata itineris*.[67] If the consignee repudiates the contract before the carrier has completed performance, the carrier may nonetheless have a legitimate interest in completing the carriage, if that is a condition of a lien or other security on the goods,[68] and on completion he may tender the goods and become entitled to the full amount of the carriage charges.

---

[67] *Appleby v. Myers* (1867) L.R. 2 C.P. 651, 661, *per* Blackburn J.

[68] See *George Barker v. Eynon* (above, para. 251). See also *Attica Sea Carriers Corp. v. Ferrostaal Poseidon Bulk Reederei GmbH* [1976] 1 Lloyd's Rep. 250, C.A.

Appendix A

CARRIAGE OF GOODS BY ROAD ACT 1965

(c. 37)

An Act to give effect to the Convention on the Contract for the International Carriage of Goods by Road signed at Geneva on 19th May 1956; and for purposes connected therewith.

[5th August 1965]

Be it enacted by the Queen's most Excellent Majesty, by and with the advice and consent of the Lords Spiritual and Temporal, and Commons, in this present Parliament assembled, and by the authority of the same, as follows:—

1. Subject to the following provisions of this Act, the provisions of the Convention on the Contract for the International Carriage of Goods by Road (in this Act referred to as "the Convention"), as set out in the Schedule to this Act, shall have the force of law in the United Kingdom so far as they relate to the rights and liabilities of persons concerned in the carriage of goods by road under a contract to which the Convention applies.

2.—(1) Her Majesty may by Order in Council from time to time certify who are the High Contracting Parties to the Convention and in respect of what territories they are respectively parties.

(2) An Order in Council under this section shall, except so far as it has been superseded by a subsequent Order, be conclusive evidence of the matters so certified.

3.—(1) A court before which proceedings are brought to enforce a liability which is limited by article 23 in the Schedule to this Act may at any stage of the proceedings make any such order as appears to the court to be just and equitable in view of the provisions of the said article 23 and of any other proceedings which have been, or are likely to be, commenced in the United Kingdom or elsewhere to enforce the liability in whole or in part.

(2) Without prejudice to the preceding subsection, a court before which proceedings are brought to enforce a liability which is limited by the said article 23 shall, where the liability is, or may be, partly enforceable in other proceedings in the United Kingdom or elsewhere, have jurisdiction to award an amount less than the court would have awarded if the limitation applied solely to the proceedings before the court, or to make any part of its award conditional on the result of any other proceedings.

4.—(1) Subject to the next following subsection, Part I of the Foreign Judgments (Reciprocal Enforcement) Act 1933 (in this section referred to as "the Act of 1933") shall apply, whether or not it would otherwise have so applied, to any judgment which—

(*a*) has been given in any such action as is referred to in paragraph 1 of article 31 in the Schedule to this Act, and
(*b*) has been so given by any court or tribunal of a territory in respect of which one of the High Contracting Parties, other than the United Kingdom, is a party to the Convention, and
(*c*) has become enforceable in that territory.

(2) In the application of Part I of the Act of 1933 in relation to any such judgment as is referred to in the preceding subsection, section 4 of that Act shall have effect with the omission of subsections (2) and (3).

(3) The registration, in accordance with Part I of the Act of 1933, of any such judgment as is referred to in subsection (1) of this section shall constitute, in relation to that judgment, compliance with the formalities for the purposes of paragraph 3 of article 31 in the Schedule to this Act.

5.—(1) Where a carrier under a contract to which the Convention applies is liable in respect of any loss or damage for which compensation is payable under the Convention, nothing in section 6(1)(c) of the Law Reform (Married Women and Tortfeasors) Act 1935, section 16(1)(c) of the Law Reform (Miscellaneous Provisions) Act (Northern Ireland) 1937, or section 3(2) of the Law Reform (Miscellaneous Provisions) (Scotland) Act 1940 shall confer on him any right to recover contribution in respect of that loss or damage from any other carrier who, in accordance with article 34 in the Schedule to this Act, is a party to the contract of carriage.

(2) The preceding subsection shall be without prejudice to the operation of article 37 in the Schedule to this Act.

6. Every High Contracting Party to the Convention shall, for the purposes of any proceedings brought in a court in the United Kingdom in accordance with the provisions of article 31 in the Schedule to this Act to enforce a claim in respect of carriage undertaken by that Party, be deemed to have submitted to the jurisdiction of that court, and accordingly rules of court may provide for the manner in which any such action is to be commenced and carried on; but nothing in this section shall authorise the issue of execution, or in Scotland the execution of diligence, against the property of any High Contracting Party.

7.—(1) Any reference in the preceding provision of this Act to a court includes a reference to an arbitration tribunal acting by virtue of article 33 in the Schedule to this Act.

(2) For the purposes of article 32 in the Schedule to this Act, as it has effect (by virtue of the said article 33) in relation to arbitrations,—

(*a*) as respects England and Wales, subsections (3) to (5) of section 27 of the Limitation Act 1939 (which determine the time at which an arbitration is deemed to be commenced) shall apply;

(*b*) as respects Northern Ireland, subsections (2) to (4) of section 72 of the Statute of Limitations (Northern Ireland) 1958 (which make similar provision) shall apply; and

(*c*) as respects Scotland, an arbitration shall be deemed to be commenced when one party to the arbitration serves on the other party or parties a notice requiring him or them to appoint an arbiter or to agree to the appointment of an arbiter or, where the arbitration agreement provides that the reference shall be to a person named or designated in the agreements, requiring him or them to submit the dispute to the person so named or designated.

8.—(1) If it appears to Her Majesty in Council that there is any conflict between the provisions of this Act (including the provisions of the Convention as set out in the Schedule to this Act) and any provisions relating to the carriage of goods for reward by land, sea or air contained in—

(*a*) any other Convention which has been signed or ratified by or on behalf of Her Majesty's Government in the United Kingdom before the passing of this Act, or

(*b*) any enactment of the Parliament of the United Kingdom giving effect to such a Convention, Her Majesty may by Order in Council make such provision as may seem to Her to be appropriate for resolving that conflict by amending or modifying this Act or any such enactment.

(2) Any statutory instrument made by virtue of this section shall be subject to annulment in pursuance of a resolution of either House of Parliament.

9. Her Majesty may by Order in Council direct that this Act shall extend, subject to such exceptions, adaptations and modifications as may be specified in the Order, to—

(*a*) the Isle of Man;
(*b*) any of the Channel Islands;
(*c*) any colony;
(*d*) any state or territory which is for the time being a protectorate or protected state for the purposes of the British Nationality Act 1948.

10. In its application to Scotland, the Schedule to this Act shall have effect as if—

(*a*) any reference therein to a plaintiff included a reference to a pursuer;
(*b*) any reference therein to a defendant included a reference to a defender; and
(*c*) any reference to security for cost included a reference to caution for expenses.

11.—(1) In the application of this Act to Northern Ireland, any reference to an enactment of the Parliament of Northern Ireland shall be construed as a reference to that enactment as amended by any Act of that

Parliament, whether passed before or after this Act, and to any enactment of that Parliament passed after this Act and re-enacting the said enactment with or without modification.

(2) In the application of section 4 of this Act to Northern Ireland, any reference to the Foreign Judgments (Reciprocal Enforcement) Act 1933 is a reference to that Act as it applies in Northern Ireland.

(3) For the purposes of section 6 of the Government of Ireland Act 1920, this Act shall, so far as it relates to matters within the powers of the Parliament of Northern Ireland, be deemed to be an Act passed before the appointed day within the meaning of that section.

12. An Order in Council made under any of the preceding provisions of this Act may contain such transitional and supplementary provisions as appear to Her Majesty to be expedient and may be varied or revoked by a subsequent Order in Council made under that provision.

13. This Act shall bind the Crown.

14.—(1) This Act may be cited as the Carriage of Goods by Road Act 1965.

(2) The persons who, for the purposes of this Act, are persons concerned in the carriage of goods by road under a contract to which the Convention applies are—

(*a*) the sender,
(*b*) the consignee,
(*c*) any carrier who, in accordance with article 34 in the Schedule to this Act or otherwise, is a party to the contract of carriage,
(*d*) any person for whom such a carrier is responsible by virtue of article 3 in the Schedule to this Act,
(*e*) any person to whom the rights and liabilities of any of the persons referred to in paragraphs (*a*) to (*d*) of this subsection have passed (whether by assignment or assignation or by operation or law).

(3) Except in so far as the context otherwise requires, any reference in this Act to an enactment shall be construed as a reference to that enactment as amended or extended by or under any other enactment.

(4) This Act shall come into operation on such day as Her Majesty may by Order in Council appoint; but nothing in this Act shall apply in relation to any contract for the carriage of goods by road made before the day so appointed.

SCHEDULE

CONVENTION ON THE CONTRACT FOR THE INTERNATIONAL CARRIAGE OF GOODS BY ROAD

CHAPTER I

SCOPE OF APPLICATION

Article 1

Section 1

1. This Convention shall apply to every contract for the carriage of goods by road in vehicles for reward, when the place of taking over of the goods and the place designated for delivery, as specified in the contract, are situated in two different countries, of which at least one is a Contracting country, irrespective of the place of residence and the nationality of the parties.

2. For the purposes of this Convention, "vehicles" means motor vehicles, articulated vehicles, trailers and semi-trailers as defined in article 4 of the Convention on Road Traffic dated 19th September 1949.

3. This Convention shall apply also where carriage coming within its scope is carried out by States or by governmental institutions or organizations.

4. This Convention shall not apply:

(*a*) to carriage performed under the terms of any international postal convention;
(*b*) to funeral consignments;
(*c*) to furniture removal.

5. The Contracting Parties agree not to vary any of the provisions of this Convention by special agreements between two or more of them, except to make it inapplicable to their frontier traffic or to authorise the use in transport operations entirely confined to their territory of consignment notes representing a title to the goods.

Article 2

1. Where the vehicle containing the goods is carried over part of the journey by sea, rail, inland waterways or air, and, except where the provisions of article 14 are applicable, the goods are not unloaded from the vehicle, this Convention shall nevertheless apply to the whole of the carriage. Provided that to the extent that it is proved that any loss, damage or delay in delivery of the goods which occurs during the carriage by the other means of transport was not caused by an act or omission of the carrier by road, but by some event which could only have occurred in the course of and by reason of the carriage by that other

means of transport, the liability of the carrier by road shall be determined not by this Convention but in the manner in which the liability of the carrier by the other means of transport would have been determined if a contract for the carriage of the goods alone had been made by the sender with the carrier by the other means of transport in accordance with the conditions prescribed by law for the carriage of goods by that means of transport. If, however, there are no such prescribed conditions, the liability of the carrier by road shall be determined by this Convention.

2. If the carrier by road is also himself the carrier by the other means of transport, his liability shall also be determined in accordance with the provisions of paragraph 1 of this article, but as if, in his capacities as carrier by road and as carrier by the other means of transport, he were two separate persons.

CHAPTER II

PERSONS FOR WHOM THE CARRIER IS RESPONSIBLE

Article 3

For the purposes of this Convention the carrier shall be responsible for the acts and omissions of his agents and servants and of any other persons of whose services he makes use for the performance of the carriage, when such agents, servants or other persons are acting within the scope of their employment, as if such act or omissions were his own.

CHAPTER III

CONCLUSION AND PERFORMANCE OF THE CONTRACT OF CARRIAGE

Article 4

The contract of carriage shall be confirmed by the making out of a consignment note. The absence, irregularity or loss of the consignment note shall not affect the existence or the validity of the contract of carriage which shall remain subject to the provisions of this Convention.

Article 5

1. The consignment note shall be made out in three original copies signed by the sender and by the carrier. These signatures may be printed or replaced by the stamps of the sender and the carrier if the law of the country in which the consignment note has been made out so permits. The first copy shall be handed to the sender, the second shall accompany the goods and the third shall be retained by the carrier.

2. When the goods which are to be carried have to be loaded in different vehicles, or are of different kinds or are divided into different

lots, the sender or the carrier shall have the right to require a separate consignment note to be made out for each vehicle used, or for each kind or lot of goods.

Article 6

1. The consignment note shall contain the following particulars:

(*a*) the date of the consignment note and the place at which it is made out;
(*b*) the name and address of the sender;
(*c*) the name and address of the carrier;
(*d*) the place and the date of taking over of the goods and the place designated for delivery;
(*e*) the name and address of the consignee;
(*f*) the description in common use of the nature of the goods and the method of packing, and, in the case of dangerous goods, their generally recognised description;
(*g*) the number of packages and their special marks and numbers;
(*h*) the gross weight of the goods or their quantity otherwise expressed;
(*i*) charges relating to the carriage (carriage charges, supplementary charges, customs duties, and other charges incurred from the making of the contract to the time of delivery);
(*j*) the requisite instructions for Customs and other formalities;
(*k*) a statement that the carriage is subject, notwithstanding any clause to the contrary, to the provisions of this Convention.

2. Where applicable, the consignment note shall also contain the following particulars:

(*a*) a statement that transhipment is not allowed;
(*b*) the charges which the sender undertakes to pay;
(*c*) the amount of "cash on delivery" charges;
(*d*) a declaration of the value of the goods and the amount representing special interest in delivery;
(*e*) the sender's instructions to the carrier regarding insurance of the goods;
(*f*) the agreed time-limit within which the carriage is to be carried out;
(*g*) a list of the documents handed to the carrier.

3. The parties may enter in the consignment note any other particulars which they may deem useful.

Article 7

1. The sender shall be responsible for all expenses, loss and damage sustained by the carrier by reason of the inaccuracy or inadequacy of:

(*a*) the particulars specified in article 6, paragraph 1, (*b*), (*d*), (*e*), (*f*), (*g*), (*h*) and (*j*);

(*b*) the particulars specified in article 6, paragraph 2;
(*c*) any other particulars or instructions given by him to enable the consignment note to be made out or for the purpose of their being entered therein.

2. If, at the request of the sender, the carrier enters in the consignment note the particulars referred to in paragraph 1 of this article, he shall be deemed, unless the contrary is proved, to have done so on behalf of the sender.

3. If the consignment note does not contain the statement specified in article 6, paragraph 1(*k*), the carrier shall be liable for all expenses, loss and damage sustained through such omission by the person entitled to dispose of the goods.

Article 8

1. On taking over the goods, the carrier shall check:

(*a*) the accuracy of the statements in the consignment note as to the number of packages and their marks and numbers, and
(*b*) the apparent condition of the goods and their packaging.

2. Where the carrier has no reasonable means of checking the accuracy of the statements referred to in paragraph 1(*a*) of this article, he shall enter his reservations in the consignment note together with the grounds on which they are based. He shall likewise specify the grounds for any reservations which he makes with regard to the apparent condition of the goods and their packaging. Such reservations shall not bind the sender unless he has expressly agreed to be bound by them in the consignment note.

3. The sender shall be entitled to require the carrier to check the gross weight of the goods or their quantity otherwise expressed. He may also require the contents of the packages to be checked. The carrier shall be entitled to claim the cost of such checking. The result of the checks shall be entered in the consignment note.

Article 9

1. The consignment note shall be *prima facie* evidence of the making of the contract of carriage, the conditions of the contract and the receipt of the goods by the carrier.

2. If the consignment note contains no specific reservations by the carrier, it shall be presumed, unless the contrary is proved, that the goods and their packaging appeared to be in good condition when the carrier took them over and that the number of packages, their marks and numbers corresponded with the statements in the consignment note.

Article 10

The sender shall be liable to the carrier for damages to persons, equipment or other goods, and for any expenses due to defective packing of the goods, unless the defect was apparent or known to the carrier at the time when he took over the goods and he made no reservations concerning it.

Article 11

1. For the purposes of the Customs or other formalities which have to be completed before delivery of the goods, the sender shall attach the necessary documents to the consignment note or place them at the disposal of the carrier and shall furnish him with all the information which he requires.

2. The carrier shall not be under any duty to enquire into either the accuracy or the adequacy of such documents and information. The sender shall be liable to the carrier for any damage caused by the absence, inadequacy or irregularity of such documents and information, except in the case of some wrongful act or neglect on the part of the carrier.

3. The liability of the carrier for the consequences arising from the loss or incorrect use of the documents specified in and accompanying the consignment note or deposited with the carrier shall be that of an agent, provided that the compensation payable by the carrier shall not exceed that payable in the event of loss of the goods.

Article 12

1. The sender has the right to dispose of the goods, in particular by asking the carrier to stop the goods in transit, to change the place at which delivery is to take place or to deliver the goods to a consignee other than the consignee indicated in the consignment note.

2. This right shall cease to exist when the second copy of the consignment note is handed to the consignee or when the consignee exercises his right under article 13, paragraph 1; from that time onwards the carrier shall obey the orders of the consignee.

3. The consignee shall, however, have the right of disposal from the time when the consignment note is drawn up, if the sender makes an entry to that effect in the consignment note.

4. If in exercising his right of disposal the consignee has ordered the delivery of the goods to another person, that other person shall not be entitled to name other consignees.

5. The exercise of the right of disposal shall be subject to the following conditions:

(*a*) that the sender or, in the case referred to in paragraph 3 of this article, the consignee who wishes to exercise the right produces the first copy of the consignment note on which the new instructions to the carrier have been entered and indemnifies the carrier against all expenses, loss and damage involved in carrying out such instructions;

(*b*) that the carrying out of such instructions is possible at the time when the instructions reach the person who is to carry them out and does not either interfere with the normal working of the carrier's undertaking or prejudice the senders or consignees of other consignments;

(*c*) that the instructions do not result in a division of the consignment.

6. When, by reason of the provisions of paragraph 5(*b*) of this article, the carrier cannot carry out the instructions which he receives, he shall immediately notify the person who gave him such instructions.

7. A carrier who has not carried out the instructions given under the conditions provided for in this article, or who has carried them out without requiring the first copy of the consignment note to be produced, shall be liable to the person entitled to make a claim for any loss or damage caused thereby.

Article 13

1. After arrival of the goods at the place designated for delivery, the consignee shall be entitled to require the carrier to deliver to him, against a receipt, the second copy of the consignment note and the goods. If the loss of the goods is established or if the goods have not arrived after the expiry of the period provided for in article 19, the consignee shall be entitled to enforce in his own name against the carrier any rights arising from the contract of carriage.

2. The consignee who avails himself of the rights granted to him under paragraph 1 of this article shall pay the charges shown to be due on the consignment note, but in the event of dispute on this matter the carrier shall not be required to deliver the goods unless security has been furnished by the consignee.

Article 14

1. If for any reason it is or becomes impossible to carry out the contract in accordance with the terms laid down in the consignment note before the goods reach the place designated for delivery, the carrier shall ask for instructions from the person entitled to dispose of the goods in accordance with the provisions of article 12.

2. Nevertheless, if circumstances are such as to allow the carriage to be carried out under conditions differing from those laid down in the consignment note and if the carrier had been unable to obtain instructions in reasonable time from the person entitled to dispose of the goods in accordance with the provisions of article 12, he shall take such steps as seem to him to be in the best interests of the person entitled to dispose of the goods.

Article 15

1. Where circumstances prevent delivery of the goods after their arrival at the place designated for delivery, the carrier shall ask the sender for his instructions. If the consignee refuses the goods the sender shall be entitled to dispose of them without being obliged to produce the first copy of the consignment note.

2. Even if he has refused the goods, the consignee may nevertheless require delivery so long as the carrier has not received instructions to the contrary from the sender.

3. When circumstances preventing delivery of the goods arise after the consignee, in exercise of his rights under article 12, paragraph 3, has given an order for the goods to be delivered to another person, paragraphs 1 and 2 of this article shall apply as if the consignee were the sender and that other person were the consignee.

Article 16

1. The carrier shall be entitled to recover the cost of his request for instructions and any expenses entailed in carrying out such instructions, unless such expenses were caused by the wrongful act or neglect of the carrier.

2. In the case referred to in article 14, paragraph 1, and in article 15, the carrier may immediately unload the goods for account of the person entitled to dispose of them and thereupon the carriage shall be deemed to be at an end. The carrier shall then hold the goods on behalf of the person so entitled. He may however entrust them to a third party, and in that case he shall not be under any liability except for the exercise of reasonable care in the choice of such third party. The charges due under the consignment note and all other expenses shall remain chargeable against the goods.

3. The carrier may sell the goods, without awaiting instructions from the person entitled to dispose of them, if the goods are perishable or their condition warrants such a course, or when the storage expenses would be out of proportion to the value of the goods. He may also proceed to the sale of the goods in other cases if after the expiry of a reasonable period he has not received from the person entitled to dispose of the goods instructions to the contrary which he may reasonably be required to carry out.

4. If the goods have been sold pursuant to this article, the proceeds of sale, after deduction of the expenses chargeable against the goods, shall be placed at the disposal of the person entitled to dispose of the goods. If these charges exceed the proceeds of sale, the carrier shall be entitled to the difference.

5. The procedure in the case of sale shall be determined by the law or custom of the place where the goods are situated.

CHAPTER IV

LIABILITY OF THE CARRIER

Article 17

1. The carrier shall be liable for the total or partial loss of the goods and for damage thereto occurring between the time when he takes over the goods and the time of delivery, as well as for any delay in delivery.

2. The carrier shall however be relieved of liability if the loss, damage or delay was caused by the wrongful act or neglect of the claimant, by the instructions of the claimant given otherwise than as the result of a wrongful act or neglect on the part of the carrier, by inherent vice of the goods or through circumstances which the carrier could not avoid and the consequences of which he was unable to prevent.

3. The carrier shall not be relieved of liability by reason of the defective condition of the vehicle used by him in order to perform the carriage, or by reason of the wrongful act or neglect of the person from whom he may have hired the vehicle or of the agents or servants of the latter.

4. Subject to article 18, paragraphs 2 to 5 the carrier shall be relieved of liability when the loss or damage arises from the special risks inherent in one or more of the following circumstances:

(*a*) Use of open unsheeted vehicles, when their use has been expressly agreed and specified in the consignment note;
(*b*) the lack of, or defective condition of packing in the case of goods which, by their nature, are liable to wastage or to be damaged when not packed or when not properly packed;
(*c*) handling, loading, stowage or unloading of the goods by the sender, the consignee or persons acting on behalf of the sender or the consignee;
(*d*) the nature of certain kinds of goods which particularly exposes them to total or partial loss or to damage, especially through breakage, rust, decay, dessication, leakage, normal wastage, or the action of moth or vermin;
(*e*) insufficiency or inadequacy of marks or numbers on the packages;
(*f*) the carriage of livestock.

5. Where under this article the carrier is not under any liability in respect of some of the factors causing the loss, damage or delay, he shall only be liable to the extent that those factors for which he is liable under this article have contributed to the loss, damage or delay.

Article 18

1. The burden of proving that loss, damage or delay was due to one of the causes specified in article 17, paragraph 2, shall rest upon the carrier.

2. When the carrier establishes that in the circumstances of the case, the loss or damage could be attributed to one or more of the special risks referred to in article 17, paragraph 4, it shall be presumed that it was so caused. The claimant shall however be entitled to prove that the loss or damage was not, in fact, attributable either wholly or partly to one of these risks.

3. This presumption shall not apply in the circumstances set out in article 17, paragraph 4(*a*), if there has been an abnormal shortage, or a loss of any package.

4. If the carriage is performed in vehicles specially equipped to protect the goods from the effects of heat, cold, variations in temperature or the humidity of the air, the carrier shall not be entitled to claim the benefit of article 17, paragraph 4(*d*), unless he proves that all steps incumbent on him in the circumstances with respect to the choice, maintenance and use of such equipment were taken and that he complied with any special instructions issued to him.

5. The carrier shall not be entitled to claim the benefit of article 17, paragraph 4(*f*), unless he proves that all steps normally incumbent on

him in the circumstances were taken and that he complied with any special instructions issued to him.

Article 19

Delay in delivery shall be said to occur when the goods have not been delivered within the agreed time-limit or when, failing an agreed time-limit, the actual duration of the carriage having regard to the circumstances of the case, and in particular, in the case of partial loads, the time required for making up a complete load in the normal way, exceeds the time it would be reasonable to allow a diligent carrier.

Article 20

1. The fact that goods have not been delivered within thirty days following the expiry of the agreed time-limit, or, if there is no agreed time-limit, within sixty days from the time when the carrier took over the goods, shall be conclusive evidence of the loss of the goods, and the person entitled to make a claim may thereupon treat them as lost.
2. The person so entitled may, on receipt of compensation for the missing goods, request in writing that he shall be notified immediately should the goods be recovered in the course of the year following the payment of compensation. He shall be given a written acknowledgment of such request.
3. Within the thirty days following receipt of such notification, the person entitled as aforesaid may require the goods to be delivered to him against payment of the charges shown to be due on the consignment note and also against refund of the compensation he received less any charges included therein but without prejudice to any claims to compensation for delay in delivery under article 23 and, where applicable, article 26.
4. In the absence of the request mentioned in paragraph 2 or of any instructions given within the period of thirty days specified in paragraph 3, or if the goods are not recovered until more than one year after the payment of compensation, the carrier shall be entitled to deal with them in accordance with the law of the place where the goods are situated.

Article 21

Should the goods have been delivered to the consignee without collection of the "cash on delivery" charge which should have been collected by the carrier under the terms of the contract of carriage, the carrier shall be liable to the sender for compensation not exceeding the amount of such charge without prejudice to his right of action against the consignee.

Article 22

1. Where the sender hands goods of a dangerous nature to the carrier, he shall inform the carrier of the exact nature of the danger and indicate, if necessary, the precautions to be taken. If this information has not been entered in the consignment note, the burden of proving, by some other means, that the carrier knew the exact nature of the danger constituted

by the carriage of the said goods shall rest upon the sender or the consignee.

2. Goods of a dangerous nature which, in the circumstances referred to in paragraph 1 of this article, the carrier did not know were dangerous, may, at any time or place, be unloaded, destroyed or rendered harmless by the carrier without compensation; further, the sender shall be liable for all expenses, loss or damage arising out of their handing over for carriage or of their carriage.

Article 23[1]

1. When, under the provisions of this Convention, a carrier is liable for compensation in respect of total or partial loss of goods, such compensation shall be calculated by reference to the value of the goods at the place and time at which they were accepted for carriage.

2. The value of the goods shall be fixed according to the commodity exchange price or, if there is no such price, according to the current market price, or, if there is no commodity exchange price or current market price, by reference to the normal value of goods of the same kind and quality.

3. Compensation shall not, however exceed 25 francs per kilogram of gross weight short. "Franc" means the gold franc weighing 10/31 of a gramme and being of millesimal fineness 900.

4. In addition, the carriage charges, Customs duties and other charges incurred in respect of the carriage of the goods shall be refunded in full in case of total loss and in proportion to the loss sustained in case of partial loss, but no further damages shall be payable.

5. In the case of delay, if the claimant proves that damage has resulted therefrom the carrier shall pay compensation for such damage not exceeding the carriage charges.

6. Higher compensation may only be claimed where the value of the goods or a special interest in delivery has been declared in accordance with articles 24 and 26.

Article 24

The sender may, against payment of a surcharge to be agreed upon, declare in the consignment note a value for the goods exceeding the limit laid down in article 23, paragraph 3, and in that case the amount of the declared value shall be substituted for that limit.

Article 25

1. In case of damage, the carrier shall be liable for the amount by which the goods have diminished in value, calculated by reference to the value of the goods fixed in accordance with article 23, paragraphs 1, 2 and 4.

---

[1] Article 23 has been altered and extended by the Carriage by Air and Road Act 1979, set out in Appendix C.

2. The compensation may not, however, exceed:

(*a*) if the whole consignment has been damaged the amount payable in the case of total loss;
(*b*) if part only of the consignment has been damaged, the amount payable in the case of loss of the part affected.

Article 26

1. The sender may, against payment of a surcharge to be agreed upon, fix the amount of a special interest in delivery in the case of loss or damage or of the agreed time-limit being exceeded, by entering such amount in the consignment note.
2. If a declaration of a special interest in delivery has been made, compensation for the additional loss or damage proved may be claimed, up to the total amount of the interest declared, independently of the compensation provided for in articles 23, 24 and 25.

Article 27

1. The claimant shall be entitled to claim interest on compensation payable. Such interest, calculated at five per centum per annum, shall accrue from the date on which the claim was sent in writing to the carrier or, if no such claim has been made, from the date on which legal proceedings were instituted.
2. When the amounts on which the calculation of the compensation is based are not expressed in the currency of the country in which payment is claimed, conversion shall be at the rate of exchange applicable on the day and at the place of payment of compensation.

Article 28

1. In cases where, under the law applicable, loss, damage or delay arising out of carriage under this Convention gives rise to an extra-contractual claim, the carrier may avail himself of the provisions of this Convention which exclude his liability or which fix or limit the compensation due.
2. In cases where the extra-contractual liability for loss, damage or delay of one of the persons for whom the carrier is responsible under the terms of article 3 is in issue, such person may also avail himself of the provisions of this Convention which exclude the liability of the carrier or which fix or limit the compensation due.

Article 29

1. The carrier shall not be entitled to avail himself of the provisions of this chapter which exclude or limit his liability or which shift the burden of proof if the damage was caused by his wilful misconduct or by such default on his part as, in accordance with the law of the court or tribunal seised of the case, is considered as equivalent to wilful misconduct.

2. The same provision shall apply if the wilful misconduct or default is committed by the agents or servants of the carrier or by any other persons of whose services he makes use for the performance of the carriage, when such agents, servants or other persons are acting within the scope of their employment. Furthermore, in such a case such agents, servants or other persons shall not be entitled to avail themselves, with regard to their personal liability, of the provisions of this chapter referred to in paragraph 1.

CHAPTER V

CLAIMS AND ACTIONS

Article 30

1. If the consignee takes delivery of the goods without duly checking their condition with the carrier or without sending him reservations giving a general indication of the loss or damage, not later than the time of delivery in the case of apparent loss or damage and within seven days of delivery, Sundays and public holidays excepted, in the case of loss or damage which is not apparent, the fact of his taking delivery shall be *prima facie* evidence that he has received the goods in the condition described in the consignment note. In the case of loss or damage which is not apparent the reservations referred to shall be made in writing.
2. When the condition of the goods has been duly checked by the consignee and the carrier, evidence contradicting the result of this checking shall only be admissible in the case of loss or damage which is not apparent and provided that the consignee has duly sent reservations in writing to the carrier within seven days, Sundays and public holidays excepted, from the date of checking.
3. No compensation shall be payable for delay in delivery unless a reservation has been sent in writing to the carrier, within twenty-one days from the time that the goods were placed at the disposal of the consignee.
4. In calculating the time-limits provided for in this article the date of delivery, or the date of checking, or the date when the goods were placed at the disposal of the consignee, as the case may be, shall not be included.
5. The carrier and the consignee shall give each other every reasonable facility for making the requisite investigations and checks.

Article 31

1. In legal proceedings arising out of carriage under this Convention, the plaintiff may bring an action in any court or tribunal of a contracting country designated by agreement between the parties and, in addition, in the courts or tribunals of a country within whose territory

(*a*) the defendant is ordinarily resident, or has his principal place of business, or the branch or agency through which the contract of carriage was made, or (*b*) the place where the goods were taken over by the carrier or the place designated for delivery is situated.

and in no other courts or tribunals.

2. Where in respect of a claim referred to in paragraph 1 of this article an action is pending before a court or tribunal competent under that paragraph, or where in respect of such a claim a judgment has been entered by such a court or tribunal no new action shall be started between the same parties on the same grounds unless the judgment of the court or tribunal before which the first action was brought is not enforceable in the country in which the fresh proceedings are brought.

3. When a judgment entered by a court or tribunal of a contracting country in any such action as is referred to in paragraph 1 of this article has become enforceable in that country, it shall also become enforceable in each of the other contracting States, as soon as the formalities required in the country concerned have been complied with. The formalities shall not permit the merits of the case to be re-opened.

4. The provisions of paragraph 3 of this article shall apply to judgments after trial, judgments by default and settlements confirmed by an order of the court, but shall not apply to interim judgments or to awards of damages, in addition to costs against a plaintiff who wholly or partly fails in his action.

5. Security for costs shall not be required in proceedings arising out of carriage under this Convention from nationals of contracting countries resident or having their place of business in one of those countries.

Article 32

1. The period of limitation for an action arising out of carriage under this Convention shall be one year. Nevertheless, in the case of wilful misconduct, or such default as in accordance with the law of the court or tribunal seised of the case, is considered as equivalent to wilful misconduct, the period of limitation shall be three years. The period of limitation shall begin to run:

(*a*) in the case of partial loss, damage or delay in delivery, from the date of delivery;
(*b*) in the case of total loss, from the thirtieth day after the expiry of the agreed time-limit or where there is no agreed time-limit from the sixtieth day from the date on which the goods were taken over by the carrier;
(*c*) in all other cases, on the expiry of a period of three months after the making of the contract of carriage.

The day on which the period of limitation begins to run shall not be included in the period.

2. A written claim shall suspend the period of limitation until such date as the carrier rejects the claim by notification in writing and returns the documents attached thereto. If a part of the claim is admitted the period of limitation shall start to run again only in respect of that part of the claim still in dispute. The burden of proof of the receipt of the claim, or of the reply and of the return of the documents shall rest with the party

relying upon these facts. The running of the period of limitation shall not be suspended by further claims having the same object.

3. Subject to the provisions of paragraph 2 above, the extension of the period of limitation shall be governed by the law of the court or tribunal seised of the case. That law shall also govern the fresh accrual of rights of action.

4. A right of action which has become barred by lapse of time may not be exercised by way of counter-claim or set-off.

Article 33

The contract of carriage may contain a clause conferring competence on an arbitration tribunal if the clause conferring competence on the tribunal provides that the tribunal shall apply this Convention.

CHAPTER VI

PROVISIONS RELATING TO CARRIAGE PERFORMED BY SUCCESSIVE CARRIERS

Article 34

If carriage governed by a single contract is performed by successive road carriers, each of them shall be responsible for the performance of the whole operation, the second carrier and each succeeding carrier becoming a party to the contract of carriage, under the terms of the consignment note, by reason of his acceptance of the goods and the consignment note.

Article 35

1. A carrier accepting the goods from a previous carrier shall give the latter a dated and signed receipt. He shall enter his name and address on the second copy of the consignment note. Where applicable, he shall enter on the second copy of the consignment note and on the receipt reservations of the kind provided for in article 8, paragraph 2.

2. The provisions of article 9 shall apply to the relations between successive carriers.

Article 36

Except in the case of a counter-claim or a set-off raised in an action concerning a claim based on the same contract of carriage, legal proceedings in respect of liability for loss, damage or delay may only be brought against the first carrier, the last carrier or the carrier who was performing that portion of the carriage during which the event causing the loss, damage or delay occurred; an action may be brought at the same time against several of these carriers.

Article 37

A carrier who has paid compensation in compliance with the provisions of this Convention, shall be entitled to recover such compensation, together with interest thereon and all costs and expenses incurred by reason of the claim, from the other carriers who have taken part in the carriage, subject to the following provisions:

(*a*) the carrier responsible for the loss or damage shall be solely liable for the compensation whether paid by himself or by another carrier;
(*b*) when the loss or damage has been caused by the action of two or more carriers, each of them shall pay an amount proportionate to his share of liability; should it be impossible to apportion the liability, each carrier shall be liable in proportion to the share of the payment for the carriage which is due to him;
(*c*) if it cannot be ascertained to which carriers liability is attributable for the loss or damage, the amount of the compensation shall be apportioned between all the carriers as laid down in (*b*) above.

Article 38

If one of the carriers is insolvent, the share of the compensation due from him and unpaid by him shall be divided among the other carriers in proportion to the share of the payment for the carriage due to them.

Article 39

1. No carrier against whom a claim is made under articles 37 and 38 shall be entitled to dispute the validity of the payment made by the carrier making the claim if the amount of the compensation was determined by judicial authority after the first mentioned carrier had been given due notice of the proceedings and afforded an opportunity of entering an appearance.
2. A carrier wishing to take proceedings to enforce his right of recovery may make his claim before the competent court or tribunal of the country in which one of the carriers concerned is ordinarily resident, or has his principal place of business or the branch or agency through which the contract of carriage was made. All the carriers concerned may be made defendants in the same action.
3. The provisions of article 31, paragraphs 3 and 4, shall apply to judgments entered in the proceedings referred to in articles 37 and 38.
4. The provisions of article 32 shall apply to claims between carriers. The period of limitation shall, however, begin to run either on the date of the final judicial decision fixing the amount of compensation payable under the provisions of this Convention, or, if there is no such judicial decision, from the actual date of payment.

Article 40

Carriers shall be free to agree among themselves on provisions other than those laid down in articles 37 and 38.

CHAPTER VII

NULLITY OF STIPULATIONS CONTRARY TO THE CONVENTION

Article 41

1. Subject to the provisions of Article 40, any stipulation which would directly or indirectly derogate from the provisions of this Convention shall be null and void. The nullity of such a stipulation shall not involve the nullity of the other provisions of the contract.

2. In particular, a benefit of insurance in favour of the carrier or any other similar clause, or any clause shifting the burden of proof shall be null and void.

[*Chapter VIII of the Convention is not reproduced. This deals with the coming into force of the Convention, the settlement of disputes between the High Contracting Parties and related matters.*]

PROTOCOL OF SIGNATURE

1. This Convention shall not apply to traffic between the United Kingdom of Great Britain and Northern Ireland and the Republic of Ireland.

APPENDIX B

CONVENTION RELATIVE AU CONTRAT DE TRANSPORT INTERNATIONAL DE MARCHANDISES PAR ROUTE (CMR)

Préambule

Les Parties contractantes,

Ayant reconnu l'utilité de régler d'une manière uniforme les conditions du contrat de transport international de marchandises par route, particulièrement en ce qui concerne les documents utilisés pour ce transport et la responsabilité du transporteur,

Sont convenues de ce qui suit:

Chapitre premier

Champ d'application

Article 1

1. La présente Convention s'applique à tout contrat de transport de marchandises par route à titre onéreux au moyen de véhicules, lorsque le lieu de la prise en charge de la marchandise et le lieu prévu pour la livraison, tels qu'ils sont indiqués au contrat, sont situés dans deux pays différents dont l'un au moins est un pays contractant. Il en est ainsi quels que soient le domicile et la nationalité des parties.

2. Pour l'application de la présente Convention, il faut entendre par "véhicules" les automobiles, les véhicules articulés, les remorques et les semi-remorques, tels qu'ils sont définis par l'article 4 de la Convention sur la circulation routière en date du 19 septembre 1949.

3. La présente Convention s'applique même si les transports rentrant dans son champ d'application sont effectués par des Etats ou par des institutions ou organisations gouvernementales.

4. La présente Convention ne s'applique pas:

(*a*) Aux transports effectués sous l'empire de conventions postales internationales;
(*b*) Aux transports funéraires;
(*c*) Aux transports de déménagement.

5. Les Parties contractantes s'interdisent d'apporter par voie d'accords particuliers conclus entre deux ou plusieurs d'entre elles toute modification à la présente Convention, sauf pour soustraire à son empire leur

trafic frontalier ou pour autoriser dans les transports empruntant exclusivement leur territoire l'emploi de la lettre de voiture représentative de la marchandise.

Article 2

1. Si le véhicule, contenant les marchandises est transporté par mer, chemin de fer, voie navigable intérieure ou air sur une partie du parcours, sans rupture de charge sauf, éventuellement, pour l'application des dispositions de l'article 14, la présente Convention s'applique, néanmoins, pour l'ensemble du transport. Cependant, dans la mesure où il est prouvé qu'une perte, une avarie ou un retard à la livraison de la marchandise qui est survenu au cours du transport par l'un des modes de transport autre que la route n'a pas été causé par un acte ou une omission du transporteur routier et qu'il provient d'un fait qui n'a pu se produire qu'au cours et en raison du transport non routier, la responsabilité du transporteur routier est determinée non par la présente Convention, mais de la façon dont la responsabilité du transporteur non routier eut été determinée si un contrat de transport avait été conclu entre l'expéditeur et le transporteur non routier pour le seul transport de la marchandise conformément aux dispositions impératives de la loi concernant le transport de marchandises par le mode de transport autre que la route. Toutefois, en l'absence de telles dispositions, la responsabilité du transporteur par route sera determinée par la présente Convention.

2. Si le transporteur routier est en même temps le transporteur non routier, sa responsabilité est également déterminée par le paragraphe 1 comme si sa fonction de transporteur routier et sa fonction de transporteur non routier étaient exercées par deux personnes différentes.

Chapitre II

Personnes dont répond le transporteur

Article 3

Pour l'application de la présente Convention, le transporteur répond, comme de ses propres actes et omissions, des actes et omissions de ses préposés et de toutes autres personnes aux services desquelles il recourt pour l'exécution du transport lorsque ces préposés ou ces personnes agissent dans l'exercise de leurs fonctions.

Chapitre III

Conclusion et exécution du contrat de transport

Article 4

Le contrat de transport est constaté par une lettre de voiture. L'absence, l'irrégularité ou la perte de la lettre de voiture n'affectent ni l'existence ni la validité du contrat de transport qui reste soumis aux dispositions de la présente Convention.

Article 5

1. La lettre de voiture est établie en trois exemplaires originaux signés par l'expéditeur et par le transporteur, ces signatures pouvant être imprimées ou remplacées par les timbres de l'expéditeur et du transporteur si la législation du pays ou la lettre de voiture établie le permet. Le premier exemplaire est remis à l'expéditeur, le deuxième accompagne la marchandise et le troisième est retenu par le transporteur.

2. Lorsque la marchandise á transporter doit étre chargée dans des véhicules différents, ou lorsqu'il s'agit de différentes espèces de marchandises ou de lots distincts, l'expéditeur ou le transporteur a le droit d'exiger l'établissement d'autant de lettres de voiture qu'il doit être utilisé de véhicules ou qu'il y a d'espèces ou de lots de marchandises.

Article 6

1. La lettre de voiture doit contenir les indications suivantes:

(*a*) Le lieu et la date de son établissement;
(*b*) Le nom et l'adresse de l'expéditeur;
(*c*) Le nom et l'adresse du transporteur;
(*d*) Le lieu et la date de la prise en charge de la marchandise et le lieu prévu pour la livraison;
(*e*) Le nom et l'adresse du destinataire;
(*f*) La dénomination courante de la nature de la marchandise et le mode d'emballage, et, pour les marchandises dangereuses, leur dénomination généralement reconnue;
(*g*) Le nombre des colis, leurs marques particulières et leurs numéros;
(*h*) Le poids brut ou la quantité autrement exprimée de la marchandise;
(*i*) Les frais afférents au transport (prix de transport, frais accessoires, droits de douane et autres frais survenant à partir de la conclusion du contrat jusqu'à la livraison);
(*j*) Les instructions requises pour les formalités de douane et autres;
(*k*) L'indication que le transport est soumis, nonobstant toute clause contraire, au régime établi par la présente Convention.

2. Le cas échéant, la lettre de voiture doit contenir, en outre, les indications suivantes:

(*a*) L'interdiction de transbordement;
(*b*) Les frais que l'expéditeur prend à sa charge;
(*c*) Le montant du remboursement à percevoir lors de la livraison de la marchandise;
(*d*) Le valeur déclarée de la marchandise et la somme représentant l'intérêt spécial à la livraison;
(*e*) Les instructions de l'expéditeur au transporteur en ce qui concerne l'assurance de la marchandise;

(*f*) Le délai convenu dans lequel le transport doit être effectué;
(*g*) La liste des documents remis au transporteur.

3. Les parties peuvent porter sur la lettre de voiture toute autre indication qu'elles jugent utile.

Article 7

1. L'expéditeur répond de tous frais et dommages que supporterait le transporteur en raison de l'inexactitude ou de l'insuffisance:

(*a*) Des indications mentionnées à l'article 6, paragraphe 1, (*b*), (*d*), (*e*), (*f*), (*g*), (*h*), et (*j*);
(*b*) Des indications mentionnées à l'article 6, paragraphe 2;
(*c*) De toute autres indications ou instructions qu'il donne pour l'établissement de la lettre de voiture ou pour y être reportées.

2. Si, à la demande de l'expéditeur, le transporteur inscrit sur la lettre de voiture les mentions visées au paragraphe 1 du présent article, il est considéré, jusqu'à preuve du contraire, comme agissant pour le compte de l'expéditeur.

3. Si la lettre de voiture ne contient pas la mention prévue à l'article 6, paragraphe 1, (*k*), le transporteur est responsable de tous frais et dommages que subirtait l'ayant droit à la marchandise en raison de cette omission.

Article 8

1. Lors de la prise en charge de la marchandise, le transporteur est tenu de vérifier:

(*a*) L'exactitude des mentions de la lettre de voiture relatives au nombre de colis, ainsi qu'à leurs marques et numéros;
(*b*) L'état apparent de la marchandise et de son emballage.

2. Si le transporteur n'a pas de moyens raisonnables de vérifier l'exactitude des mentions visées au paragraphe 1, (*a*) du présent article, il inscrit sur la lettre de voiture des réserves qui doivent être motivées. Il doit de même motiver toutes les réserves qu'il fait au suject de l'état apparent de la marchandise et de son emballage. Ces réserves n'engagent pas l'expéditeur, si celui-ci ne les a pas expressément acceptées sur la lettre de voiture.

3. L'expéditeur a le droit d'exiger la vérification par le transporteur du poids brut ou de la quantité autrement exprimée de la marchandise. Il peut aussi exiger la vérification du contenu des colis. Le transporteur peut réclamer le paiement des frais de vérification. Le résultat des vérifications est consigné sur la lettre de voiture.

Article 9

1. La lettre de voiture fait foi, jusqu'à preuve du contraire, des conditions du contrat et de la réception de la marchandise par le transporteur.

2. En l'absence d'inscription sur la lettre de voiture de réserves motivées du transporteur, il y a présomption que la marchandise et son emballage étaient en bon état apparent au moment de la prise en charge par le transporteur et que le nombre des colis ainsi que leurs marques et numéros étaient conformes aux énonciations de la lettre de voiture.

Article 10

L'expéditeur est responsable envers le transporteur des dommages aux personnes, au matériel ou à d'autres marchandises, ainsi que des frais, qui auraient pour origine la défectuosité de l'emballage de la marchandise, à moins que, la défectuosité étant apparente ou connue du transporteur au moment de la prise en charge, le transporteur n'ait pas fait de réserves à son sujet.

Article 11

1. En vue de l'accomplissement des formalités de douane et autres à remplir avant la livraison de la marchandise, l'expéditeur doit joindre à la lettre de voiture ou mettre à la disposition du transporteur les documents nécessaires et lui fournir tous renseignements voulus.
2. Le transporteur n'est pas tenu d'examiner si ces documents et renseignements sont exacts ou suffisants. L'expéditeur est responsable envers le transporteur de tous dommages qui pourraient résulter de l'absence, de l'insuffisance ou de l'irrégularité de ces documents et renseignements, sauf en cas de faute du transporteur.
3. Le transporteur est responsable au même titre qu'un commissionaire des conséquences de la perte ou de l'utilisation inexacte des documents mentionnés sur la lettre de voiture et qui accompagnent celle-ci ou qui sont déposés entre ses mains; toutefois, l'indemnité à sa charge ne dépassera pas celle qui serait due en cas de perte de la marchandise.

Article 12

1. L'expéditeur a le droit de disposer de la marchandise, notamment en demandant au transporteur d'en arrêter le transport, de modifier le lieu prévu pour la livraison ou de livrer la marchandise à un destinataire différent de celui indiqué sur la lettre de voiture.
2. Ce droit s'éteint lorsque le deuxième exemplaire de la lettre de voiture est remis au destinataire ou que celui-ci fait valoir le droit prévu à l'article 13, paragraphe 1; à partir de ce moment, le transporteur doit se conformer aux ordres du destinataire.
3. Le droit de disposition appartient toutefois au destinataire dès l'établissement de la lettre de voiture si une mention dans ce sens est faite par l'expéditeur sur cette lettre.
4. Si, en exerçant son droit de disposition, le destinataire ordonne de livrer la marchandise à une autre personne, celle-ci ne peut pas désigner d'autres destinataires.
5. L'exercice du droit de disposition est subordonné aux conditions suivantes:

(*a*) L'expéditeur ou, dans le cas visé au paragraphe 3 du présent article, le destinataire qui veut exercer ce droit doit présenter le premier exemplaire de la lettre de voiture, sur lequel doivent être inscrites les nouvelles instructions données au transporteur, et dédommager le transporteur des frais et du préjudice qu'entraîne l'exécution de ces instructions;

(*b*) Cette exécution doit être possible au moment où les instructions parviennent à la personne qui doit les exécuter et elle ne doit ni entraver l'exploitation normale de l'entreprise du transporteur, ni porter préjudice aux expéditeurs ou destinataires d'autres envois;

(*c*) Les instructions ne doivent jamais avoir pour effet de diviser l'envoi.

6. Lorsque, en raison des dispositions prévues au paragraphe 5, (*b*) du présent article, le transporteur ne peut exécuter les instructions qu'il reçoit, il doit en aviser immédiatement la personne dont émanent ces instructions.

7. Le transporteur qui n'aura pas exécuté les instructions données dans les conditions prévues au présent article ou qui se sera conformé à de telles instructions sans avoir exigé la présentation du premier exemplaire de la lettre de voiture sera responsable envers l'ayant droit du préjudice causé par ce fait.

Article 13

1. Après l'arrivée de la marchandise au lieu prévu pourla livraison, le destinataire a le droit de demander que le deuxième exemplaire de la lettre de voiture lui soit remis et que la marchandise lui soit livrée, le tout contre décharge. Si la perte de la marchandise est établie, ou si la marchandise n'est pas arrivée à l'expiration du délai prévu à l'article 19, le destinataire est autorisé à faire valoir en son propre nom vis-à-vis du transporteur les droits qui résultent du contrat de transport.

2. Le destinataire qui se prévaut des droits qui lui sont accordés aux termes du paragraphe 1 du présent article est tenu de payer le montant des créances résultant de la lettre de voiture. En cas de contestation à ce sujet, le transporteur n'est obligé d'effectuer la livraison de la marchandise que si une caution lui est fournie par le destinataire.

Article 14

1. Si, pour un motif quelconque, l'exécution du contrat dans les conditions prévues à la lettre de voiture est ou devient impossible avant l'arrivée de la marchandise au lieu prévu pour la livraison, le transporteur est tenu de demander des instructions à la personne qui a le droit de disposer de la marchandise conformément à l'article 12.

2. Toutefois, si les circonstances permettent l'exécution du transport dans des conditions différentes de celles prévues à la lettre de voiture et si le transporteur n'a pu obtenir en temps utile les instructions de la personne qui a le droit de disposer de la marchandise conformément à l'article 12, il prend les mesures qui lui paraissent les meilleures dans l'intérêt de la personne ayant le droit de disposer de la marchandise.

Article 15

1. Lorsque, après l'arrivée de la marchandise au lieu de destination, il se présente des empêchements à la livraison, le transporteur demande des instructions à l'expéditeur. Si le destinataire refuse la marchandise, l'expéditeur a le droit de disposer de celle-ci sans avoir à produire le premier exemplaire de la lettre de voiture.

2. Même s'il a refusé la marchandise, le destinataire peut toujours en demander la livraison tant que le transporteur n'a pas reçu d'instructions contraires de l'expediteur.

3. Si l'empêchement à la livraison se présente après que, conformément au droit qu'il détient en vertu de l'article 12, paragraphe 3, le destinataire a donné l'ordre de livrer la marchandise à une autre personne, le destinataire est substitué à l'expéditeur, et cette autre personne au destinataire, pour l'application des paragraphes 1 et 2 ci-dessus.

Article 16

1. Le transporteur a droit au remboursement des frais que lui cause sa demande d'instructions, ou qu'entraîne pour lui l'exécution des instructions reçues, à moins que ces frais ne soient la conséquence de sa faute.

2. Dans les cas visés à l'article 14, paragraphe 1, et à l'article 15, le transporteur peut décharger immédiatement la marchandise pour le compte de l'ayant droit; après ce déchargement, le transport est réputé terminé. Le transporteur assume alors la garde de la marchandise. Il peut toutefois confier la marchandise à un tiers et n'est alors responsable que du choix judicieux de ce tiers. La marchandise reste grevée des créances résultant de la lettre de voiture et de tous autres frais.

3. Le transporteur peut faire procéder à la vente de la marchandise sans attendre d'instructions de l'ayant droit lorsque la nature périssable ou l'état de la marchandise le justifie ou lorsque les frais de garde sont hors de proportion avec la valeur de la marchandise. Dans les autres cas, il peut également faire procéder à la vente lorsque, dans un delai raisonnable, il n'a pas reçu de l'ayant droit d'instructions contraires dont l'exécution puisse équitablement être exigée.

4. Si la marchandise a été vendue en application du présent article, le produit de la vente doit être mis à la disposition de l'ayant droit, déduction faite des frais grevant la marchandise. Si ces frais sont supérieurs au produit de la vente, le transporteur a droit à la différence.

5. La façon de procéder en cas de vente est déterminée par la loi ou les usages du lieu où se trouve la marchandise.

Chapitre IV

Responsabilité du transporteur

Article 17

1. Le transporteur est responsable de la perte totale ou partielle, ou de l'avarie, qui se produit entre le moment de la prise en charge de la marchandise et celui de la livraison, ainsi que du retard à la livraison.

2. Le transporteur est déchargé de cette responsabilité si la perte, l'avarie ou le retard a eu pour cause une faute de l'ayant droit, un ordre de celui-ci ne résultant pas d'une faute du transporteur, un vice propre de la marchandise, ou des circonstances que le transporteur ne pouvait pas éviter et aux conséquences desquelles il ne pouvait pas obvier.

3. Le transporteur ne peut exciper, pour se décharger de sa responsabilité, ni des défectuosités du véhicule dont il se sert pour effectuer le transport, ni de fautes de la personne dont il aurait loué le véhicule ou des préposés de celle-ci.

4. Compte tenu de l'article 18, paragraphs 2 à 5, le transporteur est déchargé de sa responsabilité lorsque la perte ou l'avarie résulte des risques particuliers inhérents à l'un des faits suivants ou à plusieurs d'entre eux:

(*a*) Emploi de véhicules ouverts et non bâchés, lorsque cet emploi a été convenu d'une manière expresse et mentionné dans la lettre de voiture;
(*b*) Absence ou défectuosité de l'emballage pour les marchandises exposées par leur nature à des déchets ou avaries quand elles ne sont pas emballées ou sont mal emballées;
(*c*) Manutention, chargement, arrimage ou déchargement de la marchandise par l'expéditeur ou le destinataire ou des personnes agissant pour le compte de l'expéditeur ou du destinataire;
(*d*) Nature de certaines marchandises exposées, par des causes inhérentes à cette nature même, soit à perte totale ou partielle, soit à avarie, notamment par bris, rouille, détérioration interne et spontanée, dessiccation, coulage, déchet normal ou action de la vermine et des rongeurs;
(*e*) Insuffisance ou imperfection des marques ou des numéros de colis;
(*f*) Transport d'animaux vivants.

5. Si, en vertu du présent article, le transporteur ne répond pas de certains des facteurs qui ont causé le dommage, sa responsabilité n'est engagée que dans la proportion où les facteurs dont il répond en vertu du présent article ont contribué au dommage.

Article 18

1. La preuve que la perte, l'avarie ou le retard a eu pour cause un des faits prévus à l'article 17, paragraphe 2, incombe au transporteur.

2. Lorsque le transporteur établit que, eu égard aux circonstances de fait, la perte ou l'avarie a pu résulter d'un ou de plusieurs des risques particuliers prévus à l'article 17, paragraphe 4, il y a présomption qu'elle en résulte. L'ayant droit peut toutefois faire la preuve que le dommage n'a pas eu l'un de ces risques pour cause totale ou partielle.

3. La présomption visée ci-dessus n'est pas applicable dans le cas prévu à l'article 17, paragraphe 4, a, s'il y a manquant d'une importance anormale ou perte de colis.

4. Si le transport est effectué au moyen d'un véhicule aménagé en vue de soustraire les marchandises à l'influence de la chaleur, du froid, des variations de température ou de l'humidité de l'air, le transporteur ne

peut invoquer le bénéfice de l'article 17, paragraphe 4, (*d*), que s'il fournit la preuve que toutes les mesures lui incombant, compte tenu des circonstances, ont été prises en ce qui concerne le choix, l'entretien et l'emploi de ces aménagements et qu'il s'est conformé aux instructions spéciales qui ont pu lui être données.

5. Le transporteur ne peut invoquer le bénéfice de l'article 17, paragraphe 4, (*f*), que s'il fournit la preuve que toutes les mesures lui incombant normalement, compte tenu des circonstances, ont été prises et qu'il s'est conformé aux instructions spéciales qui ont pu lui être données.

Article 19

Il y a retard à la livraison lorsque la marchandise n'a pas été livrée dans le délai convenu ou, s'il n'a pas été convenu de délai, lorsque la durée effective du transport dépasse, compte tenu des circonstances et, notamment, dans le cas d'un chargement partiel, du temps voulu pour assembler un chargement complet dans des conditions normales, le temps qu'il est raisonnable d'allouer à des transporteurs diligents.

Article 20

1. L'ayant droit peut, sans avoir à fournir d'autres preuves, considerer la marchandise comme perdu quand elle n'a pas été livrée dans les trente jours qui suivent l'expiration du délai convenu ou, s'il n'a pas été convenu de délai, dans les soixante jours qui suivent la prise en charge de la marchandise par le transporteur.

2. L'ayant droit peut, en recevant le paiement de l'indemnité pour la marchandise perdue, demander, par écrit, à être avisé immédiatement dans le cas où la marchandise serait retrouvée au cours de l'année qui suivra le paiement de l'indemnité. Il lui est donné par écrit acte de cette demande.

3. Dans les trente jours qui suivent la réception de cet avis, l'ayant droit peut exiger que la marchandise lui soit livrée contre paiement des créances résultant de la lettre de voiture et contre restitution de l'indemnité qu'il a reçue, déduction faite éventuellement des frais qui auraient été compris dans cette indemnité, et sous réserve de tous droits à l'indemnité pour retard à la livraison prévue à l'article 23 et, s'il y a lieu, à l'article 26.

4. A défaut soit de la demande prévue au paragraphe 2, soit d'instructions données dans le délai de trente jours prévu au paragraphe 2, ou encore si la marchandise n'a été retrouvée que plus d'un an après le paiement de l'indemnité, le transporteur en dispose conformément à la loi du lieu où se trouve la marchandise.

Article 21

Si la marchandise est livrée au destinataire sans encaissement du remboursement qui aurait dû être perçu par le transporteur en vertu des dispositions du contrat de transport, le transporteur est tenu d'indemniser l'expéditeur à concurrence du montant du remboursement, sauf son recours contre le destinataire.

Article 22

1. Si l'expéditeur remet au transporteur des marchandises dangereuses, il lui signale la nature exacte du danger qu'elles présentent et lui indique éventuellement les précautions à prendre. Au cas où cet avis n'a pas été consigné sur la lettre de voiture, il appartient à l'expéditeur ou au destinataire de faire la preuve, par tous autres moyens, que le transporteur a eu connaissance de la nature exacte du danger que présentait le transport desdites marchandises.

2. Les marchandises dangereuses qui n'auraient pas été connues comme telles par le transporteur dans les conditions prévues au paragraphe 1 du présent article peuvent à tout moment et en tout lieu être déchargées, détruites ou rendues inoffensives par le transporteur, et ce sans aucune indemnité; l'expéditeur est en outre responsable de tous frais et dommages résultant de leur remise au transport ou de leur transport.

Article 23

1. Quand, en vertu des dispositions de la présente Convention, une indemnité pour perte totale ou partielle de la marchandise est mise à la charge du transporteur, cette indemnité est calculée d'après la valeur de la marchandise au lieu et à l'époque de la prise en charge.

2. La valeur de la marchandise est déterminée d'apres le cours en bourse ou, à défaut, d'après le prix courant sur le marché ou, à défaut de l'un et de l'autre, d'après la valeur usuelle des marchandises de même nature et qualité.

3. Toutefois, l'indemnitè ne peut dépasser 25 francs per kilogramme du poids brut manquant. Le franc s'entend du franc-or, d'un poids de 10/31 de gramme au titre de 0,900.

4. Sont en outre remboursés le prix du transport, les droits de douane et les autres frais encourus à l'occasion du transport de la marchandise, en totalité en cas de perte totale, et au prorata en cas de perte partielle; d'autres dommages-intérêts ne sont pas dus.

5. En cas de retard, si l'ayant droit prouve qu'um préjudice en est résulté, le transporteur est tenu de payer pour ce préjudice une indemnité qui ne peut pas dépasser le prix du transport.

6. Des indemnités plus élevées ne peuvent être réclamées qu'en cas de déclaration de la valeur de la marchandise ou de déclaration d'intérêt spécial à la livraison, conformément aux articles 24 et 26.

Article 24

L'expéditeur peut déclarer dans la lettre de voiture, contre paiement d'un supplément de prix à convenir, une valeur de la marchandise excédant la limite mentionnée au paragraphe 3 de l'article 23 et, dans ce cas, le montant déclaré se substitue à cette limite.

Article 25

1. En cas d'avarie, le transporteur paie le montant de la dépréciation calculée d'après la valeur de la marchandise fixée conformément à l'article 23, paragraphes 1, 2 et 4.

2. Toutefois, l'indemnité ne peut dépasser:

(*a*) Si la totalité de l'expédition est dépréciée par l'avarie, le chiffre qu'elle aurait atteint en cas de perte totale;

(*b*) Si une partie seulement de l'expédition est dépréciée par l'avarie, le chiffre qu'elle aurait atteint en cas de perte de la partie dépréciée.

Article 26

1. L'expéditeur peut fixer, en l'inscrivant à la lettre de voiture, et contre pairment d'un supplément de prix à convenir, le montant d'un intérêt spécial à la livraison, pour le cas de perte ou d'avarie et pour celui de dépassement du délai convenu.

2. S'il y a eu déclaration d'intérêt spécial à la livraison, il peut être réclamé, indépendamment des indemnités prévues aux articles 23, 24 et 25, et à concurrence du montant de l'intérêt déclaré, une indemnité égale au dommage supplémentaire dont la preuve est apportée.

Article 27

1. L'ayant droit peut demander les intérêts de l'indemnité. Ces intérêts, calculés à raison de 5 pour 100 l'an, courent du jour de la réclamation adressée par écrit au transporteur ou, s'il n'y a pas eu de réclamation, du jour de la demande en justice.

2. Lorsque les éléments qui servent de base au calcul de l'indemnité ne sont pas exprimés dans la monnaie du pays où le paiement est réclamé, la conversion est faite d'après le cours du jour et du lieu du paiement de l'indemnité.

Article 28

1. Lorsque, d'après la loi applicable, la perte, l'avarie ou le retard survenu au cours d'un transport soumis à la présente Convention peut donner lieu à une réclamation extra-contractuelle, le transporteur peut se prévaloir des dispositions de la présente Convention qui excluent sa responsabilité ou qui déterminent ou limitent les indemnités dues.

2. Lorsque la responsabilité extra-contractuelle pour perte, avarie ou retard d'une des personnes dont le transporteur répond aux termes de l'article 3 est mise en cause, cette personne peut également se prévaloir des dispositions de la présente Convention qui excluent la responsabilité du transporteur ou qui déterminent ou limitent les indemnités dues.

Article 29

1. Le transporteur n'a pas le droit de se prévaloir des dispositions du présent chapitre qui excluent ou limitent sa responsabilité ou qui renversent le fardeau de la preuve, si le dommage provient de son dol ou d'une faute qui lui est imputable et qui, d'après la loi de la juridiction saisie, est considérée comme équivalente au dol.

2. Il en est de même si le dol ou la faute est le fait des préposés du transporteur ou de toutes autres personnes aux services desquelles il recourt pour l'exécution du transport lorsque ces préposés ou ces autres personnes agissent dans l'exercise de leurs fonctions. Dans ce cas, ces préposés ou ces autres personnes n'ont pas davantage le droit de se prévaloir, en ce qui concerne leur responsabilité personnelle, des dispositions du présent chapitre visées au paragraphe 1.

Chapitre V

Réclamations et actions

Article 30

1. Si le destinataire a pris livraison de la marchandise sans qu'il en ait constaté l'état contradictoirement avec le transporteur ou sans qu'il ait, au plus tard au moment de la livraison s'il s'agit de pertes ou avaries apparentes, ou dans les sept jours à dater de la livraison, dimanche et jours fériés non compris, lorsqu'il s'agit de pertes ou avaries non apparentes, adressé des réserves au transporteur indiquant la nature générale de la perte ou de l'avarie, il est présumé, jusqu'à preuve contraire, avoir reçu la marchandise dans l'état décrit dans la lettre de voiture. Les réserves visées ci-dessus doivent être faites par écrit lorsqu'il s'agit de pertes ou avaries non apparentes.

2. Lorsque l'état de la marchandise a été constaté contradictoirement par le destinataire et le transporteur, la preuve contraire au résultat de cette constatation ne peut être faite que s'il s'agit de pertes ou avaries non apparentes et si le destinataire a adressé des réserves écrites au transporteur dans les sept jours, dimanche et jours fériés non compris, à dater de cette constatation.

3. Un retard à la livraison no peut donner lieu à indemnité que si une réserve a été adressée par écrit dans le délai de 21 jours à dater de la mise de la marchandise à la disposition du destinataire.

4. La date de livraison ou, selon le cas, celle de la constatation ou celle de la mise à disposition n'est pas comptée dans les délais prévus au présent article.

5. Le transporteur et le destinataire se donnent réciproquement toutes facilités raisonnables pour les constations et vérifications utiles.

Article 31

1. Pour tous litiges auxquels donnent lieu les transports soumis à la présente Convention, le demandeur peut saisir, en dehors des juridictions des pays contractants désignés d'un commun accord par les parties, les juridictions du pays sur le territoire duquel:

(*a*) Le défendeur a sa résidence habituelle, son siège principal ou la succursale ou l'agence par l'intermédiaire de laquelle le contrat de transport a été conclu, ou
(*b*) Le lieu de la prise en charge de la marchandise ou celui prévu pour la livraison est situé,

et ne peut saisir que ces juridictions.

2. Lorsque dans un litige visé au paragraphe 1 du présent article une action est en instance devant une juridiction compétente aux termes de ce paragraphe, ou lorsque dans un tel litige un jugement a été prononcé par une telle juridiction, il ne peut être intenté aucune nouvelle action pour la même cause entre les même parties à moins que la décision de la juridiction devant laquelle la première action a été intentée ne soit pas susceptible d'être exécutée dans le pays où la nouvelle action est intentée.

3. Lorsque dans un litige visé au paragraphe 1 du présent article un jugement rendu par une juridiction d'un pays contractant est devenu exécutoire dans ce pays, il devient également exécutoire dans chacun des autres pays contractants aussitôt après accomplissement des formalités prescrites à cet effet dans le pays intéressé. Ces formalités ne peuvent comporter aucune révision de l'affaire.

4. Les dispositions du paragraphe 3 du présent article s'appliquent aux jugements contradictoires, aux jugements par défaut et aux transactions judiciaires, mais ne s'appliquent ni aux jugements qui ne sont exécutoires que par provision, ni aux condamnations en dommages et intérêts qui seraient prononcés en sus des dépens contre un demandeur en raison du rejet total ou partiel de sa demande.

5. Il ne peut être exigé de caution de ressortissants de pays contractants, ayant leur domicile ou un établissement dans un de ces pays, pour assurer le paiement des dépens à l'occasion des actions en justice auxquelles donnent lieu les transports soumis à la présente Convention.

Article 32

1. Les actions auxquelles peuvent donner lieu les transports soumis à la présente Convention sont prescrites dans le délai d'un an. Toutefois, dans le cas de dol ou de faute considérée, d'après la loi de la juridiction saisie, comme équivalente au dol, la prescription est de trois ans. La prescription court:

(*a*) Dans le cas de perte partielle, d'avarie ou de retard, à partir du jour où la marchandise a été livrée;
(*b*) Dans le cas de perte totale, à partir du trentième jour après l'expiration du délai convenu ou, s'il n'a pas été convenu de délai, à partir du soixantième jour après la prise en charge de la marchandise par le transporteur;
(*c*) Dans tous les autres cas, à partir de l'expiration d'un délai de trois mois à dater de la conclusion du contrat de transport.

Le jour indiqué ci-dessus comme point de départ de la prescription n'est pas comprise dans le délai.

2. Une réclamation écrite suspend la prescription jusqu'au jour où le transporteur repousse la réclamation par écrit et restitue les pièces qui y étaient jointes. En cas d'acceptation partielle de la réclamation, la prescription ne reprend son cours que pour la partie de la réclamation qui reste litigieuse. La preuve de la réception de la réclamation ou de la réponse et de la restitution des pièces est à la charge de la partie qui invoque ce fait. Les réclamations ultérieures ayant le même objet ne suspendent pas la prescription.

3. Sous réserve des dispositions du paragraphe 2 ci-dessus, la suspension de la prescription est régie par la loi de la juridiction saisie. Il en est de même en ce qui concerne l'interruption de la prescription.

4. L'action, prescrite ne peut plus ête exercée, même sous forme de demande reconventionnelle ou d'exception.

Article 33

Le contrat de transport peut contenir une clause attribuant compétence à un tribunal arbitral à condition que cette clause prévoie que le tribunal arbitral appliquera la présente Convention.

Chapitre VI

Dispositions relatives au transport effectué par transporteurs successifs

Article 34

Si un transport régi par un contrat unique est exécuté par des transporteurs routiers successifs, chacun de ceux-ci assume la responsabilité de l'execution du transport total, le second transporteur et chacun des transporteurs suivants devenant, de par leur acceptation de la marchandise et de la lettre de voiture, parties au contrat, aux conditions de la lettre de voiture.

Article 35

1. Le transporteur qui accepte la marchandise du transporteur précédent remet à celui-ci un reçu daté et signé. Il doit porter son nom et son adresse sur le deuxième exemplaire de la lettre de voiture. S'il y a lieu, il appose sur cet exemplaire, ainsi que sur le reçu, des réserves analogues à celles qui sont prévues à l'article 8, paragraphe 2.

2. Les dispositions de l'article 9 s'appliquent aux relations entre transporteurs successfis.

Article 36

A moins qu'il ne s'agisse d'une demande reconventionelle ou d'une exception formulée dans une instance relative à une demande fondée sur le même contrat de transport, l'action en responsabilité pour perte, avarie ou retard ne peut être dirigée que contre le premier transporteur, le dernier transporteur ou le transporteur qui exécutait la partie du transport au cours de laquelle s'est produit le fait ayant causé la perte, l'avarie ou le retard; l'action peut être dirigée à la fois contre plusieurs de ces transporteurs.

Article 37

Le transporteur qui a payé une indemnité en vertu des dispositions de la présente Convention a le droit d'exercer un recours en principal, intérêts et frais contre les transporteurs qui ont participé à l'exécution du contrat de transport, conformément aux dispositions suivantes:

(*a*) Le transporteur par le fait duquel le dommage a été causé doit seul supporter l'indemnité, qu'il l'ait payée lui-même ou qu'elle ait été payée par un autre transporteur;
(*b*) Lorsque le dommage a été causé par le fait de deux ou plusieurs transporteurs, chacun d'eux doit payer un montant proportionnel à sa part de responsabilité; si l'évaluation des parts de responsabilité est impossible, chacun d'eux est responsable proportionnellement à la part de rémunération du transport qui lui revient;
(*c*) Si l'on ne peut déterminer quels sont ceux des transporteurs auxquels la responsabilité n'est imputable, la charge de l'indemnité due est répartie, dans la proportion fixée en b, entre tous les transporteurs.

Article 38

Si l'un des transporteurs est insolvable, la part lui incombant et qu'il n'a pas payée est répartie entre tous les autres transporteurs proportionnellement à leur rémunération.

Article 39

1. Le transporteur contre lequel est exercé un des recours prévus aux articles 37 et 38 n'est pas recevable à contester le bien-fondé du paiement effectué par le transporteur exerçant le recours, lorsque l'indemnité a été fixée par décision de justice, pourvu qu'il ait été dûment informé du procès et qu'il ait été à même d'y intervenir.
2. Le transporteur qui veut exercer son recours peut le former devant le tribunal compétent du pays dans lequel l'un des transporteurs intéressés a sa résidence habituelle, son siège principal ou la succursale ou l'agence par l'entremise de laquelle le contrat de transport a été conclu. Le recours peut être dirigé dans une seule et même instance contre tous les transporteurs intéressés.
3. Les dispositions de l'article 31, paragraphes 3 et 4, s'appliquent aux jugements rendus sur les recours prévus aux articles 37 et 38.
4. Les dispositions de l'article 32 sont applicables aux recours entre transporteurs. La prescription court, toutefois, soit à partir du jour d'une décision de justice définitive fixant l'indemnité à payer en vertu des dispositions de la présente Convention, soit, au cas où il n'y aurait pas eu de telle décision, à partir du jour du paiement effectif.

Article 40

Les transporteurs sont libres de convenir entre eux de dispositions dérogeant aux articles 37 et 38.

Chapitre VII

Nullité des stipulations contraires à la Convention

Article 41

1. Sous réserve des dispositions de l'article 40, est nulle et de nul effet toute stipulation qui, directement ou indirectement, dérogerait aux dispositions de la présente Convention. La nullité de telles stipulations n'entraîne pas la nullité des autres dispositions du contrat.

2. En particulier, serait nulle toute clause par laquelle le transporteur se ferait céder le bénéfice de l'assurance de la marchandise ou toute autre clause analogue, ainsi que toute clause déplaçant le fardeau de la preuve.

[Chapter VIII containing the Final Provisions has been omitted]

CARRIAGE BY AIR AND ROAD ACT 1979

1979 Chapter 28

An Act to enable effect to be given to provisions of certain protocols signed at Montreal on 25th September 1975 which further amend the convention relating to carriage by air known as the Warsaw Convention as amended at The Hague 1955; to modify article 26(2) of the said convention both as in force apart from those protocols and as in force by virtue of them; to provide for the amendment of certain Acts relating to carriage by air or road in consequence of the revision of relevant conventions; and to replace references to gold francs in the Carriage of Goods by Road Act 1965 and the Carriage of Passengers by Road Act 1974 by references to special drawing rights.

[4th April 1979]

BE IT ENACTED by the Queen's most Excellent Majesty, by and with the advice and consent of the Lords Spiritual and Temporal, and Commons, in this present Parliament assembled, and by the authority of the same, as follows:—

1.—(1) For Schedule 1 to the Carriage by Air Act 1961 (which contains the English and French texts of the Warsaw Convention mentioned in the title to this Act as it has the force of law in the United Kingdom by virtue of section 1 of that Act) there shall be substituted Schedule 1 to this Act (which contains the English and French texts of that Convention as amended by provisions of protocols No. 3 and No. 4 which were signed at Montreal on 25th September 1975).

(2) The said Act of 1961 and the Carriage by Air (Supplementary Provisions) Act 1962 shall have effect with the amendments set out in Schedule 2 to this Act (which are consequential upon the changes of texts made by the preceding subsection or are connected with the coming into force of those texts).

(3) Neither of the preceding subsections shall affect rights and liabilities arising out of an occurrence which took place before the coming into force of that subsection or, if the subsection comes into force in pursuance of section 7(2) of this Act for some purposes only, arising out of an occurrence which took place before it comes into force for those purposes.

2.—(1) In the Carriage by Air Act 1961, after section 4 there shall be inserted the following section—

4A.—(1) In Article 26(2) the references to damages shall be construed as including loss of part of the baggage or cargo in question and the reference to the receipt of baggage or cargo shall, in relation to loss of part of it, be construed as receipt of the remainder of it.

(2) It is hereby declared, without prejudice to the operation of any other section of this Act, that the reference to Article 26(2) in the preceding subsection is to Article 26(2) as set out in Part I and Part II of the First Schedule to this Act.

(2) This section shall come into force at the passing of this Act but shall not apply to loss which occurred before the passing of this Act.

3.—(1) In the carriage by Air Act 1961, after section 8 there shall be inserted the following section—

8A.—(1) If at any time it appears to Her Majesty in Council that Her Majesty's Government in the United Kingdom have agreed to a revision of the Convention, Her Majesty may by Order in Council provide that this Act, the Carriage by Air (Supplementary Provisions) Act 1962 and section 5(1) of the Carriage by Air and Road Act 1979 shall have effect subject to such exceptions, adaptations and modifications as Her Majesty considers appropriate in consequence of the revision.

(2) In the preceding subsection "revision" means an omission from, addition to or alteration of the Convention and includes replacement of the Convention or part of it by another convention.

(3) An Order in Council under this section shall not be made unless a draft of the Order has been laid before Parliament and approved by a resolution of each House of Parliament.

(2) In the Carriage by Air (Supplementary Provisions) Act 1962, after section 4 there shall be inserted the following section—

4A.—(1) Section 8A of the said Act of 1961 (which among other things enables Her Majesty in Council to alter that Act and this Act in consequence of any revision of the convention to which that Act relates) shall have effect in relation to a revision of the Convention in the Schedule to this Act as it has effect in relation to a revision of the Convention mentioned in that section but as if the reference in that section to the said Act of 1961 were omitted.

(2) An order under the said section 8A may relate both to that Act and this Act; and in the preceding subsection "revision," in relation to the Convention in the Schedule to this Act, means an omission from, addition to or alteration of that Convention and includes replacement of that Convention or part of it by another convention.

(3) In the Carriage of Goods by Road Act 1965, after section 8 there shall be inserted the following section—

8A.—(1) If at any time it appears to Her Majesty in Council that Her Majesty's Government in the United Kingdom have agreed to any revision of the Convention, Her Majesty may by Order in Council make such amendment of—

(*a*) the provisions set out in the Schedule to this Act; and

(*b*) the definition of, and references in this Act to, or to particular provisions of, the Convention; and

(*c*) section 5(1) of the Carriage by Air and Road Act 1979,

as appear to Her to be appropriate in consequence of the revision.

(2) In the preceding subsection "revision" means an omission from, addition to or alteration of the Convention and includes replacement of the Convention or part of it by another convention.

(3) An Order in Council under this section shall not be made unless a draft of the Order has been laid before Parliament and approved by a resolution of each House of Parliament.

(4) In section 8 of the Carriage of Passengers by Road Act 1974 (of which subsection (1) enables amendments of the provisions of that Act mentioned in paragraphs (*a*) and (*b*) of that subsection to be made by Order in Council in consequence of any revision of the Convention mentioned in that subsection, whether the revision operates by way of amendment of the text of the Convention as then in force or takes the form of a new convention or part of a new convention having substantially the same effect as the provisions set out in the Schedule to that Act)—

(*a*) in subsection (1) the words from "whether" to "Act" where it first occurs shall be omitted;

(*b*) at the end of paragraph (*b*) of subsection (1) there shall be inserted the words "and

(*c*) of section 5(1) of the Carriage by Air and Road Act 1979"; and

(*c*) after subsection (1) there shall be inserted the following subsection—

(1A) In the preceding subsection "revision" means an omission from, addition to or alteration of the Convention and includes replacement of the Convention or part of it by another convention.

4.—(1) Schedule 1 to the Carriage by Air Act 1961 as originally enacted shall have effect with the following amendments, namely—

(*a*) in Article 22 of Part I of that Schedule (which among other things provides that the liability of a carrier is limited to two hundred and fifty thousand francs for each passenger and two hundred and fifty francs per kilogramme of cargo and registered baggage unless a higher limit is agreed and to five thousand francs for objects of which a passenger takes charge himself)—

(i) for the words "two hundred and fifty thousand francs" where they first occur and the words "two hundred and fifty francs" and "five thousand francs" there shall be substituted respectively the words "16,600 special drawing rights", "17 special drawing rights" and "332 special drawing rights",

(ii) for the words "two hundred and fifty thousand francs" in the second place where they occur there shall be substituted the words "this limit," and

(iii) for paragraph (5) there shall be substituted the following paragraph—

(5) The sums mentioned in terms of the special drawing right in this Article shall be deemed to refer to the special drawing right as defined by the International Monetary Fund. Conversion of the sums into national currencies shall, in case of judicial proceedings, be made according to the value of such currencies in terms of the special drawing right at the date of the judgment;

(*b*) in Article 22 of Part II of that Schedule (which contains the corresponding provisions of the French text)—

(i) for the words "deux cent cinquante mille francs," "deux cent cinquante francs" and "cinq mille francs" there shall be substituted respectively the words "16,600 Droits de Tirage spéciaux", "17 Droits de Tirage spéciaux" and "332 Droits de Tirage spéciaux", and

(ii) for paragraph (5) there shall be substituted the following paragraph—

(5) Les sommes indiquées en Droits de Tirage spéciaux dans le présent article sont considérées comme se rapportant au Droit de Tirage spécial tel que défini par le Fonds monétaire international. La conversion de ces sommes en monnaies nationales s'effectuera en cas d'instance judiciaire suivant la valeur de ces monnaies en Droit de Tirage spécial à la date du jugement.;

but nothing in this subsection affects the provisions of Schedule 1 to this Act.

(2) The Schedule to the Carriage of Goods by Road Act 1965 (which contains the text of the Convention on the Contract for the International Carriage of Goods by Road as it has the force of law in the United Kingdom by virtue of section 1 of that Act) shall have effect with the following amendments, namely—

(*a*) for paragraph 3 of Article 23 (which provides that compensation for loss of goods shall not exceed 25 francs per kilogram of gross weight short) there shall be substituted the following paragraph—

3. Compensation shall not, however, exceed 8.33 units of account per kilogram of gross weight short.;

(*b*) at the end of Article 23 there shall be inserted the following paragraph—

7. The unit of account mentioned in this Convention is the Special Drawing Right as defined by the International Monetary Fund. The amount mentioned in paragraph 3 of this article shall be converted into the national currency of the State of the Court seised of the case on the basis of the value of that currency on the date of the judgment or the date agreed upon by the parties.

(3) The Schedule to the Carriage of Passengers by Road Act 1974 (which contains the text of the Convention on the Contract for the International Carriage of Passengers and Luggage by Road as it has the force of law in the United Kingdom by virtue of section 1 of that Act) shall have effect with the following amendments, namely—

(*a*) in paragraph 1 of Article 13 (which among other things provides that the total damages payable by a carrier in respect of the same occurrence shall not exceed 250,000 francs for each victim) for the words "250,000 francs" there shall be substituted the words "83,333 units of account";

(*b*) in paragraph 1 of Article 16 (which among other things provides that compensation in respect of luggage shall not exceed 500 francs for each piece of luggage nor 2,000 francs for each passenger and that compensation in respect of personal effects shall not exceed 1,000 francs for each passenger) for the words "500 francs", "2,000 francs" and "1,000 francs" respectively there shall be substituted the words "166.67 units of account", 666.67 units of account" and "333.33 units of account";

(*c*) for Article 19 (which provides that the franc referred to in the Convention shall be the gold franc specified in that Article) there shall be substituted the following Article—

Article 19

The Unit of Account mentioned in this Convention is the Special Drawing Right as defined by the International Monetary Fund. The amounts mentioned in articles 13 and 16 of this Convention shall be converted into the national currency of the State of the Court seised of the case on the basis of the value of that currency on the date of the judgment or the date agreed upon by the Parties.

(4) If judgment in respect of a liability limited by the said Article 22, 23, 13 or 16 is given—

(*a*) in the case of a liability limited by the said Article 22, at a time when the amendments made by this section to that Article are in force for the purposes of the liability; or

(*b*) in any other case, at a time when the amendments made by this section to the other Article in question are in force,

then, notwithstanding that the liability arose before the amendments in question came into force, the judgment shall be in accordance with that Article as amended by this section and, in a case falling within the said Article 13 or 16, in accordance with the said Article 19 as so amended.

5.—(1) For the purposes of Articles 22 and 22A of Schedule 1 to this Act and the Articles 22, 23 and 19 mentioned in the preceding section as amended by that section, the value on a particular day of one special drawing right shall be treated as equal to such a sum in sterling as the International Monetary Fund have fixed as being the equivalent of one special drawing right—

(*a*) for that day; or

(*b*) if no sum has been so fixed for that day, for the last day before that day for which a sum has been so fixed.

(2) A certificate given by or on behalf of the Treasury stating—

(*a*) that a particular sum in sterling has been fixed as aforesaid for a particular day; or
(*b*) that no sum has been so fixed for a particular day and that a particular sum in sterling has been so fixed for a day which is the last day for which a sum has been so fixed before the particular day,

shall be conclusive evidence of those matters for the purposes of the preceding subsection; and a document purporting to be such a certificate shall in any proceedings be received in evidence and, unless the contrary is proved, be deemed to be such a certificate.

(3) The Treasury may charge a reasonable fee for any certificate given by or on behalf of the Treasury in pursuance of the preceding subsection, and any fee received by the Treasury by virtue of this subsection shall be paid into the Consolidated Fund.

6.—(1) It is hereby declared that the powers to make Orders in Council conferred by—

(*a*) sections 8A, 9 and 10 of the Carriage by Air Act 1961 (which provide for the amendment of that Act and other Acts in consequence of a revision of the relevant convention and for the application of that Act to the countries mentioned in section 9 and to such carriage by air as is mentioned in section 10); and
(*b*) sections 8, 8A and 9 of the Carriage of Goods by Road Act 1965 (which provide for the resolution of conflicts between provisions of that Act and certain other provisions relating to carriage by road, for the amendment of that Act in consequence of a revision of the relevant convention and for the application of that Act to the countries mentioned in section 9); and
(*c*) sections 7, 8 and 9 of the Carriage of Passengers by Road Act 1974 (which provide as mentioned in the preceding paragraph),

include power to make Orders in Council in respect of the Act in question as amended by this Act.

(2) It is hereby declared that Schedule 1 to the said Act of 1961 as originally enacted or, if subsection (1) of section 4 of this Act has come into force, as amended by that subsection, remains in force in relation to any matter in relation to which Schedule 1 to this Act is not for the time being in force and that the reference to Schedule 1 to the Act in section 2(1)(*b*) of the Carriage by Air (Supplementary Provisions) Act 1962 is to be construed as a reference to both the Schedules 1 aforesaid so far as each is for the time being in force.

(3) This Act binds the Crown.

(4) The following provisions (which are superseded by this Act) are hereby repealed, namely—

(*a*) section 4(4) of the said Act of 1961;

(*b*) in section 8(1) of the said Act of 1974 the words from "whether" to "Act" where it first occurs.

7.—(1) This Act may be cited as the Carriage by Air and Road Act 1979.

(2) This Act, except section 2, shall come into force on such day as Her Majesty may by Order in Council appoint, and—

(*a*) different days may be appointed in pursuance of this subsection for different provisions of this Act or for different purposes of the same provision;

(*b*) it is hereby declared that a day or days may be appointed in pursuance of this subsection in respect of subsection (1) of section 1 of this Act and Schedule 1 to this Act notwithstanding that the protocols mentioned in that subsection are not in force in accordance with the provisions in that behalf of those protocols.

APPENDIX D

BRITISH INTERNATIONAL FREIGHT ASSOCIATION (BIFA)—STANDARD TRADING CONDITIONS 1989 EDITION*

The Customer's attention is drawn to the Clauses hereof which exclude or limit the Company's liability and those which require the Customer to indemnify the Company in certain circumstances.

Definitions and application

1. In these Conditions—

"Company"	Is the BIFA Member trading under these Conditions.
"Person"	Includes persons or any Body or Bodies Corporate.
"The Owner"	Means the Owner of the goods (including any packaging, containers or equipment) to which any business concluded under these Conditions relates and any other person who is or may become interested in them.
"Customer"	Means any person at whose request or on whose behalf the Company undertakes any business or provides advice, information or services.

2. (A) Subject to Sub-Paragraph (B) below, all and any activities of the Company in the course of business whether gratuitous or not are undertaken subject to these Conditions.

(B) If any legislation is compulsorily applicable to any business undertaken, these Conditions shall, as regards such business, be read as subject to such legislation and nothing in these Conditions shall be construed as a surrender by the Company of any of its rights or immunities or as an increase of any of its responsibilities or liabilities under such legislation and if any part of these Conditions be repugnant to such legislation to any extent such part shall as regards such business be overridden to that extent and no further.

3. The Customer warrants that he is either the Owner or the authorised Agent of the Owner and also that he is accepting these Conditions not only for himself but also as Agent for and on behalf of the Owner.

4. In authorising the Customer to enter into any Contract with the Company and/or in accepting any document issued by the Company in

* These Conditions are for use by BIFA members only.

connection with such Contract, the Owner and Consignee accept these Conditions for themselves and their Agents and for any parties on whose behalf they or their Agents may act, and in particular, but without prejudice to the generality of this Clause, they accept that the Company shall have the right to enforce against them jointly and severally any liability of the Customer under these Conditions or to recover from them any sums to be paid by the Customer which upon proper demand have not been paid.

The company

5. (A) Subject to Clauses 13 and 14 below, the Company shall be entitled to procure any or all of its services as an Agent or to provide those services as a Principal.

(B) The offer and acceptance of an inclusive price for the accomplishment of any service or services shall not itself determine whether any such service is or services are to be arranged by the Company acting as Agent or to be provided by the Company acting as a Contracting Principal.

(C) When acting as an Agent the Company does not make or purport to make any Contract with the Customer for the carriage, storage, packing or handling of any goods nor for any other physical service in relation to them and acts solely on behalf of the Customer in securing services by establishing Contracts with Third Parties so that direct contractual relationships are established between the Customer and such Third Parties.

(D) The Company shall on demand by the Customer provide evidence of any Contract entered into as Agent for the Customer. Insofar as the Company may be in default of this obligation, it shall be deemed to have contracted with the Customer as a Principal for the performance of the Customer's instructions.

6. When and to the extent that the Company has contracted as Principal for the performance of any of its services, it undertakes to perform and/or in its own name to procure the performance of those services, and subject always to the totality of these Conditions and in particular to Clauses 26–29 hereof accepts liability for loss of or damage to goods taken into its charge occurring between the time when it takes the goods into its charge and the time when the Company is entitled to call upon the Customer, Consignee or Owner to take delivery of the goods.

7. When and to the extent that the Company in accordance with these Conditions is acting as an Agent on behalf of the Customer, the Company shall be entitled and the Customer hereby expressly authorises the Company to enter into Contracts on behalf of the Customer—

(A) for the carriage of goods by any route or means or person;

(B) for the storage, packing, trans-shipment, loading, unloading or handling of the goods by any person at any place and for any length of time;

(C) for the carriage or storage of goods in or on transport units as defined in Clause 19 and with other goods of whatever nature; and

(D) to do such acts as may in the opinion of the Company be reasonably necessary in the performance of its obligations in the interests of the Customer.

8. The Company reserves to itself a reasonable liberty as to the means, route and procedure to be followed in the handling, storage and transportation of goods.

9. The Company shall be entitled to perform any of its obligations herein by itself or by its parent, subsidiary or associated Companies.

In the absence of agreement to the contrary any Contract to which these Conditions apply is made by the Company on its own behalf and also as Agent for and on behalf of any such parent, subsidiary or associated Company, and any such Company shall be entitled to the benefit of these Conditions.

10. (A) Subject to Sub-Clause (B) hereof, the Company shall have a general lien on all goods and documents relating to goods in its possession, custody or control for all sums due at any time from the Customer or Owner, and shall be entitled to sell or dispose of such goods or documents as Agent for and at the expense of the Customer and apply the proceeds in or towards the payment of such sums on 28 days notice in writing to the Customer. Upon accounting to the Customer for any balance remaining after payment of any sum due to the Company and the costs of sale or disposal the Company shall be discharged of any liability whatsoever in respect of the goods or documents.

(B) When the goods are liable to perish or deteriorate, the Company's right to sell or dispose of the goods shall arise immediately upon any sum becoming due to the company subject only to the Company taking reasonable steps to bring to the Customer's attention its intention of selling or disposing of the goods before doing so.

11. The Company shall be entitled to retain and be paid all brokerages, commissions, allowances and other remunerations customarily retained by or paid to Freight Forwarders.

12. (A) If delivery of the goods or any part thereof is not taken by the Customer, Consignee or Owner, at the time and place when and where the Company is entitled to call upon such person to take delivery thereof, the Company shall be entitled to store the goods or any part thereof at the sole risk of the Customer, whereupon the liability of the Company in respect of the goods or that part thereof stored as aforesaid shall wholly cease and the cost of such storage if paid for or payable by the Company or any Agent or Sub-Contractor of the Company shall forthwith upon demand be paid by the Customer to the Company.

(B) The Company shall be entitled at the expense of the Customer to dispose of (by sale or otherwise as may be reasonable in all the circumstances):—

(i) on 28 days notice in writing to the Customer, or where the Customer cannot be traced and reasonable efforts have been made to contact any parties who may reasonably be supposed by the Company to have any interest in the goods, any goods which have been held by the Company for 90 days and which cannot be delivered as instructed; and

(ii) without prior notice, goods which have perished, deteriorated or altered or are in immediate prospect of doing so in a manner which has caused or may reasonably be expected to cause loss or damage to Third Parties or to contravene any applicable laws or regulations.

13. (A) No insurance will be effected except upon express instructions given in writing by the Customer and all insurances effected by the Company are subject to the usual exceptions and conditions of the Policies of the Insurance Company or Underwriters taking the risk. Unless otherwise agreed in writing the Company shall not be under any obligation to effect a separate insurance on each consignment but may declare it on any open or general Policy held by the Company.

(B) Insofar as the Company agrees to arrange insurance, the Company acts solely as Agent for the Customer using its best endeavours to arrange such insurance and does so subject to the limits of liability contained in Clause 29 hereof.

14. (A) Except under special arrangements previously made in writing or under the terms of a printed document signed by the Company, any instructions relating to the delivery or release of goods in specified circumstances only, such as (but without prejudice to the generality of this Clause) against payment or against surrender of a particular document, are accepted by the Company only as Agents for the Customer where Third Parties are engaged to effect compliance with the instructions.

(B) The Company shall not be under any liability in respect of such arrangements as are referred to under Sub-Clause (A) hereof save where such arrangements are made in writing.

(C) In any event, the Company's liability in respect of the performance or arranging the performance of such instructions shall not exceed that provided for in these Conditions in respect of loss or damage to goods.

15. Advice and information, in whatever form it may be given, is provided by the Company for the Customer only and the Customer shall indemnify the Company against any liability, claims, loss, damage, costs or expenses arising out of any other persons relying upon such advice or information. Except under special arrangements previously made in writing, advice and information which is not related to specific instructions accepted by the Company is provided gratuitously and without liability.

16. (A) Except under special arrangement previously made in writing the Company will not accept or deal with bullion, coin, precious stones, jewellery, valuables, antiques, pictures, human remains, livestock or plants. Should any Customer nevertheless deliver any such goods to the Company or cause the Company to handle or deal with any such goods otherwise than under special arrangements previously made in writing the Company shall be under no liability whatsoever for or in connection with such goods howsoever arising.

(B) The company may at any time waive its rights and exemptions from liability under Sub-Clause (A) above in respect of any one or more of the categories of goods mentioned herein or of any part of any category. If such waiver is not in writing, the onus of proving such waiver shall be on the Customer.

17. Except following instructions previously received in writing and accepted by the Company, the Company will not accept or deal with goods of a dangerous or damaging nature, nor with goods likely to harbour or encourage vermin or other pests, nor with goods liable to taint or affect other goods. If such goods are accepted pursuant to a special arrangement and then in the opinion of the Company they constitute a risk to other goods, property, life or health, the Company shall where reasonably practicable contact the Customer, but reserves the right at the expense of the Customer to remove or otherwise deal with the goods.

18. Where there is a choice of rates according to the extent or degree of the liability assumed by carriers, warehousemen or others, no declaration of value where optional will be made except under special arrangements previously made in writing.

The Customer

19. The Customer warrants:

(A) that the description and particulars of any goods furnished by or on behalf of the Customer are full and accurate.

(B) that all goods have been properly and sufficiently prepared, packed, stowed, labelled and/or marked, and that the preparation, packing, stowage, labelling and marking are appropriate to any operations or transactions affecting the goods and the characteristics of the goods.

(C) that where the Company receives the goods from the Customer already stowed in or on a container, trailer, tanker, or any other device specifically constructed for the carriage of goods by land, sea or air (each hereafter individually referred to as "the transport unit"), the transport unit is in good condition, and is suitable for the carriage to the intended destination of the goods loaded therein or thereon.

20. Should the Customer otherwise than under special arrangements previously made in writing as set out in Clause 17 above deliver to the Company or cause the Company to deal with or handle goods of a dangerous or damaging nature, or goods likely to harbour or encourage vermin or other pests, or goods liable to taint or affect other goods, he shall be liable for all loss or damage arising in connection with such goods and shall indemnify the Company against all penalties, claims, damages, costs and expenses whatsoever arising in connection therewith, and the goods may be dealt with in such manner as the Company or any other person in whose custody they may be at any relevant time shall think fit.

21. The Customer undertakes that no claim shall be made against any Director, Servant, or Employee of the Company which imposes or attempts to impose upon them any liability in connection with any services which are the subject of these Conditions and if any such claim should nevertheless be made to indemnify the Company against all consequences thereof.

22. The Customer shall save harmless and keep the Company indemnified from and against:—

(A) All liability, loss, damage, costs and expenses whatsoever (including without prejudice to the generality of the foregoing, all duties, taxes, imposts, levies, deposits and outlays of whatsoever nature levied by any authority in relation to the goods) arising out of the Company acting in accordance with the Customer's instructions or arising from any breach by the Customer of any Warranty contained in these Conditions or from the negligence of the Customer, and

(B) Without derogation from Sub-Clause (A) above, any liability assumed or incurred by the Company when by reason of carrying out the Customer's instructions the Company has reasonably become liable or may become liable to any other party, and

(C) All claims, costs and demands whatsoever and by whomsoever made or preferred in excess of the liability of the Company under the terms of these Conditions regardless whether such claims, costs and demands arise from or in connection with the negligence or breach of duty of the Company its Servants, Sub-Contractors or Agents, and

(D) Any claims of a General Average nature which may be made on the Company.

23. (A) The Customer shall pay to the Company in cash or as otherwise agreed all sums immediately when due without reduction or deferment on account of any claim, counterclaim or set-off.

(B) In respect of all sums which are overdue the Customer shall be liable to pay to the Company interest calculated at 4% above the Base Rate for the time being of Midland Bank Plc.

24. Despite the acceptance by the Company of instructions to collect freight, duties, charges or other expenses from the Consignee or any other person the Customer shall remain responsible for such freight, duties, charges or expenses on receipt of evidence of proper demand and in the absence of evidence of payment (for whatever reason) by such Consignee or other person when due.

25. Where liability for general Average arises in connection with the goods, the Customer shall promptly provide security to the Company or to any other party designated by the Company in a form acceptable to the Company.

Liability and limitation

26. The Company shall perform its duties with a reasonable degree of care, diligence, skill and judgement.

27. The Company shall be relieved of liability for any loss or damage if and to the extent that such loss or damage is caused by:—

(A) strike, lock-out, stoppage or restraint of labour, the consequences of which the company is unable to avoid by the exercise of reasonable diligence;

(B) any cause or event which the Company is unable to avoid and the consequences whereof the Company is unable to prevent by the exercise of reasonable diligence.

28. Except under special arrangements previously made in writing the Company accepts no responsibility for departure or arrival dates of goods.

29. (A) Subject to Clause 2(B) above and Sub-Clause (D) below the Company's liability howsoever arising and notwithstanding that the cause of loss or damage be unexplained shall not exceed

(i) in the case of claims for loss or damage to goods

(a) the value of any goods lost or damaged, or

(b) a sum at the rate of two Special Drawing Rights as defined by the International Monetary Fund (hereinafter referred to as SDR's), per kilo of gross weight of any goods lost or damaged whichever shall be the least

(ii) in the case of all other claims

(a) the value of the goods the subject of the relevant transaction between the Company and its Customer, or

(b) a sum at the rate of two SDR's per kilo of the gross weight of the goods the subject of the said transaction, or

(c) 75,000 SDR's in respect of any one transaction whichever shall be the least.

For the purposes of Clause 29(A) the value of the goods shall be their value when they were or should have been shipped. The value of SDR's shall be calculated as at the date when the claim is received by the Company in writing.

(B) Subject to Clause 2(B) above, and Sub-Clause (D) below, the Company's liability for loss or damage as a result of failure to deliver or arrange delivery of goods in a reasonable time or (where there is a special arrangement under Clause 28) to adhere to agreed departure or arrival dates shall not in any circumstances whatever exceed a sum equal to twice the amount of the Company's charges in respect of the relevant transaction.

(C) Save in respect of such loss or damage as is referred to at Sub-Clause (B) and subject to Clause 2(B) above and Sub-Clause (D) below the Company shall not in any circumstances whatsoever be liable for indirect or consequential loss such as (but not limited to) loss of profits, loss of market or the consequences of delay or deviation however caused.

(D) By special arrangement agreed in writing, the Company may accept liability in excess of the limits set out in Sub-Clauses (A) to (C) above upon the Customer agreeing to pay the Company's additional charges for accepting such increased liability. Details of the Company's additional charges will be provided upon request.

30. (A) Any claim by the Customer against the Company arising in respect of any service provided for the Customer or which the Company has undertaken to provide shall be made in writing and notified to the Company within 14 days of the date upon which the Customer became or should have become aware of any event or occurrence alleged to give rise to such claim and any claim not made and notified as aforesaid shall be deemed to be waived and absolutely barred except where the Customer can show that it was impossible for him to comply with this Time Limit and that he has made the claim as soon as it was reasonably possible for him to do so.

(B) Notwithstanding the provisions of Sub-Paragraph (A) above the Company shall in any event be discharged of all liability whatsoever howsoever arising in respect of any service provided for the Customer or which the Company has undertaken to provide unless suit be brought and written notice thereof given to the Company within nine months from the date of the event or occurrence alleged to give rise to a cause of action against the Company.

Jurisdiction and law

31. These Conditions and any act or contract to which they apply shall be governed by English Law and any dispute arising out of any act or contract to which these Conditions apply shall be subject to the exclusive jurisdiction of the English Courts.

Appendix E

Road Haulage Association Limited

CONDITIONS OF CARRIAGE 1991*

Effective from 1 June 1991

Company stamp or details

(hereinafter referred to as "the Carrier") is not a common carrier and accepts goods for carriage only upon that condition and the Conditions set out below. No servant or agent of the Carrier is permitted to alter or vary these Conditions in any way unless expressly authorised in writing to do so.

1. Definitions

In these Conditions:

"*Customer*" means the person or company who contracts for the services of the Carrier including any other carrier who gives a Consignment to the Carrier for carriage.

"*Contract*" means the contract of carriage between the Customer and the Carrier.

"*Consignee*" means the person or company to whom the Carrier contracts to deliver the goods.

road and partly by such other means of transport any loss, damage or delay shall be deemed to have occurred while the goods were being carried by road unless the contrary is proved by the Carrier.

3. Dangerous Goods

Dangerous Goods must be disclosed by the Customer and if the Carrier agrees to accept them for carriage they must be classified, packed and labelled in accordance with the statutory regulations for the carriage by road of the substance declared. Transport Emergency Cards (Tremcards) or information in writing in the manner required by the relevant statutory provisions must be provided by the Customer in respect of each substance and must accompany the Consignment.

4. Loading and Unloading

(1) Unless the Carrier has agreed in writing to the contrary with the Customer:

(a) The Carrier shall not be under any obligation to provide any plant, power or labour, other than that carried by the vehicle, required for loading or unloading the Consignment.

(b) The Customer warrants that any special appliances required for loading or unloading the Consignment which are not

"*Consignment*" means goods in bulk or contained in one parcel, package or container, as the case may be, or any number of separate parcels, packages or containers sent at one time in one load by or for the Customer from one address to one address.

"*Dangerous Goods*" means dangerous substances listed by the Health and Safety Commission in Part I of the Authorised and Approved List of Dangerous Substances, explosives, radioactive substances and any other substance presenting a similar hazard.

2. Parties and Sub-Contracting

(1) The Customer warrants that he is either the owner of the goods in any Consignment or is authorised by such owner to accept these Conditions on such owner's behalf.

(2) The Carrier and any other carrier employed by the Carriage may employ the services of any other carrier for the purpose of fulfilling the Contract in whole or in part and the name of every other such carrier shall be provided to the Customer upon request.

(3) The Carrier contracts for itself and as agent of and trustee for its servants and agents and all other carriers referred to in (2) above and such other carrier's servants and agents and every reference in Conditions 3–19 inclusive hereof "the Carrier" shall be deemed to include every other such carrier, servant and agent with the intention that they shall have the benefit of the Contract and collectively and together with the Carrier be under no greater liability to the Customer or any other party than is the Carrier hereunder.

(4) Notwithstanding Condition 2(3) the carriage of goods in any Consignment by rail, sea, inland waterway or air is arranged by the Carrier as agent of the Customer and shall be subject to the Conditions of the rail, shipping, inland waterway or air carrier contracted to carry the goods. The Carrier shall be under no liability whatever to whomsoever and however arising in respect of such carriage. Provided that where goods are carried partly by carried by the vehicle will be provided by the Customer or on the Customer's behalf.

(c) The Carrier shall be under no liability whatever to the Customer for any damage whatever, however caused, if the Carrier is instructed to load or unload goods required special appliances which, in breach of the warranty in (b) above, have not been provided by the Customer or on the Customer's behalf.

(d) The Carrier shall not be required to provide service beyond the usual place of collection or delivery but if any such service is given by the Carrier it shall be at the sole risk of the Customer.

(2) The Customer shall indemnify the Carrier against all claims and demands whatever which could not have been made if such instructions as are referred to in (1)(c) of this Condition and such service as is referred to in (1)(d) of this Condition had not been given.

5. Consignment Notes

The Carrier shall, if so required, sign a document prepared by the sender acknowledging the receipt of the Consignment but no such document shall be evidence of the condition or of the correctness of the declared nature, quantity, or weight of the Consignment at the time it is received by the Carrier.

6. Transit

(1) Transit shall commence when the Carrier takes possession of the Consignment whether at the point of collection or at the Carrier's premises.

(2) Transit shall (unless otherwise previously determined) end when the Consignment is tendered at the usual place of delivery at the Consignee's address within the customary cartage hours of the district.

Provided that:

(a) if no safe and adequate access or no adequate unloading facilities there exist then transit shall be deemed to end at the expiry of one clear day after notice in writing (or by telephone if so previously agreed in writing) of the arrival of the Consignment at the Carrier's premises has been sent to the Consignee; and

(b) when for any other reason whatever a Consignment cannot be delivered or when a Consignment is held by the Carrier 'to await order' or 'to be kept till called for' or upon any like instructions and such instructions are not given or the Consignment is not called for and removed, within a reasonable time, then transit shall be deemed to end.

7. Undelivered or Unclaimed Goods

Where the Carrier is unable for any reason to deliver a Consignment to the Consignee or as he may order, or where by virtue of the proviso to Condition 6(2) hereof transit is deemed to be at end, the Carrier may sell the goods and payment or tender of the proceeds after deduction of all proper charges and expenses in relation thereto and of all outstanding charges in relation to the carriage and storage of the goods shall (without prejudice to any claim or right which the Customer may have against the Carrier otherwise arising under these Conditions) discharge the Carrier from all liability in respect of such goods, their carriage and storage.

Provided that:

(1) the Carrier shall do what is reasonable to obtain the value of the Consignment and

(2) the power to sale shall not be exercised where the name and address of the sender or of the Consignee is known unless the Carrier shall have done what is reasonable in the circumstances to give notice to the sender or, if the name and address of the sender is not known, to the Consignee that the goods will be sold unless within the time specified in such notice, being a reasonable time in the circumstances from the giving of such notice, the goods are

(2) Subject to these Conditions the Carrier shall be liable for:

(a) loss or mis-delivery of or damage to livestock, bullion, money, securities, stamps, precious metals or precious stones only if:

- (*i*) the Carrier has specifically agreed in writing to carry any such items and
- (*ii*) the Customer has agreed in writing to reimburse the Carrier in respect of all additional costs which result from the carrying of the said items and
- (*iii*) the loss, mis-delivery or damage is occasioned during transit and results from negligent act or omission by the Carrier;

(b) any loss or mis-delivery of or damage to any other goods occasioned during transit unless the same had arisen from, and the Carrier has used reasonable care to minimise the effects of:

- (*i*) Act of God;
- (*ii*) any consequences of war, invasion, act of foreign enemy, hostilities (whether war or not), civil war, rebellion, insurrection, military or usurped power or confiscation, requisition, or destruction of or damage to property by or under the order of any government or public or local authority;
- (*iii*) seizure or forfeiture under legal process;
- (*iv*) error, act, omission, mis-statement or mis-representation by the Customer or other owner of the goods or by servants or agents of either of them;
- (*v*) inherent liability to wastage in bulk or weight, latent defect or inherent defect, vice or natural deterioration of the goods;
- (*vi*) insufficient or improper packing;
- (*vii*) insufficient or improper labelling or addressing;
- (*viii*) riot, civil commotion, strike, lockout, general or partial stoppage or restraint of labour from whatever cause;

taken away or instructions are given for their disposal.

8. Carrier's Charges

(1) The Carrier's charges shall be payable by the Customer without prejudice to the Carrier's rights against the Consignee or any other person. Provided that when goods are consigned 'carriage forward' the Customer shall not be required to pay such charges unless the consignee fails to pay after a reasonable demand has been made by the Carrier for payment thereof.

(2) Except where a quotation states otherwise all quotations based on a tonnage rate shall apply to the gross weight unless:

(a) the goods exceed 2.25 cubic metres in measurement per tonne, in which case the tonnage rate shall be computed upon and apply to each measurement of 2.25 cubic metres or any part thereof, or

(b) the size or shape of a Consignment necessitates the use of a vehicle of greater carrying capacity than the weight of the Consignment would otherwise require, in which case the tonnage rate shall be computed upon and apply to the carrying capacity of such vehicle as is reasonably required.

(3) Charges shall be payable on the expiry of any time limit previously stipulated and the Carrier shall be entitled to interest at 5 per cent above the Clearing Bank Base Rate current at this time, calculated on a daily basis on all amounts overdue to the Carrier.

9. Liability for Loss and Damage

(1) The Customer shall be deemed to have elected to accept the terms set out in (2) of this Condition unless, before the transit commences, the Customer has agreed in writing that the Carrier shall not be liable for any loss or mis-delivery of or damage to goods however or whenever caused and whether or not caused or contributed to directly or indirectly by any act, omission, neglect, default or other wrongdoing on the part of the Carrier.

(*ix*) Consignee not taking or accepting delivery within a reasonable time after the Consignment has been tendered.

(3) The Carrier shall not in any circumstances be liable for loss of or damage to goods after transit of such goods is deemed to have ended within the meaning of Condition 6(2) hereof, whether or not caused or contributed to directly or indirectly by any act, omission, neglect, default or other wrongdoing on the part of the Carrier.

10. Fraud

The Carrier shall not in any circumstances be liable in respect of a Consignment where there has been fraud on the part of the Customer or the owner of the goods or the servants or agents of either in respect of that Consignment, unless the fraud has been contributed by the complicity of the Carrier or of any servant of the Carrier acting in the course of his employment.

11. Limitation of Liability

(1) Except as otherwise provided in these Conditions the liability of the Carrier in respect of loss or mis-delivery of or damage to goods, however sustained, shall in all circumstances be limited as follows:

(a) To the value of the Consignment where, at any time prior to the commencement of transit, the Customer has given seven days' written notice to the Carrier requiring that the limit of the Carrier's liability be set at the value of the Consignment where this value exceeds **£1,300 per tonne** or, if no such notice has been given;

(b) To **£1,300 per tonne** on either the gross weight of the Consignment or, where applicable, the tonnage computed in accordance with Condition 8(2)(a) or (b) hereof; or

(c) To the proportion of the sum, ascertained in accordance with (1)(a) or (b) of this Condition, which the actual value of part of the Consignment bears to the actual value of the whole of the Consignment where loss mis-delivery or damage, however sustained, is in respect of that part of the Consignment.

Provided that:

(*i*) nothing in this Condition shall limit the liability of the Carrier to less than the sum of £10;

(*ii*) the Carrier shall be entitled to require proof of the value of the whole of the Consignment and of any part thereof lost, mis-delivered or damaged;

(*iii*) the Customer shall be required to agree with the Carrier the carriage charges appropriate to the value of the Consignment where the limit of liability is increased above **£1,300 per tonne** in accordance with (1)(a) of this Condition.

(2) Notwithstanding Condition 11(1), the liability of the Carrier in respect of the indirect or consequential loss or damage, however arising and including loss of market, shall not exceed the amount of the carriage charges in respect of the Consignment or the amount of the claimant's proved loss, whichever is the smaller, unless;

(a) at the time of entering into the Contract with the Carrier the Customer declares to the Carrier a special interest in delivery in the case of loss or damage or of an agreed time limit being exceeded and agrees to pay a surcharge calculated on the amount of that interest, and

(b) prior to the commencement of transit the Customer has delivered to the Carrier written confirmation of the special interest, agreed time limit and amount of the interest.

12. Insurance

The Carrier shall insure his liabilities arising out of the carriage of goods under these Conditions.

13. Indemnity to the Carrier

The Customer shall indemnify the Carrier against:

(1) all consequences suffered by the Carrier (including but not limited

Carrier or make a claim in writing within the time limit applicable and

(b) such advice or claim was given or made within a reasonable time, the Carrier shall not have the benefit of the exclusion of liability afforded by this Condition.

15. Lien

The Carrier shall have a general lien against the Customer, where the Customer is the owner of the goods, for any monies whatever due from the Customer to the Carrier. If such a lien is not satisfied within a reasonable time, the Carrier may, at his absolute discretion sell the goods, or part thereof, as agent for the Customer and apply the proceeds towards the monies due and the expenses of the retention, insurance and sale of the goods and shall, upon accounting to the Customer for any balance remaining, be discharged from all liability whatever in respect of the goods. Where the Customer is not the owner of the goods, the Carrier shall have a particular lien against said owner, allowing him to retain possession, but not dispose of, the goods against monies due from the Customer in respect of the Consignment.

16. Unreasonable Detention

The Customer shall be liable for the cost of unreasonable detention of any vehicle, trailer, container or sheet but the rights of the Carrier against any other person in respect thereof shall remain unaffected.

17. Computation of Time

In the computation of time where any period provided by these Conditions is seven days or less, Saturdays, Sundays and all statutory public holidays shall be excluded.

18. Loss Adjustment

The value of a Consignment or part Consignment shall be taken as its invoice value if the goods have been sold. Otherwise it shall be taken as the to claims, demands, proceedings, fines, penalties, damages, costs, expenses and loss of or damage to the carrying vehicle and to other goods carried) of any error, omission, mis-statement or misrepresentation by the Customer or other owner of the goods or by any servant or agent of either of them, insufficient or improper packing, labelling or addressing of the goods or fraud as in Condition 10;

(2) all claims and demands whatever by whomsoever made in excess of the liability of the Carrier under these Conditions;

(3) all losses suffered by and claims made against the Carrier resulting from loss of or damage to property caused by or arising out of the carriage by the Carrier of Dangerous Goods whether or not declared by the Customer as such;

(4) all claims made upon the Carrier by H.M. Customs and Excise in respect of dutiable goods consigned in bond whether or not transit has ended or been suspended.

14. Time Limits for Claims

The Carrier shall not be liable for:

(1) loss from a parcel, package or container or from an unpacked Consignment or for damage to a Consignment or any part of a Consignment unless he is advised thereof in writing otherwise than upon a consignment note or delivery document within three days, and the claim is made in writing within seven days, after the termination of transit;

(2) loss, mis-delivery or non-delivery of the whole of a Consignment or of any separate parcel, package or container forming part of a Consignment unless he is advised of the loss, mis-delivery or non-delivery in writing otherwise than upon a consignment note or delivery document within twenty-eight days, and the claim is made in writing within forty-two days, after the commencement of transit.

Provided that if the Customer proves that,

(a) it was not reasonably possible for the Customer to advise the

cost thereof to the owner.

19. Impossibility of Performance

The Carrier shall be relieved of its obligation to perform the Contract to the extent that the performance is prevented by failure of the Customer, fire, weather conditions, industrial dispute, labour disturbance or cause beyond the reasonable control of the carrier.

Road Haulage Association Limited
CONDITIONS OF CARRIAGE 1991
EXPLANATORY NOTES

STATUS OF THE CONDITIONS

The RHA Conditions of Carriage 1991 result from a review of the RHA Conditions of Carriage 1982. **They take effect from 1 June 1991** and are designed to meet the challenging needs of the industry. They also include amendments reflecting changes in statutory regulations and members' experience in the use of the RHA Conditions of Carriage 1982.

The 1991 Conditions have been submitted to the Office of Fair Trading and have been placed on the public register. This means that from 1 June 1991 members are free to operate in accordance with the new Conditions and they are recommended to do so. They are designed to provide the haulier with guidance under which to operate whilst striking a balance between his interests and those of his customers.

The Conditions are not compulsory but if any member intends to modify them, he should take the greatest care to ensure that they meet the requirement of "reasonableness" in the Unfair Contract Terms Act 1977.

The Conditions are the copyright of the RHA and may not be used by non-members.

TO USE THE CONDITIONS

A member who intends to trade under these Conditions should take the following action:–

EFFECTS OF THE CONDITIONS

The Conditions are set out in the same sequence as the preceding version, commencing with definitions and proceeding through the parties to the contract, loading, unloading, transit etc. They vary from the RHA Conditions of Carriage 1982 as follows:

Preamble. Any alteration or variation of the Conditions by a servant or agent of the Carrier must now be authorised in writing.

Condition 1. Replaces the definition of "Trader" by a definition of "Customer", defines "Consignee" and up-dates the definition of "Dangerous Goods".

Condition 2. A new Condition 2(4) covers carriage by means other than road. It also makes the Carrier responsible for proving, if necessary, that any damage, loss or delay did not occur while goods were being carried by road.

Condition 3. The requirements for the Carriage of Dangerous Goods have been up-dated to reflect current statutory provisions.

Condition 4. This Condition has been revised to facilitate the use of plant, power and labour, carried on the Carrier's vehicle, to be used for loading and unloading. It also makes wider provision for a Carrier to agree in writing to provide service beyond the usual places of collection and delivery or additional facilities.

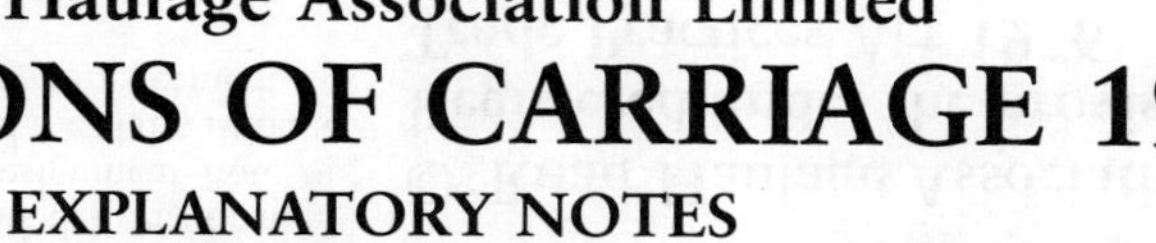

1. Refer the Conditions to his insurers or brokers and secure any necessary adjustments to existing insurance covers.

   (**N.B.** The basic liability limit, given in Condition 11, has been increased).

2. Inform existing customers, in writing, preferably by Recorded Delivery, of the intention to trade subject to the new Conditions saying, for example, "Please note that as from (date) goods will be accepted for carriage only subject to the RHA Conditions of Carriage 1991, copies of which are available free on application" (or "a copy of which is attached").

3. Inform existing sub-contractors in writing, preferably by Recorded Delivery, that as from (date), goods will be accepted for carriage and sub-contracted only subject to the RHA Conditions of Carriage 1991.

4. Retain Recorded Delivery receipts or, if the above letters are not sent by Recorded Delivery, maintain a permanent record of customers and sub-contractors and the dates on which the letters were despatched.

5. Print (or overprint) at the foot of the letter headings, quotation forms, confirmation notes, consignment notes, and invoices, etc. "Goods are accepted for carriage and sub-contracted only subject to the RHA Conditions of Carriage 1991, copies of which are available free on application".

   (**N.B.** "1991" should be included to stress that the new Conditions and not any previous editions are to apply. However, if existing letter headings etc. refer to the "Current RHA Conditions of Carriage" this reference will probably suffice until reprinting of documents becomes necessary).

6. Maintain a stock of the Conditions for issue to customers or sub-contractors as and when required.

Condition 5. No change.

Condition 6. No change.

Condition 7. No change.

Condition 8. Condition 8(3) has been amended to clarify the Carrier's entitlement to interest on outstanding payments.

Condition 9. No change.

Condition 10. No change.

Condition 11. This Condition has been redrafted to give greater prominence to the need for a Customer to give seven days' written notice when he requires the Carrier to increase his liability above the basic limit. In addition, this basic liability has been increased to £1300 per tonne. **It is essential that members operating in accordance with the RHA Conditions of Carriage 1991 make any necessary adjustment to their existing insurance cover.**

Condition 12. This new Condition requires the Carrier to insure his liabilities.

Condition 13. No change.

Condition 14. No change.

Condition 15. This Condition has been re-drafted in the light of a Court judgement concerning goods belonging to a third party. It now allows the Carrier to hold such goods against monies due but not to dispose of them.

Condition 16. No change.

Condition 17. No change.

Condition 18. This new Condition defines the value of goods in order to facilitate loss adjustment.

Condition 19. No change.

INDEX

Index